TRADITIONS & ENCOUNTERS

TRADITIONS ENCOUNTERS

A Global Perspective on the Past

VOLUME A: From the Beginning to 1000

THIRD EDITION

JERRY H. BENTLEY
University of Hawai`i

HERBERT F. ZIEGLER
University of Hawai`i

Boston   Burr Ridge, IL   Dubuque, IA   Madison, WI   New York   San Francisco   St. Louis
Bangkok   Bogotá   Caracas   Kuala Lumpur   Lisbon   London   Madrid   Mexico City
Milan   Montreal   New Delhi   Santiago   Seoul   Singapore   Sydney   Taipei   Toronto

The McGraw·Hill Companies

Published by McGraw-Hill, an imprint of The McGraw-Hill Companies, Inc. 1221 Avenue of the Americas, New York, NY, 10020. Copyright © 2006, 2003, 2000. All rights reserved. No part of this publication may be reproduced or distributed in any form or by any means, or stored in a database or retrieval system, without the prior written consent of The McGraw-Hill Companies, Inc., including, but not limited to, in any network or other electronic storage or transmission, or broadcast for distance learning.

This book is printed on acid-free paper.

1 2 3 4 5 6 7 8 9 0 VNH/VNH 0 9 8 7 6 5

ISBN 0-07-299829-6

Editor in Chief: *Emily Barrosse*
Publisher: *Lyn Uhl*
Senior Sponsoring Editor: *Jon-David Hague*
Marketing Manager: *Katherine Bates*
Director of Development: *Lisa Pinto*
Developmental Editors: *Jim Strandberg and Angela Kao*
Managing Editor: *Melissa Williams*
Senior Project Manager: *Christina Gimlin*
Manuscript Editor: *Margaret Moore*
Art Director: *Jeanne Schreiber*
Senior Design Manager: *Kim Menning*
Cover and Interior Design: *Ellen Pettengell*
Art Editor: *Katherine McNab*
Manager, Photo Research: *Brian Pecko*
Supplements Producers: *Louis Swaim and Kate Boylan*
Media Project Manager: *Kate Boylan*
Lead Production Supervisor: *Randy Hurst*

Composition: *10/12 Galliard by Thompson Type*
Printing: *50# Pub Thin, VonHoffmann*

Cover: © Erich Lessing/Art Resource, NY

Credits: The credits section for this book begins on page C-1 and is considered an extension of the copyright page.

The following Library of Congress data is for the complete edition of this title.

Library of Congress Cataloging-in-Publication Data
Bentley, Jerry H., 1949–
    Traditions & encounters : a global perspective on the past / Jerry H. Bentley, Herbert F. Ziegler.—[3rd ed].
        p. cm.
    Includes bibliographical references and index.
    ISBN 0-07-295754-9 (alk. paper)
    1. World history. 2. Intercultural communication—History. I. Title: Traditions and encounters. II. Ziegler, Herbert F., 1949– III. Title.
D20.B42 2005
909.82—dc22

2004063157

The Internet addresses listed in the text were accurate at the time of publication. The inclusion of a website does not indicate an endorsement by the authors or McGraw-Hill, and McGraw-Hill does not guarantee the accuracy of the information presented at these sites.

www.mhhe.com

BRIEF CONTENTS

Detailed Contents

PART I
THE EARLY COMPLEX SOCIETIES, 3500 TO 500 B.C.E.   2

PART II
THE FORMATION OF CLASSICAL SOCIETIES, 500 B.C.E. TO 500 C.E.   156

PART III

THE POSTCLASSICAL ERA, 500 TO 1000 C.E.   314

Maps

SOURCES FROM THE PAST

Contexts & Connections

PREFACE

❦

Since the early 1990s, journalists, politicians, scholars, and others have frequently resorted to the term *globalization* when commenting on the increasingly tight connections linking the world's lands and peoples. By the late twentieth century, global transportation and communication networks had become more intricate than ever before, and they promoted both economic integration and systematic interaction among peoples throughout the world. Trade goods and electronic currency flowed around the world, while manufacturers restlessly sought new sites to produce consumer goods. Globalization brought tremendous wealth to some, and it facilitated both commercial and cultural exchanges that enriched the lives of many peoples. Alongside opportunities, the era of globalization also brought numerous problems: widespread pollution, global warming, cultural challenges, ethnic tensions, political conflicts, and weapons of mass destruction loomed as potential threats to peoples of all world regions.

Yet even though they are more prominent today than ever before, global interactions and global problems are by no means new features of world history. To the contrary, there is a long historical context for contemporary globalization, and only in light of past experience is it possible to understand the contemporary world.

A GLOBAL PERSPECTIVE ON THE PAST

Our purpose in *Traditions & Encounters* is to offer a global perspective on the past—a vision of history that is meaningful and appropriate for the interdependent world of contemporary times. During an era when peoples from all parts of the earth meet, mingle, interact, and do business with one another, a global perspective has become an essential tool for informed and responsible citizenship. Because global interactions profoundly influence the fortunes of peoples in all lands, it is impossible to understand the contemporary world by approaching it exclusively from the viewpoint of western Europe, the United States, Japan, or any other individual society. It is equally impossible to understand the world's history by viewing it exclusively through the lenses of any particular society's historical experience.

A global perspective on the past calls for analysis that respects the historical experiences of all the world's peoples—not just one or a few—and that examines the roles of all in the making of a world inhabited by all. A global perspective calls also for analysis that goes beyond the study of individual societies to examine their larger regional, continental, hemispheric, and global contexts. A global perspective calls further for exploration of the networks and structures that have promoted interactions between peoples of different societies. A global perspective calls finally for attention to the effects of interactions on the lands, peoples, and societies that have participated in large-scale historical processes. By bringing a global perspective to the study of world history, we seek to offer an understanding of the past that places the contemporary world in meaningful historical context.

On the basis of a superficial inspection, *Traditions & Encounters* might look similar to several other textbooks that survey the world's past. Like other books, for example, *Traditions & Encounters* examines the historical development of societies in Asia, Europe, Africa, the Americas, and Oceania. Yet *Traditions & Encounters* differs from other works in two particularly important ways. First, it relies on a pair of prominent themes to bring a global perspective to the study of world history: it traces the historical development of individual societies in all world regions, and it also focuses attention systematically on interactions between peoples of different societies. Second, it organizes the human past into seven eras that represent distinct and coherent periods of global historical development.

THEMES: TRADITION AND ENCOUNTER

How is it possible to make sense of the entire human past? The study of world history is an exhilarating project that offers unparalleled opportunities to understand oneself and one's own society in relation to the larger world. Given the range of human diversity, however, world history also presents a daunting challenge. Human communities have adopted widely varying forms of political, social, and economic organization, and they have elaborated even more diverse cultural, religious, and philosophical legacies. Given the manifold diversity of human societies, it might seem that masses of unrelated detail threaten to swamp any effort to deal with all the world's history.

In this book we concentrate on two main themes—tradition and encounter—that help to bring order to world history. These two themes bring focus to some of the most important features of human experience on the earth. In combination, they account for much of the historical development of human societies.

The theme of tradition draws attention to the formation, maintenance, and sometimes collapse of individual societies. From their earliest days on earth, human groups have generated distinctive political, social, economic, and cultural traditions that have guided affairs in their own societies. Some of these traditions arose and disappeared relatively quickly, while others influenced human affairs over the centuries and millennia, sometimes down to the present day. Thus one of our principal concerns in this book is to examine the development of the diverse political, social, economic, and cultural traditions that have shaped the lives and experiences of the world's various peoples. Individual chapters explore the traditions that different peoples have relied on to organize and sustain societies in Asia, Europe, Africa, the Americas, and Oceania. Emphasis falls especially on the large, densely populated, complex, city-based societies that have most deeply influenced world affairs for the past six thousand years, but smaller and less powerful societies also receive their share of attention. This third edition of *Traditions & Encounters* draws on recent scholarship to offer updated and enhanced understanding of the world's individual societies.

While elaborating distinctive political, social, economic, and cultural traditions to organize their affairs, the world's peoples have also interacted regularly with one another since the earliest days of human history. The theme of encounter directs attention to communications, interactions, networks, and exchanges that have linked individual societies to their neighbors and others in the larger world. By systematically examining encounters among peoples of different societies, we draw attention to processes of cross-cultural interaction that have been some of the most effective agents of change in all of world history. In the form of mass migrations, campaigns of imperial expansion, long-distance trade, diffusions of food crops, the spread of infectious and contagious diseases, transfers of technological skills, and the spread of religious and cultural traditions, these interactions have profoundly influenced the experiences of individual societies and the development of the world as a whole. Thus, while presenting a wide-ranging discussion of individual societies and their traditions, this book also devotes considerable attention to the many and varied forms of interaction that have linked the fortunes of peoples from different societies. Many of the book's chapters also examine the large-scale structures of transportation, communication, and exchange that supported interactions among the world's peoples. Just as it updates treatments of individual societies, this third edition of *Traditions & Encounters* also draws on recent scholarship to enhance discussions of encounters and focus attention more clearly than before on processes of cross-cultural interaction.

ORGANIZATION: SEVEN ERAS OF GLOBAL HISTORY

While relying on the themes of tradition and encounter to bring the diversity of world history into focus, we also seek to bring about improved understanding of the world's development through time by organizing it into seven eras of global history. These eras, treated successively in the seven parts of this book, represent coherent epochs that form the larger architecture of world history as we see it. The seven eras do not reflect the particular experience of any single society so much as the common experiences of all societies participating in processes of cross-cultural interaction. Thus our seven eras of global history owe their coherence particularly to patterns in the networks of transportation, communication, and exchange that have linked peoples of different societies at different times in the past. Even in ancient times these networks supported interactions that shaped the experiences of peoples from different lands, and with the development of increasingly effective technologies of transportation and communication, interactions have grown more frequent, systematic, and intense over time. By studying the world's peoples in the framework of the seven eras of global history, we seek to offer meaningful comparisons between different societies and also to highlight the role of cross-cultural interactions in shaping the experiences of individual societies and influencing the development of the world as a whole.

Thus from the beginning to the end of this book we focus on the twin themes of tradition and encounter, which in combination go a long way toward accounting for the historical development of the human species on planet earth, and we situate the experiences of individual societies in their larger regional, continental, hemispheric, and global contexts. By bringing a global perspective to the study of humanity's common historical experience, we seek to offer a vision of the past that is both meaningful and appropriate for the interdependent world of contemporary times. We hope that *Traditions & Encounters* will enable readers to understand the development of human societies through time and also to place the contemporary world in its proper historical context.

CHANGES FOR THE THIRD EDITION

In preparing this third edition of *Traditions & Encounters*, we have paid close attention to recent scholarship that has transformed historians' understanding of the global past—sometimes dramatically so. This effort has resulted in revised, updated, and expanded treatments of societies in all world regions. In addition to reflecting the best recent scholarship, we have also sought to enhance the book's global perspective by emphasizing historical comparisons and by bringing clearer focus to historical processes that have linked the world's peoples and societies. Thus we have reorganized the treatment of the early modern era (Part V) so as to integrate Russian experience more clearly into both

European history and world history. Similarly, we have reorganized the treatment of the twentieth century (Part VII) so as to explain more clearly the roles of developing societies in the modern world. This effort has led us to include a new chapter discussing nationalism and political identities in Asian, African, and Latin American lands (Chapter 36).

Two additional features that are new to this third edition of *Traditions & Encounters* also merit mention. First, we have added questions for reflection at the end of all the excerpts from primary sources in the "Sources from the Past" boxes. Second, we have included a new series of brief essays in "Contexts & Connections" boxes. These essays take a specific issue from an individual chapter as a point of departure, then venture widely through time and space in seeking to understand the larger contexts of particular historical experiences. We hope that both "Sources from the Past" boxes and "Contexts & Connections" essays will promote improved understanding of the world and its development through time.

TOOLS FOR THE STUDENT

McGraw-Hill's *Primary Source Investigator* (PSI) CD-ROM is bound into each copy of *Traditions & Encounters* text and provides students with instant access to hundreds of world history documents, images, artifacts, audio recordings, and videos. PSI helps students practice the art of "doing history" on a real archive of historical sources. Students follow the three basic steps of *Ask, Research,* and *Argue* to examine sources, take notes on them, and then save or print copies of the sources as evidence for their papers or presentations. After researching a particular theme, individual, or time period, students can use PSI's writing guide to walk them through the steps of developing a thesis, organizing their evidence, and supporting their conclusion.

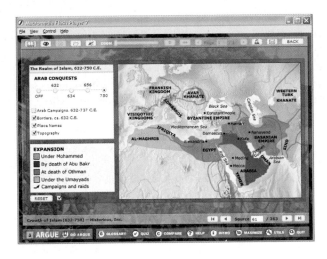

More than just a history or writing tool, the PSI is also a student study tool that contains 43 interactive maps, quiz questions, and an interactive glossary with audio pronunciation guide. The maps and glossary may also be found on the student website www.mhhe.com/bentley3 with additional supporting materials such as part timelines, chapter summaries, and multiple choice quizzes.

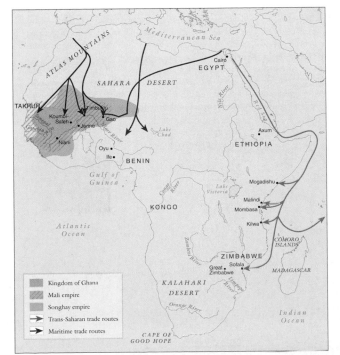

As we strengthened the substantive content of *Traditions & Encounters,* we also worked to produce a book more accessible and useful for readers. The entire map program has been revised for clarity, greater detail, and more topographical information. Any map with a global Online Learning Center (OLC) icon also has an interactive counterpart on the book's website and on the PSI CD.

The interactive maps offer a variety of learning functions. Students can use the maps to view topography, territories, borders, developing trends, and other topics. Visit the site at www.mhhe.com/bentley3.

New to this edition are *Contexts & Connections* essays which appear in about half of the chapters. Each essay highlights historical subjects with interesting links across different geographic regions and eras. Many of these essays utilize objects of material culture as clues to discerning the past or to examining historical issues in detail with a view toward present-day relevance. They were written to capture the imagination, to bring the past closer to the present, and to provide a basis for classroom discussion.

Contexts & Connections

The World's First Coins

When relating the story of Cyrus's victory over King Croesus of Lydia, the Greek historian Herodotus offered a description of Croesus's kingdom. He characterized the Lydians as an exceptionally prosperous people. "So far as we have any knowledge," he reported, "they were the first nation to introduce the use of gold and silver coin, and the first who sold goods by retail." The king himself had a reputation as the wealthiest person in the world—a view reflected in the popular expression that particularly wealthy individuals are "as rich as Croesus." The wealth of the Lydian kingdom arose partly from use of the coins that Herodotus mentioned.

Mesopotamian and Egyptian peoples had long used silver and gold fashioned into rings, rods, and ingots as currency to facilitate exchanges of goods. It was much simpler to purchase goods for a certain quantity of silver than to barter goods directly for one another. Yet silver and gold currencies had their own problems. Careful merchants had to weigh tokens in their scales to make sure they came to the right amount. Even then it was possible for unscrupulous individuals to dilute the silver or gold content of a token by alloying it with some cheaper metal.

Beginning about 640 B.C.E. the kings of Lydia issued the first coins of precisely measured metal bearing guarantees of their value. They minted their early coins from electrum, a rare but naturally occurring alloy of gold and silver found in local rivers. Croesus later minted coins of pure gold and silver. These coins immediately caught the attention of Lydia's trading partners, and officially spon- sored coins were soon in use throughout the eastern Mediterranean region. (Chinese rulers independently is- sued bronze coins about the same time.)

The availability of officially minted coins with guaranteed values provided a tremendous boost to trade. The earliest beneficiary was the kingdom of Lydia itself, which drew crowds of foreign merchants to vast markets in the capital at Sardis. There Lydians traded merchandise that they obtained from Mesopotamia, Egypt, and the eastern Mediterranean region, as well as the highly prized perfumes that were the most famous products of Lydian manufacturers. This bustling trade in large, officially sponsored marketplaces is what Herodotus had in mind when he said the Lydians were "the first who sold goods by retail." In later centuries, Greeks, Romans, and others made use of their own minted coins as they built commercial empires throughout the Mediterranean basin.

Coins did not entirely displace other currencies: in various world regions, cattle, cowry shells, cacao beans, and other items functioned as mediums of exchange long after the invention of coins. Even in regions where they were in common use, coins have not always dominated economic exchange: after the invention of printed paper money, and especially after the more recent development of electronic currency, coins increasingly became impractical except for small-scale transactions. Meanwhile, however, for two millennia and more, officially minted coins lubricated trade and facilitated economic transactions throughout much of the world.

GLOSSARY AND PRONUNCIATION KEY

AH *a* sound, as in *car, father*
IH short *i* sound, as in *fit, bit, mirror*
OO long *u* sound, as in *mte, tool, crew*
UH short *u* sound, as in *up, cut, color*
A short *a* sound, as in *ap, fat, parrot*
EE long *e* sound, as in *cren, meet, money*
OH long *o* sound, as in *open, po, tone*
EH short *e* sound, as in *ten, elf, berry*
AY long *a* sound, as in *ape, date, play*
EYE long *i* sound, as in *ice, high, bite*
OW diphthong *a* sound, as in *cow, how, low*
AW diphthong *a* sound, as in *awful, paw, law*

Note on emphasis: Syllables in capital letters receive the accent. If there is no syllable in capitals, then all syllables get equal accent.

Abbasid (ah-BAH-sihd) Cosmopolitan Arabic dynasty (750–1258) that replaced the Umayyads; founded by Abu al-Abbas and reached its peak under Harun al-Rashid.
Abolitionism Antislavery movement.
Absolutism Political philosophy that stressed the divine right theory of kingship; the French king Louis XIV was the classic example.
Abu Bakr (ah-BOO BAHK-uhr) First caliph after the death of Muhammad.
Achaemenid empire (ah-KEE-muh-nid) First great Persian empire (558–330 B.C.E.), which began under Cyrus and reached its peak under Darius.
Aeshylus (ES-kuh-luhs) Greek tragedian, author of the *Oresteia*.
Age grades Bantu institution in which individuals of roughly the same age carried out communal tasks appropriate for that age.
Ahimsa (uh-HIM-suh) Jain term for the principle of nonviolence to other living things or their souls.
Ahmosis (AH-moh-sis) Egyptian pharaoh (c. 1500 B.C.E.), founder of the New Kingdom.
Ahura Mazda (uh-HOORE-uh MAHZ-duh) Main god of Zoroastrianism who

represented truth and goodness and was perceived to be in an eternal struggle with the malign spirit Angra Mainyu.
Al-Andalus (al-ANN-duh-luhs) Islamic Spain.
Allah (AH-lah) God of the monotheistic religion of Islam.
Ali'i nui Hawaiian class of high chiefs.
Amon-Re (AH-muhn RAY) Egyptian god, combination of the sun god Re and the air god Amon.
Angkor (AHN-kohr) Southeast Asian Khmer kingdom (889–1432) that was centered around the temple cities of Angkor Thom and Angkor Wat.
Anti-Semitism Term coined in late nineteenth century that was associated with a prejudice against Jews and the political, social, and economic actions taken against them.
Antonianism African syncretic religion, founded by Dona Beatriz, that taught that Jesus Christ was a black African man and that heaven was for Africans.
Apartheid (ah-PAHR-teyed) South African system of "separateness" that was implemented in 1948 and that maintained the black majority in a position of political, social, and economic subordination.
Appeasement British and French policy in the 1930s that tried to maintain peace in Europe in the face of German aggression by making concessions.
Arianism Early Christian heresy that centered around teaching of Arius (250–336 C.E.) and contained the belief that Jesus was a mortal human being and not coeternal with God; Arianism was the focus of Council of Nicaea.
Artha Hindu concept for the pursuit of economic well-being and honest prosperity.
Arthashastra (AR-thah-sha-strah) Ancient Indian political treatise from the time of Chandragupta Maurya; its authorship was traditionally ascribed to Kautalya, and it stressed that war was inevitable.

Aryans (AIR-ee-anns) Indo-European tribes who settled in India after 1500 B.C.E.; their union with indigenous Dravidians formed the basis of Hinduism.
Association of Southeast Asian Nations (ASEAN.) Regional organization established in 1967 by Thailand, Malaysia, Singapore, Indonesia, and the Philippines; the organization was designed to promote economic progress and political stability; it later became a free-trade zone.
Assyrians (uh-SEAR-ee-uhns) Southwest Asian people who built an empire that reached its height during the eighth and seventh centuries B.C.E.; it was known for a powerful army and a well-structured state.
Astrolabe Navigational instrument for determining latitude.
Aten Monotheistic god of Egyptian pharaoh Akhenaten (r. 1353–1335 B.C.E.) and a very early example of monotheism.
Audiencias Spanish courts in Latin America.
Australopithecus (ah-strah-loh-PITH-uh-kuhs) "Southern ape," oldest known ancestor of humans; it lived from around four million down to around one million years ago, and it could walk on hind legs, freeing up hands for use of simple tools.
Austronesians People who as early as 2000 B.C.E. began to explore and settle islands of the Pacific Ocean basin.
Avesta Book that contain the holy writings of Zoroastrianism.
Aztec empire Central American empire constructed by the Mexica and expanded greatly during the fifteenth century during the reigns of Itzcoatl and Motecuzoma I.
Axum African kingdom centered in Ethiopia that became an early and lasting center of Coptic Christianity.
Balfour Declaration British declaration from 1917 that supported the creation of a Jewish homeland in Palestine.
Bantu (BAN-too) African peoples who originally lived in the area of present-day Nigeria; around 2000 B.C.E. they

We have taken the book's glossary and pronunciation guide one step further by rendering it interactive. A multimedia version of this glossary is available on the book's website www.mhhe.com/bentley3 and on the *Primary Source Investigator* CD-ROM packaged with the book. Students and teachers can now listen to hard-to-pronounce words, and students can switch to the flashcard feature to quiz themselves on important terms. For reminders of these study tools, new PSI and OLC icons appear at the end of each chapter.

PART I

THE EARLY COMPLEX SOCIETIES, 3500 TO 500 B.C.E.

For thousands of years after the emergence of the human species, human beings lived in tiny communities with no permanent home. They formed compact, mobile societies, each consisting of a few dozen people, and they traveled regularly in pursuit of game and edible plants. From the vantage point of the fast-moving present, that long first stage of human experience on the earth might seem slow paced and almost changeless. Yet intelligence set human beings apart from the other members of the animal kingdom and enabled human groups to invent tools and techniques that enhanced their ability to exploit the natural environment. Human beings gradually emerged as the most dynamic species of the animal kingdom, and even in remote prehistoric times they altered the face of the earth to suit their needs.

Yet humans' early exploitation of the earth's resources was only a prologue to the extraordinary developments that followed the introduction of agriculture. About twelve thousand years ago human groups began to experiment with agriculture, and it soon became clear that cultivation provided a larger and more reliable food supply than did foraging. Groups that turned to agriculture experienced rapid population growth, and they settled in permanent communities. The world's first cities, which appeared about six thousand years ago, quickly came to dominate political and economic affairs in their respective regions. Indeed, since the appearance of cities, the earth and its creatures have fallen progressively under the influence of complex societies organized around cities.

The term *complex society* refers to a form of large-scale social organization that emerged in several parts of the ancient world. Early complex societies all depended on robust agricultural economies in which cultivators produced more food than they needed for their own subsistence. This agricultural surplus enabled many individuals to congregate in urban settlements, where they devoted their time and energy to specialized tasks other than food production. Political authorities, government officials, military experts, priests, artisans, craftsmen, and merchants all lived off this surplus agricultural production. Through their organization of political, economic, social, and cultural affairs, complex societies had the capacity to shape the lives of large populations over extensive territories.

During the centuries from 3500 to 500 B.C.E., complex societies arose independently in several widely scattered regions of the world, including Mesopotamia, Egypt, northern India, China, Mesoamerica, and the central Andean region of South America. Most complex societies sprang from small agricultural communities situated either in river valleys or near sources of water that cultivators could tap to irrigate their crops. All established political authorities, built states with formal governmental institutions, collected surplus agricultural production in the form of taxes or tribute, and distributed it to those who worked at tasks other than agriculture. Complex societies

Effective pedagogical features from the first edition have been retained. Each of the book's seven parts opens with an introduction that outlines the themes running through all the chapters in that part. This information creates a strong framework for understanding the details of individual chapters.

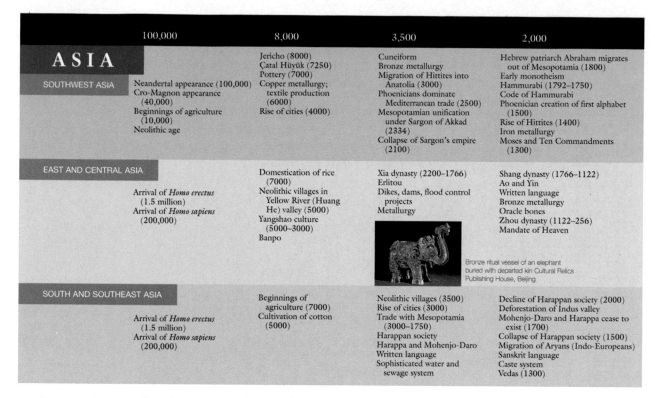

	100,000	8,000	3,500	2,000
ASIA				
SOUTHWEST ASIA	Neandertal appearance (100,000) Cro-Magnon appearance (40,000) Beginnings of agriculture (10,000) Neolithic age	Jericho (8000) Çatal Hüyük (7250) Pottery (7000) Copper metallurgy; textile production (6000) Rise of cities (4000)	Cuneiform Bronze metallurgy Migration of Hittites into Anatolia (3000) Phoenicians dominate Mediterranean trade (2500) Mesopotamian unification under Sargon of Akkad (2334) Collapse of Sargon's empire (2100)	Hebrew patriarch Abraham migrates out of Mesopotamia (1800) Early monotheism Hammurabi (1792–1750) Code of Hammurabi Phoenician creation of first alphabet (1500) Rise of Hittites (1400) Iron metallurgy Moses and Ten Commandments (1300)
EAST AND CENTRAL ASIA	Arrival of *Homo erectus* (1.5 million) Arrival of *Homo sapiens* (200,000)	Domestication of rice (7000) Neolithic villages in Yellow River (Huang He) valley (5000) Yangshao culture (5000–3000) Banpo	Xia dynasty (2200–1766) Erlitou Dikes, dams, flood control projects Metallurgy	Shang dynasty (1766–1122) Ao and Yin Written language Bronze metallurgy Oracle bones Zhou dynasty (1122–256) Mandate of Heaven
SOUTH AND SOUTHEAST ASIA	Arrival of *Homo erectus* (1.5 million) Arrival of *Homo sapiens* (200,000)	Beginnings of agriculture (7000) Cultivation of cotton (5000)	Neolithic villages (3500) Rise of cities (3000) Trade with Mesopotamia (3000–1750) Harappan society Harappa and Mohenjo-Daro Written language Sophisticated water and sewage system	Decline of Harappan society (2000) Deforestation of Indus valley Mohenjo-Daro and Harappa cease to exist (1700) Collapse of Harappan society (1500) Migration of Aryans (Indo-Europeans) Sanskrit language Caste system Vedas (1300)

Bronze ritual vessel of an elephant buried with departed kin Cultural Relics Publishing House, Beijing

Part opening timelines have been revised and are now available with each book as a mini-poster.

Each chapter opens with a story of individual experiences that draw students into the chapter and illustrate its main themes.

CHAPTER 2

EARLY SOCIETIES IN SOUTHWEST ASIA AND THE INDO-EUROPEAN MIGRATIONS

By far the best-known individual of ancient Mesopotamian society was a man named Gilgamesh. According to historical sources, Gilgamesh was the fifth king of the city of Uruk. He ruled about 2750 B.C.E.—for a period of 126 years, according to one semilegendary source—and he led his community in its conflicts with Kish, a nearby city that was the principal rival of Uruk. Historical sources record very little additional detail about Gilgamesh's life and deeds.

But Gilgamesh was a figure of Mesopotamian mythology and folklore as well as history. He was the subject of numerous poems and legends, and Mesopotamian bards made him the central figure in a cycle of stories known collectively as the *Epic of Gilgamesh*. As a figure of legend, Gilgamesh became the greatest hero figure of ancient Mesopotamia. According to the stories, the gods granted Gilgamesh a perfect body and endowed him with superhuman strength and courage. He was "the man to whom all things were known," a supremely wise individual who "saw mysteries and knew secret things." The legends declare that he constructed the massive city walls of Uruk as well as several of the city's magnificent temples to Mesopotamian deities.

The stories that make up the *Epic of Gilgamesh* recount the adventures of this hero and his cherished friend Enkidu as they sought fame. They killed an evil monster, rescued Uruk from a ravaging bull, and matched wits with the gods. In spite of their heroic deeds, Enkidu offended the gods and fell under a sentence of death. His loss profoundly affected Gilgamesh, who sought for some means to cheat death and gain eternal life. He eventually found a magical plant that had the power to confer immortality, but a serpent stole the plant and carried it away, forcing Gilgamesh to recognize that death is the ultimate fate of all human beings. Thus, while focusing on the activities of Gilgamesh and Enkidu, the stories explored themes of friendship, loyalty, ambition, fear of death, and longing for immortality. In doing so they reflected the interests and concerns of the complex, urban-based society that had recently emerged in Mesopotamia.

Productive agricultural economies supported the development of the world's first complex societies, in which sizable numbers of people lived in cities and extended their political, social, economic, and cultural influence over large regions. The earliest urban societies so far known emerged during the early fourth millennium B.C.E. in southwest Asia, particularly in Mesopotamia.

As people congregated in cities, they needed to find ways to resolve disputes—sometimes between residents within individual settlements, other times between

THE QUEST FOR ORDER
Mesopotamia: "The Land between the Rivers"
The Course of Empire
The Later Mesopotamian Empires

THE FORMATION OF A COMPLEX SOCIETY AND SOPHISTICATED CULTURAL TRADITIONS
Economic Specialization and Trade
The Emergence of a Stratified Patriarchal Society
The Development of Written Cultural Traditions

THE BROADER INFLUENCE OF MESOPOTAMIAN SOCIETY
Hebrews, Israelites, and Jews
The Phoenicians

THE INDO-EUROPEAN MIGRATIONS
Indo-European Origins
Indo-European Expansion and Its Effects

31

Sources from the Past

The Wealth and Commerce of Constantinople

The Spanish rabbi Benjamin of Tudela traveled throughout Europe, north Africa, and southwest Asia between 1165 and 1173 C.E. He may have ventured as far as India, and he mentioned both India and China in his travel account. His main purpose was to record the conditions of Jewish communities, but he also described the many lands and about three hundred cities that he visited. His travels took place during an era of political decline for the Byzantine empire, yet he still found Constantinople a flourishing and prosperous city.

The circumference of the city of Constantinople is eighteen miles; half of it is surrounded by the sea, and half by land, and it is situated upon two arms of the sea, one coming from the sea of Russia [the Black Sea], and one from the sea of Sepharad [the Mediterranean].

All sorts of merchants come here from the land of Babylon, from the land of Shinar [Mesopotamia], from Persia, Media [western Iran], and all the sovereignty of the land of Egypt, from the land of Canaan [Palestine], and the empire of Russia, from Hungary, Patzinakia [Ukraine], Khazaria [southern Russia], and the land of Lombardy [northern Italy] and Sepharad [Spain].

Constantinople is a busy city, and merchants come to it from every country by sea or land, and there is none like it in the world except Baghdad, the great city of Islam. In Constantinople is the church of Hagia Sophia, and the seat of the pope of the Greeks, since Greeks do not obey the pope of Rome. There are also as many churches as there are days of the year. . . . And in this church [Hagia Sophia] there are pillars of gold and silver, and lamps of silver and gold more than a man can count.

Close to the walls of the palace is also a place of amusement belonging to the emperor, which is called the Hippodrome, and every year on the anniversary of the birth of Jesus the emperor gives a great entertain-

ment there. And in that place men from all the races of the world come before the emperor and empress with jugglery and without jugglery, and they introduce lions, leopards, bears, and wild asses, and they engage them in combat with one another; and the same thing is done with birds. No entertainment like this is to be found in any other land. . . .

From every part of the Byzantine empire tribute is brought here every year, and they fill strongholds with garments of silk, purple, and gold. Like unto these storehouses and this wealth there is nothing in the whole world to be found. It is said that the tribute of the city amounts every year to 20,000 gold pieces, derived both from the rents of shops and markets and from the tribute of merchants who enter by sea or land.

The Greek inhabitants are very rich in gold and precious stones, and they go clothed in garments of silk and gold embroidery, and they ride horses and look like princes. Indeed, the land is very rich in all cloth stuffs and in bread, meat, and wine.

Wealth like that of Constantinople is not to be found in the whole world. Here also are men learned in all the books of the Greeks, and they eat and drink, every man under his vine and his fig-tree.

SOURCE: Benjamin of Tudela. *The Itinerary of Benjamin of Tudela.* Trans. by M. N. Adler. London: H. Frowde, 1907. (Translation slightly modified.)

How is it possible to account for the prosperity that Benjamin of Tudela found in Constantinople?

The Sources from the Past boxes bring the past to life, spotlighting significant primary source documents relevant to the chapter, such as poems, journal accounts, religious writings, and letters. Introductions place the documents in context and explain their significance; new thought provoking questions prompt readers to contextualize and think critically about key issues raised in the document.

Marginal notes highlight key terms, events, and concepts as they appear within the narrative.

Muhammad's time. Although he was not deeply knowledgeable about Judaism or Christianity, Muhammad had a basic understanding of both faiths. He may even have traveled by caravan to Syria, where he would certainly have dealt with Jewish and Christian merchants.

Muhammad's Spiritual Transformation

About 610 C.E., as he approached age forty, Muhammad underwent a profound spiritual experience that transformed his life and left a deep mark on world history. His experience left him with the convictions that in all the world there was only one true deity, Allah ("God"), that he ruled the universe, that idolatry and the recognition of other gods amounted to wickedness, and that Allah would soon bring his judgment on the world, rewarding the righteous and punishing the wicked. Muhammad experienced visions, which he understood as messages or revelations from Allah, delivered through the archangel Gabriel (also recognized by Jews and Christians as a special messenger of God), instructing him to explain his faith to others. He did not set out to construct a new religion by combining elements of Arab, Jewish, and Christian beliefs. In light of his cultural context, however, it is not surprising that he shared numerous specific beliefs with Jews and Christians—and indeed also with Zoroastrians, whose views had profoundly influenced the development of both Judaism and Christianity. In any case, in accordance with instructions transmitted to him by Gabriel, Muhammad began to expound his faith to his family and close friends. Gradually, others showed interest in his message, and by about 620 C.E. a zealous and expanding minority of Mecca's citizenry had joined his circle.

The Quran

Muhammad originally presented oral recitations of the revelations he received during his visions. As the Islamic community grew, his followers prepared written texts of his teachings. During the early 650s devout Muslims compiled these written versions of Muhammad's revelations and issued them as the Quran ("recitation"), the holy book of Islam. A work of magnificent poetry, the Quran communicates in powerful and moving terms Muhammad's understanding of Allah and his relation to the world, and it serves as the definitive authority for Islamic religious doctrine and social organization.

Apart from the Quran, several other sources have provided moral and religious guidance for the Islamic community. Most important after the Quran itself are traditions known as *hadith*, which include sayings attributed to Muhammad and accounts of the prophet's deeds. Several collections of *hadith* appeared between the ninth and eleventh century C.E., and Muslim scholars have often taken them as guides for interpretation of the Quran. Regarded as less authoritative than the Quran and the *hadith*, but still important as inspirations for Islamic thought, were early works describing social and legal customs, biographies of Muhammad, and pious commentaries on the Quran.

Muhammad's Migration to Medina

Conflict at Mecca

The growing popularity of Muhammad's preaching brought him into conflict with the ruling elites at Mecca. Conflict centered on religious issues. Muhammad's insistence that Allah was the only divine power in the universe struck many polytheistic Arabs as offensive and dangerous as well, since it disparaged long-recognized deities and spirits thought to wield influence over human affairs. The tensions also had a personal dimension. Mecca's ruling elites, who were also the city's wealthiest merchants, took it as a personal affront and a threat to their position when Muhammad denounced greed as moral wickedness that Allah would punish.

Muhammad's attack on idolatry also represented an economic threat to those who owned and profited from the many shrines to deities that attracted merchants

A concise chronological table summarizes the critical events covered in the chapter.

CHRONOLOGY	
589–618	Sui dynasty (China)
602–664	Life of Xuanzang
604–618	Reign of Sui Yangdi
618–907	Tang dynasty (China)
627–649	Reign of Tang Taizong
669–935	Silla dynasty (Korea)
710–794	Nara period (Japan)
755–757	An Lushan's rebellion
794–1185	Heian period (Japan)
875–884	Huang Chao's rebellion
960–1279	Song dynasty (China)
960–976	Reign of Song Taizu
1024	First issuance of government-sponsored paper money
1130–1200	Life of Zhu Xi
1185–1333	Kamakura period (Japan)
1336–1573	Muromachi period (Japan)

A paragraph summary at the end of each chapter reinforces the chapter's key points, making student review easier.

The revival of centralized imperial rule in China had profound implications for all of east Asia and indeed for most of the eastern hemisphere. When the Sui and Tang dynasties imposed their authority throughout China, they established a powerful state that guided political affairs throughout east Asia. Tang armies extended Chinese influence to Korea, Vietnam, and central Asia. They did not invade Japan, but the impressive political organization of China prompted the islands' rulers to imitate Tang examples. Moreover, the Sui and Tang dynasties laid a strong political foundation for rapid economic development. Chinese society prospered throughout the postclassical era, partly because of technological and industrial innovation. Tang and Song prosperity touched all of China's neighbors, since it encouraged surging commerce in east Asia. Chinese silk, porcelain, and lacquerware were prized commodities among trading peoples from southeast Asia to east Africa. Chinese inventions such as paper, printing, gunpowder, and the magnetic compass found a place in societies throughout the eastern hemisphere as they diffused across the silk roads and sea lanes. The postclassical era was an age of religious as well as commercial and technological exchanges: Nestorian Christians, Zoroastrians, Manichaeans, and Muslims all maintained communities in Tang China, and Buddhism became the most popular religious faith in all of east Asia. During the postclassical era, Chinese social organization and economic dynamism helped to sustain interactions between the peoples of the eastern hemisphere on an unprecedented scale.

Each chapter concludes with a For Further Reading section that contains a list and brief description of the most important books available about topics discussed in the chapter. This list can help students get started with research projects or follow up on subjects that they find especially interesting.

FOR FURTHER READING

Kenneth Ch'en. *Buddhism in China: A Historical Survey.* Princeton, 1964. A clear and detailed account by an eminent scholar.

Hugh R. Clark. *Community, Trade, and Networks: Southern Fujian Province from the Third to the Thirteenth Century.* Cambridge, 1991. Excellent scholarly study exploring the transformation of a region by trade and market forces.

Peter Duus. *Feudalism in Japan.* 2nd ed. New York, 1976. A brief survey of early Japanese political history, concentrating on the Kamakura and Muromachi periods.

Patricia Buckley Ebrey. *Chinese Civilization: A Sourcebook.* 2nd ed. New York, 1993. A splendid collection of documents in translation.

Patricia Buckley Ebrey and Peter N. Gregory, eds. *Religion and Society in T'ang and Sung China.* Honolulu, 1993. Important collection of scholarly essays dealing with the early entry of Buddhism in China.

Mark Elvin. *The Pattern of the Chinese Past.* Stanford, 1973. A brilliant analysis of Chinese history, concentrating particularly on economic, social, and technological themes.

Jacques Gernet. *Buddhism in Chinese Society: An Economic History from the Fifth to the Tenth Century.* Trans. by F. Verellen. New York, 1995. An important study emphasizing the economic and social significance of Buddhist monasteries in the Chinese countryside.

———. *Daily Life in China on the Eve of the Mongol Invasion, 1250–1276.* Trans. by H. M. Wright. New York, 1962. Rich portrait of Southern Song China, emphasizing social history.

Ivan Morris. *The World of the Shining Prince: Court Life in Ancient Japan.* Harmondsworth, 1964. Vividly reconstructs the court life of Heian Japan.

Joseph Needham. *Science in Traditional China.* Cambridge, Mass., 1981. Essays on the history of Chinese science and technology.

Edward H. Schafer. *The Golden Peaches of Samarkand: A Study of T'ang Exotics.* Berkeley, 1963. Deals with relations between China and central Asian lands during the Tang dynasty.

———. *The Vermilion Bird: T'ang Images of the South.* Berkeley, 1967. Evocative study of relations between China and Vietnam during the Tang dynasty.

SUPPLEMENTS

The supplements listed here may accompany *Traditions & Encounters: A Global Perspective on the Past*. Please contact your local McGraw-Hill representative for details concerning policies, prices, and availability, as some restrictions may apply.

For the Instructor

- **The Instructor's Resource CD-ROM (or IRCD)** contains several instructor tools in one location. For lecture preparation, teachers will find an Instructor's Manual and PowerPoint samples by chapter with over 100 images, maps, graphs, and tables. For quizzes and tests, the IRCD also contains a Test Bank and Computerized Test Bank.
- **The Instructor's Manual and Test Bank** have both been heavily revised for clarity and consistency. The Instructor's Manual was prepared by Rose Mary Sheldon and Timothy Dowling at the Virginia Military Institute. The Test Bank was prepared by Eric Osborne and Douglas Harmon at the Virginia Military Institute.
- **A Computerized Test Bank** is available on the Instructor's Resource CD-ROM in Brownstone Diploma for Windows and Macintosh. This version of the Test Bank allows instructors to customize each test to suit any course syllabus.
- **A Set of Overhead Transparencies** is available to adopters of the book. It contains over 120 maps, charts, and illustrations, organized by chapter.
- **The Online Learning Center for Instructors** at www.mhhe.com/bentley3. At the homepage for the text-specific website, instructors will find a series of online tools to meet a wide range of classroom needs. The Instructor's Manual, PowerPoint presentations, and blank maps can be downloaded by instructors, but are password-protected to prevent tampering. Instructors can create web-based homework assignments or classroom activities by linking to the student's side of the Online Learning Center. Instructors can also create an interactive course syllabus using McGraw-Hill's PageOut (www.mhhe.com/pageout).
- **PageOut** at www.mhhe.com/pageout. On the PageOut website, instructors can create their own course websites. PageOut requires no prior knowledge of HTML, no long hours of coding, and no design skills on the instructor's part. Simply plug the course information into a template and click on one of sixteen designs. The process takes no time at all and leaves instructors with a professionally designed website. Powerful features include an interactive course syllabus that lets instructors post content and links, an online gradebook, lecture notes, bookmarks, and even a discussion board where instructors and students can discuss course-related topics.
- **Videos** on topics in world history is available through the Films for the Humanities and Sciences collection. Contact your local McGraw-Hill sales representative for further information.
- **Readers.** McGraw-Hill offers a number of readers that complement this text. Visit our online catalogue at www.mhhe.com.
- **Advanced Placement Instructor's Manual.** Written by Ane Lintvedt, Bard Keeler, and Joan Arno, the Instructor's Manual for Advanced Placement teachers contains lecture topics, teaching strategies, group activities, world history skills, and habits of mind specifically tailored around the six themes. Visit the book website at www.mhhe.com/bentley3 for more information.
- **Classroom Performance System (CPS).** The Classroom Performance System brings ultimate interactivity to *Traditions & Encounters*. CPS is a wireless response

system that gives you immediate feedback from every student in the class. With CPS you can ask subjective and objective questions during your lecture, prompting every student to respond with their individual, wireless response pad, and providing you with instant results. A complete CPS Tutorial is at www.einstruction.com.

For the Student

- **The Online Learning Center for Students** at www.mhhe.com/bentley3 provides students with a wide range of tools for students to use in testing their knowledge of the book. It includes chapter overviews, more new interactive maps, multiple choice and essay quizzes, matching and identification games, as well as primary source indexes for further research. This new edition also contains a new feature based on the book's "Contexts & Connections" box, an interactive timeline, and an interactive glossary with an audio pronunciation guide.
- Each chapter of the **Student Study Guide with Map Exercises** includes a synopsis of the chapter, an outline, student quizzes, map identification exercises, primary source documents, and other resources to help students master the material covered in the text. New to this edition of the study guide are matching and sequencing exercises and group activities.
- **Map Workbooks** test students' knowledge of the geography relevant to each chapter. Exercises require students to fill in important items on a blank map or to answer questions by interpreting a completed map.
- *History and the Internet: A Guide* is a brief guide that explores the many ways that the World Wide Web facilitates the study of history. It also includes a history of the Internet, instructions for searching and navigating the Web, a glossary of Web jargon, and lists of significant websites in history.
- **PowerWeb: World History,** an online supplement, is a collection of readings delivered electronically, along with other tools for conducting research in history. In addition, student study tools, web research tips and exercises, and free access to the global content provider Factiva are included. A card with a password for accessing PowerWeb has been packaged free with the textbook.
- Two **After the Fact Interactive** units are available for use with *Traditions & Encounters:* "After the Fact Interactive: Tracing the Silk Roads" for volume 1, and "After the Fact Interactive: Envisioning the Atlantic World" for volume 2. These rich, visually appealing modules on CD-ROM allow students to be apprentice historians, examining a variety of multimedia primary source materials and constructing arguments based on their research.

A Brief Note on Usage

This book qualifies dates as B.C.E. ("Before the Common Era") or C.E. ("Common Era"). In practice, B.C.E. refers to the same epoch as B.C. ("Before Christ"), and C.E. refers to the same epoch as A.D. (*Anno Domini,* a Latin term meaning "in the year of the Lord"). As historical study becomes a global, multicultural enterprise, however, scholars increasingly prefer terminology that does not apply the standards of one society to all the others. Thus reference in this book to B.C.E. and C.E. reflects emerging scholarly convention concerning the qualification of historical dates.

Measurements of length and distance appear here according to the metric system, followed by their English-system equivalents in parentheses.

The book transliterates Chinese names and terms into English according to the *pinyin* system, which has largely displaced the more cumbersome Wade-Giles system. Transliteration of names and terms from other languages follows contemporary scholarly conventions.

ABOUT THE AUTHORS

Jerry H. Bentley is professor of history at the University of Hawai`i and editor of the *Journal of World History*. He has written extensively on the cultural history of early modern Europe and on cross-cultural interactions in world history. His research on the religious, moral, and political writings of the Renaissance led to the publication of *Humanists and Holy Writ: New Testament Scholarship in the Renaissance* (1983) and *Politics and Culture in Renaissance Naples* (1987). His more recent research has concentrated on global history and particularly on processes of cross-cultural interaction. His book *Old World Encounters: Cross-Cultural Contacts and Exchanges in Pre-Modern Times* (1993) studies processes of cultural exchange and religious conversion before modern times, and his pamphlet *Shapes of World History in Twentieth-Century Scholarship* (1996) discusses the historiography of world history. His current interests include processes of cross-cultural interaction and cultural exchange in modern times.

Herbert F. Ziegler is an associate professor of history at the University of Hawai`i. He has taught world history since 1980 and currently serves as director of the world history program at the University of Hawai`i. He also serves as book review editor of the *Journal of World History*. His interest in twentieth-century European social and political history led to the publication of *Nazi Germany's New Aristocracy* (1990). He is at present working on a study that explores from a global point of view the demographic trends of the past ten thousand years, along with their concomitant technological, economic, and social developments. His other current research project focuses on the application of complexity theory to a comparative study of societies and their internal dynamics.

ACKNOWLEDGMENTS

Many individuals have contributed to this book, and the authors take pleasure in recording deep thanks for all the comments, criticism, advice, and suggestions that helped to improve the work. The editorial team at McGraw-Hill did an outstanding job of keeping the authors focused on the project. Special thanks go to Lyn Uhl, Jon-David Hague, Katherine Bates, Jim Strandberg, Angela Kao, and Christina Gimlin, who provided crucial support by helping the authors work through difficult issues and solve the innumerable problems of content, style and organization that arise in any project to produce a history of the world. Many colleagues at the University of Hawai`i and elsewhere aided and advised the authors on matters of organization and composition. Mimi Henriksen was especially generous with her time and advice. Finally, we would like to express our appreciation for the advice of the following individuals who read and commented on the original manuscript and previous editions of this text:

Henry Abramson
Florida Atlantic University

Roger Adelson
Arizona State University

William Alexander
Norfolk State University

Alfred Andrea
University of Vermont

Ed Anson
University of Arkansas at Little Rock

Henry Antkiewicz
East Tennessee State University

Maria Arbelaez
University of Nebraska at Omaha

Peter Arnade
University of California—San Marcos

Karl Bahm
University of Wisconsin, Superior

Vaughan Baker
University of Louisiana at Lafayette

Ian Barrow
Middlebury College

Dixee Bartholomew-Feis
Buena Vista University

Guy Beckwith
Auburn University

Lynda Bell
University of California—Riverside

Norman Bennett
Boston University

Houri Berberian
California State University, Long Beach

Robert Blackey
California State University—San Bernardino

Wayne Bodle
Indiana University of Pennsylvania

Michael Brescia
State University of New York, Fredonia

Samuel Brunk
University of Texas, El Paso

Deborah Buffton
University of Wisconsin, La Crosse

Maureen Burgess
Colorado State University

Rainer Buschmann
Hawaii Pacific University

Sharon L. Bush
LeMoyne-Owen College

Antonio Calabria
University of Texas, San Antonio

Lewis Call
California Polytechnic State University, San Luis Obispo

Thomas Callahan, Jr.
Rider University

Alice-Catherine Carls
University of Tennessee at Martin

Kay Carr
Southern Illinois University

James Carroll
Iona College

Tom Carty
Springfield College

Bruce Castleman
San Diego State University

Douglas Catterall
Cameron University

Douglas Chambers
University of Southern Mississippi Hattiesburg

Choi Chatterjee
California State University, Los Angeles

Orazio Ciccarelli
University of Southern Mississippi

Andrew Clark
University of North Carolina at Wilmington

Hugh R. Clark
Usrinus College

Tim Coates
College of Charleston

Joan Coffey
Sam Houston State University

Daniel Connerton
North Adams State

Bruce Cruikshank
Hastings College

Graciella Cruz-Tara
Florida Atlantic University

Richard Cusimano
University of Louisiana at Lafayette

Ken Czech
St. Cloud State University

Touraj Daryaee
California State University, Fullerton

Jon Davidann
Hawaii Pacific University

Allen Davidson
Georgia Southern University

Brian Davies
University of Texas, San Antonio

John Davis
Radford University

Thomas Davis
Virginia Military Institute

Elisa Denlinger
University of Wisconsin, LaCrosse

Stewart Dippel
University of the Ozarks

Ross Doughty
Ursinus College

Cathi Dunkle
Mid-Michigan Community College

Ross Dunn
San Diego State University

Lane Earns
University of Wisconsin, Oshkosh

Christopher Ehret
University of California, Los Angeles

Laura Endicott
Southwestern Oklahoma State

Nancy Erickson
Erskine College

James Evans
Southeastern Community College

David Fahey
Miami University

Edward Farmer
University of Minnesota

James David Farthing
Oklahoma Baptist University

Lanny Fields
California State University—San Bernardino

Robert Frankle
University of Memphis

Bonnie Frederick
Washington State University

Karl Friday
University of Georgia

Amy Froide
University of Tennessee, Chattanooga

James Fuller
University of Indianapolis

Robert Gomez
San Antonio College

Paul Goodwin
University of Connecticut, Storrs

Matthew Gordon
Miami University of Ohio

Steve Gosch
University of Wisconsin, Eau Claire

Joseph Gowaskie
Rider University

John Haag
University of Georgia

Jeffrey Hamilton
Baylor University

Michael Hamm
Centre College

Travis Hanes III
University of North Carolina—Wilmington

Preston Hardy, Jr.
University of Tennessee, Martin

Russell Hart
Hawaii Pacific University

John Hayden
Southwestern Oklahoma State

Randolph Head
University of California, Riverside

Mary Hedberg
Saginaw Valley State University

Gerald Herman
Northeastern University

David Hertzel
Southwestern Oklahoma State

Udo Heyn
California State University—Los Angeles

Kathryn Hodgkinson
The Hockaday School

Peter Hoffenberg
University of Hawaii, Manoa

Blair Holmes
Brigham Young University

Mary Hovanec
Cuyahoga Community College

Scott Howlett
Saddleback Community College

Kailai Huang
Massachusetts College of Liberal Arts

J. Sanders Huguenin
University of Science and Arts of Oklahoma

Richard Hume
Washington State University

Carol Sue Humphrey
Oklahoma Baptist University

Alfred Hunt
State University of New York

Raymond Hylton
J. Sergeant Reynolds Community College

Phyllis Jestice
University of Southern Mississippi, Hattiesburg

Cheryl Johnson-Odim
Loyola University

Kimberley Jones-de Oliveira
Long Island University

Jonathan Judaken
University of Memphis

Alan Karras
University of California, Berkeley

Thomas Kay
Wheaton College

Charles Keller
Pittsburgh State University

Winston Kinsey
Appalachian State University

Cengiz Kirli
Purdue University

Paul Knoll
University of Southern California

Keith Knuuti
University of Hawaii, Hilo

Kenneth Koons
Virginia Military Institute

Cheryl Koos
California State University, Los Angeles

Cynthia Kosso
Northern Arizona University

Zoltan Kramer
Central Washington University

James Krokar
DePaul University

Glenn Lamar
University of Louisiana at Lafayette

Lisa Lane
Miracosta College

George Lankevich
Bronx Community College

Dennis Laumann
University of Memphis

Donald Layton
Indiana State University

Loyd Lee
SUNY-New Paltz

Jess LeVine
Brookdale Community College

Richard Lewis
St. Cloud State University

Yi Li
Tacoma Community College

Tony Litherland
Oklahoma Baptist University

James Long
Colorado State University

David Longfellow
Baylor University

Ben Lowe
Florida Atlantic University

Jared Ludlow
Brigham Young University, Hawaii

Herbert Luft
Pepperdine Univeristy

Lu Lui
University of Tennessee—Knoxville

Paul Madden
Hardin-Simmons University

Farid Mahdavi
San Diego State University

Dorothea A. L. Martin
Appalachian State University

Tracey Martin
Benedictine University

Ken Mason
Santa Monica College

Robert Mathews
Northshore Community College

William Maynard
Arkansas State University

Robert McCormick
University of South Carolina—Spartanburg

Jeff McEwen
Chattanooga State Technical College

Randall McGowen
University of Oregon

Adam McKeown
Columbia University

John McNeill
Georgetown University

James McSwain
Tuskegee University

Pamela McVay
Ursuline College

John Mears
Southern Methodist University

Daniel Miller
Calvin College

Monserrat Miller
Marshall University

Laura Mitchell
University of Texas, San Antonio

David Montgomery
Brigham Young University

Garth Montgomery
Radford University

George Moore
San Jose State University

Gloria Morrow
Morgan State University

David Mungello
Baylor University

Jeffrey Myers
Avila College

Peter Nayenga
Saint Cloud State University

Ruth Necheles-Jansyn
Long Island University

Marian Nelson
University of Nebraska

Janise Nuckols
Windward Community College

Deanne Nuwer
University of Southern Mississippi, Hattiesburg

Greg O'Brien
University of Southern Mississippi, Hattiesburg

Veena Talwar Oldenburg
Baruch College

Brian O'Neil
University of Southern Mississippi

Patricia O'Niell
Central Oregon Community College

Samuel Oppenheim
California State University, Stanislaus

John Oriji
California Polytechnic State University, San Luis Obispo

Anne Osborne
Rider University

James Overfield
University of Vermont

Keith Pacholl
State University of West Georgia

Melvin Page
East Tennessee State University

Loretta Pang
Kapiolani Community College

Jean Paquette
Lander University

Jotham Parsons
University of Delaware

Denis Paz
University of North Texas

Patrick Peebles
University of Missouri—Kansas City

Peter W. Petschauer
Appalachian State University

Phyllis Pobst
Arkansas State University

Jon Porter
Franklin College

Clifton Potter
Lynchburg College

David Price
Santa Fe Community College

Alfonso Quiroz
Bernard M. Baruch College, CUNY

Stephen Rapp
Georgia State University

Vera Reber
Shippensburg University

John Reid
Georgia Southern University

Thomas Renna
Saginaw Valley State University

Diana Reynolds
Point Loma Nazarene University

Douglas Reynolds
Georgia State University

Ira Rice
Ball State University

Cheryl Riggs
California State University—San Bernardino

John Ritter
Chemeketa Community College

Bill Rodner
Tidewater Community College, Virginia Beach

Dan Russell
Springfield College

Eric Rust
Baylor University

John Ryan
Kansas City Kansas Community College

William Schell
Murray State University

Daryl Schuster
University of Central Florida

Jane Scimeca
Brookdale Community College

Gary Scudder
Georgia Perimiter College

Kimberly Sebold
University of Maine, Presque Isle

Tara Sethia
California State University, Pomona

Howard Shealy
Kennesaw State College

Nancy Shoemaker
University of Connecticut, Storrs

MaryAnn Sison
*University of Southern Mississippi,
Hattiesburg*

Jonathan Skaff
Shippensburg University

David Smith
*California State Polytechnic
University, Pomona*

Michael Smith
Purdue University

Roland Spickerman
University of Detroit—Mercy

Wendy St. Jean
Springfield College

Michelle Staley
East Mississippi Community College

Tracy Steele
Sam Houston State University

Richard Steigmann-Gall
Kent State University, Kent

John Steinberg
Georgia Southern University

Heather Streets
Washington State University

Laichen Sun
California State University, Fullerton

Roshanna Sylvester
California State University, Fullerton

John Thornton
Millersville University

Robert Tignor
Princeton University

James Tueller
Brigham Young University, Hawaii

Kirk Tyvela
Ohio University

Sandra Wagner-Wright
University of Hawaii, Hilo

Jeff Wasserstrom
Indiana University—Bloomington

Watrous-Schlesinger
Washington State University, Pullman

Theodore Weeks
Southern Illinois University

Robert Wenke
University of Washington

Sally West
Truman State University

Sherri West
Brookdale Community College

Scott Wheeler
West Point

Joe Whitehorne
Lord Fairfax Community College

S. Jonathan Wiesen
*Southern Illinois University,
Carbondale*

Anne Will
Skagit Valley Community College

Richard Williams
Washington State University

Allen Wittenborn
San Diego State University

David Wittner
Utica College

William Wood
Point Loma Nazarene University

John Woods
University of Chicago

John Voll
Georgetown University

Anand Yang
University of Utah

Ping Yao
*California State University,
Los Angeles*

C. K. Yoon
James Madison University

Herb Zettl
Springfield College

THE EARLY COMPLEX SOCIETIES, 3500 TO 500 B.C.E.

For thousands of years after the emergence of the human species, human beings lived in tiny communities with no permanent home. They formed compact, mobile societies, each consisting of a few dozen people, and they traveled regularly in pursuit of game and edible plants. From the vantage point of the fast-moving present, that long first stage of human experience on the earth might seem slow paced and almost changeless. Yet intelligence set human beings apart from the other members of the animal kingdom and enabled human groups to invent tools and techniques that enhanced their ability to exploit the natural environment. Human beings gradually emerged as the most dynamic species of the animal kingdom, and even in remote prehistoric times they altered the face of the earth to suit their needs.

Yet humans' early exploitation of the earth's resources was only a prologue to the extraordinary developments that followed the introduction of agriculture. About twelve thousand years ago human groups began to experiment with agriculture, and it soon became clear that cultivation provided a larger and more reliable food supply than did foraging. Groups that turned to agriculture experienced rapid population growth, and they settled in permanent communities. The world's first cities, which appeared about six thousand years ago, quickly came to dominate political and economic affairs in their respective regions. Indeed, since the appearance of cities, the earth and its creatures have fallen progressively under the influence of complex societies organized around cities.

The term *complex society* refers to a form of large-scale social organization that emerged in several parts of the ancient world. Early complex societies all depended on robust agricultural economies in which cultivators produced more food than they needed for their own subsistence. This agricultural surplus enabled many individuals to congregate in urban settlements, where they devoted their time and energy to specialized tasks other than food production. Political authorities, government officials, military experts, priests, artisans, craftsmen, and merchants all lived off this surplus agricultural production. Through their organization of political, economic, social, and cultural affairs, complex societies had the capacity to shape the lives of large populations over extensive territories.

During the centuries from 3500 to 500 B.C.E., complex societies arose independently in several widely scattered regions of the world, including Mesopotamia, Egypt, northern India, China, Mesoamerica, and the central Andean region of South America. Most complex societies sprang from small agricultural communities situated either in river valleys or near sources of water that cultivators could tap to irrigate their crops. All established political authorities, built states with formal governmental institutions, collected surplus agricultural production in the form of taxes or tribute, and distributed it to those who worked at tasks other than agriculture. Complex societies traded enthusiastically with peoples who had access to scarce resources, and in an effort to ensure stability and economic productivity in neighboring regions, they often sought to extend their authority to surrounding territories.

Complex societies generated much more wealth than did hunting and gathering groups or small agricultural communities. Because of their high levels of organization, they also were able to preserve wealth and pass it along to their heirs. Some individuals and families accumulated great personal wealth, which enhanced their social status. When bequeathed to heirs and held within particular families, this accumulated wealth became the foundation for social distinctions. These societies developed different kinds of social distinctions, but all recognized several classes of people, including ruling elites, common people, and slaves. Some societies also recognized distinct classes of aristocrats, priests, merchants, artisans, free peasants, and semifree peasants.

All complex societies required cultivators and individuals of lower classes to support the more privileged members of society by paying taxes or tribute (often in the form of surplus agricultural production) and also by providing labor and military service. Cultivators often worked not only their own lands but also those belonging to the privileged classes. Individuals from the lower classes made up the bulk of their societies' armies and contributed the labor for large construction projects such as city walls, irrigation and water control systems, roads, temples, palaces, pyramids, and royal tombs.

The early complex societies also created sophisticated cultural traditions. Most of them either invented or borrowed a system of writing that made it possible to record information and store it for later use. They first used writing to keep political, administrative, and business records, but they soon expanded on these utilitarian applications and used writing to construct traditions of literature, learning, and reflection.

Cultural traditions took different forms in different complex societies. Some societies devoted resources to organized religions that sought to mediate between human communities and the gods, whereas others left religious observances largely in the hands of individual family groups. All of them paid close attention to the heavens, however, since they needed to gear their agricultural labors to the changing seasons.

All the complex societies organized systems of formal education that introduced intellectual elites to skills such as writing and astronomical observation deemed necessary for their societies' survival. In many cases reflective individuals also produced works that explored the nature of humanity and the relationship between human beings, the world, and the gods. Some of these works inspired religious and philosophical traditions for two millennia or more.

Complex society was not the only form of social organization that early human groups constructed, but it was an unusually important and influential type of society. Complex societies produced much more wealth and harnessed human resources on a much larger scale than did bands of hunting and gathering peoples, small agricultural communities, or nomadic groups that herded domesticated animals. As a result, complex societies deployed their power, pursued their interests, and promoted their values over much larger regions than did smaller societies. Indeed, most of the world's peoples have led their lives under the influence of complex societies.

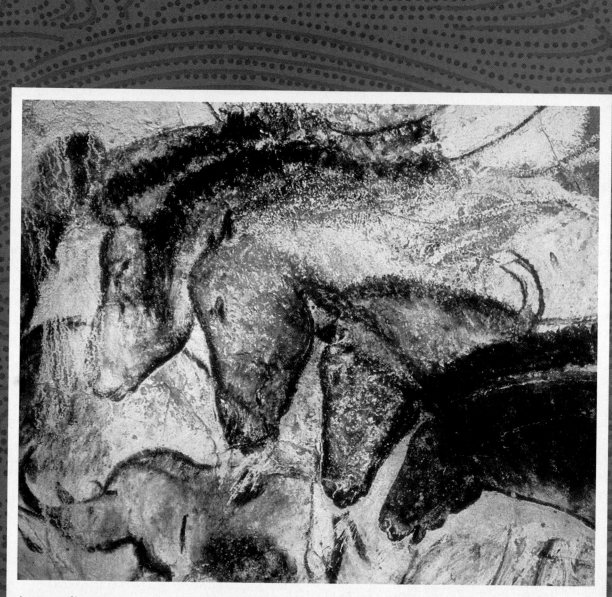

A quartet of horses depicted about thirty thousand years ago in a painting from the Chauvet cave in southern France.

CHAPTER 1

BEFORE HISTORY

Throughout the evening of 30 November 1974, a tape player in an Ethiopian desert blared the Beatles' song "Lucy in the Sky with Diamonds" at top volume. The site was an archaeological camp at Hadar, a remote spot about 160 kilometers (100 miles) northeast of Addis Ababa. The music helped fuel a spirited celebration: earlier in the day, archaeologists had discovered the skeleton of a woman who died 3.5 million years ago. Scholars refer to this woman's skeleton as AL 288-1, but the woman herself has become by far the world's best-known prehistoric individual under the name Lucy.

At the time of her death, from unknown causes, Lucy was twenty-five to thirty years of age. She stood just over 1 meter (about 3.5 feet) tall and probably weighed about 25 kilograms (55 pounds). After she died, sand and mud covered Lucy's body, hardened gradually into rock, and entombed her remains. By 1974, however, rain waters had eroded the rock and exposed Lucy's fossilized skeleton. The archaeological team working at Hadar eventually found 40 percent of Lucy's bones, which together form the most complete and best-preserved skeleton of any early human ancestor. Later searches at Hadar turned up bones belonging to perhaps as many as sixty-five additional individuals, although no other collection of bones rivals Lucy's skeleton for completeness.

Analysis of Lucy's skeleton and other bones found at Hadar demonstrates that the earliest ancestors of modern human beings walked upright on two feet. Erect walking is crucial for human beings because it frees their arms and hands for other tasks. Lucy and her contemporaries did not possess large or well-developed brains—Lucy's skull was about the size of a small grapefruit—but unlike the neighboring apes, which used their forelimbs for locomotion, Lucy and her companions could carry objects with their arms and manipulate tools with their dexterous hands. These abilities enabled Lucy and her companions to survive better than many other species. As the brains of our human ancestors grew larger and more sophisticated—a process that gradually occurred over several million years—human beings learned to take even better advantage of their arms and hands and established flourishing communities throughout the world.

According to geologists the earth came into being some five billion years ago. The first living organisms made their appearance hundreds of millions of years later. In their wake came increasingly complex creatures such as fish, birds, reptiles, and mammals. About thirty million years ago, short, hairy, monkeylike animals began to populate tropical regions of the world. Humanlike cousins to these animals began to appear

THE EVOLUTION OF *HOMO SAPIENS*
The Hominids
Homo Sapiens

PALEOLITHIC SOCIETY
Economy and Society of Hunting and Gathering Peoples
Paleolithic Culture

THE NEOLITHIC ERA AND THE TRANSITION TO AGRICULTURE
The Origins of Agriculture
Early Agricultural Society
Neolithic Culture
The Origins of Urban Life

only four or five million years ago, and modern human beings only about forty thousand years ago.

Even the most sketchy review of the earth's natural history clearly shows that human society has not developed in a vacuum. The earliest human beings inhabited a world already well stocked with flora and fauna, a world shaped for countless eons by natural rhythms that governed the behavior of all the earth's creatures. Human beings made a place for themselves in this world, and over time they learned to take advantage of the earth's resources more successfully than any other creature. Indeed, it has become clear in recent years that the human animal has exploited the natural environment so thoroughly that the earth has undergone irreversible changes.

A discussion of such early times might seem peripheral to a book that deals with the history of human societies, their origins, development, and interactions. In conventional terminology, *prehistory* refers to the period before writing, while *history* refers to the era after the invention of writing enabled human communities to record and store information. It is certainty true that the availability of written documents vastly enhances the ability of scholars to understand past ages, but recent research by archaeologists and evolutionary biologists has brightly illuminated the physical and social development of early human beings. It is now clear that long before the invention of writing, human beings made a place for their species in the natural world and laid the social, economic, and cultural foundations on which their successors built increasingly complex societies.

THE EVOLUTION OF *HOMO SAPIENS*

During the past century or so, archaeologists, evolutionary biologists, and other scholars have vastly increased the understanding of human origins and the lives our distant ancestors led. Their work has done much to clarify the relationship between human beings and other animal species. On one hand, researchers have shown that human beings share some remarkable similarities with the large apes. This point is true not only of external features, such as physical form, but also of the basic elements of genetic makeup and body chemistry—DNA, chromosomal patterns, life-sustaining proteins, and blood types. In the case of some of these elements, scientists have been able to observe a difference of only 1.6 percent between the DNA of human beings and chimpanzees. Biologists therefore place human beings in the order of primates, along with monkeys, chimpanzees, gorillas, and the various other large apes.

On the other hand, human beings clearly stand out as the most distinctive of the primate species. Small differences in genetic makeup and body chemistry have led to enormous differences in levels of intelligence and ability to exercise control over the natural world. Human beings developed an extraordinarily high order of intelligence, which enabled them to devise tools, technologies, language skills, and other means of communication and cooperation. Whereas other animal species adapted physically and genetically to their natural environment, human beings altered the natural environment to suit their own needs and desires—a process that began in remote prehistory and continues in the present day. Over the long run, too, intelligence endowed humans with immense potential for social and cultural development.

The Hominids

A series of spectacular discoveries in east Africa has thrown valuable light on the evolution of the human species. In Tanzania, Kenya, Ethiopia, and other places, archaeologists have unearthed bones and tools of human ancestors going back about five million years. The Olduvai Gorge in Tanzania and Hadar in Ethiopia have yielded especially rich remains of individuals like the famous Lucy. These individuals probably represented several different species belonging to the genus *Australopithecus* ("the southern ape"), which flourished in east Africa during the long period from about four million to one million years ago.

In spite of its name, *Australopithecus* was not an ape but rather a hominid—a creature belonging to the family Hominidae, which includes human and humanlike species. Evolutionary biologists recognize *Australopithecus* as a genus standing alongside *Homo* (the genus in which biologists place modern human beings) in the family of hominids. Compared to our own species, *Homo sapiens,* Lucy and other australopithecines would seem short, hairy, and limited in intelligence. They stood something over one meter (three feet) tall, weighed 25 to 55 kilograms (55 to 121 pounds), and had a brain size of about 500 cubic centimeters. (The brain size of modern humans averages about 1,400 cc.)

Australopithecus

Compared to other ape and animal species, however, australopithecines were sophisticated creatures. They walked upright on two legs, which enabled them to use their arms independently for other tasks. They had well-developed hands with opposable thumbs, which enabled them to grasp tools and perform intricate operations. They almost certainly had some ability to communicate verbally, although analysis of their skulls suggests that the portion of the brain responsible for speech was not very large or well developed.

The intelligence of australopithecines was sufficient to allow them to plan complex ventures. They often traveled deliberately—over distances of 15 kilometers (9.3 miles) and more—to obtain the particular kinds of stone that they needed to fashion tools. Chemical analyses show that the stone from which australopithecines made tools was often available only at sites distant from the camps where archaeologists discovered the finished tools. These tools included choppers, scrapers, and other implements for food preparation. With the aid of their tools and intelligence, australopithecines established themselves securely throughout most of eastern and southern Africa.

By about one million years ago, australopithecines had disappeared as new species of hominids possessing greater intelligence evolved and displaced their predecessors. The new species belonged to the genus *Homo* and thus represented creatures considerably different from the australopithecines. Most important of them was *Homo erectus*—"upright-walking

Homo Erectus

Fossilized footprints preserved near Olduvai Gorge in modern Tanzania show that hominids walked upright some 3.5 million years ago.

MAP [1.1]
Global spread of hominids
and *Homo sapiens*.

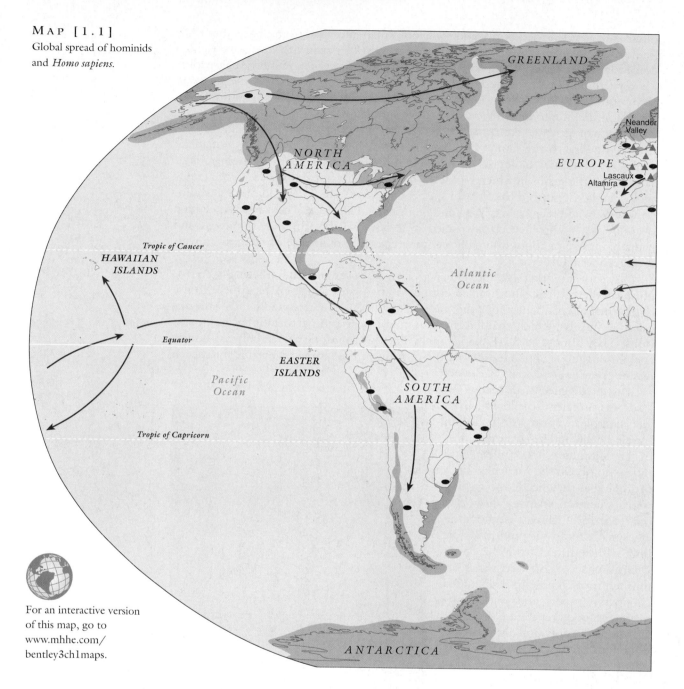

For an interactive version
of this map, go to
www.mhhe.com/
bentley3ch1maps.

human"—who flourished from about 2.5 million to 200,000 years ago. *Homo erectus*
possessed a larger brain than the australopithecines—the average capacity was about
1,000 cc—and fashioned more sophisticated tools as well. To the australopithecine
choppers and scrapers, *Homo erectus* added cleavers and hand axes, which not only
were useful in hunting and food preparation but also provided protection against
predators. *Homo erectus* also knew how to tend a fire, which furnished the species with
a means to cook food, a defense against large animals, and a source of artificial heat.

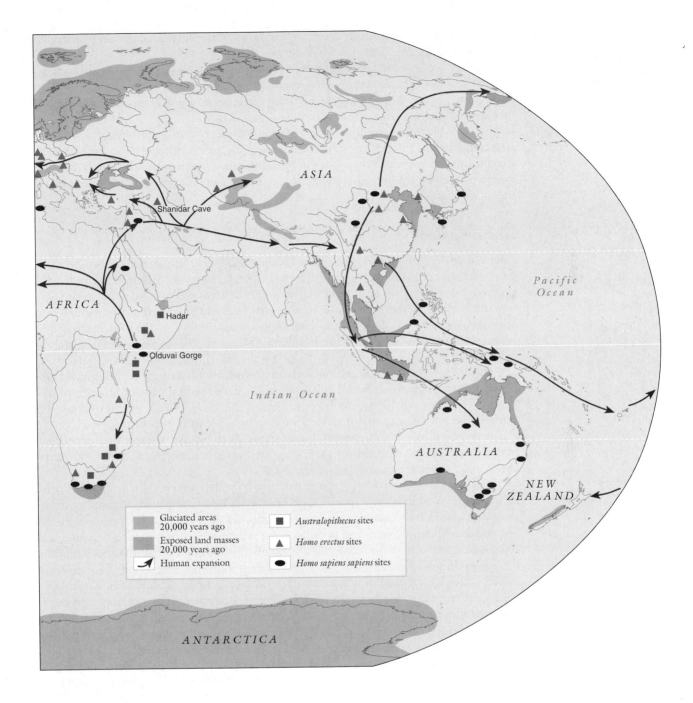

Even more important than tools and fire were intelligence and language skills, which enabled individuals to communicate complex ideas to each other. Archaeologists have determined, for example, that bands of *Homo erectus* men conducted their hunts in well-coordinated ways that presumed prior communication. Many sites associated with *Homo erectus* served as camps for communities of hunters. The quantities of animal remains found at those sites—particularly bones of large and dangerous animals such as elephant, rhinoceros, and bear—provide evidence that hunters worked in

Migrations of
Homo Erectus

groups and brought their prey back to their camps. Cooperation of this sort presumed both high intelligence and effective language skills.

With effective tools, fire, intelligence, and language, *Homo erectus* gained increasing control over the natural environment and introduced the human species into widely scattered regions. Whereas australopithecines had not ventured beyond eastern and southern Africa, *Homo erectus* migrated to north Africa and the Eurasian landmass. Almost two million years ago, *Homo erectus* groups moved to southwest Asia and beyond to Europe, south Asia, east Asia, and southeast Asia. By two hundred thousand years ago they had established themselves throughout the temperate zones of the eastern hemisphere, where archaeologists have unearthed many specimens of their bones and tools.

Homo Sapiens

Like *Australopithecus,* though, *Homo erectus* faded with the arrival of more intelligent and successful human species. *Homo sapiens* ("consciously thinking human") evolved about two hundred thousand years ago and has skillfully adapted to the natural environment ever since. Early *Homo sapiens* already possessed a large brain—one approaching the size of modern human brains. More important than the size of the brain, though, is its structure: the modern human brain is especially well developed in the frontal regions, where conscious and reflective thought takes place. This physical feature provided *Homo sapiens* with an enormous advantage. Although not endowed with great strength and not equipped with natural means of attack and defense—claws, beaks, fangs, shells, venom, and the like—*Homo sapiens* possessed a remarkable intelligence that provided a powerful edge in the contest for survival. It enabled individuals to understand the structure of the world around them, to organize more efficient methods of exploiting natural resources, and to communicate and cooperate on increasingly complex tasks.

Migrations
of Homo Sapiens

Intelligence enabled *Homo sapiens* to adapt to widely varying environmental conditions and to establish the species securely throughout the world. Beginning more than one hundred thousand years ago, communities of *Homo sapiens* spread throughout the eastern hemisphere and populated the temperate lands of Africa, Europe, and Asia, where they encountered *Homo erectus* groups that had inhabited those regions for several hundred thousand years. *Homo sapiens* soon moved beyond the temperate zones, though, and established communities in progressively colder regions—migrations that were possible because their intelligence allowed *Homo sapiens* to fashion warm clothes from animal skins and to build effective shelters against the cold.

Between sixty thousand and fifteen thousand years ago, *Homo sapiens* extended the range of human population even further. Several ice ages cooled the earth's temperature during that period, resulting in the concentration of water in massive glaciers, the lowering of the world's sea levels, and the exposure of land bridges that linked Asia with regions of the world previously uninhabited by humans. Small bands of individuals crossed those bridges and established communities in the islands of Indonesia and New Guinea, and some of them went farther to cross the temporarily narrow straits of water separating southeast Asia from Australia.

Homo sapiens arrived in Australia about sixty thousand years ago, perhaps even earlier. Somewhat later, beginning as early perhaps as twenty-five thousand years ago, other groups took advantage of land bridges linking Siberia with Alaska and established human communities in North America. From there they migrated throughout the western hemisphere. About fifteen thousand years ago, communities of *Homo sapiens* had appeared in almost every habitable region of the world.

Contexts & Connections

The Wandering Animal

Currently, about 150 million people, who account for some 2.5 percent of the world's population, live outside the countries of their birth, while more than a billion others are descendants of individuals who left their homelands within the past three centuries. The high incidence of mobility in modern times reflects the fact that cheap and reliable means of transportation have facilitated large-scale movements for the world's peoples. Since the 1960s many governments have relaxed controls over movements across their borders, and some have intentionally sought to attract students and workers to their lands. As a result, the past fifty years have witnessed human migrations on an unprecedented scale.

Yet human mobility is by no means a recent development. To the contrary, the migratory impulse is a distinctively human trait that has shaped human experience on planet earth for the past two million years. Soon after human species evolved in east Africa, they left behind their homeland and established colonies throughout the world. Only the highest mountains, the driest deserts, and the coldest climes have resisted human encroachment, and even those regions have frequently seen temporary human visitors. No other species of animal has independently made its way to all corners of the world, although many species have established a presence in distant lands after humans transported them to new homes.

Recent archaeological discoveries have shed stunning light on the early migrations of *Homo erectus* individuals. From remains unearthed in China, Java, and other places, scholars have long known that *Homo erectus* traveled overland to many sites in the eastern hemisphere about two million years before the present. From recent excavations on Flores Island in modern-day Indonesia, it is now clear that Homo erectus not only traveled by foot but also used some sort of watercraft to make crossings of at least 25 kilometers (15.5 miles) about eight hundred thousand years before the present. Unlike many other southeast Asian islands, Flores Island was never connected to the Eurasian continent by a land bridge, even during the coldest ice ages, because a deep underwater trench separates the island from the continent. Thus, in order to establish a presence on Flores Island, *Homo erectus* had to cross a sizable body of water. (The earliest previously known evidence of human reliance on watercraft dated only to about sixty thousand years before the present, when *Homo sapiens* individuals made their way to Australia.)

Homo erectus did not venture beyond the eastern hemisphere. Only after the evolution of *Homo sapiens* did human beings establish their presence in the western hemisphere and Oceania, as well as the northerly reaches

(continued)

The Natural Environment

Their intellectual abilities enabled members of the *Homo sapiens* species to recognize problems and possibilities in their environment and then to take action that favored their survival. At sites of early settlements, archaeologists have discovered increasingly sophisticated tools that reflect *Homo sapiens'* progressive control over the environment. In addition to the choppers, scrapers, axes, and other tools that earlier species possessed, *Homo sapiens* used knives, spears, bows, and arrows. Individuals made dwellings for themselves in caves and in hutlike shelters fabricated from wood, bones, and animal skins. In cold regions *Homo sapiens* warmed themselves with fire and cloaked themselves in the skins of animals. Mounds of ashes discovered at their campsites show that in especially cold regions, they kept fires burning continuously during the winter months. In all parts of the earth, members of the species learned to use spoken

Contexts & Connections

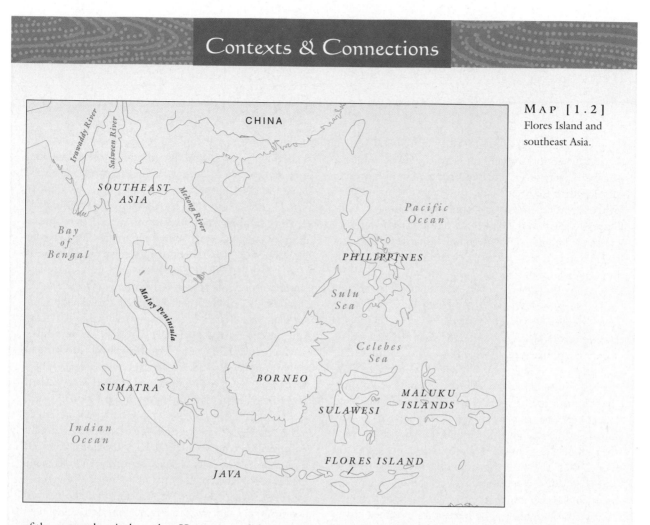

MAP [1.2]
Flores Island and
southeast Asia.

of the eastern hemisphere that *Homo erectus* did not visit. Nevertheless, the extensive travels of *Homo erectus* as well as *Homo sapiens* demonstrate that human beings have been wandering animals for a very long time indeed.

Their far-flung migrations constitute a deep historical context for rampant human mobility in both ancient and modern times.

languages to communicate complex ideas and coordinate their efforts in the common interest. *Homo sapiens* used superior intelligence, sophisticated tools, and language to exploit the natural world more efficiently than any other species the earth had seen.

Indeed, intelligent, tool-bearing humans competed so successfully in the natural world that they brought tremendous pressure to bear on other species. As the population of *Homo sapiens* increased, large mammal species in several parts of the world became extinct. Mammoths and the woolly rhinoceros disappeared from Europe, giant kangaroos from Australia, and mammoths, mastodons, and horses from the

Sources from the Past

Richard E. Leakey on the Nature of *Homo Sapiens Sapiens*

Richard E. Leakey (1944–) has spent much of his life searching for the fossilized remains of early hominids in east Africa. While seeking to explain the evolutionary biology of hominids, Leakey offered some reflections on the nature and distinctive characteristics of our own species.

What are we? To the biologist we are members of a sub-species called *Homo sapiens sapiens*, which represents a division of the species known as *Homo sapiens*. Every species is unique and distinct: that is part of the definition of a species. But what is particularly interesting about our species? . . .

Our forelimbs, being freed from helping us to get about, possess a very high degree of manipulative skill. Part of this skill lies in the anatomical structure of the hands, but the crucial element is, of course, the power of the brain. No matter how suitable the limbs are for detailed manipulation, they are useless in the absence of finely tuned instructions delivered through nerve fibres. The most obvious product of our hands and brains is technology. No other animal manipulates the world in the extensive and arbitrary way that humans do. The termites are capable of constructing intricately structured mounds which create their own "air-conditioned" environment inside. But the termites cannot choose to build a cathedral instead. Humans are unique because they have the capacity to *choose* what they do.

Communication is a vital thread of all animal life. Social insects such as termites possess a system of communication that is clearly essential for their complex labours: their language is not verbal but is based upon an exchange of chemicals between individuals and on certain sorts of signalling with the body. In many animal groups, such as birds and mammals, communicating by sound is important, and the posture and movement of the body can also transmit messages. The tilting of the head, the staring or averted eyes, the arched back, the bristled hair or feathers: all are part of an extensive repertoire of animal signals. In animals that live in groups, the need to be able to communicate effectively is paramount.

For humans, body language is still very important but the voice has taken over as the main channel of information-flow. Unlike any other animal, we have a spoken language which is characterized by a huge vocabulary and a complex grammatical structure. Speech is an unparalleled medium for exchanging complex information, and it is also an essential part of social interaction in that most social of all creatures, *Homo sapiens sapiens*.

All the points I have mentioned are characteristics of a very intelligent creature, but humans are more than just intelligent. Our sense of justice, our need for aesthetic pleasure, our imaginative flights, and our penetrating self-awareness, all combine to create an indefinable spirit which I believe is the "soul."

SOURCE: Richard E. Leakey. *The Making of Mankind.* New York: E. P. Dutton, 1981, pp. 18, 20.

Granting that Homo sapiens sapiens *possesses distinctive characteristics and enjoys unique abilities, as Leakey has eloquently suggested, to what extent does human membership in the larger animal kingdom help explain human experiences in the world?*

Americas. Archaeologists believe that changes in the earth's climate might have altered the natural environment enough to harm these species. In most cases, however, human hunting probably helped push large animals into extinction. Thus, from their earliest days on earth, members of the species *Homo sapiens* became effective and efficient competitors in the natural world—to the point that they threatened the very survival of other large but less intelligent species.

PALEOLITHIC SOCIETY

By far the longest portion of the human experience on earth is the period historians and archaeologists call the paleolithic era, the "old stone age." The principal characteristic of the paleolithic era was that human beings foraged for their food: they hunted wild animals or gathered edible products of naturally growing plants. The paleolithic era extended from the evolution of the first hominids until about twelve thousand years ago, when groups of *Homo sapiens* in several parts of the world began to rely on cultivated crops to feed themselves.

Economy and Society of Hunting and Gathering Peoples

In the absence of written records, scholars have drawn inferences about paleolithic economy and society from other kinds of evidence. Archaeologists have excavated many sites that open windows on paleolithic life, and anthropologists have carefully studied hunting and gathering societies in the contemporary world. In the Amazon basin of South America, the tropical forests of Africa and southeast Asia, the deserts of Africa and Australia, and a few other regions as well, small communities of hunters and gatherers follow the ways of our common paleolithic ancestors. Although contemporary hunting and gathering communities reflect the influence of the modern world—they are by no means exact replicas of paleolithic societies—they throw important light on the economic and social dynamics that shaped the experiences of prehistoric foragers. In combination, then, the studies of both archaeologists and anthropologists help to illustrate how the hunting and gathering economy decisively influenced all dimensions of the human experience during the paleolithic era.

Relative Social Equality

A hunting and gathering economy virtually prevents individuals from accumulating private property and basing social distinctions on wealth. In order to survive, most hunters and gatherers must follow the animals that they stalk, and they must move with the seasons in search of edible plant life. Given their mobility, it is easy to see that for them, the notion of private, landed property has no meaning at all. Individuals possess only a few small items like weapons and tools that they can carry easily as they move. In the absence of accumulated wealth, hunters and gatherers of paleolithic times, like their contemporary descendants, probably lived a relatively egalitarian existence. Social distinctions no doubt arose, and some individuals became influential because of their age, strength, courage, intelligence, fertility, force of personality, or some other trait. But personal or family wealth could not have served as a basis for permanent social differences.

Some scholars believe that this relative social equality in paleolithic times extended even further, to relations between the sexes. All members of a paleolithic group made important contributions to the survival of the community. Men traveled on sometimes distant hunting expeditions in search of large animals while women and children gathered edible plants, roots, nuts, and fruits from the area near the group's camp. Meat from the hunt was the most highly prized item in the paleolithic diet, but plant foods were essential to survival. Anthropologists calculate that in modern hunting and gathering societies, women contribute more calories to the community's diet than do the men. As a source of protein, meat represents a crucial supplement to the diet. But plant products sustain the men during hunting expeditions and feed the entire community when the hunt does not succeed. Because of the thorough interdependence of the sexes from the viewpoint of food production, paleolithic society probably did not encourage the domination of one sex by the other—certainly not to the extent that became common later.

Artist's conception of food preparation in a *Homo erectus* community.

A hunting and gathering economy has implications not only for social and sexual relations but also for community size and organization. The foraging lifestyle of hunters and gatherers dictates that they mostly live in small bands, which today include about thirty to fifty members. Larger groups could not move efficiently or find enough food to survive over a long period. During times of drought or famine, even small bands have trouble providing for themselves. Individual bands certainly have relationships with their neighbors—agreements concerning the territories that the groups exploit, for example, or arrangements to take marriage partners from each others' groups—but the immediate community is the focus of social life.

The survival of hunting and gathering bands depends on a sophisticated understanding of their natural environment. In contemporary studies, anthropologists have found that hunting and gathering peoples do not wander aimlessly about hoping to find a bit of food. Instead, they exploit the environment systematically and efficiently by timing their movements to coincide with the seasonal migrations of the animals they hunt and the life cycles of the plant species they gather.

Archaeological remains show that early peoples also went about hunting and gathering in a purposeful and intelligent manner. As early as three hundred thousand years ago, for example, *Homo erectus* had learned to hunt big game successfully. Although almost anyone could take a small, young, or wounded animal, the hunting of big game posed difficult problems. Large animals such as elephant, mastodon, rhinoceros, bison, and wild cattle were not only strong and fast but also well equipped to defend themselves and even attack their human hunters. *Homo erectus* and *Homo sapiens* fashioned special tools, such as sharp knives, spears, and bows and arrows, and devised special tactics for hunting these animals. The hunters wore disguises such as animal skins and coordinated their movements so as to attack game simultaneously from several directions. They sometimes even started fires or caused disturbances to stampede herds into swamps or enclosed areas where hunters could kill them more easily. Paleolithic hunting was a complicated venture. It clearly demonstrated the capacity of early human communities to pool their uniquely human traits—high intelligence, ability to make complicated plans, and sophisticated language and communications skills—to exploit the environment.

Big-Game Hunting

Paleolithic Settlements

Statue of a Neandertal man based on the study of recently discovered bones.

In regions where food resources were especially rich, a few peoples in late paleolithic times abandoned the nomadic lifestyle and established permanent settlements. The most prominent paleolithic settlements were those of Natufian society in the eastern Mediterranean (modern-day Israel and Lebanon), Jomon society in central Japan, and Chinook society in the Pacific northwest region of North America (including the modern states of Oregon and Washington and the Canadian province of British Columbia). As early as 13,500 B.C.E., Natufians collected wild wheat and took animals from abundant antelope herds. From 10,000 to 300 B.C.E., Jomon settlers harvested wild buckwheat and developed a productive fishing economy. Chinook society emerged after 3000 B.C.E. and flourished until the mid-nineteenth century C.E., principally on the basis of wild berries, acorns, and massive salmon runs in local rivers. Paleolithic settlements had permanent dwellings, sometimes in the form of long houses that accommodated several hundred people, but often in the form of smaller structures for individual families. Many settlements had populations of a thousand or more individuals. As archaeological excavations continue, it is becoming increasingly clear that paleolithic peoples organized complex societies with specialized rulers and craftsmen in many regions where they found abundant food resources.

Paleolithic Culture

Neandertal Peoples

Paleolithic individuals did not limit their creative thinking to strictly practical matters of subsistence and survival. Instead, they reflected on the nature of human existence and the world around them. The earliest evidence of reflective thought comes from sites associated with Neandertal peoples, named after the Neander valley in western Germany where their remains first came to light. Neandertal peoples flourished in Europe and southwest Asia between about two hundred thousand and thirty-five thousand years ago, and Neandertal remains have turned up also in Africa and east Asia.

At several Neandertal sites archaeologists have discovered signs of careful, deliberate burial accompanied by ritual observances. Perhaps the most notable is that of Shanidar cave, located about 400 kilometers (250 miles) north of Baghdad in modern-day Iraq, where survivors laid the deceased to rest on beds of freshly picked wild flowers and then covered the bodies with shrouds and garlands of other flowers. At other Neandertal sites in France, Italy, and central Asia, survivors placed flint tools and animal bones in and around the graves of the deceased. It is impossible to know precisely what Neandertal peoples were thinking when they buried their dead in this fashion. Possibly they simply wanted to honor the memory of the departed, or perhaps they wanted to prepare the dead for a new dimension of existence, a life beyond the grave. Whatever their intentions, Neandertal peoples apparently recognized a significance in the life and death of individuals that none of their ancestors had appreciated. They had developed a capacity for emotions and feelings, and they cared for each other even to the extent of preparing elaborate resting places for the departed.

Cro-Magnon Peoples

Another sign of reflective thought occurs in the creative achievements of paleolithic peoples. The responsible parties in this case were Cro-Magnon peoples, the first human beings of the fully modern type, who appeared on the earth about forty thousand years ago. If dressed in modern clothes and groomed in modern fashion, they would be physically indistinguishable from contemporary human beings. Some archaeologists and evolutionary biologists classify Cro-Magnon peoples as *Homo sapiens sapiens*—our own subspecies—to distinguish them from other *Homo sapiens* subspecies such as the Neandertal. More intelligent than their predecessors, Cro-Magnon peoples gradually displaced their Neandertal neighbors, whose communities gradually died out and disappeared.

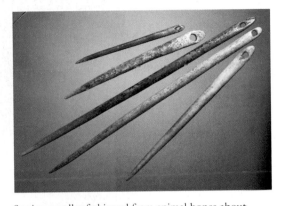

Sewing needles fashioned from animal bones about fifteen thousand years ago.

Many scholars believe the high intelligence of Cro-Magnon peoples was due to physiological changes that enhanced their ability to speak and communicate complex ideas. Whatever the explanation, the increased intelligence of Cro-Magnon peoples sparked an explosion of creativity. Cro-Magnon hunters devised finer and more sophisticated weapons, for example, than any of their ancestors. They invented harpoons, bows and arrows, and spear-throwers—small slings that enabled hunters to hurl spears at speeds upwards of 160 kilometers (100 miles) per hour. From antlers and bones they crafted tools such as awls and needles, with which they then sewed animal skins into garments tailored to individual sizes. Cro-Magnon peoples also displayed a noticeable interest in fashion and artistic production. They adorned themselves with jewelry such as necklaces, bracelets, and beads, and they produced decorative pieces of furniture for use in their dwellings.

More important than jewelry and furniture, however, are the Venus figurines and cave paintings found at Cro-Magnon sites. Archaeologists use the term *Venus figurines*—named after the Roman goddess of love—to refer to small sculptures of women, usually depicted with exaggerated sexual features. Hundreds of these statuettes survive, many of them from Cro-Magnon sites in central Europe.

Venus Figurines

Venus figurine from Austria. The exaggerated sexual features suggest that paleolithic peoples fashioned such figurines out of an interest in fertility.

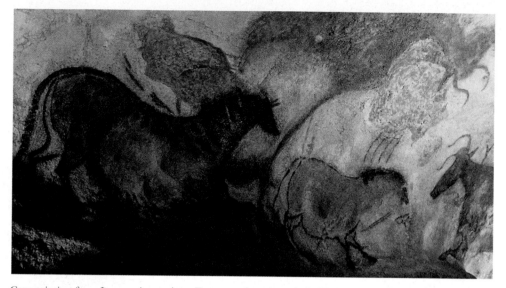

Cave painting from Lascaux in southern France, perhaps intended to help hunters gain control over the spirits of large game animals.

Most scholars believe that the figures reflect a deep interest in fertility. The prominent sexual features of the Venus figurines suggest that the sculptors' principal interests were fecundity and the generation of new life—matters of immediate concern to paleolithic societies. Some interpreters even speculate that the figures had a place in ritual observances intended to increase fertility.

Cave Paintings   Paintings in caves inhabited or frequented by Cro-Magnon peoples are the most dramatic examples of prehistoric art. The known examples of cave art date from about thirty-four thousand to twelve thousand years ago, and most of them come from caves in southern France and northern Spain. In that region alone, archaeologists have discovered more than one hundred caves bearing prehistoric paintings. The best-known are Lascaux in France and Altamira in Spain. There prehistoric peoples left depictions of remarkable sensitivity and power. Most of the subjects were animals, especially large game such as mammoth, bison, and reindeer, although a few human figures also appear.

As in the case of the Venus figurines, the explanation for the cave paintings involves a certain amount of educated guesswork. It is conceivable that Cro-Magnon artists sometimes worked for purely aesthetic reasons—to beautify their living quarters. But many examples of cave art occur in places that are almost inaccessible to human beings—deep within remote chambers, for example, or at the end of long and constricted passages. Paintings in such remote locations presumably had some other purpose. Most analysts believe that the prominence of game animals in the paintings reflects the artists' interest in successful hunting expeditions. Thus cave paintings may have represented efforts to exercise "sympathetic magic"—to gain control over subjects (in this case, game animals) by capturing their spirits (by way of accurate representations of their physical forms). Although not universally accepted, this interpretation accounts reasonably well for a great deal of the evidence and has won widespread support among scholars.

Whatever the explanation for prehistoric art, the production of the works themselves represented conscious and purposeful activity of a high order. Cro-Magnon artists compounded their own pigments and manufactured their own tools. They made paints from minerals, plants, blood, saliva, water, animal fat, and other available ingredients. They used mortar and pestle for grinding pigments and mixing paints, which they applied with moss, frayed twigs and branches, or primitive brushes fabricated from hair. The simplicity and power of their representations have left deep impressions on modern critics ever since the early twentieth century, when their works became widely known. The display of prehistoric artistic talent clearly testifies once again to the remarkable intellectual power of the human species.

THE NEOLITHIC ERA AND THE TRANSITION TO AGRICULTURE

A few societies of hunting and gathering peoples inhabit the contemporary world, although most of them do not thrive because agricultural and industrial societies have taken over environments best suited to a foraging economy. Demographers estimate the current number of hunters and gatherers to be about thirty thousand, a tiny fraction of the world's human population of more than six billion. The vast majority of the world's peoples, however, have crossed an economic threshold of immense significance. When human beings brought plants under cultivation and animals under domestication, they dramatically altered the natural world and steered human societies in new directions.

The Origins of Agriculture

The term *neolithic era* means "new stone age," as opposed to the old stone age of paleolithic times. Archaeologists first used the term *neolithic* because of refinements in tool-making techniques: they found polished stone tools in neolithic sites, rather than the chipped implements characteristic of paleolithic sites. Gradually, however, archaeologists became aware that something more fundamental than tool production distinguished the paleolithic from the neolithic era. Polished stone tools occurred in sites where peoples relied on cultivation, rather than foraging, for their subsistence. Today the term *neolithic era* refers to the early stages of agricultural society, from about twelve thousand to six thousand years ago.

Neolithic Era

Because they depended on the bounty of nature, foraging peoples faced serious risks. Drought, famine, disease, floods, extreme temperatures, and other natural disasters could annihilate entire communities. Even in good times, many hunting and gathering peoples had to limit their populations so as not to exceed the capacity of their lands to support them. They most likely resorted routinely to infanticide in order to control their numbers.

Neolithic peoples sought to ensure themselves of more regular food supplies by encouraging the growth of edible crops and bringing wild animals into dependence on human keepers. Many scholars believe that women most likely began the systematic care of plants. As the principal gatherers in foraging communities, women became familiar with the life cycles of plants and noticed the effects of sunshine, rain, and temperature on vegetation. Hoping for larger and more reliable supplies of food, women in neolithic societies probably began to nurture plants instead of simply collecting available foods in the wild. Meanwhile, instead of just stalking game with the intention of killing it for meat, neolithic men began to capture animals and domesticate them by providing for their needs and supervising their breeding. Over a period of decades and centuries, these practices gradually led to the formation of agricultural economies.

By suggesting that agriculture brought about an immediate transformation of human society, the popular term *agricultural revolution* is somewhat misleading. The

Two cave paintings produced five to six thousand years ago illustrate the different roles played by men and women in the early days of agriculture. Here women harvest grain.

Men herd domesticated cattle in the early days of agriculture. This painting and the previous one both came from a cave at Tassili n'Ajjer in modern-day Algeria.

establishment of an agricultural economy was not an event that took place at a given date but, rather, a process that unfolded over many centuries, as human beings gradually learned how to cultivate crops and keep animals. It would be more appropriate to speak of an "agricultural transition"—leading from paleolithic experiments with cultivation to early agricultural societies in the neolithic era—rather than an agricultural revolution.

Independent Inventions of Agriculture

Agriculture—including both the cultivation of crops and the domestication of animals—emerged independently in several different parts of the world. The earliest evidence of agricultural activity discovered so far dates to the era after 9000 B.C.E., when peoples of southwest Asia (modern-day Iraq, Syria, and Turkey) cultivated wheat and barley while domesticating sheep, goats, pigs, and cattle. Between 9000 and 7000 B.C.E., African peoples inhabiting the southeastern margin of the Sahara desert (modern-day Sudan) domesticated cattle, sheep, and goats while cultivating sorghum. Between 8000 and 6000 B.C.E., peoples of sub-Saharan west Africa (in the vicinity of modern Nigeria) also began independently to cultivate yams, okra, and black-eyed peas. In east Asia, residents of the Yangzi River valley began to cultivate rice as early as 6500 B.C.E., while their neighbors to the north in the Yellow River valley raised crops of millet and soybeans after 5500 B.C.E. East Asian peoples also kept pigs and chickens from an early date, perhaps 6000 B.C.E., and they later added water buffaloes to their domesticated stock. In southeast Asia the cultivation of taro, yams, coconut, breadfruit, bananas, and citrus fruits, including oranges, lemons, limes, tangerines, and grapefruit, dates from an indeterminate but very early time, probably 3000 B.C.E. or earlier.

Peoples of the western hemisphere also turned independently to agriculture. Inhabitants of Mesoamerica (central Mexico) cultivated maize (corn) as early as 4000 B.C.E., and they later added a range of additional food crops, including beans, peppers, squashes, and tomatoes. Residents of the central Andean region of South America (modern Peru) cultivated potatoes after 3000 B.C.E., and they later added maize and beans to their diets. It is possible that the Amazon River valley was yet another site of independently invented agriculture, this one centering on the cultivation of manioc, sweet potatoes, and peanuts. Domesticated animals were much less prominent in the Americas than in the eastern hemisphere. Paleolithic peoples had hunted many large species to extinction: mammoths, mastodons, and horses had all disappeared from the Americas by 7000 B.C.E. (The horses that have figured so prominently in the modern history of the Americas all descended from animals introduced to the western hemisphere during the past five hundred years.) With the exception of llamas, alpacas, and guinea pigs of the Andean regions, most other American animals were not well suited to domestication.

Once established, agriculture spread rapidly, partly because of the methods of early cultivators. One of the earliest techniques, known as slash-and-burn cultivation, involved frequent movement on the part of farmers. To prepare a field for cultivation, a community would slash the bark on a stand of trees in a forest and later burn the dead trees to the ground. The resulting weed-free patch was extremely fertile and produced abundant harvests. After a few years, however, weeds invaded the field, and the soil lost its original fertility. The community then moved to another forest region and repeated the procedure. Migrations of slash-and-burn cultivators helped spread agriculture throughout both eastern and western hemispheres. By 6000 B.C.E., for example, agriculture had spread from its southwest Asian homeland to the eastern shores of the Mediterranean and the Balkan region of eastern Europe, and by 4000 B.C.E. it had spread farther to western Europe north of the Mediterranean.

The Early Spread of Agriculture

While agriculture radiated out from its various hearths, foods originally cultivated in only one region also spread widely, as merchants, migrants, or other travelers carried knowledge of these foods to agricultural lands that previously had relied on different crops. Wheat, for example, spread from its original homeland in southwest Asia to Iran and northern India after 5000 B.C.E. and farther to northern China perhaps by 3000 B.C.E. Meanwhile, rice spread from southern China to southeast Asia by 3000 B.C.E. and to the Ganges River valley in India by 1500 B.C.E. African sorghum reached India by 2000 B.C.E., while southeast Asian bananas took root in tropical lands throughout the Indian Ocean basin. In the western hemisphere, maize spread from Mesoamerica to the southwestern part of the United States by 1200 B.C.E. and farther to the eastern woodlands region of North America by 100 C.E.

MAP [1.3]
Origins and early spread of agriculture.

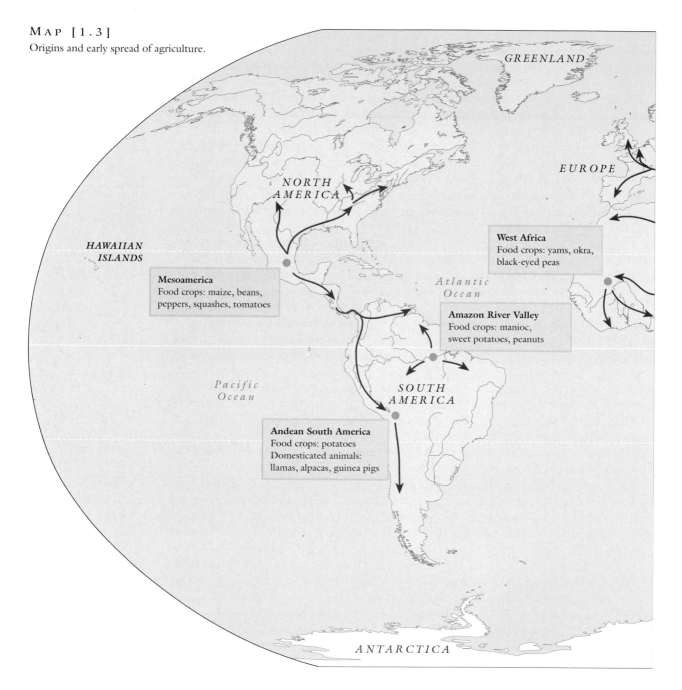

Agriculture involved long hours of hard physical labor—clearing land, preparing fields, planting seeds, pulling weeds, and harvesting crops. Indeed, agriculture probably required more work than paleolithic foraging: anthropologists calculate that modern hunting and gathering peoples spend about four hours per day in providing themselves with food and other necessities, devoting the remainder of their time to rest, leisure, and social activities. Yet agriculture had its own appeal in that it made possible the production of abundant food supplies. Thus agriculture spread widely, eventually influencing the lives and experience of almost all human beings.

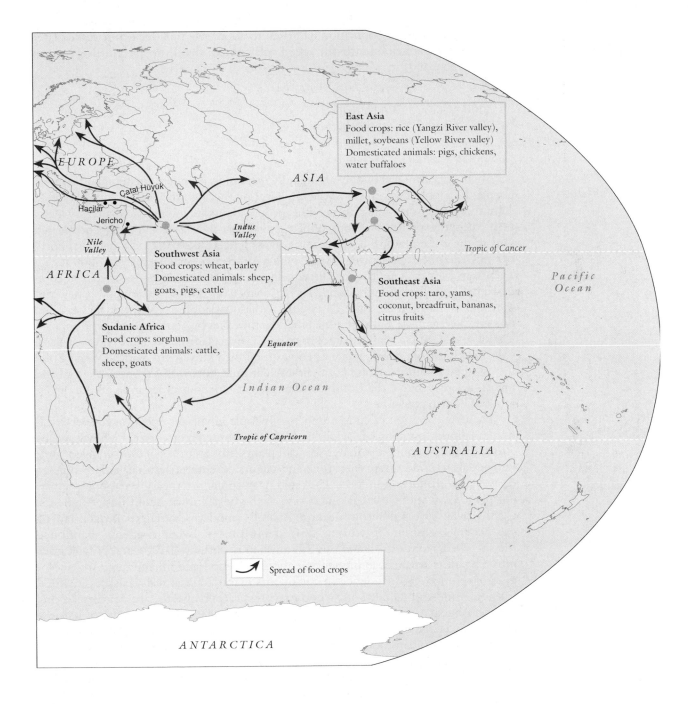

East Asia
Food crops: rice (Yangzi River valley), millet, soybeans (Yellow River valley)
Domesticated animals: pigs, chickens, water buffaloes

Southwest Asia
Food crops: wheat, barley
Domesticated animals: sheep, goats, pigs, cattle

Southeast Asia
Food crops: taro, yams, coconut, breadfruit, bananas, citrus fruits

Sudanic Africa
Food crops: sorghum
Domesticated animals: cattle, sheep, goats

Spread of food crops

Early Agricultural Society

In the wake of agriculture came a series of social and cultural changes that transformed human history. Perhaps the most important change associated with agriculture was a population explosion. Spread thinly across the earth in paleolithic times, the human species multiplied prodigiously after agriculture increased the supply of food. Historians estimate that before agriculture, about 10,000 B.C.E., the earth's human population was about four million. By 5000 B.C.E., when agriculture had appeared in a few world regions, human population had risen to about five million. Estimates for later dates demonstrate eloquently the speed with which, thanks to agriculture, human numbers increased:

Year	Human Population
3000 B.C.E.	14 million
2000 B.C.E.	27 million
1000 B.C.E.	50 million
500 B.C.E.	100 million

Emergence of Villages and Towns

Their agricultural economy and rapidly increasing numbers encouraged neolithic peoples to adopt new forms of social organization. Because they devoted their time to cultivation rather than foraging, neolithic peoples did not continue the migratory life of their paleolithic predecessors but, rather, settled near their fields in permanent villages. One of the earliest known neolithic villages was Jericho, site of a freshwater oasis north of the Dead Sea in present-day Israel, which came into existence before 8000 B.C.E. Even in its early days, Jericho may have had two thousand residents—a vast crowd compared to a paleolithic hunting band. The residents farmed mostly wheat and barley with the aid of water from the oasis. During the earliest days of the settlement, they kept no domesticated animals, but they added meat to their diet by hunting local game animals. They also engaged in a limited amount of trade, particularly in salt and obsidian, a hard, volcanic glass from which ancient peoples fashioned knives and blades. About 7000 B.C.E., the residents surrounded their circular mud huts with a formidable wall and moat—a sure sign that the wealth concentrated at Jericho had begun to attract the interest of human predators.

Specialization of Labor

The concentration of large numbers of people in villages encouraged specialization of labor. Most people in neolithic villages cultivated crops or kept animals. Many also continued to hunt and forage for wild plants. But a surplus of food enabled some individuals to concentrate their time and talents on enterprises that had nothing to do with the production of food. The rapid development of specialized labor is apparent from excavations carried out at one of the best-known neolithic settlements, Çatal Hüyük. Located in south-central Anatolia (modern-day Turkey), Çatal Hüyük was occupied continuously from 7250 to 5400 B.C.E., when residents abandoned the site. Originally a small and undistinguished neolithic village, Çatal Hüyük grew into a bustling town, accommodating about five thousand inhabitants. Archaeologists have uncovered evidence that residents manufactured pots, baskets, textiles, leather, stone and metal tools, wood carvings, carpets, beads, and jewelry among other products. Çatal Hüyük became a prominent village partly because of its close proximity to large obsidian deposits. The village probably was a center of production and trade in obsidian tools: archaeologists have discovered obsidian that originated near Çatal Hüyük at sites throughout much of the eastern Mediterranean region.

Three early craft industries—pottery, metallurgy, and textile production—illustrate the potential of specialized labor in neolithic times. Neolithic craftsmen were not always the original inventors of the technologies behind these industries: the Jomon society of central Japan produced the world's first known pottery, for example, about 10,000 B.C.E. But neolithic craftsmen expanded dramatically on existing practices and supplemented them with new techniques to fashion natural products into useful items. Their enterprises reflected the conditions of early agricultural society: either the craft industries provided tools and utensils needed by cultivators, or they made use of cultivators' and herders' products in new ways.

Pottery

The earliest of the three craft industries to emerge was pottery. Paleolithic hunters and gatherers had no use for pots. They did not store food for long periods of time, and in any case lugging heavy clay pots around as they moved from one site to another would have been inconvenient. A food-producing society, however, needs containers to store surplus foods. By about 7000 B.C.E. neolithic villagers in several parts of the world had discovered processes that transformed malleable clay into permanent, fire-hardened, waterproof pottery capable of storing dry or liquid products. Soon thereafter, neolithic craftsmen discovered that they could etch designs into their clay that fire would harden into permanent decorations and furthermore that they could color their products with glazes. As a result, pottery became a medium of artistic expression as well as a source of practical utensils.

Pottery vessel from Haçilar in Anatolia in the shape of a reclining deer, produced about the early sixth millennium B.C.E.

Metalworking

Metallurgy soon joined pottery as a neolithic industry. The earliest metal that humans worked with systematically was copper. In many regions of the world, copper occurs naturally in relatively pure and easily malleable form. By simply hammering the cold metal it was possible to turn it into jewelry and simple tools. By 6000 B.C.E., though, neolithic villagers had discovered that when heated to high temperatures, copper became much more workable and that they could use heat to extract copper from its ores. By 5000 B.C.E., they had raised temperatures in their furnaces high enough to melt copper and pour it into molds. With the technology of smelting and casting copper, neolithic communities were able to make not only jewelry and decorative items but also tools such as knives, axes, hoes, and weapons. Moreover, copper metallurgy served as a technological foundation on which later neolithic craftsmen developed expertise in the working of gold, bronze, iron, and other metals.

Textile Production

Because natural fibers decay more easily than pottery or copper, the dating of textile production is not certain, but fragments of textiles survive from as early as 6000 B.C.E. As soon as they began to raise crops and keep animals, neolithic peoples experimented with techniques of selective breeding. Before long they had bred strains of plants and animals that provided long, lustrous, easily worked fibers. They then developed technologies for spinning the fibers into threads and weaving the threads into cloth. The invention of textiles was probably the work of women, who were able to spin thread and weave fabrics at home while nursing and watching over small children. In any case, textile production quickly became one of the most important enterprises in agricultural society.

Social Distinctions

The concentration of people into permanent settlements and the increasing specialization of labor provided the first opportunity for individuals to accumulate considerable wealth. Individuals could trade surplus food or manufactured products for gems, jewelry, and other valuable items. The institutionalization of privately owned landed property—which occurred at an uncertain date after the introduction of agriculture—enhanced the significance of accumulated wealth. Because land was (and remains) the ultimate source of wealth in any agricultural society, ownership of land carried enormous economic power. When especially successful individuals managed to consolidate wealth in their families' hands and kept it there for several generations, clearly defined social classes emerged. Already at Çatal Hüyük, for example, differences in wealth and social status are clear from the quality of interior decorations in houses and the value of goods buried with individuals from different social classes.

Neolithic Culture

Quite apart from its social effects, agriculture left its mark on the cultural dimension of the human experience. Because their lives and communities depended on the successful cultivation of crops, neolithic farmers closely observed the natural world around them and noted the conditions that favored successful harvests. In other words, they developed a kind of early applied science. From experience accumulated over the generations, they acquired an impressive working knowledge of the earth and its rhythms. Agricultural peoples had to learn when changes of season would take place: survival depended upon the ability to predict when they could reasonably expect sunshine, rain, warmth, and freezing temperatures. They learned to associate the seasons with the different positions of the sun, moon, and stars. As a result, they accumulated a store of knowledge concerning relationships between the heavens and the earth, and they made the first steps toward the elaboration of a calendar, which would enable them to predict with tolerable accuracy the kind of weather they could expect at various times of the year.

Religious Values   The workings of the natural world also influenced neolithic religion. Paleolithic communities had already honored, and perhaps even worshiped, Venus figurines in hopes of ensuring fertility. Neolithic religion reflected the same interest in fertility, but it celebrated particularly the rhythms that governed agricultural society—birth, growth, death, and regenerated life. Archaeologists have unearthed thousands of neolithic representations of gods and goddesses in the form of clay figurines, drawings on pots and vases, decorations on tools, and ritual objects.

The neolithic gods included not only the life-bearing, Venus-type figures of paleolithic times but also other deities associated with the cycle of life, death, and regeneration. A pregnant goddess of vegetation, for example, represented neolithic hopes for fertility in the fields. Sometimes neolithic worshipers associated these goddesses with animals like frogs or butterflies that dramatically changed form during the course of their lives, just as seeds of grain sprouted, flourished, died, and produced new seed for another agricultural cycle. Meanwhile, young male gods associated with bulls and goats represented the energy and virility that participates in the creation of life.

Some deities were associated with death: many neolithic goddesses possessed the power to bring about decay and destruction. Yet physical death was not an absolute end. The procreative capacities of gods and goddesses resulted in the births of infant deities who represented the regeneration of life—freshly sprouted crops, replenished stocks of domestic animals, and infant human beings to inaugurate a new biological cycle. Thus neolithic religious thought clearly reflected the natural world of early agricultural society.

The Origins of Urban Life

Within four thousand years of its introduction, agriculture had dramatically transformed the face of the earth. Human beings multiplied prodigiously, congregated in densely populated quarters, placed the surrounding lands under cultivation, and domesticated several species of animals. Besides altering the physical appearance of the earth, agriculture also transformed the lives of human beings. Even a modest neolithic village dwarfed a paleolithic band of a few dozen hunters and gatherers. In larger villages and towns, such as Jericho and Çatal Hüyük, with their populations of several thousand people, their specialized labor, and their craft industries, social relationships became more complex than would have been conceivable during paleolithic times. Gradually, dense populations, specialized labor, and complex social relations gave rise to an altogether new form of social organization—the city.

Like the transition from foraging to agricultural society, the development of cities *Emergence of Cities* and complex societies organized around urban centers was a gradual process rather than a well-defined event. Because of favorable location, some neolithic villages and towns attracted more people and grew larger than others. Over time, some of these settlements evolved into cities. What distinguished early cities from their predecessors, the neolithic villages and towns?

Even in their early days, cities differed from neolithic villages and towns in two principal ways. In the first place, cities were larger and more complex than neolithic villages and towns. Çatal Hüyük featured an impressive variety of specialized crafts and industries. With progressively larger populations, cities fostered more intense specialization than any of their predecessors among the neolithic villages and towns. Thus it was in cities that large classes of professionals emerged—individuals who devoted all their time to efforts other than the production of food. Professional craft workers refined existing technologies, invented new ones, and raised levels of quality and production. Professional managers also appeared—governors, administrators, military strategists, tax collectors, and the like—whose services were necessary to the survival of the community. Cities also gave rise to professional cultural specialists such as priests, who maintained their communities' traditions, transmitted their values, organized public rituals, and sought to discover meaning in human existence.

In the second place, whereas neolithic villages and towns served the needs of their inhabitants and immediate neighbors, cities decisively influenced the political, economic, and cultural life of large regions. Cities established marketplaces that attracted buyers and sellers from distant parts. Brisk trade, conducted over increasingly longer distances, promoted economic integration on a much larger scale than was possible in neolithic times. To ensure adequate food supplies for their large populations, cities also extended their claims to authority over their hinterlands, thus becoming centers of political and military control as well as economic influence. In time, too, the building of temples and schools in neighboring regions enabled the cities to extend their cultural traditions and values to surrounding areas.

The earliest known cities grew out of agricultural villages and towns in the valleys of the Tigris and Euphrates rivers in modern-day Iraq. These communities crossed the urban threshold during the period about 4000 to 3500 B.C.E. and soon dominated their regions. During the following centuries cities appeared in several other parts of the world, including Egypt, northern India, northern China, central Mexico, and the central Andean region of South America. Cities became the focal points of public affairs—the sites from which leaders guided human fortunes, supervised neighboring regions, and organized the world's earliest complex societies.

In many ways the world of prehistoric human beings seems remote and even alien. Yet the evolution of the human species and the development of human society during the paleolithic and neolithic eras have profoundly influenced the lives of all the world's peoples during the past six millennia. Paleolithic peoples enjoyed levels of intelligence that far exceeded those of other animals, and they invented tools and languages that enabled them to flourish in all regions of the world. Indeed, they thrived so well that they threatened their sources of food. Their neolithic descendants began to cultivate food in order to sustain their communities, and the agricultural societies that they built transformed the world. Human population rose dramatically, and human groups congregated in villages, towns, and eventually cities. There they engaged in specialized labor and launched industries that produced pottery, metal goods, and textiles as well as tools and decorative items. Thus intelligence, language, reflective thought, agriculture, urban settlements, and craft industries all figure in the legacy that prehistoric human beings left for their descendants.

CHRONOLOGY

4 million–1 million years ago	Era of *Australopithecus*
3.5 million years ago	Era of Lucy
2.5 million–200,000 years ago	Era of *Homo erectus*
200,000 B.C.E.	Early evolution of *Homo sapiens*
200,000–35,000 B.C.E.	Era of Neandertal peoples
40,000 B.C.E.	First appearance of Cro-Magnon peoples *(Homo sapiens sapiens)*
13,500–10,500 B.C.E.	Natufian society
10,000–8000 B.C.E.	Early experimentation with agriculture
10,000–300 B.C.E.	Jomon society
8000 B.C.E.	Appearance of agricultural villages
4000–3500 B.C.E.	Appearance of cities
3000 B.C.E.–1850 C.E.	Chinook society

FOR FURTHER READING

Elizabeth Wayland Barber. *Women's Work: The First 20,000 Years.* New York, 1994. Fascinating study of prehistoric and ancient textiles, which the author argues was a craft industry dominated by women from the earliest times.

V. Gordon Childe. *What Happened in History?* Baltimore, 1964. Survey of human experience from paleolithic times to early urban societies by a distinguished anthropologist.

David Christian. *Maps of Time: An Introduction to Big History.* Berkeley, 2004. A brilliant study that considers human history in the context of natural history since the big bang.

Mark Nathan Cohen. *The Food Crisis in Prehistory: Overpopulation and the Origins of Agriculture.* New Haven, 1977. Contends that overpopulation and food shortages encouraged human communities to resort to cultivation.

———. *Health and the Rise of Civilization.* New Haven, 1989. Argues that human groups faced new dietary problems and diseases as they relied on agriculture and congregated in urban settings.

Jared Diamond. *The Third Chimpanzee: The Evolution and Future of the Human Animal.* New York, 1992. An insightful guide to human evolution and its significance for human behavior.

———. *Guns, Germs, and Steel: The Fates of Human Societies.* New York, 1997. A wide-ranging book that throws fresh light particularly on the invention and early spread of agriculture.

Margaret Ehrenberg. *Women in Prehistory*. London, 1989. Brings archaeological discoveries to bear on questions of sex and gender relations in prehistoric times.

Clive Gamble. *Timewalkers: The Prehistory of Global Civilization*. Cambridge, Mass., 1994. Examines the migration of human beings to all parts of the world in the context of human evolution.

Marija Gimbutas. *The Goddesses and Gods of Old Europe*. London, 1982. A provocative examination of the religions of paleolithic Europe.

———. *The Civilization of the Goddess*. San Francisco, 1991. A controversial but often insightful book especially valuable for its analysis of prehistoric art and religion.

Donald C. Johanson and Maitland A. Edey. *Lucy: The Beginnings of Humankind*. New York, 1981. Fascinating account of the discovery of Lucy and the scholarly controversies that ensued.

Richard E. Leakey. *The Making of Mankind*. New York, 1981. A richly illustrated volume that outlines the evolutionary history of early hominids for a popular audience.

James Mellaart. *Çatal Hüyük: A Neolithic Town in Anatolia*. New York, 1967. Discussion of Çatal Hüyük by its excavator.

John E. Pfeiffer. *The Creative Explosion: An Inquiry into the Origins of Art and Religion*. New York, 1982. Focuses attention on the late paleolithic era when human groups developed sophisticated hunting tools and began to produce works of art.

Kathy D. Schick and Nicholas Toth. *Making Silent Stones Speak: Human Evolution and the Dawn of Technology*. New York, 1993. Fascinating examination of stone tools and paleolithic technology.

Andrew Sherratt. *Economy and Society in Prehistoric Europe: Changing Perspectives*. Princeton, 1997. Collection of brilliant essays by a prominent scholar who places archaeological discoveries in larger social context and emphasizes interactions between prehistoric societies.

Bruce D. Smith. *The Emergence of Agriculture*. New York, 1995. Concentrates on the initial domestication of plant and animal species in world regions where agriculture originated.

Christopher Stringer and Clive Gamble. *In Search of the Neanderthals: Solving the Puzzle of Human Origins*. New York, 1993. Excellent, well-illustrated study of Neandertal peoples and their relationship to modern human beings.

Christopher Stringer and Robin McKie *African Exodus: The Origins of Modern Humanity*. New York, 1996. Offers a contemporary interpretation of human evolution that draws on both archaeological discoveries and recent genetic studies.

Erik Trinkaus and Pat Shipman. *The Neandertals: Changing the Image of Mankind*. New York, 1993. Insightful account of the discovery, study, and interpretation of Neandertal remains.

Peter J. Ucko and Andrée Rosenfeld. *Paleolithic Cave Art*. New York, 1967. Careful, scholarly study of paleolithic art with reflections on artists and their motives.

See our **Online Learning Center** at www.mhhe.com/bentley3 for additional readings, practice maps, quizzes, and internet activities.

Unfamiliar words? Check out the **Primary Source Investigator CD-ROM** for an interactive glossary, interactive maps, more images, and primary sources.

The Royal Standard of Ur, a painting dating from about 2700 B.C.E., depicts scenes from daily life in the Sumerian city-state of Ur.

EARLY SOCIETIES IN SOUTHWEST ASIA AND THE INDO-EUROPEAN MIGRATIONS

By far the best-known individual of ancient Mesopotamian society was a man named Gilgamesh. According to historical sources, Gilgamesh was the fifth king of the city of Uruk. He ruled about 2750 B.C.E.—for a period of 126 years, according to one semilegendary source—and he led his community in its conflicts with Kish, a nearby city that was the principal rival of Uruk. Historical sources record very little additional detail about Gilgamesh's life and deeds.

But Gilgamesh was a figure of Mesopotamian mythology and folklore as well as history. He was the subject of numerous poems and legends, and Mesopotamian bards made him the central figure in a cycle of stories known collectively as the *Epic of Gilgamesh*. As a figure of legend, Gilgamesh became the greatest hero figure of ancient Mesopotamia. According to the stories, the gods granted Gilgamesh a perfect body and endowed him with superhuman strength and courage. He was "the man to whom all things were known," a supremely wise individual who "saw mysteries and knew secret things." The legends declare that he constructed the massive city walls of Uruk as well as several of the city's magnificent temples to Mesopotamian deities.

The stories that make up the *Epic of Gilgamesh* recount the adventures of this hero and his cherished friend Enkidu as they sought fame. They killed an evil monster, rescued Uruk from a ravaging bull, and matched wits with the gods. In spite of their heroic deeds, Enkidu offended the gods and fell under a sentence of death. His loss profoundly affected Gilgamesh, who sought for some means to cheat death and gain eternal life. He eventually found a magical plant that had the power to confer immortality, but a serpent stole the plant and carried it away, forcing Gilgamesh to recognize that death is the ultimate fate of all human beings. Thus, while focusing on the activities of Gilgamesh and Enkidu, the stories explored themes of friendship, loyalty, ambition, fear of death, and longing for immortality. In doing so they reflected the interests and concerns of the complex, urban-based society that had recently emerged in Mesopotamia.

Productive agricultural economies supported the development of the world's first complex societies, in which sizable numbers of people lived in cities and extended their political, social, economic, and cultural influence over large regions. The earliest urban societies so far known emerged during the early fourth millennium B.C.E. in southwest Asia, particularly in Mesopotamia.

As people congregated in cities, they needed to find ways to resolve disputes—sometimes between residents within individual settlements, other times between whole settlements themselves—that inevitably arose as individual and group interests conflicted. In search of order, settled agricultural peoples recognized political authorities and built states throughout Mesopotamia. The establishment of states encouraged the creation of empires, as some states sought to extend their power and enhance their security by imposing their rule on neighboring lands.

Apart from stimulating the establishment of states, urban society in Mesopotamia also promoted the emergence of social classes, thus giving rise to increasingly complex social and economic structures. Cities fostered specialized labor, and the efficient production of high-quality goods in turn stimulated trade. Furthermore, early Mesopotamia also developed distinctive cultural traditions as Mesopotamians invented a system of writing and supported organized religions.

Mesopotamian and other peoples regularly interacted with one another. Mesopotamian prosperity attracted numerous migrants, such as the ancient Hebrews, who settled in the region's cities and adopted Mesopotamian ways. Merchants like the Phoenicians, who also embraced Mesopotamian society, built extensive maritime trade networks that linked southwest Asia with lands throughout the Mediterranean basin. Some Indo-European peoples also had direct dealings with their Mesopotamian contemporaries, with effects crucial for both Indo-European and Mesopotamian societies. Other Indo-European peoples never heard of Mesopotamia, but they employed Mesopotamian inventions like wheels and metallurgy when undertaking extensive migrations that profoundly influenced historical development throughout much of Eurasia from western Europe to India and beyond. Even in the earliest days of city life, the world was the site of frequent and intense interaction between peoples of different societies.

THE QUEST FOR ORDER

During the fourth millennium B.C.E., human population increased rapidly in Mesopotamia. Inhabitants had few precedents to guide them in the organization of a large-scale society. At most they inherited a few techniques for keeping order in the small agricultural villages of neolithic times. By experimentation and adaptation, however, they created states and governmental machinery that brought political and social order to their territories. Moreover, effective political and military organization enabled them to build regional empires and extend their authority to neighboring peoples.

Mesopotamia: "The Land between the Rivers"

The place-name *Mesopotamia* comes from two Greek words meaning "the land between the rivers," and it refers specifically to the fertile valleys of the Tigris and Euphrates rivers in modern-day Iraq. Mesopotamia receives little rainfall, but the Tigris and Euphrates brought large volumes of fresh water to the region. Early cultivators realized that by tapping these rivers, building reservoirs, and digging canals, they could irrigate fields of barley, wheat, and peas. Small-scale irrigation began in Mesopotamia soon after 6000 B.C.E.

Sumer   Artificial irrigation led to increased food supplies, which in turn supported a rapidly increasing human population and attracted migrants from other regions. Human numbers grew especially fast in the land of Sumer in the southern half of Mesopotamia. It is possible that the people known as the Sumerians already inhabited this

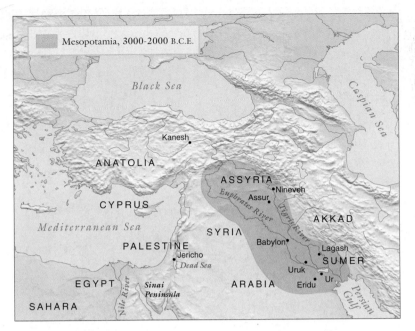

M A P [2 . 1]

Early Mesopotamia, 3000–2000 B.C.E.

land in the sixth millennium B.C.E., but it is perhaps more likely that they were later migrants attracted to the region by its agricultural potential. In either case, by about 5000 B.C.E. the Sumerians were constructing elaborate irrigation networks that helped them realize abundant agricultural harvests. By 3000 B.C.E. the population of Sumer approached one hundred thousand—an unprecedented concentration of people in ancient times—and the Sumerians were the dominant people of Mesopotamia.

Semitic Migrants

While supporting a growing population, the wealth of Sumer also attracted migrants from other regions. Most of the new arrivals were Semitic peoples—so called because they spoke tongues in the Semitic family of languages, including Akkadian, Aramaic, Hebrew, and Phoenician. (Semitic languages spoken in the world today include Arabic and Hebrew, and African peoples speak many other languages related to Semitic tongues.) Semitic peoples were nomadic herders who went to Mesopotamia from the Arabian and Syrian deserts to the south and west. They often intermarried with the Sumerians, and they largely adapted to Sumerian ways.

Beginning around 4000 B.C.E., as human numbers increased in southern Mesopotamia, the Sumerians built the world's first cities. These cities differed markedly from the neolithic villages that preceded them. Unlike the earlier settlements, the Sumerian cities were centers of political and military authority, and their jurisdiction extended into the surrounding regions. Moreover, bustling marketplaces that drew buyers and sellers from near and far turned the cities into economic centers as well. Finally, the cities also served as cultural centers where priests maintained organized religions and scribes developed traditions of writing and formal education.

Sumerian City-States

For almost a millennium, from 3200 to 2350 B.C.E., a dozen Sumerian cities—Eridu, Ur, Uruk, Lagash, Nippur, Kish, and others—dominated public affairs in

The massive temple of the moon god Nanna-Suen (sometimes known as Sin) dominated the Sumerian city of Ur. Constructing temples of this size required a huge investment of resources and thousands of laborers.

Mesopotamia. These cities all experienced internal and external pressures that prompted them to establish states—formal governmental institutions that wielded authority throughout their territories. Internally, the cities needed to maintain order and ensure that inhabitants cooperated on community projects. With their expanding populations, the cities also needed to prevent conflicts between urban residents from escalating into serious civic disorder. Moreover, because agriculture was crucial to the welfare of urban residents, the cities all became city-states: they not only controlled public life within the city walls but also oversaw affairs in surrounding agricultural regions.

While preserving the peace, government authorities also organized work on projects of value to the entire community. Palaces, temples, and defensive walls dominated all the Sumerian cities, and all were the work of laborers recruited and coordinated by government authorities like Gilgamesh, whom legendary accounts credit with the building of city walls and temples at Uruk. Particularly impressive were the ziggurats—distinctive stepped pyramids that housed temples and altars to the principal local deity. In the city of Uruk, a massive ziggurat and temple complex went up about 3200 B.C.E. to honor the fertility goddess Inanna. Scholars have calculated that its construction required the services of fifteen hundred laborers working ten hours per day for five years.

Even more important than buildings were the irrigation systems that supported productive agriculture and urban society. As their population grew, the Sumerians

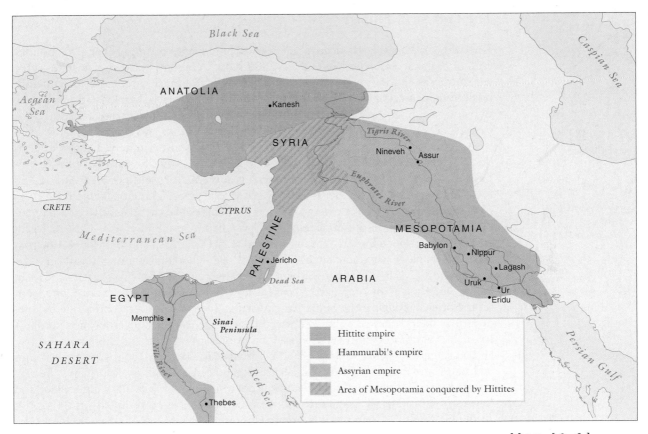

MAP [2.2]

Mesopotamian empires, 1800–600 B.C.E.

For an interactive version of this map, go to www.mhhe.com/ bentley3ch2maps.

expanded their networks of reservoirs and canals. The construction, maintenance, and repair of the irrigation systems required the labor of untold thousands of workers. Only recognized government authorities had the standing to draft workers for this difficult labor and order them to participate in such large-scale projects. Even when the irrigation systems functioned perfectly, recognized authority was still necessary to ensure equitable distribution of water and to resolve disputes.

In addition to their internal pressures, the Sumerian cities also faced external problems. The wealth stored in Sumerian cities attracted the interest of peoples outside the cities. Mesopotamia is a mostly flat land with few natural geographic barriers. It was a simple matter for raiders to attack the Sumerian cities and take their wealth. The cities responded to this threat by building defensive walls and organizing military forces. The need to recruit, train, equip, maintain, and deploy military forces created another demand for recognized authority.

Sumerian Kings

The earliest Sumerian governments were probably assemblies of prominent men who made decisions on behalf of the whole community. When crises arose, assemblies yielded their power to individuals who possessed full authority during the period of emergency. These individual rulers gradually usurped the authority of the assemblies and established themselves as monarchs. By about 3000 B.C.E. all Sumerian cities had kings who claimed absolute authority within their realms. In fact, however, the kings generally ruled in cooperation with local nobles, who came mostly from the ranks of military leaders who had displayed special valor in battle. By 2500 B.C.E. city-states dominated public life in Sumer, and city-states like Assur and Nineveh had also begun to emerge in northern Mesopotamia.

The Course of Empire

Once they had organized effective states, Mesopotamians ventured beyond the boundaries of their own societies. As early as 2800 B.C.E., conflicts between city-states often led to war, as aggrieved or ambitious kings sought to punish or conquer their neighbors. Sumerian accounts indicate that the king of Kish, a city-state located just east of Babylon, extended his rule to much of southern Mesopotamia after 2800 B.C.E., for example, while Sumerian poems praised King Gilgamesh for later liberating Uruk from Kish's control. In efforts to move beyond these constant conflicts, a series of conquerors worked to establish order on a scale larger than the city-state by building empires that supervised the affairs of numerous subject cities and peoples. After 2350 B.C.E. Mesopotamia fell under the control of several powerful regional empires.

Sargon of Akkad

-first imperialist

These regional empires emerged as Semitic peoples like the Akkadians and Babylonians of northern Mesopotamia began to overshadow the Sumerians. The creator of empire in Mesopotamia was Sargon of Akkad, a city near Kish and Babylon whose precise location has so far eluded archaeologists. A talented administrator and brilliant warrior, Sargon (2370–2315 B.C.E.) began his career as a minister to the king of Kish. About 2334 B.C.E. he organized a coup against the king, recruited an army, and went on the offensive against the Sumerian city-states. He conquered the cities one by one, destroyed their defensive walls, and placed them under his own governors and administrators. As Sargon's conquests mounted, his armies grew larger and more professional, and no single city-state could withstand his forces. He also seized control of trade routes and supplies of natural resources like silver, tin, and cedar wood. By controlling and taxing trade, Sargon obtained financial resources to maintain his military juggernaut and transform his capital of Akkad into the wealthiest and most powerful city in the world. At the high point of his reign, his empire embraced all of Mesopotamia, and his armies had ventured as far afield as the Mediterranean and Black Sea.

For several generations Sargon's successors maintained his empire. Gradually, though, it weakened, partly because of chronic rebellion in city-states that resented imperial rule, partly also because of invasions by peoples hoping to seize a portion of Mesopotamia's fabulous wealth. By about 2150 B.C.E. Sargon's empire had collapsed altogether. Yet the memory of his deeds, recorded in legends and histories as well as in his own works of propaganda, inspired later conquerors to follow his example.

Hammurabi and the Babylonian Empire

Most prominent of the later conquerors was the Babylonian Hammurabi (reigned 1792–1750 B.C.E.), who styled himself "king of the four quarters of the world." The Babylonian empire dominated Mesopotamia until about 1600 B.C.E. Hammurabi improved on Sargon's administrative techniques by relying on centralized bureaucratic rule and regular taxation. Instead of traveling from city to city with an army both large and hungry, Hammurabi and his successors ruled from Babylon (located near modern Baghdad) and stationed deputies in

Bronze bust of a Mesopotamian king often thought to represent Sargon of Akkad. The sculpture dates to about 2350 B.C.E. and reflects high levels of expertise in the working of bronze.

the territories they controlled. Instead of confiscating supplies and other wealth in the unfortunate regions their armies visited, Hammurabi and later rulers instituted less ruinous but more regular taxes collected by their officials. By these means Hammurabi developed a more efficient and predictable government than his predecessors and also spread its costs more evenly over the population.

Hammurabi also sought to maintain his empire by providing it with a code of law. Sumerian rulers had promulgated laws perhaps as early as 2500 B.C.E., and Hammurabi borrowed liberally from his predecessors in compiling the most extensive and most complete Mesopotamian law code. In the prologue to his laws, Hammurabi proclaimed that the gods had chosen him "to promote the welfare of the people, . . . to cause justice to prevail in the land, to destroy the wicked and evil, [so] that the strong might not oppress the weak, to rise like the sun over the people, and to light up the land." Hammurabi's laws established high standards of behavior and stern punishments for violators. They prescribed death penalties for murder, theft, fraud,

Hammurabi's Laws

This handsome basalt stele shows Hammurabi receiving his royal authority from the sun god, Shamash. Some four thousand lines of Hammurabi's laws are inscribed below.

false accusations, sheltering of runaway slaves, failure to obey royal orders, adultery, and incest. Civil laws regulated prices, wages, commercial dealings, marital relationships, and the conditions of slavery.

The code relied heavily on the principle of *lex talionis,* the "law of retaliation," whereby offenders suffered punishments resembling their violations. But the code also took account of social standing when applying this principle. It provided, for example, that a noble who destroyed the eye or broke the bone of another noble would have his own eye destroyed or bone broken, but if a noble destroyed the eye or broke the bone of a commoner, the noble merely paid a fine in silver. Local judges did not always follow the prescriptions of Hammurabi's code: indeed, they frequently relied on their own judgment when deciding cases that came before them. Nevertheless, Hammurabi's laws established a set of common standards that lent some degree of cultural unity to the far-flung Babylonian empire.

Despite Hammurabi's administrative efficiencies and impressive law code, the wealth of the Babylonian empire attracted invaders, particularly the Hittites, who had built a powerful empire in Anatolia (modern-day Turkey), and about 1595 B.C.E. the Babylonian empire crumbled before Hittite assaults. For several centuries after the fall of Babylon, southwest Asia was a land of considerable turmoil, as regional states competed for power and position while migrants and invaders struggled to establish footholds for themselves in Mesopotamia and neighboring regions.

The Later Mesopotamian Empires

Imperial rule returned to Mesopotamia with the Assyrians, a hardy people from northern Mesopotamia who had built a compact state in the Tigris River valley during the nineteenth century B.C.E. Taking advantage of their location on trade routes running both north-south and east-west, the Assyrians built flourishing cities at Assur and Nineveh. They built a powerful and intimidating army by organizing their forces into standardized units and placing them under the command of professional officers. The Assyrians appointed these officers because of merit, skill, and bravery rather than noble birth or family connections. They supplemented infantry with cavalry forces and light, swift, horse-drawn chariots, which they borrowed from the Hittites. These chariots were devastating instruments of war that allowed archers to attack their enemies from rapidly moving platforms. Waves of Assyrian chariots stormed their opponents with a combination of high speed and withering firepower that unnerved the opponents and left them vulnerable to the Assyrian infantry and cavalry forces.

The Assyrian Empire   After the collapse of the Babylonian empire, the Assyrian state was one among many jockeying for power and position in northern Mesopotamia. After about 1300 B.C.E., however, Assyrians gradually extended their authority to much of southwest Asia. They made use of recently invented iron weapons to strengthen their army, which pushed relentlessly in all directions. At its high point, during the eighth and seventh centuries B.C.E., the Assyrian empire embraced not only Mesopotamia but also Syria, Palestine, much of Anatolia, and most of Egypt.

Like most other Mesopotamian peoples, the Assyrians relied on the administrative techniques pioneered by their Babylonian predecessors, and they followed laws much like those enshrined in the code of Hammurabi. They also preserved a great deal of Mesopotamian literature in huge libraries maintained at their large and lavish courts. Yet Assyrian domination was extremely unpopular. Assyrian rulers faced intermittent rebellion by subjects in one part or another of their far-flung empire, which was too large for them to administer effectively. A combination of internal unrest and external assault brought their empire down in 612 B.C.E.

Nebuchadnezzar and the New Babylonian Empire   For half a century, from 600 to 550 B.C.E., Babylon once again dominated Mesopotamia during the New Babylonian empire, sometimes called the Chaldean empire. King Nebuchadnezzar (reigned 605–562 B.C.E.) lavished wealth and resources on his capital city. Babylon occupied some 850 hectares (more than 2,100 acres), and the city's defensive walls were reportedly so thick that a four-horse chariot could turn around on top of them. Within the walls there were enormous palaces and 1,179 temples, some of them faced with gold and decorated with thousands of statues. When one of the king's wives longed for flowering shrubs from her mountain homeland, Nebuchadnezzar had them planted in terraces above the city walls, and the hanging gardens of Babylon have symbolized the city's luxuriousness ever since.

By this time, however, peoples beyond Mesopotamia had acquired advanced weapons and experimented with techniques of administering large territories. By the mid-sixth century B.C.E. Mesopotamians largely lost control of their affairs, as foreign conquerors absorbed them into their own empires.

A relief sculpture from the seventh century B.C.E. depicts the Assyrian king Ashurbanipal on a hunting expedition. Here the king spears a lion.

THE FORMATION OF A COMPLEX SOCIETY AND SOPHISTICATED CULTURAL TRADITIONS

With the emergence of cities and the congregation of dense populations in urban spaces, specialized labor proliferated. The Mesopotamian economy became increasingly diverse, and trade linked the region with distant peoples. Clearly defined social classes emerged, as small groups of people concentrated wealth and power in their own hands, and Mesopotamia developed into a patriarchal society that vested authority largely in adult males. While building a complex society, Mesopotamians also allocated some of their resources to individuals who worked to develop sophisticated cultural traditions. They invented systems of writing that enabled them to record information for future retrieval. Writing soon became a foundation for education, science, literature, and religious reflection.

Economic Specialization and Trade

When large numbers of people began to congregate in cities and work at tasks other than agriculture, they vastly expanded the stock of human skills. Craftsmen refined techniques inherited from earlier generations and experimented with new ways of doing things. Pottery, textile manufacture, woodworking, leather production, brick making, stonecutting, and masonry all became distinct occupations in the world's earliest cities.

Bronze Metallurgy

Metallurgical innovations ranked among the most important developments that came about because of specialized labor. Already in neolithic times, craftsmen had fashioned copper into tools and jewelry. In pure form, however, copper is too soft for use as an effective weapon or as a tool for heavy work. About 4000 B.C.E. Mesopotamian metalworkers discovered that if they alloyed copper with tin, they could make much harder and stronger implements. Experimentation with copper metallurgy thus led to the invention of bronze. Because both copper and tin were relatively rare and hence expensive, most people could not afford bronze implements. But bronze had an immediate impact on military affairs, as craftsmen turned out swords, spears, axes, shields, and armor made of the recently invented metal. Over a longer period, bronze also had an impact on agriculture. Mesopotamian farmers began to use bronze knives and bronze-tipped plows instead of tools made of bone, wood, stone, or obsidian.

Iron Metallurgy

After about 1000 B.C.E. Mesopotamian craftsmen began to manufacture effective tools and weapons with iron as well as bronze. Experimentation with iron metallurgy began as early as the fourth millennium B.C.E., but early efforts resulted in products that were too brittle for heavy-duty uses. About 1300 B.C.E. craftsmen from Hittite society in Anatolia (discussed later in this chapter) developed techniques of forging exceptionally strong iron tools and weapons. Iron metallurgy soon spread throughout Anatolia, Mesopotamia, and other regions as well, and Assyrian conquerors made particularly effective use of iron weapons in building their empire. Because iron deposits are much cheaper and more widely available than copper and tin, the ingredients of bronze, iron quickly became the metal of choice for weapons and tools.

The Wheel

While some craftsmen refined the techniques of bronze and iron metallurgy, others devised efficient means of transportation based on wheeled vehicles and sailing ships, both of which facilitated long-distance trade. The first use of wheels probably took place about 3500 B.C.E., and Sumerians were building wheeled carts by 3000 B.C.E. Wheeled carts and wagons enabled people to haul heavy loads of bulk goods—such as grain, bricks, or metal ores—over much longer distances than human porters or draft animals could manage. The wheel rapidly diffused from Sumer to neighboring lands, and within a few centuries it had become a standard means of overland transportation.

Shipbuilding

Sumerians also experimented with technologies of maritime transportation. By 3500 B.C.E. they had built watercraft that allowed them to venture into the Persian Gulf and beyond. By 2300 B.C.E. they were trading regularly with merchants of Harappan society in the Indus River valley of northern India (discussed in chapter 4), which they reached by sailing through the Persian Gulf and the Arabian Sea. Until about 1750 B.C.E. Sumerian merchants shipped woolen textiles, leather goods, sesame oil, and jewelry to India in exchange for copper, ivory, pearls, and semiprecious stones. During the time of the Babylonian empire, Mesopotamians traded extensively with peoples in all directions: they imported silver from Anatolia, cedar wood from Lebanon, copper from Arabia, gold from Egypt, tin from Persia, lapis lazuli from Afghanistan, and semiprecious stones from northern India.

Trade Networks

Archaeological excavations have shed bright light on one Mesopotamian trade network in particular. During the early second millennium B.C.E., Assyrian merchants traveled regularly by donkey caravan some 1,600 kilometers (1,000 miles) from their home of Assur in northern Mesopotamia to Kanesh (modern Kültepe) in Anatolia. Surviving correspondence shows that during the forty-five years from 1810 to 1765 B.C.E. merchants transported at least eighty tons of tin and one hundred thousand textiles from Assur and returned from Kanesh with no less than ten tons of silver. The correspondence also shows that the merchants and their families operated a well-organized business. Merchants' wives and children manufactured textiles in Assur and sent them to their menfolk who lived in trading colonies at Kanesh. The merchants responded with orders for textiles in the styles desired at Kanesh.

The Emergence of a Stratified Patriarchal Society

Social Classes

Agriculture enabled human groups to accumulate wealth, and clear distinctions between the more and less wealthy appeared already in neolithic villages like Jericho and Çatal Hüyük. With increasingly specialized labor and long-distance trade, however, cities provided many more opportunities for the accumulation of wealth. Social distinctions in Mesopotamia became much more sharply defined than those of neolithic villages.

In early Mesopotamia the ruling classes consisted of kings and nobles who won their positions because of their valor and success as warriors. Community members

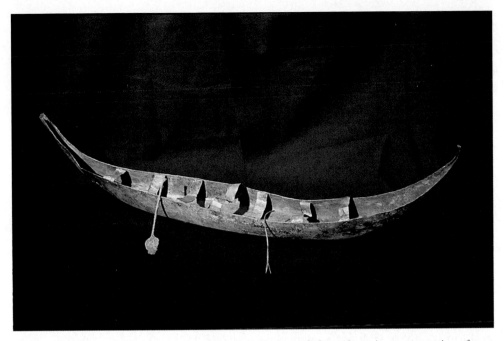

A silver model of a boat discovered in a royal tomb at Ur throws light on Sumerian transportation of grain and other goods on the rivers, canals, and marshes of southern Mesopotamia about 2700 B.C.E.

originally elected their kings, but royal status soon became hereditary, as kings arranged for their sons to succeed them. Nobles were mostly members of royal families and other close supporters of the kings.

The early kings of the Sumerian cities made such a deep impression on their contemporaries that legends portrayed them as offspring of the gods. According to many legends, for example, Gilgamesh of Uruk, the son of a goddess and a king, was two-thirds divine and one-third human. Some legends recognized him as a full-fledged god. Large-scale construction projects ordered by the kings and the lavish decoration of capital cities also reflected the high status of the Mesopotamian ruling classes. All the Mesopotamian cities boasted massive city walls and imposing public buildings.

Closely allied with the ruling elites were priests and priestesses, many of whom were younger relatives of the rulers. The principal role of the priestly elites was to intervene with the gods to ensure good fortune for their communities. In exchange for these services, priests and priestesses lived in temple communities and received offerings of food, drink, and clothing from city inhabitants. Temples also generated their own income from vast tracts of land that they owned and large workshops that they maintained. One temple community near the city of Lagash employed six thousand textile workers between 2150 and 2100 B.C.E. Other temple communities cultivated grains, herded sheep and goats, and manufactured leather, wood, metal, and stone goods. Because of their wealth, temples provided comfortable livings for their inhabitants, and they also served the needs of the larger community. Temples functioned as banks where individuals could store wealth, and they helped underwrite trading ventures to distant lands. They also helped those in need by taking in orphans, supplying grain in times of famine, and providing ransoms for community members captured in battle.

Apart from the ruling and priestly elites, Mesopotamian society included less privileged classes of free commoners, dependent clients, and slaves. Free commoners mostly worked as peasant cultivators in the countryside on land owned by their families,

Temple Communities

Gypsum carving of an elderly couple from the city of Nippur about 2500 B.C.E.

although some also worked in the cities as builders, craftsmen, or professionals, such as physicians or engineers. Dependent clients had fewer options than free commoners because they possessed no property. Dependent clients usually worked as agricultural laborers on estates owned by others, including the king, nobles, or priestly communities, and they owed a portion of their production to the landowners. Free commoners and dependent clients all paid taxes—usually in the form of surplus agricultural production—that supported the ruling classes, military forces, and temple communities. In addition, when conscripted by ruling authorities, free commoners and dependent clients also provided labor services for large-scale construction projects involving roads, city walls, irrigation systems, temples, and public buildings.

Slaves

Slaves came from three main sources: prisoners of war, convicted criminals, and heavily indebted individuals who sold themselves into slavery in order to satisfy their obligations. Some slaves worked as agricultural laborers on the estates of nobles or temple communities, but most were domestic servants in wealthy households. Many masters granted slaves their freedom, often with a financial bequest, after several years of good service. Slaves with accommodating masters sometimes even engaged in small-scale trade and earned enough money to purchase their own freedom.

Patriarchal Society

While recognizing differences of rank, wealth, and social status, Mesopotamians also built a patriarchal society that vested authority over public and private affairs in adult men. Within their households men decided the work that family members would perform and made marriage arrangements for their children as well as any others who came under their authority. Men also dominated public life. Men ruled as kings, and decisions about policies and public affairs rested almost entirely in men's hands.

Hammurabi's laws throw considerable light on sex and gender relations in ancient Mesopotamia. The laws recognized men as heads of their households and entrusted all major family decisions to their judgment. Men even had the power to sell their wives and children into slavery to satisfy their debts. In the interests of protecting the reputations of husbands and the legitimacy of offspring, the laws prescribed death by drowning as the punishment for adulterous wives, as well as for their partners, while permitting men to engage in consensual sexual relations with concubines, slaves, or prostitutes without penalty.

Women's Roles

In spite of their subordinate legal status, women made their influence felt in Mesopotamian society. At ruling courts women sometimes advised kings and their governments. A few women wielded great power as high priestesses who managed the enormous estates belonging to their temples. Others obtained a formal education and worked as scribes—literate individuals who prepared administrative and legal documents for governments and private parties. Women also pursued careers as midwives, shopkeepers, brewers, bakers, tavern keepers, and textile manufacturers.

During the second millennium B.C.E., Mesopotamian men progressively tightened their control over the social and sexual behavior of women. To protect family fortunes and guarantee the legitimacy of heirs, Mesopotamians insisted on the virginity of brides at marriage, and they forbade casual socializing between married women and men outside their family. By 1500 B.C.E. and probably even earlier, married women in Mesopotamian cities had begun to wear veils when they ventured beyond their own households in order to discourage the attention of men from other families. This concern to control women's social and sexual behavior spread throughout much of southwest Asia and the Mediterranean basin, where it reinforced patriarchal social structures.

The Development of Written Cultural Traditions

The world's earliest known writing came from Mesopotamia. Sumerians invented a system of writing about the middle of the fourth millennium B.C.E. to keep track of

Sources from the Past

Hammurabi's Laws on Family Relationships

By the time of Hammurabi, Mesopotamian marriages had come to represent important business and economic relationships between families. Hammurabi's laws reflect a concern to ensure the legitimacy of children and to protect the economic interests of both marital partners and their families. While placing women under the authority of their fathers and husbands, the laws also protected women against unreasonable treatment by their husbands or other men.

128: If a seignior acquired a wife, but did not draw up the contracts for her, that woman is no wife.

129: If the wife of a seignior has been caught while lying [i.e., having sexual relations] with another man, they shall bind them and throw them into the water. If the husband of the woman wishes to spare his wife, then the king in turn may spare his subject.

130: If a seignior bound the (betrothed) wife of a(nother) seignior, who had no intercourse with a male and was still living in her father's house, and he has lain in her bosom and they have caught him, that seignior shall be put to death, while that woman shall go free.

131: If a seignior's wife was accused by her husband, but she was not caught while lying with another man, she shall make affirmation by god and return to her house. . . .

138: If a seignior wishes to divorce his wife who did not bear him children, he shall give her money to the full amount of her marriage-price [money or goods that the husband paid to the bride's family in exchange for the right to marry her] and he shall also make good to her the dowry [money or goods that the bride brought to the marriage] which she brought from her father's house and then he may divorce her.

139: If there was no marriage-price, he shall give her one mina of silver as the divorce-settlement.

140: If he is a peasant, he shall give her one-third mina of silver.

141: If a seignior's wife, who was living in the house of the seignior, has made up her mind to leave in order that she may engage in business, thus neglecting her house (and) humiliating her husband, they shall prove it against her; and if her husband has then decided on her divorce, he may divorce her, with nothing to be given her as her divorce-settlement upon her departure. If her husband has not decided on her divorce, her husband may marry another woman, with the former woman living in the house of her husband like a maidservant.

142: If a woman so hated her husband that she has declared, "You may not have me," her record shall be investigated at her city council, and if she was careful and was not at fault, even though her husband has been going out and disparaging her greatly, that woman, without incurring any blame at all, may take her dowry and go off to her father's house.

143: If she was not careful, but was a gadabout, thus neglecting her house (and) humiliating her husband, they shall throw that woman into the water.

SOURCE: James B. Pritchard, ed. *Ancient Near Eastern Texts Relating to the Old Testament.* Princeton: Princeton University Press, 1955, pp. 171–72.

Discuss the extent to which Hammurabi's various provisions on family relationships protected the interests of different groups—husbands, wives, and the family itself.

commercial transactions and tax collections. They first experimented with pictographs representing animals, agricultural products, and trade items—such as sheep, oxen, wheat, barley, pots, and fish—that figured prominently in tax and commercial transactions. By 3100 B.C.E. conventional signs representing specific words had spread throughout Mesopotamia.

A writing system that depends on pictures is useful for purposes such as keeping records, but it is a cumbersome way to communicate abstract ideas. Beginning about

Cuneiform Writing

Cuneiform tablet from Ur dating from the period 2900 to 2600 B.C.E. It records deliveries of barley to a temple.

2900 B.C.E. the Sumerians developed a more flexible system of writing that used graphic symbols to represent sounds, syllables, and ideas as well as physical objects. By combining pictographs and other symbols, the Sumerians created a powerful writing system.

When writing, a Sumerian scribe used a stylus fashioned from a reed to impress symbols on wet clay. Because the stylus left lines and wedge-shaped marks, Sumerian writing is known as *cuneiform,* a term that comes from two Latin words meaning "wedge-shaped." When dried in the sun or baked in an oven, the clay hardened and preserved a permanent record of the scribe's message. Many examples of early Sumerian writing survive to the present day. Babylonians, Assyrians, and other peoples later adapted the Sumerians' script to their own languages, and the tradition of cuneiform writing continued for more than three thousand years. Although it entered a period of decline in the fourth century B.C.E. after the arrival of Greek alphabetic script, in which each written symbol represents a distinct, individual sound, scribes continued to produce cuneiform documents into the early centuries C.E.

Education   Most education in ancient times was vocational instruction designed to train individuals to work in specific trades and crafts. Yet Mesopotamians also established formal schools, since it required a great deal of time and concentrated effort to learn cuneiform writing. Most of those who learned to read and write became scribes or government officials. A few pursued their studies further and became priests, physicians, or professionals such as engineers and architects. Formal education was by no means common, but already by 3000 B.C.E., literacy was essential to the smooth functioning of Mesopotamian society.

Though originally invented for purposes of keeping records, writing clearly had potential that went far beyond the purely practical matter of storing information. Mesopotamians relied on writing to communicate complex ideas about the world, the gods, human beings, and their relationships with one another. Indeed, writing made possible the emergence of a distinctive cultural tradition that shaped Mesopotamian values for almost three thousand years.

Astronomy and Mathematics   Literacy led to a rapid expansion of knowledge. Mesopotamian scholars devoted themselves to the study of astronomy and mathematics—both important sciences for agricultural societies. Knowledge of astronomy helped them prepare accurate calendars, which in turn enabled them to chart the rhythms of the seasons and determine the appropriate times for planting and harvesting crops. They used their mathematical skills to survey agricultural lands and allocate them to the proper owners or tenants. Some Mesopotamian conventions persist to the present day: Mesopotamian scientists divided the year into twelve months, for example, and they divided the hours of the day into sixty minutes, each composed of sixty seconds.

The Epic of Gilgamesh   Mesopotamians also used writing to communicate abstract ideas, investigate intellectual problems, and reflect on human beings and their place in the world. Best known of the reflective literature from Mesopotamia is the *Epic of Gilgamesh*. Parts of this work came from the Sumerian city-states, but the whole epic, as known today, was the work of compilers who lived after 2000 B.C.E. during the days of the Babylonian empire. In recounting the experiences of Gilgamesh and Enkidu, the epic explored themes of friendship, relations between humans and the gods, and especially the meaning of life and death. The stories of Gilgamesh and Enkidu resonated so widely that for some two thousand years—from the time of the Sumerian city-states to the fall of the Assyrian empire—they were the principal vehicles for Mesopotamian reflections on moral issues.

THE BROADER INFLUENCE OF MESOPOTAMIAN SOCIETY

While building cities and regional states, Mesopotamians deeply influenced the development and experiences of peoples living far beyond their own lands. Often their wealth and power attracted the attention of neighboring peoples. Sometimes Mesopotamians projected their power to foreign lands and imposed their ways by force. Occasionally migrants left Mesopotamia and carried their inherited traditions to new lands. Mesopotamian influence did not completely transform other peoples and turn them into carbon copies of Mesopotamians. To the contrary, other peoples adopted Mesopotamian ways selectively and adapted them to their own needs and interests. Yet the broader impact of Mesopotamian society shows that even in early times, complex agricultural societies organized around cities had strong potential to influence the development of distant human communities.

Hebrews, Israelites, and Jews

The best-known cases of early Mesopotamian influence involved Hebrews, Israelites, and Jews, who preserved memories of their historical experiences in an extensive collection of sacred writings. Hebrews were speakers of the ancient Hebrew language. Israelites formed a branch of Hebrews who settled in Palestine (modern-day Israel) after 1300 B.C.E. Jews descended from southern Israelites who inhabited the kingdom of Judah. For more than two thousand years, Hebrews, Israelites, and Jews interacted constantly with Mesopotamians and other peoples as well, with profound consequences for the development of their own societies.

The Early Hebrews

The earliest Hebrews were pastoral nomads who inhabited lands between Mesopotamia and Egypt during the second millennium B.C.E. As Mesopotamia prospered, some of the Hebrews settled in the region's cities. According to the Hebrew scriptures (the Old Testament of the Christian Bible), the Hebrew patriarch Abraham came from the Sumerian city of Ur, but he migrated to Palestine about 1850 B.C.E., perhaps because of disorder in Sumer. Abraham's descendants continued to recognize many of the deities, values, and customs common to Mesopotamian peoples. Hebrew law, for example, borrowed the principle of *lex talionis* from Hammurabi's code. The Hebrews also told the story of a devastating flood that had destroyed all early human society. Their account was a variation on similar flood stories related from the earliest days of Sumerian society. One early version of the story made its way into the *Epic of Gilgamesh*. The Hebrews altered the story and adapted it to their own interests and purposes, but their familiarity with the flood story shows that they participated fully in the larger society of Mesopotamia.

MAP [2.3]
Israel and Phoenicia,
1500–600 B.C.E.

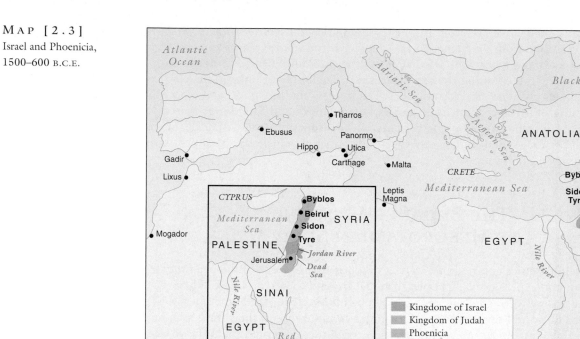

*Migrations
and Settlement
in Palestine*

According to their scriptures, some Hebrews migrated from Palestine to Egypt during the eighteenth century B.C.E. About 1300 B.C.E., however, this branch of the Hebrews departed under the leadership of Moses and went to Palestine. Organized into a loose federation of twelve tribes, these Hebrews, known as the Israelites, fought bitterly with other inhabitants of Palestine and carved out a territory for themselves. Eventually the Israelites abandoned their inherited tribal structure in favor of a Mesopotamian-style monarchy that brought all their twelve tribes under unified rule. During the reigns of King David (1000–970 B.C.E.) and King Solomon (970–930 B.C.E.), Israelites dominated the territory between Syria and the Sinai peninsula. They built an elaborate and cosmopolitan capital city at Jerusalem and entered into diplomatic and commercial relations with Mesopotamians, Egyptians, and Arabian peoples. Like other peoples of southwest Asia, the Israelites made use of iron technology to strengthen their military forces and produce tough agricultural implements.

*Moses and
Monotheism*

After the time of Moses, the religious beliefs of the Israelites developed along increasingly distinctive lines. The early Hebrews had recognized many of the same gods as their Mesopotamian neighbors: they believed that nature spirits inhabited trees, rocks, and mountains, for example, and they honored various deities as patrons or protectors of their clans. Moses, however, embraced monotheism: he taught that there was only one god, known as Yahweh, who was a supremely powerful deity, the creator and sustainer of the world. All other gods, including the various Mesopotamian deities, were false imposters—figments of the human imagination rather than true and powerful gods. When the kings of the Israelites established their capital at Jerusalem, they did not build a ziggurat, which they associated with false Mesopotamian gods but, rather, a magnificent, lavishly decorated temple in honor of Yahweh.

Although he was the omnipotent creator of the universe, Yahweh was also a very personal god. He expected his followers to worship him alone, and he demanded that they observe high moral and ethical standards. In the Ten Commandments, a set of religious and ethical principles that Moses announced to the Israelites, Yahweh warned his followers against destructive and antisocial behavior like lying, theft, adul-

An Assyrian relief sculpture depicts King Jehu of Israel paying tribute to King Shalmaneser III of Assyria about the middle of the ninth century B.C.E.

tery, and murder. A detailed and elaborate legal code prepared after Moses's death instructed the Israelites further to provide relief and protection for widows, orphans, slaves, and the poor. Between about 1000 and 400 B.C.E., the Israelites' religious leaders compiled their teachings in a set of holy scriptures known as the Torah (Hebrew for "doctrine" or "teaching"), which laid down Yahweh's laws and outlined his role in creating the world and guiding human affairs. The Torah taught that Yahweh would reward individuals who obeyed his will and punish those who did not. It also taught that Yahweh would reward or punish the whole community collectively, according to its observance of his commandments.

Assyrian and Babylonian Conquests

After the tenth century, the Israelites experienced a series of political and military setbacks. Following King Solomon's reign, tribal tensions led to the division of the community into a large kingdom of Israel in the north and a smaller kingdom of Judah in the land known as Judea to the south. During the ninth century B.C.E. the kingdom of Israel came under pressure of the expanding Assyrian empire and even had to pay tribute to Assyrian rulers. In 722 B.C.E. Assyrian forces conquered the northern kingdom and deported many of its inhabitants to other regions. Many of these exiles assimilated into other communities and lost their identity as Israelites. The kingdom of Judah retained its independence only temporarily: founders of the New Babylonian empire toppled the Assyrians, then looked south, conquered the kingdom of Judah, and destroyed Jerusalem in 586 B.C.E. Again, the conquerors forced many residents into exile. Unlike their cousins to the north, however, most of these Israelites maintained their religious identity, and many of the deportees eventually returned to Judea, where they became known as Jews.

Ironically, perhaps, the Israelites' devotion to Yahweh intensified during this era of turmoil. Between the ninth and sixth centuries B.C.E., a series of prophets urged the Israelites to rededicate themselves to their faith and obey Yahweh's commandments. These prophets were moral and social critics who blasted their compatriots for their materialism, their neglect of the needy, and their abominable interest in the fertility gods and nature deities worshiped by neighboring peoples. The prophets warned the Israelites that unless they mended their ways, Yahweh would punish them by sending conquerors to humiliate and enslave them. Many Israelites took the Assyrian and Babylonian conquests as proof that the prophets accurately represented Yahweh's mind and will.

*The Early Jewish
Community*

The exiles who returned to Judea after the Babylonian conquest did not abandon hope for a state of their own, and indeed they organized several small Jewish states as tributaries to the great empires that dominated southwest Asia after the sixth century B.C.E. But the returnees also built a distinctive religious community based on their conviction that they had a special relationship with Yahweh, their devotion to Yahweh's teachings as expressed in the Torah, and their concern for justice and righteousness. These elements enabled the Jews to maintain a strong sense of identity as a people distinct from Mesopotamians and others, even as they participated fully in the development of a larger complex society in southwest Asia. Over the longer term, Jewish monotheism, scriptures, and moral concerns also profoundly influenced the development of Christianity and Islam.

The Phoenicians

North of the Israelites' kingdom in Palestine, the Phoenicians occupied a narrow coastal plain between the Mediterranean Sea and the Lebanon Mountains. They spoke a Semitic language, referring to themselves as Canaanites and their land as Canaan. (The term *Phoenician* comes from early Greek references.)

*The Early
Phoenicians*

Ancestors of the Phoenicians migrated to the Mediterranean coast and built their first settlements sometime after 3000 B.C.E. They did not establish a unified monarchy but rather organized a series of independent city-states ruled by local kings. The major cities—Tyre, Sidon, Beirut, and Byblos—had considerable influence over their smaller neighbors, and during the tenth century B.C.E. Tyre dominated southern Phoenicia. Generally speaking, however, the Phoenicians showed more interest in pursuing commercial opportunities than in state building or military expansion. Indeed, Phoenician cities were often subject to imperial rule from Egypt or Mesopotamia.

*Phoenician Trade
Networks*

Though not a numerous or militarily powerful people, the Phoenicians influenced societies throughout the Mediterranean basin because of their maritime trade and communication networks. Their meager lands did not permit development of a large agricultural society, so after about 2500 B.C.E. the Phoenicians turned increasingly to industry and trade. They traded overland with Mesopotamian and other peoples, and they provided much of the cedar timber, furnishings, and decorative items that went into the Israelites' temple in Jerusalem. Soon the Phoenicians ventured onto the seas and engaged also in maritime trade. They imported food and raw materials in exchange for high-quality metal goods, textiles, pottery, glass, and works of art that they produced for export. They enjoyed a special reputation for brilliant red and purple textiles colored with dyes extracted from several species of mollusc that were common in waters near Phoenicia. They also supplied Mesopotamians and Egyptians with cedar logs from the Lebanon Mountains for construction and shipbuilding.

The Phoenicians were excellent sailors, and they built the best ships of their times. Between 1200 and 800 B.C.E., they dominated Mediterranean trade. They established

A relief sculpture from an Assyrian palace depicts Phoenician ships transporting massive cedar logs, sometimes by towing them, sometimes by hauling them on top of the boats.

commercial colonies in Rhodes, Cyprus, Sicily, Sardinia, Spain, and north Africa. They sailed far and wide in search of raw materials like copper and tin, which they used to make bronze, as well as more exotic items like ivory and semiprecious stones, which they fashioned into works of decorative art. Their quest for raw materials took them well beyond the Mediterranean: Phoenician merchant ships visited the Canary Islands, coastal ports in Portugal and France, and even the distant British Isles, and adventurous Phoenician mariners made exploratory voyages to the Azores Islands and down the west coast of Africa as far as the Gulf of Guinea.

Like the Hebrews, the Phoenicians largely adapted Mesopotamian cultural traditions to their own needs. Their gods, for example, mostly came from Mesopotamia. The Phoenicians' most prominent female deity was Astarte, a fertility goddess known in Babylon and Assyria as Ishtar. Like the Mesopotamians, the Phoenicians associated other deities with mountains, the sky, lightning, and other natural phenomena. Yet the Phoenicians did not blindly follow Mesopotamian examples: each city built temples to its own favored deities and devised its own rituals and ceremonies to honor the gods.

The Phoenicians' tradition of writing also illustrates their creative adaptation of Mesopotamian practices to their own needs. For a millennium or more, they relied on cuneiform writing to preserve information, and they compiled a vast collection of religious, historical, and literary writings. (Most Phoenician writing has perished, although some fragments have survived.) After 2000 B.C.E. Syrian, Phoenician, and other peoples began experimenting with simpler alternatives to cuneiform. By 1500 B.C.E. Phoenician scribes had devised an early alphabetic script consisting of twenty-two symbols representing consonants—the Phoenician alphabet had no symbols for vowels.

Alphabetic Writing

Sources from the Past

Israelites' Relations with Neighboring Peoples

When Solomon succeeded David and assumed the Israelites' throne, he inherited a state of peace with neighboring peoples, and he was able to construct a temple to Yahweh. In order to do so, however, he needed to establish trade relations with neighboring peoples, since the Israelites did not have the raw materials or construction skills to build a large and magnificent temple. Thus he dealt with Hiram, king of the Phoenician city of Tyre, who provided timber and construction workers and also helped Solomon obtain gold, precious stones, and decorative items for the temple.

And Hiram king of Tyre sent his servants unto Solomon, for he had heard that they had anointed him king in the room of his father, for Hiram was ever a lover of David. And Solomon sent to Hiram, saying, "Thou knowest how David my father could not build a house [temple] in the name of the Lord his God because of the wars which were about him on every side, until the Lord put [his enemies] under the soles of his feet. But now the Lord my God hath given me rest on every side, so that there is neither adversary nor evil occurring. And behold, I plan to build a house in the name of the Lord my God. . . . Now therefore command thou that they hew me cedar trees out of Lebanon, and my servants shall be with thy servants, and unto thee will I give hire for thy servants according to all that thou shalt appoint, for thou knowest that there is not among us any that has skill to hew timber like the Sidonians [Phoenicians]". . . .

And Hiram sent to Solomon, saying, "I have considered the things which thou sent to me for, and I will do all thy desire concerning timber of cedar, and concerning timber of fir. My servants shall bring them down from Lebanon unto the sea, and I will convey them by sea in floats unto the place that thou shalt appoint me, and will cause them to be discharged there, and thou shalt receive them, and thou shalt accomplish my desire, in giving food for my household." So Hiram gave Solomon cedar trees and fir trees according to all his desire. And Solomon gave Hiram twenty thousand measures of wheat for food for his household, and twenty measures of pure oil. Thus gave Solomon to Hiram year by year. And the Lord gave Solomon wisdom, as he promised him, and there was peace between Hiram and Solomon, and they two made a league together.

And king Solomon raised a levy out of all Israel, and the levy was thirty thousand men. And he sent them to Lebanon, ten thousand a month in turns. A month they were in Lebanon, and two months at home. . . . And the king commanded, and they brought great stones, costly stones, and hewed stones, to lay the foundation of the house. And Solomon's builders and Hiram's builders did hew them, and the stonemasons. So they prepared timber and stones to build the house. . . .

And king Solomon made a navy of ships in Ezion-geber [a port on the Gulf of Aqaba]. And Hiram sent in the navy his servants, shipmen that had knowledge of the sea, with the servants of Solomon. And they came to Ophir [probably southern Arabia or Ethiopia], and fetched from thence gold, four hundred and twenty talents, and brought it to king Solomon. . . .

And the navy of Hiram, that brought gold from Ophir, brought in from Ophir great plenty of almug trees and precious stones. And the king made of the almug trees pillars for the house of the Lord.

SOURCE: 1 Kings 5:1–18, 9:26–28, 10:11–12 (Authorized Version). (Translation slightly modified.)

In what ways does the Hebrew scriptural discussion of Solomon's temple portray the Israelites as participants in a larger world of diplomatic, commercial, and cultural interaction?

Learning twenty-two letters and building words with them was much easier than memorizing the hundreds of symbols employed in cuneiform. Because alphabetic writing required much less investment in education than did cuneiform writing, more people were able to become literate than ever before.

NORTH SEMITIC			GREEK		ETRUSCAN	LATIN	
EARLY PHOENICIAN	EARLY HEBREW	PHOENICIAN	EARLY	CLASSICAL	EARLY	EARLY	CLASSICAL
K	K	X	A	A	A	A	A
9	9	9	B	B	B		B
1	1	1	1	Γ	7		C
△	9	4	△	△	∩	∆	D

Phoenician, Greek, Hebrew, and Roman letters.

Alphabetic writing spread widely as the Phoenicians traveled and traded throughout the Mediterranean basin. About the ninth century B.C.E., for example, Greeks modified the Phoenician alphabet and added symbols representing vowels. Romans later adapted the Greek alphabet to their own language and passed it along to their cultural heirs in Europe. In later centuries alphabetic writing spread to central Asia, south Asia, southeast Asia, and ultimately throughout most of the world.

THE INDO-EUROPEAN MIGRATIONS

After 3000 B.C.E. Mesopotamia was a prosperous, productive region where peoples from many different communities mixed and mingled. But Mesopotamia was only one region in a much larger world of interaction and exchange. Mesopotamians and their neighbors all dealt frequently with peoples from regions far beyond southwest Asia. Among the most influential of these peoples in the third and second millennia B.C.E. were those who spoke various Indo-European languages. Their migrations throughout much of Eurasia profoundly influenced historical development in both southwest Asia and the larger world as well.

Indo-European Origins

During the eighteenth and nineteenth centuries, linguists noticed that many languages of Europe, southwest Asia, and India featured remarkable similarities in vocabulary and grammatical structure. Ancient languages displaying these similarities included Sanskrit (the sacred language of ancient India), Old Persian, Greek, and Latin. Modern descendants of these languages include Hindi and other languages of northern India, Farsi (the language of modern Iran), and most European languages, excepting only a few, such as Basque, Finnish, and Hungarian. Because of the geographic regions where these tongues are found, scholars refer to them as Indo-European languages. Major subgroups of the Indo-European family of languages include Indo-Iranian, Greek, Balto-Slavic, Germanic, Italic, and Celtic. English belongs to the Germanic subgroup of the Indo-European family of languages.

After noticing linguistic similarities, scholars sought a way to explain the close relationship between the Indo-European languages. It was inconceivable that speakers of all these languages independently adopted similar vocabularies and grammatical structures. The only persuasive explanation for the high degree of linguistic coincidence was

Indo-European Languages

SIMILARITIES IN VOCABULARY INDICATING CLOSE RELATIONSHIPS BETWEEN SELECT INDO-EUROPEAN LANGUAGES					
English	**German**	**Spanish**	**Greek**	**Latin**	**Sanskrit**
father	vater	padre	pater	pater	pitar
one	ein	uno	hen	unus	ekam
fire	feuer	fuego	pyr	ignis	agnis
field	feld	campo	agros	ager	ajras
sun	sonne	sol	helios	sol	surya
king	könig	rey	basileus	rex	raja
god	gott	dios	theos	deus	devas

that speakers of Indo-European languages were all descendants of ancestors who spoke a common tongue and migrated from their original homeland. As migrants established their own separate communities and lost touch with one another, their languages evolved along different lines, adding new words and expressing ideas in different ways. Yet they retained the basic grammatical structure of their original speech, and they also kept much of their ancestors' vocabulary, even though they often adopted different pronunciations (and consequently different spellings) of the words they inherited from the earliest Indo-European language.

The Indo-European Homeland

The original homeland of Indo-European speakers was probably the steppe region of modern-day Ukraine and southern Russia, the region just north of the Black Sea and the Caspian Sea. The earliest Indo-European speakers built their society there between about 4500 and 2500 B.C.E. They lived mostly by herding cattle, sheep, and goats, while cultivating barley and millet at least in small quantities. They also hunted horses, which flourished in the vast grasslands of the Eurasian steppe stretching from Hungary in the west to Mongolia in the east.

Horses

Because they had observed horses closely and learned the animals' behavioral patterns, Indo-European speakers were able to domesticate horses about 4000 B.C.E. They probably used horses originally as a source of food, but they also began to ride them soon after domesticating them. By 3000 B.C.E. Sumerian knowledge of bronze metallurgy and wheels had spread north to the Indo-European homeland, and soon thereafter Indo-European speakers devised ways to hitch horses to carts, wagons, and chariots. The earliest Indo-European language had words not only for cattle, sheep, goats, and horses, but also for wheels, axles, shafts, harnesses, hubs, and linchpins—all of the latter learned from Mesopotamian examples.

The possession of domesticated horses vastly magnified the power of Indo-European speakers. Once they had domesticated horses, Indo-European speakers were able to exploit the grasslands of southern Russia, where they relied on horses and wheeled vehicles for transport and on cattle and sheep for meat, milk, and wool. Horses also enabled them to develop transportation technologies that were much faster and more efficient than alternatives that relied on cattle, donkey, or human power. Furthermore, because of their strength and speed, horses provided Indo-European speakers with a tremendous military advantage over peoples they encountered. It is perhaps significant that many groups of Indo-European speakers considered themselves superior to other peoples: the terms *Aryan, Iran,* and *Eire* (the official name of the modern Republic of Ireland) all derive from the Indo-European word *aryo,* meaning "nobleman" or "lord."

Indo-European Expansion and Its Effects

Horses also provided Indo-European speakers with a means of expanding far beyond their original homeland. As they flourished in southern Russia, Indo-European speakers experienced a population explosion, which prompted some of them to move into the sparsely inhabited eastern steppe or even beyond the grasslands altogether. The earliest Indo-European society began to break up about 3000 B.C.E., as migrants took their horses and other animals and made their way to new lands. Intermittent migrations of Indo-European peoples continued until about 1000 C.E. Like early movements of other peoples, these were not mass migrations so much as gradual and incremental processes that resulted in the spread of Indo-European languages and ethnic communities, as small groups of people established settlements in new lands, which then became foundations for further expansion.

The Nature of Indo-European Migrations

The most influential Indo-European migrants in ancient times were the Hittites. About 1900 B.C.E. the Hittites migrated to the central plain of Anatolia, where they imposed their language and rule on the region's inhabitants. During the seventeenth and sixteenth centuries B.C.E., they built a powerful kingdom and established close relations with Mesopotamian peoples. They traded with Babylonians and Assyrians, adapted cuneiform writing to their Indo-European language, and accepted many Mesopotamian deities into their own pantheon. In 1595 B.C.E. the Hittites toppled the mighty Babylonian empire of Mesopotamia, and for several centuries thereafter they were the dominant power in southwest Asia. Between 1450 and 1200 B.C.E. their authority extended to eastern Anatolia, northern Mesopotamia, and Syria down to Phoenicia. After 1200 B.C.E. the unified Hittite state dissolved, as waves of invaders attacked societies throughout the eastern Mediterranean region. Nevertheless, a Hittite identity survived, along with the Hittite language, throughout the era of the Assyrian empire and beyond.

The Hittites

MAP [2.4]

Indo-European migrations, 3000–1000 B.C.E.

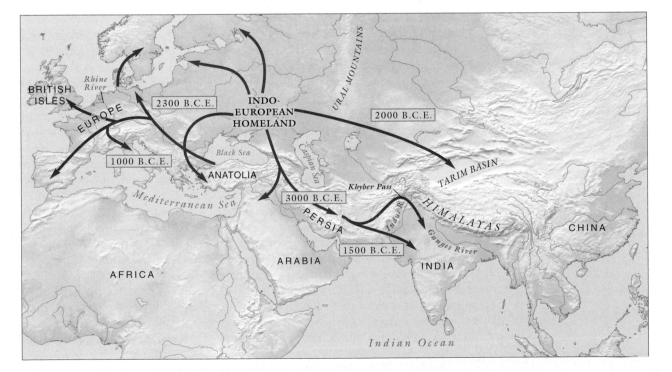

War Chariots

The Hittites were responsible for two technological innovations—the construction of light, horse-drawn war chariots and the refinement of iron metallurgy—that greatly strengthened their own society and influenced other peoples throughout much of the ancient world. Sumerian armies had sometimes used heavy chariots with solid wooden wheels, but they were so slow and cumbersome that they had limited military value. About 2000 B.C.E. Hittites fitted chariots with recently invented spoked wheels, which were much lighter and more maneuverable than Sumerian wheels. The Hittites' speedy chariots were crucial in their campaign to establish a state in Anatolia. Following the Hittites' example, Mesopotamians soon added chariot teams to their own armies, and Assyrians made especially effective use of chariots in building their empire. Indeed, chariot warfare was so effective—and its techniques spread so widely—that charioteers became the elite strike forces in armies throughout much of the ancient world from Rome to China.

Iron Metallurgy

After about 1300 B.C.E. the Hittites also refined the technology of iron metallurgy, which enabled them to produce effective weapons cheaply and in large quantities. Other peoples had tried casting iron into molds, but cast iron was too brittle for use as tools or weapons. Hittite craftsmen discovered that by heating iron in a bed of charcoal, then hammering it into the desired shape, they could forge tough, strong implements. Hittite methods of iron production diffused rapidly—especially after the collapse of their kingdom in 1200 B.C.E. and the subsequent dispersal of Hittite craftsmen—and eventually spread throughout all of Eurasia. (Peoples of sub-Saharan Africa independently invented iron metallurgy.) Hittites were not the original inventors either of horse-drawn chariots or of iron metallurgy: in both cases they built on Mesopotamian precedents. But in both cases they clearly improved on existing technologies and introduced innovations that other peoples readily adopted.

Indo-European Migrations to the East

While the Hittites were building a state in Anatolia, other Indo-European speakers migrated from the steppe to different regions. Some went east into central Asia, venturing as far as the Tarim Basin (now western China) by 2000 B.C.E. Stunning evidence of these migrations came to light recently when archaeologists excavated burials of individuals with European features in China's Xinjiang province. Because of the region's extremely dry atmosphere, the remains of some deceased individuals are so well preserved that their fair skin, light hair, and brightly colored garments are still clearly visible. Descendants of these migrants survived in central Asia and spoke Indo-European languages until well after 1000 C.E., but most of them were later absorbed into societies of Turkish-speaking peoples.

Indo-European Migrations to the West

Meanwhile, other Indo-European migrants moved west. One wave of migration took Indo-European speakers into Greece after 2200 B.C.E., with their descendants moving into central Italy by 1000 B.C.E. Another migratory wave established an Indo-European presence farther to the west. By 2300 B.C.E. some Indo-European speakers had made their way from southern Russia into central Europe (modern Germany and Austria), by 1200 B.C.E. to western Europe (modern France), and shortly thereafter to the British Isles, the Baltic region, and the Iberian peninsula. These migrants depended on a pastoral and agricultural economy: none of them built cities or organized large states. For most of the first millennium B.C.E., however, Indo-European Celtic peoples largely dominated Europe north of the Mediterranean, speaking related languages and honoring similar deities throughout the region. They recognized three principal social groups: a military ruling elite, a small group of priests, and a large class of commoners. Most of the commoners tended herds and cultivated crops, but some also worked as miners, craftsmen, or producers of metal goods. Even without large states, Celtic peoples traded copper, tin, and handicrafts throughout much of Europe.

Yet another, later wave of migrations established an Indo-European presence in Iran and India. About 1500 B.C.E the Medes and Persians migrated into the Iranian plateau, while the Aryans began filtering into northern India. Like the Indo-European Celts in Europe, the Medes, Persians, and Aryans herded animals, cultivated grains, and divided themselves into classes of rulers, priests, and commoners. Unlike the Celts, though, the Medes, Persians, and Aryans soon built powerful states (discussed in later chapters) on the basis of their horse-based military technologies and later their possession also of iron weapons.

Indo-European Migrations to the South

Building on neolithic foundations, Mesopotamian peoples constructed societies much more complex, powerful, and influential than those of their predecessors. Through their city-states, kingdoms, and regional empires, Mesopotamians created formal institutions of government that extended the authority of ruling elites to all corners of their states, and they occasionally mobilized forces that projected their power to distant lands. They generated several distinct social classes. Specialized labor fueled productive economies and encouraged the establishment of long-distance trade networks. They devised systems of writing, which enabled them to develop sophisticated cultural traditions. They deeply influenced other peoples, such as the Hebrews and Phoenicians, throughout southwest Asia and the eastern Mediterranean basin. They had frequent dealings also with Indo-European peoples. Although Indo-European society emerged far to the north of Mesopotamia, speakers of Indo-European languages migrated widely and established societies throughout much of Eurasia. Sometimes they drew inspiration from Mesopotamian practices, and sometimes they developed their own practices that influenced Mesopotamians and others as well. Thus, already in remote antiquity, the various peoples of the world profoundly influenced one another through cross-cultural interaction and exchange.

CHRONOLOGY

3200–2350 B.C.E.	Era of Sumerian dominance in Mesopotamia
3000 B.C.E.–1000 C.E.	Era of Indo-European migrations
2350–1600 B.C.E.	Era of Babylonian dominance in Mesopotamia
2334–2315 B.C.E.	Reign of Sargon of Akkad
1792–1750 B.C.E.	Reign of Hammurabi
1450–1200 B.C.E.	Hittite state based in Anatolia
1000–612 B.C.E.	Era of Assyrian dominance in Mesopotamia
1000–970 B.C.E.	Reign of Hebrew King David
970–930 B.C.E.	Reign of Hebrew King Solomon
722 B.C.E.	Assyrian conquest of the kingdom of Israel
605–562 B.C.E.	Reign of Nebuchadnezzar
600–550 B.C.E.	New Babylonian empire
586 B.C.E.	New Babylonian conquest of the kingdom of Judah

FOR FURTHER READING

Maria Eugenia Aubet. *The Phoenicians and the West: Politics, Colonies, and Trade*. Trans. by M. Turton. Cambridge, 1993. A scholarly synthesis based on archaeological finds as well as written records.

Elizabeth Wayland Barber. *The Mummies of Ürümchi*. New York, 1999. Brings archaeological evidence to bear on the early Indo-European migrations, especially those to the Tarim Basin.

———. *Women's Work: The First 20,000 Years*. New York, 1994. Fascinating study of ancient textiles, which the author argues was a craft industry dominated by women from the earliest times.

John Bright. *A History of Israel*. 3rd ed. Philadelphia, 1981. A reliable historical survey that draws profitably on scholarship.

Andrew George, trans. *The Epic of Gilgamesh*. London, 1999. A careful study and fresh translation of the best-known Mesopotamian literary work prepared on the basis of recently discovered texts.

Michael Grant. *The History of Ancient Israel*. New York, 1984. A lively and accessible popular account by a leading historian of the ancient world.

William H. McNeill and Jean Sedlar, eds. *The Ancient Near East*. New York, 1968. A collection of primary sources in translation, concentrating on Mesopotamia and Egypt.

———, eds. *The Origins of Civilization*. New York, 1968. Like its companion volume just cited, a collection of translated sources concentrating on Mesopotamia and Egypt.

J. P. Mallory. *In Search of the Indo-Europeans: Language, Archaeology, and Myth*. London, 1989. Carefully reviews modern theories about early Indo-European speakers in light of both the linguistic and the archaeological evidence.

——— and Victor H. Mair. *The Tarim Mummies: Ancient China and the Mystery of the Earliest Peoples from the West*. London, 2000. A cautious analysis of the Indo-European migrants to the Tarim Basin, drawing heavily on linguistic evidence.

Sabatino Moscati, ed. *The Phoenicians*. New York, 1988. A lavishly illustrated volume with essays by experts on all dimensions of Phoenician society and history.

Hans J. Nissen. *The Early History of the Ancient Near East, 9000–2000 B.C.* Trans. by E. Lutzeier. Chicago, 1988. A brilliant synthesis of scholarship on the development of cities and complex society in Mesopotamia and neighboring regions.

Joan Oates. *Babylon*. London, 1979. Well-illustrated and authoritative examination of ancient Babylonian society.

J. N. Postgate. *Early Mesopotamia: Society and Economy at the Dawn of History*. London, 1992. Outstanding synthesis that draws on both archaeological and textual sources.

James B. Pritchard, ed. *Ancient Near Eastern Texts Relating to the Old Testament.* 2 vols. 3rd ed. Princeton, 1975. Important collection of primary sources in translation, emphasizing parallels between the ancient Hebrews and other peoples.

Colin Renfrew. *Archaeology and Language: The Puzzle of Indo-European Origins.* Cambridge, 1987. Presents a controversial argument concerning the origins and migrations of Indo-European peoples.

Michael Roaf. *Cultural Atlas of Mesopotamia and the Ancient Near East.* New York, 1990. Richly illustrated volume with well-informed essays on all dimensions of Mesopotamian history.

Georges Roux. *Ancient Iraq.* 3rd ed. London, 1992. A well-written and engaging survey of Mesopotamian political, social, economic, and cultural history.

See our **Online Learning Center at www.mhhe.com/bentley3** for additional readings, practice maps, quizzes, and internet activities.

Unfamiliar words? Check out the **Primary Source Investigator CD-ROM** for an interactive glossary, interactive maps, more images, and primary sources.

Excavations surrounding the pyramids as seen from the air.

CHAPTER 3

EARLY AFRICAN SOCIETIES AND THE BANTU MIGRATIONS

For almost three thousand years, Egyptian embalmers preserved the bodies of deceased individuals through a process of mummification. Egyptian records rarely mention the techniques of mummification, but the Greek historian Herodotus traveled in Egypt about 450 B.C.E. and briefly explained the craft. The embalmer first used a metal hook to draw the brain of the deceased out through a nostril, then removed the internal organs through an incision made alongside the abdomen, washed them in palm wine, and sealed them with preservatives in stone vessels. Next, the embalmer washed the body, filled it with spices and aromatics, and covered it for about two months with natron, a naturally occuring salt substance. When the natron had extracted all moisture from the body, the embalmer cleansed it again and wrapped it with strips of fine linen covered with resin. Adorned with jewelry, the preserved body then went into a coffin bearing a painting or sculpted likeness of the deceased.

Careful preservation of the body was only a part of the funerary ritual for prominent Egyptians. Ruling elites, wealthy individuals, and sometimes common people as well laid their deceased to rest in expensive tombs equipped with furniture, tools, weapons, and ornaments that the departed would need in their next lives. Relatives periodically brought food and wine to nourish the deceased, and archaeologists have discovered soups, beef ribs, pigeons, quail, fish, bread, cakes, and fruits among these offerings. Artists decorated some tombs with elegant paintings of family members and servants, whose images accompanied the departed into a new dimension of existence.

Egyptian funerary customs were reflections of a prosperous agricultural society. Food offerings consisted mostly of local agricultural products, and scenes painted on tomb walls often depicted workers preparing fields or cultivating crops. Moreover, bountiful harvests explained the accumulation of wealth that supported elaborate funerary practices, and they also enabled some individuals to devote their efforts to specialized tasks like embalming. Agriculture even influenced religious beliefs. Many Egyptians believed fervently in a life beyond the grave, and they likened the human experience of life and death to the agricultural cycle in which crops grow, die, and come to life again in another season.

As Mesopotamians built a productive agricultural society in southwest Asia and as Indo-European peoples introduced domesticated horses to much of Eurasia, cultivation and herding also transformed African societies. African agriculture first took root in the Sudan, then moved into the Nile River valley and also to most parts of sub-Saharan Africa. Agriculture flourished particularly in the fertile Nile valley, and abundant harvests soon supported fast-growing populations. This agricultural bounty underwrote the development of Egypt, the most prosperous and powerful of the early agricultural societies in Africa, and also of Nubia, Egypt's neighbor to the south.

Distinctive Egyptian and Nubian societies began to take shape in the valley of the Nile River during the late fourth millennium B.C.E., shortly after the emergence of complex society in Mesopotamia. Like their Mesopotamian counterparts, Egyptians and Nubians drew on agricultural surpluses to organize formal states, support specialized laborers, and develop distinctive cultural traditions. Like Mesopotamians again, Egyptian and Nubian residents of the Nile valley had regular dealings with peoples from other societies. They drew inspiration for political and social organization both from Mesopotamia and from their African neighbors to the south. They also traded actively with Mesopotamians, Phoenicians, Africans, and others as well. Political and economic competition sometimes led to military conflicts with peoples of other societies: on several occasions when they enjoyed great wealth and power, both Egyptians and Nubians embarked on campaigns of imperial conquest, but when their power waned, they found themselves intermittently under attack from the outside.

Indeed, like their counterparts in Mesopotamia, Egyptian and Nubian societies developed from their earliest days in a larger world of interaction and exchange. Just as Mesopotamians, Hittites, Hebrews, and Phoenicians influenced one another in southwest Asia, inhabitants of the Nile valley mixed and mingled with Mesopotamians, Phoenicians, and other peoples from the eastern Mediterranean, southwest Asia, and sub-Saharan Africa. Just as Indo-European peoples migrated to new lands and established communities that transformed much of Eurasia, Bantu peoples migrated from their original homeland in west Africa and established settlements that brought profound change to much of sub-Saharan Africa. By no means were Egypt and Nubia isolated centers of social development. Like Mesopotamia, Egypt in particular was a spectacularly prosperous society, but like Mesopotamia again, Egypt was only one part of a much larger world of interacting societies.

EARLY AGRICULTURAL SOCIETY IN AFRICA

Egypt was the most prominent of early African societies, but it was by no means the only agricultural society, nor even the only complex, city-based society of ancient Africa. To the contrary, Egypt emerged alongside Nubia and other agricultural societies in sub-Saharan Africa. Indeed, agricultural crops and domesticated animals reached Egypt from sub-Saharan Africa by way of Nubia as well as from southwest Asia. Favorable geographic conditions enabled Egyptians to build an especially productive agricultural economy that supported a powerful state, while Nubia became home to a somewhat less prosperous but nonetheless sophisticated society. After taking shape as distinctive societies, Egypt had regular dealings with both eastern Mediterranean and southwest Asian peoples, while Nubia linked Egypt and the eastern Mediterranean basin with the peoples and societies of sub-Saharan Africa.

Climatic Change and the Development of Agriculture in Africa

African agriculture emerged in the context of gradual but momentous changes in climatic conditions. About 10,000 B.C.E., after the end of the last ice age, the area now occupied by the Sahara desert was mostly a grassy steppe land with numerous lakes, rivers, and streams. Climatic and geographic conditions were much like those of the Sudan region—not the modern state of Sudan but, rather, the extensive transition zone of savanna and grassland that stretches across the African continent between the Sahara to the north and the tropical rain forest to the south. Grasses and cattle flourished in this environment. Many human inhabitants of the region lived by hunting wild cattle and collecting wild grains, while others subsisted on fish and aquatic resources from the region's waters.

After about 9000 B.C.E., peoples of the eastern Sudan domesticated cattle and became nomadic herders, while they continued to collect wild grains. After 7500 B.C.E. they established permanent settlements and began to cultivate sorghum, a grain still widely grown in the contemporary world for human and animal consumption. Meanwhile, after about 8000 B.C.E., inhabitants of the western Sudan began to cultivate yams in the region between the Niger and Congo rivers. Sudanic agriculture became increasingly diverse over the following centuries: sheep and goats arrived from southwest Asia after 7000 B.C.E., and Sudanic peoples began to cultivate gourds, watermelons, and cotton after 6500 B.C.E.

Early Sudanic Agriculture

Agricultural productivity enabled Sudanic peoples to organize small-scale states. By about 5000 B.C.E. many Sudanic peoples had formed small monarchies ruled by kings who were viewed as divine or semidivine beings. For several thousand years, when Sudanic peoples buried their deceased kings, they also routinely executed a group of royal servants and entombed them along with the kings so that they could continue to meet their masters' needs in another life. Sudanic peoples also developed religious beliefs that reflected their agricultural society. They recognized a single divine force as the source of good and evil, and they associated it with rain—a matter of concern for any agricultural society.

After 5000 B.C.E. the northern half of Africa experienced a long-term climatic change that profoundly influenced social organization and agriculture throughout the region. Although there was considerable fluctuation, the climate generally became much hotter and drier than before. The Sahara desert, which as late as 5000 B.C.E. had been cool and well watered enough to support human, animal, and vegetable life, became increasingly arid and uninhabitable. This process of desiccation turned rich grasslands into barren desert, and it drove both humans and animals to more hospitable regions. Many Sudanic cultivators and herders gathered around remaining bodies of water such as Lake Chad. Some moved south to the territory that is now northern Uganda. Others congregated in the valley of the Nile River, the principal source of water flowing through north Africa.

Climatic Change

Fed by rain and snow in the high mountains of east Africa, the Nile, which is the world's longest river, courses some 6,695 kilometers (4,160 miles) from its source at Lake Victoria to its outlet through the delta to the Mediterranean Sea. Each spring, rain and melting snow swell the river, which surges north through the Sudan and Egypt. Until the completion of the high dam at Aswan in 1968, the Nile's accumulated waters annually flooded the plains downstream. When the waters receded, they left behind a layer of rich, fertile muck, and these alluvial deposits supported a remarkably productive agricultural economy throughout the Nile River valley.

The Nile River Valley

Egypt and Nubia: "Gifts of the Nile"

Agriculture transformed the entire Nile River valley, with effects that were most dramatic in Egypt. In ancient times, Egypt referred not to the territory embraced by the modern state of Egypt but, rather, to the ribbon of land bordering the lower third of

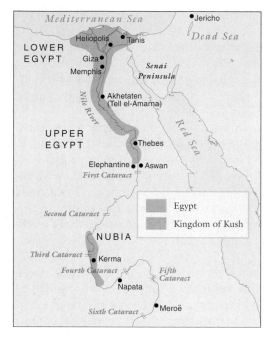

M A P [3 . 1]
The Nile valley, 3000–2000 B.C.E.

Early Agriculture in the Nile Valley

the Nile between the Mediterranean and the river's first cataract (an unnavigable stretch of rapids and waterfalls) near Aswan. Egypt enjoyed a much larger floodplain than most of the land to the south known as Nubia, the middle stretches of the Nile valley between the river's first and sixth cataracts. As the Sahara became increasingly arid, cultivators flocked to the Nile valley and established societies that depended on intensive agriculture. Because of their broad floodplains, Egyptians were able to take better advantage of the Nile's annual floods than their neighbors to the south, and they turned Egypt into an especially productive agricultural region that was capable of supporting a much larger population than were Nubian lands. Because of its prosperity, the Greek historian Herodotus proclaimed Egypt "the gift of the Nile." If he had known more about Nubia, Herodotus might well have realized that it too was a gift of the Nile, even if it was a less prosperous land than its neighbor to the north.

Geography ensured that both Egypt and Nubia would come under the influence of both sub-Saharan Africa and the eastern Mediterranean basin, since the Nile River links the two regions. About 10,000 B.C.E., migrants from the Red Sea hills in northern Ethiopia traveled down the Nile valley and introduced to Egypt and Nubia the practice of collecting wild grains. They also introduced a language ancestral to Coptic, the language of ancient Egypt, to the lower reaches of the Nile valley. After 5000 B.C.E., as the African climate grew hotter and drier, Sudanic cultivators and herders moved down the Nile, introducing Egypt and Nubia to African crops like gourds and watermelons as well as animals domesticated in the Sudan, particularly cattle and donkeys. About the same time, wheat and barley from Mesopotamia reached Egypt and Nubia by traveling up the Nile from the Mediterranean.

Both Egyptians and Nubians relied heavily on agriculture at least by 5000 B.C.E. Egyptian cultivators went into the floodplains in the late summer, after the recession of the Nile's annual flood, sowed their seeds without extensive preparation of the soil, allowed their crops to mature during the cool months of the year, and harvested them during the winter and early spring. With less extensive floodplains, Nubians relied more on prepared fields and irrigation by waters diverted from the Nile. As in Mesopotamia, high agricultural productivity led to a rapid increase in population throughout the Nile valley. Demographic pressures soon forced Egyptians in particular to develop more intense and sophisticated methods of agriculture. Cultivators moved beyond the Nile's immediate floodplains and began to grow crops on higher ground that required plowing and careful preparation. They built dikes to protect their fields from floods and catchment basins to store water for irrigation. By 4000 B.C.E. agricultural villages dotted the Nile's shores from the Mediterranean in the north to the river's fourth cataract in the south.

As in Mesopotamia, dense human population in Egypt and Nubia brought a need for formal organization of public affairs. Neither Egypt nor Nubia faced the external dangers that threatened Mesopotamia, since the Red Sea, the Mediterranean Sea, and hostile deserts discouraged foreign invaders in ancient times. Nevertheless, the need to maintain order and organize community projects led both Egyptians and Nubians to create states and recognize official authorities. By 4000 B.C.E. agricultural villages along the Nile traded regularly with one another and cooperated in building irrigation networks.

A painting from the tomb of a priest who lived about the fifteenth century B.C.E. depicts agricultural workers plowing and sowing crops in southern Egypt.

Political Organization

The earliest Egyptian and Nubian states were small kingdoms much like those instituted in the Sudan after 5000 B.C.E. Indeed, it is likely that the notion of divine or semidivine rulers reached Egypt and Nubia from the eastern and central Sudan, where rulers had earlier founded small kingdoms to govern their agricultural and herding communities. In any case, small kingdoms appeared first in southern Egypt and Nubia after 4000 B.C.E. During the following centuries, residents living farther down the Nile (to the north) founded similar states so that by 3300 B.C.E. small local kingdoms organized public life throughout Egypt as well as Nubia. As in the earlier Sudanic states, royal servants in these Nile kingdoms routinely accompanied deceased rulers to their graves.

The Unification of Egypt

By 3500 B.C.E. political and economic competition fueled numerous skirmishes and small-scale wars between the Nile kingdoms. Some kingdoms overcame their neighbors and gradually expanded until they controlled sizable territories. One expansive kingdom was Ta-Seti, a strong Nubian realm that flourished about 3400 to 3200 B.C.E. and extended its rule north of the Nile's first cataract into Egypt. When Ta-Seti declined, the local kingdoms of southern Egypt were in a strong position to increase their own power, since Egypt's broad floodplains offered much more arable land and supported much larger populations than Nubian territories to the south.

After 3100 B.C.E. Egypt followed a path quite different from those of the smaller Nubian kingdoms. Drawing on agricultural and demographic advantages, Egyptian rulers forged all the territory between the Nile delta and the river's first cataract into a unified kingdom much larger and more powerful than any other Nile state. Tradition holds that unified rule came to Egypt about 3100 B.C.E. in the person of a conqueror named Menes (sometimes identified with an early Egyptian ruler called Narmer). Menes was an ambitious minor official from southern Egypt (known as Upper Egypt, since the Nile flows north) who rose to power and extended his authority north and into the delta (known as Lower Egypt). According to tradition, Menes founded the city of Memphis, near modern Cairo, which stood at the junction of Upper and Lower Egypt. Memphis served as Menes' capital and eventually became the cultural as well as the political center of ancient Egypt.

Menes

Menes, unifier of Egypt, prepares to sacrifice an enemy. He wears the crown of Upper Egypt, and the falcon representing the god Horus oversees his actions in this relief carving on a votive tablet. Two fallen enemies lie at the bottom of the tablet.

Menes and his successors built a centralized state ruled by the pharaoh, the Egyptian king. The early pharaohs claimed to be gods living on the earth in human form, the owners and absolute rulers of all the land. In this respect, they continued the tradition of divine kingship inherited from the early agricultural societies of the Sudan. Indeed, as late as 2600 B.C.E., deceased pharaohs took royal servants with them to the grave. Egyptians associated the early pharaohs with Horus, the sky god, and they often represented the pharaohs together with a falcon or a hawk, the symbol of Horus. Later they viewed rulers as offspring of Amon, a sun god, so that the pharaoh was a son of the sun. They considered the ruling pharaoh a human sun overseeing affairs on the earth, just as Amon was the sun supervising the larger cosmos, and they believed that after his death the pharaoh actually merged with Amon. Artistic representations also depict pharaohs as enormous figures towering over their human subjects.

The Archaic Period and the Old Kingdom

The power of the pharaohs was greatest during the first millennium of Egyptian history—the eras known as the Archaic Period (3100–2660 B.C.E.) and the Old Kingdom (2660–2160 B.C.E.). The most enduring symbols of their authority and divine status are the massive pyramids constructed during the Old Kingdom as royal tombs, most of them during the century from 2600 to 2500 B.C.E. These enormous monuments stand today at Giza, near Cairo, as testimony to the pharaohs' ability to marshal Egyptian resources. The largest is the pyramid of Khufu (also known as Cheops), which involved the precise cutting and fitting of 2.3 million limestone blocks weighing up to 15 tons, with an average weight of 2.5 tons. Scholars estimate that construction of Khufu's pyramid required the services of some eighty-four thousand laborers working eighty days per year (probably during the late fall and winter, when the demand for agricultural labor was light) for twenty years. Apart from the laborers, hundreds of architects, engineers, craftsmen, and artists also contributed to the construction of the pyramids.

Relations between Egypt and Nubia

Even after the emergence of the strong pharaonic state that took Egypt on a path different from those followed by other Nile societies, the fortunes of Egypt and Nubia remained closely intertwined. Egyptians had strong interests in Nubia for both political and commercial reasons: they were wary of Nubian kingdoms that might threaten Upper Egypt, and they desired products like gold, ivory, ebony, and precious stones that were available only from southern lands. Meanwhile, Nubians had equally strong interests in Egypt: they wanted to protect their independence from their massive and powerful neighbor to the north, and they sought to profit by controlling trade down the Nile.

The Early Kingdom of Kush

Tensions led to frequent violence between Egypt and Nubia throughout the Archaic Period and the Old Kingdom. The early pharaohs organized at least five military campaigns to Nubia between 3100 and 2600 B.C.E. Pharaonic forces destroyed the Nubian kingdom of Ta-Seti soon after the unification of Egypt, leading to Egyptian domination of Lower Nubia (the land between the first and second cataracts of

Sources from the Past

Harkhuf's Expeditions to Nubia

Many Egyptians wrote brief autobiographies that they or their descendants had carved into their tombs. One of the most famous autobiographies from the Old Kingdom is that of Harkhuf, a royal official who became governor of Upper Egypt before 2300 B.C.E. The inscriptions in his tomb mention his four expeditions to Nubia to seek valuable items and report on political conditions there. The inscriptions also include the text of a letter from the boy-pharaoh Neferkare expressing his appreciation for Harkhuf's fourth expedition and his desire to see the dancing dwarf that Harkhuf brought back from Nubia.

The majesty of [Pharaoh] Mernere, my lord, sent me together with my father . . . to [the Upper Nubian kingdom of] Yam to open the way to that country. I did it in seven months; I brought from it all kinds of beautiful and rare gifts, and was praised for it greatly.

His majesty sent me a second time alone. . . . I came down [the Nile] bringing gifts from that country in great quantity, the likes of which had never before been brought back to this land [Egypt]. . . .

Then his majesty sent me a third time to Yam. . . . I came down with three hundred donkeys laden with incense, ebony, . . . panther skins, elephant's tusks, throw sticks, and all sorts of good products.

[The letter of Pharaoh Neferkare to Harkhuf:] Notice has been taken of this dispatch of yours which you made for the King at the Palace, to let one know that you have come down in safety from Yam with the army that was with you. You have said in this dispatch of yours that you have brought all kinds of great and beautiful gifts. . . . You have said in this dispatch of yours that you have brought a pygmy of the god's dances from the land of the horizon-dwellers [the region of Nubia southeast of Egypt], like the pygmy whom the [royal official] Bawerded brought from Punt [Ethiopia and Somalia] in the time of King Isesi. You have said to my majesty that his like has never been brought by anyone who [visited] Yam previously.

Truly you know how to do what your lord loves and praises. Truly you spend day and night planning to do what your lord loves, praises, and commands. His majesty will provide you many worthy honors for the benefit of your son's son for all time, so that all people will say, when they hear what my majesty did for you: "Does anything equal what was done for the sole companion Harkhuf when he came down from Yam, on account of the vigilance he showed in doing what his lord loved, praised, and commanded?"

Come north to the residence at once! Hurry and bring with you this pygmy whom you brought from the land of the horizon-dwellers live, hale, and healthy, for the dances of the god, to gladden the heart, to delight the heart of King Neferkare who lives forever! When he goes down with you into the ship, get worthy men to be around him on deck, lest he fall into the water! When he lies down at night, get worthy men to lie around him in his tent. Inspect ten times at night! My majesty desires to see this pygmy more than the gifts of the mineland [the Sinai peninsula] and of Punt!

When you arrive at the residence and this pygmy is with you live, hale, and healthy, my majesty will do great things for you, more than was done for the [royal official] Bawerded in the time of King Isesi, in accordance with my majesty's wish to see this pygmy. Orders have been brought to the chief of the new towns and the companion, overseer of priests to command that supplies be furnished from what is under the charge of each from every storage depot and every temple that has not been exempted.

SOURCE: Miriam Lichtheim, ed. *Ancient Egyptian Literature*, 3 vols. Berkeley: University of California Press, 1973, 1: 25–27.

How does Harkhuf's autobiography illuminate early Egyptian interest in Nubia and the processes by which Egyptians of the Old Kingdom developed knowledge about Nubia?

the Nile) for more than half a millennium, from about 3000 to 2400 B.C.E. This Egyptian presence in the north forced Nubian leaders to concentrate their efforts at political organization farther to the south in Upper Nubia. By about 2500 B.C.E. they had established a powerful kingdom, called Kush, with a capital at Kerma, about 700 kilometers (435 miles) south of Aswan. Though not as powerful as united Egypt, the kingdom of Kush was a formidable and wealthy state that dominated the upper reaches of the Nile and occasionally threatened southern Egypt.

In spite of constant tension and frequent hostilities, numerous diplomats and explorers traveled from Egypt to Nubia in search of political alliances and commercial relationships, while many Nubians sought improved fortunes in Egypt. Around 2300 B.C.E., for example, the Egyptian explorer Harkhuf made four expeditions to Nubia. He returned from one of his trips with a caravan of some three hundred donkeys bearing exotic products from tropical Africa, as well as a dancing dwarf, and his cargo stimulated Egyptian desire for trade with southern lands. Meanwhile, Nubian peoples looked for opportunities to pursue in Egypt. By the end of the Old Kingdom, Nubian mercenaries were quite prominent in Egyptian armies. Indeed, they often married Egyptian women and assimilated into Egyptian society.

Turmoil and Empire

The Middle Kingdom

Toward the end of the Old Kingdom, high agricultural productivity made several regions of Egypt so prosperous and powerful that they were able to ignore the pharaohs and pursue their own interests. As a result, the central state declined and eventually disappeared altogether during a long season of political upheaval and social unrest (2160–2040 B.C.E.). Pharaonic authority returned with the establishment of the Middle Kingdom (2040–1640 B.C.E.). Pharaohs of the Middle Kingdom were not as powerful as their predecessors of the Old Kingdom, but they effectively stabilized Egypt and supervised relations with neighboring lands of Nubia, north Africa, and Syria.

The Hyksos

Gradually, however, Egypt came under the pressure of foreign peoples from southwest Asia, particularly a Semitic people whom Egyptians called the Hyksos ("foreign rulers"). Little information survives about the Hyksos, but it is clear that they were horse-riding nomads. Indeed, they probably introduced horses to Egypt, and their horse-drawn chariots, which they learned about from Hittites and Mesopotamians, provided them with a significant military advantage over Egyptian forces. They enjoyed an advantage also in their weaponry: the Hyksos used bronze weapons and bronze-tipped arrows, while Egyptians relied mostly on wooden weapons and arrows with stone heads. About 1674 B.C.E. the Hyksos captured Memphis and levied tribute throughout Egypt. The Hyksos themselves probably did not often travel south of the Nile delta in large numbers, but they claimed authority over the whole of Egypt and ruled the land through Egyptian intermediaries.

Hyksos rule provoked a strong reaction especially in Upper Egypt, where disgruntled nobles organized revolts against the foreigners. They adopted horses and chariots for their own military forces. They also equipped their troops with bronze weapons. Working from Thebes and later from Memphis, Egyptian leaders gradually pushed the Hyksos out of the Nile delta and founded a powerful state known as the New Kingdom (1550–1070 B.C.E.).

The New Kingdom

Pharaohs of the New Kingdom presided over a prosperous and productive society. Agricultural surpluses supported a population of perhaps four million people as well as an army and an elaborate bureaucracy that divided responsibilities among different offices. One department oversaw the court and royal estates, for example, while others dealt with military forces, state-recognized religious cults, the treasury,

Funerary sculpture from a tomb in Upper Egypt dating from about 2200–2000 B.C.E. depicts Nenu, a Nubian mercenary soldier who served in the Egyptian army, together with his Egyptian wife, their two sons, a servant, and two pet dogs.

agricultural affairs, local government, and the administration of conquered territories. Pharaohs of the New Kingdom did not build enormous pyramids like their predecessors of the Old Kingdom, but they erected numerous temples, palaces, and monumental statues to advertise their power and authority.

Pharaohs of the New Kingdom also worked to extend Egyptian authority well beyond the Nile valley and the delta. After expelling the Hyksos, they sought to prevent new invasions by seizing control of regions that might pose threats in the future. Most vigorous of the New Kingdom pharaohs was Tuthmosis III (reigned 1479–1425 B.C.E.). After seventeen campaigns that he personally led to Palestine and Syria, Tuthmosis dominated the coastal regions of the eastern Mediterranean as well as north Africa. Rulers of the New Kingdom also turned their attention to the south and restored Egyptian dominance in Nubia. Campaigning as far south as the Nile's fifth cataract, Egyptian armies destroyed Kerma, the capital of the kingdom of Kush, and crushed a series of small Nubian states that had arisen during the period

Egyptian Imperialism

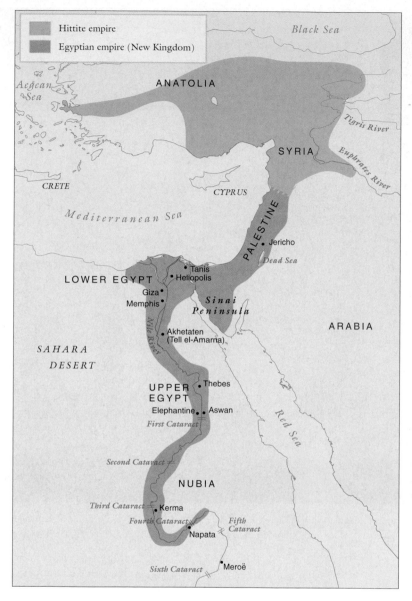

	Hittite empire
	Egyptian empire (New Kingdom)

M A P [3 . 2]

Imperial Egypt, 1400 B.C.E.

of Hyksos rule. Thus for half a millennium Egypt was an imperial power throughout much of the eastern Mediterranean basin and southwest Asia as well as most of the Nile River valley.

After the New Kingdom, Egypt entered a long period of political and military decline. Just as Hyksos rule provoked a reaction in Egypt, Egyptian rule provoked reactions in the regions subdued by pharaonic armies. Local resistance drove Egyptian forces out of Nubia and southwest Asia, then Kushite and Assyrian armies invaded Egypt itself.

A wall painting from the tomb of an Egyptian imperial official in Nubia depicts a delegation of Nubians bringing tribute in the forms of exotic beasts, animal skins, and rings of gold.

By 1100 B.C.E. Egyptian forces were in full retreat from Nubia. After they vacated the region, about the tenth century B.C.E., Nubian leaders organized a new kingdom of Kush with a capital at Napata, located just below the Nile's fourth cataract. By the eighth century B.C.E., rulers of this revived kingdom of Kush were powerful enough to invade Egypt, which at the time was in the grip of religious and factional disputes. King Kashta conquered Thebes about 760 B.C.E. and founded a Kushite dynasty that ruled Egypt for almost a century. Kashta's successors consolidated Kushite authority in Upper Egypt, claimed the title of pharaoh, and eventually extended their rule to the Nile delta and beyond.

The Revived Kingdom of Kush

Meanwhile, as Kushites pushed into Egypt from the south, Assyrian armies equipped with iron weapons bore down from the north. During the mid-seventh century B.C.E., while building their vast empire, the Assyrians invaded Egypt, campaigned as far south as Thebes, drove out the Kushites, and subjected Egypt to Assyrian rule. After the mid-sixth century B.C.E., like Mesopotamia, Egypt fell to a series of foreign conquerors who built vast empires throughout southwest Asia and the eastern Mediterranean region, including Egypt and north Africa.

THE FORMATION OF COMPLEX SOCIETIES AND SOPHISTICATED CULTURAL TRADITIONS

As in Mesopotamia, cities and the congregation of dense populations encouraged the emergence of specialized labor in the early agricultural societies of Africa. This development was particularly noticeable in Egypt, but specialized labor was a prominent feature also of societies in the southern reaches of the Nile River valley. Clearly defined social classes emerged throughout the Nile valley, and both Egypt and Nubian lands built patriarchal societies that placed authority largely in the hands of their adult males. The Egyptian economy was especially productive, and because of both its prosperity and its geographic location, Egypt figured as a center of trade, linking lands in southwest Asia, the eastern Mediterranean, and sub-Saharan Africa. Meanwhile, like southwest Asia, the Nile valley was a site of sophisticated cultural development. Writing systems appeared in both Egypt and Nubia, and writing soon became a principal medium of literary expression and religious reflection as well as a means for preserving governmental records and commercial information.

The Emergence of Cities and Stratified Societies

Cities of the Nile Valley

Cities were not as prominent in early societies of the Nile River valley as they were in ancient Mesopotamia. In the Nile valley, populations clustered mostly in numerous agricultural villages that traded regularly with their neighbors up and down the river. Nevertheless, several major cities emerged and guided affairs in both Egypt and Nubia. The conqueror Menes founded Memphis as early as 3100 B.C.E. Because of its location at the head of the Nile delta, Memphis was a convenient site for a capital: Menes and many later pharaohs as well ruled over a unified Egypt from Memphis. Besides the capital, other cities also played important roles in Egyptian affairs. Thebes, for example, was a prominent political center even before the unification of Egypt. After unification, Thebes became the administrative center of Upper Egypt, and several pharaohs even took the city as their capital. Heliopolis, meaning "City of the Sun," was the headquarters of a sun cult near Memphis and a principal cultural center of ancient Egypt. Founded about 2900 B.C.E., Heliopolis reached the height of its influence during the New Kingdom, when it was the site of an enormous temple to the sun god Re. Yet another important city was Tanis on the Nile delta. At least by the time of the Middle Kingdom, and perhaps even earlier, Tanis was a bustling port and Egypt's gateway to the Mediterranean.

Nubian cities are not so well known as those of Egypt, but written records and archaeological excavations both make it clear that powerful and prosperous cities emerged in the southern Nile valley as well as in Egypt. The most prominent Nubian cities of ancient times were Kerma, Napata, and Meroë. Kerma, located just above the Nile's third cataract, was the capital of the earliest kingdom of Kush. For a millennium after its foundation about 2500 B.C.E., Kerma dominated both river and overland routes between Egypt to the north and Sudanic regions to the south. The fortunes of Kerma waxed and waned as Egypt and Kush contested one another for power in Nubia, but it remained an influential site until its destruction about 1450 B.C.E. by the aggressive armies of Egypt's expansive New Kingdom. About the tenth century B.C.E., Napata emerged as the new political center of Nubia. Located just below the Nile's fourth cataract, Napata was more distant from Egypt than Kerma and hence less vulnerable to threats from the north. After King Kashta and his successors conquered Egypt, Napata enjoyed tremendous prosperity because of the wealth that flowed up the Nile to the Kushite capital. About the middle of the seventh century B.C.E., after Assyrian forces expelled the Kushites and asserted their own imperial control in Egypt, the capital of Kush moved farther south, this time to Meroë, located between the Nile's fifth and sixth cataracts about 1,600 kilometers (1,000 miles) from the southern border of Egypt. Meroë presided over a flourishing kingdom of Kush that enjoyed great prosperity because of its participation in Nile trade networks until its gradual decline after about 100 C.E.

Social Classes

In Egypt and Nubia alike, ancient cities were centers of considerable accumulated wealth, which encouraged the development of social distinctions and hierarchies. Like the Mesopotamians, ancient Egyptians recognized a series of well-defined social classes. Egyptian peasants and slaves played roles in society similar to those of their

Building pyramids and other large structures involved heavy work, especially by the less privileged classes. Here an Egyptian manuscript painting produced about 1000 B.C.E. depicts a supervisor overseeing a group of laborers as they drag a sled loaded with building blocks.

Mesopotamian counterparts: they supplied the hard labor that made complex agricultural society possible. The organization of the ruling classes, however, differed considerably between Mesopotamia and Egypt. Instead of a series of urban kings, as in Mesopotamia, Egyptians recognized the pharaoh as a supreme central ruler. Because the pharaoh was theoretically an absolute ruler, Egyptian society had little room for a noble class like that of Mesopotamia. Instead of depending on nobles who owed their positions to their birth, Egypt relied on professional military forces and an elaborate bureaucracy of administrators and tax collectors who served the central government. Thus, in Egypt much more than in Mesopotamia, individuals of common birth could attain high positions in society through government service.

Surviving information illuminates Egyptian society much better than Nubian, but it is clear that Nubia also was the site of a complex, hierarchical society in ancient times. Meroë, for example, was home to government officials, priests, craftsmen, merchants, laborers, and slaves. Cemeteries associated with Nubian cities clearly reveal social and economic distinctions. Tombs of wealthy and powerful individuals were often elaborate structures—comfortable dwelling places tastefully decorated with paintings and filled with expensive goods such as gold jewelry, gems, fine furniture, and abundant supplies of food. In keeping with the traditions of Sudanic kingship, many royal tombs became the final resting places also of servants ritually executed so that they could tend to the needs of their masters in death. Graves of commoners were much simpler, although they usually contained jewelry, pottery, personal ornaments, and other goods to accompany the departed.

Like their Mesopotamian counterparts, both Egyptian and Nubian peoples built patriarchal societies that vested authority over public and private affairs in their men. Men governed their households and also dominated public life. With rare exceptions men were the rulers in both Egyptian and Nubian states, and decisions about government policies and public affairs rested mostly in men's hands.

Patriarchal Society

Yet women made their influence felt in ancient Egyptian and Nubian societies much more than in contemporary Mesopotamia. In Egypt, women of the royal family frequently served as regents for young rulers. In one notable case, a woman took power as pharaoh herself: Queen Hatshepsut (reigned 1473–1458 B.C.E.) served as coruler with her stepson Tuthmosis III. The notion of a female ruler was unfamiliar and perhaps somewhat unsettling to many Egyptians. In an effort to present her in unthreatening guise, a monumental statue of Queen Hatshepsut depicts her wearing the stylized beard traditionally associated with the pharaohs. In Nubia, by contrast, there is abundant evidence of many women rulers in the kingdom of Kush, particularly during the period when Meroë was the capital. Some ruled in their own right, while others reigned jointly with male kings, and many governed also in the capacity of a regent known as the *kandake* (root of the name Candace). Meanwhile, other women wielded considerable power as priestesses in the numerous religious cults observed in Egypt and Nubia. A few women also obtained a formal education and worked as scribes who prepared administrative and legal documents for governments and private parties.

Economic Specialization and Trade

With the formation of complex, city-based societies, peoples of the Nile valley were able to draw on a rapidly expanding stock of human skills. Bronze metallurgy made its way from Mesopotamia to both Egypt and Nubia, and Sudanic peoples independently developed a technology of iron production that eventually spread to most parts of sub-Saharan Africa. Pottery, textile manufacture, woodworking, leather production, stonecutting, and masonry all became distinct occupations in cities throughout the Nile valley. Specialized labor and the invention of efficient transportation technologies encouraged the development of trade networks that linked the Nile valley to a much larger world.

Bronze Metallurgy   Nile societies were much slower than their Mesopotamian counterparts to adopt metal tools and weapons. Whereas the production of bronze flourished in Mesopotamia by 3000 B.C.E., use of bronze implements became widespread in Egypt only after the seventeenth century B.C.E., when the Hyksos relied on bronze weapons to impose their authority on the Nile delta. After expelling the Hyksos, Egyptians equipped their own forces with bronze weapons, and the imperial armies of Tuthmosis and other pharaohs of the New Kingdom carried up-to-date bronze weapons like those used in Mesopotamia and neighboring lands. As in Mesopotamia and other lands as well, the high cost of copper and tin kept bronze out of the hands of most people.

A wall painting produced about 1300 B.C.E. shows Egyptian goldsmiths fashioning jewelry and decorative objects for elite patrons. Early experience with gold metallurgy prepared craftsmen to work with bronze and iron when knowledge of those metals reached Egypt.

Royal workshops closely monitored supplies of the valuable metal: officers weighed the bronze tools issued to workers at royal tombs, for example, to ensure that craftsmen did not shave slivers off them and divert expensive metal to personal uses.

Iron Metallurgy

Bronze was even less prominent in Nubian societies than in Egypt. Indeed, Nubia produced little bronze since the region was poor in copper and tin resources and so relied on imports from the north. During the centuries after 1000 B.C.E., however, the southern Nile societies made up for their lack of bronze with the emergence of large-scale production of iron. The Hittites had developed techniques for forging iron in Anatolia about 1300 B.C.E., but iron metallurgy in Africa arose independently from local experimentation with iron ores, which are plentiful in sub-Saharan Africa. The earliest traces of African iron production discovered by archaeologists date from about 900 B.C.E. in the Great Lakes region of east Africa (modern-day Burundi and Rwanda) and also on the southern side of Lake Chad (in modern-day Cameroon). It is quite possible that African peoples produced iron before 1000 B.C.E. From the Great Lakes region and the Sudan, iron metallurgy quickly spread throughout most of sub-Saharan Africa. Furnaces churned out iron implements both in Nubia and in west Africa at least by 500 B.C.E. Meroë in particular became a site of large-scale iron production. Indeed, archaeologists who excavated Meroë in the early twentieth century C.E. found enormous mounds of slag still remaining from ancient times.

Transportation

Nile craftsmen also worked from the early days of agricultural society to devise efficient means of transportation. Within Egypt, the Nile River greatly facilitated transportation, and Egyptians traveled up and down the river before 3500 B.C.E. Because the Nile flows north, boats could ride the currents from Upper to Lower Egypt. Meanwhile, prevailing winds blow almost year-round from the north, so that by raising a sail, boats could easily make their way upriver from Lower to Upper Egypt. Soon after 3000 B.C.E. Egyptians sailed beyond the Nile into the Mediterranean, and by about 2000 B.C.E. they had also thoroughly explored the waters of the Red Sea, the Gulf of Aden, and the western portion of the Arabian Sea. Egyptians also made use of Mesopotamian-style wheeled vehicles for local transport, and they relied on donkey caravans for transport between the Nile valley and ports on the Red Sea.

In Nubia, navigation on the Nile was less convenient than in Egypt because unnavigable cataracts made it necessary to transport goods overland before continuing on the river. Moreover, sailing ships heading upriver could not negotiate a long stretch of the Nile around the fourth cataract because winds blow the same direction as the currents. Thus, while Nubian societies were able to make some use of the Nile for purposes of transportation, they had to rely more than Egyptians on overland transport by wheeled vehicles and donkey caravan.

Trade Networks

In both Egypt and Nubia, specialized labor and efficient means of transportation encouraged the development of long-distance trade. Egypt was in special need of trade because the land enjoys few natural resources other than the Nile. Irregular exchanges of goods between Egypt and Nubia took place at very early times, perhaps 4000 B.C.E. or even before. By the time of the Old Kingdom, trade flowed regularly between Egypt and Nubia. The cities of Aswan and Elephantine at the southern border of Egypt reflected this trade in their very names: Aswan took its name from the ancient Egyptian word *swene*, meaning "trade," while Elephantine owed its name to the large quantities of elephant ivory that passed through it while traveling down the Nile from Nubia to Egypt. Apart from ivory, exotic African goods such as ebony, leopard skins, ostrich feathers, gemstones, gold, and slaves went down the Nile in exchange for pottery, wine, honey, and finished products from Egypt. Among the most prized Egyptian exports were fine linen textiles woven from the flax that flourished in the Nile valley as well as high-quality decorative and ornamental objects like

A wooden model found in a tomb shows how Egyptians traveled up and down the Nile River. Produced about 2000 B.C.E., this sculpture depicts a relatively small boat with a mast, sail, rudder, and poles to push the vessel through shallow waters. Many wall and tomb paintings confirm the accuracy of this model.

boxes, furniture, and jewelry produced by skilled artisans. Commerce linked Egypt and Nubia throughout ancient times, even when tensions or hostilities complicated relations between the two societies.

Egyptian merchants looked north as well as south. They traded with Mesopotamians as early as 3500 B.C.E., and after 3000 B.C.E. they were active throughout the eastern Mediterranean basin. Egyptian commerce in the Mediterranean sometimes involved massive transfers of goods. Since Egypt has very few trees, for example, all wood came from abroad. Pharaohs especially prized aromatic cedar for their tombs, and Egyptian ships regularly imported huge loads from Lebanon. One record of about 2600 B.C.E. mentions an expedition of forty ships hauling cedar logs. In exchange for cedar Egyptians offered gold, silver, linen textiles, leather goods, and dried foods such as lentils.

After the establishment of the New Kingdom, Egyptians also traded through the Red Sea and the Gulf of Aden with an east African land they called Punt—probably modern-day Somalia and Ethiopia. From Punt they imported gold, ebony, ivory, cattle, aromatics, and human slaves. The tomb of Queen Hatshepsut bears detailed illustrations of a trading expedition to Punt about 1450 B.C.E. Paintings in the tomb show large Egyptian ships bearing jewelry, tools, and weapons to Punt and then loading the exotic products of the southern land, including apes, monkeys, dogs, a live panther, and

Queen Hatshepsut's fleet takes on cargo at Punt. Stevedores carry jars of aromatics and trees with carefully wrapped roots onto the Egyptian vessels. In the bottom panel, ships loaded with cargo prepare to depart.

live myrrh trees with their roots carefully bound in bags. Thus, as in southwest Asia, specialization of labor and efficient technologies of transportation not only quickened the economies of complex societies in Egypt and Nubia but also encouraged their interaction with peoples of distant lands.

Early Writing in the Nile Valley

Hieroglyphic Writing

Writing appeared in Egypt at least by 3200 B.C.E., possibly as a result of Mesopotamian influence. As in Mesopotamia, the earliest Egyptian writing was pictographic, but Egyptians soon supplemented their pictographs with symbols representing sounds and ideas. Early Greek visitors to Egypt marveled at the large and handsome pictographs that adorned Egyptian monuments and buildings. Since the symbols were particularly prominent on temples, the visitors called them hieroglyphs, from two Greek words meaning "holy inscriptions." Quite apart from monumental inscriptions, hieroglyphic writing survives also on sheets of papyrus, a paper-like material fashioned from the insides of papyrus reeds, which flourish along the Nile River. The hot, dry climate of Egypt has preserved not only mummified bodies but also large numbers of papyrus texts bearing administrative and commercial records as well as literary and religious texts.

Although striking and dramatic, hieroglyphs were also somewhat cumbersome. Egyptians went to the trouble of using hieroglyphs for formal writing and monumental inscriptions, but for everyday affairs they commonly relied on the hieratic ("priestly") script, a simplified, cursive form of hieroglyphs. Hieratic appeared in the early centuries of the third millennium B.C.E., and Egyptians made extensive use of the script for more than three thousand years, from about 2600 B.C.E. to 600 C.E. Hieratic largely disappeared after the middle of the first millennium C.E., when Egyptians adapted the Greek alphabet to their own language and developed alphabetic scripts known as the demotic ("popular") and Coptic ("Egyptian") scripts. Hieratic, demotic, and Coptic scripts all survive mostly in papyrus texts but occasionally also in inscriptions.

Contexts & Connections

Deciphering Hieroglyphic Writing

How do you figure out how to read a complicated script that has fallen out of use? This was the question addressed by thousands of scholars over the centuries who sought to crack the code of hieroglyphic, the majestic script used in formal writings and also in carved texts that adorned monuments and temples in ancient Egypt. Hieroglyphic script was in use well before 3000 B.C.E., while the latest datable example came from temple carvings of 394 C.E. After the early centuries C.E., education in hieroglyphics disappeared, and by the early sixth century, even scholars were unable to read the script.

Over the centuries, untold numbers of individuals gazed upon hieroglyphic writing and generated theories about its origin, meaning, and influence. One popular line of thought held that hieroglyphic writing was a mysterious and possibly even divinely created script that was capable of conveying esoteric wisdom that alphabetic writing

The Rosetta stone, with hieroglyphic text at the top, demotic in the middle, and Greek at the bottom.

could not transmit—a theory that was particularly difficult to challenge at a time when no one was able to read hieroglyphs. Another speculation held that Egyptian hieroglyphs were the source of inspiration for the characters used in Chinese writing. Before the nineteenth century, most if not all commentators assumed that hieroglyphic writing was an entirely pictographic rather than alphabetic or phonetic script.

The key to the decipherment of hieroglyphic writing came to light in July 1799 with the discovery of an inscribed stele known as the Rosetta stone, which is now one of the most famous items in the collections of the British Museum in London. The discovery followed the invasion of Egypt by the French general Napoleon Bonaparte in 1798. While digging the foundation for a fort in the Nile delta, Bonaparte's forces found the stele in the town of Rashid, known as Rosetta in ancient times. Inscriptions on the Rosetta stone convey the same message in three different scripts: hieroglyphic, demotic, and Greek. In the late eighteenth century, many scholars knew how to read Greek, so they were able to take the Greek text as a guide to decipher the hieroglyphic and demotic scripts. They used the Rosetta stone as a key to open the door to the understanding of ancient Egyptian writing.

Principal credit for this feat belongs to the brilliant French linguist Jean-François Champollion (1790–1832). Through diligent comparison of hieroglyphic and Greek scripts on the Rosetta stone, together with adroit reasoning about his observations, Champollion realized that ancient Egypt writing was fundamentally phonetic, not pictographic, as earlier theories had assumed. Some symbols were indeed physical representations: various hieroglyphs were stylized depictions of a hawk, a serpent, a human face, a pair of walking legs, and the like. In most cases, however, these symbols had phonetic values and thus represented the sounds of vowels, consonants, syllables, or clusters of letters rather than the objects they depicted. From that realization, Champollion was able to rebuild comprehension of hieroglyphic writing. Champollion's studies deprived hieroglyphic writing of its mystery, but they opened the way to a richer and deeper understanding of ancient Egyptian society.

Formal education and literacy brought handsome rewards in ancient Egypt. The *Education* privileged life of a scribe comes across clearly in a short work known as "The Satire of the Trades." Written during the Middle Kingdom by a scribe exhorting his son to study diligently, the work detailed all the miseries associated with eighteen different professions: metalsmiths stunk like fish; potters grubbed in the mud like pigs; fishermen ran the risk of sudden death in the jaws of the Nile's ferocious crocodiles. Only the scribe led a comfortable, honorable, and dignified life.

Nubian peoples spoke their own languages, although many individuals were fully conversant in Egyptian as well as their native tongues, but all early writing in Nubia was Egyptian hieroglyphic writing. Indeed, over the centuries Egypt wielded great cultural influence in Nubia, especially during times when Egyptian political and military influence was strong in southern lands. Egyptian political and military officials often erected monuments and inscribed them with accounts in hieroglyphics of their deeds in Nubia. Similarly, Egyptian priests traveled regularly to Nubia, organized temples devoted to Egyptian gods, and promoted their beliefs in hieroglyphics. Egyptian influence was very strong in Nubia also during the eighth and seventh centuries B.C.E. when the kings of Kush ruled Egypt as pharaohs and sponsored extensive trade, travel, and communication between Egypt and Nubia.

Nubian inscriptions continued to appear in Egyptian hieroglyphic writing as late as *Meroitic Writing* the first century C.E. After about the fifth century B.C.E., however, Egyptian cultural influence declined noticeably in Nubia. After the transfer of the Kushite capital from Napata to Meroë, Nubian scribes even devised an alphabetic script for the Meroitic language. They borrowed Egyptian hieroglyphs but used them to represent sounds rather than ideas and so created a flexible writing system. Many Meroitic inscriptions survive, both on monuments and on papyrus. To date, however, scholars have not been able to understand Meroitic writing. Although they have ascertained the sound values of the alphabet, the Meroitic language itself is so different from other known languages that no one has been able to decipher Meroitic texts.

The Development of Organized Religious Traditions

Like their counterparts in other world regions, Egyptians and Nubians believed that *Amon and Re* deities played prominent roles in the world and that proper cultivation of the gods was an important community responsibility. The principal gods revered in ancient Egypt were Amon and Re. Amon was originally a local Theban deity associated with the sun, creation, fertility, and reproductive forces, while Re was a sun god worshiped at Heliopolis. During the Old Kingdom and Middle Kingdom, priests increasingly associated the two gods with one another and honored them in the combined cult of Amon-Re. At Heliopolis, a massive temple complex supported priests who tended to the cult of Amon-Re and studied the heavens for astronomical purposes. When Egypt became an imperial power during the New Kingdom, some devotees suggested that Amon-Re might even be a universal god who presided over all the earth.

For a brief period the cult of Amon-Re faced a monotheistic challenge from the *Aten and Monotheism* god Aten, another deity associated with the sun. Aten's champion was Pharaoh Amenhotep IV (reigned 1353–1335 B.C.E.), who changed his name to Akhenaten in honor of his preferred deity. Akhenaten considered Aten the world's "sole god, like whom there is no other." Thus, unlike the priests of Amon-Re, most of whom viewed their god as one among many, Akhenaten and others devoted to Aten considered their deity the one and only true god. Their faith represented one of the world's earliest expressions of monotheism—the belief that a single god rules over all creation.

Akhenaten built a new capital city called Akhetaten ("Horizon of Aten," located at modern Tell el-Amarna), where broad streets, courtyards, and open temples allowed unobscured vision and constant veneration of the sun. He also dispatched agents to all parts of Egypt with instructions to encourage the worship of Aten and to chisel out the names of Amon, Re, and other gods from inscriptions on temples and public buildings. As long as Akhenaten lived, the cult of Aten flourished. But when the pharaoh died, traditional priests mounted a fierce counterattack, restored the cult of Amon-Re to privileged status, and nearly annihilated the worship and even the memory of Aten.

Mummification

Whereas Mesopotamians believed with Gilgamesh that death brought an end to an individual's existence, many Egyptians believed that death was not an end so much as a transition to a new dimension of existence. The yearning for immortality helps to explain the Egyptian practice of mummifying the dead. During the Old Kingdom, Egyptians believed that only the ruling elites would survive the grave, so they mummified only pharaohs and their close relatives. Later, however, other royal officials and wealthy individuals merited the posthumous honor of mummification. During the Middle and New Kingdoms, Egyptians came to think of eternal life as a condition available to normal mortals as well as members of the ruling classes. By the time the Greek historian Herodotus described the process of mummification in the fifth century B.C.E., many wealthy families were able to help their deceased relatives attain immortality by preserving their bodies. Mummification never became general practice in Egypt, but with or without preservation of the body, a variety of religious cults promised to lead individuals of all classes to immortality.

Cult of Osiris

The cult of Osiris attracted particularly strong popular interest. According to the myths surrounding the cult, Osiris's evil brother Seth murdered him and scattered his dismembered parts throughout the land, but the victim's loyal wife, Isis, retrieved his parts and gave her husband a proper burial. Impressed by her devotion, the gods restored Osiris to life—not to physical human life among mortals, however, but to a different kind of existence as god of the underworld, the dwelling place of the departed. Because of his death and resurrection, Egyptians associated Osiris with the Nile (which flooded, retreated, and then flooded again the following year) and with their crops (which similarly grew, died, and then sprouted again.)

Osiris (seated at right) receives a recently deceased individual, while attendants weigh the heart of another individual against a feather. This illustration comes from a papyrus copy of the *Book of the Dead* that was buried with a royal mummy.

Sources from the Past

The Great Hymn to Aten

After the death of Pharaoh Akhenaten, priests of Amon destroyed temples to Aten and all public inscriptions singing his praises. Yet many private inscriptions survived in tombs of priests and royal officials who died while in service at the new royal capital of Akhetaten. In excavating these tombs, archaeologists have brought to light many texts praising Aten and outlining the monotheistic beliefs surrounding his cult. Most famous of these inscriptions is the text known as "The Great Hymn to Aten."

Splendid you rise in heaven's lightland,
O living Aten, creator of life!
When you have dawned in eastern lightland,
You fill every land with your beauty.
You are beauteous, great radiant,
High over every land;
Your rays embrace the lands,
To the limit of all that you made. . . .

When you set in western lightland,
Earth is in darkness as if in death;
One sleeps in chambers, heads covered,
One eye does not see another.
Were they robbed of their goods,
That are under their heads,
People would not remark it.
Every lion comes from its den,
All the serpents bite;
Darkness hovers, earth is silent,
As their maker rests in lightland.

Earth brightens when you dawn in lightland.
When you shine as Aten of daytime;
As you dispel the dark,
As you cast your rays,
The Two Lands [of Upper Egypt and Lower Egypt]
   are in festivity.
Awake they stand on their feet,

You have roused them;
Bodies cleansed, clothed,
Their arms adore your appearance.
The entire land sets out to work. . . .
How many are your deeds,
Though hidden from sight,
O Sole God beside whom there is none!
You made the earth as you wished, you alone,
All peoples, herds, and flocks;
All upon earth that walk on legs,
All on high that fly on wings,
The lands of Khor and Kush,
The land of Egypt. . . .

Your rays nurse all fields,
When you shine they live, they grow for you;
You made the seasons to foster all that you made,
Winter to cool them, heat that they taste you.
You made the far sky to shine therein,
To behold all that you made;
You alone, shining in your form of living Aten,
Risen, radiant, distant, near.
You made millions of forms from yourself alone,
Towns, villages, fields, the river's course;
All eyes observe you upon them,
For you are the Aten of daytime on high.

SOURCE: Miriam Lichtheim, ed. *Ancient Egyptian Literature*, 3 vols. Berkeley: University of California Press, 1976, 2: 96–99.

As conceived in "The Great Hymn to Aten," what was the role of Aten as creator and sustainer of life on earth?

Egyptians also associated Osiris with immortality and honored him through a religious cult that demanded observance of high moral standards. As lord of the underworld, Osiris had the power to determine who deserved the blessing of immortality and

An elaborate gold ring from a tomb at Meroë, dating probably to the third century C.E., depicts a deity named Sebiumeker (sometimes referred to as Sebewyemeker). Although often associated with Osiris, Sebiumeker was a Meroitic god with no exact counterpart in Egypt.

who did not. Following their deaths, individual souls faced the judgment of Osiris, who had their hearts weighed against a feather symbolizing justice. Those with heavy hearts carrying a burden of evil and guilt did not merit immortality, whereas those of pure heart and honorable deeds gained the gift of eternal life. Thus Osiris's cult held out hope of eternal reward for those who behaved according to high moral standards, and it cast its message in terms understandable to cultivators in early agricultural society.

Nubian Religious Beliefs

Nubian peoples observed their own religious traditions, some of which they probably inherited from the early agricultural societies of the Sudan, but very little written information survives to throw light on their religious beliefs. The most prominent of the Nubian deities was the lion-god Apedemak, often depicted with a bow and arrows, who served as war god for the kingdom of Kush. Another deity, Sebiumeker, was a creator god and divine guardian of his human devotees.

Alongside native traditions, Egyptian religious cults were quite prominent in Nubia, especially after the aggressive pharaohs of the New Kingdom imposed Egyptian rule on the southern lands. Nubian peoples did not mummify the remains of their deceased, but they built pyramids similar to those of Egypt, although smaller, and they embraced several Egyptian gods. Amon was the preeminent Egyptian deity in Nubia as in Egypt itself: many Nubian temples honored Amon, and the kings of Kush portrayed themselves as champions of the Egyptian god. Osiris was also popular in Nubia, where he sometimes appeared in association with the native deity Sebiumeker. In the early days after their introduction, Egyptian cults were most prominent among the Nubian ruling classes. Gradually, however, Egyptian gods attracted a sizable following, and they remained popular in Nubia until the sixth century C.E. They did not displace native gods so much as they joined them in the Nubian pantheon. Indeed, Nubians often identified Egyptian gods with their own deities or endowed the foreign gods with traits important in Nubian society.

BANTU MIGRATIONS AND EARLY AGRICULTURAL SOCIETIES OF SUB-SAHARAN AFRICA

Like their counterparts in southwest Asia, Egyptian and Nubian societies participated in a much larger world of interaction and exchange. Mesopotamian societies developed under the strong influences of long-distance trade, diffusions of technological innovations, the spread of cultural traditions, and the far-flung migrations of Semitic and Indo-European peoples. Similarly, quite apart from their dealings with southwest Asian and Mediterranean peoples, Egyptian and Nubian societies developed in the context of widespread interaction and exchange in sub-Saharan Africa. The most prominent processes unfolding in sub-Saharan Africa during ancient times were the migrations of Bantu-speaking peoples and the establishment of agricultural societies in regions where Bantu speakers settled. Just as Sudanic agriculture spread to the Nile valley and provided an economic foundation for the development of Egyptian and Nubian societies, it also spread to most other regions of Africa south of the Sahara and supported the emergence of distinctive agricultural societies.

The Dynamics of Bantu Expansion

The Bantu

Among the most influential peoples of sub-Saharan Africa in ancient times were those who spoke Bantu languages. The original Bantu language was one of many related tongues in the larger Niger-Congo family of languages widely spoken in west Africa after 4000 B.C.E. (Niger-Congo languages include also those spoken by Mande, Kru, Wolof, Yoruba, Igbo, and other peoples.) The earliest Bantu speakers inhabited a region embracing the eastern part of modern Nigeria and the southern part of modern Cameroon. Members of this community referred to themselves as *bantu* (meaning "persons" or "people"). The earliest Bantu speakers settled mostly along the banks of rivers, which they navigated in canoes, and in open areas of the region's forests. They cultivated yams and oil palms, which first came under cultivation by early agricultural peoples in the western Sudan, and in later centuries they also adopted crops that reached them from the eastern and central Sudan, particularly millet and sorghum. They also kept goats and raised guinea fowl. They lived in clan-based villages headed by chiefs who conducted religious rituals and represented their communities in dealings with neighboring villages. They traded regularly with hunting and gathering peoples who inhabited the tropical forests. Formerly called pygmies, these peoples are now referred to as forest peoples. Bantu cultivators provided these forest peoples with pottery and stone axes in exchange for meat, honey, and other forest products.

Unlike most of their neighbors, the Bantu displayed an early readiness to migrate to new territories. By 3000 B.C.E. they were slowly spreading south into the west African forest, and after 2000 B.C.E. they expanded rapidly to the south toward the Congo River basin and east toward the Great Lakes, absorbing local populations of hunting, gathering, and fishing peoples into their own agricultural societies. Over the centuries, as some groups of Bantu speakers settled and others moved on to new territories, their languages differentiated into more than five hundred distinct but related tongues. (Today, more than ninety million people speak Bantu languages, which collectively constitute the most prominent family of languages in sub-Saharan Africa.) Like the Indo-European migrations discussed in chapter 2, the Bantu migrations were not mass movements of peoples. Instead, they were intermittent and incremental processes that resulted in the gradual spread of Bantu languages and ethnic communities, as small groups moved to new territories and established settlements, which then became foundations for further expansion. By 1000 C.E. Bantu-speaking peoples occupied most of Africa south of the equator.

The precise motives of the early Bantu migrants remain shrouded in the mists of time, but it seems likely that population pressures drove the migrations.

Bantu Migrations

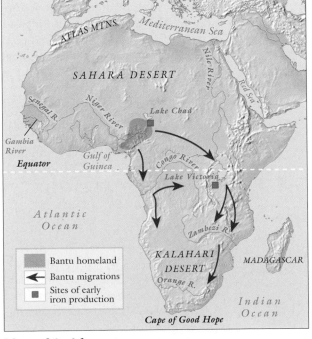

MAP [3.3]

Bantu migrations, 2000 B.C.E.–1000 C.E.

Two features of Bantu society were especially important for the earliest migrations. First, Bantu peoples made effective use of canoes in traveling the networks of the Niger, Congo, and other rivers. Canoes enabled Bantu to travel rapidly up and down the rivers, leapfrogging established communities and establishing new settlements at inviting spots on riverbanks. Second, agricultural surpluses enabled the Bantu population to increase more rapidly than the populations of hunting, gathering, and fishing peoples whom they encountered as they moved into new regions. When settlements grew uncomfortably large and placed strains on available resources, small groups left their parent communities and moved to new territories. Sometimes they moved to new sites along the rivers, but they often moved inland as well, encroaching on territories occupied by forest peoples. Bantu migrants placed pressures on the forest dwellers, and they most likely clashed with them over land resources. They learned a great deal about local environments from the forest peoples, however, and they also continued to trade regularly with them. Indeed, they often intermarried and absorbed forest peoples into Bantu agricultural society.

Iron and Migration   After about 1000 B.C.E., the pace of Bantu migrations quickened, as Bantu peoples began to produce iron tools and weapons. Iron tools enabled Bantu cultivators to clear land and expand the zone of agriculture more effectively than before, while iron weapons strengthened the hand of Bantu groups against adversaries and competitors for lands or other resources. Thus iron metallurgy supported rapid population growth among the Bantu while also lending increased momentum to their continuing migrations, which in turn facilitated the spread of iron metallurgy throughout most of sub-Saharan Africa.

Early Agricultural Societies of Sub-Saharan Africa

Several smaller migrations took place alongside the spread of Bantu peoples in sub-Saharan Africa. Between 3500 and 1000 B.C.E., southern Kushite herders pushed into parts of east Africa (modern-day Kenya and Tanzania), while Sudanese cultivators and herders moved into the upper reaches of the Nile River (now southern Sudan and northern Uganda). Meanwhile, Mande-speaking peoples who cultivated African rice established communities along the Atlantic estuaries of west Africa, and other peoples speaking Niger-Congo languages spread the cultivation of okra from forest regions throughout much of west Africa.

Spread of Agriculture   Among the most important effects of Bantu and other migrations was the establishment of agricultural societies throughout most of sub-Saharan Africa. Between 1000 and 500 B.C.E., cultivators extended the cultivation of yams and grains deep into east and south Africa (modern-day Kenya, Malawi, Mozambique, Zimbabwe, and South Africa), while herders introduced sheep and cattle to the region. About the same time, Bantu and other peoples speaking Niger-Congo languages spread the intensive cultivation of yams, oil palms, millet, and sorghum throughout west and central Africa while also introducing sheep, pigs, and cattle to the region. By the late centuries B.C.E., agriculture had reached almost all of sub-Saharan Africa except for densely forested regions and deserts.

As cultivation and herding spread throughout sub-Saharan Africa, agricultural peoples built distinctive societies and cultural traditions. Most Bantu and other peoples as well lived in communities of a few hundred individuals led by chiefs. Many peoples recognized groups known as age sets, or age grades, consisting of individuals born within a few years of one another. Members of each age set jointly assumed responsibility for tasks appropriate to their levels of strength, energy, maturity, and experience. During their early years, for example, members of an age set might perform light public chores. At maturity, members jointly underwent elaborate initiation rites that introduced them to adult society. Older men cultivated fields and provided military service, while women tended to domestic chores and sometimes traded at markets. In later years, members of age sets served as community leaders and military officers.

Religious Beliefs

African cultivators and herders also developed distinctive cultural and religious traditions. Both Sudanic and Niger-Congo peoples (including Bantu speakers), for example, held monotheistic religious beliefs by 5000 B.C.E. Sudanic peoples recognized a single, impersonal divine force that they regarded as the source of both good and evil. They believed that this divine force could take the form of individual spirits, and they often addressed the divine force through prayers to intermediary spirits. The divine force itself, however, was ultimately responsible for rewards and punishments meted out to human beings. For their part, Niger-Congo peoples recognized a single god originally called Nyamba who created the world and established the principles that would govern its development, then stepped back and allowed the world to proceed on its own. Individuals did not generally address this distant creator god directly but, rather, offered their prayers to ancestor spirits and local territorial spirits believed to inhabit the world and influence the fortunes of living humans. Proper attention to these spirits would ensure them good fortune, they believed, while their neglect would bring punishment or adversity from disgruntled spirits.

Individual communities did not always hold religious beliefs in the precise forms just outlined. Rather, they frequently borrowed elements from other communities and adapted their beliefs to changing circumstances or fresh understandings of the world. Migrations of Bantu and other peoples in particular resulted in a great deal of cultural mixing and mingling, and religious beliefs often spread to new communities in the wake of population movements. After 1000 B.C.E., for example, as they encountered Sudanic peoples and their reverence of a single divine force that was the source of good and evil, many Bantu peoples associated the god Nyamba with goodness. As a result, this formerly distant creator god took on a new moral dimension that brought him closer to the lives of individuals. Thus changing religious beliefs sometimes reflected widespread interactions among African societies.

Like other world regions, Africa was a land in which peoples of different societies regularly traded, communicated, and interacted with one another from ancient times. African agriculture and herding first emerged in the Sudan, then spread both to the Nile River valley and to arable lands throughout sub-Saharan Africa. Agricultural crops and domesticated animals from southwest Asia soon made their way into the Nile valley. With its broad floodplains, Egypt became an especially productive land, while Nubia supported a smaller but flourishing society. Throughout the Nile valley, abundant agricultural surpluses supported dense populations and supported the construction of prosperous societies with sophisticated cultural traditions. Elsewhere in sub-Saharan Africa, populations were less dense, but the migrations of Bantu and other peoples facilitated the spread of agriculture, and later iron metallurgy as well, throughout most of the region. Meanwhile, the Nile River served as a route of trade and communication linking Egypt and the Mediterranean basin to the north with the Sudan and sub-Saharan Africa to the south. Only in the context of migration, trade, communication, and interaction is it possible to understand the early development of African societies.

CHRONOLOGY

9000 B.C.E.	Origins of Sudanic herding
7500 B.C.E.	Origins of Sudanic cultivation
3100 B.C.E.	Unification of Egypt
3100–2660 B.C.E.	Archaic Period of Egyptian history
2660–2160 B.C.E.	Egyptian Old Kingdom
2600–2500 B.C.E.	Era of pyramid building in Egypt
2500–1450 B.C.E.	Early kingdom of Kush with capital at Kerma
2040–1640 B.C.E.	Egyptian Middle Kingdom
2000 B.C.E.	Beginnings of Bantu migrations
1550–1070 B.C.E.	Egyptian New Kingdom
1479–1425 B.C.E.	Reign of Pharaoh Tuthmosis III
1473–1458 B.C.E.	Reign of Queen Hatshepsut (coruler with Tuthmosis III)
1353–1335 B.C.E.	Reign of Pharaoh Amenhotep IV (Akhenaten)
900 B.C.E.	Invention of iron metallurgy in sub-Saharan Africa
760 B.C.E.	Conquest of Egypt by King Kashta of Kush

FOR FURTHER READING

Cyril Aldred. *The Egyptians*. Rev. ed. New York, 1984. A popular, well-illustrated, and reliable survey of ancient Egyptian history.

Elizabeth Wayland Barber. *Women's Work: The First 20,000 Years*. New York, 1994. Fascinating study of ancient textiles, which the author argues was a craft industry dominated by women from the earliest times.

Stanley Burstein, ed. *Ancient African Civilizations: Kush and Axum*. Princeton, 1998. Brings together the principal Greek and Latin writings on the kingdoms of Kush and Axum.

Basil Davidson. *Lost Cities of Africa*. Rev. ed. Boston, 1970. Popular account with discussions of Kush and Meroë.

Christopher Ehret. *An African Classical Age: Eastern and Southern Africa in World History, 1000 B.C. to A.D. 400*. Charlottesville, Va., 1998. A pathbreaking volume focusing on eastern and southern Africa and drawing on both linguistic and archaeological evidence.

———. *The Civilizations of Africa: A History to 1800*. Charlottesville, Va., 2001. An important contribution that views Africa in the context of world history.

T. G. H. James. *Pharaoh's People: Scenes from Life in Imperial Egypt*. London, 1984. Draws on archaeological and literary scholarship in reconstructing daily life in ancient Egypt.

Robert W. July. *Precolonial Africa: An Economic and Social History.* New York, 1975. Excellent short analysis of African social and economic history.

Timothy Kendall, ed. *Kerma and the Kingdom of Kush, 2500–1500 B.C.: The Archaeological Discovery of an Ancient Nubian Empire.* Washington, D.C., 1997. Well-illustrated volume that focuses on the city of Kerma and its role in ancient Nubian society.

Miriam Lichtheim, ed. *Ancient Egyptian Literature.* 3 vols. Berkeley, 1973–80. An important collection of primary sources in translation that reflects the results of recent scholarship.

Roderick James McIntosh. *The Peoples of the Middle Niger: The Island of Gold.* Oxford, 1998. Fascinating volume emphasizing the environmental context of west African history.

William H. McNeill and Jean Sedlar, eds. *The Ancient Near East.* New York, 1968. A collection of primary sources in translation that concentrates on Mesopotamia and Egypt.

———, eds. *The Origins of Civilization.* New York, 1968. Like its companion volume just cited, a collection of translated sources that concentrates on Mesopotamia and Egypt.

James B. Pritchard, ed. *Ancient Near Eastern Texts Relating to the Old Testament.* 2 vols. 3rd ed. Princeton, 1975. Important collection of primary sources in translation that emphasizes parallels between the ancient Hebrews and other peoples.

Jan Vansina. *Paths in the Rainforests: Toward a History of Political Tradition in Equatorial Africa.* Madison, 1990. A brilliant synthesis concentrating on central Africa by one of the world's foremost historians of Africa.

Derek A. Welsby. *The Kingdom of Kush: The Napatan and Meroitic Empires.* London, 1996. Draws on both written and archaeological sources in tracing the development of ancient Nubia and charting its relationship with Egypt.

See our **Online Learning Center** at www.mhhe.com/bentley3 for additional readings, practice maps, quizzes, and internet activities.

Unfamiliar words? Check out the **Primary Source Investigator CD-ROM** for an interactive glossary, interactive maps, more images, and primary sources.

Sandstone bust of a distinguished man, perhaps a priest-king, from Mohenjo-daro.

CHAPTER 4

EARLY SOCIETIES IN SOUTH ASIA

For a god, Indra was a very rambunctious fellow. According to the stories told about him by the Aryans, Indra had few if any peers in fighting, feasting, or drinking. The Aryans were a herding people who spoke an Indo-European language and who migrated to south Asia in large numbers after 1500 B.C.E. In the early days of their migrations they took Indra as their chief deity. The Aryans told dozens of stories about Indra and sang hundreds of hymns in his honor.

One story had to do with a war between the gods and the demons. When the gods were flagging, they appointed Indra as their leader, and soon they had turned the tide against their enemies. Another story, a favorite one of the Aryans, had to do with Indra's role in bringing rain to the earth—a crucial concern for any agricultural society. According to this story, Indra did battle with a dragon who lived in the sky and hoarded water in the clouds. Indra first slaked his thirst with generous drafts of *soma,* a hallucinogenic potion consumed by Aryan priests, and then attacked the dragon, which he killed by hurling thunderbolts at it. The dragon's heavy fall caused turmoil both on earth and in the atmosphere, but afterward the rains filled seven rivers that flowed through northern India and brought life-giving waters to inhabitants of the region.

The Aryans took Indra as a leader against earthly as well as heavenly foes. They did not mount a planned invasion of India, but as they migrated in sizable numbers into south Asia, they came into conflict with Dravidian peoples already living there. When they clashed with the Dravidians, the Aryans took the belligerent Indra as their guide. Aryan hymns praised Indra as the military hero who trampled enemy forces and opened the way for the migrants to build a new society.

For all his contributions, Indra did not survive permanently as a prominent deity. As Aryan and Dravidian peoples mixed, mingled, interacted, and intermarried, tensions between them subsided. Memories of the stormy and violent Indra receded into the background, and eventually they faded almost to nothing. For a thousand years and more, however, Aryans looked upon the rowdy, raucous war god as a ready source of inspiration as they sought to build a society in an already occupied land.

Tools excavated by archaeologists show that India was a site of paleolithic communities at least two hundred thousand years ago, long before the Aryans introduced Indra to south Asia. Between 8000 and 5000 B.C.E., cultivators built a neolithic society west of the Indus River, in the region bordering on the Iranian plateau, probably as a result of Mesopotamian influence. By 7000 B.C.E. agriculture had taken root in the Indus River valley. Thereafter agriculture spread rapidly, and by about 3000 B.C.E. Dravidian peoples had established neolithic communities throughout much of the Indian subcontinent. The earliest neolithic settlers cultivated wheat, barley, and cotton, and they also kept herds of cattle, sheep, and goats. Agricultural villages were especially numerous in the valley of the Indus River. As the population of the valley swelled and as people interacted with increasing frequency, some of these villages evolved into bustling cities, which served as the organizational centers of Indian society.

As in Mesopotamia and Egypt, early cities in India stood at the center of an impressive political, social, and cultural order built by Dravidian peoples on the foundation of an agricultural economy. The earliest urban society in India, known as Harappan society, brought wealth and power to the Indus River valley. Eventually, however, it fell into decline, possibly because of environmental problems, just as large numbers of Indo-European migrants moved into India from central Asia and built a very different society. For half a millennium, from about 1500 to 1000 B.C.E., the Indian subcontinent was a site of turmoil as the migrants struggled with Dravidian peoples for control of the land and its resources. Gradually, however, stability returned with the establishment of numerous agricultural villages and regional states. During the centuries after 1000 B.C.E., Aryan and Dravidian peoples increasingly interacted and intermarried, and their combined legacies led to the development of a distinctive society and a rich cultural tradition.

HARAPPAN SOCIETY

Like societies in Mesopotamia and Egypt, Harappan society—named after Harappa, one of its two chief cities—developed in the valley of a river, the Indus, whose waters were available for irrigation of crops. As agricultural yields increased, the population also grew rapidly, and by about 3000 B.C.E. neolithic villages were evolving into thriving cities.

Unfortunately, it is impossible to follow the development of Harappan society in detail for two reasons. One is that many of the earliest Harappan physical remains are inaccessible. Silt deposits have raised the level of the land in the Indus valley, and the water table has risen correspondingly. Because the earliest Harappan remains lie below the water table, archaeologists cannot excavate them or study them systematically. The earliest accessible remains date from about 2500 B.C.E., when Harappan society was already well established. As a result, scholars have learned something about Harappa at its high point, but very little about the circumstances that brought it into being or the conditions of life during its earliest days.

A second problem that handicaps scholars who study Harappan society is the lack of deciphered written records. Harappans had a system of writing that used about four hundred symbols to represent sounds and words, and archaeologists have discovered thousands of clay seals, copper tablets, and other artifacts with Harappan inscriptions. Scholars consider the language most likely a Dravidian tongue related to those currently spoken in central and southern India, but they have not yet succeeded in deciphering the script. As a result, the details of Harappan life remain hidden behind the veil of an elaborate pictographic script. The understanding of Harappan society depends entirely on the study of material remains that archaeologists have uncovered since the 1920s.

Foundations of Harappan Society

If the Greek historian Herodotus had known of Harappan society, he might have called it "the gift of the Indus." Like the Nile, the Indus draws its waters from rain and melting snow in towering mountains—in this case, the Hindu Kush and the Himalayas, the world's highest peaks. As the waters charge downhill, they pick up enormous quantities of silt, which they carry for hundreds of kilometers. Like the Nile again, the Indus then deposits its burden of rich soil as it courses through lowlands and loses its force. Today, a series of dams has largely tamed the Indus, but for most of history it spilled its waters annually over a vast floodplain, sometimes with devastating effect. Much less predictable than the Nile, the Indus has many times left its channel altogether and carved a new course to the sea.

The Indus River

Despite its occasional ferocity, the Indus made agricultural society possible in northern India. Early cultivators sowed wheat and barley in September, after the flood receded, and harvested their crops the following spring. Inhabitants of the valley supplemented their harvests of wheat and barley with meat from herds of cattle, sheep, and goats. Their diet also included poultry: cultivators in the Indus valley kept flocks of the world's first domesticated chickens. Indus valley inhabitants cultivated cotton probably before 5000 B.C.E., and fragments of dyed cloth dating to about 2000 B.C.E. testify to the existence of a cotton textile industry.

As in Mesopotamia and Egypt, agricultural surpluses in India vastly increased the food supply, stimulated population growth, and supported the establishment of cities and specialized labor. Between 3000 and 2500 B.C.E., Dravidian peoples built a complex society that dominated the Indus River valley until its decline after 1900 B.C.E. The agricultural surplus of the Indus valley fed two large cities, Harappa and Mohenjo-daro, as well as subordinate cities and a vast agricultural hinterland. Archaeologists have excavated about seventy Harappan settlements along the Indus River. Harappan society embraced much of modern-day Pakistan and a large part of northern India as well—a territory about 1.3 million square kilometers (502,000 square miles)—and thus was considerably larger than either Mesopotamian or Egyptian society.

No evidence survives concerning the Harappan political system. Archaeological excavations have turned up no evidence of a royal or imperial authority. It is possible that, like the early Sumerian city-states, the Harappan cities were economic and political centers for their own regions. Because of their large size, however, Harappa and Mohenjo-daro were especially prominent in Harappan society even if they did not dominate the Indus valley politically or militarily. The population of Mohenjo-daro was thirty-five to forty thousand, while Harappa was probably slightly smaller. Archaeologists have discovered the sites of about 1,500 Harappan settlements, but none of the others approached the size of Harappa or Mohenjo-daro.

Political Organization

Both Harappa and Mohenjo-daro had city walls, a fortified citadel, and a large granary, suggesting that they served as centers of political authority and sites for the collection and redistribution of taxes paid in the form of grain. The two cities represented a considerable investment of human labor and other resources: both featured marketplaces, temples, public buildings, extensive residential districts, and broad streets laid out on a carefully planned grid so that they ran north-south or east-west. Mohenjo-daro also had a large pool, perhaps used for religious or ritual purposes, with private dressing rooms for bathers.

Harappa and Mohenjo-Daro

The two cities clearly established the patterns that shaped the larger society: weights, measures, architectural styles, and even brick sizes were consistent throughout the land, even though the Harappan society stretched almost 1,500 kilometers

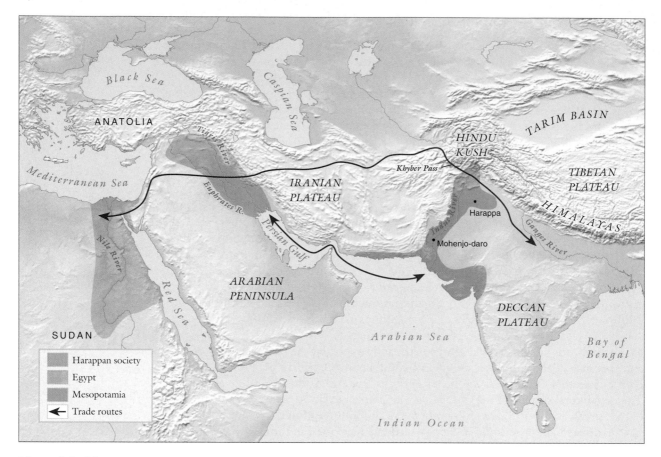

MAP [4.1]

Harappan society and its neighbors, ca. 2000 B.C.E.

Specialized Labor and Trade

(932 miles) from one end to the other. This standardization no doubt reflects the prominence of Harappa and Mohenjo-daro as powerful and wealthy cities whose influence touched all parts of Harappan society. The high degree of standardization was possible also because the Indus River facilitated trade, travel, and communications among the far-flung regions of Harappan society.

Like all complex societies in ancient times, Harappa depended on a successful agricultural economy. But Harappans also engaged in trade, both domestic and foreign. Pottery, tools, and decorative items produced in Harappa and Mohenjo-daro found their way to all corners of the Indus valley. From neighboring peoples in Persia and the Hindu Kush mountains, the Harappans obtained gold, silver, copper, lead, gems, and semiprecious stones. During the period about 2300 to 1750 B.C.E., they also traded with Mesopotamians, exchanging Indian copper, ivory, pearls, and semiprecious stones for Sumerian wool, leather, and olive oil. Some of this trade might have gone by land over the Iranian plateau, but most of it probably traveled by ships that followed the coastline of the Arabian Sea between the mouth of the Indus River and the Persian Gulf.

Harappan Society and Culture

Like societies in Mesopotamia and Egypt, Harappan society generated considerable wealth. Excavations at Mohenjo-daro show that at its high point, from about 2500

This aerial view of the excavations at Mohenjo-daro illustrates the careful planning and precise layout of the city.

to 2000 B.C.E., the city was a thriving economic center with a population of about forty thousand. Goldsmiths, potters, weavers, masons, and architects, among other professionals, maintained shops that lined Mohenjo-daro's streets. Other cities also housed communities of jewelers, artists, and merchants.

Social Distinctions

The wealth of Harappan society, like that in Mesopotamia and Egypt, encouraged the formation of social distinctions. Harappans built no pyramids, palaces, or magnificent tombs, but their rulers wielded great authority from the citadels at Harappa and Mohenjo-daro. It is clear from Harappan dwellings that rich and poor lived in very different styles. In Mohenjo-daro, for example, many people lived in one-room tenements in barrackslike structures, but there were also individual houses of two and three stories with a dozen rooms and an interior courtyard, as well as a few very large houses with several dozen rooms and multiple courtyards. Most of the larger houses had their own wells and built-in brick ovens. Almost all houses had private bathrooms with showers and toilets that drained into city sewage systems. The water and sewage systems of Mohenjo-daro were among the most sophisticated of the ancient world, and they represented a tremendous investment of community resources.

In the absence of deciphered writing, Harappan beliefs and values are even more difficult to interpret than politics and society. Archaeologists have discovered samples of Harappan writing dating as early as 3300 B.C.E., and they have recovered hundreds of seals bearing illustrations and written inscriptions. Scholars have been able to identify several symbols representing names or words, but not enough to understand the significance of the texts. Even without written texts, however, material remains shed

Fertility Cults

Bronze statuette of a dancing girl from Mohenjo-daro.

some tantalizing light on Harappan society. A variety of statues, figurines, and illustrations carved onto seals reflect a tradition of representational art as well as expertise in gold, copper, and bronze metallurgy. A particularly striking statue is a bronze figurine of a dancing girl discovered at Mohenjo-daro. Provocatively posed and clad only in bracelets and a necklace, the figure expresses a remarkable suppleness and liveliness.

Harappan religion reflected a strong concern for fertility. Like other early agricultural societies, Harappans venerated gods and goddesses whom they associated with creation and procreation. They recognized a mother goddess and a horned fertility god, and they held trees and animals sacred because of their associations with vital forces. For lack of written descriptions, it is impossible to characterize Harappan religious beliefs more specifically. Many scholars believe, however, that some Harappan deities survived the collapse of the larger society and found places later in the Hindu pantheon. Fertility and procreation are prominent concerns in popular Hinduism, and scholars have often noticed similarities between Harappan and Hindu deities associated with these values.

Harappan Decline

Sometime after 1900 B.C.E., Harappan society entered a period of decline. One cause was ecological degradation: Harappans deforested the Indus valley in order to clear land for cultivation and to obtain firewood. Deforestation led to erosion of topsoil and also to reduced amounts of rainfall. Over hundreds of years—perhaps half a millennium or more—most of the Indus valley became a desert, and agriculture is possible there today only with the aid of artificial irrigation. These climatic and ecological changes reduced agricultural yields, and Harappan society faced a subsistence crisis during the centuries after 1900 B.C.E.

It is also possible that natural catastrophes—periodic flooding of the Indus River or earthquakes—might have weakened Harappan society. Archaeologists found more than thirty unburied human skeletons scattered about the streets and buildings of Mohenjo-daro. No sign of criminal or military violence accounts for their presence, but a sudden flood or earthquake could have trapped some residents who were unable to flee the impending disaster. In any case, by about 1700 B.C.E., the populations of Harappa and Mohenjo-daro had abandoned the cities as mounting difficulties made it impossible to sustain complex urban societies. Some of the smaller, subordinate cities outlived Harappa and Mohenjo-daro, but by about 1500 B.C.E., Harappan cities had almost entirely collapsed.

Decline of the cities, however, did not mean the total disappearance of Harappan social and cultural traditions. In many ways, Harappan traditions survived the decline of the cities, because peoples from other societies adopted Harappan ways for their

The carving on a seal discovered at Mohenjo-daro depicts a man wearing cattle horns and meditating while surrounded by both domestic and wild animals. The figure may well represent a Harappan deity.

own purposes. Cultivation of wheat, barley, and cotton continued to flourish in the Indus valley long after the decline of Harappan society. Harappan deities and religious beliefs intrigued migrants to India and found a home in new societies. Eventually, cities themselves returned to south Asia, and in some cases, Harappan urban traditions may even have inspired the establishment of new cities.

THE INDO-EUROPEAN MIGRATIONS AND EARLY ARYAN INDIA

During the second millennium B.C.E., as Harappan society declined, bands of foreigners filtered into the Indian subcontinent and settled throughout the Indus valley and beyond. Most prominent were nomadic and pastoral peoples speaking Indo-European languages who called themselves Aryans ("noble people"). By 1500 B.C.E. or perhaps somewhat earlier, they had begun to file through the passes of the Hindu Kush mountains and establish small herding and agricultural communities throughout northern India.

Their migrations took place over several centuries: by no means did the arrival of the Aryans constitute an invasion or an organized military campaign. It is likely that Indo-European migrants clashed with Dravidians and other peoples already settled in India, but there is no indication that the Aryans conquered or destroyed Harappan society. By the time the Indo-Europeans entered India, internal problems had already brought Harappan society to the point of collapse. During the centuries after 1500 B.C.E., Dravidian and Indo-European peoples intermarried, interacted, and laid social and cultural foundations that would influence Indian society to the present day.

The Aryans and India

The Early Aryans

When they entered India, the Aryans practiced a limited amount of agriculture, but they depended much more heavily on a pastoral economy. They kept sheep and goats, but they especially prized their horses and herds of cattle. Horses were quite valuable because of their expense and relative rarity: horses do not breed well in India, so it was necessary for Aryans to replenish their supplies of horseflesh by importing animals from central Asia. Like their Indo-European cousins to the north, the Aryans harnessed horses to carts or wagons to facilitate transportation, and they also hitched them to chariots, which proved to be devastating war machines when deployed against peoples who made no use of horsepower. Meanwhile, cattle became the principal measure of wealth in early Aryan society. The Aryans consumed both dairy products and beef—cattle did not become sacred, protected animals (as they are today among Hindus) until many centuries after the Aryans' arrival—and they often calculated prices in terms of cattle. Wealthy individuals in early Aryan society usually owned their fortunes due to extensive herds of cattle.

The Vedas

The early Aryans did not use writing, but they composed numerous poems and songs. Indeed, they preserved extensive collections of religious and literary works by memorizing them and transmitting them orally from one generation to another in their sacred language, Sanskrit. (For everyday communication, the Aryans relied on a related but less formal tongue known as Prakrit, which later evolved into Hindi, Bengali, Urdu, and other languages currently spoken in northern India.) The earliest of these orally transmitted works were the Vedas, which were collections of hymns, songs, prayers, and rituals honoring the various gods of the Aryans. There are four Vedas, the earliest and most important of which is the *Rig Veda*, a collection of some 1,028 hymns addressed to Aryan gods. Aryan priests compiled the *Rig Veda* between about 1400 and 900 B.C.E., and they committed it to writing, along with the three later Vedas, about 600 B.C.E.

The Vedas represent a priestly perspective on affairs: the word *veda* means "wisdom" or "knowledge" and refers to the knowledge that priests needed to carry out their functions. While transmitting religious knowledge, however, the Vedas also shed considerable light on early Aryan society in India. In view of their importance as historical sources, scholars refer to Indian history during the millennium between 1500 and 500 B.C.E. as the Vedic age.

The Vedic Age

The Vedas reflect a boisterous society in which the Aryans clashed repeatedly with the Dravidians and other peoples already living in India. The Vedas refer frequently to conflicts between Aryans and indigenous peoples whom the Aryans called *dasas,* meaning "enemies" or "subject peoples." The Vedas identify Indra, the Aryan war god and military hero, as one who ravaged citadels, smashed dams, and destroyed forts the way age consumes cloth garments. These characterizations suggest that the Aryans clashed repeatedly with the Dravidians of the Indus valley, attacking their cities and wrecking the irrigation systems that had supported agriculture in Harappan society. It is clear that Aryans often had friendly relations with Dravidian peoples: they learned about the land, for example, and adopted Dravidian agricultural techniques when they settled in villages. Nevertheless, competition over land and resources fueled intermittent conflict between Aryan and Dravidian peoples.

The Aryans also fought ferociously among themselves. They did not have a state or common government but, rather, formed hundreds of chiefdoms organized around herding communities and agricultural villages. Most of the chiefdoms had a leader known as a *raja*—a Sanskrit term related to the Latin word *rex* ("king")—who governed in collaboration with a council of village elders. Given the large number of chiefdoms, there was enormous potential for conflict in Aryan society. The men of one village often raided the herds of their neighbors—an offense of great significance, since the Aryans regarded cattle as the chief form of wealth in their society. Occasionally, too, ambitious chiefs sought to extend their authority by conquering neighbors and dominating the regions surrounding their own communities.

Aryan Migrations in India

During the early centuries of the Vedic age, Aryan groups settled in the Punjab, the upper Indus River valley that straddles the modern-day border between northern India and Pakistan. These migrations were some of the most prominent waves in the larger process of early Indo-European migrations (discussed in chapter 2). After establishing themselves in the Punjab, Aryan migrants spread east and south and established communities throughout much of the Indian subcontinent. After 1000 B.C.E. they began to settle in the area between the Himalayan foothills and the Ganges River. About that same time they learned to make iron tools, and with axes and iron-tipped plows they cleared forests and established agricultural communities in the Ganges valley. Iron implements enabled them to produce more food and support larger populations, which in turn encouraged them to push farther into India. By about 750 B.C.E., populations had increased enough that Aryans had established the first small cities in the Ganges River valley. Indeed, population became so dense in northern India that some Aryans decided to move along and seek their fortunes elsewhere. By 500 B.C.E. Aryan groups had migrated as far south as the northern Deccan, a plateau region in the southern cone of the Indian subcontinent about 1,500 kilometers (950 miles) south of the Punjab.

Changing Political Organization

As they settled into permanent communities and began to rely more on agriculture than herding, the Aryans gradually lost the tribal political organization that they had brought into India and evolved more formal political institutions. In a few places, especially in the isolated

This bronze sword manufactured by Aryan craftsmen was a much stronger and more effective weapon than those available to Harappan defenders.

hilly and mountainous regions of northern India, councils of elders won recognition as the principal sources of political authority. They directed the affairs of small republics—states governed by representatives of the citizens. In most places, though, chiefdoms developed into regional kingdoms. Between 1000 and 500 B.C.E., tribal chiefs worked increasingly from permanent capitals and depended on the services of professional administrators. They did not build large imperial states: not until the fourth century B.C.E. did an Indian state embrace as much territory as Harappan society. But they established regional kingdoms as the most common form of political organization throughout most of the subcontinent.

Origins of the Caste System

Although they did not build a large-scale political structure, the Aryans constructed a well-defined social order. Indeed, in some ways their social hierarchy served to maintain the order and stability that states and political structures guaranteed in other societies, such as Mesopotamia, Egypt, and China. The Aryan social structure rested on sharp hereditary distinctions between individuals and groups, according to their occupations and roles in society. These distinctions became the foundation of the caste system, which largely determined the places that individuals and groups occupied in society.

The term *caste* comes from the Portuguese word *casta,* and it refers to a social class of hereditary and usually unchangeable status. When Portuguese merchants and mariners visited India during the sixteenth century C.E., they noticed the sharp, inherited distinctions between different social groups, which they referred to as castes. Scholars have employed the term *caste* ever since in reference to the Indian social order.

Caste and Varna

Caste identities developed gradually as the Aryans established settlements throughout India. When the Aryans first entered India, they probably had a fairly simple society consisting of herders and cultivators led by warrior chiefs and priests. As they settled in India, however, growing social complexity and interaction with Dravidian peoples prompted them to refine their social distinctions. The Aryans used the term *varna,* a Sanskrit word meaning "color," to refer to the major social classes. This terminology suggests that social distinctions arose partly from differences in complexion between the Aryans, who referred to themselves as "wheat-colored," and the darker-skinned Dravidians. Over time Aryans and Dravidians mixed, mingled, interacted, and intermarried to the point that distinguishing between them was impossible. Nevertheless, in early Vedic times differences between the two peoples probably prompted Aryans to base social distinctions on Aryan or Dravidian ancestry.

Social Distinctions in the Late Vedic Age

After about 1000 B.C.E. the Aryans increasingly recognized four main *varnas:* priests *(brahmins);* warriors and aristocrats *(kshatriyas);* cultivators, artisans, and merchants *(vaishyas);* and landless peasants and serfs *(shudras).* Some centuries later, probably about the end of the Vedic age, they added the category of the untouchables—people who performed dirty or unpleasant tasks, such as butchering animals or handling dead bodies, and who theoretically became so polluted from their work that their very touch could defile individuals of higher status. A late hymn of the *Rig Veda,* composed probably around 1000 B.C.E., offers a priestly view of *varna* distinctions. According to the hymn, the gods created the four *varnas* during the early days of the world and produced *brahmins* and *kshatriyas* as the most honorable human groups that would lead their societies. Thus during the late Vedic age the recognition of *varnas* and theories of their origins had the effect of enhancing the status and power of priestly and aristocratic classes.

Subcastes and Jati

Until about the sixth century B.C.E., the four *varnas* described Vedic society reasonably well. Because they did not live in cities and did not yet pursue many specialized occupations, the Aryans had little need for a more complicated social order. Over the longer term, however, a much more elaborate scheme of social classification emerged. As Vedic society became more complex and generated increasingly specialized occupations, the caste system served as the umbrella for a complicated hierarchy of subcastes known as *jati*. Occupation largely determined an individual's *jati:* people working at the same or similar tasks in a given area belonged to the same subcaste, and their offspring joined them in both occupation and *jati* membership. By the eighteenth and nineteenth centuries C.E., in its most fully articulated form, the system featured several thousand *jati*, which prescribed individuals' roles in society in minute detail. *Brahmins* alone divided themselves into some 1,800 *jati*. Even untouchables belonged to *jati,* and some of them looked down upon others as far more miserable and polluted than themselves.

Castes and subcastes deeply influenced the lives of individual Indians through much of history. Members of a *jati* ate with one another and intermarried, and they cared for those who became ill or fell on hard times. Elaborate rules dictated forms of address and specific behavior appropriate for communication between members of different castes and subcastes. Violation of *jati* rules could result in expulsion from the larger group. This penalty was serious, since an outcaste individual could not function well and sometimes could not even survive when shunned by all members of the larger society.

The caste system never functioned in an absolutely rigid or inflexible manner but, rather, operated so as to accommodate social change. Indeed, if the system had entirely lacked the capacity to change and reflect new social conditions, it would have disappeared. Individual *vaishyas* or *shudras* occasionally turned to new lines of work and prospered on the basis of their own initiative, for example, while individual *brahmins* or *kshatriyas* sometimes fell on hard times, lost their positions of honor, and moved down in the social hierarchy. More often, however, social mobility came about as the result of group rather than individual efforts, as members of *jati* improved their condition collectively. Achieving upward mobility was not an easy matter—it often entailed moving to a new area, or at least taking on a new line of work—but the possibility of improving individual or group status helped to dissipate tensions that otherwise might have severely tested Indian society.

Caste and Social Mobility

The caste system also enabled foreign peoples to find a place in Indian society. The Aryans were by no means the only foreigners to cross the passes of the Hindu Kush and enter India. Many others followed them over the course of the centuries and, upon arrival, sooner or later organized themselves into well-defined groups and adopted caste identities.

By the end of the Vedic age, caste distinctions had become central institutions in Aryan India. Whereas in other lands, states and empires maintained public order, in India the caste system served as a principal foundation of social stability. Individuals have often identified more closely with their *jati* than with their cities or states, and castes have played a large role in maintaining social discipline in India.

The Development of Patriarchal Society

While building an elaborate social hierarchy on the foundations of caste and *varna* distinctions, the Aryans also constructed a strongly patriarchal social order on the basis of gender distinctions. At the time of their migrations into India, men already dominated Aryan society. All priests, warriors, and tribal chiefs were men, and the Aryans recognized descent through the male line. Women influenced affairs within their own families but enjoyed no public authority. By maintaining and reinforcing

Sources from the Past

The *Rig Veda* on the Origin of the Castes

Priests compiled the Rig Veda *over a period of half a millennium, and the work inevitably reflects changing conditions of Aryan India. One of the later hymns of the* Rig Veda *offers a brief account of the world's creation and the origin of the four castes (varnas). The creation came when the gods sacrificed Purusha, a primeval being who existed before the universe, and brought the world with all its creatures and features into being. The late date of this hymn suggests that the Aryans began to recognize the four castes about 1000 B.C.E. The hymn clearly reflects the interests of the brahmin priests who composed it.*

A thousand heads hath Purusha, a thousand eyes, a thousand feet.

He covered earth on every side and spread ten finger's breadth beyond.

This Purusha is all that hath been and all that is to be,
The Lord of Immortality which waxes greater still by food.

So mighty is his greatness; yea, greater than this is Purusha.

All creatures are one-fourth of him, [the other] three-fourths [of him are] eternal life in heaven. . . .

When the gods prepared the sacrifice with Purusha as their offering,

Its oil was spring, the holy gift was autumn; summer was the wood. . . .

From that great general sacrifice the dripping fat was gathered up.

He formed the creatures of the air, and animals both wild and tame.

From that great general sacrifice [sages] and [ritual hymns] were born.

Therefrom were [spells and charms] produced; the Yajas [a book of ritual formulas] had its birth from it.

From it were horses born; from it all creatures with two rows of teeth.

From it were generated [cattle], from it the goats and sheep were born.

When they divided Purusha, how many portions did they make?

What do they call his mouth, his arms? What do they call his thighs and feet?

The *brahmin* was his mouth, of both his arms was the *kshatriya* made.

His thighs became the *vaishya*, from his feet the *shudra* was produced.

The moon was gendered from his mind, and from his eye the sun had birth;

Indra and Agni [the god of fire] from his mouth were born, and Vayu [the wind] from his breath.

Forth from his navel came mid-air; the sky was fashioned from his head;

Earth from his feet, and from his ear the regions. Thus they formed the worlds.

SOURCE: Ralph T. Griffith, trans. *The Hymns of the Rigveda*, 4 vols., 2nd ed. Benares: E. J. Lazarus, 1889–92, 4:289–93. (Translation slightly modified.)

How does this passage from the Rig Veda *compare with accounts of the world's creation offered by other religious and scientific traditions?*

these gender distinctions, the Aryans established a patriarchal social order that stood alongside the caste system and *varna* hierarchy as a prominent feature of their society.

As the Aryans settled in agricultural communities throughout India, they maintained a thoroughly patriarchal society. Only males could inherit property, unless a family had no male heirs, and only men could preside over family rituals that honored departed ancestors. Because they had no priestly responsibilities, women rarely learned the Vedas, and formal education in Sanskrit remained almost exclusively a male preserve.

The patriarchal spokesmen of Vedic society sought to place women explicitly under the authority of men. During the first century B.C.E. or perhaps somewhat later, an anonymous sage prepared a work and attributed it to Manu, founder of the human race according to Indian mythology. Much of the work, known as the *Lawbook of Manu,* dealt with proper moral behavior and social relationships, including sex and gender relationships. Although composed after the Vedic age, the *Lawbook of Manu* reflected the society constructed earlier under Aryan influence. The author advised men to treat women with honor and respect, but he insisted that women remain subject to the guidance of the principal men in their lives—first their fathers, then their husbands, and finally, if they survived their husbands, their sons. The *Lawbook* also specified that the most important duties of women were to bear children and maintain wholesome homes for their families.

The Lawbook of Manu

Sati

This greenish-blue schist carving illustrates the devotion of a mother to her child.

Thus, like Mesopotamian, Egyptian, and other early agricultural societies, Vedic India constructed and maintained a deeply patriarchal social order. One Indian custom demonstrated in especially dramatic fashion the dependence of women on their men—the practice of *sati* (sometimes spelled *suttee*), by which a widow voluntarily threw herself on the funeral pyre of her deceased husband to join him in death. Although widows occasionally entered the fires during the Vedic age and in later centuries, *sati* never became a popular or widely practiced custom in India. Nevertheless, moralists often recommended *sati* for widows of socially prominent men, since their example would effectively illustrate the devotion of women to their husbands and reinforce the value that Indian society placed on the subordination of women.

RELIGION IN THE VEDIC AGE

As the caste system emerged and helped to organize Indian society, distinctive cultural and religious traditions also took shape. The Aryans entered India with traditions and beliefs that met the needs of a mobile and often violent society. During the early centuries after their arrival in India, these inherited traditions served them well as they fought to establish a place for themselves in the subcontinent. As they spread throughout India and mixed with the Dravidians, however, the Aryans encountered new religious ideas that they considered intriguing and persuasive. The resulting fusion of Aryan traditions with Dravidian beliefs and values laid the foundation for Hinduism, a faith immensely popular in India and parts of southeast Asia for more than two millennia.

Aryan Religion

As in Mesopotamia, Egypt, and other lands, religious values in India reflected the larger society. During the early centuries following their migrations, for example, the Aryans spread through the Punjab and other parts of India, often fighting with the Dravidians and even among themselves. The hymns, songs, and prayers collected in the *Rig Veda* throw considerable light on Aryan values during this period.

Aryan Gods

The chief deity of the *Rig Veda* was Indra, the boisterous and often violent character who was partial both to fighting and to strong drink. Indra was primarily a war god. The Aryans portrayed him as the wielder of thunderbolts who led them into battle against their enemies. Indra also had a domestic dimension: the Aryans associated him with the weather and especially with the coming of rain to water the crops and the land. The Aryans also recognized a host of other deities, including gods of the sun, the sky, the moon, fire, health, disease, dawn, and the underworld. The preeminence of Indra, however, reflects the instability and turbulence of early Vedic society.

Although the Aryans accorded high respect to Indra and his military leadership, their religion did not neglect ethics. They believed that the god Varuna presided over the sky from his heavenly palace, where he oversaw the behavior of mortals and preserved the cosmic order. Varuna and his helpers despised lying and evil deeds of all sorts, and they afflicted malefactors with severe punishments, including disease and death. They dispatched the souls of serious evildoers to the subterranean House of Clay, a dreary and miserable realm of punishment, while allowing souls of the virtuous to enter the Aryan heaven known as the World of the Fathers.

Ritual Sacrifices

Yet this ethical concern was a relatively minor aspect of Aryan religion during early Vedic times. Far more important from a practical point of view was the proper performance of ritual sacrifices by which the Aryans hoped to win the favor of the gods. By the time the Aryans entered India, these sacrifices had become complex and elaborate affairs. They involved the slaughter of dozens and sometimes even hundreds of specially prepared animals—cattle, sheep, goats, and horses from the Aryans' herds—as priests spoke the sacred and mysterious chants and worshipers partook of *soma,* a hallucinogenic concoction that produced sensations of power and divine inspiration. The Aryans believed that during the sacrificial event their gods visited the earth and joined the worshipers in ritual eating and drinking. By pleasing the gods with frequent and large sacrifices, the Aryans expected to gain divine support that would ensure military success, large families, long life, and abundant herds of cattle. But these rewards required constant attention to religious ritual: proper honor for the gods called for households to have *brahmins* perform no less than five sacrifices per day—a time-consuming and expensive obligation.

Spirituality

Later in the Vedic age, Aryan religious thought underwent a remarkable evolution. As the centuries passed, many Aryans became dissatisfied with the sacrificial cults of the Vedas, which increasingly seemed like sterile rituals rather than a genuine means of communicating with the gods. Even *brahmins* sometimes became disenchanted with rituals that did not satisfy spiritual longings. Beginning about 800 B.C.E. many thoughtful individuals left their villages and retreated to the forests of the Ganges valley, where they lived as hermits and reflected on the relationships between human beings, the world, and the gods. They contemplated the Vedas and sought mystical understandings of the texts, and they attracted disciples who also thirsted for a spiritually fulfilling faith.

These mystics drew considerable inspiration from the religious beliefs of Dravidian peoples, who often worshiped nature spirits that they associated with fertility and the generation of new life. Dravidians also believed that human souls took on new physical forms after the deaths of their bodily hosts. Sometimes souls returned as plants or animals, sometimes in the bodily shell of newborn humans. The notion that souls could experience transmigration and reincarnation—that an individual soul could depart one body at death and become associated with another body through a new birth—intrigued thoughtful people and encouraged them to try to understand the principles that governed the fate of souls. As a result, a remarkable tradition of religious speculation emerged.

The Blending of Aryan and Dravidian Values

Traces of this tradition appear in the Vedas, but it achieved its fullest development in a body of works known as the Upanishads, which began to appear late in the Vedic age, about 800 to 400 B.C.E. (Later Upanishads continued to appear until the fifteenth century C.E., but the most important were those composed during the late Vedic age.) The word *upanishad* literally means "a sitting in front of," and it refers to the practice of disciples gathering before a sage for discussion of religious issues. Most of the disciples were men, but not all. Gargi Vakaknavi, for example, was a woman who drove the eminent sage Yajnavalkya to exasperation because he could not answer her persistent questions. The Upanishads often took the form of dialogues that explored the Vedas and the religious issues that they raised.

The Upanishads

Accompanied by an attendant bearing his banner and weapons, Indra rides an elephant that carries him through the clouds, while a king and a crowd of people in the landscape below worship a sacred tree.

The Upanishads taught that appearances are deceiving, that individual human beings in fact are not separate and autonomous creatures. Instead, each person participates in a larger cosmic order and forms a small part of a universal soul, known as *Brahman*. Whereas the physical world is a theater of change, instability, and illusion, Brahman is an eternal, unchanging, permanent foundation for all things that exist—hence the only genuine reality. The authors of the Upanishads believed that individual souls were born into the physical world not once, but many times: they believed that souls appeared most often as humans, but sometimes as animals, and possibly even occasionally as plants or other vegetable matter. The highest goal of the individual soul, however, was to escape this cycle of birth and rebirth and enter into permanent union with Brahman.

Brahman, the Universal Soul

The Upanishads developed several specific doctrines that helped to explain this line of thought. One was the doctrine of *samsara*, which held that upon death, individual souls go temporarily to the World of the Fathers and then return to earth in a new incarnation. Another was the doctrine of *karma*, which accounted for the specific incarnations that souls experienced. The *Brhadaranyaka Upanishad* offers a succinct explanation of the workings of karma: "Now as a man is like this or like that, according as he acts and according as he behaves, so will he be: a man of good acts will become good, a man of bad acts, bad. He becomes pure by pure deeds, bad by bad deeds." Thus individuals who lived virtuous lives and fulfilled all their duties could expect rebirth into a purer and more honorable existence—for example, into a higher and more

Teachings of the Upanishads

Sources from the Past

The *Mundaka Upanishad* on the Nature of Brahman

Indian commentators often spoke of the Mundaka Upanishad *as "the shaving Upanishad" because, like a razor, it cut off errors arising in the mind. Its purpose was to teach knowledge of Brahman, which it held was not accessible through sacrifices, rites, or even worship. Only proper instruction would bring understanding of Brahman.*

Brahma was before the gods were, the Creator of all, the Guardian of the Universe. The vision of Brahman, the foundation of all wisdom, he gave in revelation to his first-born son Atharvan.

That vision and wisdom of Brahman given to Atharvan, he in olden times revealed to Angira. And Angira gave it to Satyavaha, who in succession revealed it to Angiras.

Now there was a man whose name was Saunaka, owner of a great household, who, approaching one day Angiras with reverence, asked him this question: "Master, what is that which, when known, all is known?" The Master replied: Sages say there are two kinds of wisdom, the higher and the lower.

The lower wisdom is in the four sacred *Vedas,* and in the six kinds of knowledge that help to know, to sing, and to use the *Vedas:* definition and grammar, pronunciation and poetry, ritual and the signs of heaven. But the higher wisdom is that which leads to the Eternal [i.e., Brahman].

He is beyond thought and invisible, beyond family and colour. He has neither eyes nor ears; he has neither hands nor feet. He is everlasting and omnipresent, infinite in the great and infinite in the small. He is the Eternal whom the sages see as the source of all creation.

Even as a spider sends forth and draws in its thread, even as plants arise from the earth and hairs from the body of man, even so the whole creation arises from the Eternal.

By *Tapas,* the power of meditation, Brahman attains expansion and then comes primeval matter. And from this comes life and mind, the elements and the worlds and the immortality of ritual action.

From that Spirit [Brahman] who knows all and sees all, whose *Tapas* is pure vision, from him comes [the god] Brahma, the creator, name and form and primal matter. . . .

This is the truth: As from a fire aflame thousands of sparks come forth, even so from the Creator an infinity of beings have life and to him return again.

But the spirit of light above form, never-born, within all, outside all, is in radiance above life and mind, and beyond this creation's Creator.

From him comes all life and mind, and the senses of all life. From him comes space and light, air and fire and water, and this earth that holds us all.

The head of his body is fire, and his eyes the sun and the moon; his ears, the regions of heaven, and the sacred *Vedas* his word. His breath is the wind that blows, and this whole universe is his heart. The earth is his footstool. He is the Spirit that is in all things.

From him comes the sun, and the source of all fire is the sun.

From him comes the moon, and from this comes the rain and all herbs that grow upon earth. And man comes from him, and man unto woman gives seed; and thus an infinity of beings come from the Spirit supreme. . . .

From him the oceans and mountains; and all rivers come from him. And all herbs and the essence of all whereby the Inner Spirit dwells with the elements: all come from him.

SOURCE: Juan Mascaró, trans. *The Upanishads.* London: Penguin, 1965, pp. 75–78.

How does the understanding of the world as articulated in the Mundaka Upanishad *compare and contrast with the view outlined in the story of Purusha's sacrifice as told in the selection from the* Rig Veda *presented earlier?*

A cave painting from an undetermined age, perhaps several thousand years ago, shows that early inhabitants of India lived in close company with other residents of the natural world.

distinguished caste. Those who accumulated a heavy burden of karma, however, would suffer in a future incarnation by being reborn into a difficult existence, or perhaps even into the body of an animal or an insect.

Even under the best of circumstances, the cycle of rebirth involved a certain amount of pain and suffering that inevitably accompany human existence. The authors of the Upanishads sought to escape the cycle altogether and attain the state of *moksha,* which they characterized as a deep, dreamless sleep that came with permanent liberation from physical incarnation. This goal was difficult to reach, since it entailed severing all ties to the physical world and identifying with the ultimate reality of Brahman, the universal soul. The two principal means to the goal were asceticism and meditation. By embarking upon a regime of extreme asceticism—leading extremely simple lives and denying themselves all pleasure—individuals could purge themselves of desire for the comforts of the physical world. By practicing yoga, a form of intense and disciplined meditation, they could concentrate on the nature of Brahman and its relationship to their own souls. Diligent efforts, then, would enable individuals to achieve *moksha* by separating themselves from the physical world of change, illusion, and incarnation. Then their souls would merge with Brahman, and they would experience eternal, peaceful ecstasy.

Just as *brahmin* theories about the origins of *varna* distinctions reflected Aryan society about 1000 B.C.E., so the religious views of the Upanishads dovetailed with the social order of the late Vedic age. Indeed, modern commentators have sometimes interpreted the worldview of the Upanishads—particularly the doctrines of samsara and karma—as a cynical ideology designed to justify the social inequalities imposed by the caste system. The doctrines of samsara and karma certainly reinforced the Vedic social order: they explained why individuals were born into their castes—because they had behaved virtuously or badly during a previous incarnation—and

Religion and Vedic Society

they encouraged individuals to observe their caste duties in hopes of enjoying a more comfortable and honorable incarnation in the future.

It would be overly simplistic, however, to consider these doctrines merely efforts of a hereditary elite to justify its position and maintain its hegemony over other classes of society. The sages who gave voice to these doctrines were conscientiously attempting to deal with genuine spiritual and intellectual problems. To them the material world seemed supremely superficial—a realm of constant change and illusion offering no clear sign as to the nature of ultimate reality. It seemed logical to suppose that a more real and substantial world stood behind the one that they inhabited. Greek philosophers, Christian theologians, and many others have arrived at similar positions during the course of the centuries. It should come as no great surprise, then, that the authors of the Upanishads sought ultimate truth and certain knowledge in an ideal world that transcends our own. Their formulation of concepts like samsara and karma represented efforts to characterize the relationship between the world of physical incarnation and the realm of ultimate truth and reality.

The Upanishads not only influenced Indian thought about the nature of the world but also called for the observance of high ethical standards. They discouraged greed, envy, gluttony, and all manner of vice, since these traits indicated excessive attachment to the material world and insufficient concentration on union with the universal soul. The Upanishads advocated honesty, self-control, charity, and mercy. Most of all, they encouraged the cultivation of personal integrity—a self-knowledge that would incline individuals naturally toward both ethical behavior and union with Brahman. The Upanishads also taught respect for all living things, animal as well as human. Animal bodies, after all, might well hold incarnations of unfortunate souls suffering the effects of a heavy debt of karma. Despite the evil behavior of these souls in their earlier incarnations, devout individuals would not wish to cause them additional suffering or harm. A vegetarian diet thus became a common feature of the ascetic regime.

Like sub-Saharan African and other regions of Eurasia, south Asia was a land of cross-cultural interaction and exchange even in ancient times. Knowledge of agriculture made its way to the Indian subcontinent as early as 7000 B.C.E., probably from southwest Asia, and a productive agricultural economy made it possible for Dravidian peoples to build a sophisticated society in the Indus River valley and to trade with peoples as far away as Mesopotamia. The arrival of Aryan migrants led to intense and systematic interactions between peoples of markedly different social and cultural traditions. While they no doubt often engaged in conflicts, they also found ways of dealing with one another and living together in a common land. By the end of the Vedic age, the merging of Aryan and Dravidian traditions had generated a distinctive Indian society. Agriculture and herding had spread with the Aryans to most parts of the Indian subcontinent. Regional states maintained order over substantial territories and established kingship as the most common form of government. The caste system not only endowed social groups with a powerful sense of identity but also helped to maintain public order. Finally, a distinctive set of religious beliefs explained the world and the role of human beings in it, and the use of writing facilitated the further reflection on spiritual and intellectual matters.

CHRONOLOGY

8000–7000 B.C.E.	Beginnings of agriculture in south Asia
2500–2000 B.C.E.	High point of Harappan society
1900 B.C.E.	Beginning of Harappan decline
1500 B.C.E.	Beginning of Aryan migration to India
1500–500 B.C.E.	Vedic age
1400–900 B.C.E.	Composition of the *Rig Veda*
1000 B.C.E.	Aryan migrations into the Ganges River valley
1000 B.C.E.	Emergence of *varna* distinctions
1000–500 B.C.E.	Formation of regional kingdoms in northern India
800–400 B.C.E.	Composition of the principal Upanishads
750 B.C.E.	Establishment of first Aryan cities in the Ganges valley
500 B.C.E.	Aryan migrations to the Deccan Plateau

FOR FURTHER READING

Bridget and Raymond Allchin. *The Rise of Civilization in India and Pakistan.* Cambridge, 1982. A detailed and authoritative survey of early Indian society based largely on archaeological evidence.

F. R. Allchin. *The Archaeology of Early Historic South Asia: The Emergence of Cities and States.* Cambridge, 1995. A collection of scholarly essays on the roles of cities and states in ancient India.

A. L. Basham. *The Wonder That Was India.* New York, 1954. A popular survey by a leading scholar of ancient India.

Ainslie T. Embree, ed. *Sources of Indian Tradition.* 2 vols. 2nd ed. New York, 1988. An important collection of primary sources in translation.

Walter A. Fairservis. *The Roots of Ancient India.* 2nd ed. Chicago, 1975. A judicious analysis of ancient Indian society, especially Harappan society, based on archaeological excavations.

Jonathan Mark Kenoyer. *Ancient Cities of the Indus Valley Civilization.* Oxford, 1998. A well-illustrated volume that synthesizes recent archaeological and linguistic scholarship on Harappan society.

J. P. Mallory. *In Search of the Indo-Europeans: Language, Archaeology, and Myth.* London, 1989. Carefully reviews modern theories about early Indo-European speakers in light of both the linguistic and the archaeological evidence.

Juan Mascaró, trans. *The Upanishads.* London, 1965. A superb English version of selected Upanishads by a gifted translator.

William H. McNeill and Jean W. Sedlar, eds. *Classical India.* Oxford, 1969. A useful collection of primary sources in translation.

Stuart Piggott. *Prehistoric India.* Harmondsworth, 1950. An older but still useful survey.

Gregory Possehl, ed. *Ancient Cities of the Indus.* New Delhi, 1979. Collection of scholarly essays that bring the results of archaeological research to bear on Harappan society.

———, ed. *Harappan Civilization: A Recent Perspective.* 2nd ed. New Delhi, 1993. Offers a variety of revisionist interpretations of Harappan society.

Shereen Ratnagar. *Encounters: The Westerly Trade of the Harappan Civilization.* Delhi, 1981. Relies on archaeological discoveries in examining commercial relations between Harappan society and Mesopotamia.

Colin Renfrew. *Archaeology and Language: The Puzzle of Indo-European Origins.* Cambridge, 1987. Presents a controversial argument concerning the origins and migrations of Indo-European peoples.

Romila Thapar. *A History of India.* Vol. 1. Harmondsworth, 1966. A sound, reliable, popular survey by a leading scholar of early Indian history.

———, ed. *Recent Perspectives of Early Indian History.* New Delhi, 1995. A valuable collection of essays discussing recent scholarship on early Indian history.

Mortimer Wheeler. *The Indus Civilization.* Cambridge, 1953. Like Piggott's work, an older but still useful study.

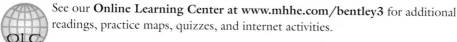

See our **Online Learning Center** at www.mhhe.com/bentley3 for additional readings, practice maps, quizzes, and internet activities.

Unfamiliar words? Check out the **Primary Source Investigator CD-ROM** for an interactive glossary, interactive maps, more images, and primary sources.

Bronze axe featuring a ferocious human face from the late Shang dynasty.

CHAPTER 5

EARLY SOCIETY IN EAST ASIA

Ancient Chinese legends tell the stories of heroic figures who invented agriculture, domesticated animals, taught people to marry and live in families, created music, introduced the calendar, and instructed people in the arts and crafts. Most important of these heroes were three sage-kings—Yao, Shun, and Yu—who laid the foundations of Chinese society. King Yao was a towering figure, sometimes associated with a mountain, who was extraordinarily modest, sincere, and respectful. Yao's virtuous influence brought harmony to his own family, the larger society, and ultimately all the states of China. King Shun succeeded Yao and continued his work by ordering the four seasons of the year and instituting uniform weights, measures, and units of time.

Most dashing of the sage-kings was Yu, a vigorous and tireless worker who rescued China from the raging waters of the flooding Yellow River. Before Yu, according to the legends, experts tried to control the Yellow River's floods by building dikes to contain its waters. The river was much too large and strong for the dikes, however, and when it broke through them it unleashed massive floods. Yu abandoned the effort to dam the Yellow River and organized two alternative strategies. He dredged the river so as to deepen its channel and minimize the likelihood of overflows, and he dug canals parallel to the river so that flood waters would flow harmlessly to the sea without devastating the countryside.

The legends say that Yu worked on the river for thirteen years without ever returning home. Once he passed by the gate to his home and heard his wife and children crying out of loneliness, but he continued on his way rather than interrupt his flood-control work. Because he tamed the Yellow River, Yu became a popular hero, and poets praised the man who protected fields and villages from deadly and destructive floods. Eventually Yu succeeded King Shun as leader of the Chinese people. Indeed, he founded the Xia dynasty, the first ruling house of ancient China.

The legends of Yao, Shun, and Yu no doubt exaggerated the virtues and deeds of the sage-kings. Agriculture, arts, crafts, marriage, family, government, and means of water control developed over an extended period of time, and no single individual was responsible for introducing them into China. Yet legends about early heroic figures reflected the interest of a people in the practices and customs that defined their society. At the same time, the moral thinkers who transmitted the legends used them to advocate values they considered beneficial for their society. By exalting Yao, Shun, and Yu as exemplars of virtue, Chinese moralists promoted the values of social harmony and selfless, dedicated work that the sage-kings represented.

Human beings appeared in east Asia as early as four hundred thousand years ago. At that early date they used stone tools and relied on a hunting and gathering economy like their counterparts in other regions of the earth. As in Mesopotamia, Egypt, and India, however, population pressures in east Asia encouraged communities to experiment with agriculture. Peoples of southern China and southeast Asia domesticated rice after about 7000 B.C.E., and by 5000 B.C.E. neolithic villages throughout the valley of the Yangzi River (Chang Jiang) depended on rice as the staple item in their diet. During the same era, millet came under cultivation farther north, in the valley of the Yellow River (Huang He), where neolithic communities flourished by 5000 B.C.E. In later centuries wheat and barley made their way from Mesopotamia to northern China, and by 2000 B.C.E. they supplemented millet as staple foods of the region.

Agricultural surpluses supported numerous neolithic communities throughout east Asia. During the centuries after 3000 B.C.E., residents of the Yangzi River and Yellow River valleys lived in agricultural villages and communicated and traded with others throughout the region. During the second millennium B.C.E., they began to establish cities, build large states, and construct distinctive social and cultural traditions. Three dynastic states based in the Yellow River valley brought much of China under their authority and forged many local communities into a larger Chinese society. Sharp social distinctions emerged in early Chinese society, and patriarchal family heads exercised authority in both public and private affairs. A distinctive form of writing supported the development of sophisticated cultural traditions. Meanwhile, Chinese cultivators had frequent dealings with peoples from other societies, particularly with nomadic herders inhabiting the grassy steppes of central Asia. Migrating frequently on the steppes, nomadic peoples linked China with lands to the west and brought knowledge of bronze and iron metallurgy, horse-drawn chariots, and wheeled vehicles to east Asia. As in early Mesopotamia, Egypt, and India, then, complex society in east Asia promoted the development of distinctive social and cultural traditions in the context of cross-cultural interaction and exchange.

POLITICAL ORGANIZATION IN EARLY CHINA

As agricultural populations expanded, villages and towns flourished throughout the Yellow River and Yangzi River valleys. Originally, these settlements looked after their own affairs and organized local states that maintained order in small territories. By the late years of the third millennium B.C.E., however, much larger regional states began to emerge. Among the most important were those of the Xia, Shang, and Zhou dynasties, which progressively brought much of China under their authority and laid a political foundation for the development of a distinctive Chinese society.

Early Agricultural Society and the Xia Dynasty

The Yellow River

Like the Indus, the Yellow River is boisterous and unpredictable. It rises in the mountains bordering the high plateau of Tibet, and it courses almost 4,700 kilometers (2,920 miles) before emptying into the Yellow Sea. It takes its name, Huang He, meaning "Yellow River," from the vast quantities of light-colored loess soil that it picks up along its route. Loess is an extremely fine, powderlike soil that was deposited on the plains of northern China, as well as in several other parts of the world, after the retreat of the glaciers at the end of the last ice age, about twelve thousand to fifteen thousand years ago. So much loess becomes suspended in the Yellow River that the water turns yellow and the river takes on the consistency of a soup. The soil gradually builds up, raising the river bed and forcing the water out of its established path. The Yellow River periodically unleashes a tremendous flood that devastates fields, communities, and anything else in its way. The Yellow River has altered its course many times and has caused so much destruction that it has earned the nickname "China's Sorrow."

Yet geographic conditions have also supported the development of complex society in China. During most years, there is enough rainfall for crops, so early cultivators had no need to build complex irrigation systems like those of Mesopotamia. They invested a great deal of labor, however, in dredging the river and building dikes, in a partially successful effort to limit the flood damage. Loess soil is extremely fertile and easy to work, so even before the introduction of metal tools, cultivators using wooden implements could bring in generous harvests.

Yangshao Society and Banpo Village

Abundant harvests in northern China supported the development of several neolithic societies during the centuries after 5000 B.C.E. Each developed its own style of pottery and architecture, and each likely had its own political, social, and cultural traditions. Yangshao society, which flourished from about 5000 to 3000 B.C.E. in the middle region of the Yellow River valley, is especially well known from the discovery in 1952 of an entire neolithic village at Banpo, near modern Xi'an. Excavations at Banpo unearthed a large quantity of fine painted pottery and bone tools used by early cultivators in the sixth and fifth millennia B.C.E.

As human population increased, settlements like that at Banpo cropped up throughout much of China, in the valley of the Yangzi River as well as the Yellow River. In east Asia, as in other parts of the world, the concentration of people in small areas brought a need for recognized authorities who could maintain order, resolve disputes, and organize public works projects. Village-level organization sufficed for purely local affairs, but it did little to prevent or resolve conflicts between villages and did not have the authority to organize large-scale projects in the interests of the larger community.

Chinese legends speak of three ancient dynasties—the Xia, Shang, and Zhou—that arose before the Qin and Han dynasties brought China under unified rule in the third century B.C.E. The Xia, Shang, and Zhou dynasties were hereditary states that extended their control over progressively larger regions, although none of them embraced all the territory claimed by later Chinese dynasties. Large numbers of written accounts survive to throw light on the Zhou dynasty, which scholars have long recognized as a historical ruling house. Until recently, however, information about the Xia and Shang dynasties came from legendary accounts that scholars mostly did not trust. As a result, many historians dismissed reports of the Xia and Shang dynasties as mythical fantasies. Only in the later twentieth century did archaeological excavations turn up evidence that the Xia and Shang were indeed historical dynasties rather than figments of ancient imaginations.

Archaeological study of the Xia dynasty is still in its early stages. Nevertheless, during the past few decades, archaeological discoveries have suggested that the Xia dynasty made one of the first efforts to organize public life in China on a large scale. Although it was not the only early state in

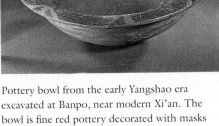

The Xia Dynasty

Pottery bowl from the early Yangshao era excavated at Banpo, near modern Xi'an. The bowl is fine red pottery decorated with masks and fishnets in black.

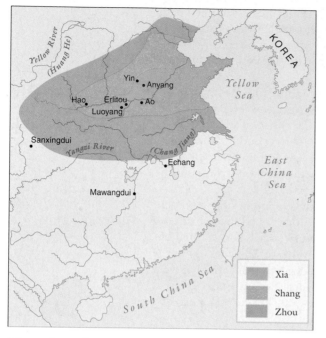

M A P [5 . 1]

The Xia, Shang, and Zhou dynasties, 2200–256 B.C.E.

China, the Xia was certainly one of the more vigorous states of its time. Most likely the dynasty came into being about 2200 B.C.E. in roughly the same region as the Yangshao society. By extending formal control over this region, the Xia dynasty established a precedent for hereditary monarchical rule in China.

Ancient legends credit the dynasty's founder, the sage-king Yu, with the organization of effective flood-control projects: thus here, as in Mesopotamia and Egypt, the need to organize large-scale public works projects helped to establish recognized authorities and formal political institutions. Although no information survives about the political institutions of the Xia, the dynasty's rulers probably exercised power throughout the middle Yellow River valley by controlling the leaders of individual villages. The dynasty encouraged the founding of cities and the development of metallurgy, since the ruling classes needed administrative centers and bronze weapons to maintain their control. The recently excavated city of Erlitou, near Luoyang, might well have been the capital of the Xia dynasty. Excavations have shown that the city featured a large, palace-type structure as well as more modest houses, pottery workshops, and a bronze foundry.

The Shang Dynasty

According to the legends, the last Xia king was an oppressive despot who lost his realm to the founder of the Shang dynasty. In fact, the Xia state did not entirely collapse and did not disappear so much as it gave way gradually before the Shang, which arose in a region to the south and east of the Xia realm. Tradition assigns the Shang dynasty to the period 1766 to 1122 B.C.E., and archaeological discoveries have largely confirmed these dates. Because the Shang dynasty left written records as well as material remains, the basic features of early Chinese society come into much clearer focus than they did during the Xia.

Bronze Metallurgy and Horse-Drawn Chariots

Technology helps to explain the rise and success of the Shang dynasty. Bronze metallurgy transformed Chinese society during Shang times and indeed may well have enabled Shang rulers to displace the Xia dynasty. Bronze metallurgy went to China from southwest Asia, together with horses, horse-drawn chariots, and other wheeled vehicles. This collection of related technologies traveled to China as well as India with the early Indo-European migrants (discussed in chapter 2), some of whom made their way to the Tarim Basin (now Xinjiang province in western China) as early as 2000 B.C.E. Early Chinese chariots were close copies of Indo-European chariots from the Iranian plateau, and ancient Chinese words for wheels, spokes, axles, and chariots all derived from Indo-European roots.

Bronze metallurgy and horse-drawn chariots reached China at least by 1200 B.C.E., and the Xia dynasty already made limited use of bronze tools and weapons. But Shang ruling elites managed to monopolize the production of bronze in the Yellow River valley by controlling access to copper and tin ores and by employing craftsmen to produce large quantities of bronze axes, spears, knives, and arrowheads exclusively for their own use. Control over bronze production strengthened Shang forces against those of the Xia and provided them with arms far superior to stone, wood, and bone weapons wielded by their rivals. Shang nobles also used bronze to make fittings for their horse-drawn chariots. Like the Aryans in India, they used these vehicles to devastating effect against adversaries who lacked horses and chariots. With their arsenal of bronze weapons, Shang armies had little difficulty imposing their rule on agricultural villages and extending their influence throughout much of the Yellow River valley. Meanwhile, because the ruling elites did not permit free production of bronze, potential rebels or competitors had little hope of resisting Shang forces and even less possibility of displacing the dynasty.

Shang kings extended their rule to a large portion of northeastern China centered on the modern-day province of Henan. Like state builders in other parts of the world, the kings claimed a generous portion of the surplus agricultural production from the regions they controlled and then used that surplus to support military forces, political allies, and others who could help them maintain their rule. Shang rulers clearly had abundant military force at their disposal. Surviving records mention armies of 3,000, 5,000, 10,000, and even 13,000 troops, and one report mentions the capture of 30,000 enemy troops. Al-

A tomb from the early Zhou dynasty containing the remains of horses and war chariots, which transformed military affairs in ancient China.

though these numbers are probably somewhat inflated, they still suggest that Shang rulers maintained a powerful military machine.

Like their Xia predecessors, Shang rulers also relied on a large corps of political allies. The Shang state rested on a vast network of walled towns whose local rulers recognized the authority of the Shang kings. During the course of the dynasty, Shang kings may have controlled one thousand or more towns. Apart from local rulers of these towns, others who shared the agricultural surplus of Shang China included advisors, ministers, craftsmen, and metalsmiths, who in their various ways helped Shang rulers shape policy or spread their influence throughout their realm.

Shang Political Organization

Shang society revolved around several large cities. According to tradition, the Shang capital moved six times during the course of the dynasty. Though originally chosen for political and military reasons, in each case the capital also became an important social, economic, and cultural center—the site not only of administration and military command but also of bronze foundries, arts, crafts, trade, and religious observances.

Excavations at two sites have revealed much about the workings of the Shang dynasty. The Shang named one of its earliest capitals Ao, and archaeologists have found its remains near modern Zhengzhou. The most remarkable feature of this site is the city wall, which originally stood at least 10 meters (33 feet) high, with a base some 20 meters (66 feet) thick. The wall consisted of layer upon layer of pounded earth—soil

The Shang Capital at Ao

packed firmly between wooden forms and then pounded with mallets until it reached rocklike hardness before the addition of a new layer of soil on top. This building technique, still used in the countryside of northern China, can produce structures of tremendous durability. Even today, for example, parts of the wall of Ao survive to a height of 3 to 4 meters (10 to 13 feet). The investment in labor required to build this wall testifies to Shang power and a high degree of centralized rule: modern estimates suggest that the wall required the services of some ten thousand laborers working almost twenty years.

The Shang Capital at Yin

Even more impressive than Ao is the site of Yin, near modern Anyang, which was the capital during the last two or three centuries of the Shang dynasty. Archaeologists working at Yin have identified a complex of royal palaces, archives with written documents, several residential neighborhoods, two large bronze foundries, several workshops used by potters, woodworkers, bone carvers, and other craftsmen, and scattered burial grounds.

Eleven large and lavish tombs constructed for Shang kings, as well as other more modest tombs, have received particular attention. Like the resting places of the Egyptian pharaohs, most of these tombs attracted grave robbers soon after their construction. Enough remains, however, to show that the later Shang kings continued to command the high respect enjoyed by their predecessors at Ao. The graves included thousands of objects—chariots, weapons, bronze goods, pottery, carvings of jade and ivory, cowry shells (which served both as money and as exotic ornamentation), and sacrifical victims, including dogs, horses, and scores of human beings intended to serve the deceased royals in another existence. One tomb alone contained skeletons of more than three hundred sacrificial victims—probably wives, servants, friends, and hunting companions—who joined the Shang king in death.

Beyond the Yellow River Valley

Like the Xia state, the Shang realm was only one of many that organized public life in ancient China. Legendary and historical accounts paid special attention to the Xia and Shang dynasties because of their location in the Yellow River valley, where the first Chinese imperial states rose in later times. But archaeological excavations are making it clear that similar states dominated other regions at the same time the Xia and Shang ruled the Yellow River valley. Recent excavations, for example, have unearthed evidence of a very large city at Sanxingdui in modern-day Sichuan province (southwestern China). Occupied about 1700 to 1000 B.C.E., the city was roughly contemporaneous with the Shang dynasty, and it probably served as capital of a regional kingdom. Like their Xia and Shang counterparts, tombs at Sanxingdui held large quantities of bronze, jade, stone, and pottery objects, as well as cowry shells and elephant tusks, that indicate close relationships with societies in the valleys of both the Yangzi River and the Yellow River.

A life-size bronze statue, produced about 1200 to 1000 B.C.E., from a tomb at Sanxingdui in southwestern China. Recent archaeological discoveries have turned up plentiful evidence of early political and social organization outside the Yellow River valley.

The Zhou Dynasty

Very little information survives to illustrate the principles of law, justice, and administration by which Shang rulers maintained order. They did not promulgate law codes such as those issued in Mesopotamia but, rather, ruled by proclamation or decree, trusting their military forces and political allies to enforce their will. The principles of ancient Chinese politics and statecraft become more clear in the practices of the Zhou dynasty, which succeeded the Shang as the preeminent political authority in northern China. Dwelling in the Wei River valley of northwestern China (modern Shaanxi province), the Zhou were a tough and sinewy people who battled Shang forces in the east and nomadic raiders from the steppes in the west. Eventually the Zhou allied with the Shang and won recognition as kings of the western regions. Because they organized their allies more effectively than the Shang, however, they gradually eclipsed the Shang dynasty and ultimately displaced it altogether.

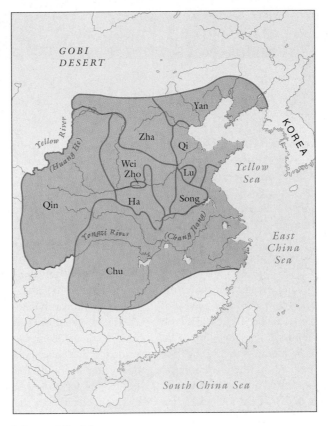

M A P [5 . 2]

China during the Period of the Warring States, 403–221 B.C.E.

The Rise of the Zhou

Shang and Zhou ambitions collided in the late twelfth century B.C.E. According to Zhou accounts, the last Shang king was a criminal fool who gave himself over to wine, women, tyranny, and greed. As a result, many of the towns and political districts subject to the Shang transferred their loyalties to the Zhou. After several unsuccessful attempts to discipline the Shang king, Zhou forces toppled his government in 1122 B.C.E. and replaced it with their own state. They allowed Shang heirs to continue governing small districts but reserved for themselves the right to oversee affairs throughout the realm. The new dynasty ruled most of northern and central China, at least nominally, until 256 B.C.E.

The Mandate of Heaven

In justifying the deposition of the Shang, spokesmen for the Zhou dynasty articulated a set of principles that have influenced Chinese thinking about government and political legitimacy over the long term. The Zhou theory of politics rested on the assumption that earthly events were closely related to heavenly affairs. More specifically, heavenly powers granted the right to govern—"the mandate of heaven"—to an especially deserving individual known as the son of heaven. The ruler then served as a link between heaven and earth. He had the duty to govern conscientiously, observe high standards of honor and justice, and maintain order and harmony within his realm. As long as he did so, the heavenly powers would approve of his work, the cosmos would enjoy a harmonious and well-balanced stability, and the ruling dynasty would retain its mandate to govern. If a ruler failed in his duties, however, chaos and suffering would afflict his realm, the cosmos would fall out of balance, and the displeased heavenly

Contexts & Connections

The Tomb of Fu Hao

Excavations of tombs have thrown enormous light on the Shang dynasty, since survivors often buried food, documents, tools, weapons, furniture, jewelry, decorative objects, and other valuable items along with their departed kin. Unfortunately, grave robbers soon broke into most tombs and carried off much of the portable wealth buried there. Over time, determined thieves were even able to loot carefully constructed and closely guarded royal tombs.

One notable royal sepulcher escaped this fate: the tomb of Fu Hao, one of sixty-four consorts (wives) of the Shang king Wu Ding, who ruled in the thirteenth century B.C.E. It is possible that thieves overlooked Fu Hao's tomb because it was located in the Shang palace at Yin rather than the cemetery that held other royal tombs. In any case, after her burial about 1250 B.C.E., Fu Hao's tomb remained undisturbed for more than three thousand years until Chinese archaeologists discovered it and excavated it in 1976. The unlooted tomb represents a valuable portal offering modern scholars access to the royal court of Shang China.

Fu Hao was King Wu Ding's favorite consort, and her tomb reflected her status. It contained 468 bronze objects, including 130 weapons, 23 bells, and 4 mirrors. In combination, the bronze items in her tomb weighed about 1,600 kilograms (3,500 pounds). Metalsmiths would have required some eleven tons of ore to produce these objects. In an age when bronze was very expensive, Fu Hao and the Shang royal family were conspicuous consumers of the valuable commodity. Quite apart from bronze wares, Fu Hao's tomb contained 755 jade carvings, 564 bone carvings, 5 finely carved ivory cups, 11 pottery objects, and 6,900 cowry shells. Moreover, the tomb held the remains of six dogs and the skeletons of sixteen human beings—sacrificial victims buried with Fu Hao to guard her and attend to her needs after death.

Documents from the tomb indicate that unlike most women of her time, Fu Hao ventured beyond the corridors of the Shang palace to play prominent roles in public life. She supervised her own estate and presided over sacrificial ceremonies that were usually the responsibility of men who were heads of their households. She even served as a general on several military campaigns and once led thirteen thousand troops in a successful operation against a neighboring state.

Fu Hao's resting place is much smaller than the eleven large tombs of Shang kings that archaeologists have excavated near modern-day Anyang. Because it escaped the

---

powers would withdraw the mandate to rule and transfer it to a more deserving candidate. On the basis of this reasoning, spokesmen for the new dynasty explained the fall of the Shang and the transfer of the mandate of heaven to the Zhou. Until the twentieth century, Chinese ruling houses emulated the Zhou dynasty by claiming the mandate of heaven for their rule, and emperors took the title "son of heaven."

Political Organization   The Zhou state was much larger than the Shang. In fact, it was so extensive that a single central court could not rule the entire land effectively, at least not with the transportation and communication technologies available during the second and first millennia B.C.E. As a result, Zhou rulers relied on a decentralized administration: they entrusted power, authority, and responsibility to subordinates who in return owed allegiance, tribute, and military support to the central government.

During the early days of the dynasty, this system worked reasonably well. The conquerors themselves continued to rule the Zhou ancestral homeland from their capital at Hao, near modern Xi'an, but they allotted possessions in conquered territories to relatives and other allies. The subordinates ruled their territories with lim-

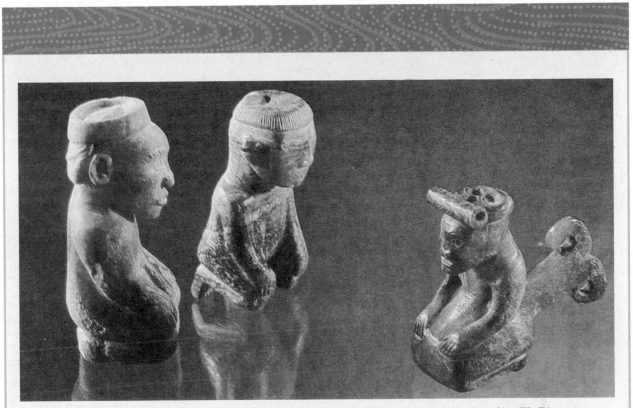

Jade figurines excavated at Anyang from the tomb of Fu Hao, who was one of the consorts of the Shang king Wu Ding. The carvings represent servants who would tend to Fu Hao's needs after death.

attention of grave robbers, however, Fu Hao's tomb has contributed more to the understanding of Shang times than the tombs of the Shang kings themselves. By shedding light on the Shang ruling class and the roles that women were able to play in Shang affairs, an archaeological discovery of the late twentieth century has opened a window on the early days of Chinese society.

ited supervision from the central government. In return for their political rights, they visited the Zhou royal court on specified occasions to demonstrate their continued loyalty to the dynasty, they delivered taxes and tribute that accounted for the major part of Zhou finances, and they provided military forces that the kings deployed in the interests of the Zhou state as a whole. When not already related to their subordinates, the Zhou rulers sought to arrange marriages that would strengthen their ties to their political allies.

Weakening of the Zhou

Despite their best efforts, however, the Zhou kings could not maintain control indefinitely over this decentralized political system. Subordinates gradually established their own bases of power: they ruled their territories not only as allies of the Zhou kings but also as long-established and traditional governors. They set up regional bureaucracies, armies, and tax systems, which allowed them to consolidate their rule and to exercise their authority. They promulgated law codes and enforced them with their own forces. As they became more secure in their rule, they also became more independent of the Zhou dynasty itself. Subordinates sometimes ignored

Iron Metallurgy

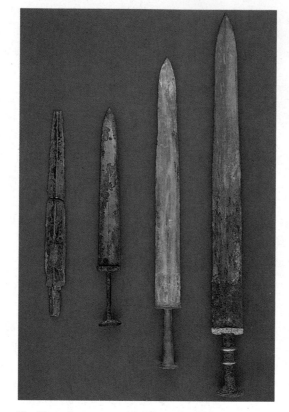

The Zhou dynasty saw a development of sword design that resulted in longer, stronger, and more lethal weapons. The iron swords depicted here reflect the political instability and chronic warfare of the late Zhou dynasty.

their obligations to appear at the royal court or to deliver tax proceeds. Occasionally, they refused to provide military support or even turned their forces against the dynasty in an effort to build up their own regional states.

Technological developments also worked in favor of subordinate rulers. The Zhou kings were not able to control the production of bronze as closely as their Shang predecessors had, and subordinates built up their own stockpiles of weapons. Moreover, during the first millennium B.C.E., the technology of iron metallurgy spread to China, and the production of iron expanded rapidly. Because iron ores are both cheaper and more abundant than copper and tin, the Zhou kings simply could not monopolize iron production. As a result, subordinates outfitted their forces with iron weapons that enabled them to resist the central government and pursue their own interests.

In the early eighth century B.C.E., the Zhou rulers faced severe problems that brought the dynasty to the point of collapse. In 771 B.C.E. nomadic peoples invaded China from the west. They came during the rule of a particularly ineffective king who did not enjoy the respect of his political allies. When subordinates refused to support the king, the invaders overwhelmed the Zhou capital at Hao. Following this disaster, the royal court moved east to Luoyang in the Yellow River valley, which served as the Zhou capital until the end of the dynasty.

In fact, the political initiative had passed from the Zhou kings to their subordinates, and the royal court never regained its authority. By the fifth century B.C.E., territorial princes ignored the central government and used their resources to build, strengthen, and expand their own states. They fought ferociously with one another in hopes of establishing themselves as leaders of a new political order. So violent were the last centuries of the Zhou dynasty that they are known as the Period of the Warring States (403–221 B.C.E.). In 256 B.C.E. the Zhou dynasty ended when the last king abdicated his position under pressure from his ambitious subordinate the king of Qin. Only with the establishment of the Qin dynasty in 221 B.C.E. did effective central government return to China.

SOCIETY AND FAMILY IN ANCIENT CHINA

In China, as in other parts of the ancient world, the introduction of agriculture enabled individuals to accumulate wealth and preserve it within their families. Social distinctions began to appear during neolithic times, and after the establishment of the Xia, Shang, and Zhou dynasties the distinctions became even sharper. Throughout China the patriarchal family emerged as the institution that most directly influenced individuals' lives and their roles in the larger society.

The Social Order

Ruling Elites

Already during the Xia dynasty, but especially under the Shang and early Zhou, the royal family and allied noble families occupied the most honored positions in Chinese society. They resided in large, palatial compounds made of pounded earth, and they lived on the agricultural surplus and taxes delivered by their subjects. Because of the high cost of copper and tin, bronze implements were beyond the means of all but the wealthy, so the conspicuous consumption of bronze by ruling elites clearly set them apart from less privileged classes. Ruling elites possessed much of the bronze weaponry that ensured military strength and political hegemony, and through their subordinates and retainers they controlled most of the remaining bronze weapons available in northern China. They also supplied their households with cast-bronze utensils—pots, jars, wine cups, plates, serving dishes, mirrors, bells, drums, and vessels used in ritual ceremonies—which were beyond the means of less privileged people. These utensils often featured elaborate, detailed decorations that indicated remarkable skill on the part of the artisans who built the molds and cast the metal. Expensive bronze utensils bore steamed rice and rich dishes of fish, pheasant, poultry, pork, mutton, and rabbit to royal and aristocratic tables, whereas less privileged classes relied on clay pots and consumed much simpler fare, such as vegetables and porridges made of millet, wheat, or rice. Ruling elites consumed bronze in staggering quantities: the tomb of Marquis Yi of Zeng, a provincial governor of the late Zhou dynasty, contained a collection of bronze weapons and decorative objects that weighed almost eleven tons.

A privileged class of hereditary aristocrats rose from the military allies of Shang and Zhou rulers. Aristocrats possessed extensive land holdings, and they worked at administrative and military tasks. By Zhou times many of them lived in cities where they obtained at least an elementary education, and their standard of living was much more refined than that of the commoners and slaves who worked their fields and served their needs. Manuals of etiquette from Zhou times instructed the privileged classes in decorous behavior and outlined the proper way to carry out rituals. When dining in polite company, for example, the cultivated aristocrat should show honor to the host and refrain from gulping down food, swilling wine, making unpleasant noises, picking teeth at the table, and playing with food by rolling it into a ball.

The delicate design of this bronze wine vessel displays the high level of craftsmanship during the late Shang dynasty.

Sources from the Past

Peasants' Protest

Peasants in ancient China mostly did not own their own land. Instead, they worked as tenants on plots allotted to them by royal or aristocratic owners, who took sizable portions of the harvest for their own uses. In the following poem from the Book of Songs, *a collection of verses dating from Zhou times, peasants liken their lords to rodents, protest the bite lords take from the peasants' agricultural production, and threaten to abandon the lords' lands for a neighboring state where conditions were better.*

Large rats! Large rats!
Do not eat our millet.
Three years have we had to do with you.
And you have not been willing to show any regard for us.
We will leave you,
And go to that happy land.
Happy land! Happy land!
There shall we find our place.

Large rats! Large rats!
Do not eat our wheat.
Three years have we had to do with you.
And you have not been willing to show any kindness
    to us.

We will leave you,
And go to that happy state.
Happy state! Happy state!
There shall we find ourselves aright.

Large rats! Large rats!
Do not eat our springing grain!
Three years have we had to do with you,
And you have not been willing to think of our toil.
We will leave you,
And go to those happy borders.
Happy borders! Happy borders!
Who will there make us always to groan?

SOURCE: James Legge, trans. *The Chinese Classics*, 5 vols. London: Henry Frowde, 1893, 4:171–72.

How might you go about judging the extent to which these verses throw reliable light on class relations in ancient China?

Specialized Labor

A small class of free artisans and craftsmen plied their trades in the cities of ancient China. Some, who worked almost exclusively for the privileged classes, enjoyed a reasonably comfortable existence. During the Shang dynasty, for example, bronzesmiths often lived in houses built of pounded earth. Although their dwellings were modest, they were also sturdy and relatively expensive to build because of the amount of labor required for pounded-earth construction. Jewelers, jade workers, embroiderers, and manufacturers of silk textiles also benefited socially because of their importance to the ruling elites.

Merchants and Trade

There is very little information about merchants and trade in ancient China until the latter part of the Zhou dynasty, but archaeological discoveries show that long-distance trade routes reached China during Shang and probably Xia times as well. Despite the high mountain ranges and forbidding deserts that stood between China and complex societies in India and southwest Asia, trade networks linked China with lands to the west and south early in the third millennium B.C.E. Jade in Shang tombs came from central Asia, and military technology involving horse-drawn chariots came through central Asia from Mesopotamia. Shang bronzesmiths worked with tin that came from the Malay peninsula in southeast Asia, and cowry shells came through southeast Asia from Burma and the Maldive Islands in the Indian Ocean. The identity of the most important trade items that went from China to other lands is not clear, but archaeologists have unearthed a few pieces of Shang pottery from Mohenjo-daro and other Harappan sites.

Meanwhile, Chinese mariners began to probe nearby waters for profitable sea routes. Legendary accounts credit King Yu, the supposed founder of the Xia dynasty, with the invention of sails. There is no archaeological indication of Chinese sails before about 500 B.C.E., but there is abundant evidence that Chinese mariners used large oar-propelled vessels before 2000 B.C.E. These watercraft supported fishing and trade with offshore islands even before the emergence of the Xia dynasty. By the time of the Shang dynasty, Chinese ships were traveling across the Yellow Sea to Korea. During the Zhou dynasty, shipbuilding emerged as a prominent business all along coastal China, and mariners had discovered how to navigate their vessels by the stars and other heavenly bodies.

A wooden digging stick with two prongs was the agricultural tool most commonly used for cultivation of loess soils in the Yellow River valley.

Peasants

Back on the land, a large class of semiservile peasants populated the Chinese countryside. They owned no land but provided agricultural, military, and labor services for their lords in exchange for plots to cultivate, security, and a portion of the harvest. They lived like their neolithic predecessors in small subterranean houses excavated to a depth of about one meter (three feet) and protected from the elements by thatched walls and roofs. Women's duties included mostly indoor activities such as wine making, weaving, and cultivation of silkworms, whereas men spent most of their time outside working in the fields, hunting, and fishing.

Few effective tools were available to cultivators until the late Zhou dynasty. They mostly relied on wooden digging sticks and spades with bone or stone tips, which were strong enough to cultivate the powdery loess soil of northern China, since bronze tools were too expensive for peasant cultivators. Beginning about the sixth century B.C.E., however, iron production increased dramatically in China, and iron plows, picks, spades, hoes, sickles, knives, and rakes all came into daily use in the countryside.

Slaves

Finally, there was a sizable class of slaves, most of whom were enemy warriors captured during battles between the many competing states of ancient China. Slaves performed hard labor, such as the clearing of new fields or the building of city walls, that required a large workforce. During the Shang dynasty, but rarely thereafter, hundreds of slaves also figured among the victims sacrificed during funerary, religious, and other ritual observances.

Family and Patriarchy

Throughout human history the family has served as the principal institution for the socialization of children and the preservation of cultural traditions. In China the extended family emerged as a particularly influential institution during neolithic times, and it continued to play a prominent role in the shaping of both private and public affairs after the appearance of the Xia, Shang, and Zhou states. Indeed, the early dynasties ruled their territories largely through family and kinship groups.

Sources from the Past

Family Solidarity in Ancient China

A poem from the Book of Songs *illustrates clearly the importance of family connections in ancient China.*

The flowers of the cherry tree—
Are they not gorgeously displayed?
Of all the men in the world
There are none equal to brothers.

On the dreaded occasions of death and burial,
It is brothers who greatly sympathize.
When fugitives are collected on the heights and low
    grounds,
They are brothers who will seek one another out.

There is the wagtail on the level height—
When brothers are in urgent difficulties,
Friends, though they may be good
Will only heave long sighs.

Brothers may quarrel inside the walls [of their own
    home],
But they will oppose insult from without,
When friends, however good they may be,
Will not afford help.

When death and disorder are past,
And there are tranquillity and rest,
Although they have brothers,
Some reckon them not equal to friends.

Your dishes may be set in array,
And you may drink to satiety.
But it is when your brothers are all present
That you are harmonious and happy, with child-like joy.

Loving union with wife and children
Is like the music of lutes.
But it is the accord of brothers
That makes the harmony and happiness lasting.

For the ordering of your family,
For the joy in your wife and children,
Examine this and study it—
Will you not find that it is truly so?

SOURCE: James Legge, trans. *The Chinese Classics*, 5 vols. London: Henry Frowde, 1893, 4:250–53.
(Translation slightly modified.)

To what extent does other archaeological and historical evidence corroborate the views expressed in these verses about the importance of family in ancient China?

Veneration of Ancestors

One reason for the pronounced influence of the Chinese family is the veneration of ancestors, a practice with roots in neolithic times. In those early days agricultural peoples in China diligently tended the graves and memories of their departed ancestors. They believed that spirits of their ancestors passed into another realm of existence from which they had the power to support and protect their surviving families if the descendants displayed proper respect and ministered to the spirits' needs. Survivors buried tools, weapons, jewelry, and other material goods along with their dead. They also offered sacrifices of food and drink at the graves of departed relatives. The strong sense of ancestors' presence and continuing influence in the world led to an equally strong ethic of family solidarity. A family could expect to prosper only if all its members—the dead as well as the living—worked cooperatively toward common interests. The family became an institution linking departed generations to the living and even to those yet unborn—an institution that wielded enormous influence over both the private and the public lives of its members.

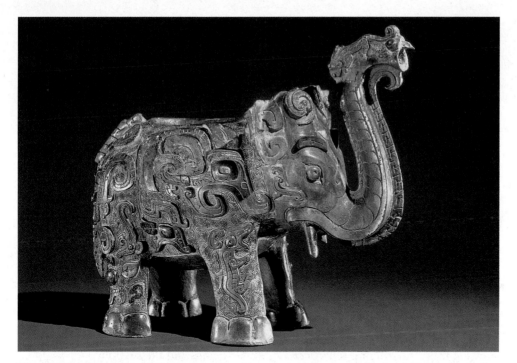

When burying their departed kin, survivors placed bronze ritual vessels with food and drink in the tombs. In the tombs of wealthy individuals, these vessels sometimes took elaborate shapes.

In the absence of organized religion or official priesthood in ancient China, the patriarchal head of the family presided at rites and ceremonies honoring ancestors' spirits. As mediator between the family's living members and its departed relatives, the family patriarch possessed tremendous authority. He officiated not only at ceremonies honoring ancestors of his own household but also at memorials for collateral and subordinate family branches that might include hundreds of individuals.

Patriarchal Society

Chinese society vested authority principally in elderly males who headed their households. Like its counterparts in other regions, Chinese society took on a strongly patriarchal character—one that intensified with the emergence of large states. During neolithic times Chinese men wielded public authority, but they won their rights to it by virtue of the female line of their descent. Even if it did not vest power and authority in women, this system provided solid reasons for a family to honor its female members. As late as Shang times, two queens posthumously received the high honor of having temples dedicated to their memories.

Women occasionally played prominent roles in public life during Shang times. Fu Hao, for example, the consort of King Wu Ding whose tomb has thrown important light on Shang royal society, performed sacrificial rites and led troops in battle. During the later Shang and Zhou dynasties, however, women lived increasingly in the shadow of men. Large states brought the military and political contributions of men into sharp focus. The ruling classes performed elaborate ceremonies publicly honoring the spirits of departed ancestors, particularly males who had guided their families and led especially notable lives. Gradually, the emphasis on men became so intense that Chinese society lost its matrilineal character. After the Shang dynasty, not even queens and empresses merited temples dedicated exclusively to their memories: at most, they had the honor of being remembered in association with their illustrious husbands.

EARLY CHINESE WRITING AND CULTURAL DEVELOPMENT

Organized religion did not play as important a role in ancient China as it did in other early societies. Early Chinese myths and legends explained the origins of the world, the human race, agriculture, and the various arts and crafts. But Chinese thinkers saw no need to organize these ideas into systematic religious traditions. They often spoke of an impersonal heavenly power—*tian* ("heaven"), the agent responsible for bestowing and removing the mandate of heaven on rulers—but they did not recognize a personal supreme deity who intervened in human affairs or took special interest in human behavior. Nor did ancient China support a large class of priests like those of Mesopotamia, Egypt, and India who mediated between human beings and the gods. A few priests conducted ritual observances in honor of royal ancestors at royal courts, but for the most part family patriarchs represented the interests of living generations to the spirits of departed ancestors.

In this environment, then, writing served as the foundation for a distinctive secular cultural tradition in ancient China. Chinese scribes may have used written symbols to keep simple records during Xia times, but surviving evidence suggests that writing came into extensive use only during the Shang dynasty. As in other lands, writing in east Asia quickly became an indispensable tool of government as well as a means of expressing ideas and offering reflections on human beings and their world.

Oracle Bones and Early Chinese Writing

In Mesopotamia and India merchants pioneered the use of writing. In China, however, the earliest known writing served the interests of rulers rather than traders. Writing in China goes back at least to the early part of the second millennium B.C.E. Surviving records indicate that scribes at the Shang royal court kept written accounts of important events on strips of bamboo or pieces of silk. Unfortunately, almost all of these materials have perished, along with their messages. Yet one medium employed by ancient Chinese scribes has survived the ravages of time to prove beyond doubt that writing figured prominently in the political life of the Shang dynasty. Recognized just over a century ago, inscriptions on so-called oracle bones have thrown tremendous light both on the Shang dynasty and on the early stages of Chinese writing.

Oracle Bones

Oracle bones were the principal instruments used by fortune-tellers in ancient China. In other early societies, specialists forecast the future by examining the entrails of sacrificed animals, divining the meaning of omens or celestial events such as eclipses, studying the flight of birds, or interpreting weather patterns. In China, diviners used specially prepared broad bones, such as the shoulder blades of sheep or turtle shells. They inscribed a question on the bone and then subjected it to heat, either by placing it into a fire or by scorching it with an extremely hot tool. When heated, the bone developed networks of splits and cracks. The fortune-teller then studied the patterns and determined the answer to the question inscribed on the bone. Often the diviner recorded the answer on the bone, and later scribes occasionally added further information about the events that actually came to pass.

During the nineteenth century C.E., peasants working in the fields around Anyang discovered many oracle bones bearing inscriptions in archaic Chinese writing. They did not recognize the writing, but they knew they had found an unusual and valuable commodity. They called their finds "dragon bones" and sold them to druggists, who ground them into powder that they resold as an especially potent medicine. Thus an untold number of oracle bones went to the relief of aches, pains, and ills before scholars recognized their true nature. During the late 1890s dragon bones came to the attention of historians and literary scholars, who soon determined that the inscriptions represented an early and previously unknown form of Chinese writing. Since then, more than one hundred thousand oracle bones have come to light.

Most of the oracle bones have come from royal archives, and the questions posed on them clearly reveal the day-to-day concerns of the Shang royal court. Will the season's harvest be abundant or poor? Should the king attack his enemy or not? Will the queen bear a son or a daughter? Would it please the royal ancestors to receive a sacrifice of animals—or perhaps of human slaves? Taken together, bits of information preserved on the oracle bones have allowed historians to piece together an understanding of the political and social order of Shang times.

Oracle bone from Shang times with an inscribed question and cracks caused by exposure of the bone to heat.

Even more important, the oracle bones offer the earliest glimpse into the tradition of Chinese writing. The earliest form of Chinese writing, like Sumerian and Egyptian writing, was the pictograph—a conventional or stylized representation of an object. To represent complex or abstract notions, the written language often combined various pictographs into an ideograph. Thus, for example, the combined pictographs of a mother and child mean "good" in written Chinese. Unlike most other languages, written Chinese did not include an alphabetic or phonetic component.

The characters used in contemporary Chinese writing are direct descendants of those used in Shang times. Scholars have identified more than two thousand characters inscribed on oracle bones, most of which have a modern counterpart. (Contemporary Chinese writing regularly uses about five thousand characters, although thousands of additional characters are also used for technical and specialized purposes.) Over the centuries written Chinese characters have undergone considerable modification: generally speaking, they have become more stylized, conventional, and abstract. Yet the affinities between Shang and later Chinese written characters are apparent at a glance.

Thought and Literature in Ancient China

The political interests of the Shang kings may have accounted for the origin of Chinese writing, but once established, the technology was available for other uses. Because Shang writing survives only on oracle bones and a small number of bronze inscriptions—all products that reflected the interests of the ruling elite that commissioned them—evidence for the expanded uses of writing comes only from the Zhou dynasty and later times.

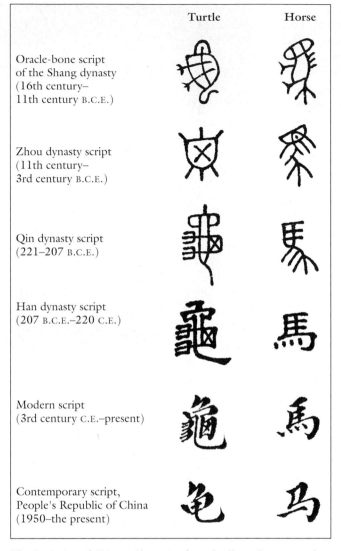

	Turtle	Horse
Oracle-bone script of the Shang dynasty (16th century–11th century B.C.E.)		
Zhou dynasty script (11th century–3rd century B.C.E.)		
Qin dynasty script (221–207 B.C.E.)		
Han dynasty script (207 B.C.E.–220 C.E.)		
Modern script (3rd century C.E.–present)		
Contemporary script, People's Republic of China (1950–the present)		

The Evolution of Chinese Characters from the Shang Dynasty to the Present

A few oracle bones survive from Zhou times, along with a large number of inscriptions on bronze ceremonial utensils that the ruling classes used during rituals venerating their ancestors. Apart from these texts, the Zhou dynasty also produced books of poetry and history, manuals of divination and ritual, and essays dealing with moral, religious, philosophical, and political themes. Best known of these works are the reflections of Confucius and other late Zhou thinkers (discussed in chapter 8), which served as the intellectual foundation of classical Chinese society. But many other less famous works show that Zhou writers, mostly anonymous, were keen observers of the world and subtle commentators on human affairs.

Several writings of the Zhou dynasty won recognition as works of high authority, and they exercised deep influence because they served as textbooks in Chinese schools. Among the most popular of these works in ancient

Zhou Literature

times was the *Book of Changes,* which was a manual instructing diviners in the art of foretelling the future. Zhou ruling elites also placed great emphasis on the *Book of History,* a collection of documents that justified the Zhou state and called for subjects to obey their overlords. Zhou aristocrats learned the art of polite behavior and the proper way to conduct rituals from the *Book of Etiquette,* also known as the *Book of Rites.*

The Book of Songs

Most notable of the classic works, however, was the *Book of Songs,* also known as the *Book of Poetry* and the *Book of Odes,* a collection of verses on themes both light and serious. Though compiled and edited after 600 B.C.E., many of the 311 poems in the collection date from a much earlier period and reflect conditions of the early Zhou dynasty. Some of the poems had political implications because they recorded the illustrious deeds of heroic figures and ancient sage-kings, and others were hymns sung at ritual observances. Yet many of them are charming verses about life, love, family, friendship, eating, drinking, work, play, nature, and daily life that offer reflections on human affairs without particular concern for political or social conditions. One poem, for example, described a bride about to join the household of her husband:

> The peach tree is young and elegant;
> Brilliant are its flowers.
> This young lady is going to her future home,
> And will order well her chamber and house.
>
> The peach tree is young and elegant;
> Abundant will be its fruit.
> This young lady is going to her future home,
> And will order well her house and chamber.
>
> The peach tree is young and elegant;
> Luxuriant are its leaves.
> This young lady is going to her future home,
> And will order well her family.

The *Book of Songs* and other writings of the Zhou dynasty offer only a small sample of China's earliest literary tradition, for most Zhou writings have perished. Those written on delicate bamboo strips and silk fabrics have deteriorated: records indicate that the tomb of one Zhou king contained hundreds of books written on bamboo strips, but none of them survive. Other books fell victim to human enemies. When the imperial house of Qin ended the chaos of the Period of the Warring States and brought all of China under tightly centralized rule in 221 B.C.E., the victorious emperor ordered the destruction of all writings that did not have some immediate utilitarian value. He spared works on divination, agriculture, and medicine, but he condemned those on poetry, history, and philosophy, which he feared might inspire doubts about his government or encourage an independence of mind. Only a few items escaped, hidden away for a decade or more until scholars and writers could once again work without fear of persecution. These few survivors represent the earliest development of Chinese literature and moral thought.

Destruction of Early Chinese Literature

ANCIENT CHINA AND THE LARGER WORLD

High mountain ranges, forbidding deserts, and turbulent seas stood between China and other early societies of the eastern hemisphere. These geographic features did not entirely prevent communication between China and other lands, but they hindered the establishment of direct long-distance trade relations such as those linking Mesopotamia with Harappan India or those between the Phoenicians and other peoples of the Mediterranean basin. Nevertheless, like other early societies, ancient China developed in the context of a larger world of interaction and exchange. Trade, migration, and the expansion of Chinese agricultural society all ensured that peoples of the various east Asian and central Asian societies would have regular dealings with one another. Chinese cultivators had particularly intense relations—sometimes friendly and sometimes hostile—with their neighbors to the north, the west, and the south.

Chinese Cultivators and Nomadic Peoples of Central Asia

From the valley of the Yellow River, Chinese agriculture spread to the north and west. The dry environment of the steppes limited expansion in these directions, however, since harvests progressively diminished to the point that agriculture became impractical.

Steppe Nomads

During the Zhou dynasty, the zone of agriculture extended about 300 kilometers (186 miles) west of Xi'an, to the eastern region of modern Gansu province.

As they expanded to the north and west, Chinese cultivators encountered nomadic peoples who had built pastoral societies in the grassy steppe lands of central Asia. These lands were too arid to sustain large agricultural societies, but their grasses supported large herds of horses, cattle, sheep, goats, and yaks. After Indo-European peoples in the western steppes began to ride domesticated horses, about 4000 B.C.E., they were able to herd their other animals more effectively and push deeper into the steppes. By 2900 B.C.E., after learning the techniques of bronze metallurgy, they had introduced heavy wagons into the steppes, and by 2200 B.C.E. their wagons were increasingly prominent in the steppe lands east of the Ural Mountains. After about 1000 B.C.E. several clusters of nomadic peoples organized powerful herding societies on the Eurasian steppes.

Nomadic Society

Nomadic peoples did little farming, since the arid steppe did not reward efforts at cultivation. Instead, the nomads concentrated on herding their animals, driving them to regions where they could find food and water. The herds provided meat and milk as well as skins and bones from which the nomads fashioned clothes and tools. Because nomadic peoples ranged widely over the grassy steppes of central Asia, they served as links between agricultural societies to the east and west. They were prominent intermediaries in trade networks spanning central Asia. They also brought knowledge of bronze metallurgy and horse-drawn chariots from southwest Asia. Nomadic peoples depended on agricultural societies for grains and finished products, such as textiles and metal goods, which they could not readily produce for themselves. In exchange for these products, they offered horses, which flourished on the steppes, and their services as links to other societies.

Despite this somewhat symbiotic arrangement, Chinese and nomadic peoples always had tense relations. Indeed, they often engaged in bitter wars, since the relatively poor but hardy nomads frequently fell upon the rich agricultural society at their doorstep and sought to seize its wealth. At least from the time of the Shang dynasty, and probably from the Xia as well, nomadic raids posed a constant threat to the northern and western regions of China. The Zhou state grew strong enough to overcome the Shang partly because Zhou military forces honed their skills waging campaigns against nomadic peoples to the west. Later, however, the Zhou state almost crumbled under the pressure of nomadic incursions compounded by disaffection among Zhou allies and subordinates.

Nomadic peoples did not imitate Chinese ways. The environment of the steppe prevented them from cultivating crops, and the need to herd their animals made it impossible for them to settle permanently in towns or to build cities. Nomadic peoples did not adopt Chinese political or social traditions but, rather, organized themselves into clans under the leadership of charismatic warrior chiefs. Nor did they use writing until about the seventh century C.E. Yet pastoral nomadism was an economic and social adaptation to agricultural society: the grains and manufactured goods available from agricultural lands enabled nomadic peoples to take advantage of the steppe environment by herding animals.

The Southern Expansion of Chinese Society

The Yangzi Valley

Chinese influence spread to the south as well as to the north and west. There was no immediate barrier to cultivation in the south: indeed, the valley of the Yangzi River supports even more intensive agriculture than is possible in the Yellow River basin. Known in China as the Chang Jiang ("Long River"), the Yangzi carries enormous

Terraced rice paddies in the river valleys of southern China have long produced abundant harvests.

volumes of water some 6,300 kilometers (3,915 miles) from its headwaters in the lofty Qinghai mountains of Tibet to its mouth near the modern Chinese cities of Nanjing and Shanghai, where it empties into the East China Sea. The moist, subtropical climate of southern China lent itself readily to the cultivation of rice: ancient cultivators sometimes raised two crops of rice per year.

There was no need for King Yu to tame the Yangzi River, which does not bring devastating floods like those of the Yellow River. But intensive cultivation of rice depended on the construction and maintenance of an elaborate irrigation system that allowed cultivators to flood their paddies and release the waters at the appropriate time. The Shang and Zhou states provided sources of authority that could supervise a complex irrigation system, and harvests in southern China burgeoned during the second and first millennia B.C.E. The populations of cultivators' communities surged along with their harvests.

As their counterparts did in lands to the north and west of the Yellow River valley, the indigenous peoples of southern China responded in two ways to the increasing prominence of agriculture in the Yangzi River valley. Many became cultivators themselves and joined Chinese agricultural society. Others continued to live by hunting and gathering: some moved into the hills and mountains, where conditions did not favor agriculture, and others migrated to Taiwan or southeast Asian lands like Vietnam and Thailand, where agriculture was more limited.

Agricultural surpluses and growing populations led to the emergence of cities, states, and complex societies in the Yangzi as well as the Yellow River valley. During

The State of Chu

the late Zhou dynasty, the powerful state of Chu, situated in the central region of the Yangzi, governed its affairs autonomously and challenged the Zhou for supremacy. By the end of the Zhou dynasty, Chu and other states in southern China were in regular communication with their counterparts in the Yellow River valley. They adopted Chinese political and social traditions as well as Chinese writing, and they built societies closely resembling those of the Yellow River valley. Although only the northern portions of the Yangzi River valley fell under the authority of the Shang and Zhou states, by the end of the Zhou dynasty all of southern China formed part of an emerging larger Chinese society.

Agricultural peoples in east Asia built complex societies that in broad outline were much like those to the west. Particularly in the valleys of the Yellow River and the Yangzi River, early Chinese cultivators organized powerful states, developed social distinctions, and established sophisticated cultural traditions. Their language, writing, beliefs, and values differed considerably from those of their contemporaries in other societies, and these cultural elements lent a distinctiveness to Chinese society. In spite of formidable geographic obstacles in the form of deserts, mountain ranges, and extensive bodies of water, inhabitants of ancient China managed to trade and communicate with peoples of other societies. As a result, wheat cultivation, bronze and iron metallurgy, horse-drawn chariots, and wheeled vehicles all made their way from southwest Asia to China in ancient times. Thus in east Asia as in other parts of the eastern hemisphere, agriculture demonstrated its potential to provide a foundation for large-scale social organization and to support interaction and exchange between peoples of different societies.

CHRONOLOGY	
5000–3000 B.C.E.	Yangshao society
2200–1766 B.C.E.	Xia dynasty
1766–1122 B.C.E.	Shang dynasty
1122–256 B.C.E.	Zhou dynasty
1403–221 B.C.E.	Period of the Warring States

FOR FURTHER READING

Cyril Birch, ed. *Anthology of Chinese Literature*. 2 vols. New York, 1965. Collection of primary sources in translation.

Kwang-chih Chang. *The Archaeology of Ancient China*. 4th ed. New Haven, 1986. Brings the results of archaeological excavations to bear on ancient Chinese history.

———. *Early Chinese Civilization: Anthropological Perspectives*. Cambridge, Mass., 1976. Essays by a distinguished archaeologist.

———. *Shang Civilization*. New Haven, 1980. Based on archaeological research.

H. G. Creel. *The Birth of China: A Study of the Formative Period of Chinese Civilization*. New York, 1954. An older popular account, well written though somewhat dated, by a leading scholar.

Nicola di Cosmo. *Ancient China and Its Enemies: The Rise of Nomadic Power in East Asian History*. Cambridge, 2002. An insightful study analyzing the emergence of pastoral nomadism and relations between Chinese cultivators and nomadic peoples in ancient times.

Jacques Gernet. *Ancient China from the Beginnings to the Empire*. Trans. by R. Rudorff. London, 1968. A brief popular survey of early Chinese society.

Cho-yun Hsu. *Ancient China in Transition: An Analysis of Social Mobility, 722–222 B.C.* Stanford, 1965. A scholarly examination of social change during the later Zhou dynasty.

Cho-yun Hsu and Katheryn M. Linduff. *Western Chou Civilization*. New Haven, 1988. Draws on both literary sources and archaeological discoveries in offering a comprehensive study of the early Zhou dynasty.

David N. Keightley, ed. *The Origins of Chinese Civilization*. Berkeley, 1983. An important collection of scholarly articles dealing with all aspects of early Chinese society.

Owen Lattimore. *Inner Asian Frontiers of China*. 2nd ed. New York, 1951. Fascinating analysis of the relationship between Chinese and nomadic peoples of central Asia by a geographer who traveled through much of central Asia.

Jessica Rawson. *Ancient China: Art and Archaeology*. New York, 1980. An outstanding and well-illustrated volume with especially strong treatment of archaeological discoveries.

William Watson. *Early Civilization in China*. New York, 1966. Well-illustrated popular account dealing with the period from prehistoric times to the Zhou dynasty.

See our **Online Learning Center** at www.mhhe.com/bentley3 for additional readings, practice maps, quizzes, and internet activities.

Unfamiliar words? Check out the **Primary Source Investigator CD-ROM** for an interactive glossary, interactive maps, more images, and primary sources.

Conflict between Maya deities from a manuscript book on calendrical matters.

CHAPTER 6

EARLY SOCIETIES IN THE AMERICAS AND OCEANIA

In early September of the year 683 C.E., a Maya man named Chan Bahlum grasped a sharp obsidian knife and cut three deep slits into the skin of his penis. He inserted into each slit a strip of paper made from beaten tree bark so as to encourage a continuing flow of blood. His younger brother Kan Xul performed a similar rite, while other members of his family also drew blood from their own bodies.

The bloodletting observances of September 683 C.E. were political and religious rituals, acts of deep piety performed as Chan Bahlum presided over funeral services for his recently deceased father, Pacal, king of the Maya city of Palenque in the Yucatan peninsula. The Maya believed that the shedding of royal blood was essential to the world's survival. Thus, as Chan Bahlum prepared to succeed his father as king of Palenque, he let his blood flow copiously.

Throughout Mesoamerica, Maya and other peoples performed similar rituals for a millennium and more. Maya rulers and their family members regularly spilled their own blood by opening wounds with obsidian knives, stingray spines, or sharpened bones. Men commonly drew blood from the penis, like Chan Bahlum, while women often drew from the tongue. Both sexes occasionally drew blood also from the earlobes, lips, or cheeks, and they sometimes increased the flow by pulling long, thick cords through their wounds.

This shedding of blood was so crucial to Maya rituals because of its association with rain and agriculture. According to Maya priests, the gods had shed their own blood to water the earth and nourish crops of maize, and they expected human beings to honor them by imitating their sacrifice. By spilling human blood the Maya hoped to please the gods and ensure that life-giving waters would bring bountiful harvests to their fields. By inflicting painful wounds not just on their enemies, but on their own bodies as well, the Maya demonstrated their conviction that bloodletting rituals were essential to the coming of rain and the survival of their agricultural society.

This agricultural society was the product of a distinctive tradition. Human groups migrated to the Americas and Oceania long after they had established communities throughout most of the eastern hemisphere, but long before any people began to experiment with agriculture. Their migrations took place during ice ages when glaciers locked up much of the earth's water, causing sea levels all over the world to decline precipitously—sometimes by as much as 300 meters (984 feet). For thousands of years, temporary land bridges joined regions that both before and after the ice ages were separated by the seas. One land bridge linked Siberia with Alaska. Another joined the continent of Australia to the island of New Guinea. Low sea levels also exposed large stretches of land that connected Sumatra, Java, and other Indonesian islands to the peninsula of southeast Asia. Human groups took advantage of these bridges by migrating to new lands. Their movements represented continuations of the migratory flows that earlier had resulted in the establishment of human communities throughout the eastern hemisphere.

When the earth's temperature rose and the glaciers melted, beginning about eighteen thousand years ago, the waters returned and flooded low-lying lands around the world. Eventually, the seas once again divided Asia from America by the body of water known as the Bering Strait, and they also separated Australia, New Guinea, and the islands of Indonesia. By that time, however, human communities had become well established in the Americas, the islands of southeast Asia, and Australia, where they independently built distinctive societies.

The return of high waters did not put an end to human migrations. Human groups fanned out from Alaska and ventured to all corners of North America, Central America, and South America. Beginning about 3000 B.C.E. coastal peoples of southeast Asia built large sailing canoes and established human settlements in the previously uninhabited islands of the Pacific Ocean. By about 700 C.E. human beings had established communities in almost every habitable part of the world.

High sea levels did not prevent human groups from migrating to new lands, but they sometimes made it difficult for peoples to maintain ties with others separated by large bodies of water. By no means did human migrants to the Americas and Oceania lead completely isolated lives. To the contrary, there were frequent and sometimes regular interactions between peoples of different societies within the Americas and within Oceania. Moreover, there were sporadic but significant contacts between Asian peoples and Pacific islanders and also between Pacific islanders and native peoples of the Americas. It is likely that at least fleeting encounters took place as well between peoples of the eastern and western hemispheres, although very little evidence survives to throw light on the nature of these encounters in early times. Yet even as they dealt frequently with peoples of other societies, the first inhabitants of the Americas and Oceania also established distinctive societies of their own, like their counterparts in the eastern hemisphere.

Indeed, despite their different origins and their distinctive political, social, and cultural traditions, peoples of the Americas and Oceania built societies that in some ways resembled those of the eastern hemisphere. Human communities independently discovered agriculture in several regions of North America and South America, and migrants introduced cultivation to the inhabited Pacific islands as well. With agriculture came increasing populations, settlement in towns, specialized labor, formal political authorities, hierarchical social orders, long-distance trade, and organized religious traditions. The Americas also generated large, densely populated societies featuring cities, monumental public works, imperial states, and sometimes traditions of writing as well. Thus, like their counterparts in the eastern hemisphere, the earliest societies of the Americas and Oceania reflected a common human tendency toward the development of increasingly complex social forms.

EARLY SOCIETIES OF MESOAMERICA

Much is unclear about the early population of the Americas by human communities. The first large wave of migration from Siberia to Alaska probably took place about 13,000 B.C.E. But small numbers of migrants may have crossed the Bering land bridge earlier, and it is also possible that some migrants reached the western hemisphere by watercraft, sailing or drifting with the currents from northeast Asia down the west coast of North America. Several archaeological excavations have yielded remains that scholars date to 15,000 B.C.E. or earlier, suggesting that at least a few human groups made their way to the Americas before the beginning of large-scale migration from Siberia. In any case, after 13,000 B.C.E. migrants arrived in large numbers, and they quickly populated all habitable regions of the western hemisphere. By 9500 B.C.E. they had reached the southernmost part of South America, more than 17,000 kilometers (10,566 miles) from the Bering land bridge.

The earliest human inhabitants of the Americas lived exclusively by hunting and gathering. Beginning about 8,000 B.C.E., however, it became increasingly difficult for them to survive by foraging. Large game animals became scarce, partly because they did not adapt well to the rapidly warming climate and partly because of overhunting by expanding human communities. By 7500 B.C.E. many species of large animals in the Americas were well on the road to extinction. Some human communities relied on fish and small game to supplement foods that they gathered. Others turned to agriculture, and they gave rise to the first complex societies in the Americas.

The Olmecs

By 8000 to 7000 B.C.E. the peoples of Mesoamerica—the region from the central portion of modern Mexico to Honduras and El Salvador—had begun to experiment with the cultivation of beans, chili peppers, avocados, squashes, and gourds. By 4000 B.C.E. they had discovered the agricultural potential of maize, which soon became the staple food of the region. Later they added tomatoes to the crops they cultivated. Agricultural villages appeared soon after 3000 B.C.E., and by 2000 B.C.E. agriculture had spread throughout Mesoamerica.

Early Agriculture in Mesoamerica

Early Mesoamerican peoples had a diet rich in cultivated foods, but they did not keep as many animals as their counterparts in the eastern hemisphere. Their domesticated animals included turkeys and small, barkless dogs, both of which they consumed as food. But most large animals of the western hemisphere were not susceptible to domestication, so Mesoamericans were unable to harness animal energy. Human laborers prepared fields for cultivation, and human porters carried trade goods on their backs. Mesoamericans had no need for wheeled vehicles, which would have been useful only if draft animals were available to pull them.

Toward the end of the second millennium B.C.E., the tempo of Mesoamerican life quickened as elaborate ceremonial centers with monumental pyramids, temples, and palaces arose alongside the agricultural villages. The first of these centers were not cities like those of early societies in the eastern hemisphere. Permanent residents of the ceremonial centers included members of the ruling elite, priests, and a few artisans and craftsmen who tended to the needs of the ruling and priestly classes. Large numbers of people gathered in the ceremonial centers on special occasions to observe rituals or on market days to exchange goods, but most people then returned to their homes in neighboring villages and hamlets.

Ceremonial Centers

The earliest known ceremonial centers of the ancient Americas appeared on the coast of the Gulf of Mexico, near the modern Mexican city of Veracruz, and they served as the nerve center of the first complex society of the Americas, that of the Olmecs. Historians and archaeologists have systematically studied Olmec society only since the 1940s, and many questions about them remain unanswered. Even their proper name is unknown: the term *Olmec* (meaning "rubber people") did not come from the ancient people themselves, but derives instead from the rubber trees that flourish in the region they inhabited. Nevertheless, some of the basic features of Olmec society have become reasonably

Olmecs: The "Rubber People"

MAP [6.1]

Early Mesoamerican
societies, 1200 B.C.E.–
1100 C.E.

Olmec Society

clear, and it is certain that Olmec cultural traditions influenced all complex societies of
Mesoamerica until the arrival of European peoples in the sixteenth century C.E.

The first Olmec ceremonial center arose about 1200 B.C.E. on the site of the
modern town of San Lorenzo, and it served as their capital for some four hundred
years. When the influence of San Lorenzo waned, leadership passed to new ceremonial centers at La Venta (800–400 B.C.E.) and Tres Zapotes (400–100 B.C.E.). These
sites defined the heartland of Olmec society, where agriculture produced rich harvests. The entire region receives abundant rainfall, so there was no need to build extensive systems of irrigation. Like the Harappans, however, the Olmecs constructed
elaborate drainage systems to divert waters that otherwise might have flooded their
fields or destroyed their settlements. Some Olmec drainage construction remains visible and effective today.

Olmec society was probably authoritarian in nature. Untold thousands of laborers
participated in the construction of the ceremonial centers at San Lorenzo, La Venta,
and Tres Zapotes. Each of the principal Olmec sites featured an elaborate complex of
temples, pyramids, altars, stone sculptures, and tombs for rulers. Common subjects delivered a portion of their harvests for the maintenance of the elite classes living in the
ceremonial centers and provided labor for the various large-scale construction projects.

Indeed, common subjects labored regularly on behalf of the Olmec elite—not
only in building drainage systems and ceremonial centers but also in providing appropriate artistic adornment for the capitals. The most distinctive artistic creations of
the Olmecs were colossal human heads—possibly likenesses of rulers—sculpted from
basalt rock. The largest of these sculptures stands 3 meters (almost 10 feet) tall and
weighs some twenty tons. In the absence of draft animals and wheels, human laborers dragged enormous boulders from quarries, floated them on rafts to points near
their destinations, dragged them to their intended sites, and then positioned them
for the sculptors. The largest sculptures required the services of about one thousand
laborers. Apart from the colossal heads, the Olmec capitals featured many other large
stone sculptures and monumental buildings that required the services of laborers by
the hundreds and thousands. Construction of the huge pyramid at La Venta, for ex-

ample, required some eight hundred thousand man-days of labor.

Olmec influence extended to much of the central and southern regions of modern Mexico and beyond that to modern Guatemala and El Salvador. The Olmecs spread their influence partly by military force, but trade was a prominent link between the Olmec heartland and the other regions of Mesoamerica. The Olmecs produced large numbers of decorative objects from jade, which they had to import. In the absence of any metal technology, they also made extensive use of obsidian from which they fashioned knives and axes with wickedly sharp cutting edges. Like jade, obsidian came to the Gulf coast from distant regions in the interior of Mesoamerica. In exchange for the imports, the Olmecs traded small works of art fashioned from jade, basalt, or ceramics and perhaps also local products such as animal skins.

Trade in Jade and Obsidian

Colossal Olmec head carved from basalt rock between 1000 and 600 B.C.E. and discovered at La Venta. Olmecs carved similar heads for their ceremonial centers at San Lorenzo and Tres Zapotes.

Among the many mysteries surrounding the Olmecs, one of the most perplexing concerns the decline and fall of their society. The Olmecs systematically destroyed their ceremonial centers at both San Lorenzo and La Venta and then deserted the sites. Archaeologists studying these sites found statues broken and buried, monuments defaced, and the capitals themselves burned. Although intruders may have ravaged the ceremonial centers, many scholars believe that the Olmecs deliberately destroyed their capitals, perhaps because of civil conflicts or doubts about the effectiveness and legitimacy of the ruling classes. In any case, by about 400 B.C.E. Olmec society had fallen on hard times, and soon thereafter societies in other parts of Mesoamerica eclipsed it altogether.

Yet later Mesoamerican societies adopted several Olmec traditions. They cultivated maize, built ceremonial centers with temple pyramids, and maintained a calendar based on one inherited from Olmec priests. They also borrowed Olmec ball games and rituals involving human sacrifice. Because the Olmecs left no written records beyond calendrical inscriptions, however, the exact roles that ball games and human sacrifices played in their society are not clear.

Heirs of the Olmecs: The Maya

During the thousand years following the Olmecs' disappearance about 100 B.C.E., complex societies arose in several Mesoamerican regions. Human population grew dramatically, and ceremonial centers cropped up at sites far removed from the Olmec heartland. Some of them evolved into genuine cities: they attracted large populations of permanent residents, embarked on ambitious programs of construction, maintained large markets, and encouraged increasing specialization of labor. Networks of long-distance trade linked the new urban centers and extended their influence to all parts of Mesoamerica. Within the cities themselves, priests devised written languages and compiled a body of astronomical knowledge. In short, Mesoamerican societies developed in a manner roughly parallel to their counterparts in the eastern hemisphere.

The earliest heirs of the Olmecs were the Maya, who created a remarkable society in the region now occupied by southern Mexico, Guatemala, Belize, Honduras, and

The Maya

Olmec ceremonial axe head carved from jade about 800 to 400 B.C.E. Jaguar features, such as those depicted here, are prominent in Olmec art.

El Salvador. The highlands of Guatemala offer fertile soil and excellent conditions for agriculture. Permanent villages began to appear there during the third century B.C.E. The most prominent of them was Kaminaljuyú, located on the site of modern Guatemala City. Like the Olmec capitals, Kaminaljuyú was a ceremonial center rather than a true city, but it dominated the life of other communities in the region. Some twelve thousand to fifteen thousand laborers worked to build its temples, and its products traveled the trade routes as far as central Mexico. During the fourth century C.E., Kaminaljuyú fell under the economic and perhaps also the political dominance of the much larger city of Teotihuacan in central Mexico and lost much of its influence in Maya society.

After the fourth century, Maya society flourished mostly in the poorly drained Mesoamerican lowlands, where thin, tropical soils quickly lost their fertility. To enhance the agricultural potential of the region, the Maya built terraces designed to trap silt carried by the numerous rivers passing through the lowlands. By artificially retaining rich earth, they dramatically increased the agricultural productivity of their lands. They harvested maize in abundance, and they also cultivated cotton from which they wove fine textiles highly prized both in their own society and by trading partners in other parts of Mesoamerica. Maya cultivators also raised cacao, the large bean that is the source of chocolate. Cacao was a precious commodity consumed mostly by nobles in Maya society. They whisked powdered cacao into water to create a stimulating beverage, and they sometimes even ate the bitter cacao beans as snacks. The product was so valuable that Maya used cacao beans as money.

Tikal

From about 300 to 900 C.E., the Maya built more than eighty large ceremonial centers in the lowlands—all with pyramids, palaces, and temples—as well as numerous smaller settlements. Some of the larger centers attracted dense populations and evolved into genuine cities. Foremost among them was Tikal, the most important Maya political center between the fourth and the ninth centuries C.E. At its height, roughly 600 to 800 C.E., Tikal was a wealthy and bustling city with a population approaching forty thousand. It boasted enormous paved plazas and scores of temples, pyramids, palaces, and public buildings. The Temple of the Giant Jaguar, a stepped pyramid rising sharply to a height of 47 meters (154 feet), dominated the skyline and represented Tikal's control over the surrounding region, which had a population of about five hundred thousand.

The Maya organized themselves politically into scores of small city-kingdoms. Tikal was probably the largest, but Palenque and Chichén Itzá also were sizable states. The smaller kingdoms had populations between ten thousand and thirty thousand. Maya kings often bore menacing names like Curl Snout, Smoking Frog, and Stormy Sky. Especially popular were names associated with the jaguar, the most dangerous predator of the Mesoamerican forests. Prominent Maya kings included Great Jaguar Paw, Shield Jaguar, Bird Jaguar, and Jaguar Penis (meaning the progenitor of other jaguar-kings).

Maya Warfare

The Maya kingdoms fought constantly with each other. Victors generally destroyed the peoples they defeated and took over their ceremonial centers, but the purpose of Maya warfare was not so much to kill enemies as to capture them in hand-to-hand combat on the battlefield. Warriors won enormous prestige when they brought back important captives from neighboring kingdoms. They stripped captives of their fine dress and symbols of rank, and sometimes they kept high-ranking captives alive for years, displaying them as trophies. Ultimately, however, most captives ended their lives either as slaves or as sacrificial victims to Maya gods. High-ranking captives in particular often underwent ritual torture and sacrifice in public ceremonies on important occasions.

Bitter conflicts between small kingdoms were sources of constant tension in Maya society. Only about the ninth century C.E. did the state of Chichén Itzá in the northern Yucatan peninsula seek to dampen hostile instincts and establish a larger political framework for Maya society. The rulers of Chichén Itzá preferred to absorb captives and integrate them into their own society rather than annihilate them or offer them up as sacrificial victims. Some captives refused the opportunity and went to their deaths as proud warriors, but many agreed to recognize the authority of Chichén Itzá and participate in the construction of a larger society. Be-

Chichén Itzá

Temple of the Giant Jaguar at Tikal, which served as funerary pyramid for Lord Cacao, a prominent Maya ruler of the late sixth and early seventh centuries C.E.

tween the ninth and eleventh centuries C.E., Chichén Itzá organized a loose empire that brought a measure of political stability to the northern Yucatan.

By about 800 C.E., however, most Maya populations had begun to desert their *Maya Decline* cities. Within a century Maya society was in full decline everywhere except the northern Yucatan, where Chichén Itzá continued to flourish. Historians have suggested many possible causes of the decline, including invasion by foreigners from Mexico, internal dissension and civil war, failure of the system of water control leading to diminished harvests and demographic collapse, ecological problems caused by destruction of the forests, the spread of epidemic diseases, and natural catastrophes such as earthquakes. Possibly several problems combined to destroy Maya society. It is likely that debilitating civil conflict and excessive siltation of agricultural terraces caused particularly difficult problems for the Maya. In any case the population declined, the people abandoned their cities, and long-distance trade with central Mexico came to a halt. Meanwhile, the tropical jungles of the lowlands encroached upon human settlements and gradually smothered the cities, temples, pyramids, and monuments of a once-vibrant society.

Maya Society and Religion

Apart from the kings and ruling families, Maya society included a large class of priests who maintained an elaborate calendar and transmitted knowledge of writing, astronomy,

In this extraordinarily well-preserved mural, musicians celebrate the designation of an heir to the Maya king at Bonampak (located in the southern part of modern Mexico).

and mathematics. A hereditary nobility owned most land and cooperated with the kings and priests by organizing military forces and participating in religious rituals. Maya merchants came from the ruling and noble classes. Their travels had strong political overtones, since they served not only as traders but also as ambassadors to neighboring lands and allied peoples. Moreover, they traded mostly in exotic and luxury goods, such as rare animal skins, cacao beans, and finely crafted works of art, which rulers coveted as signs of special status. Apart from the ruling and priestly elites, Maya society generated several other distinct social classes. Professional architects and sculptors oversaw construction of large monuments and public buildings. Artisans specialized in the production of pottery, tools, and cotton textiles. Finally, large classes of peasants and slaves fed the entire society and provided physical labor for the construction of cities and monuments.

The Maya built upon the cultural achievements of their Olmec predecessors. Maya priests studied astronomy and mathematics, and they devised both a sophisticated calendar and an elaborate system of writing. They understood the movements of heavenly bodies well enough to plot planetary cycles and predict eclipses of the sun and moon. They invented the concept of zero and used a symbol to represent zero mathematically, which facilitated their manipulation of large numbers. By combining their astronomical observations and mathematical reasoning, Maya priests calculated the length of the solar year at 365.242 days—about seventeen seconds shorter than the figure reached by modern astronomers.

The Maya Calendar

Maya priests constructed the most elaborate calendar of the ancient Americas. Its complexity reflected a powerful urge to identify meaningful cycles of time and to understand human events in the context of those cycles. The Maya calendar interwove two kinds of year: a solar year of 365 days governed the agricultural cycle, and a ritual year of 260 days governed daily affairs by organizing time into twenty "months" of thirteen days apiece. The Maya believed that each day derived certain specific characteristics from its position in both the solar and the ritual calendar and that the combined attributes of each day would determine the fortune of activities undertaken on that day. It took fifty-two years for the two calendars to work through all possible combinations of days and return simultaneously to their respective starting points, so 18,980 different combinations of characteristics could influence the prospects of an individual day. Maya priests carefully studied the various opportunities and dangers that would come together on a given day in hopes that they could determine which activities were safe to initiate. Apart from calculating the prospects of individual days, the Maya attributed especially great significance to the fifty-two-year periods in which the two calendars ran. They believed that the end of a cycle would bring monumental changes and that ultimately the world would end after one such cycle.

Maya Writing

While building on the calendrical calculations of the Olmecs, the Maya also expanded upon their predecessors' tradition of written inscriptions. In doing so they created the most flexible and sophisticated of all the early American systems of writing. The Maya script contained both ideographic elements (like Chinese characters) and symbols for syllables. Scholars have begun to decipher this script only since the 1960s, and it has become clear that writing was just as important to the Maya as it was to early complex societies in the eastern hemisphere. Maya scribes wrote works of history, poetry, and myth, and they also kept genealogical, administrative, and astronomical records. Most Maya writing survives today in the form of inscriptions on temples and monuments, but scribes produced untold numbers of books written on paper made from beaten tree bark or on vellum made from deerskin. When Spanish conquerors and missionaries arrived in Maya lands in the sixteenth century C.E., however, they destroyed all the books they could find in hopes of undermining native religious beliefs. Today only four books of the ancient Maya survive, all dealing with astronomical and calendrical matters.

In this stone relief sculpture, a Maya king from Yaxchilán (between Tikal and Palenque in the southern Yucatan peninsula) holds a torch over a woman from the royal family as she draws a thorn-studded rope through a hole in her tongue, so as to shed her blood in honor of the Maya gods.

Maya Religious Thought

Surviving inscriptions and other writings shed considerable light on Maya religious and cultural traditions. The *Popol Vuh,* a Maya creation myth, taught that the gods had created human beings out of maize and water, the ingredients that became human flesh and blood. Thus Maya religious thought reflected the fundamental role of agriculture in their society, much like religious thought in early complex societies of the eastern hemisphere. Maya priests also taught that the gods kept the world going and maintained the agricultural cycle in exchange for honors and sacrifices performed for them by human beings.

Bloodletting Rituals

The most important of these sacrifices involved the shedding of human blood, which the Maya believed would prompt the gods to send rain to water their crops of maize. Some bloodletting rituals centered on war captives. Before sacrificing the victims by decapitation, their captors cut off the ends of their fingers or lacerated their bodies so as to cause a copious flow of blood in honor of the gods. Yet the Maya did not look upon these rituals simply as opportunities to torture their enemies. The frequent and voluntary shedding of royal blood, as in the case of Chan Bahlum's self-sacrifice at Palenque, testifies to the depth of Maya convictions that they inhabited a world created and sustained by deities who expected honor and reverence from their human subjects.

The Maya Ball Game

Apart from the calendar and sacrificial rituals, the Maya also inherited a distinctive ball game from the Olmecs. The game sometimes pitted two men against each other, but it often involved teams of two to four members apiece. (There is no evidence that women played the game.) The object of the game was for players to score points by propelling a rubber ball through a ring or onto a marker without using their hands. The Maya used a ball about 20 centimeters (8 inches) in diameter. Made of solid baked rubber, the ball was both heavy and hard—a blow to the head could easily cause a concussion—and players needed great dexterity and skill to maneuver it accurately using only their feet, legs, hips, torso, shoulders, or elbows. The game was extremely popular: almost all Maya ceremonial centers, towns, and cities had stone-paved courts on which players performed publicly.

The Maya played the ball game for several reasons. Sometimes individuals competed for sporting purposes, and sometimes players or spectators laid bets on the outcome of contests between professionals. The ball game figured also in Maya political affairs as a ritual that honored the conclusion of treaties. High-ranking captives often engaged in forced public competition in which the stakes were their very lives: losers became sacrificial victims and faced torture and execution immediately following the match. Alongside some ball courts were skull racks that bore the decapitated heads of losing players. Thus Maya concerns to please the gods by shedding human blood extended even to the realm of sport.

Heirs of the Olmecs: Teotihuacan

While the Maya flourished in the Mesoamerican lowlands, a different society arose to the north in the highlands of Mexico. For most of human history, the valley of central Mexico, situated some two kilometers (more than a mile) above sea level, was the site of several large lakes fed by the waters coming off the surrounding mountains. Most of the lakes have disappeared during the past two or three centuries as a result of environmental changes and deliberate draining of their waters. In earlier times, however, their abundant supplies of fish and waterfowl attracted human settlers. The lakes also served as sources of fresh water and as transportation routes linking communities situated on their shores.

A limestone altar carved in 796 C.E. depicts two Maya kings playing a ritual ball game to celebrate the negotiation of an agreement.

Sources from the Past

The *Popol Vuh* on the Creation of Human Beings

The Popol Vuh *outlines traditional Maya views on the creation of the world and human beings. The version of the work that survives today dates from the mid-sixteenth century, but it reflects beliefs of a much earlier era. According to the* Popol Vuh, *the gods wanted to create intelligent beings that would recognize and praise them. Three times they tried to fashion such beings out of animals, mud, and wood, but without success. Then they decided to use maize and water as their ingredients.*

And here is the beginning of the conception of humans, and of the search for the ingredients of the human body. So they spoke, the [gods] Bearer, Begetter, the Makers, Modelers named Sovereign Plumed Serpent:

"The dawn has approached, preparations have been made, and morning has come for the provider, nurturer, born in the light, begotten in the light. Morning has come for humankind, for the people of the face of the earth," they said. It all came together as they went on thinking in the darkness, in the night, as they searched and they sifted, they thought and they wondered.

And here their thoughts came out in clear light. They sought and discovered what was needed for human flesh. . . . Broken Place, Bitter Water Place is the name: the yellow corn, white corn came from there. . . .

And these were the ingredients for the flesh of the human work, the human design, and the water was for the blood. It became human blood, and corn was also used by the Bearer, Begetter. . . .

And then the yellow corn and white corn were ground, and Xmucane did the grinding nine times. Corn was used, along with the water she rinsed her hands with, for the creation of grease; it became human fat when it was worked by the Bearer, Begetter, Sovereign Plumed Serpent, as they are called. . . .

It was staples alone that made up their flesh.

These are the names of the first people who were made and modeled.

This is the first person: Jaguar Quitze.

And now the second: Jaguar Night.

And now the third: Mahucutah.

And the fourth: True Jaguar.

And these are the names of our first mother-fathers. They were simply made and modeled, it is said; they had no mother and no father. We have named the men by themselves. No woman gave birth to them, nor were they begotten by the builder, sculptor, Bearer, Begetter. By sacrifice alone, by genius alone they were made, they were modeled by the Maker, Modeler, Bearer, Begetter, Sovereign Plumed Serpent. And when they came to fruition, they came out human:

They talked and they made words.

They looked and they listened.

They walked, they worked. . . .

And then their wives and women came into being. Again, the same gods thought of it. It was as if they were asleep when they received them, truly beautiful women were there with Jaguar Quitze, Jaguar Night, Mahucutah, and True Jaguar. With their women there they became wider awake. Right away they were happy at heart again, because of their wives.

Celebrated Seahouse is the name of the wife of Jaguar Quitze.

Prawn House is the name of the wife of Jaguar Night.

Hummingbird House is the name of the wife of Mahucutah.

Macaw House is the name of the wife of True Jaguar.

So these are the names of their wives, who became ladies of rank, giving birth to the people of the tribes, small and great.

SOURCE: Dennis Tedlock, trans. *Popol Vuh: The Definitive Edition of the Mayan Book of the Dawn of Life and the Glories of Gods and Kings.* New York: Simon and Schuster, 1985, pp.163–65, 167.

Discuss the extent to which this account of human creation reflects the influences on Maya society of both agriculture and the untamed natural world.

The earliest settlers in the valley of Mexico did not build extensive irrigation systems, but they channeled some of the waters from the mountain streams into their fields and established a productive agricultural society. Expanding human population led to the congregation of people in cities and the emergence of a complex society in the Mesoamerican highlands. The earliest center of this society was the large and bustling city of Teotihuacan, located about 50 kilometers (31 miles) northeast of modern Mexico City.

The City of Teotihuacan

Teotihuacan was probably a large agricultural village by 500 B.C.E. It expanded rapidly after about 200 B.C.E., and by the end of the millennium its population approached fifty thousand. By the year 100 C.E., the city's two most prominent monuments, the colossal pyramids of the sun and the moon, dominated the skyline. The Pyramid of the Sun is the largest single structure in Mesoamerica. It occupies nearly as much space as the pyramid of Khufu in Egypt, though it stands only half as tall. At its high point, about 400 to 600 C.E., Teotihuacan was home to almost two hundred thousand inhabitants, a thriving metropolis with scores of temples, several palatial residences, neighborhoods with small apartments for the masses, busy markets, and hundreds of workshops for artisans and craftsmen.

The organization of a large urban population, along with the hinterland that supported it, required a recognized source of authority. Although Teotihuacan generated large numbers of books and records that perhaps would have shed light on the character of this authority, they unfortunately perished when the city itself declined. Paintings and murals suggest that Teotihuacan was a theocracy of sorts. Priests figure prominently in the works of art, and scholars interpret many figures as representations of deities. Priests were crucial to the survival of the society, since they kept the calendar and ensured that planting and harvesting took place at the appropriate seasons. Thus it would not have been unusual for them to govern Teotihuacan in the name of the gods, or at least to cooperate closely with a secular ruling class.

Aerial view of Teotihuacan, looking toward the Pyramid of the Moon (top center) from the Pyramid of the Sun (bottom left). Shops and residences occupied the spaces surrounding the main street and the pyramids.

Apart from rulers and priests, Teotihuacan's population included cultivators, artisans, and merchants. Perhaps as many as two-thirds of the city's inhabitants worked during the day in fields surrounding Teotihuacan and returned to their small apartments in the city at night. Artisans of Teotihuacan were especially famous for their obsidian tools and fine orange pottery, and scholars have identified numerous workshops and stores where toolmakers and potters produced and marketed their goods within the city itself. The residents of Teotihuacan also participated in extensive trade and exchange networks. Professional merchants traded their products throughout Mesoamerica. Archaeologists have found numerous samples of the distinctive obsidian tools and orange pottery at sites far distant from Teotihuacan, from the region of modern Guatemala City in the south to Durango and beyond in the north.

The Society of Teotihuacan

Until about 500 C.E. there was little sign of military organization in Teotihuacan. The city did not have defensive walls, and works of art rarely depicted warriors. Yet the influence of Teotihuacan extended to much of modern Mexico and beyond. The Maya capital of Kaminaljuyú, for example, fell under the influence of Teotihuacan during the fourth century C.E. Although the rulers of Teotihuacan may have established colonies to protect their sources of obsidian and undertaken military expeditions to back up their authority throughout central Mexico, the city's influence apparently derived less from military might than from its ability to produce fine manufactured goods that appealed to consumers in distant markets.

Like the Maya, the residents of Teotihuacan built on cultural foundations established by the Olmecs. They played the ball game, adapted the Olmec calendar to their own uses, and expanded the Olmecs' graphic symbols into a complete system of writing. Unfortunately, only a few samples of their writing survive in stone carvings. Because their books have all perished, it is impossible to know exactly how they viewed the world and their place in it. Works of art suggest that they recognized an earth god and a rain god, and it is certain that they carried out human sacrifices during their religious rituals.

Cultural Traditions

Teotihuacan began to experience increasing military pressure from other peoples around 500 C.E. Works of art from this period frequently depicted eagles, jaguars, and coyotes—animals that Mesoamericans associated with fighting and military conquest. After about 650 C.E. Teotihuacan entered a period of decline. About the middle of the eighth century invaders sacked and burned the city, destroying its books and monuments. After that catastrophe most residents deserted Teotihuacan, and the city slowly fell into ruin.

Decline of Teotihuacan

EARLY SOCIETIES OF SOUTH AMERICA

By about 12,000 B.C.E. hunting and gathering peoples had made their way across the narrow isthmus of Central America and into South America. Those who migrated into the region of the northern and central Andes mountains hunted deer, llama, alpaca, and other large animals. Both the mountainous highlands and the coastal regions below benefited from a cool and moist climate that provided natural harvests of squashes, gourds, and wild potatoes. Beginning about 8000 B.C.E., however, the climate of this whole region became increasingly warm and dry, and the changes placed pressure on natural food supplies. To maintain their numbers, the human communities of the region began to experiment with agriculture. Here, as elsewhere, agriculture encouraged population growth, the establishment of villages and cities, the building of states, and the elaboration of organized cultural traditions.

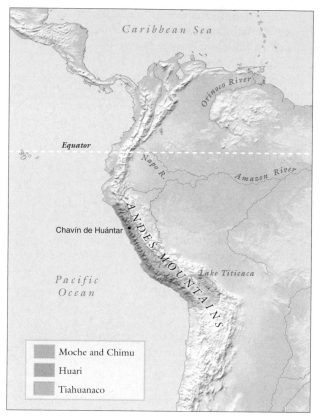

MAP [6.2]

Early societies of Andean South America, 1000 B.C.E.–700 C.E.

For an interactive version
of this map, go to
www.mhhe.com/
bentley3ch6maps.

*Early Agriculture
in South America*

The Chavín Cult

During the centuries after 1000 B.C.E., the central Andean region generated complex societies parallel to those of Mesoamerica.

Early Andean Society and the Chavín Cult

Although they were exact contemporaries, early Meso-american and Andean societies developed largely independently. The heartland of early Andean society was the region now occupied by the states of Peru and Bolivia. Geography discouraged the establishment of communications between the Andean region and Meso-america because neither society possessed abundant pack animals or a technology to facilitate long-distance transportation. Neither the Andes mountains nor the lowlands of modern Panama and Nicaragua offered an attractive highway linking the two regions. Several agricultural products and technologies diffused slowly from one area to the other: cultivation of maize and squashes spread from its Mesoamerican home to the central Andean region while Andean gold, silver, and copper metallurgy traveled north to Mesoamerica.

Geography even conspired against the establishment of communications within the central Andean region. Deep valleys crease the western flank of the Andes mountains, as rivers drain waters from the highlands to the Pacific Ocean, so transportation and communication between the valleys has always been very difficult. Nevertheless, powerful Andean states sometimes overcame the difficulties and influenced human affairs as far away as modern Ecuador and Colombia to the north and northern Chile to the south.

Most of the early Andean heartland came under cultivation between 2500 and 2000 B.C.E., and permanent settlements dotted the coastal regions in particular. The earliest cultivators of the region relied on beans, peanuts, and sweet potatoes as their main food crops. They also cultivated cotton, which they used to make fishnets and textiles. The rich marine life of the Pacific Ocean supplemented agricultural harvests, enabling coastal peoples to build an increasingly complex society. Settlements probably appeared later in the Andean highlands than in the coastal regions, but many varieties of potato supported agricultural communities in the highlands after about 2000 B.C.E. By 1800 B.C.E. peoples in all the Andean regions had begun to fashion distinctive styles of pottery and to build temples and pyramids in large ceremonial centers.

Shortly after the year 1000 B.C.E., a new religion appeared suddenly in the central Andes. The Chavín cult, which enjoyed enormous popularity during the period 900 to 800 B.C.E., spread through most of the territory occupied by modern Peru and then vanished about 300 B.C.E. Unfortunately, no information survives to indicate the precise significance of the cult, nor even its proper name: scholars have named it after the modern town of Chavín de Huántar, one of the cult's most prominent sites. One theory suggests that the cult arose when maize became an important crop in South America. The capacity of maize to support large populations might well have served as the stimulus for the emergence of a cult designed to promote fertility and abundant harvests. In any case the large temple complexes and elaborate works of art that accompanied the cult demonstrate its importance to those who honored it. Devotees produced intricate stone carvings representing their deities with the features of humans and wild animals such as jaguars, hawks, eagles, and snakes. The extensive distribution of the temples and carvings shows that the Chavín cult seized the imagination of agricultural peoples throughout the central Andean region.

During the era of the Chavín cult, Andean society became increasingly complex. Weavers devised techniques of producing elaborate cotton textiles, some with intricate patterns and designs. Artisans manufactured large, light, and strong fishnets from cotton string. Craftsmen experimented with minerals and discovered techniques of gold, silver, and copper metallurgy. They mostly fashioned metals into pieces of jewelry or other decorative items but also made small tools out of copper.

Early Cities

There is no evidence to suggest that Chavín cultural and religious beliefs led to the establishment of a state or any organized political order. Indeed, they probably inspired the building of ceremonial centers rather than the making of true cities. As the population increased and society became more complex, however, cities began to appear shortly after the disappearance of the Chavín cult. Beginning about 200 B.C.E. large cities emerged at the modern-day sites of Huari, Pucara, and Tiahuanaco. Each of these early Andean cities had a population exceeding ten thousand, and each also featured large public buildings, ceremonial plazas, and extensive residential districts.

Early Andean States: Mochica

Along with cities there also appeared regional states. The earliest Andean states arose in the many valleys on the western side of the mountains. These states emerged when conquerors unified the individual valleys and organized them into integrated societies. They coordinated the building of irrigation systems so that the lower valleys could support intensive agriculture, and they established trade and exchange networks that tied the highlands, central valleys, and coastal regions together. Each region contributed its own products to the larger economy of the valley: from the highlands came potatoes, llama meat, and alpaca wool; the central valleys supplied maize, beans, and squashes; and the coasts provided sweet potatoes, fish, and cotton.

This organization of the Andean valleys into integrated economic zones did not come about by accident. Builders of early Andean states worked deliberately and did not hesitate to use force to consolidate their domains. Surviving stone fortifications and warriors depicted in works of art testify that the early Andean states relied heavily on arms to introduce order and maintain stability in their small realms.

The Mochica State

Because early Andean societies did not make use of writing, their beliefs, values, and ways of life remain largely hidden behind veils of time. One of the early Andean states, however, left a remarkable artistic legacy that allows a glimpse into the life of a society otherwise almost entirely lost. The Mochica state had its base in the valley of the Moche River, and it dominated the coasts and valleys of northern Peru during the period about 300 to 700 C.E. Mochica painting survives largely on pottery vessels, and it offers a detailed and expressive depiction of early Andean society in all its variety.

Many Mochica ceramics take the form of portraits of individuals' heads. Others represent the major gods and the various subordinate deities and demons. Some of the most interesting depict scenes in the everyday life of the Mochica people: aristocrats embarking on a hunting party, warriors leading captives bound by ropes, women working in a textile factory under the careful eye of a supervisor, rulers receiving messengers or ambassadors from neighboring states, and beggars looking for handouts on a busy

Many Mochica pots portray human figures and often depict distinctive characteristics of individuals or typical scenes from daily life. This pot represents two women helping a man who consumed a little too much maize beer.

street. Even in the absence of writing, Mochica artists left abundant evidence of a complex society with considerable specialization of labor.

Mochica was only one of several large states that dominated the central Andean region during the first millennium C.E. Although they integrated the regional economies of the various Andean valleys, none of these early states was able to impose order on the entire region or even to dominate a portion of it for very long. The exceedingly difficult geographical barriers posed by the Andes mountains presented challenges that ancient technology and social organization simply could not meet. As a result, at the end of the first millennium C.E., Andean society exhibited regional differences much sharper than those of Mesoamerica and early complex societies in the eastern hemisphere.

EARLY SOCIETIES OF OCEANIA

Human migrants entered Australia and New Guinea at least by 60,000 years before the present, and possibly earlier than that. They arrived in watercraft—probably canoes fitted with sails—but because of the low sea levels of that era, the migrants did not have to cross large stretches of open ocean. These earliest inhabitants of Oceania also migrated—perhaps over land when sea levels were still low—to the Bismarcks, Solomons, and other small island groups near New Guinea. Beginning about 5,000 years ago, seafaring peoples from southeast Asia visited the northern coast of New Guinea for purposes of trade. Some of them settled there, but many others ventured farther and established communities in the island groups of the western Pacific Ocean. During the centuries that followed, their descendants sailed large, oceangoing canoes throughout the Pacific basin, and by the middle centuries of the first millennium C.E., they had established human communities in all the habitable islands of the Pacific Ocean.

Early Societies in Australia and New Guinea

Human migrants reached Australia and New Guinea long before any people had begun to cultivate crops or keep herds of domesticated animals. Inevitably, then, the earliest inhabitants of Australia and New Guinea lived by hunting and gathering their food. For thousands of years, foraging peoples probably traveled back and forth between Australia and New Guinea. These migrations ceased about ten thousand years ago when rising seas separated the two lands. After that time human societies in Australia and New Guinea followed radically different paths. The aboriginal peoples of Australia maintained hunting and gathering societies until large numbers of European migrants established settler communities there in the nineteenth and twentieth centuries C.E. In New Guinea, however, human communities turned to agriculture: beginning about 3000 B.C.E. the cultivation of root crops like yams and taro and the keeping of pigs and chickens spread rapidly throughout the island.

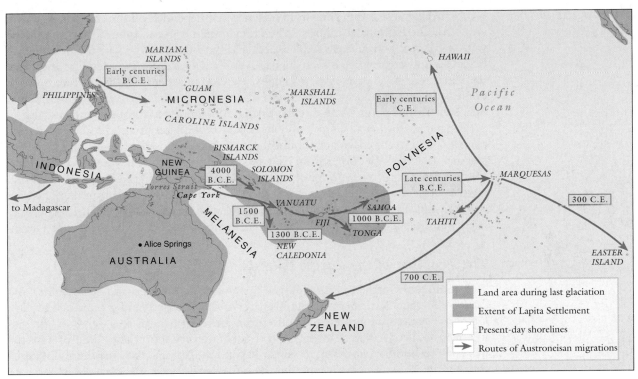

MAP [6.3]
Early societies of Oceania,
1500 B.C.E.–700 C.E.

Like hunting and gathering peoples elsewhere, the aboriginal Australians lived in small, mobile communities that undertook seasonal migrations in search of food. Over the centuries, they learned to exploit the resources of the various ecological regions of Australia. Plant foods, including fruits, berries, roots, nuts, seeds, shoots, and green leaves, constituted the bulk of their diet. In the tropical region of Cape York in northern Australia, they consumed no fewer than 141 different species of plants. Aboriginal peoples found abundant plant life even in the harsh desert regions of interior Australia. In the vicinity of modern Alice Springs in central Australia, for example, they included about twenty species of greens and forty-five kinds of seeds and nuts in their diet. They also used at least 124 plants as medicines, ointments, and drugs. To supplement their plant-based diet, they used axes, spears, clubs, nets, lassos, snares, and boomerangs to bring down animals ranging in size from rats to giant kangaroos, which grew to a height of 3 meters (almost 10 feet), and to catch fish, waterfowl, and small birds.

Early Hunting and Gathering Societies in Australia

The earliest inhabitants of New Guinea foraged for food, like their neighbors to the south. About five thousand years ago, however, a process of social and economic change began to unfold in New Guinea. The agents of change were seafaring peoples from southeast Asia speaking Austronesian languages, whose modern linguistic relatives include Malayan, Indonesian, Filipino, Polynesian, and other Oceanic languages as well as the Malagasy language of Madagascar and the tongues spoken by the indigenous peoples of Taiwan and southern China. Austronesian-speaking peoples possessed remarkable seafaring skills. They sailed the open ocean in large canoes equipped with outriggers, which stabilized their craft and reduced the risks of long voyages. By paying close attention to winds, currents, stars, cloud formations, and other natural indicators, they learned how to find distant lands reliably and return home safely. Beginning about 3000 B.C.E. these mariners visited the northern coast of New Guinea, where they traded with the indigenous peoples and established their own communities.

Austronesian Peoples

*Early Agriculture
in New Guinea*

Austronesian seafarers came from societies that depended on the cultivation of root crops and the herding of animals. When they settled in New Guinea, they introduced yams, taro, pigs, and chickens to the island, and the indigenous peoples themselves soon began to cultivate crops and keep animals. Within a few centuries agriculture and herding had spread to all parts of New Guinea. Here, as in other lands, agriculture brought population growth and specialization of labor: after the change to agriculture, permanent settlements, pottery, and carefully crafted tools appeared throughout the island.

Separated from New Guinea only by the narrow Torres Strait, the aboriginal peoples of northern Australia knew about the cultivation of foodstuffs, since they had occasional dealings with traders from New Guinea. Agriculture even spread to the islands of the Torres Strait, but it did not take root in Australia until the arrival of European peoples in the late eighteenth century C.E. Meanwhile, Austronesian-speaking peoples who introduced agriculture and herding to New Guinea sailed their outrigger canoes farther and established the first human settlements in the islands of the Pacific Ocean.

The Peopling of the Pacific Islands

The hunting and gathering peoples who first inhabited Australia and New Guinea also established a few settlements in the Bismarck and Solomon island groups east of New Guinea. They ventured to these islands during the era when the seas were low and sailing distances from New Guinea were consequently very short. They did not have the maritime technology, however, to sail far beyond the Solomons to the more distant islands in the Pacific Ocean. Even if they had, the small Pacific islands, with limited supplies of edible plants and animals, would not have supported communities of foragers.

*Austronesian
Migrations to
Polynesia*

Austronesian-speaking peoples possessed a sophisticated maritime technology as well as agricultural expertise, and they established human settlements in the islands of the Pacific Ocean. Their outrigger canoes enabled them to sail safely over long distances of open ocean, and their food crops and domesticated animals enabled them to establish agricultural societies in the islands. Once they had established

Austronesian mariners sailed double-hulled voyaging canoes much like this one from Ra'iatea in the Society Islands drawn in 1769 by an artist who accompanied Captain James Cook on his first voyage in the Pacific Ocean.

coastal settlements in New Guinea, Austronesian seafarers sailed easily to the Bismarck and Solomon islands, perhaps in the interests of trade. From there they undertook exploratory voyages that led them to previously unpopulated islands.

By about 1500 B.C.E. Austronesian mariners had arrived at Vanuatu (formerly called New Hebrides) and New Caledonia, by 1300 B.C.E. at Fiji, and by 1000 B.C.E. at Tonga and Samoa. During the late centuries of the first millennium B.C.E., they established settlements in Tahiti and the Marquesas. From there they launched ventures that took them to the most remote outposts of Polynesia—the territory falling in the triangle with Hawai`i, Easter Island, and New Zealand at the points—which required them to sail over thousands of nautical miles of blue water. They reached the islands of Hawai`i in the early centuries C.E., Easter Island by 300 C.E., and the large islands of New Zealand by 700 C.E.

While one branch of the Austronesian-speaking peoples populated the islands of Polynesia, other branches sailed in different directions. From the Philippines some ventured to the region of Micronesia, which includes small islands and atolls such as the Mariana, Caroline, and Marshall islands of the western Pacific. Yet others looked west from their homelands in Indonesia, sailed throughout the Indian Ocean, and became the first human settlers of the large island of Madagascar off the east African coast. Malagasy, the principal language of modern-day Madagascar, is clearly identifiable as an Austronesian tongue.

Austronesian Migrations to Micronesia and Madagascar

The earliest Austronesian migrants to sail out into the blue water of the Pacific Ocean and establish human settlements in Pacific islands are known as the Lapita peoples. No one knows what they called themselves: the name *Lapita* comes from a beach in New Caledonia where some of the earliest recognizable Lapita artifacts came to the attention of archaeologists. It is clear, however, that between about 1500 and 500 B.C.E., Lapita peoples maintained communication and exchange networks throughout a large region extending about 4,500 kilometers (2,800 miles) from New Guinea and the Bismarck Archipelago to Samoa and Tonga.

The Lapita Peoples

Wherever they settled, Lapita peoples established agricultural villages where they raised pigs and chickens and introduced the suite of crops they inherited from their Austronesian ancestors, including yams, taro, breadfruit, and bananas. They supplemented their crops and domesticated animals with fish and seaweed from nearby waters, and they soon killed off most of the large land animals and birds (some of which, in the absence of natural predators, had evolved into flightless species) that were suitable for human consumption. They left abundant evidence of their presence in the form of their distinctive pottery decorated with stamped geometric designs.

For about one thousand years, Lapita peoples maintained extensive networks of trade and communication across vast stretches of open ocean. Their agricultural settlements were largely self-sufficient, but they placed high value on some objects from distant islands. Their pottery was a principal item of long-distance exchange, as was high-quality obsidian, which they sometimes transported over thousands of kilometers, since it was available at only a few sites of Lapita settlement. Other trade items brought to light by archaeologists include

This reconstructed Lapita pot discovered in New Caledonia features the distinctive stamped design characteristic of all Lapita pottery.

Sources from the Past

The Voyage of Ru

Numerous chants and stories of Pacific islanders preserve the memory of ancient seafarers who built ocean-going canoes, equipped them with supplies, and sailed off in search of new lands. Many of the mariners mentioned in these stories set out from Havai`i (modern-day Ra`iatea near Tahiti). The stories mention several motives for the voyages: overpopulation, social tensions, and thirst for adventure. The following selection explains how the navigator Ru undertook a voyage from Havai`i to the previously uninhabited island of Aitutaki in the Southern Cook Islands.

Although not of royal blood, Ru was a man of good standing. He was a peace-loving man, but ambitious of becoming a leader, and [he] viewed with concern the quickly-increasing population of the island.

Moved by a quarrel over the headship of his clan, Ru began to make plans. He decided to build a large seaworthy canoe and call together his friends and relations, and try to persuade enough of them to join him in searching for an uninhabited island somewhere toward the setting sun, where he felt sure he would find land and become a great chief. [He persuaded his four younger brothers, his four wives, and twenty young women from the ruling family of Havai'i to accompany him] . . .

A search was then made for two large *tamanu* trees suitable for a canoe for the voyage. The making of this canoe was a lengthy process, for the trees had to be felled and hewn out with stone adzes. When finished to Ru's satisfaction, the two hulls were hauled down to the beach and lashed together. . . . Some further days were spent training for the coming voyage. The canoe and the mat-sails were tested, and much time was spent handling and paddling the canoe until the crew were proficient. For two days friends and relatives assisted in gathering enough food for the voyage. *Taro, puraka* [pig], *kuru* [breadfruit], and a large supply of water were put on board. All record of how the water was carried has been lost. Some say it was carried in coconuts.

The next morning, the wind being favorable, Ru decided to set sail. The whole island came to say farewell to the twenty-nine voyagers. The reef was cleared, the sails were hoisted, and the canoe was headed toward the west, Ru taking the steering oar, and his brother Veri-tuamaroa standing in the bows as pilot. Though conditions were favorable for the first two days, the women were sick as soon as the canoe was out of sight of the land. On the third day heavy clouds banked up, the wind, which had changed round, now blew strongly from the west, and the sea was so rough that the women and men had to take turns bailing the canoe; she was riding heavily owing to the hulls being new and deeply laden. [The voyaging party survived the storm] . . .

Favorable weather was met for the next two days and each night Ru checked his course by a star. On the third afternoon after the storm, Verituamaroa, who was still in the bows of the canoe, cried out that he could see land ahead. It was thought that he might have been deceived by a bank of clouds, but soon they could clearly see the break of waves on the reef. All now gazed eagerly at the new land. After a search a suitable passage was found [through the reef], the sails were taken down, and the women were ordered to paddle the canoe in. . . .

Finding the island uninhabited, Ru divided it among the twenty young women, as they were of royal blood and consequently had first claim to the land. Ru told them that they were as mats on the floor, as other canoes were bound to come sooner or later bringing men with them. On these mats the men would sleep, and from them this new land would be populated.

SOURCE: Drury Low. "The Story of Ru's Canoe and the Discovery and Settlement of Aitutaki." *Journal of the Polynesian Society* 43 (1934): 17–24.

What does Ru's story suggest about the nature of social and gender relations in early Pacific islands populations?

shell jewelry and stone tools. It is likely that Lapita peoples also traded feathers, foodstuffs, and spouses, although evidence for these exchanges does not survive in the archaeological record. In any case, it is clear that like their counterparts in other regions of the world, the earliest inhabitants of the Pacific islands maintained regular contacts with peoples well beyond their own societies.

Chiefly Political Organization

After about 500 B.C.E. Lapita trade networks fell into disuse, probably because the various Lapita settlements had grown large enough that they could supply their own needs and concentrate on the development of their own societies. By the middle part of the first millennium B.C.E., Lapita and other Austronesian peoples had established hierarchical chiefdoms in the Pacific islands. Leadership passed from a chief to his eldest son, and near relatives constituted a local aristocracy. Contests for power and influence between ambitious subordinates frequently caused tension and turmoil, but the possibility of migration offered an alternative to conflict. Dissatisfied or aggrieved parties often built voyaging canoes, recruited followers, and set sail with the intention of establishing new settlements in uninhabited or lightly populated islands. Indeed, the spread of Austronesian peoples throughout the Pacific islands came about partly because of population pressures and conflicts that encouraged small parties to seek fresh opportunities in more hospitable lands.

Over the longer term, descendants of Lapita peoples built strong, chiefly societies, particularly on large islands with relatively dense populations like those of the Tongan, Samoan, and Hawaiian groups. In Hawai`i, for example, militarily skilled chiefs cooperated closely with priests, administrators, soldiers, and servants in ruling their districts, which might include a portion of an island, an entire island, or even several islands. Chiefs and their retinues claimed a portion of the agricultural surplus produced by their subjects, and they sometimes required subjects to deliver additional products, such as fish, birds, or timber. Apart from organizing public life in their own districts, chiefs and their administrators vied with the ruling classes of neighboring districts, led public ritual observances, and oversaw irrigation systems that watered the taro plants that were crucial to the survival of Hawaiian society. Eventually, the chiefly and aristocratic classes became so entrenched and powerful that they regarded themselves as divine or semidivine, and the law of the land prohibited common subjects from even gazing directly at them.

Very little writing survives to illuminate the historical development of early societies in the Americas and Oceania. Thus it is impossible to offer the sort of richly detailed account of their political organization, social structures, and cultural traditions that historians commonly provide for societies of the eastern hemisphere. Nevertheless, it is clear that migrations to the Americas and Oceania represented continuations of population movements that began with *Homo erectus* and early *Homo sapiens,* resulting eventually in the establishment of human communities in almost all habitable parts of the earth. Moreover, it is clear also that the earliest inhabitants of the Americas and Oceania built productive and vibrant societies whose development roughly paralleled that of their counterparts in the eastern hemisphere. Many communities depended on an agricultural economy, and with their surplus production they supported dense populations, engaged in specialized labor, established formal political authorities, constructed hierarchical social orders, carried on long-distance trade, and formed distinctive cultural traditions. The early historical development of the Americas and Oceania demonstrates once again the tendency of agriculture to encourage human communities to construct ever more elaborate and complex forms of social organization.

CHRONOLOGY

	AMERICAS
13,000 B.C.E.	Human migration to North America from Siberia
8000–7000 B.C.E.	Origins of agriculture in Mesoamerica
4000 B.C.E.	Origins of maize cultivation in Mesoamerica
3000 B.C.E.	Origins of agriculture in South America
1200–100 B.C.E.	Olmec society
1000–300 B.C.E.	Chavín cult
200 B.C.E.–750 C.E.	Teotihuacan society
300–1100 C.E.	Maya society
300–700 C.E.	Mochica society
	OCEANIA
60,000 B.C.E.	Human migration to Australia and New Guinea
3000 B.C.E.	Origins of agriculture in New Guinea
3000 B.C.E.	Austronesian migrations to New Guinea
1500–500 B.C.E.	Lapita society
1500 B.C.E.–700 C.E.	Austronesian migrations to Pacific islands

FOR FURTHER READING

Robert McC. Adams. *The Evolution of Urban Society.* Chicago, 1966. Provocative analysis comparing the development of Mesopotamian and Mesoamerican societies by a leading archaeologist.

Peter Bellwood. *The Polynesians: Prehistory of an Island People.* Rev. ed. London, 1987. Well-illustrated popular account em-

phasizing the origins and early development of Polynesian societies.

Ignacio Bernal. *Mexico before Cortez: Art, History, and Legend.* Trans. by W. Barnstone. Garden City, 1963. Judicious survey by a leading student of ancient Mesoamerica.

————. *The Olmec World*. Trans. by D. Heyden and F. Horcasitas. Berkeley, 1969. The best general study of the Olmecs.

Geoffrey Blainey. *Triumph of the Nomads: A History of Aboriginal Australia*. Melbourne, 1975. A sympathetic account of Australia before European arrival, well informed by archaeological discoveries.

Michael D. Coe. *The Maya*. 4th ed. London, 1987. Well-illustrated popular account by one of the world's leading scholars of the Maya.

Nigel Davies. *The Ancient Kingdoms of Mexico*. Harmondsworth, 1983. Popular account that reflects archaeological discoveries.

David Freidel, Linda Schele, and Joy Parker. *Maya Cosmos: Three Thousand Years on the Shaman's Path*. New York, 1993. Fascinating investigation of Maya conceptions of the world and their continuing influence in the present day.

K. R. Howe. *The Quest for Origins: Who First Discovered and Settled the Pacific Islands?* Honolulu, 2003. Reviews the numerous theories advanced to explain the arrival of human populations and the establishment of human societies in the remote islands of the Pacific Ocean.

Jesse D. Jennings, ed. *The Prehistory of Polynesia*. Cambridge, Mass., 1979. Brings together essays by prominent scholars on Polynesia before the arrival of Europeans in the Pacific Ocean.

Friedrich Katz. *The Ancient American Civilizations*. Trans. by K. M. L. Simpson. New York, 1972. Detailed survey that compares the experiences of Mesoamerica and Andean South America.

Patrick V. Kirch. *The Lapita Peoples: Ancestors of the Oceanic World*. Cambridge, Mass., 1997. Thorough discussion of Lapita society based on the author's own studies and other recent scholarship.

————. *On the Road of the Winds: An Archaeological History of the Pacific Islands before European Contact*. Berkeley, 2000. A valuable synthesis of recent scholarship by the foremost contemporary archaeologist of the Pacific islands.

Edward P. Lanning. *Peru before the Incas*. Englewood Cliffs, 1967. Summarizes the results of archaeological research that has transformed scholars' understanding of ancient Andean societies.

David Lewis. *We, the Navigators: The Ancient Art of Landfinding in the Pacific*. Honolulu, 1973. Fascinating reconstruction of traditional methods of noninstrumental navigation used by seafaring peoples of the Pacific islands.

Linda Schele and David Freidel. *A Forest of Kings: The Untold Story of the Ancient Maya*. New York, 1990. Draws heavily on deciphered inscriptions in reconstructing the history of the ancient Maya.

Linda Schele and Mary Ellen Miller. *The Blood of Kings: Dynasty and Ritual in Maya Art*. New York, 1986. A richly illustrated volume that explores Maya society through works of art and architecture as well as writing.

Dennis Tedlock, trans. *Popol Vuh: The Definitive Edition of the Mayan Book of the Dawn of Life and the Glories of Gods and Kings*. New York, 1985. The best translation of the *Popol Vuh*, with an excellent introduction.

Muriel Porter Weaver. *The Aztecs, Maya, and Their Predecessors: Archaeology of Mesoamerica*. 3rd ed. San Diego, 1993. An up-to-date survey based on recent historical and archaeological research.

See our **Online Learning Center** at www.mhhe.com/bentley3 for additional readings, practice maps, quizzes, and internet activities.

Unfamiliar words? Check out the **Primary Source Investigator CD-ROM** for an interactive glossary, interactive maps, more images, and primary sources.

PART II

THE FORMATION OF CLASSICAL SOCIETIES, 500 B.C.E. TO 500 C.E.

Shortly after *Homo sapiens sapiens* turned to agriculture, human communities began to experiment with methods of social organization. In several cases the experimentation encouraged the development of complex societies that integrated the lives and livelihoods of peoples over large regions. These early complex societies launched human history on a trajectory that it continues to follow today. States, social classes, technological innovation, specialization of labor, trade, and sophisticated cultural traditions rank among the most important legacies of these societies.

Toward the end of the first millennium B.C.E., several early societies achieved particularly high degrees of internal organization, extended their authority over extremely large regions, and elaborated especially influential cultural traditions. The most prominent of these societies developed in Persia, China, India, and the Mediterranean basin. Because their legacies have endured so long and have influenced the ways that literally billions of people have led their lives, historians often refer to them as classical societies.

The classical societies of Persia, China, India, and the Mediterranean basin differed from one another in many ways. They raised different food crops, constructed buildings out of different materials, lived by different legal and moral codes, and recognized different gods. Classical China and India depended on the cultivation of rice, millet, and wheat, while in Persia and the Mediterranean wheat was the staple food crop. In China, packed earth and wood served as the principal construction material even for large public buildings; in India, wood was the most common building material; and in Persia and the Mediterranean, architects designed buildings of brick and stone. The classical societies differed even more strikingly when it came to beliefs and values. They generated a wide variety of ideas about the organization of family and society, the understanding of what constituted proper public and private behavior, the nature of the gods or other powers thought to influence human affairs, and proper relationships among human beings, the natural world, and the gods.

Despite these differences, these societies faced several common problems. They all confronted the challenge, for example, of administering vast territories without advanced technologies of transportation and communication. Rulers built centralized imperial states on a scale much larger than their predecessors in earlier societies. They constructed elaborate systems of bureaucracy and experimented with administrative organization in an effort to secure influence for central governments and extend imperial authority to the far reaches of their realms. To encourage political and economic integration of their lands, classical rulers built roads and supported networks of trade and communication that linked the sometimes far-flung regions under their authority.

The classical societies all faced military challenges, and they raised powerful armies for both defensive and offensive purposes. Military challenges frequently arose from within classical societies themselves in the form of rebellion, civil war, or conflict between powerful factions. External threats came from nomadic and migratory peoples who sought to share in the wealth generated by the productive agricultural economies of classical societies. Sometimes mounted nomadic warriors charged into settlements, seized what they wished, and departed before the victims could mount a defense. In other cases, migratory peoples moved into classical societies in such large numbers that they disrupted the established political and social order. In hopes of securing their borders and enhancing the welfare of their lands, rulers of most classical societies launched campaigns of expansion that ultimately produced massive imperial states.

The bureaucracies and armies that enabled classical societies to address some problems effectively created difficulties as well. One pressing problem revolved around the maintenance of the bureaucracies and armies. To finance administrative and military machinery, rulers of the classical societies all claimed some portion of the agricultural and industrial surplus of their lands in the form of taxes or tribute. Most of them also required their subjects to provide compulsory, uncompensated labor services for large-scale public projects involving the building and maintenance of structures such as defensive walls, highways, bridges, and irrigation systems.

The classical societies also faced the challenge of trying to maintain an equitable distribution of land and wealth. As some individuals flourished and accumulated land and wealth, they enjoyed economic advantages over their neighbors. Increasingly sharp economic distinctions gave rise to tensions that fueled bitter class conflict. In some cases, conflicts escalated into rebellions and civil wars that threatened the very survival of the classical societies.

All the classical societies engaged in long-distance trade. This trade encouraged economic integration within the societies, since their various regions came to depend on one another for agricultural products and manufactured items. Long-distance trade led also to the establishment of regular commerce between peoples of different societies and cultural regions. The volume of trade increased dramatically when classical empires pacified large stretches of the Eurasian landmass. Long-distance trade became common enough that a well-established network of land and sea routes, known collectively as the silk roads, linked lands as distant as China and Europe.

Finally, all the classical societies generated sophisticated cultural and religious traditions. Different societies held widely varying beliefs and values, but their cultural and religious traditions offered guidance on moral, religious, political, and social issues. These traditions often served as foundations for educational systems that prepared individuals for careers in government. As a result, they shaped the values of people who made law and implemented policy. Several cultural and religious traditions also attracted large popular followings and created institutional structures that enabled them to survive over a long term and extend their influence through time.

Over the centuries, specific political, social, economic, and cultural features of the classical societies have disappeared. Yet their legacies deeply influenced future societies and in many ways continue to influence the lives of the world's peoples. Appreciation of the legacies of classical societies in Persia, China, India, and the Mediterranean basin is crucial for the effort to understand the world's historical development.

Gold plaque depicting a figure who was perhaps a priest in Achaemenid times.

CHAPTER 7

THE EMPIRES OF PERSIA

T he Greek historian Herodotus relished a good story, and he related many a tale about the Persian empire and its conflicts with other peoples, including Greeks. One story had to do with a struggle between Cyrus, leader of the expanding Persian realm, and Croesus, ruler of the powerful and wealthy kingdom of Lydia in southwestern Anatolia. Croesus noted the growth of Persian influence with concern and asked the Greek oracle at Delphi whether to go to war against Cyrus. The oracle responded that an attack on Cyrus would destroy a great kingdom.

Overjoyed, Croesus lined up his allies and prepared for war. In 546 B.C.E. he launched an invasion and seized a small town, provoking Cyrus to engage the formidable Lydian cavalry. The resulting battle was hard fought but inconclusive. Because winter was approaching, Croesus disbanded his troops and returned to his capital at Sardis, expecting Cyrus to retreat as well. But Cyrus was a vigorous and unpredictable warrior, and he pursued Croesus to Sardis. When he learned of the pursuit, Croesus hastily assembled an army to confront the invaders. Cyrus threw it into disarray, however, by advancing a group of warriors mounted on camels, which spooked the Lydian horses and sent them into headlong flight. Cyrus's army then surrounded Sardis and took the city after a siege of only two weeks. Croesus narrowly escaped death in the battle, but he was taken captive and afterward became an advisor to Cyrus. Herodotus could not resist pointing out that events proved the Delphic oracle right: Croesus's attack on Cyrus did indeed lead to the destruction of a great kingdom—his own.

The victory over Lydia was a major turning point in the development of the Persian empire. Lydia had a reputation as a kingdom of fabulous wealth, partly because it was the first land to use standardized coins with values guaranteed by the state. Taking advantage of its coins and its geographic location on the Mediterranean, Lydia conducted maritime trade with Greece, Egypt, and Phoenicia as well as overland trade with Mesopotamia and Persia. Lydian wealth and resources gave Cyrus tremendous momentum as he extended Persian authority to new lands and built the earliest of the vast imperial states of classical times.

Classical Persian society began to take shape during the sixth century B.C.E. when warriors conquered the region from the Indus River to Egypt and southeastern Europe. Their conquests yielded an enormous realm much larger than the earlier Babylonian or Assyrian empires. The very size of the Persian empire created political and administrative problems for its rulers. Once they solved those problems, however, a series of Persian-based empires governed much of the territory between India and the

Mediterranean Sea for more than a millennium—from the mid-sixth century B.C.E. until the early seventh century C.E.—and brought centralized political organization to many distinct peoples living over vast geographic spaces.

In organizing their realm, Persian rulers relied heavily on Mesopotamian techniques of administration, which they adapted to their own needs. Yet they did not hesitate to create new institutions or adopt new administrative procedures. In the interest of improved communications and military mobility, they also invested resources in the construction of roads and highways linking the regions of the empire. As a result of these efforts, central administrators were able to send instructions throughout the empire, dispatch armies in times of turmoil, and ensure that local officials would carry out imperial policies.

The organization of the vast territories embraced by the classical Persian empires had important social, economic, and cultural implications. High agricultural productivity enabled many people to work at tasks other than cultivation: classes of bureaucrats, administrators, priests, craftsmen, and merchants increased in number as the production and distribution of food became more efficient. Meanwhile, social extremes became more pronounced: a few individuals and families amassed enormous wealth, many led simple lives, and some fell into slavery. Good roads fostered trade within imperial borders, and Persian society itself served as a commercial and cultural bridge between Indian and Mediterranean societies. As a crossroads, Persia served not only as a link in long-distance trade networks but also as a conduit for the exchange of philosophical and religious ideas. Persian religious traditions did not attract many adherents beyond the imperial boundaries, but they inspired religious thinkers subject to Persian rule and deeply influenced Judaism, Christianity, and Islam.

THE RISE AND FALL OF THE PERSIAN EMPIRES

The empires of Persia arose in the arid land of Iran. For centuries Iran had developed under the shadow of the wealthier and more productive Mesopotamia to the west while absorbing intermittent migrations and invasions of nomadic peoples coming out of central Asia to the northeast. During the sixth century B.C.E., rulers of the province of Persia in southwestern Iran embarked on a series of conquests that resulted in the formation of an enormous empire. For more than a millennium, four ruling dynasties—the Achaemenids (558–330 B.C.E.), Seleucids (323–83 B.C.E.), Parthians (247 B.C.E.–224 C.E.), and Sasanids (224–651 C.E.)—maintained a continuous tradition of imperial rule in much of southwest Asia.

The Achaemenid Empire

The Medes and the Persians

The origins of classical Persian society trace back to the late stages of Mesopotamian society. During the centuries before 1000 B.C.E., two closely related peoples known as the Medes and the Persians migrated from central Asia to Persia (the southwestern portion of the modern-day state of Iran), where they lived in loose subjection to the Babylonian and Assyrian empires. The Medes and Persians spoke Indo-European languages, and their movements were part of the larger Indo-European migrations. They shared many cultural traits with their distant cousins, the Aryans, who migrated into India. They were mostly pastoralists, although they also practiced a limited amount of agriculture. They organized themselves by clans rather than by states or formal political institutions, but they recognized leaders who collected taxes and delivered tribute to their Mesopotamian overlords.

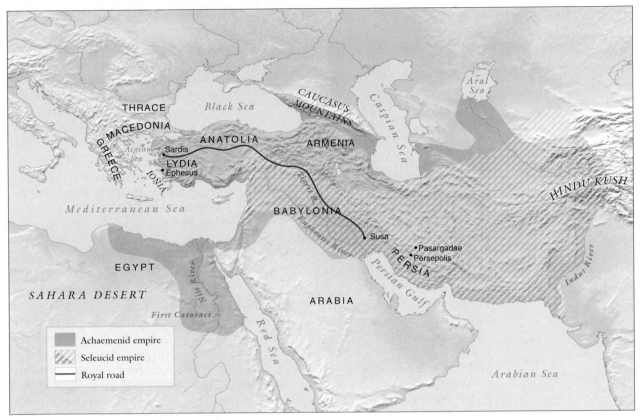

MAP [7.1]
The Achaemenid and Seleucid empires, 558–83 B.C.E.

For an interactive version of this map, go to www.mhhe.com/ bentley3ch7maps.

Though not tightly organized politically, the Medes and Persians were peoples of considerable military power. As descendants of nomadic peoples from central Asia, they possessed the equestrian skills common to many steppe peoples. They were expert archers, even when mounted on their horses, and they frequently raided the wealthy lands of Mesopotamia. When the Assyrian and Babylonian empires weakened in the sixth century B.C.E., the Medes and Persians embarked on a vastly successful imperial venture of their own.

Cyrus

Cyrus the Achaemenid (reigned 558–530 B.C.E.) launched the Persians' imperial venture. In some ways Cyrus was an unlikely candidate for this role. He came from a mountainous region of southwestern Iran, and in reference to the region's economy, his contemporaries often called him Cyrus the Shepherd. Yet Cyrus proved to be a tough, wily leader and an outstanding military strategist. His conquests laid the foundation of the first Persian empire, also known as the Achaemenid empire because its rulers claimed descent from Cyrus's Achaemenid clan.

Cyrus's Conquests

In 558 B.C.E. Cyrus became king of the Persian tribes, which he ruled from his mountain fortress at Pasargadae. In 553 B.C.E. he initiated a rebellion against his Median overlord, whom he crushed within three years. By 548 B.C.E. he had brought all of Iran under his control, and he began to look for opportunities to expand his influence. In 546 B.C.E. he conquered the powerful kingdom of Lydia in Anatolia (modern-day Turkey). Between 545 B.C.E. and 539 B.C.E. he campaigned in central Asia and Bactria (modern Afghanistan). In a swift campaign of 539 B.C.E., he seized Babylonia, whose vassal states immediately recognized him as their lord. Within twenty years Cyrus went from minor regional king to ruler of an empire that

The tomb of Cyrus at Pasargadae—one of very few Achaemenid monuments that have survived to the present.

Darius

stretched from India to the borders of Egypt.

Cyrus no doubt would have mounted a campaign against Egypt, the largest and wealthiest neighboring state outside his control, had he lived long enough. But in 530 B.C.E. he fell, mortally wounded, while protecting his northeastern frontier from nomadic raiders. His troops recovered his body and placed it in a simple tomb, which still stands, that Cyrus had prepared for himself at his palace in Pasargadae.

Cyrus's empire survived and expanded during the reigns of his successors. His son Cambyses (reigned 530–522 B.C.E.) conquered Egypt in 525 B.C.E. and brought its wealth into Persian hands. The greatest of the Achaemenid emperors, Darius (reigned 521–486 B.C.E.), a younger kinsman of Cyrus, extended the empire both east and west. His armies pushed into northwestern India as far as the Indus River, absorbing the northern Indian kingdom of Gandhara, while also capturing Thrace, Macedonia, and the western coast of the Black Sea in southeastern Europe. By the late sixth century, Darius presided over an empire stretching some 3,000 kilometers (1,865 miles) from the Indus River in the east to the Aegean Sea in the west and 1,500 kilometers (933 miles) from Armenia in the north to the first cataract of the Nile River in the south. This empire embraced mountains, valleys, plateaus, jungles, deserts, and arable land, and it touched the shores of the Arabian Sea, Aral Sea, Persian Gulf, Caspian Sea, Black Sea, Red Sea, and Mediterranean Sea. With a population of some thirty-five million, Darius's realm was by far the largest empire the world had yet seen.

Yet Darius was more important as an administrator than as a conqueror. Governing a far-flung empire was a much more difficult challenge than conquering it. The Achaemenid rulers presided over more than seventy distinct ethnic groups, including peoples who lived in widely scattered regions, spoke many different languages, and observed a profusion of religious and cultural traditions. To maintain their empire, the Achaemenids needed to establish lines of communication with all parts of their realm and design institutions that would enable them to tax and administer their territories. In doing so, they not only made it possible for the Achaemenid empire to survive but also pioneered administrative techniques that would outlast their own dynasty and influence political life in southwestern Asia for centuries to come.

Persepolis

Soon after his rise to power, Darius began to centralize his administration. About 520 B.C.E. he started to build a new capital of astonishing magnificence at Persepolis, near Pasargadae. Darius intended Persepolis to serve not only as an administrative center but also as a monument to the Achaemenid dynasty. Structures at Persepolis included vast reception halls, lavish royal residences, and a well-protected treasury. From the time of Darius to the end of the Achaemenid dynasty in 330 B.C.E., Persepolis served as the nerve center of the Persian empire—a resplendent capital bustling with advisors, ministers, diplomats, scribes, accountants, translators, and bureaucratic officers of all descriptions. Even today, massive columns and other ruins bespeak the grandeur of Darius's capital.

Ruins of Persepolis, showing the imperial reception hall and palaces.

The government of the Achaemenid empire depended on a finely tuned balance between central initiative and local administration. The Achaemenid rulers made great claims to authority in their official title—"The Great King, King of Kings, King in Persia, King of Countries." Like their Mesopotamian predecessors, the Achaemenids appointed governors to serve as agents of the central administration and oversee affairs in the various regions. Darius divided his realm into twenty-three satrapies—administrative and taxation districts governed by satraps. Yet the Achaemenids did not try to push direct rule on their subjects: most of the satraps were Persians, but the Achaemenids recruited local officials to fill almost all administrative posts below the level of the satrap.

Achaemenid Administration: The Satrapies

Because the satraps often held posts distant from Persepolis, there was always a possibility that they might ally with local groups and become independent of Achaemenid authority, or even threaten the empire itself. The Achaemenid rulers relied on two measures to discourage this possibility. First, each satrapy had a contingent of military officers and tax collectors who served as checks on the satraps' power and independence. Second, the rulers created a new category of officials—essentially imperial spies—known as "the eyes and ears of the king." These agents traveled throughout the empire with their own military forces conducting surprise audits of accounts and procedures in the provinces and collecting intelligence reports. The division of provincial responsibilities and the institution of the eyes and ears of the king helped the Achaemenid rulers maintain control over a vast empire that otherwise might easily have split into a series of independent regional kingdoms.

Darius also sought to improve administrative efficiency by regularizing tax levies and standardizing laws. Cyrus and Cambyses had accepted periodic "gifts" of tribute from subject lands and cities. Though often lavish, the gifts did not provide a consistent and reliable source of income for rulers who needed to finance a large bureaucracy and army. Darius replaced irregular tribute payments with formal tax levies. He

Taxes, Coins, and Laws

required each satrapy to pay a set quantity of silver—and in some cases a levy of horses or slaves as well—deliverable annually to the imperial court. To expedite the payment of taxes, Darius followed the example of the Lydian rulers and issued standardized coins—a move that also fostered trade throughout his empire. In an equally important initiative begun in the year 520 B.C.E., he sought to bring the many legal systems of his empire closer to a single standard. He did not abolish the existing laws of individual lands or peoples, nor did he impose a uniform law code on his entire empire. But he directed legal experts to study and codify the laws of his subject peoples, modifying them when necessary to harmonize them with the legal principles observed in the empire as a whole.

Roads and Communications

Alongside their administrative and legal policies, the Achaemenid rulers took other measures to knit their far-flung realm into a coherent whole. They built good roads across their realm, notably the so-called Persian Royal Road—parts of it paved with stone—that stretched some 2,575 kilometers (1,600 miles) from the Aegean port of Ephesus to Sardis in Anatolia, through Mesopotamia along the Tigris River, to Susa in Iran, with an extension to Pasargadae and Persepolis. Caravans took some ninety days to travel this road, lodging at inns along the well-policed route.

The imperial government also organized a courier service and built 111 postal stations at intervals of 40 to 50 kilometers (25 to 30 miles) along the Royal Road. Each station kept a supply of fresh horses, enabling couriers to speed from one end of the Royal Road to the other in a week's time. The Greek historian Herodotus spoke highly of these imperial servants, and even today the United States Postal Service takes his description of their efforts as a standard for its own employees: "Neither snow nor rain nor heat nor gloom of night stays these couriers from the swift completion of their appointed rounds." The Achaemenids also improved existing routes between Mesopotamia and Egypt, and they built a new road between Persia and the Indus River to link the imperial center with the satrapy of Gandhara in northwestern India. In addition to improving communications, these roads facilitated trade, which helped to integrate the empire's various regions into a larger economy.

Decline and Fall of the Achaemenid Empire

The Achaemenid Commonwealth

The Achaemenids' roads and administrative machinery enabled them to govern a vast empire and extend Persian influences throughout their territories. Persian concepts of law and justice administered by trained imperial officials linked peoples from the Mediterranean Sea to the Indus River in a larger Persian society. Political stability made it possible to undertake massive public works projects such as the construction of *qanat* (underground canals), which led to enhanced agricultural production and population growth. Iron metallurgy spread to all parts of the empire, and by the end of the Achaemenid dynasty, iron tools were common in Persian agricultural communities. Peoples in the various regions of the Achaemenid empire maintained their ethnic identities, but all participated in a larger Persian commonwealth.

Eventually, however, difficulties between rulers and subject peoples undermined the integrity of the Achaemenid empire. Cyrus and Darius both consciously pursued a policy of toleration in administering their vast multicultural empire: they took great care to respect the values and cultural traditions of the peoples they ruled. In Mesopotamia, for example, they did not portray themselves as Persian conquerors but, rather, as legitimate Babylonian rulers and representatives of Marduk, the patron deity of Babylon. Darius also won high praise from Jews in the Achaemenid empire, since he allowed them to return to Jerusalem and rebuild the temple that Babylonian conquerors had destroyed in 587 B.C.E.

Carving from Persepolis showing an enthroned Darius (with his son Xerxes standing behind him) receiving a high court official, as incense burners perfume the air.

Darius's successor, Xerxes (reigned 486–465 B.C.E.), retreated from this policy of toleration, however, flaunted his Persian identity, and sought to impose his own values on conquered lands. This policy caused enormous ill will, especially in Mesopotamia and Egypt where peoples with their own cultural traditions resented Xerxes' pretensions. Xerxes successfully repressed rebellions against his rule in Mesopotamia and Egypt. Yet resentment of Persian conquerors continued to fester, and it caused serious problems for the later Achaemenids as they tried to hold their empire together.

The Persian Wars

The Achaemenids had an especially difficult time with their ethnic Greek subjects, and efforts to control the Greeks helped to bring about the collapse of the Achaemenid empire. Ethnic Greeks inhabited many of the cities in Anatolia—particularly in the region of Ionia on the Aegean coast of western Anatolia—and they maintained close economic and commercial ties with their cousins in the peninsula of Greece itself. The Ionian Greeks fell under Persian domination during the reign of Cyrus. They became restive under Darius's Persian governors—"tyrants," the Greeks called them—who oversaw their affairs. In 500 B.C.E. the Ionian cities rebelled, expelled or executed their governors, and asserted their independence. Their rebellion launched a series of conflicts known as the Persian Wars (500–479 B.C.E.).

The conflict between the Ionian Greeks and the Persians expanded considerably when the cities of peninsular Greece sent fleets to aid their kinsmen in Ionia. Darius managed to put down the rebellion and reassert Achaemenid authority, but he and his successors became entangled in a difficult and ultimately destructive effort to extend their authority to the Greek peninsula. In 490 B.C.E. Darius attempted to forestall future problems by mounting an expedition to conquer the wealthy Greek cities and absorb them into his empire. Though larger and much more powerful than the forces of the disunited Greek city-states, the Persian army had to contend with long and fragile lines of supply as well as a hostile environment. After some initial successes the Persians suffered a rout at the battle of Marathon (490 B.C.E.), and they returned home without achieving their goals. Xerxes sent another expedition ten years later, but within eighteen months, it too had suffered defeat both on land and at sea and had returned to Persia.

For almost 150 years the Persian empire continued to spar intermittently with the Greek cities. The adversaries mounted small expeditions against each other, attacking individual cities or fleets, but they did not engage in large-scale campaigns. The Greek cities were too small and disunited to pose a serious challenge to the enormous Persian empire. Meanwhile, for their part, the later Achaemenids had to concentrate on the other restive and sometimes rebellious regions of their own empire and could not embark on new rounds of expansion.

Alexander of Macedon

The standoff ended with the rise of Alexander of Macedon, often called Alexander the Great (discussed more fully in chapter 10). In 334 B.C.E. Alexander invaded Persia with an army of some forty-eight thousand tough, battle-hardened Macedonians. Though far smaller than the Persian army in numbers, the well-disciplined Macedonians carried heavier arms and employed more sophisticated military tactics than their opponents. As a result, they sliced through the Persian empire, advancing almost at will and dealing their adversaries a series of devastating defeats. In 331 B.C.E. Alexander shattered Achaemenid forces at the battle of Gaugamela, and within a year the empire founded by Cyrus the Shepherd had dissolved.

Alexander led his forces into Persepolis, confiscated the wealth stored in the imperial treasury there, paid his respects at the tomb of Cyrus in Pasargadae, and proclaimed himself heir to the Achaemenid rulers. After a brief season of celebration, Alexander and his forces ignited a blaze—perhaps intentionally—that destroyed Persepolis. The conflagration was so great that when archaeologists first began to explore the ruins of Persepolis in the eighteenth century, they found layers of ash and charcoal up to 1 meter (3 feet) deep.

A coin issued by Alexander with an image of the conqueror.

The Achaemenid empire had crumbled, but its legacy was by no means exhausted. Alexander portrayed himself in Persia and Egypt as a legitimate successor of the Achaemenids who observed their precedents and deserved their honors. He retained the Achaemenid administrative structure, and he even confirmed the appointments of many satraps and other officials. As it happened, Alexander had little time to enjoy his conquests, because he died in 323 B.C.E. after a brief effort to extend his empire to India. But the states that succeeded him—the Seleucid, Parthian, and Sasanid empires—continued to employ a basically Achaemenid structure of imperial administration.

The Seleucid, Parthian, and Sasanid Empires

The Seleucids

After Alexander died, his chief generals carved his empire into three large realms, which they divided among themselves. The choicest realm, which included most of the former Achaemenid empire, went to Seleucus (reigned 305–281 B.C.E.), formerly commander of an elite corps of guards in Alexander's army. Like Alexander, Seleucus and his successors retained the Achaemenid systems of administration and taxation as well as the imperial roads and postal service. The Seleucids also founded new cities throughout the realm and attracted Greek colonists to occupy them. The migrants, who represented only a fraction of the whole population of the empire, largely adapted to their new environment. Nonetheless, the establishment of cities greatly stimulated trade and economic development both within the Seleucid empire and beyond.

As foreigners, the Seleucids faced opposition from native Persians and especially their ruling classes. Satraps often revolted against Seleucid rule, or at least worked to build power bases that would enable them to establish their independence. The Seleucids soon lost their holdings in northern India, and the seminomadic Parthians progressively took over Iran during the third century B.C.E. The Seleucids continued to rule a truncated empire until 83 B.C.E., when Roman conquerors put an end to their empire.

The Parthians

Meanwhile, the Parthians established themselves as lords of a powerful empire based in Iran that they extended to wealthy Mesopotamia. The Parthians had occupied the region of eastern Iran around Khurasan since Achaemenid times. They retained many of the customs and traditions of nomadic peoples from the steppes of central Asia. They did not have a centralized government, for example, but organized themselves politically through a federation of leaders who met in councils and jointly determined policy for all allied groups. They were skillful warriors, accustomed to defending themselves against constant threats from nomadic peoples farther east.

Gold sculpture of a nomadic horseman discharging an arrow. This figurine dates from the fifth or fourth century B.C.E. and might well represent a Parthian.

As they settled and turned increasingly to agriculture, the Parthians also devised an effective means to resist nomadic invasions. Because they had no access to feed grains, nomadic peoples allowed their horses to forage for food on the steppes during the winter. The Parthians discovered that if they fed their horses on alfalfa during the winter, their animals would grow much larger and stronger than the small horses and ponies of the steppes. Their larger animals could then support heavily armed warriors outfitted with metal armor, which served as an effective shield against the arrows of the steppe nomads. Well-trained forces of heavily armed cavalry could usually put nomadic raiding parties to flight. Indeed, few existing forces could stand up to Parthian heavy cavalry.

As early as the third century B.C.E., the Parthians began to wrest their independence from the Seleucids. The Parthian satrap revolted against his Seleucid overlord in 238 B.C.E., and during the following decades his successors gradually enlarged their holdings. Mithradates I, the Parthians' greatest conqueror, came to the throne about 171 B.C.E. and transformed his state into a mighty empire. By about 155 B.C.E. he had consolidated his hold on Iran and had also extended Parthian rule to Mesopotamia.

Parthian Conquests

The Parthians portrayed themselves as enemies of the foreign Seleucids, as restorers of rule in the Persian tradition. To some extent this characterization was accurate. The Parthians largely followed the example of the Achaemenids in structuring their empire: they governed through satraps, employed Achaemenid techniques of administration and taxation, and built a capital city at Ctesiphon on the Euphrates River near modern Baghdad. But the Parthians also retained elements of their own steppe traditions. They did not develop nearly so centralized a regime as the Achaemenids or Seleucids but, rather, vested a great deal of authority and responsibility in their clan leaders. These men often served as satraps, and they regularly worked to build independent bases of power in their regions. They frequently mounted rebellions against the imperial government, though without much success.

Parthian Government

For about three centuries the Parthians presided over a powerful empire between India and the Mediterranean. Beginning in the first century C.E., they faced pressure in the west from the expanding Roman empire. The Parthian empire as a whole never stood in danger of falling to the Romans, but on three occasions in the second century C.E. Roman armies captured the Parthian capital at Ctesiphon. Combined with internal difficulties caused by the rebellious satraps, Roman pressure contributed to the weakening of the Parthian state. During the early third century C.E., internal rebellion brought it down.

The Sasanids

Once again, though, the tradition of imperial rule continued, this time under the Sasanids, who came from Persia and claimed direct descent from the Achaemenids. The Sasanids toppled the Parthians in 224 C.E. and ruled until the year 651, recreating much of the splendor of the Achaemenid empire. From their cosmopolitan capital at Ctesiphon, the Sasanid "king of kings" provided strong rule from Parthia to Mesopotamia while also rebuilding an elaborate system of administration and founding or refurbishing numerous cities. Sasanid merchants traded actively with peoples to both east and west, and they introduced into Iran the cultivation of crops like rice, sugarcane, citrus fruits, eggplant, and cotton that came west over the trade routes from India and China.

During the reign of Shapur I (239–272 C.E.), the Sasanids stabilized their western frontier and created a series of buffer states between themselves and the Roman empire. Shapur even defeated several Roman armies and settled the prisoners in Iran, where they devoted their famous engineering skills to the construction of roads and dams. After Shapur, the Sasanids did not expand militarily, but entered into a standoff relationship with the Kushan empire in the east and the Roman and Byzantine empires in the west. None of these large empires was strong enough to overcome the others, but they contested border areas and buffer states, sometimes engaging in lengthy and bitter disputes that sapped the energies of all involved.

These continual conflicts seriously weakened the Sasanid empire in particular. The empire came to an end in 651 C.E. when Arab warriors killed the last Sasanid ruler, overran his realm, and incorporated it into their rapidly expanding Islamic empire. Yet even conquest by external invaders did not end the legacy of classical Persia, since Persian administrative techniques and cultural traditions were so powerful that the Arab conquerors adopted them for their own use in building a new Islamic society.

IMPERIAL SOCIETY AND ECONOMY

Throughout the eastern hemisphere during the classical era, public life and social structure became much more complicated than they had been during the days of the early complex societies. Centralized imperial governments needed large numbers of administrative officials, which led to the emergence of educated classes of bureaucrats. Stable empires enabled many individuals to engage in trade or other specialized labor as artisans, craftsmen, or professionals of various kinds. Some of them accumulated vast wealth, which led to increased distance and tensions between rich and poor. Meanwhile, slavery became more common than in earlier times. The prominence of slavery had to do partly with the expansion of imperial states, which often enslaved conquered foes, but it also reflected the increasing gulf between rich and poor, which placed such great economic pressure on some individuals that they had to give up their freedom in order to survive. All these developments had implications for the social structures of classical societies in Persia as well as China, India, and the Mediterranean basin.

Social Development in Classical Persia

During the early days of the Achaemenid empire, Persian society reflected its origins on the steppes of central Asia. When the Medes and Persians migrated to Iran, their social structure was very similar to that of the Aryans in India, consisting primarily of warriors, priests, and peasants. For centuries, when they lived on the periphery and in the shadow of the Mesopotamian empires, the Medes and Persians maintained

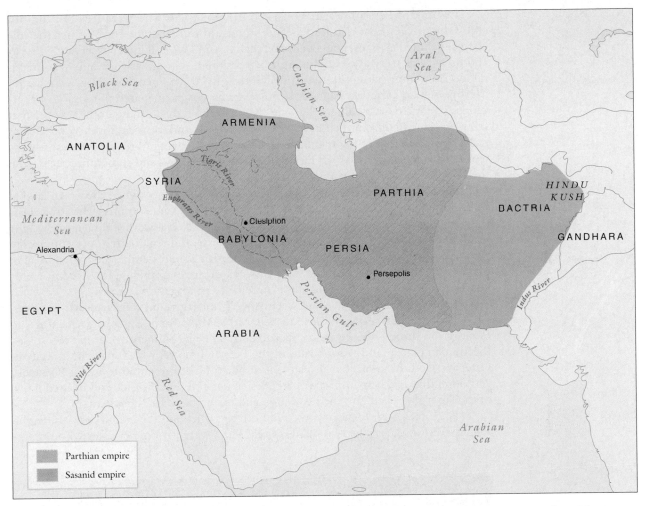

MAP [7.2]
The Parthian and Sasanid
empires, 247 B.C.E.–651 C.E.

steppe traditions. Even after the establishment of the Achaemenid empire, some of them followed a seminomadic lifestyle and maintained ties with their cousins on the steppes. Family and clan relationships were extremely important in the organization of Persian political and social affairs. Male warriors headed the clans, which retained much of their influence long after the establishment of the Achaemenid empire.

Imperial Bureaucrats

The development of a cosmopolitan empire, however, brought considerable complexity to Persian society. The requirements of imperial administration, for example, called for a new class of educated bureaucrats who to a large extent undermined the position of the old warrior elite. The bureaucrats did not directly challenge the patriarchal warriors and certainly did not seek to displace them from their privileged position in society. Nevertheless, the bureaucrats' crucial role in running the day-to-day affairs of the empire guaranteed them a prominent and comfortable place in Persian society. By the time of the later Achaemenids and the Seleucids, Persian cities were home to masses of administrators, tax collectors, and record keepers. The bureaucracy even included a substantial corps of translators, who facilitated communications among the empire's many linguistic groups. Imperial survival depended on these literate professionals, and high-ranking bureaucrats came to share power and influence with warriors and clan leaders.

Free Classes

The bulk of Persian society consisted of individuals who were free but did not enjoy the privileges of clan leaders and important bureaucrats. In the cities the free classes included artisans, craftsmen, merchants, and low-ranking civil servants. Priests and priestesses were also prominent urban residents, along with servants who maintained the temple communities in which they lived. In Persian society, as in earlier Mesopotamian societies, members of the free classes participated in religious observances conducted at local temples, and they had the right to share in the income that temples generated from their agricultural operations and from craft industries such as textile production that the temples organized. The weaving of textiles was mostly the work of women, who received rations of grain, wine, beer, and sometimes meat from the imperial and temple workshops that employed them.

In the countryside the free classes included peasants who owned their own land as well as landless cultivators who worked as laborers or tenants on properties owned by the state, temple communities, or other individuals. Free residents of rural areas had the right to marry and move as they wished, and they could seek better opportunities in the cities or in military service. Because the Persian empires embraced a great deal of parched land that received little rainfall, work in the countryside involved not only cultivation but also the building and maintenance of irrigation systems.

The most remarkable of these systems were underground canals known as *qanat*, which allowed cultivators to distribute water to fields without losing large quantities to evaporation through exposure to the sun and open air. Numerous *qanat* crisscrossed the Iranian plateau in the heartland of the Persian empire, where extreme scarcity of water justified the enormous investment of human labor required to build the canals. Although they had help from slaves, free residents of the countryside contributed much of the labor that went into the excavation and maintenance of the *qanat*.

Slaves

A large class of slaves also worked in both the cities and the countryside. Individuals passed into slavery by two main routes. Most were prisoners of war who became

In this sculpture from Persepolis, Persian nobles dressed in fine cloaks and hats ascend the staircase leading to the imperial reception hall.

slaves as the price of survival. These prisoners usually came from military units, but the Persians also enslaved civilians who resisted their advance or who rebelled against imperial authorities. Other slaves came from the ranks of free subjects who accumulated debts that they could not satisfy. In the cities, for example, merchants, artisans, and craftsmen borrowed funds to purchase goods or open shops, while in the countryside small farmers facing competition from large-scale cultivators borrowed against their property and liberty to purchase tools, seed, or food. Failure to repay these debts in a timely fashion often forced the borrowers not only to forfeit their property but also to sell their children, their spouses, or themselves into slavery.

Slave status deprived individuals of their personal freedom. Slaves became the property of an individual, the state, or an institution such as a temple community: they worked at tasks set by their owners, and they could not move or marry at will, although existing family units usually stayed together. Most slaves probably worked as domestic servants or skilled laborers in the households of the wealthy, but at least some slaves cultivated their owners' fields in the countryside. State-owned slaves provided much of the manual labor for large-scale construction projects such as roads, irrigation systems, city walls, and palaces.

In Mesopotamia, temple communities owned many slaves who worked at agricultural tasks and performed administrative chores for their priestly masters. During the mid to late sixth century B.C.E., a slave named Gimillu served the temple community of Eanna in Uruk, and his career is relatively well-known because records of his various misadventures survive in archives. Gimillu appeared in numerous legal cases because he habitually defrauded his masters, pocketed bribes, and embezzled temple funds. Yet he held a high position in the temple community and always managed to escape serious punishment. His career reveals that slaves sometimes had administrative talents and took on tasks involving considerable responsibility. Gimillu's case clearly shows that slaves sometimes enjoyed close relationships with powerful individuals who could protect them from potential enemies.

Economic Foundations of Classical Persia

Agriculture was the economic foundation of classical Persian society. Like other classical societies, Persia needed large agricultural surpluses to support military forces and administrative specialists as well as residents of cities who were artisans, craft workers, and merchants rather than cultivators. The Persian empires embraced several regions of exceptional fertility—notably Mesopotamia, Egypt, Anatolia, and northern India—and they prospered by mobilizing the agricultural surpluses of these lands.

Agricultural Production

Barley and wheat were the grains cultivated most commonly in the Persian empires. Peas, lentils, mustard, garlic, onions, cucumbers, dates, apples, pomegranates, pears, and apricots supplemented the cereals in diets throughout Persian society, and beer and wine were the most common beverages. In most years agricultural production far exceeded the needs of cultivators, making sizable surpluses available for sale in the cities or for distribution to state servants through the imperial bureaucracy. Vast quantities of produce flowed into the imperial court from state-owned lands cultivated by slaves or leased out to tenants in exchange for a portion of the annual harvest. Even though they are incomplete, surviving records show that, for example, in 500 B.C.E., during the middle period of Darius's reign, the imperial court received almost eight hundred thousand liters of grain, quite apart from vegetables, fruits, meat, poultry, fish, oil, beer, wine, and textiles. Officials distributed some of this produce to the imperial staff as wages in kind, but much of it also found its way into the enormous banquets that Darius organized for as many as ten thousand guests. Satraps and

Trade

other high officials lived on a less lavish scale than the Persian emperors but also bene-fited from agricultural surpluses delivered to their courts from their own lands.

Agriculture was the foundation of the Persian economy, but long-distance trade grew rapidly during the course of the Persian empires and linked lands from India to Egypt in a vast commercial zone. Several conditions promoted the growth of trade: the relative political stability maintained by the Persian empires, the general prosper-ity of the realm, the use of standardized coins, and the availability of good trade routes, including long-established routes, newly constructed highways such as the Persian Royal Road, and sea routes through the Red Sea, Persian Gulf, and Arabian Sea. Markets operated regularly in all the larger cities of the Persian empires, and the largest cities, such as Babylon, also were home to banks and companies that invested in commercial ventures.

As trade grew, the regions of the Persian empires all contributed particular prod-ucts to the larger imperial economy. India supplied gold, ivory, and aromatics. Iran and central Asia provided lapis lazuli, turquoise, and other semiprecious stones. Mesopotamia and Iran were sources of finished products like textiles, mirrors, and jewelry. Anatolia supplied gold, silver, iron, copper, and tin. Phoenicia contributed glass, cedar, timber, and richly dyed woolen fabrics. Spices and aromatics came from Arabia. Egypt provided grain, linen textiles, and papyrus writing materials as well as gold, ebony, and ivory obtained from Nubia. Greek oil, wine, and ceramics also made their way throughout the empire and even beyond its borders.

Long-distance trade of this sort became especially prominent during the reigns of Alexander of Macedon and his Seleucid successors. The cities they established and the colonists they attracted stimulated trade throughout the whole region from the Mediterranean to northern India. Indeed, Greek migrants facilitated cultural as well as commercial exchanges by encouraging the mixing and mingling of religious faiths, art styles, and philosophical speculation throughout the Persian realm.

Tribute bearers from lands subject to Achaemenid rule bring rams, horses, and fabrics to the imperial court at Persepolis.

Contexts & Connections

The World's First Coins

When relating the story of Cyrus's victory over King Croesus of Lydia, the Greek historian Herodotus offered a description of Croesus's kingdom. He characterized the Lydians as an exceptionally prosperous people. "So far as we have any knowledge," he reported, "they were the first nation to introduce the use of gold and silver coin, and the first who sold goods by retail." The king himself had a reputation as the wealthiest person in the world—a view reflected in the popular expression that particularly wealthy individuals are "as rich as Croesus." The wealth of the Lydian kingdom arose partly from use of the coins that Herodotus mentioned.

Mesopotamian and Egyptian peoples had long used silver and gold fashioned into rings, rods, and ingots as currency to facilitate exchanges of goods. It was much simpler to purchase goods for a certain quantity of silver than to barter goods directly for one another. Yet silver and gold currencies had their own problems. Careful merchants had to weigh tokens in their scales to make sure they came to the right amount. Even then it was possible for unscrupulous individuals to dilute the silver or gold content of a token by alloying it with some cheaper metal.

Beginning about 640 B.C.E. the kings of Lydia issued the first coins of precisely measured metal bearing guarantees of their value. They minted their early coins from electrum, a rare but naturally occurring alloy of gold and silver found in local rivers. Croesus later minted coins of pure gold and silver. These coins immediately caught the attention of Lydia's trading partners, and officially sponsored coins were soon in use throughout the eastern Mediterranean region. (Chinese rulers independently issued bronze coins about the same time.)

The availability of officially minted coins with guaranteed values provided a tremendous boost to trade. The earliest beneficiary was the kingdom of Lydia itself, which drew crowds of foreign merchants to vast markets in the capital at Sardis. There Lydians traded merchandise that they obtained from Mesopotamia, Egypt, and the eastern Mediterranean region, as well as the highly prized perfumes that were the most famous products of Lydian manufacturers. This bustling trade in large, officially sponsored marketplaces is what Herodotus had in mind when he said the Lydians were "the first who sold goods by retail." In later centuries, Greeks, Romans, and others made use of their own minted coins as they built commercial empires throughout the Mediterranean basin.

Coins did not entirely displace other currencies: in various world regions, cattle, cowry shells, cacao beans, and other items functioned as mediums of exchange long after the invention of coins. Even in regions where they were in common use, coins have not always dominated economic exchange: after the invention of printed paper money, and especially after the more recent development of electronic currency, coins increasingly became impractical except for small-scale transactions. Meanwhile, however, for two millennia and more, officially minted coins lubricated trade and facilitated economic transactions throughout much of the world.

RELIGIONS OF SALVATION IN CLASSICAL PERSIAN SOCIETY

Cross-cultural influences were especially noticeable in the development of Persian religion. Persians came from the family of peoples who spoke Indo-European languages, and their earliest religion closely resembled that of the Aryans of India. During the classical era, however, the new faith of Zoroastrianism emerged and became widely popular in Iran and to a lesser extent also in the larger Persian empires. Zoroastrianism reflected the cosmopolitan society of the empires, and it profoundly influenced the beliefs and values of Judaism, Christianity, and Islam. During the late centuries of the classical era, from about 100 to 500 C.E., three missionary religions—Buddhism, Christianity, and Manichaeism—also found numerous converts in the Persian empire.

Zarathustra and His Faith

The earliest Persian religion centered on cults that celebrated outstanding natural elements and geographic features such as the sun, the moon, water, and especially fire. Persians recognized many of the same gods as the ancient Aryans, and their priests performed sacrifices similar to those conducted by the *brahmins* in India. The priests even made ceremonial use of a hallucinogenic agent called *haoma* in the same way that the Aryans used *soma,* and indeed the two concoctions were probably the same substance. Like the Aryans, the ancient Persians glorified strength and martial virtues, and the cults of both peoples sought principally to bring about a comfortable material existence for their practitioners.

Zarathustra

During the classical era Persian religion underwent considerable change, as moral and religious thinkers sought to adapt their messages to the circumstances of a complex, cosmopolitan society. One result was the emergence of Zoroastrianism, which emerged from the teachings of Zarathustra. Though Zarathustra was undoubtedly a historical person and the subject of many early stories, little certain information survives about his life and career. It is not even clear when he lived, though most scholars date his life to the late seventh and early sixth centuries B.C.E. He came from an aristocratic family, and he probably was a priest who became disenchanted with the traditional religion and its concentration on bloody sacrifices and mechanical rituals. In any case, when he was about twenty years old, Zarathustra left his family and home in search of wisdom. After about ten years of travel, he experienced a series of visions and became convinced that the supreme god, whom he called Ahura Mazda ("the wise lord"), had chosen him to serve as his prophet and spread his message.

The Gathas

Like his life, Zarathustra's doctrine has also proven to be somewhat elusive for modern analysts. Many of the earliest Zoroastrian teachings have perished, because the priests, known as *magi,* at first transmitted them orally. Only during the Seleucid dynasty did *magi* begin to preserve religious texts in writing, and only under the Sasanids did they compile their scriptures in a holy book known as the Avesta. Nevertheless, many of Zarathustra's own compositions survive, since *magi* preserved them with special diligence through oral transmission. Known as the *Gathas,* Zarathustra's works were hymns that he composed in honor of the various deities that he recognized. Apart from the *Gathas,* ancient Zoroastrian literature included a wide variety of hymns, liturgical works, and treatises on moral and theological themes. Though some of these works survive, the arrival of Islam in the seventh century C.E. and the subsequent decline of Zoroastrianism resulted in the loss of most of the Avesta and later Zoroastrian works.

Zoroastrian Teachings

Zarathustra and his followers were not strict monotheists. They recognized Ahura Mazda as a supreme deity, an eternal and beneficent spirit, and the creator of all good things. But Zarathustra also spoke of six lesser deities, whom he praised in the *Gathas.* Furthermore, he believed that Ahura Mazda engaged in a cosmic conflict with an independent adversary, an evil and malign spirit known as Angra Mainyu ("the destructive spirit" or "the hostile spirit"). Following a struggle of some twelve thousand years, Zarathustra believed, Ahura Mazda and the forces of good would ultimately prevail, and Angra Mainyu and the principle of evil would disappear forever. At that time individual human souls would undergo judgment and would experience rewards or punishments according to the holiness of their thoughts, words, and deeds. Honest and moral individuals would enter into a heavenly paradise, whereas demons would fling their evil brethren into a hellish realm of pain and suffering.

Zarathustra did not call for ascetic renunciation of the world in favor of a future heavenly existence. To the contrary, he considered the material world a blessing that reflected the benevolent nature of Ahura Mazda. His moral teachings allowed human beings to enjoy the world and its fruits—including wealth, sexual pleasure, and social prestige—as long as they did so in moderation and behaved honestly toward others. Zoroastrians have often summarized their moral teachings in the simple formula "good words, good thoughts, good deeds."

A gold clasp or button of the fifth century B.C.E. with the symbol of Ahura Mazda as a winged god.

Popularity of Zoroastrianism

Zarathustra's teachings began to attract large numbers of followers during the sixth century B.C.E., particularly among Persian aristocrats and ruling elites. Wealthy patrons donated land and established endowments for the support of Zoroastrian temples. The Achaemenid era saw the emergence of a sizable priesthood, whose members conducted religious rituals, maintained a calendar, taught Zoroastrian values, and preserved Zoroastrian doctrine through oral transmission.

Cyrus and Cambyses probably observed Zoroastrian rites, although little evidence survives to illustrate their religious preferences. Beginning with Darius, however, the Achaemenid emperors closely associated themselves with Ahura Mazda and claimed divine sanction for their rule. Darius ordered stone inscriptions celebrating his achievements, and in these monuments he clearly revealed his devotion to Ahura Mazda and his opposition to the principle of evil. He did not attempt to suppress other gods or religions, but tolerated the established faiths of the various peoples in his empire. Yet he personally regarded Ahura Mazda as a deity superior to all others.

In one of his inscriptions, Darius praised Ahura Mazda as the great god who created the earth, the sky, and humanity and who moreover elevated Darius himself to the imperial honor. With the aid of imperial sponsorship, Zoroastrian temples cropped up throughout the Achaemenid realm. The faith was most popular in Iran, but it attracted sizable followings also in Mesopotamia, Anatolia, Egypt, and other parts of the Achaemenid empire even though there was no organized effort to spread it beyond its original homeland.

Religions of Salvation in a Cosmopolitan Society

The arrival of Alexander of Macedon inaugurated a difficult era for the Zoroastrian community. During his Persian campaign, Alexander's forces burned many temples and killed numerous *magi*. Because at that time the *magi* still transmitted Zoroastrian doctrines orally, an untold number of hymns and holy verses disappeared. The Zoroastrian faith survived, however, and the Parthians cultivated it in order to rally support against the Seleucids. Once established in power, the Parthians observed Zoroastrian rituals, though they did not support the faith as enthusiastically as their predecessors had done.

During the Sasanid dynasty, however, Zoroastrianism experienced a revival. As self-proclaimed heirs to the Achaemenids, the Sasanids identified closely with Zoroastrianism

Officially Sponsored Zoroastrianism

Sources from the Past

Zarathustra on Good and Evil

Like many other religious faiths of classical times, Zoroastrianism encouraged the faithful to observe high moral and ethical standards. In this hymn from the Gathas, *Zarathustra relates how Ahura Mazda and Angra Mainyu—representatives of good and evil, respectively—made choices about how to behave based on their fundamental natures. Human beings did likewise, according to Zarathustra, and ultimately all would experience the rewards and punishments that their choices merited.*

In the beginning, there were two Primal Spirits, Twins
  spontaneously active;
These are the Good and the Evil, in thought, and in
  word, and in deed:
Between these two, let the wise choose aright;
Be good, not base.

And when these Twin Spirits came together at first,
They established Life and Non-Life,
And so shall it be as long as the world shall last;
The worst existence shall be the lot of the followers of
  evil,
And the Good Mind shall be the reward of the
  followers of good.

Of these Twin Spirits, the Evil One chose to do the
  worst;
While the bountiful Holy Spirit of Goodness,
Clothing itself with the mossy heavens for a garment,
  chose the Truth;
And so will those who [seek to] please Ahura Mazda with
  righteous deeds, performed with faith in Truth. . . .

And when there cometh Divine Retribution for the Evil
  One,
Then at Thy command shall the Good Mind establish
  the Kingdom of Heaven, O Mazda,
For those who will deliver Untruth into the hands of
  Righteousness and Truth.

Then truly cometh the blow of destruction on
  Untruth,
And all those of good fame are garnered up in the Fair
  Abode,
The Fair Abode of the Good Mind, the Wise Lord, and
  of Truth!

O ye mortals, mark these commandments—
The commandments which the Wise Lord has given,
  for Happiness and for Pain;
Long punishment for the evil-doer, and bliss for the
  follower of Truth,
The joy of salvation for the Righteous ever afterwards!

SOURCE: D. J. Irani. *The Divine Songs of Zarathustra*. London: George Allen & Unwin, 1924.

What assumptions does Zarathustra make about human nature and the capacity of human beings to make morally good choices out of their own free will?

and supported it zealously. Indeed, the Sasanids often persecuted other faiths if they seemed likely to become popular enough to challenge the supremacy of Zoroastrianism. With generous imperial backing, the Zoroastrian faith and the *magi* flourished as never before. Theologians prepared written versions of the holy texts and collected them in the Avesta. They also explored points of doctrine and addressed difficult questions of morality and theology. Most people probably did not understand the theologians' reflections, but they flocked to Zoroastrian temples where they prayed to Ahura Mazda and participated in rituals.

The Zoroastrian faith faced severe difficulties in the seventh century C.E. when Islamic conquerors toppled the Sasanid empire. The conquerors did not outlaw the

Darius faces Ahura Mazda, to whom he attributed his authority, as the various kings subject to him acknowledge him as their lord.

religion altogether, but they placed political and financial pressure on the *magi* and Zoroastrian temples. Some Zoroastrians fled their homeland and found refuge in India, where their descendants, known as Parsis ("Persians"), continue even today to observe Zoroastrian traditions. But most Zoroastrians remained in Iran and eventually converted to Islam. As a result, Zoroastrian numbers progressively dwindled. Only a few thousand faithful maintain a Zoroastrian community in modern-day Iran.

Meanwhile, even though Zoroastrianism ultimately declined in its homeland, the cosmopolitan character of the Persian realm offered it opportunities to influence other religious faiths. Numerous Jewish communities had become established in Mesopotamia, Anatolia, and Persia after the Hebrew kingdom of David and Solomon fell in 930 B.C.E. During the Seleucid, Parthian, and Sasanid eras, the Persian empire attracted merchants, emissaries, and missionaries from the whole region between the Mediterranean and India. Three religions of salvation—Buddhism, Christianity, and Manichaeism, all discussed in later chapters—found a footing alongside Judaism and attracted converts. Indeed, Christianity and Manichaeism became extremely popular faiths in spite of intermittent rounds of persecution organized by Sasanid authorities.

Other Faiths

While foreign faiths influenced religious developments in classical Persian society, Zoroastrianism also left its mark on the other religions of salvation. Jews living in Persia during Achaemenid times adopted several specific teachings of Zoroastrianism, which later found their way into the faiths of Christianity and Islam as well. These teachings included the notion that an omnipotent and beneficent deity was responsible for all creation, the idea that a purely evil being worked against the creator god, the conviction that the forces of good will ultimately prevail over the power of evil after a climactic struggle, the belief that human beings must strive to observe the highest moral standards, and the doctrine that individuals will undergo judgment, after which the morally upright will experience rewards in paradise while evildoers will suffer punishments in hell. These teachings, which have profoundly influenced Judaism, Christianity, and Islam, all derived ultimately from the faith of Zarathustra and his followers.

Influence of Zoroastrianism

The Achaemenid empire inaugurated a new era of world history. The Achaemenids borrowed military and administrative techniques devised earlier by Babylonian and Assyrian rulers, but they applied those techniques on a much larger scale than did any of their Mesopotamian predecessors. In doing so they conquered a vast empire and then governed its diverse lands and peoples with tolerable success for more than two centuries. The Achaemenids demonstrated how it was possible to build and maintain a massive imperial state, and their example inspired later efforts to establish similar large-scale imperial states based in Persia and other Eurasian lands as well. The Achaemenid and later Persian empires integrated much of the territory from the Mediterranean Sea to the Indus River into a commonwealth in which peoples of different regions and ethnic groups participated in a larger economy and society. By sponsoring regular and systematic interactions between peoples of different communities, the Persian empires wielded tremendous cultural as well as political, social, and economic influence. Indeed, Persian religious beliefs helped to shape moral and religious thought throughout much of southwest Asia and the Mediterranean basin. Zoroastrian teachings were particularly influential: although Zoroastrianism declined after the Sasanid dynasty, its doctrines decisively influenced the fundamental teachings of Judaism, Christianity, and Islam.

CHRONOLOGY

7th–6th centuries B.C.E.(?)	Life of Zarathustra
558–330 B.C.E.	Achaemenid dynasty
558–530 B.C.E.	Reign of Cyrus the Achaemenid
521–486 B.C.E.	Reign of Darius
334–330 B.C.E.	Invasion and conquest of the Achaemenid empire by Alexander of Macedon
323–83 B.C.E.	Seleucid dynasty
247 B.C.E.–224 C.E.	Parthian dynasty
224–651 C.E.	Sasanid dynasty

FOR FURTHER READING

Mary Boyce, ed. *Textual Sources for the Study of Zoroastrianism*. Totowa, N.J., 1984. Sources in translation with numerous explanatory comments by the author.

———. *Zoroastrians: Their Religious Beliefs and Practices*. London, 1979. A survey of Zoroastrian history by a leading revisionist scholar.

Maria Brosius. *Women in Ancient Persia, 559-331 B.C.* Oxford, 1996. Carefully examines both Persian and Greek sources for information about women and their role in Achaemenid society.

J. M. Cook. *The Persian Empire*. New York, 1983. A popular account of the Achaemenid empire.

William Culican. *The Medes and the Persians*. New York, 1965. Well-illustrated survey with generous attention to art and architecture.

Muhammad A. Dandamaev and Vladimir G. Lukonin. *The Culture and Social Institutions of Ancient Iran*. Ed. by P. L. Kohl. Cambridge, 1989. Scholarly account that brings the results of Russian research to bear on the Achaemenid empire.

Jacques Duchesne-Guillemin. *The Hymns of Zarathustra*. London, 1952. A translation and commentary of Zarathustra's most important *Gathas*.

Richard C. Foltz. *Spirituality in the Land of the Noble: How Iran Shaped the World's Religions*. Oxford, 2004. Includes an accessible discussion of the Zoroastrian faith.

Richard N. Frye. *The Heritage of Central Asia: From Antiquity to the Turkish Expansion*. Princeton, 1996. Briefly sketches the history of various Iranian-speaking peoples in the steppes of central Asia as well as on the Iranian plateau.

———. *The Heritage of Persia*. Cleveland, 1963. A leading scholar's solid survey of Persia up to the Islamic conquest.

R. Ghirshman. *Iran*. Harmondsworth, 1954. An older work but still valuable for the archaeological information it provides.

William W. Malandra. *An Introduction to Ancient Iranian Religion*. Minneapolis, 1983. Careful study of Zoroastrian textual sources.

A. T. Olmstead. *History of the Persian Empire (Achaemenid Period)*. Chicago, 1948. An older study concentrating on political history; exceptionally well written and still valuable.

Susan Sherwin-White and Amélie Kuhrt. *From Samarkhand to Sardis: A New Approach to the Seleucid Empire*. Berkeley, 1993. Detailed scholarly analysis of the Seleucid empire concentrating on political and economic matters.

Mortimer Wheeler. *Flames over Persepolis*. New York, 1968. Deals with Alexander's conquest of the Achaemenid empire and especially the spread of Greek art styles throughout the Persian empire.

Robert C. Zaehner. *The Dawn and Twilight of Zoroastrianism*. London, 1961. An important interpretation of Zoroastrianism that concentrates on the Achaemenid and Sasanid periods.

———, ed. *The Teachings of the Magi: A Compendium of Zoroastrian Beliefs*. London, 1956. Translations of texts by later Zoroastrian theologians.

See our **Online Learning Center** at www.mhhe.com/bentley3 for additional readings, practice maps, quizzes, and internet activities.

Unfamiliar words? Check out the **Primary Source Investigator CD-ROM** for an interactive glossary, interactive maps, more images, and primary sources.

The Han emperor discusses classical texts with Confucian scholars.

CHAPTER 8

THE UNIFICATION OF CHINA

In the year 99 B.C.E., Chinese imperial officials sentenced the historian Sima Qian to punishment by castration. For just over a decade Sima Qian had worked on a project that he had inherited from his father, a history of China from earliest times to his own day. This project brought Sima Qian high prominence at the imperial court. When he spoke in defense of a dishonored general, his views attracted widespread attention. The emperor reacted furiously when he learned that Sima Qian had publicly expressed opinions that contradicted the ruler's judgment and ordered the historian to undergo his humiliating punishment.

Human castration was by no means uncommon in premodern times. Thousands of boys and young men of undistinguished birth underwent voluntary castration in China and many other lands as well in order to pursue careers as eunuchs. Ruling elites often appointed eunuchs, rather than nobles, to sensitive posts because eunuchs did not sire families and so could not build power bases to challenge established authorities. As personal servants of ruling elites, eunuchs sometimes came to wield enormous power because of their influence with rulers and their families.

Exemplary punishment was not an appealing alternative, however, to educated elites and other prominent individuals: when sentenced to punitive castration, Chinese men of honor normally avoided the penalty by taking their own lives. Yet Sima Qian chose to endure his punishment. In a letter to a friend he explained that an early death by suicide would mean that a work that only he was capable of producing would go forever unwritten. To transmit his understanding of the Chinese past, then, Sima Qian opted to live and work in disgrace until his death about 90 B.C.E.

During his last years Sima Qian completed a massive work consisting of 130 chapters, most of which survive. He consulted court documents and the historical works of his predecessors, and when writing about his own age he supplemented these sources with personal observations and information gleaned from political and military figures who played leading roles in Chinese society. He composed historical accounts of the emperors' reigns and biographical sketches of notable figures, including ministers, statesmen, generals, empresses, aristocrats, scholars, officials, merchants, and rebels. He even described the societies of neighboring peoples with whom Chinese sometimes conducted trade and sometimes made war. The work of the disgraced but conscientious scholar Sima Qian provides the best information available about the development of early imperial China.

A rich body of political and social thought prepared the way for the unification of China under the Qin and Han dynasties. Confucians, Daoists, Legalists, and others formed schools of thought and worked to bring political and social stability to China during the chaotic years of the late Zhou dynasty and the Period of the Warring States. Legalist ideas contributed directly to unification by outlining means by which rulers could strengthen their states. The works of the Confucians and Daoists did not lend themselves so readily to the unification process, but both schools of thought survived over the long term and profoundly influenced Chinese political and cultural traditions.

Rulers of the Qin and Han dynasties adopted Legalist principles and imposed centralized imperial rule on all of China. Like the Achaemenids of Persia, the Qin and Han emperors ruled through an elaborate bureaucracy, and they built roads that linked the various regions of China. They went further than the Persian emperors in their efforts to foster cultural unity in their realm. They imposed a common written language throughout China and established an educational system based on Confucian thought and values. For almost 450 years the Qin and Han dynasties guided the fortunes of China and established a strong precedent for centralized imperial rule.

Especially during the Han dynasty, political stability was the foundation of economic prosperity. High agricultural productivity supported the development of iron and silk industries, and Chinese goods found markets in central Asia, India, the Persian empire, and even the Mediterranean basin. In spite of economic prosperity, however, later Han society experienced deep divisions between the small class of extremely wealthy landowners and the masses of landless poor. These divisions eventually led to civil disorder and the emergence of political factions, which ultimately brought the Han dynasty to an end.

IN SEARCH OF POLITICAL AND SOCIAL ORDER

The late centuries of the Zhou dynasty brought political confusion to China and led eventually to the chaos associated with the Period of the Warring States (403–221 B.C.E.). During those same centuries, however, there also took place a remarkable cultural flowering that left a permanent mark on Chinese history. In a way, political turmoil helps to explain the cultural creativity of the late Zhou dynasty and the Period of the Warring States because it forced thoughtful people to reflect on the nature of society and the proper roles of human beings in society. Some sought to identify principles that would restore political and social order. Others concerned themselves with a search for individual tranquility apart from society. Three schools of thought that emerged during those centuries of confusion and chaos—Confucianism, Daoism, and Legalism—exercised a particularly deep influence on Chinese political and cultural traditions.

Confucius and His School

Confucius

The first Chinese thinker who addressed the problem of political and social order in a straightforward and self-conscious way was Kong Fuzi (551–479 B.C.E.)—"Master Philosopher Kong," as his disciples called him, or Confucius, as he is known in English. He came from an aristocratic family in the state of Lu in northern China, and for many years he sought an influential post at the Lu court. But Confucius was a strong-willed man who often did not get along well with others. He could be quite cantankerous: he was known to lodge bitter complaints, for example, if someone undercooked or overcooked his rice. Not surprisingly, then, he refused to compromise his beliefs in the interest of political expediency, and he insisted on observing principles that frequently clashed with state policy. When he realized that he would never obtain anything more than a minor post in Lu, Confucius left in search of a more prestigious appointment elsewhere. For about ten years he traveled to courts throughout northern China, but he found none willing to accept his services. In 484 B.C.E., bitterly disappointed, he returned to Lu, where he died five years later.

Confucius never realized his ambition to become a powerful minister. Throughout his career, however, he served as an educator as well as a political advisor, and in this capacity he left an enduring mark on Chinese society. He attracted numerous disciples who aspired to political careers. Some of his pupils compiled the master's sayings and teachings in a book known as the *Analects,* a work that has profoundly influenced Chinese political and cultural traditions.

Confucian Ideas

No contemporary portrait of Confucius survives, but artists have used their imaginations and depicted him in many ways over the years. This portrait of 1735 identifies Confucius as "the Sage and Teacher" and represents him in the distinctive dress of an eighteenth-century Confucian scholar-bureaucrat.

Confucius's thought was fundamentally moral, ethical, and political in character. It was also thoroughly practical: Confucius did not address abstruse philosophical questions, because he thought they would not help to solve the political and social problems of his day. Nor did he deal with religious questions, because he thought they went beyond the capacity of mortal human intelligence. He did not even concern himself much with the structure of the state, because he thought political and social harmony arose from the proper ordering of human relationships rather than the establishment of state offices. In an age when bureaucratic institutions were not yet well developed, Confucius believed that the best way to promote good government was to fill official positions with individuals who were both well educated and extraordinarily conscientious. Thus Confucius concentrated on the formation of what he called *junzi*—"superior individuals"—who took a broad view of public affairs and did not allow personal interests to influence their judgments.

In the absence of an established educational system and a formal curriculum, Confucius had his disciples study works of poetry and history produced during the Zhou dynasty, since he believed that they provided excellent insight into human nature. He carefully examined the *Book of Songs,* the *Book of History,* the *Book of Rites,* and other works with his students, concentrating especially on their practical value for prospective administrators. As a result of Confucius's influence, literary works of the Zhou

Sources from the Past

Confucius on Good Government

Confucius never composed formal writings, but his disciples collected his often pithy remarks into a work known as the Analects ("sayings"). Referred to as "the Master" in the following excerpts from the Analects, Confucius consistently argued that only good men possessing moral authority could rule effectively.

The Master said, "He who exercises government by means of his virtue may be compared to the north polar star, which keeps its place, while all the stars turn toward it. . . ."

The Master said, "If the people be led by laws, and uniformity be imposed on them by punishments, they will try to avoid the punishment, but will have no sense of shame.

"If they be led by virtue, and uniformity be provided for them by the rules of propriety, they will have the sense of shame, and moreover will become good. . . ."

The duke Ai asked, saying, "What should be done in order to secure the submission of the people?" Confucius replied, "Advance the upright and set aside the crooked, and then the people will submit. Advance the crooked and set aside the upright, and then the people will not submit."

Ji Kang asked how to cause the people to reverence their ruler, to be faithful to him, and to go on to seek virtue. The Master said, "Let him preside over them with gravity; then they will reverence him. Let him be filial and kind to all; then they will be faithful to him. Let him advance the good and teach the incompetent; then they will eagerly seek to be virtuous. . . ."

Zigong asked about government. The Master said, "The requisites of government are that there be suffi-

ciency of food, sufficiency of military equipment, and the confidence of the people in their ruler."

Zigong said, "If it cannot be helped, and one of these must be dispensed with, which of the three should be foregone first?" "The military equipment," said the Master.

Zigong again asked, "If it cannot be helped, and one of the remaining two must be dispensed with, which of them should be foregone?" The Master answered, "Part with the food. From olden times, death has been the lot of all men; but if the people have no faith in their rulers, there is no standing for the state. . . ."

Ji Kang asked Confucius about government, saying, "What do you say to killing the unprincipled for the good of the principled?" Confucius replied, "Sir, in carrying on your government, why should you use killing at all? Let your evinced desires be for what is good, and the people will be good. The relation between superiors and inferiors is like that between the wind and the grass. The grass must bend when the wind blows across it. . . ."

The Master said, "When a prince's personal conduct is correct, his government is effective without the issuing of orders. If his personal conduct is not correct, he may issue orders, but they will not be followed."

SOURCE: James Legge, trans. *The Chinese Classics,* 7 vols. Oxford: Clarendon Press, 1893, 1:145, 146, 152, 254, 258–59, 266. (Translations slightly modified.)

Compare Confucius's understanding of moral virtue with Zarathustra's notion of morality discussed in the previous chapter.

dynasty became the core texts of the traditional Chinese education. For more than two thousand years, until the early twentieth century C.E., talented Chinese seeking government posts proceeded through a cycle of studies deriving from the one developed by Confucius in the fifth century B.C.E.

For Confucius, though, an advanced education represented only a part of the preparation needed by the ideal government official. More important than formal learning was the possession of a strong sense of moral integrity and a capacity to deliver wise and fair judgments. Thus Confucius encouraged his students to cultivate high ethical standards and to hone their faculties of analysis and judgment.

Confucius emphasized several qualities in particular. One of them he called *ren*, by which he meant an attitude of kindness and benevolence or a sense of humanity. Confucius explained that individuals possessing *ren* were courteous, respectful, diligent, and loyal, and he considered *ren* a characteristic desperately needed in government officials. Another quality of central importance was *li*, a sense of propriety, which called for individuals to behave in conventionally appropriate fashion: they should treat all other human beings with courtesy, while showing special respect and deference to elders or superiors. Yet another quality that Confucius emphasized was *xiao*, filial piety, which reflected the high significance of the family in Chinese society. The demands of filial piety obliged children to respect their parents and other family elders, look after their welfare, support them in old age, and remember them along with other ancestors after their deaths.

Confucian Values

Confucius emphasized personal qualities like *ren*, *li*, and *xiao* because he believed that individuals who possessed these traits would gain influence in the larger society. Those who disciplined themselves and properly molded their own characters would not only possess personal self-control but also have the power of leading others by example. Only through enlightened leadership by morally strong individuals, Confucius believed, was there any hope for the restoration of political and social order in China. Thus his goal was not simply the cultivation of personal morality for its own sake but, rather, the creation of *junzi* who could bring order and stability to China.

Because Confucius expressed his thought in general terms, later disciples could adapt it to the particular problems of their times. Indeed, the flexibility of Confucian thought helps to account for its remarkable longevity and influence in China. Two later disciples of Confucius—Mencius and Xunzi—illustrate especially well the ways in which Confucian thought lent itself to elaboration and adaptation.

Mencius (372–289 B.C.E.) was the most learned man of his age and the principal spokesman for the Confucian school. During the Period of the Warring States, he traveled widely throughout China, consulting with rulers and offering advice on political issues. Mencius firmly believed that human nature was basically good, and he argued for policies that would allow it to influence society as a whole. Thus he placed special emphasis on the Confucian virtue of *ren* and advocated government by benevolence and humanity. This principle implied that rulers would levy light taxes, avoid wars, support education, and encourage harmony and cooperation. Critics charged that Mencius held a naively optimistic view of human nature, arguing that his policies would rarely succeed in the real world where human interests, wills, and ambitions constantly clash. Indeed, Mencius's advice had little practical effect during his lifetime. Over the long term, however, his ideas deeply influenced the Confucian tradition. Since about the tenth century C.E., many Chinese scholars have considered Mencius the most authoritative of Confucius's early expositors.

Mencius

Like Confucius and Mencius, Xunzi (298–238 B.C.E.) was a man of immense learning, but unlike his predecessors, he also served for many years as a government administrator. His practical experience encouraged him to develop a view of human nature that was less rosy than Mencius's view. Xunzi believed that human beings selfishly pursued their own interests, no matter what effects their actions had on others, and resisted making any contribution voluntarily to the larger society. He considered strong social discipline the best means to bring order to society. Thus whereas Mencius emphasized the Confucian quality of *ren*, Xunzi emphasized *li*. He advocated the establishment of clear, well-publicized standards of conduct that would set limits on the

Xunzi

pursuit of individual interests and punish those who neglected their obligations to the larger society. Xunzi once likened human beings to pieces of warped lumber: just as it was possible to straighten out bad wood, so too it was possible to turn selfish and recalcitrant individuals into useful, contributing members of society. But the process involved harsh social discipline similar to the steam treatments, heat applications, hammering, bending, and forcible wrenching that turned warped wood into useful lumber.

Like Confucius and Mencius, however, Xunzi also believed that it was possible to improve human beings and restore order to society. This fundamental optimism was a basic characteristic of Confucian thought. It explains the high value that Confucian thinkers placed on education and public behavior, and it accounts also for their activist approach to public affairs. Confucians involved themselves in society: they sought government positions and made conscientious efforts to solve political and social problems and to promote harmony in public life. By no means, however, did the Confucians win universal praise for their efforts: to some of their contemporaries, Confucian activism represented little more than misspent energy.

Daoism

The Daoists were the most prominent critics of Confucian activism. Like Confucianism, Daoist thought developed in response to the turbulence of the late Zhou dynasty and the Period of the Warring States. But unlike the Confucians, the Daoists considered it pointless to waste time and energy on problems that defied solution. Instead of Confucian social activism, the Daoists devoted their energies to reflection and introspection, in hopes that they could understand the natural principles that governed the world and could learn how to live in harmony with them. The Daoists believed that over a long term, this approach would bring harmony to society as a whole, as people ceased to meddle in affairs that they could not understand or control.

Laozi and the Daodejing

According to Chinese tradition, the founder of Daoism was a sage named Laozi who lived during the sixth century B.C.E. Although there probably was a historical Laozi, it is almost certain that several hands contributed to the *Daodejing* (*Classic of the Way and of Virtue*), the basic exposition of Daoist beliefs traditionally ascribed to Laozi, and that the book acquired its definitive form over several centuries. After the *Daodejing*, the most important Daoist work was the *Zhuangzi*, named after its author, the philosopher Zhuangzi (369–286 B.C.E.), who provided a well-reasoned compendium of Daoist views.

The Dao

Daoism represented an effort to understand the fundamental character of the world and nature. The central concept of Daoism is *dao*, meaning "the way," more specifically "the way of nature" or "the way of the cosmos." *Dao* is an elusive concept, and the Daoists themselves did not generally characterize it in positive and forthright terms. In the *Daodejing*, for example, *dao* figures as the original force of the cosmos, an eternal and unchanging principle that governs all the workings of the world. Yet the *Daodejing* envisioned *dao* as a supremely passive force and spoke of it mostly in negative terms: *dao* does nothing, and yet it accomplishes everything. *Dao* resembles water, which is soft and yielding, yet is also so powerful that it eventually erodes even the hardest rock placed in its path. *Dao* also resembles the cavity of a pot or the hub of a wheel: although they are nothing more than empty spaces, they make the pot and the wheel useful tools.

If the principles of *dao* governed the world, it followed that human beings should tailor their behavior to its passive and yielding nature. To the Daoists, living in harmony with *dao* meant retreating from engagement in the world of politics and admin-

A jade statue produced about the tenth century C.E. depicts the sage Laozi on an ox. Legends reported that Laozi rode a blue ox from China to central Asia when spreading his teachings.

istration. Ambition and activism had not solved political and social problems. Far from it: human striving had brought the world to a state of chaos. The proper response to this situation was to cease frantic striving and live in as simple a manner as possible.

The Doctrine of Wuwei

Thus early Daoists recognized as the chief moral virtue the trait of *wuwei*—disengagement from the competitive exertions and active involvement in affairs of the world. *Wuwei* required that individuals refrain from advanced education (which concentrated on abstruse trivialities) and from personal striving (which indicated excessive concern with the tedious affairs of the world). *Wuwei* called instead for individuals to live simply, unpretentiously, and in harmony with nature.

Wuwei also had implications for state and society: the less government, the better. Instead of expansive kingdoms and empires, the *Daodejing* envisioned a world of tiny, self-sufficient communities where people had no desire to conquer their neighbors or to trade with them. Indeed, even when people lived so close to the next community that they could hear the dogs barking and cocks crowing, they would be so content with their existence that they would not even have the desire to visit their neighbors!

Political Implications of Daoism

By encouraging the development of a reflective and introspective consciousness, Daoism served as a counterbalance to the activism and extroversion of the Confucian tradition. Indeed, Daoism encouraged the cultivation of self-knowledge in a way that appealed strongly to Confucians as well as to Daoists. Because neither Confucianism nor Daoism was an exclusive faith that precluded observance of the other, it has been possible through the centuries for individuals to study the Confucian curriculum and take administrative posts in the government while devoting their private hours to reflection on human nature and the place of humans in the larger world—to live as Confucians by day, as it were, and Daoists by night.

Sources from the Past

Laozi on Living in Harmony with *Dao*

Committed Daoists mostly rejected opportunities to play active roles in government. Yet like the Confucians, the Daoists held strong views on virtuous behavior, and their understanding of dao *had deep political implications, as exemplified by the following excerpts from the* Daodejing.

The highest goodness is like water, for water is excellent in benefitting all things, and it does not strive. It occupies the lowest place, which men abhor. And therefore it is near akin to the *dao*. . . .

In governing men and in serving heaven, there is nothing like moderation. For only by moderation can there be an early return to the normal state of humankind. This early return is the same as a great storage of virtue. With a great storage of virtue there is nothing that may not be achieved. If there is nothing that may not be achieved, then no one will know to what extent this power reaches. And if no one knows to what extent a man's power reaches, that man is fit to be the ruler of a state. Having the secret of rule, his rule shall endure. Setting the tap-root deep, and making the spreading roots firm: this is the way to ensure long life to the tree. . . .

Use uprightness in ruling a state; employ indirect methods in waging war; practice non-interference in order to win the empire. . . .

The greater the number of laws and enactments, the more thieves and robbers there will be. Therefore the Sage [Laozi] says: "So long as I do nothing, the people will work out their own reformation. So long as I love calm, the people will right themselves. If only I keep from meddling, the people will grow rich. If only I am free from desire, the people will come naturally back to simplicity. . . ."

There is nothing in the world more soft and weak than water, yet for attacking things that are hard and strong, there is nothing that surpasses it, nothing that can take its place.

The soft overcomes the hard; the weak overcomes the strong. There is no one in the world but knows this truth, and no one who can put it into practice.

SOURCE: Lionel Giles, trans. *The Sayings of Lao Tzu.* London: John Murray, 1905, pp. 26, 29–30, 41, 50. (Translations slightly modified.)

To what extent did Daoists offer useful or practical political alternatives in the Period of the Warring States?

Legalism

Ultimately, neither Confucian activism nor Daoist retreat was able to solve the problems of the Period of the Warring States. Order returned to China only after the emergence of a third school of thought—that of the Legalists—which promoted a practical and ruthlessly efficient approach to statecraft. Unlike the Confucians, the Legalists did not concern themselves with ethics, morality, or propriety. Unlike the Daoists, the Legalists cared nothing about principles governing the world or the place of human beings in nature. Instead, they devoted their attention exclusively to the state, which they sought to strengthen and expand at all costs.

Shang Yang   Legalist doctrine emerged from the insights of men who participated actively in Chinese political affairs during the late fourth century B.C.E. Most notable of them was Shang Yang (ca. 390–338 B.C.E.), who served as chief minister to the duke of the Qin state in western China. His policies survive in a work entitled *The Book of*

Lord Shang, which most likely includes contributions from other ministers as well as from Shang Yang himself. Though a clever and efficient administrator, Shang Yang also was despised and feared because of his power and ruthlessness. Upon the death of his patron, the duke of Qin, Shang Yang quickly fell: his enemies at court executed him, mutilated his body, and annihilated his family.

The most systematic of the Legalist theorists was Han Feizi (ca. 280–233 B.C.E.), a student of the Confucian scholar Xunzi. Han Feizi carefully reviewed Legalist ideas from political thinkers in all parts of China and synthesized them in a collection of powerful and well-argued essays on statecraft. Like Shang Yang, Han Feizi served as an advisor at the Qin court, and he too fell afoul of other ambitious men, who forced him to end his life by taking poison. The Legalist state itself consumed the two foremost exponents of Legalist doctrine.

Han Feizi

Shang Yang, Han Feizi, and other Legalists reasoned that the foundations of a state's strength were agriculture and armed forces. Thus Legalists sought to channel as many individuals as possible into cultivation or military service while discouraging them from pursuing careers as merchants, entrepreneurs, scholars, educators, philosophers, poets, or artists, since those lines of work did not directly advance the interests of the state.

Legalist Doctrine

The Legalists expected to harness subjects' energy by means of clear and strict laws—hence the name "Legalist." Their faith in laws distinguished the Legalists clearly from the Confucians, who relied on ritual, custom, education, a sense of propriety, and the humane example of benevolent *junzi* administrators to induce individuals to behave appropriately. The Legalists believed that these influences were not powerful enough to persuade subjects to subordinate their self-interest to the needs of the state. They imposed a strict legal regimen that clearly outlined expectations and provided severe punishment, swiftly administered, for violators. They believed that if people feared to commit small crimes, they would hesitate all the more before committing great crimes. Thus Legalists imposed harsh penalties even for minor infractions: individuals could suffer amputation of their hands or feet, for example, for disposing of ashes or trash in the street. The Legalists also established the principle of collective responsibility before the law. They expected all members of a family or community to observe the others closely, forestall any illegal activity, and report any infractions. Failing these obligations, all members of a family or community were liable to punishment along with the actual violator.

The Legalists' principles of government did not win them much popularity. Over the course of the centuries, Chinese moral and political philosophers have had little praise for the Legalists, and few have openly associated themselves with the Legalist school. Yet Legalist doctrine lent itself readily to practical application, and Legalist principles of government quickly produced remarkable results for rulers who adopted them. In fact, Legalist methods put an end to the Period of the Warring States and brought about the unification of China.

THE UNIFICATION OF CHINA

During the Period of the Warring States, rulers of several regional states adopted elements of the Legalist program. Legalist doctrines met the most enthusiastic response in the state of Qin, in western China, where Shang Yang and Han Feizi oversaw the implementation of Legalist policies. The Qin state soon dominated its neighbors and imposed centralized imperial rule throughout China. Qin rule survived only for a few years, but the succeeding Han dynasty followed the Qin example by governing China through a centralized imperial administration.

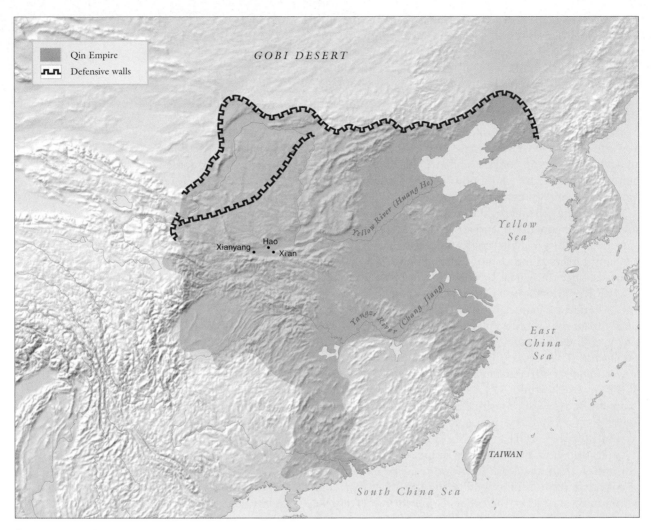

MAP [8.1]
China under the Qin
dynasty, 221–207 B.C.E.

For an interactive version
of this map, go to
www.mhhe.com/
bentley3ch8maps.

The Kingdom of Qin

The Qin Dynasty

During the fourth and third centuries B.C.E., the Qin state underwent a remarkable round of economic, political, and military development. Shang Yang encouraged peasant cultivators to migrate to the sparsely populated state. By granting them private plots and allowing them to enjoy generous profits, his policy dramatically boosted agricultural production. By granting land rights to individual cultivators, his policy also weakened the economic position of the hereditary aristocratic classes. This approach allowed Qin rulers to establish centralized, bureaucratic rule throughout their state. Meanwhile, they devoted the newfound wealth of their state to the organization of a powerful army equipped with the most effective iron weapons available. During the third century B.C.E., the kingdom of Qin gradually but consistently grew at the expense of the other Chinese states. Qin rulers attacked one state after another, absorbing each new conquest into their centralized structure, until finally they had brought China for the first time under the sway of a single state.

The First Emperor

In the year 221 B.C.E., the king of Qin proclaimed himself the First Emperor and decreed that his descendants would follow him and reign for thousands of generations. The First Emperor, Qin Shihuangdi (reigned 221–210 B.C.E.), could not know that his dynasty would last only fourteen years and in 207 B.C.E. would dissolve because of civil insurrections. Yet the Qin dynasty had a significance out of proportion to its short life. Like the Achaemenid empire in Persia, the Qin dynasty established a tradition of centralized imperial rule that provided large-scale political organization over the long term of Chinese history.

Like his ancestors in the kingdom of Qin, the First Emperor of China ignored the nobility and ruled his empire through a centralized bureaucracy. He governed from his capital at Xianyang, near the early Zhou capital of Hao and the modern city of Xi'an. The remainder of China he

A life-size model of an infantryman suggests the discipline that drove the armies of Qin Shihuangdi.

divided into administrative provinces and districts, and he entrusted the communication and implementation of his policies to officers of the central government who served at the pleasure of the emperor himself. He disarmed regional military forces and destroyed fortresses that might serve as points of rebellion or resistance. He built roads to facilitate communications and the movement of armies. He also drafted laborers by the hundreds of thousands to build defensive walls. Regional kings in northern and western regions of China had already constructed many walls in their own realms in an effort to discourage raids by nomadic peoples. Qin Shihuangdi ordered workers to link the existing sections into a massive defensive barrier that was a precursor to the Great Wall of China.

Resistance to Qin Policies

It is likely that many Chinese welcomed the political stability introduced by the Qin dynasty, but by no means did the new regime win universal acceptance. Confucians, Daoists, and others launched a vigorous campaign of criticism. In an effort to reassert his authority, Qin Shihuangdi ordered execution for those who criticized his regime, and he demanded the burning of all books of philosophy, ethics, history, and literature. His decree exempted works on medicine, fortune-telling, and agriculture on the grounds that they had some utilitarian value. The emperor also spared the official history of the Qin state. Other works, however, largely went into the flames during the next few years.

The Burning of the Books

The First Emperor took his policy seriously and enforced it earnestly. In the year following his decree, Qin Shihuangdi sentenced some 460 scholars residing in the capital to be buried alive for their criticism of his regime, and he forced many other critics from the provinces into the army and dispatched them to dangerous frontier posts. For the better part of a generation, there was no open discussion of classical literary or philosophical works. When it became safe again to speak openly, scholars began a long and painstaking task of reconstructing the suppressed texts. In some cases scholars had managed, at great personal risk, to hide copies of the forbidden books, which they retrieved and recirculated. In other cases they reassembled texts that they had committed to memory. In many cases, however, works suppressed by Qin Shihuangdi simply disappeared.

Qin Centralization

The First Emperor launched several initiatives that enhanced the unity of China. In keeping with his policy of centralization, he standardized the laws, currencies, weights, and measures of the various regions of China. Previously, regional states had organized their own legal and economic systems, which often conflicted with one another and hampered commerce and communications across state boundaries. Uniform coinage and legal standards encouraged the integration of China's various regions into a more tightly knit society than had ever been conceivable before. The roads and bridges that Qin Shihuangdi built throughout his realm, like those built in other classical societies, also encouraged economic integration: though constructed largely with military uses in mind, they served as fine highways for interregional commerce.

Standardized Script

Perhaps even more important than his legal and economic policies was the First Emperor's standardization of Chinese script. Before the Qin dynasty, all regions of China used scripts derived from the one employed at the Shang court, but they had developed along different lines and had become mutually unrecognizable. In hopes of ensuring better understanding and uniform application of his policies, Qin Shihuangdi mandated the use of a common script throughout his empire. The regions of China continued to use different spoken languages, as they do even today, but they wrote these languages with a common script—just as if Europeans spoke English, French, German, Italian, Russian, Spanish, and other languages but wrote them all down in Latin. In China, speakers of different languages use the same written symbols, but pronounce them and process them mentally in different ways. Nevertheless, the common script enables them to communicate in writing across linguistic boundaries.

In spite of his ruthlessness, Qin Shihuangdi ranks as one of the most important figures in Chinese history. The First Emperor established a precedent for centralized imperial rule, which remained the norm in China until the early twentieth century. He also pointed China in the direction of political and cultural unity, and with some periods of interruption, China has remained politically and culturally unified to the present day.

Tomb of the First Emperor

Qin Shihuangdi died in 210 B.C.E. His final resting place was a lavish tomb constructed by some seven hundred thousand drafted laborers as a permanent monument to the First Emperor. Rare and expensive grave goods accompanied the emperor in burial, along with sacrificed slaves, concubines, and many of the craftsmen who designed and built the tomb. Qin Shihuangdi was laid to rest in an elaborate underground palace lined with bronze and protected by traps and crossbows rigged to fire at intruders. The ceiling of the palace featured paintings of the stars and planets, while a vast map of the First Emperor's realm, with flowing mercury representing its rivers and seas, decorated the floor. Buried in the vicinity of the tomb itself was an entire army of life-size pottery figures to guard the emperor in death. Since 1974, when scholars began to excavate the area around Qin Shihuangdi's tomb, more than fifteen thousand terra-cotta sculptures have come to light, including magnificently detailed soldiers, horses, and weapons.

One detachment of the formidable, life-size, terra-cotta army buried in the vicinity of Qin Shihuangdi's tomb to protect the emperor after his death.

The terra-cotta army of Qin Shihuangdi protected his tomb until recent times, but it could not save his successors or his empire. The First Emperor had conscripted millions of laborers from all parts of China to work on massive public works projects such as palaces, roads, bridges, irrigation systems, defensive walls, and his own tomb. While these projects increased productivity and promoted the integration of China's various regions, they also generated tremendous ill will among laborers compelled to leave their families and their lands. Revolts began in the year after Qin Shihuangdi's death, and in 207 B.C.E. waves of rebels overwhelmed the Qin court, slaughtering government officials and burning state buildings. The Qin dynasty quickly dissolved in chaos.

The Early Han Dynasty

Liu Bang

The bloody end of the Qin dynasty might well have ended the experiment with centralized imperial rule in China. Although ambitious governors and generals could have carved China into regions and contested one another for hegemony in a reprise of the Period of the Warring States, centralized rule returned almost immediately, largely because of a determined commander named Liu Bang. Judging from the historian Sima Qian's account, Liu Bang was not a colorful or charismatic figure, but he was a persistent man and a methodical planner. He surrounded himself with brilliant advisors and enjoyed the unwavering loyalty of his troops. By 206 B.C.E. he had restored order throughout China and established himself at the head of a new dynasty.

Liu Bang called the new dynasty the Han, in honor of his native land. The Han dynasty turned out to be one of the longest and most influential in all of Chinese history. It lasted for more than four hundred years, from 206 B.C.E. to 220 C.E., although for a brief period (9–23 C.E.) a usurper temporarily displaced Han rule. Thus historians conventionally divide the dynasty into the Former Han (206 B.C.E.–9 C.E.) and the Later Han (25–220 C.E.).

The Han dynasty consolidated the tradition of centralized imperial rule that the Qin dynasty had pioneered. During the Former Han, emperors ruled from Chang'an, a cosmopolitan city near modern Xi'an that became the cultural capital of China. They mostly used wood as a building material, and later dynasties built over their city, so nothing of Han-era Chang'an survives. Contemporaries described Chang'an as a thriving metropolis with a fine imperial palace, busy markets, and expansive parks. During the Later Han, the emperors moved their capital east to Luoyang, also a cosmopolitan city second in importance only to Chang'an throughout much of Chinese history.

Early Han Policies

During the early days of the Han dynasty, Liu Bang attempted to follow a middle path between the decentralized network of political alliances of the Zhou dynasty and the tightly centralized state of the Qin. Zhou decentralization encouraged political chaos, he thought, because regional governors were powerful enough to resist the emperor and pursue their own ambitions. Liu Bang thought that Qin centralization created a new set of problems, however, because it provided little incentive for imperial family members to support the dynasty.

Liu Bang tried to save the advantages and avoid the excesses of both Zhou and Qin dynasties. On the one hand, he allotted large landholdings to members of the imperial family, in the expectation that they would provide a reliable network of support for his rule. On the other hand, he divided the empire into administrative districts governed by officials who served at the emperor's pleasure in the expectation that he could exercise effective control over the development and implementation of his policies.

Liu Bang learned quickly that reliance on his family did not guarantee support for the emperor. In 200 B.C.E. an army of nomadic Xiongnu warriors besieged Liu Bang and almost captured him. He managed to escape—but without receiving the support he had expected from his family members. From that point forward, Liu Bang and his successors followed a policy of centralization. They reclaimed lands from family members, absorbed those lands into the imperial domain, and entrusted political responsibilities to an administrative bureaucracy. Thus, despite a brief flirtation with a decentralized government, the Han dynasty left as its principal political legacy a tradition of centralized imperial rule.

The Martial Emperor, Han Wudi

Much of the reason for the Han dynasty's success was the long reign of the dynasty's greatest and most energetic emperor, Han Wudi, the "Martial Emperor," who occupied the imperial throne for fifty-four years, from 141 to 87 B.C.E. Han Wudi ruled his empire with vision and vigor. He pursued two policies in particular: administrative centralization and imperial expansion.

Han Centralization

Domestically, Han Wudi worked strenuously to increase the authority and prestige of the central government. He built an enormous bureaucracy to administer his empire, and he relied on Legalist principles of government. Like Qin Shihuangdi, Han Wudi sent imperial officers to implement his policies and maintain order in administrative provinces and districts. He also continued the Qin policy of building roads and canals to facilitate trade and communication between China's regions. To finance the vast machinery of his government, he levied taxes on agriculture, trade, and craft industries, and he established imperial monopolies on the production of

Model of a chariot of the kind used by high imperial officials in the Qin and Han dynasties. Crafted from bronze with silver inlay, this model is about one-third life size.

essential goods such as iron and salt while placing the lucrative liquor industry under state supervision.

In building such an enormous governmental structure, Han Wudi faced a serious problem of recruitment. He needed thousands of reliable, intelligent, educated individuals to run his bureaucracy, but education in China took place largely on an individual, ad hoc basis. Men such as Confucius, Mencius, and Xunzi accepted students and tutored them, but there was no system to provide a continuous supply of educated candidates for office.

The Confucian Educational System

Han Wudi addressed this problem in 124 B.C.E. by establishing an imperial university that prepared young men for government service. Personally, the Martial Emperor was a practical man of affairs who cared little for learning. In this respect he resembled all the other early Han emperors: Liu Bang once emptied his bladder in the distinctive cap worn by Confucian scholars in order to demonstrate his contempt for academic pursuits! Yet Han Wudi recognized that the success of his efforts at bureaucratic centralization would depend on a corps of educated officeholders. The imperial university took Confucianism—the only Chinese cultural tradition developed enough to provide rigorous intellectual discipline—as the basis for its curriculum. Ironically, then, while he relied on Legalist principles of government, Han Wudi ensured the long-term survival of the Confucian tradition by establishing it as the official imperial ideology. By the end of the Former Han dynasty, the imperial university enrolled more than three thousand students, and by the end of the Later Han, the student population had risen to more than thirty thousand.

Han Imperial Expansion

While he moved aggressively to centralize power and authority at home, Han Wudi pursued an equally vigorous foreign policy of imperial expansion. He invaded northern Vietnam and Korea, subjected them to Han rule, and brought them into

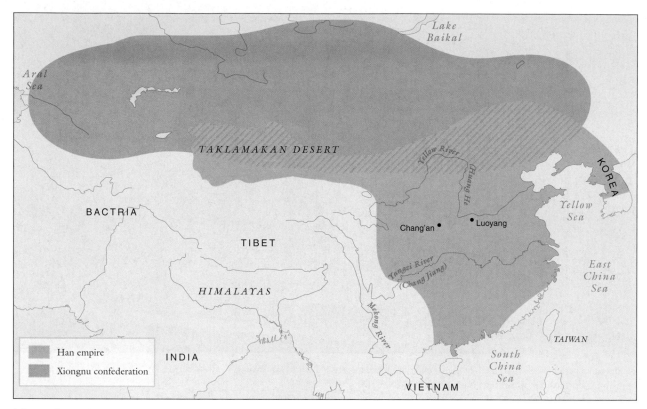

MAP [8.2]

East Asia and central Asia at the time of Han Wudi, ca. 87 B.C.E.

The Xiongnu

the orbit of Chinese society. He ruled both lands through a Chinese-style government, and Confucian values followed the Han armies into the new colonies. Over the course of the centuries, the educational systems of both northern Vietnam and Korea drew their inspiration almost entirely from Confucianism.

The greatest foreign challenge that Han Wudi faced came from the Xiongnu, a nomadic people from the steppes of central Asia who spoke a Turkish language. Like most of the other nomadic peoples of central Asia, the Xiongnu were superb horsemen. Xiongnu boys learned to ride sheep and shoot rodents at an early age, and as they grew older they graduated to larger animals and aimed their bows and arrows at larger prey. Their weaponry was not as sophisticated as that of the Chinese: their bows and arrows were not nearly as lethal as the ingenious and powerful crossbows wielded by Chinese warriors. But their mobility offered the Xiongnu a distinct advantage. When they could not satisfy their needs and desires through peaceful trade, they mounted sudden raids into villages or trading areas, where they commandeered food supplies or manufactured goods and then rapidly departed. Because they had no cities or settled places to defend, the Xiongnu could quickly disperse when confronted by a superior force.

During the reign of Maodun (210–174 B.C.E.), their most successful leader, the Xiongnu ruled a vast federation of nomadic peoples that stretched from the Aral Sea to the Yellow Sea. Maodun brought strict military discipline to the Xiongnu. According to Sima Qian, Maodun once instructed his forces to shoot their arrows at whatever target he himself selected. He aimed in succession at his favorite horse, one of his wives, and his father's best horse, and he summarily executed those who failed to discharge their arrows. When his forces reliably followed his orders, Maodun targeted his father, who immediately fell under a hail of arrows, leaving Maodun as the Xiongnu chief.

With its highly disciplined army, the Xiongnu empire was a source of concern to the Han emperors. During the early days of the dynasty, they attempted to pacify the Xiongnu by paying them tribute—providing them with food and finished goods in hopes that they would refrain from mounting raids in China—or by arranging marriages between the ruling houses of the two peoples in hopes of establishing peaceful diplomatic relations. Neither method succeeded for long.

Ultimately, Han Wudi decided to go on the offensive against the Xiongnu. He invaded central Asia with vast armies—sometimes including as many as one hundred thousand troops—and brought much of the Xiongnu empire under Chinese military control. He pacified a long central Asian corridor extending almost to Bactria, which prevented the Xiongnu from maintaining the integrity of their empire and which served also as the lifeline of a trade network that linked much of the Eurasian landmass. He even planted colonies of Chinese cultivators in the oasis communities of central Asia. As a result of these efforts, the Xiongnu empire soon fell into disarray. For the moment, the Han state enjoyed uncontested hegemony in both east Asia and central Asia. Before long, however, economic and social problems within China brought serious problems for the Han dynasty itself.

Han Expansion into Central Asia

FROM ECONOMIC PROSPERITY TO SOCIAL DISORDER

Already during the Xia, Shang, and Zhou dynasties, a productive agricultural economy supported the emergence of complex society in China. High agricultural productivity continued during the Qin and Han dynasties, and it supported the development of craft industries such as the forging of iron tools and the weaving of silk textiles. During the Han dynasty, however, China experienced serious social and economic problems as land became concentrated in the hands of a small, wealthy elite class. Social tensions generated banditry, rebellion, and even the temporary deposition of the Han state itself. Although Han rulers regained the throne, they presided over a much-weakened realm. By the early third century C.E., social and political problems had brought the Han dynasty to an end.

Productivity and Prosperity during the Former Han

The structure of Chinese society during the Qin and Han dynasties was very similar to that of the Zhou era. Patriarchal households averaged five inhabitants, although several generations of aristocratic families sometimes lived together in large compounds. During the Han dynasty, moralists sought to enhance the authority of patriarchal family heads by emphasizing the importance of filial piety and women's subordination to their menfolk. The anonymous Confucian *Classic of Filial Piety,* composed probably in the early Han dynasty, taught that children should obey and honor their parents as well as other superiors and political authorities. Similarly, Ban Zhao, a well-educated woman from a prominent Han family, wrote a widely read treatise entitled *Admonitions for Women* that emphasized humility, obedience, subservience, and devotion to their husbands as the virtues most appropriate for women. To Confucian moralists and government authorities alike, orderly, patriarchal families were the foundations of a stable society.

Patriarchal Social Order

The vast majority of the Chinese population worked in the countryside cultivating grains and vegetables, which they harvested in larger quantities than ever before. In late Zhou times, cultivators often strengthened their plows with iron tips, but metalworkers did not produce enough iron to provide all-metal tools. During the Han dynasty the

Clay model of an aristocratic house of the sort inhabited by a powerful clan during the Han dynasty. This model came from a tomb near the city of Guangzhou in southern China.

Iron Metallurgy

iron industry entered a period of rapid growth—partly because Han rulers favored the industry and encouraged its expansion—and cultivators soon used not only plows but also shovels, picks, hoes, sickles, and spades with iron parts. The tougher implements enabled cultivators to produce more food and support larger populations than ever before. The agricultural surplus allowed many Chinese to produce fine manufactured goods and to engage in trade.

The significance of the iron industry went far beyond agriculture. Han artisans experimented with production techniques and learned to craft fine utensils for both domestic and military uses. Iron pots, stoves, knives, needles, axes, hammers, saws, and other tools became standard fixtures in households that could not have afforded more expensive bronze utensils. The ready availability of iron also had important military implications. Craftsmen designed suits of iron armor to protect soldiers against arrows and blows, and the strength and sharpness of Han swords, spears, and arrowheads help to explain the success of Chinese armies against the Xiongnu and other nomadic peoples.

Silk Textiles

Textile production—particularly sericulture, the manufacture of silk—became an especially important industry. The origins of sericulture date to the fourth millennium B.C.E., long before the ancient Xia dynasty, but only in Han times did sericulture expand from its original home in the Yellow River valley to most parts of China. It developed especially rapidly in the southern regions known today as Sichuan and Guangdong provinces, and the industry thrived after the establishment of long-distance trade relations with western lands in the second century B.C.E.

Although silkworms inhabited much of Eurasia, Chinese silk was especially fine because of advanced sericulture techniques. Chinese producers bred their silkworms, fed them on finely chopped mulberry leaves, and carefully unraveled their cocoons so as to obtain long fibers of raw silk that they wove into light, strong, lustrous fabrics. (In other lands, producers relied on wild silkworms that ate a variety of leaves and chewed through their cocoons, leaving only short fibers that yielded lower-quality fabrics.) Chinese silk became a prized commodity in India, Persia, Mesopotamia, and even the distant Roman empire. Commerce in silk and other products led to the establishment of an intricate network of trade routes known collectively as the silk roads (discussed in chapter 12).

Paper

While expanding the iron and silk industries, Han craftsmen also invented paper. In earlier times Chinese scribes had written mostly on bamboo strips and silk fabrics but also inscribed messages on oracle bones and bronze wares. Probably before 100 C.E.

Han gentlemen sport luxurious silk gowns as they engage in sophisticated conversation. Wealthy individuals and ruling elites commonly dressed in silk, but peasants and others of the lower classes rarely if ever donned silk garments.

Chinese craftsmen began to fashion hemp, bark, and textile fibers into sheets of paper, which was less expensive than silk and easier to write on than bamboo. Although wealthy elites continued to read books written on silk rolls, paper soon became the preferred medium for most writing.

High agricultural productivity supported rapid demographic growth and general prosperity during the early part of the Han dynasty. Historians estimate that in about 220 B.C.E., just after the founding of the Qin dynasty, the Chinese population was about twenty million. By the year 9 C.E., at the end of the Former Han dynasty, it had tripled to sixty million. Meanwhile, taxes claimed only a small portion of production, yet state granaries bulged so much that their contents sometimes spoiled before they could be consumed.

Population Growth

Economic and Social Difficulties

In spite of general prosperity, China began to experience economic and social difficulties in the Former Han period. The military adventures and the central Asian policy of Han Wudi caused severe economic strain. Expeditions against the Xiongnu and the establishment of agricultural colonies in central Asia were extremely expensive undertakings, and they rapidly consumed the empire's surplus wealth. To finance his ventures, Han Wudi raised taxes and confiscated land and personal property from wealthy individuals, sometimes on the pretext that they had violated imperial laws. These measures did not kill industry and commerce in China, but they discouraged investment in manufacturing and trading enterprises, which in turn had a dampening effect on the larger economy.

In Han times the wealthiest classes enjoyed the privilege of being buried in suits of jade plaques sewn together with gold threads, like the burial dress of Liu Sheng, who died in 113 B.C.E. at Manzheng in Hebei Province. Legend held that jade prevented decomposition of the deceased's body. Scholars have estimated that a jade burial suit like this one required ten years' worth of labor.

Social Tensions

Distinctions between rich and poor hardened during the course of the Han dynasty. Wealthy individuals wore fine silk garments, leather shoes, and jewelry of jade and gold, whereas the poor classes made do with rough hemp clothing and sandals. Tables in wealthy households held pork, fish, fowl, and fine aged wines, but the diet of the poor consisted mostly of grain or rice supplemented by small quantities of vegetables or meat. By the first century B.C.E., social and economic differences had generated serious tensions, and peasants in hard-pressed regions began to organize rebellions in hopes of gaining a larger share of Han society's resources.

Land Distribution

A particularly difficult problem concerned the distribution of land. Individual economic problems brought on by poor harvests, high taxes, or crushing burdens of debt forced many small landowners to sell their property under unfavorable conditions or even to forfeit it in exchange for cancellation of their debts. In extreme cases, individuals had to sell themselves and their families into slavery to satisfy their creditors. Owners of large estates not only increased the size of their holdings by absorbing the property of their less fortunate neighbors but also increased the efficiency of their operations by employing cheap labor. Sometimes cheap laborers came in the form of slaves, other times in the form of tenant farmers who had to deliver as much as half their produce to the landowner for the right to till his property. In either case the laborers worked on terms that favored the landlords.

By the end of the first century B.C.E., land had accumulated in the hands of a relatively small number of individuals who owned vast estates, while ever-increasing numbers of peasant cultivators led difficult lives with few prospects for improvement. Landless peasants became restive, and Chinese society faced growing problems of banditry and sporadic rebellion. Because the Han emperors depended heavily on the political cooperation of large landowners, however, they did not attempt any serious reform of the landholding system.

The Reign of Wang Mang

Tensions came to a head during the early first century C.E. when a powerful and respected Han minister named Wang Mang undertook a thoroughgoing program of reform. In 6 C.E. a two-year-old boy inherited the Han imperial throne. Because the boy was unable to govern, Wang Mang served as his regent. Many officials regarded Wang as more capable than members of the Han family and urged him to claim the imperial honor for himself. In 9 C.E. he did just that: announcing that the mandate

A painted brick depicts a peasant working in the fields with a team of oxen and a wooden harrow. By the Han dynasty, many plows of this type had iron teeth. Produced in the third or fourth century C.E., this brick painting came from a tomb in Gansu Province in western China.

of heaven had passed from the Han to his own family, he seized the throne. Wang Mang then introduced a series of wide-ranging reforms that have prompted historians to refer to him as the "socialist emperor."

The most important reforms concerned landed property: Wang Mang limited the amount of land that a family could hold and ordered officials to break up large estates, redistribute them, and provide landless individuals with property to cultivate. Despite his good intentions, the socialist emperor attempted to impose his policy without adequate preparation and communication. The result was confusion: landlords resisted a policy that threatened their holdings, and even peasants found its application inconsistent and unsatisfactory. After several years of chaos, Wang Mang faced the additional misfortune of poor harvests and famine, which sparked widespread revolts against his rule. In 23 C.E. a coalition of disgruntled landlords and desperate peasants ended both his dynasty and his life.

The Later Han Dynasty

Within two years a recovered Han dynasty returned to power, but it ruled over a weakened realm. The Later Han emperors even decided to abandon Chang'an, which had suffered grave damage during the years of chaos and rebellion, and establish a new capital at Luoyang. Nevertheless, during the early years of the Later Han, emperors ruled vigorously in the manner of Liu Bang and Han Wudi. They regained control of the centralized administration and reorganized the state bureaucracy. They also maintained the Chinese presence in central Asia, continued to keep the Xiongnu in submission, and exercised firm control over the silk roads.

The Later Han emperors did not seriously address the problem of land distribution that had helped to bring down the Former Han dynasty. The wealthy classes still lived in relative luxury while peasants worked under difficult conditions. The empire continued to suffer the effects of banditry and rebellions organized by desperate peasants with few opportunities to improve their lot. The Yellow Turban uprising—so named because of the distinctive headgear worn by the rebels—was a particularly serious revolt that raged throughout China and tested the resilience of the Han state during the

The Yellow Turban Uprising

Though it dates from a somewhat later era about the sixth century C.E., this cave painting from Dunhuang in Gansu Province (western China) offers some idea of the chaos that engulfed China as the Han dynasty crumbled.

Collapse of the Han Dynasty

late second century C.E. Although the Later Han dynasty possessed the military power required to keep civil disorder under reasonable control, rebellions by the Yellow Turbans and others weakened the Han state during the second and third centuries C.E.

The Later Han emperors were unable, however, to prevent the development of factions at court that paralyzed the central government. Factions of imperial family members, Confucian scholar bureaucrats, and court eunuchs sought to increase their influence, protect their own interests, and destroy their rivals. On several occasions relations between the various factions became so strained that they made war against each other. In 189 C.E., for example, a faction led by an imperial relative descended on the Han palace and slaughtered more than two thousand beardless men in an effort to destroy the eunuchs as a political force. In this respect the attack succeeded. From the unmeasured violence of the operation, however, it is clear that the Later Han dynasty had reached a point of internal weakness from which it could not easily recover. Indeed, early in the next century, the central government disintegrated, and for almost four centuries China remained divided into several large regional kingdoms.

The Qin state lasted for a short fourteen years, but it opened a new era in Chinese history. Qin conquerors imposed unified rule on a series of politically independent kingdoms and launched an ambitious program to forge culturally distinct regions into a larger Chinese society. The Han dynasty endured for more than four centuries and largely completed the project of unifying China. Han rulers built a centralized bureaucracy that administered a unified empire, thus establishing a precedent for centralized imperial rule in China. They also entered into a close alliance with Confucian moralists who organized a system of advanced education that provided recruits for the imperial bureaucracy. Moreover, on the basis of a highly productive economy stimulated by technological innovations, Han rulers projected Chinese influence abroad to Korea, Vietnam, and central Asia. Thus, like classical societies in Persia, India, and the Mediterranean basin, Han China produced a set of distinctive political and cultural traditions that shaped Chinese and neighboring societies over the long term.

CHRONOLOGY

sixth century B.C.E.(?)	Laozi
551–479 B.C.E.	Confucius
403–221 B.C.E.	Period of the Warring States
390–338 B.C.E.	Shang Yang
372–289 B.C.E.	Mencius
298–238 B.C.E.	Xunzi
280–233 B.C.E.	Han Feizi
221–207 B.C.E.	Qin dynasty
206 B.C.E.–9 C.E.	Former Han dynasty
141–87 B.C.E.	Reign of Han Wudi
9–23 C.E.	Reign of Wang Mang
25–220 C.E.	Later Han dynasty

FOR FURTHER READING

Thomas J. Barfield. *The Perilous Frontier: Nomadic Empires and China*. Cambridge, Mass., 1989. A provocative analysis of the relations between Chinese and central Asian peoples.

Derk Bodde. *China's First Unifier: A Study of the Ch'in Dynasty as Seen in the Life of Li Ssu*. Leiden, 1938. Important study of the minister responsible for much of the Qin dynasty's policy.

H. G. Creel. *The Birth of China*. New York, 1937. An older work offering a lively and well-written popular account.

Sebastian De Grazia, ed. *Masters of Chinese Political Thought from the Beginnings to the Han Dynasty*. New York, 1973. A valuable collection of primary sources in translation, all of them bearing on political themes.

Mark Elvin. *The Pattern of the Chinese Past*. Stanford, 1973. A remarkable analysis of Chinese history by an economic historian who brings a comparative perspective to his work.

Cho-yun Hsu. *Han Agriculture: The Formation of Early Chinese Agrarian Economy (206 B.C.–A.D. 220)*. Seattle, 1980. Studies the development of intensive agriculture in Han China and provides English translations of more than two hundred documents illustrating the conditions of rural life.

Michael Loewe. *Everyday Life in Early Imperial China*. London, 1968. Deals with the social, economic, and cultural history of China during the Han dynasty.

Victor H. Mair, trans. *Tao Te Ching: The Classic Book of Integrity and the Way*. New York, 1990. A fresh and lively translation of the Daoist classic *Daodejing,* based on recently discovered manuscripts.

Frederick W. Mote. *Intellectual Foundations of China*. 2nd ed. New York, 1989. A compact and concise introduction to the cultural history of classical China.

Michele Pirazzoli-t'Serstevens. *The Han Dynasty*. Trans. by J. Seligman. New York, 1982. An excellent and well-illustrated survey of Han China that draws on archaeological discoveries.

Benjamin I. Schwartz. *The World of Thought in Ancient China*. Cambridge, Mass., 1985. A synthesis of classical Chinese thought by a leading scholar.

Arthur Waldron. *The Great Wall of China: From History to Myth*. Cambridge, 1989. Places the modern Great Wall in the tradition of Chinese wall building from Qin times forward.

Arthur Waley, trans. *The Analects of Confucius*. New York, 1938. An English version of Confucius's sayings by a gifted translator.

———, trans. *Three Ways of Thought in Ancient China*. New York, 1940. Translations and comments on works from Confucian, Daoist, and Legalist traditions.

Burton Watson, trans. *Basic Writings of Mo Tzu, Hsün Tzu, and Han Fei Tzu*. New York, 1967. Translations of important political and social treatises from classical China.

———, trans. *Records of the Grand Historian*. Rev. ed. 2 vols. New York, 1993. Excellent translation of Sima Qian's history, the most important narrative source for Han China.

Wang Zhongshu. *Han Civilization*. Trans. by K. C. Chang. New Haven, 1982. A scholarly work that draws on both historical and archaeological research.

See our **Online Learning Center** at www.mhhe.com/bentley3 for additional readings, practice maps, quizzes, and internet activities.

Unfamiliar words? Check out the **Primary Source Investigator CD-ROM** for an interactive glossary, interactive maps, more images, and primary sources.

Head of the Buddha carved in limestone.

CHAPTER 9

STATE, SOCIETY, AND THE QUEST FOR SALVATION IN INDIA

The earliest description of India by a foreigner came from the pen of a Greek ambassador named Megasthenes. As the diplomatic representative of the Seleucid emperor, Megasthenes lived in India for many years during the late fourth and early third centuries B.C.E., and he traveled throughout much of northern India. Although Megasthenes' book, the *Indika,* has long been lost, many quotations from it survive in Greek and Latin literature. These fragments clearly show that Megasthenes had great respect for the Indian land, people, and society.

Like travel writers of all times, Megasthenes included a certain amount of spurious information in his account of India. He wrote, for example, of ants the size of foxes that mined gold from the earth and fiercely defended their hoards from any humans who tried to steal them. Only by distracting them with slabs of meat, Megasthenes said, could humans safely make away with their treasure. He also reported races of monstrous human beings: some with no mouth who survived by breathing in the odors of fruits, flowers, and roots, others with feet pointing backwards and eight toes per foot, and yet others with the heads of dogs who communicated by barking.

Beyond the tall tales, Megasthenes offered a great deal of reliable information. He portrayed India as a fertile land that supported two harvests of grain per year. He described the capital of Pataliputra as a rectangle-shaped city situated along the Ganges River and surrounded by a moat and a massive timber wall with 570 towers and sixty-four gates. He mentioned large armies that used elephants as war animals. He pointed out the strongly hierarchical character of Indian society (although he incorrectly held that there were seven instead of four main castes). He noted that two main schools of "philosophers" (Hindus and Buddhists) enjoyed special prominence as well as exemption from taxes, and he described the ascetic lifestyles and vegetarian diets followed by particularly devout individuals. In short, Megasthenes portrayed India as a wealthy land that supported a distinctive society with well-established cultural traditions.

In India as in Persia and China, the centuries after 500 B.C.E. witnessed the development of a classical society whose influence has persisted over the centuries. Its most prominent features were a well-defined social structure, which left individuals with few doubts about their position and role in society, and several popular religious traditions that helped to shape Indian beliefs and values. Two religions, Buddhism and Hinduism, also appealed strongly to peoples beyond the subcontinent.

THE FORTUNES OF EMPIRE IN CLASSICAL INDIA
The Mauryan Dynasty and the Temporary Unification of India
The Emergence of Regional Kingdoms and the Revival of Empire

ECONOMIC DEVELOPMENT AND SOCIAL DISTINCTIONS
Towns and Trade
Family Life and the Caste System

RELIGIONS OF SALVATION IN CLASSICAL INDIA
Jainism and the Challenge to the Established Cultural Order
Early Buddhism
Mahayana Buddhism
The Emergence of Popular Hinduism

Efforts to maintain an imperial government did not succeed nearly as well in India as they did in Persia and China. For the most part, classical India fell under the sway of regional kingdoms rather than centralized empires. Imperial regimes were crucial for the consolidation of Indian cultural traditions, however, because they sponsored cultural leaders and promoted their ideals throughout the subcontinent and beyond. The spread of Buddhism is a case in point: imperial support helped the faith secure its position in India and attract converts in other lands. Thus, even in the absence of a strong and continuing imperial tradition like that of Persia or China, the social and cultural traditions of classical India not only shaped the lives and experiences of the subcontinent's inhabitants but also influenced peoples in distant lands.

THE FORTUNES OF EMPIRE IN CLASSICAL INDIA

Following their migrations to India after 1500 B.C.E., the Aryans established a series of small kingdoms throughout the subcontinent. For centuries the rulers of these kingdoms fought constantly among themselves and sought to expand their states by absorbing others. By the sixth century B.C.E., wars of expansion had resulted in the consolidation of several large regional kingdoms that dominated much of the subcontinent. Despite strenuous efforts, none of these kingdoms was able to establish hegemony over the others. During the classical era, the Mauryan and the Gupta dynasties founded centralized, imperial states that embraced much of India, but neither empire survived long enough to establish centralized rule as a lasting feature of Indian political life.

The Mauryan Dynasty and the Temporary Unification of India

The unification of India came about partly as a result of intrusion from beyond the subcontinent. About 520 B.C.E. the Persian emperor Darius crossed the Hindu Kush mountains, conquered parts of northwestern India, and made the kingdom of Gandhara in the northern Punjab (the northern part of modern-day Pakistan) a province of the Achaemenid empire. The establishment of Achaemenid authority in India introduced local rulers to Persian techniques of administration. Almost two centuries later, in 327 B.C.E., after overrunning the Persian empire, Alexander of Macedon crossed the Indus River and crushed the states he found there. Alexander remained in India only for a short time, and he did not make a deep impression on the Punjabi people: he departed after his forces mutinied in the year 325 B.C.E., and contemporary Indian sources did not even mention his name. Yet his campaign had an important effect on Indian politics and history, since he created a political vacuum in northwestern India by destroying the existing states and then withdrawing his own forces.

Kingdom of Magadha

Poised to fill the vacuum was the dynamic kingdom of Magadha, located in the central portion of the Ganges plain. Several regional kingdoms in the valley of the Ganges had become wealthy as workers turned forests into fields and trade became an increasingly prominent feature of the local economy. By about 500 B.C.E. Magadha had emerged as the most important state in northeastern India. During the next two centuries, the kings of Magadha conquered the neighboring states and gained control of Indian commerce passing through the Ganges valley as well as overseas trade between India and Burma passing across the Bay of Bengal. The withdrawal of Alexander from the Punjab presented Magadha with a rare opportunity to expand.

Chandragupta Maurya

During the late 320s B.C.E., an ambitious adventurer named Chandragupta Maurya exploited that opportunity and laid the foundation for the Mauryan empire, the first

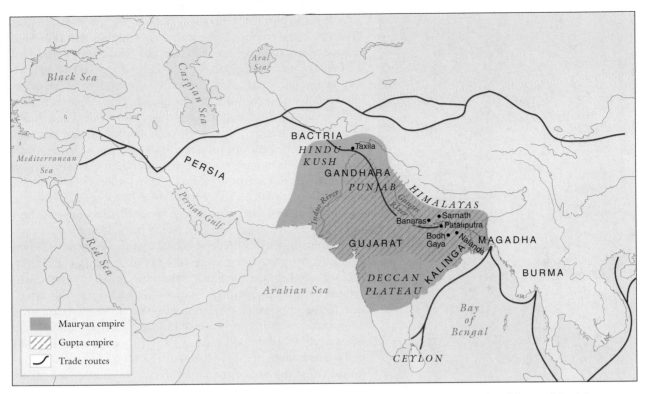

MAP [9.1]
The Mauryan and Gupta empires, 321 B.C.E.–550 C.E.

For an interactive version of this map, go to www.mhhe.com/bentley3ch9maps.

state to bring a centralized and unified government to most of the Indian subcontinent. Chandragupta began by seizing control of small, remote regions of Magadha and then worked his way gradually toward the center. By 321 B.C.E. he had overthrown the ruling dynasty and consolidated his hold on the kingdom. He then moved into the Punjab and brought northwestern India under his control. Next he ventured beyond the Indus River and conquered the Greek state in Bactria—a large region straddling the border between modern Pakistan and Afghanistan, where Alexander of Macedon's Greek successors maintained a kingdom during the Seleucid era. By the end of the fourth century B.C.E., Chandragupta's empire embraced all of northern India from the Indus to the Ganges.

Chandragupta's Government

A careful and systematic advisor named Kautalya devised procedures for the governance of Chandragupta's realm. Some of Kautalya's advice survives in the ancient Indian political handbook known as the *Arthashastra,* a manual offering detailed instructions on the uses of power and the principles of government. The *Arthashastra* outlined methods of administering the empire, overseeing trade and agriculture, collecting taxes, maintaining order, conducting foreign relations, and waging war. Kautalya also advised Chandragupta to make abundant use of spies, and he even included prostitutes in his stable of informants. Like the emperors of Persia and China, Chandragupta and Kautalya built a bureaucratic administrative system that enabled them to implement policies throughout the state.

Ashoka Maurya

Tradition holds that Chandragupta abdicated his throne to become a monk and led such an ascetic life that he starved himself to death. Whether this report is true or not, it is certain that his son succeeded him in 297 B.C.E. and added most of southern India to the growing empire. The high point of the Mauryan empire, however, came during the reign of Chandragupta's grandson Ashoka.

As a symbol of his rule, Ashoka had this sculpture of four lions mounted atop a column about 20 meters (66 feet) tall. The lion capital is the official symbol of the modern Republic of India.

Ashoka began his reign (268–232 B.C.E.) as a conqueror. When he came to power, the only major region that remained independent of the Mauryan empire was the kingdom of Kalinga (modern Orissa) in the east-central part of the subcontinent. In fact, Kalinga was not only independent of Mauryan rule but also actively hostile to its spread. The kingdom's resistance created difficulties for Ashoka because Kalinga controlled the principal trade routes, both by land and by sea, between the Ganges plain and southern India. Thus Ashoka's first major undertaking as emperor was to conquer Kalinga and bring it under Mauryan control, which he did in a bloody campaign in 260 B.C.E. By Ashoka's estimate, 100,000 Kalingans died in the fighting, 150,000 were driven from their homes, and untold numbers of others perished in the ruined land.

In spite of this campaign, Ashoka is much better known as a governor than as a conqueror. With Kalinga subdued, Ashoka ruled almost the entire subcontinent—only the southernmost region escaped his control—and he turned his attention to the responsible government of his realm. As heir to the administrative structure that Chandragupta and Kautalya had instituted, Ashoka ruled through a tightly organized bureaucracy. He established his capital at the fortified city of Pataliputra (near modern Patna), where a central administration developed policies for the whole empire. Pataliputra was a thriving and cosmopolitan city: Megasthenes reported that a local committee looked after the interests of foreigners in the city—and also carefully observed their movements. Ashoka went to great pains to ensure that his local subordinates implemented his policies. A central treasury oversaw the efficient collection of taxes—a hallmark of Kautalya's influence—which supported legions of officials, accountants, clerks, soldiers, and other imperial employees. Ashoka communicated his policies throughout his realm by inscribing edicts in natural stone formations or on pillars that he ordered erected. In these promulgations, known as the rock and pillar edicts, Ashoka issued imperial decrees, encouraged his subjects to observe Buddhist values, and expressed his intention to serve as a fair, just, and humane ruler.

As a result of Ashoka's policies, the various regions of India became well integrated, and the subcontinent benefited from both an expanding economy and a stable government. Ashoka encouraged the expansion of agriculture—the foundation of the empire's wealth—by building irrigation systems. He encouraged trade by building roads, most notably a highway of more than 1,600 kilometers (1,000 miles) linking Pataliputra with Taxila, the chief political and commercial center of northern India, which offered access to Bactria, Persia, and other points west. Ashoka also provided comforts for administrators, merchants, and other travelers by planting banyan trees to offer shade, digging wells, and establishing inns along the roads.

Decline of the Mauryan Empire

Ashoka's policies did not long survive his rule, nor did his empire. Ashoka died in 232 B.C.E., and decline set in almost immediately. During its later years the Mauryan empire suffered from acute financial and economic difficulties. The empire depended on a strong army and a large corps of officials to administer imperial policy. Salaries for soldiers and bureaucrats were very expensive: Megasthenes said that in times of peace, military forces spent their time in idleness and drinking bouts while continuing to draw

Archaeological excavations have unearthed parts of the defensive palisade, constructed of timbers almost 5 meters (16 feet) tall, that surrounded Pataliputra during Mauryan times.

their pay. Eventually, these administrative costs outstripped the revenues that flowed into the central treasury. The later Mauryan emperors often resorted to the tactic of debasing their currency—reducing the amount of precious metal in a coin without reducing its nominal value. Because of their financial difficulties, they were unable to hold the realm together. They maintained control of the Ganges valley for some fifty years after Ashoka's death, but eventually they lost their grip even on this heartland of the Mauryan empire. By about 185 B.C.E. the Mauryan empire had disappeared.

The Emergence of Regional Kingdoms and the Revival of Empire

Although the Mauryan empire came to an end, India did not crumble into anarchy. Instead, local rulers formed a series of kingdoms that brought order to large regions. Although regional kingdoms emerged throughout the subcontinent, historical records and archaeological excavations have thrown clearest light on developments in northern India. For almost two centuries after the collapse of the Mauryan empire, northwestern India fell under the rule of Greek-speaking conquerors from Bactria—Alexander of Macedon's imperial heirs who had mingled with local populations since establishing an independent Bactrian kingdom in the third century B.C.E. Indo-Greek forces invaded northern India as early as 182 B.C.E. and seized a large territory extending as far south

Bactrian Rule in Northwestern India

as Gujarat. Bactria was a thriving commercial center linking lands from China in the east to the Mediterranean basin in the west, so Bactrian rule had the effect of promoting cross-cultural interaction and exchange in northern India. Large volumes of trade provided sources of revenue for the Bactrian rulers, and the city of Taxila flourished because of its strategic location on trade routes leading from northern India to Bactria. The northern region of Gandhara became a site of intense cultural as well as commercial exchange.

The Kushan Empire   Beginning in the late second century B.C.E., several groups of nomadic conquerors from central Asia attacked Bactria and eventually put an end to the Indo-Greek kingdom there. The most successful of these conquerors were the Kushans, who ruled a sizable empire embracing much of northern India and central Asia from about 1 to 300 C.E. Under Kanishka, the most prominent of the Kushan emperors (reigned 78–103 C.E.), the Kushan empire embraced modern-day Pakistan, Afghanistan, and northern India to Gujarat and the central part of the Ganges valley. Like the Indo-Greek Bactrians, the Kushans facilitated commerce between India and lands to the north. Indeed, the Kushan empire played a crucial role in the silk roads network (discussed in chapter 12) by pacifying much of the large region between Persia and China, thus making it possible for merchants to travel safely across long distances. On several occasions the Kushans and other rulers of northern India faced ambitious kings who sought to expand their realms and imitate the Mauryas by building an empire based in the Indian subcontinent. Only with the Guptas, however, did any of them approach the realization of their imperial ambitions.

The Gupta Dynasty

Erected about 400 C.E., this iron pillar commemorates a mighty king of the Gupta dynasty, probably Chandra Gupta II. The pillar is 7.5 meters (25 feet) tall and still stands, barely rusted, near Delhi.

Like the Mauryas, the Guptas based their state in Magadha, a crucial region because of its wealth, its dominance of the Ganges valley, and its role as intermediary between the various regions of the subcontinent. The new empire arose on foundations laid by Chandra Gupta (not related to Chandragupta Maurya), who forged alliances with powerful families in the Ganges region and established a dynamic kingdom about the year 320 C.E. His successors, Samudra Gupta (reigned 335–375 C.E.) and Chandra Gupta II (reigned 375–415 C.E.), made the Magadhan capital of Pataliputra once again the center of a large empire. Between the two of them, Samudra Gupta and Chandra Gupta II conquered many of the regional kingdoms of India, and they established tributary alliances with others that elected not to fight. Only the Deccan Plateau and the southernmost part of the subcontinent remained outside the orbit of Gupta influence.

The Gupta empire was somewhat smaller in size than the Mauryan, and it also differed considerably in organization. Ashoka had insisted on knowing the details of regional affairs, which he closely monitored from his court at Pataliputra. The Guptas left local government and administration, and even the making of basic policy, in the hands of their allies in the various regions of their empire. When nomadic invaders threatened the empire during the later fifth century C.E., it split easily along the fault lines of the administrative regions. But during the late fourth and early fifth centuries C.E., the Gupta dynasty brought stability and prosperity to the subcontinent. A Chinese Buddhist monk named Faxian traveled widely in India searching for texts of the Buddhist scriptures during the reign of Chandra Gupta II. In an account of his travels, Faxian reported that India was a prosperous land with little crime. It was possible to travel throughout the country, he said, without fear of molestation and even without official travel documents.

Gupta Decline

Gupta administrative talents were not a match, however, for the invasions of the White Huns, a nomadic people from central Asia who occupied Bactria during the fourth century C.E., and then prepared to cross the Hindu Kush mountains into India. For the first half of the fifth century, the Guptas repelled the Huns, but the defense cost them dearly in resources and eventually weakened their state. By the end of the fifth century, the Huns moved across the Hindu Kush almost at will and established several kingdoms in northern and western India.

The Gupta dynasty continued in name only: regional governors progressively usurped imperial rights and powers, and contemporary documents do not even record the names of all the later Gupta emperors. Once again, imperial government survived only for a short term in India. Not until the establishment of the Mughal dynasty in the sixteenth century C.E. did any state rule as much of India as the Mauryan and Gupta empires ruled. Memories of empire remained, to be sure, and there were periodic efforts to bring all of the subcontinent again under the control of a unified regime. But for the most part, large regional kingdoms dominated political life in India during the millennium between the Gupta and the Mughal dynasties.

ECONOMIC DEVELOPMENT AND SOCIAL DISTINCTIONS

After spreading through the subcontinent, Aryan migrants turned increasingly from herding to agriculture. After about 1000 B.C.E., when they learned the techniques of iron metallurgy, they used iron axes and tools to advance into regions previously inaccessible to them, notably the jungle-covered valley of the Ganges River. The Aryans dispatched *shudras,* semifree serfs, to work in recently cleared fields, and from fertile lands they reaped large harvests. Agricultural surpluses supported the large-scale states such as the regional kingdoms and the Mauryan and Gupta empires that organized Indian public life. Agricultural surpluses also encouraged the emergence of towns, the growth of trade, and further development of the caste system.

Towns and Trade

After about 600 B.C.E. towns dotted the Indian countryside, especially in the northwestern corner of the subcontinent. These towns served the needs of a productive agricultural society by providing manufactured products for local consumption—pots, textiles, iron tools, and other metal utensils—as well as luxury goods such as jewelry destined for the wealthy and elite classes. Demand for manufactured products was very high, and some entrepreneurs organized businesses on a large scale. During Mauryan times, for example, a pottery manufacturer named Saddalaputta

Towns and Manufacturing

Jewel-bedecked flying goddesses drop flowers on the earth from their perch in the heavens. Their gems and personal adornments reflect the tastes of upper-class women during the Gupta dynasty. This painting on a rock wall, produced about the sixth century C.E., survives in modern Sri Lanka.

owned about five hundred workshops, whose products he distributed throughout the Ganges valley in his own fleet of boats.

Flourishing towns maintained marketplaces and encouraged the development of trade. Within the subcontinent itself trade was most active along the Ganges River, although trade routes also passed through the Ganges delta east to Burma and down the east Indian coast to the Deccan and southern India. Roads built by Ashoka also facilitated overland commerce within the subcontinent.

Long-Distance Trade   Meanwhile, the volume of long-distance trade also grew as large imperial states in China, southwest Asia, and the Mediterranean basin provided a political foundation enabling merchants to deal with their counterparts in distant lands. Direct political and military links with foreign peoples drew Indians into long-distance commercial relations. Beginning with Cyrus, the Achaemenid rulers of Persia coveted the wealth of India and included the northern kingdom of Gandhara as a province of their empire. The presence of Persian administrators in India and the building of roads between Persia and India facilitated commerce between the two lands. Alexander of Macedon's conquests helped to establish even more extensive trade networks by forging links between India and the Mediterranean basin by way of Bactria, Persia, and Anatolia.

From India, long-distance trade passed overland in two directions: through the Hindu Kush mountains and the Gandharan capital of Taxila to Persia and the Mediterranean basin, and across the silk roads of central Asia to markets in China. Cotton, aromatics, black pepper, pearls, and gems were the principal Indian exports, in exchange for which Indian merchants imported horses and bullion from western lands and silk from China.

During the Mauryan era merchants continued to use land routes, but they increasingly turned to the sea to transport their goods. Seaborne trade benefited especially from the rhythms of the monsoon winds that govern weather and the seasons in the Indian Ocean basin. During the spring and summer the winds blow from the southwest, and during the fall and winter they come from the northeast. Once mariners recognized these rhythms, they could sail easily and safely before the wind to any part of the Indian Ocean basin.

Trade in the Indian Ocean Basin

Many surviving gold coins reflect the commercial vitality of northern India in the late first and early second centuries C.E. This one depicts the Buddha gesturing to his followers.

As early as the fifth century B.C.E., Indian merchants had traveled to the islands of Indonesia and the southeast Asian mainland, where they exchanged pearls, cotton, black pepper, and Indian manufactured goods for spices and exotic local products. Many of these goods did not remain in India but, instead, traveled west through the Arabian Sea to the lands bordering the Persian Gulf and the Red Sea. Indian products also found markets in the Mediterranean basin. Indian pepper became so popular there that the Romans established direct commercial relations and built several trading settlements in southern India. Archaeologists working in southern India have unearthed hoards of Roman coins that testify to the large volume of trade between classical India and Mediterranean lands.

Family Life and the Caste System

In the midst of urban growth and economic development, Indian moralists sought to promote stability by encouraging respect for strong patriarchal families and to promote the maintenance of a social order in which all members played well-defined roles. Most people lived with members of their nuclear family. Particularly among higher castes, however, several generations of a family often lived in large compounds ruled by powerful patriarchs. Literary works suggest that women were largely subordinate to men. The two great Indian epics, the *Mahabharata* and the *Ramayana*, commonly portrayed women as weak-willed and emotional creatures and exalted wives who devoted themselves to their husbands. In the *Ramayana*, for example, the beautiful Sita loyally followed her husband Rama into undeserved exile in a wild forest and remained faithful to him even during a long separation.

Gender Relations

During the early centuries C.E., patriarchal dominance became more pronounced in India. By the Gupta era child marriage was common: when girls were eight or nine years of age, their parents betrothed them to men in their twenties. Formal marriage took place just after the girls reached puberty. Wives often came to dominate domestic affairs in their households, but the practice of child marriage placed them under the control of older men and encouraged them to devote themselves to family matters rather than to public affairs in the larger society.

Social Order

Castes and Guilds

Buddhist art often depicted individuals as models of proper social relationships. Here a sculpture from a Buddhist temple at Karli, produced about the first century C.E., represents an ideal Buddhist married couple.

After their arrival in India, the Aryans recognized four main castes or classes of people: priests *(brahmins)*, warriors and aristocrats *(kshatriyas)*, peasants and merchants *(vaishyas)*, and serfs *(shudras)*. *Brahmins* in particular endorsed this social order, which brought them honor, prestige, and sometimes considerable wealth as well. The growth of trade and the proliferation of industries, however, had deep implications for the larger structure of Indian society, since they encouraged further development of the caste system.

As trade and industrial activity expanded, new groups of artisans, craftsmen, and merchants appeared, many of whom did not fit easily in the established structure. Individuals working in the same craft or trade usually joined together to form a guild, a corporate body that supervised prices and wages in a given industry and provided for the welfare of members and their families. Guild members lived in the same quarter of town, socialized with each other, intermarried, and cared for the group's widows, orphans, and needy.

In effect, the guilds functioned as subcastes, known as *jati,* based on occupation. In fact, *jati* assumed much of the responsibility for maintaining social order in India. *Jati* regularly organized their own courts, through which they disciplined guild members, resolved differences, and regulated community affairs. Individuals who did not abide by group rules were liable to expulsion from the community. These outcastes then had to make their way through life—often by working as butchers, leather tanners, or undertakers or in other occupations deemed low and unclean—without the networks of support provided by *jati*. Thus Indian guilds and *jati* performed services that central governments provided in other lands. The tendency for individuals and their families to associate closely with others of the same occupation remained a prominent feature of Indian society well into modern times.

Wealth and the Social Order

Beyond encouraging further development of the caste system, economic development in the subcontinent also generated tremendous wealth, which posed a serious challenge to the social order that arose in India following the Aryan migrations. Traditional social theory accorded special honor to the *brahmins* and *kshatriyas* because of the worthy lives they had led during previous incarnations and the heavy responsibilities they assumed as priests, warriors, and rulers during their current incarnations. Members of the *vaishya* and *shudra* castes, on the other hand, merited no special respect but, rather, had the obligation to work as directed by the higher castes. During the centuries after 600 B.C.E., however, trade and industry brought prosperity to many *vaishyas* and even *shudras,* who sometimes became wealthier and more influential in society than their *brahmin* and *kshatriya* contemporaries.

Economic development and social change in classical India had profound implications for the established cultural as well as the social order. The beliefs, values, and rituals that were meaningful in early Aryan society seemed increasingly irrelevant during the centuries after 600 B.C.E. Along with emerging towns, growing trade, increasing wealth, and a developing social structure, classical India also saw the appearance of new religions that addressed the needs of the changing times.

RELIGIONS OF SALVATION IN CLASSICAL INDIA

Ancient Indian religion revolved around ritual sacrifices offered by *brahmin* priests in hopes that the gods would reward their loyal human servants with large harvests and abundant herds. Because the *brahmins* performed services deemed crucial for the survival of society, they enjoyed exemption from taxation. They also received hefty fees and generous gifts in return for their services. As the Indian economy developed, however, these services seemed less meaningful than they had before, especially to the newly wealthy classes of merchants and artisans. Many of these individuals came from the lower castes, and they resented the *brahmins'* pretensions to superiority.

During the sixth and fifth centuries B.C.E., a rash of new religions and philosophies rejected the *brahmins'* cults and appealed to the interests of new social classes. Some of them tended toward atheistic materialism: members of the Charvaka sect, for example, believed that the gods were figments of the imagination, that *brahmins* were charlatans who enriched themselves by hoodwinking others, and that human beings came from dust and returned to dust like any other animal in the natural world. The Charvakas' beliefs clearly reflected the increasingly materialistic character of Indian society and economy. Others, like the Jains, Buddhists, and Hindus, turned to intense spirituality as an alternative to the mechanical rituals of the *brahmins*.

Jainism and the Challenge to the Established Cultural Order

Among the most influential of the new religions was Jainism. Although Jainist doctrines first appeared during the seventh century B.C.E., they became popular only when the great teacher Vardhamana Mahavira turned to Jainism in the late sixth century B.C.E. Mahavira ("the great hero") was born in northern India about 540 B.C.E. to a prominent *kshatriya* family. According to the semilegendary accounts of his life, he left home at the age of thirty to seek salvation by escaping from the cycle of incarnation. For twelve years he led an ascetic life wandering throughout the Ganges valley, after which he gained enlightenment. He abandoned all his worldly goods, even his clothes, and taught an ascetic doctrine of detachment from the world. For the next thirty years, until his death about 468 B.C.E., he expounded his thought to a group of dedicated disciples who formed a monastic order to perpetuate and spread his message. These disciples referred to Mahavira as *Jina* ("the conqueror"), and borrowing from this title his followers referred to themselves as *Jains*.

Vardhamana Mahavira

Much of the inspiration for Jainist doctrine came from the Upanishads. Jains believed that everything in the universe—humans, animals, plants, the air, bodies of water, and even inanimate physical objects such as rocks—possessed a soul. As long as they remained trapped in terrestrial bodies, these souls experienced both physical and psychological suffering. Only by purification from selfish behavior could souls gain release from their imprisonment, shed the burdens of karma that they had accumulated during their various incarnations, and attain a state of bliss.

Individuals underwent purification by observing the principle of *ahimsa*, or nonviolence to other living things or their souls. Devout Jain monks went to extremes to

Jainist Ethics

Appeal of Jainism

Mahavira with one of his disciples. Representations of the early Jains often depicted them in the nude because of their ascetic way of life.

avoid harming the millions of souls they encountered each day. They swept the ground before them as they walked to avoid causing harm to invisible insects; they strained their drinking water through cloth filters to remove tiny animals they might unwittingly consume; they followed an abstemious and strictly vegetarian diet; they even wore masks and avoided making sudden movements so that they would not bruise or otherwise disturb the tiny souls inhabiting the surrounding air.

Jainist ethics were so demanding that few people other than devout monks could hope to observe them closely. The Jains believed that almost all occupations inevitably entailed violence of some kind: farming involved the killing of pests and the harvesting of living plants, for example, while crafts like leather tanning depended on the slaughter of animals. Thus for most people Jainism was not a practical alternative to the religion of the *brahmins*.

For certain groups, however, Jainism represented an attractive alternative to the traditional cults. Jainist values and ethics had significant social implications. If all creatures possessed souls and participated in the ultimate reality of the world, it made little sense to draw sharp distinctions between different classes of human beings. As a result, the Jains did not recognize social hierarchies based on caste or *jati*. It is not surprising, then, that their faith became popular especially among members of lower castes who did not command much respect in the traditional social order, including merchants, scholars, and literary figures. In a typical day, individuals in these classes did little overt violence to other creatures or their souls, and they appreciated the spiritual sensitivity and the high moral standards that Jainism encouraged. They provided substantial lay support for the Jainist monks and helped to maintain the ideal of *ahimsa* as a prominent concern of Indian ethics. Indeed, the doctrine of *ahimsa* has been an especially influential teaching over the long term, both in India and beyond. Quite apart from some two million Indian individuals who maintain Jainist traditions in the present day, many Buddhists and Hindus recognize *ahimsa* as a fundamental element of their beliefs, and prominent reformers of the twentieth century C.E. such as Mohandas K. Gandhi and Martin Luther King Jr. relied on the doctrine of *ahimsa* when promoting social reform by nonviolent means.

In spite of the moral respect it has commanded and the influence it has wielded through the centuries, however, Jainism has always been the faith of a small minority. It has simply been too difficult—or even impossible—for most people to observe. A more popular and practical alternative to the *brahmins'* cults came in the form of Buddhism.

Early Buddhism

Like Mahavira, the founder of Buddhism came from a *kshatriya* family, but he gave up his position and inheritance in order to seek salvation. His name was Siddhartha Gautama, born about 563 B.C.E. in a small tribal state governed by his father in the foothills of the Himalayas. According to early accounts, Gautama lived a pampered and sheltered life in palaces and parks, because his father had determined that Gautama would experience only happiness and would never know misery. He married his cousin and excelled in the program of studies that would prepare him to succeed his father as governor.

Siddhartha Gautama

Eventually, however, Gautama became dissatisfied with his comfortable life. One day, according to an early legend, while riding toward a park in his chariot, Gautama saw a man made miserable by age and infirmity. When he asked for an explanation of this unsettling sight, Gautama learned from his chariot driver that all human beings grow old and weak. On later outings Gautama saw a sick man and a corpse, from whose fates he learned that disease and death were also inevitable features of the human condition. Finally Gautama noticed a monk traveling by foot in his distinctive dress, and he learned that some individuals withdraw from the active life of the world to lead holy lives and to perfect their spiritual qualities. In light of the misery he had previously witnessed, Gautama considered the monk a noble character and determined to take up an ascetic, wandering life for himself in the hope that it would help him to understand the phenomenon of suffering. Though not a strictly historical account, this story conveys well the Buddhist concern with suffering.

About 534 B.C.E. Gautama left his wife, family, and the comforts of home to lead the existence of a holy man. He wandered throughout the Ganges valley searching for spiritual enlightenment and an explanation for suffering. He survived for a while by begging for his food but then abandoned society altogether to live as a hermit. He sought enlightenment first by means of intense meditation and later through the rigors of extreme asceticism. None of these tactics satisfied him. Then, according to Buddhist legends, as he sat one day beneath a large bo tree in Bodh Gaya, southwest of Pataliputra, Gautama decided that he would remain exactly where he was until he understood the problem of suffering. For forty-nine days he sat in meditation as various demons tempted him with pleasures and threatened him with terrors in efforts to shake his resolution. Eventually the demons withdrew, and Gautama prevailed. After forty-nine days under the bo tree, he received enlightenment: he understood both the problem of suffering and the means by which humans could eliminate it from the world. At that point, Gautama became the Buddha—"the enlightened one."

Gautama's Search for Enlightenment

The Buddha publicly announced his doctrine for the first time about 528 B.C.E. at the Deer Park of Sarnath, near the Buddhist holy city of Banaras (modern Varanasi), in a sermon delivered to friends who had formerly been his companions in asceticism. Buddhists refer to this sermon as the "Turning of the Wheel of the Law" because it represented the beginning of the Buddha's quest to promulgate the law of righteousness. His teachings quickly attracted attention, and disciples came from all parts of the Ganges valley. He organized them into a community of monks who owned only their yellow robes and their begging bowls. They traveled on foot, preaching the Buddha's doctrine and seeking handouts for their meals. For more than forty years, the Buddha himself led his disciples throughout much of northern India in hopes of bringing spiritual enlightenment to others. About 483 B.C.E., at an age of some eighty years, he died after leaving his companions with a final message: "Decay is inherent in all component things! Work out your salvation with diligence!"

The Buddha and His Followers

The core of the Buddha's doctrine, known as the Four Noble Truths, teaches that all life involves suffering; that desire is the cause of suffering; that elimination of desire

Buddhist Doctrine: The Dharma

brings an end to suffering; and that a disciplined life conducted in accordance with the Noble Eightfold Path brings the elimination of desire. The Noble Eightfold Path calls for individuals to lead balanced and moderate lives, rejecting both the devotion to luxury often found in human society and the regimes of extreme asceticism favored by hermits and Jains. Specifically, the Noble Eightfold Path demands right belief, right resolve, right speech, right behavior, right occupation, right effort, right contemplation, and right meditation.

A moderate lifestyle characterized by quiet contemplation, thoughtful reflection, and disciplined self-control would enable Buddhists to reduce their desires for material goods and other worldly attractions, resulting eventually in detachment from the world itself. Ultimately, they believed that this lifestyle would lead them to personal salvation, which for Buddhists meant an escape from the cycle of incarnation and attainment of *nirvana*, a state of perfect spiritual independence. Taken together, the teachings of the Four Noble Truths and the Noble Eightfold Path constitute the Buddhist *dharma*—the basic doctrine shared by Buddhists of all sects.

A confident and serene Buddha preaches his first sermon after his enlightenment at the Deer Park of Sarnath.

Appeal of Buddhism

Like the Jains, the Buddhists sought to escape the cycle of incarnation without depending on the services of the *brahmins*. Like the Jains, too, they did not recognize social distinctions based on caste or *jati*. As a result, their message appealed strongly to members of lower castes. Because it did not demand the rigorous asceticism of Jainism, Buddhism became far more popular. Merchants were especially prominent in the ranks of the early Buddhists, and they often used Buddhist monasteries as inns when they traveled through northern India.

Apart from the social implications of the doctrine, there were several other reasons for the immense popularity of early Buddhism in India. One has to do with language. Following the example of the Buddha himself, early Buddhist monks and preachers avoided the use of Sanskrit, the literary language of the Vedas that the *brahmins* employed in their rituals, in favor of vernacular tongues that reached a much larger popular audience. Furthermore, early Buddhists recognized holy sites that served as focal points for devotion. Even in the early days of Buddhism, pilgrims flocked to Bodh Gaya, where Gautama received enlightenment, and the Deer Park of Sarnath, where as the Buddha he preached his first sermon. Also popular with the faithful were stupas—shrines housing relics of the Buddha and his first disciples that pilgrims venerated while meditating on Buddhist values.

Yet another reason for the early popularity of Buddhism was the organization of the Buddhist movement. From the days of the Buddha himself, the most enthusiastic and highly motivated converts joined monastic communities where they dedicated their lives to the search for enlightenment and salvation. Gifts and grants from pious lay supporters provided for the land, buildings, finances, and material needs of the

The famous Buddhist stupa at Sanchi, originally built by Ashoka and enlarged in later times.

monasteries. The monks themselves spent much of their time preaching, explaining the *dharma* to lay audiences, and encouraging their listeners to follow the Noble Eightfold Path in their daily lives. During the centuries following the Buddha's death, this monastic organization proved to be extremely efficient at spreading the Buddhist message and winning converts to the faith.

Ashoka's Support

The early Buddhist movement also benefited from the official patronage and support of the Mauryan dynasty. The precise reason for Ashoka's conversion to Buddhism is unclear. Early legends held that a devout Buddhist monk brought about Ashoka's conversion by dazzling him with supernatural powers. Ashoka's own account, as preserved in one of his edicts, explains that the emperor adopted Buddhism about 260 B.C.E. after the war against Kalinga. Saddened by the violence of the war and the suffering of the Kalingans, Ashoka said that he decided to pursue his aims henceforth by means of virtue, benevolence, and humanity rather than arms. Quite apart from his sincere religious convictions, it is also likely that Ashoka found Buddhism appealing as a faith that could lend unity to his culturally diverse and far-flung realm. In any case, in honor of *ahimsa*, the doctrine of nonviolence, Ashoka banned animal sacrifices in Pataliputra, gave up his beloved hunting expeditions, and eliminated most meat dishes from the tables of his court. Ashoka rewarded Buddhists with grants of land, and he encouraged them to spread their faith throughout India. He built monasteries and stupas and made pilgrimages to the holy sites of Buddhism. Ashoka also sent missionaries to Bactria and Ceylon (modern Sri Lanka), thus inaugurating a process by which Buddhism attracted large followings in central Asia, east Asia, and southeast Asia.

Mahayana Buddhism

From its earliest days Buddhism attracted merchants, artisans, and others of low rank in the traditional Indian social order. Its appeal was due both to its disregard for social classes and to its concern for ethical behavior instead of complicated ceremonies that seemed increasingly irrelevant to the lives and experiences of most people. Yet, even though it vastly simplified religious observances, early Buddhism made heavy demands on individuals seeking to escape from the cycle of incarnation. A truly righteous existence involved considerable sacrifice: giving up personal property, forsaking the search for social standing, and resolutely detaching oneself from the charms of family and the world. The earliest Buddhists thought that numerous physical incarnations, stretching over thousands of years, might be necessary before an individual soul would become pure enough to achieve salvation and pass into nirvana. While perhaps more attractive than the religion of the *brahmins,* Buddhism did not promise to make life easy for its adherents.

Development of Buddhism

King Ashoka erected many stone pillars such as this handsome column, which stands 10 meters (32 feet) tall, to promote Buddhist teachings, direct travelers to holy sites, or commemorate significant events of the Buddha's life.

Between the third century B.C.E. and the first century C.E., however, three new developments in Buddhist thought and practice reduced obligations of believers, opened new avenues to salvation, and brought explosive popularity to the faith. In the first place, whereas the Buddha had not considered himself divine, some of his later followers began to worship him as a god. Thus Buddhism acquired a devotional focus that helped converts channel their spiritual energies and identify more closely with their faith. In the second place, theologians articulated the notion of the *boddhisatva* ("an enlightened being"). *Boddhisatvas* were individuals who had reached spiritual perfection and merited the reward of nirvana, but who intentionally delayed their entry into nirvana in order to help others who were still struggling. Some theologians taught that *boddhisatvas* could even perform good deeds on behalf of their less spiritually inclined brethren. Like Christian saints, *boddhisatvas* served as examples of spiritual excellence, and they provided a source of inspiration. Finally, Buddhist monasteries began to accept gifts from wealthy individuals and to regard the bequests as acts of generosity that merited salvation. Thus wealthy individuals could enjoy the comforts of the world, avoid the sacrifices demanded by early Buddhist teachings, and still ensure their salvation.

The Spread of Mahayana Buddhism

Because these innovations opened the road to salvation for large numbers of people, their proponents called their faith the *Mahayana* ("the greater vehicle," which could carry more people to salvation), as opposed to the *Hinayana* ("the lesser vehicle"), a pejorative term for the earlier and stricter doctrine known also as Theravada Buddhism. During the early centuries C.E., Mahayana Buddhism spread rapidly throughout India and attracted many converts from lay and wealthy classes. In later centuries Mahayana Buddhism became established also in central Asia, China, Japan, and Korea. The stricter Theravada faith did not disappear: it remained the dominant school of Buddhism in Ceylon, and in later centuries it spread also to Burma, Thailand, and other parts of southeast Asia. Since the first century C.E., however, most of the world's Buddhists have sought to ride the greater vehicle to salvation.

Sources from the Past

Ashoka as a Teacher of Humility and Equality According to the *Ashokavadana*

Following Ashoka's death, many legends circulated about the emperor, his life, his rule, and his devotion to Buddhism. About the second century C.E., anonymous editors collected many of these legends in a work known as the Ashokavadana (The Legend of Ashoka). Though not historically reliable, the legend is valuable as a work showing how later generations revered Ashoka and made a hero of the Buddhist emperor. The following selection celebrates Ashoka's efforts to promote the Buddhist values of humility and the equality of believers in spite of their different caste origins.

Not long after King Ashoka had come to have faith in the Teaching of the Buddha, he started honoring Buddhist monks, throwing himself at their feet wherever he saw them, in a crowd, or in a deserted place.

Now Ashoka had a minister named Yasas, and although he had the utmost faith in the Blessed One [the Buddha], he said, one day, to the king: "Your majesty, you ought not to prostrate yourself before wandering mendicants of every caste, and the Buddhist monks do come from all four castes."

To this Ashoka did not immediately respond. Sometime later, however, he told all his ministers that he needed to have the heads of various sorts of creatures, and he asked one of them to bring him the head of such and such an animal, and another to bring him the head of another animal, and so on. Finally, he ordered Yasas to bring him the head of a human being.

Now when the ministers had gathered all these heads, Ashoka ordered them to go to the market place and sell them. Soon, all of the heads had been sold, except Yasas's human head that no one would buy. Ashoka then told Yasas to give his head away, but, even though it was gratis, still no one would take it.

Ashamed at his lack of success, Yasas came back to Ashoka and said: "O king, the heads of cows, asses, sheep, deer, and birds—all were sold to people for a price; but no one would take this worthless human head, even free of charge."

"Why is that?" Ashoka asked his minister, "why wouldn't anyone accept this human head?"

"Because it disgusted them," Yasas replied.

"Oh?" said the king, "is it just this head that is disgusting or the heads of all human beings?"

"The heads of all humans," answered Yasas.

"What?" said Ashoka, "is my head disgusting as well?"

Out of fear, Yasas did not want to tell him the real fact of the matter, but the king ordered him to speak the truth, and finally he answered: "Yes."

After forcing this admission out of his minister, Ashoka then revealed to him his purpose in doing so: "You, sir, are obsessed with matters of form and superiority, and because of this attachment you seek to dissuade me from bowing down at the feet of the monks. But if I acquire some merit by bowing down a head so disgusting that no one on earth would take it, even free of charge, what harm is there in that? You, sir, look at the caste *(jati)* and not at the inherent qualities of the monks. Haughty, deluded, and obsessed with caste, you harm yourself and others."

SOURCE: John S. Strong. *The Legend of King Ashoka: A Study and Translation of the* Ashokavadana. Princeton: Princeton University Press, 1983, pp. 234–36. (Translation slightly modified.)

In what ways and for what reasons might this story from the Ashokavadana *have appealed to various groups of early Buddhists?*

Nalanda

Mahayana Buddhism flourished partly because of educational institutions that efficiently promoted the faith. During the Vedic era, Indian education was mostly an informal affair involving a sage and his students. When Jains and Buddhists organized monasteries, however, they began to offer regular instruction and established educational institutions. Most monasteries provided basic education, and larger communities

Carving of a *boddhisatva* from the second or third century C.E. This carving perhaps represents Avalokitesvara, also known as the Lord of Compassion. Almost as perfect as the Buddha, Avalokitesvara had a reputation for protecting merchants and sailors, helping women conceive, and turning enemies into kindhearted friends.

offered advanced instruction as well. Best known of all was the Buddhist monastery at Nalanda, founded during the Gupta dynasty in the Ganges River valley near Pataliputra. At Nalanda it was possible to study not only Buddhism but also the Vedas, Hindu philosophy, logic, mathematics, astronomy, and medicine. Nalanda soon became so famous as an educational center that pilgrims and students from foreign lands traveled there to study with the most renowned masters of Buddhist doctrine. By the end of the Gupta dynasty, several thousand students may have been in residence there.

The Emergence of Popular Hinduism

As Buddhism generated new ideas and attracted widespread popular interest, Hinduism underwent a similar evolution that transformed it into a popular religion of salvation. While drawing inspiration from the Vedas and Upanishads, popular Hinduism increasingly departed from the older traditions of the *brahmins*. Like Mahayana Buddhism, Hinduism experienced changes in doctrine and observances that resulted in a faith that addressed the interests and met the needs of ordinary people.

The Epics

The great epic poems, the *Mahabharata* and the *Ramayana,* illustrate the development of Hindu values. Both works originated as secular tales transmitted orally during the late years of the Vedic age (1500–500 B.C.E.). *Brahmin* scholars revised them and committed them to writing probably during the early centuries C.E. The *Mahabharata* dealt with a massive war for the control of northern India between two groups of cousins. Though originally a purely secular work, the *brahmins* made a prominent place in the poem for the god Vishnu, the preserver of the world who intervened frequently on behalf of virtuous individuals.

The *Ramayana* too was originally a love and adventure story involving the trials faced by the legendary Prince Rama and his loyal wife, Sita. Rama went to great lengths to rescue Sita after the demon king of Ceylon kidnapped her, and his alliance with Hanuman, general of the monkeys, led to exciting clashes with his enemies. Later *brahmin* editors made Rama an incarnation of Vishnu, and they portrayed Rama and Sita as the ideal Hindu husband and wife, devoted and loyal to each other even in times of immense difficulty.

The Bhagavad Gita

A short poetic work known as the *Bhagavad Gita* ("song of the lord") best illustrates both the expectations that Hinduism made of individuals and the promise of salvation that it held out to them. The *Gita* was the work of many hands, and the date of its composition is uncertain. Scholars have placed it at various points between 300 B.C.E. and 300 C.E., and it most likely underwent several rounds of revision before taking on its final form about 400 C.E. Yet it eloquently evokes the cultural climate of India between the Mauryan and the Gupta dynasties.

The work is a self-contained episode of the *Mahabharata*. It presents a dialogue between Arjuna, a *kshatriya* warrior about to enter battle, and his charioteer Krishna, who was in fact a human incarnation of the god Vishnu. The immediate problem addressed in the work was Arjuna's reluctance to fight: the enemy included many of his friends and relatives, and even though he recognized the justice of his cause, he

Contexts & Connections

The Indian Invention of "Arabic" Numerals

Quite apart from its elaboration of reflective religious traditions, India was notable also for the development of a very sophisticated body of mathematical thought in classical times. Mathematical reasoning itself was not unusual: Babylonians, Egyptians, Greeks, and Maya all generated rich traditions of mathematics. Both Babylonians and Maya also used symbols for zero, which simplified calculations. During the Gupta era, though, Indian scholars created a body of mathematical thought so powerful that it remains the basis of computational sciences in the contemporary world.

The development of an advanced Indian mathematics was possible because of the symbols used to represent numbers and reliance on place-value notation. The symbols used by Indian mathematicians were direct ancestors of the figures in almost universal use in the present day: 1, 2, 3, 4, 5, 6, 7, 8, 9, and 0. The last symbol is particularly important. Although it stands literally for nothing, the symbol for zero, which Indian mathematicians seem to have invented independently, facilitates adoption of a system of place-value notation, in which the value of a symbol depends on its place in the representation of a number. In the number 123, for example, the symbol 1 stands in the hundreds column and represents not the number 1 but the number 100, while the symbol 2 stands in the tens column and represents not the number 2 but the number 20, and the symbol 3 stands on the ones column, representing the number 3. With the availability of a symbol for zero, it is possible to take place-value notation further and represent very different numbers with the same symbols: 1,023, 1,203, and 1,230, for example.

With their distinctive numerical symbols and place-value notation, Indian mathematicians were able to make routine calculations that would be extremely difficult in systems that relied on other symbols (such as let-ters of the alphabet, as in the case of Roman numerals) or other systems of notation. Consider the two following calculations, one using Roman numerals, the other using Indian numerals:

CCLIX	259
MII	1,002
DLXXII	572
MDCCCXXXIII	1,833

If rudimentary addition is cumbersome with Roman numerals, a simple operation involving the multiplication of quantities would be nightmarish. Would you rather multiply 19×84 or $XIX \times LXXXIV$? With their flexible numerals and place-value notation, Indian mathematicians were able to carry out advanced algebraic calculations and anticipate the invention of calculus.

If Indian mathematicians invented the numerals in common use today, why do we call them "Arabic" numerals? When scholars from other lands learned about Indian mathematics, they immediately recognized the power and precision of Indian calculations and adopted them for use in their own societies. Foreign Buddhist monks who studied at Nalanda, for example, learned Indian mathematics and astronomy as well as Buddhist theology. They took Indian numerals to southeast Asia by the seventh century C.E. and soon thereafter to China as well. In the eighth century, Muslim Arabs and Persians encountered Indian mathematics and adopted what they called "Hindi" numerals. In the twelfth century, western Europeans learned about the very sophisticated tradition of mathematics that Muslim scholars had built and gradually replaced Roman symbols with what they called "Arabic" numerals. Thus Indian numerals acquired a misleading name.

shrank from the conflict. In an effort to persuade the warrior to fight, Krishna presented Arjuna with several lines of argument. In the first place, he said, Arjuna must not worry about harming his friends and relatives, because the soul does not die with the human body. Arjuna's weapons did not have the power to touch the soul, so he could never harm or kill another person in any meaningful way.

Krishna also held that Arjuna's caste imposed specific moral duties and social responsibilities upon him. The duty of *shudras* was to serve, of *vaishyas* to work, of *brahmins* to learn the scriptures and seek wisdom. Similarly, Krishna argued, the duty of *kshatriyas* was to govern and fight. Indeed, Krishna went further and held that an individual's social responsibilities had spiritual significance. He told Arjuna that failure to fulfill caste duties was a grievous sin, whereas their observance brought spiritual benefits.

Finally, Krishna taught that Arjuna would attain everlasting peace and blessedness if he devoted himself to the love, adoration, and service of Krishna himself. Arjuna should abandon his selfish and superficial personal concerns and surrender to the deeper wisdom of the god. As a reward, wholehearted worship would bring Arjuna eternal salvation through unity with his god. Alongside understanding of the soul and caste duties, then, unquestioning faith and devotion would put Arjuna in the proper state of mind for the looming conflict by aligning his actions with divine wisdom and will. Krishna's teaching that faith would bring salvation helped inspire a tradition of ecstatic and unquestioning devotion in popular Hinduism.

Hindu Ethics

Hindu ethics thus differed considerably from those of earlier Indian moralists. The Upanishads had taught that only through renunciation and detachment from the world could individuals escape the cycle of incarnation. As represented in the *Bhagavad Gita,* however, Hindu ethical teachings made life much easier for the lay classes by holding out the promise of salvation precisely to those who participated actively in the world and met their caste responsibilities. To be sure, Krishna taught that individuals should meet their responsibilities in detached fashion: they should not become personally or emotionally involved in their actions, and they especially should not strive for material reward or recognition. Rather, they should perform their duties faithfully, concentrating on their actions alone, with no thought as to their consequences.

Other works by early Hindu moralists acknowledged even more openly than did the *Bhagavad Gita* that individuals could lead honorable lives in the world. Indeed, Hindu ethics commonly recognized four principal aims of human life: obedience to religious and moral laws *(dharma),* the pursuit of economic well-being and honest prosperity *(artha),* the enjoyment of social, physical, and sexual pleasure *(kama),* and the salvation of the soul *(moksha).* According to Hindu moral precepts, a proper balance of *dharma, artha,* and *kama* would help an individual to attain *moksha.*

As devotional Hinduism evolved and became increasingly distinct from the teachings of the Upanishads and the older traditions of the *brahmins,* it also enhanced its appeal to all segments of Indian society. Hinduism offered salvation to masses of people who, as a matter of practical necessity, had to lead active lives in the world and thus could not even hope to achieve the detachment envisioned in the Upanishads.

Popularity of Hinduism

Hinduism gradually displaced Buddhism as the most popular religion in India. Buddhism remained strong through much of the first millennium C.E., and until about the eighth century pilgrims traveled to India from as far away as China to visit the holy sites of Buddhism and learn about the faith in its original homeland. Within India itself, however, Buddhism grew remote from the popular masses. Later Buddhist monks did not seek to communicate their message to the larger society in the zealous way of their predecessors, but increasingly confined themselves to the comforts of monasteries richly endowed by wealthy patrons.

Meanwhile, devotional Hinduism also attracted political support and patronage, particularly from the Gupta emperors. The Guptas and their successors bestowed grants of land on Hindu *brahmins* and supported an educational system that promoted Hindu values. Just as Ashoka Maurya had advanced the cause of Buddhism, the Guptas and their successors later helped Hinduism become the dominant reli-

Sources from the Past

Caste Duties According to the *Bhagavad Gita*

In urging Arjuna to enter battle, Krishna pointed out that Arjuna could not harm the immortal souls of his family and friends on the other side. Beyond that, however, Krishna emphasized the duty to fight that Arjuna inherited as a member of the kshatriya *caste. Yet Krishna also counseled Arjuna to perform his duty in a spirit of detachment, not caring for victory or defeat.*

As a man, casting off old clothes, puts on others and new ones, so the embodied self, casting off old bodies, goes to others and new ones. Weapons do not divide the self into pieces; fire does not burn it; waters do not moisten it; the wind does not dry it up. It is not divisible; it is not combustible; it is not to be moistened; it is not to be dried up. It is everlasting, all-pervading, stable, firm, and eternal. It is said to be unperceived, to be unthinkable, to be unchangeable. Therefore knowing it to be such, you ought not to grieve. But even if you think that the self is constantly born, and constantly dies, still, O you of mighty arms, you ought not to grieve thus. For to one that is born, death is certain; and to one that dies, birth is certain. Therefore about this unavoidable thing, you ought not to grieve. . . .

Having regard to your own duty, you ought not to falter, for there is nothing better for a *kshatriya* than a righteous battle. Happy those *kshatriyas* who can find such a battle—an open door to heaven! But if you will not fight this righteous battle, then you will have abandoned your own duty and your fame, and you will incur sin. All beings, too, will tell of your everlasting infamy; and to one who has been honored, infamy is a greater evil than death. Warriors who are masters of great chariots will think that you have abstained from the battle through fear, and having been highly thought of by them, you will fall down to littleness. Your enemies, too, decrying your power, will speak much about you that should not be spoken. And what, indeed, could be more lamentable than that? Killed, you will obtain heaven; victorious, you will enjoy the earth. Therefore arise, resolved to engage in battle. Looking on pleasure and pain, on gain and loss, on victory and defeat as the same, prepare for battle, and thus you will not incur sin. . . .

The state of mind that consists in firm understanding regarding steady contemplation does not belong to those who are strongly attached to worldly pleasures and power, and whose minds are drawn away by that flowery talk that is full of specific acts for the attainment of pleasures and power, and that promises birth as the fruit of actions— that flowery talk uttered by unwise ones who are enamored of Vedic words, who say there is nothing else, who are full of desires, and whose goal is heaven. . . .

Your business is with action alone, not by any means with the fruit of the action. Let not the fruit of action be your motive to action. Let not your attachment be fixed on inaction. Having recourse to devotion, perform actions, casting off all attachment, and being equable in success or ill success.

SOURCE: *The Bhagavad Gita.* Trans. by Kashinath Trimbak Telang. In F. Max Müller, ed., *The Sacred Books of the East,* vol. 8. Oxford: Clarendon Press, 1908, pp. 45–48. (Translation slightly modified.)

How do these reflections on caste duties and detachment in the Bhagavad Gita *compare and contrast with the moral and ethical teachings of Zarathustra and Confucius discussed in earlier chapters?*

gious and cultural tradition in India. By about 1000 C.E., Buddhism had entered a noticeable decline in India while Hinduism grew in popularity. Within a few centuries devotional Hinduism and the more recently introduced faith of Islam almost completely eclipsed Buddhism in its homeland.

In India, as in classical Persia and China, a robust agricultural economy supported the creation of large-scale states and interregional trade. Although an imperial state did not become a permanent feature of Indian political life, the peoples of the subcontinent maintained an orderly society based on the caste system and regional states. Indian cultural and religious traditions reflected the conditions of the larger society in which they developed. Mahayana Buddhism and devotional Hinduism in particular addressed the needs of the increasingly prominent lay classes, and the two faiths profoundly influenced the religious life of Asian peoples over the long term of history.

CHRONOLOGY

563–483 B.C.E.	Life of Siddartha Gautama, the Buddha
540–468 B.C.E.	Life of Vardhamana Mahavira
520 B.C.E.	Invasion of India by Darius of Persia
327 B.C.E.	Invasion of India by Alexander of Macedon
321–185 B.C.E.	Mauryan dynasty
321–297 B.C.E.	Reign of Chandragupta Maurya
268–232 B.C.E.	Reign of Ashoka Maurya
182 B.C.E.–1 C.E.	Bactrian rule in northern India
1–300 C.E.	Kushan empire in northern India and central Asia
78–103 C.E.	Reign of Kushan emperor Kanishka
320–550 C.E.	Gupta dynasty

FOR FURTHER READING

Roy C. Amore and Larry D. Shinn. *Lustful Maidens and Ascetic Kings*. New York, 1981. Translations of stories and moral tales from Hindu and Buddhist writings.

Jeannine Auboyer. *Daily Life in Ancient India*. Trans. by S. W. Taylor. New York, 1965. An excellent and well-researched, though somewhat dated, introduction to Indian social history during the classical era.

A. L. Basham. *The Wonder That Was India*. New York, 1954. Popular survey by a leading scholar of early Indian history.

Edward Conze. *Buddhism: Its Essence and Development*. New York, 1959. Systematic account of Buddhism from a theological point of view.

William Theodore De Bary, ed. *Sources of Indian Tradition*. 2 vols. 2nd ed. New York, 1988. Important collection of sources in translation.

Kautalya. *The Kautilya Arthashastra*. 3 vols. 2nd ed. Ed. by R. P. Kangle. Bombay, 1960–69. Translation of the most important political treatise of classical India.

Xinru Liu. *Ancient India and Ancient China: Trade and Religious Exchanges, A.D. 1–600*. Delhi, 1988. Important study exploring the early spread of Buddhism from India to central Asia and China.

Juan Mascaró, trans. *The Bhagavad Gita*. Harmondsworth, 1962. Brilliant and evocative English version by a gifted translator.

William H. McNeill and Jean W. Sedlar, eds. *Classical India*. New York, 1969. Collection of primary sources in translation.

Jean W. Sedlar. *India and the Greek World: A Study in the Transmission of Culture*. Totowa, N.J., 1980. Important study of relations between India and Greece, based on solid research.

John S. Strong. *The Legend of King Ashoka: A Study and Translation of the* Ashokavadana. Princeton, 1983. Valuable translation of an important early Buddhist account of King Ashoka's life and reign.

Romila Thapar. *Ashoka and the Decline of the Mauryas*. London, 1961. The best scholarly study of Ashoka and his reign.

———. *A History of India*, vol. 1. Harmondsworth, 1966. Popular account by one of the leading scholars of early Indian history.

———, ed. *Recent Perspectives of Early Indian History*. New Delhi, 1995. A valuable collection of essays discussing recent scholarship on early Indian history.

Mortimer Wheeler. *Flames over Persepolis*. New York, 1968. Examines the influence of Greek and Persian traditions in northern India after the time of Alexander of Macedon.

See our **Online Learning Center** at www.mhhe.com/bentley3 for additional readings, practice maps, quizzes, and internet activities.

Unfamiliar words? Check out the **Primary Source Investigator CD-ROM** for an interactive glossary, interactive maps, more images, and primary sources.

The theater at Delphi.

MEDITERRANEAN SOCIETY: THE GREEK PHASE

For a man who perhaps never existed, Homer has been a profoundly influential figure. According to tradition, Homer composed the two great epic poems of ancient Greece, the *Iliad* and the *Odyssey*. In fact, scholars now know that bards recited both poems for generations before Homer lived—the mid-eighth century B.C.E., if he was indeed a historical figure. Some experts believe that Homer was not a real man so much as a convenient name for several otherwise anonymous scribes who committed the *Iliad* and the *Odyssey* to writing. Others believe that a man named Homer had a part in preparing a written version of the epics, but that others also contributed significantly to his work.

Whether Homer ever really lived or not, the epics attributed to him deeply influenced the development of classical Greek thought and literature. The *Iliad* offered a Greek perspective on a campaign waged by a band of Greek warriors against the city of Troy in Anatolia during the twelfth century B.C.E. The *Odyssey* recounted the experiences of the Greek hero Odysseus as he sailed home after the Trojan war. The two works described scores of difficulties faced by Greek warriors—not only battles with Trojans but also challenges posed by deities and monsters, conflicts among themselves, and even psychological barriers that individuals had to surmount. Between them, the two epics preserved a rich collection of stories that literary figures mined for more than a millennium, reworking Homer's material and exploring his themes from fresh perspectives.

Quite apart from their significance as literary masterpieces, the *Iliad* and the *Odyssey* also testify to the frequency and normality of travel, communication, and interaction in the Mediterranean basin during the second and first millennia B.C.E. Both works portray Greeks as expert and fearless seamen, almost as comfortable aboard their ships as on land, who did not hesitate to venture into the waters of what Homer called the "wine-dark sea" in pursuit of their goals. Homer lovingly described the sleek galleys in which Greek warriors raced across the waters, sometimes to plunder the slower but heavily laden cargo vessels that plied the Mediterranean sea lanes, more often to launch strikes at enemy targets. He even had Odysseus construct a sailing ship single-handedly when he found himself shipwrecked on an island inhabited only by a goddess. The *Iliad* and the *Odyssey* make it clear that maritime links touched peoples throughout the Mediterranean basin in Homer's time and, further, that Greeks were among the most prominent seafarers of the age.

Already during the second millennium B.C.E., Phoenician merchants had established links between lands and peoples at the far ends of the Mediterranean Sea. During the classical era, however, the Mediterranean basin became much more tightly integrated than before as Greeks, and later Romans as well, organized commercial exchange and sponsored interaction throughout the region. Under Greek and Roman supervision, the Mediterranean served not as a barrier but, rather, as a highway linking Anatolia, Egypt, Greece, Italy, France, Spain, north Africa, and even southern Russia (by way of routes through the Black Sea).

Ancient Greece differed from classical societies in other lands. Early in the classical era, the Greeks lived in independent, autonomous city-states. Only after the late third century B.C.E. did they play prominent roles in the large, centralized empire established by their neighbors to the north in Macedon. Yet from the seventh through the second centuries B.C.E., the Greeks integrated the societies and economies of distant lands through energetic commercial activity over the Mediterranean sea lanes. They also generated a remarkable body of moral thought and philosophical reflection. Just as the traditions of classical Persia, China, and India shaped the cultural experiences of those lands, the traditions of the Greeks profoundly influenced the long-term cultural development of the Mediterranean basin, Europe, and southwest Asia as well.

EARLY DEVELOPMENT OF GREEK SOCIETY

Humans inhabited the Balkan region and the Greek peninsula from an early but indeterminate date. During the third millennium B.C.E., they increasingly met and mingled with peoples from different societies who traveled and traded in the Mediterranean basin. As a result, early inhabitants of the Greek peninsula built their societies under the influence of Mesopotamians, Egyptians, Phoenicians, and others active in the region. Beginning in the ninth century B.C.E., the Greeks organized a series of city-states, which served as the political context for the development of classical Greek society.

Minoan and Mycenaean Societies

Knossos

During the late third millennium B.C.E., a sophisticated society arose on the island of Crete. Scholars refer to it as Minoan society, after Minos, a legendary king of ancient Crete. Between 2000 and 1700 B.C.E., the inhabitants of Crete built a series of lavish palaces throughout the island, most notably the enormous complex at Knossos decorated with vivid frescoes depicting Minoans at work and play. These palaces were the nerve centers of Minoan society: they were residences of rulers, and they also served as storehouses where officials collected taxes in kind from local cultivators. Palace officials devised a script known as Linear A, in which written symbols stood for syllables rather than words, ideas, vowels, or consonants. Although linguists have not yet been able to decipher Linear A, it is clear that Cretan administrators used the script to keep detailed records of economic and commercial matters.

Between 2200 and 1450 B.C.E., Crete was a principal center of Mediterranean commerce. Due to its geographic location in the east-central Mediterranean, Crete received early influences from Phoenicia and Egypt. By 2200 B.C.E. Cretans were traveling aboard advanced sailing craft of Phoenician design. Minoan ships sailed to Greece, Anatolia, Phoenicia, and Egypt, where they exchanged Cretan wine, olive oil, and wool for grains, textiles, and manufactured goods. Archaeologists have discovered pottery vessels used as storage containers for Minoan wine and olive oil as far away as Sicily. After 1600 B.C.E. Cretans established colonies on Cyprus and many islands in the Aegean Sea, probably to mine local copper ores and gain better access to markets where tin was available.

A magnificent fresco from the town of Akrotiri on the island of Thera depicts a busy harbor, showing that Akrotiri traded actively with Crete and other Minoan sites. The volcanic eruption of Thera about 1628 B.C.E. destroyed Akrotiri.

Decline of Minoan Society

After 1700 B.C.E. Minoan society experienced a series of earthquakes, volcanic eruptions, and tidal waves. Most destructive was a massive volcanic eruption about 1628 B.C.E. on the island of Thera (Santorini) north of Crete. Between 1600 and 1450 B.C.E., Cretans embarked on a new round of palace building to replace structures destroyed by these natural catastrophes: they built luxurious complexes with indoor plumbing and drainage systems and even furnished some of them with flush toilets. After 1450 B.C.E., however, the wealth of Minoan society attracted a series of invaders, and by 1100 B.C.E. Crete had fallen under foreign domination. Yet the Minoan traditions of maritime trade, writing, and construction deeply influenced the inhabitants of nearby Greece.

Mycenaean Society

Beginning about 2200 B.C.E. migratory Indo-European peoples filtered over the Balkans and into the Greek peninsula. By 1600 B.C.E. they had begun to trade with Minoan merchants and visit Crete, where they learned about writing and large-scale construction. They adapted Minoan Linear A to their own language, which was an early form of Greek, and devised a syllabic script known as Linear B. After 1450 B.C.E. they also built massive stone fortresses and palaces throughout the southern part of the Greek peninsula, known as the Peloponnesus. Because the fortified sites offered protection, they soon attracted settlers who built small agricultural communities. Their society is known as Mycenaean, after Mycenae, one of their most important settlements.

From 1500 to 1100 B.C.E., the Mycenaeans expanded their influence beyond peninsular Greece. They largely overpowered Minoan society, and they took over the Cretan palaces, where they established craft workshops. Archaeologists have unearthed thousands of clay tablets in Linear B that came from the archives of Mycenaean rulers in Crete as well as peninsular Greece. The Mycenaeans also established settlements in Anatolia, Sicily, and southern Italy.

Chaos in the Eastern Mediterranean

About 1200 B.C.E. the Mycenaeans engaged in a conflict with the city of Troy in Anatolia. This Trojan war, which Homer recalled from a Greek perspective in his

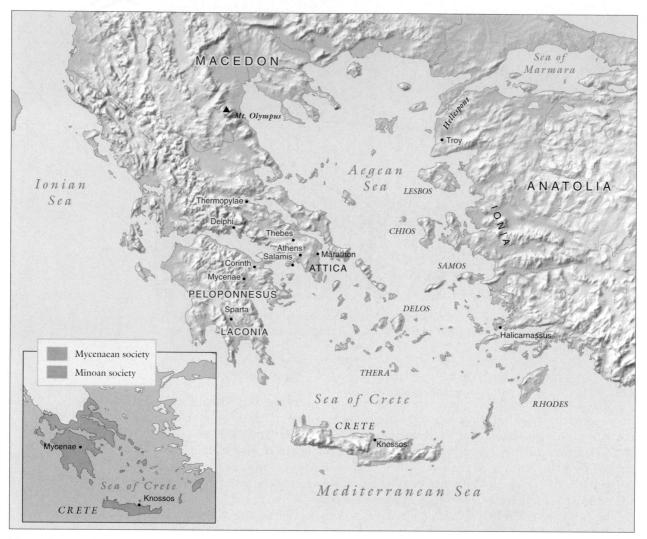

MAP [10.1]
Classical Greece,
800–350 B.C.E.

Iliad, coincided with invasions of foreign mariners in the Mycenaean homeland. Indeed, from 1100 to 800 B.C.E. chaos reigned throughout the eastern Mediterranean region. Invasions and civil disturbances made it impossible to maintain stable governments or even productive agricultural societies. Mycenaean palaces fell into ruin, the population sharply declined, and people abandoned most settlements. Many inhabitants of the Greek peninsula fled to the islands of the Aegean Sea, Anatolia, or Cyprus. Writing in both Linear A and Linear B disappeared. The boisterous character of the era comes across clearly in Homer's works. Though set in an earlier era, both the *Iliad* and the *Odyssey* reflect the tumultuous centuries after 1100 B.C.E. They portray a society riven with conflict, and they recount innumerable episodes of aggression, treachery, and violence alongside heroic bravery and courage.

The World of the Polis

The Polis

In the absence of a centralized state or empire, local institutions took the lead in restoring political order in Greece. The most important institution was the city-state, or polis. The term *polis* originally referred to a citadel or fortified site that offered refuge for local communities during times of war or other emergencies. These sites attracted increasing populations, and many of them gradually became lively commercial centers. They took on an increasingly urban character and extended their authority over surrounding regions. They levied taxes on their hinterlands and appropriated a portion of the agricultural surplus to support the urban population. By about 800 B.C.E. many poleis (the plural of polis) had become bustling city-states that functioned as the principal centers of Greek society.

The poleis took various political forms. Some differences reflected the fact that poleis emerged independently and elaborated their traditions with little outside influence. Others arose from different rates of economic development. A few poleis developed as small monarchies, but most were under the collective rule of local notables. Many fell into the hands of generals or ambitious politicians—called "tyrants" by the Greeks—who gained power by irregular means. (The tyrants were not necessarily oppressive despots: indeed, many of

The Lion Gate at Mycenae illustrates the heavy fortifications built by Myceneans to protect their settlements.

them were extremely popular leaders. The term *tyrant* referred to their routes to power rather than their policies.) The most important of the poleis were Sparta and Athens, whose contrasting constitutions help to illustrate the variety of political styles in classical Greece.

Sparta

Sparta was situated in a fertile region of the Peloponnesus. As their population and economy expanded during the eighth and seventh centuries B.C.E., the Spartans progressively extended their control over the Peloponnesus. In doing so, they reduced neighboring peoples to the status of *helots*, servants of the Spartan state. Although they were not chattel slaves, the helots also were not free. They could form families, but they could not leave the land. Their role in society was to provide agricultural labor and keep Sparta supplied with food. By the sixth century B.C.E., the helots probably outnumbered the Spartan citizens themselves by more than ten to one. With their large subject population, the Spartans were able to cultivate the Peloponnesus efficiently, but they also faced the constant threat of rebellion. As a result, the Spartans devoted most of their resources to maintaining a powerful and disciplined military machine.

Spartan Society

In theory, Spartan citizens were equal in status. To discourage the development of economic and social distinctions, Spartans observed an extraordinarily austere

A painted cup produced in Sparta about 550 B.C.E. depicts hunters attacking a boar. Spartans regarded hunting as an exercise that helped to sharpen fighting skills and aggressive instincts.

lifestyle as a matter of policy. They did not wear jewelry or elaborate clothes, nor did they pamper themselves with luxuries or accumulate private wealth on a large scale. They generally did not even circulate coins made of precious metals but, instead, used iron bars for money. It is for good reason, then, that our adjective *spartan* refers to a lifestyle characterized by simplicity, frugality, and austerity.

Distinction among the ancient Spartans came not by wealth or social status, but by prowess, discipline, and military talent, which the Spartan educational system cultivated from an early age. All boys from families of Spartan citizens left their homes at age seven and went to live in military barracks, where they underwent a rigorous regime of physical training. At age twenty they began active military service, which they continued until retirement. Spartan authorities also prescribed vigorous physical exercise for girls in hopes that they would bear strong children. When they reached eighteen to twenty years of age, young women married and had occasional sexual relations, but did not live with their husbands. Only at about age thirty did men leave the barracks and set up a household with their wives and children.

By the fourth century B.C.E., Spartan society had lost much of its ascetic rigor. Aristocratic families had accumulated great wealth, and Spartans had developed a taste for luxury in food and dress. Nevertheless, Spartan society stood basically on the foundation of military discipline, and its institutions both reflected and reinforced the larger society's commitment to military values. In effect, Sparta sought to maintain public order—and discourage rebellion by the helots—by creating a military state that could crush any threat.

Athens

In Athens as in Sparta, population growth and economic development caused political and social strain, but the Athenians relieved tensions by establishing a government based on democratic principles. Whereas Sparta sought to impose order by military means, Athens sought to negotiate order by considering the interests of the polis's various constituencies. Citizenship was by no means open to all residents: only free adult males from Athens played a role in public affairs, leaving foreigners, slaves, and women with no direct voice in government. In seeking to resolve social problems, Athenians opened government offices to all citizens and broadened the base of political participation in classical Greece.

Athenian Society

During the seventh century B.C.E., an increasing volume of maritime trade brought prosperity to Attica, the region around Athens. The principal beneficiaries of this prosperity were aristocratic landowners, who also controlled the Athenian government. As their wealth grew, the aristocrats increased their landholdings and cultivated them with greater efficiency. Owners of small plots could not compete and fell heavily into debt. Competitive pressures often forced them to sell their holdings to aristocrats, and debt burdens sometimes overwhelmed them and pushed them into slavery.

By the early sixth century B.C.E., Attica had a large and growing class of people extremely unhappy with the structure of their society and poised to engage in war against their wealthy neighbors. Many poleis that experienced similar economic conditions suffered decades of brutal civil war between aristocrats and less privileged classes. In Athens, however, an aristocrat named Solon served as a mediator between classes, and he devised a solution to class conflict in Attica.

Solon forged a compromise between the classes. He allowed aristocrats to keep their lands—rather than confiscate them and redistribute them to landless individuals, as many of the less privileged preferred—but he cancelled debts, forbade debt slavery, and liberated those already enslaved for debt. To ensure that aristocrats would not undermine his reforms, Solon also provided representation for the common classes in the Athenian government by opening the councils of the polis to any citizen wealthy enough to devote time to public affairs, regardless of his lineage. Later reformers went even further. During the late sixth and fifth centuries B.C.E., Athenian leaders increased opportunities for commoners to participate in government, and they paid salaries to officeholders so financial hardship would not exclude anyone from service.

Solon and Athenian Democracy

These reforms gradually transformed Athens into a democratic state. The high tide of Athenian democracy came under the leadership of the statesman Pericles. Though he was of aristocratic birth, Pericles was the most popular Athenian leader from 461 B.C.E. until his death in 429 B.C.E. He wielded enormous personal influence in a government with hundreds of officeholders from the common classes, and he supported building programs that provided employment for thousands of construction workers and laborers. Under the leadership of Pericles, Athens became the most sophisticated of the poleis, with a vibrant community of scientists, philosophers, poets, dramatists, artists, and architects. Little wonder, then, that in a moment of civic pride, Pericles boasted that Athens was "the education of Greece."

Pericles

GREECE AND THE LARGER WORLD

As the poleis prospered, Greeks became increasingly prominent in the larger world of the Mediterranean basin. They established colonies along the shores of the Mediterranean and the Black Sea, and they traded throughout the region. Eventually, their political and economic interests brought them into conflict with the expanding Persian empire. During the fifth century B.C.E., a round of intermittent war between the Greeks and Persians ended in stalemate, but in the next century Alexander of Macedon toppled the Achaemenid empire. Indeed, Alexander built an empire stretching from India to Egypt and Greece. His conquests created a vast zone of trade and communication that encouraged commercial and cultural exchange on an unprecedented scale.

Greek Colonization

By about 800 B.C.E. the poleis were emerging as centers of political organization in Greece. During the next century increasing population strained the resources available in the rocky and mountainous Greek peninsula. To relieve population pressures, the Greeks began to establish colonies in other parts of the Mediterranean basin. Between the mid-eighth and the late sixth

The image of Pericles, wearing a helmet that symbolizes his post as Athenian leader, survives in a Roman copy of a Greek statue.

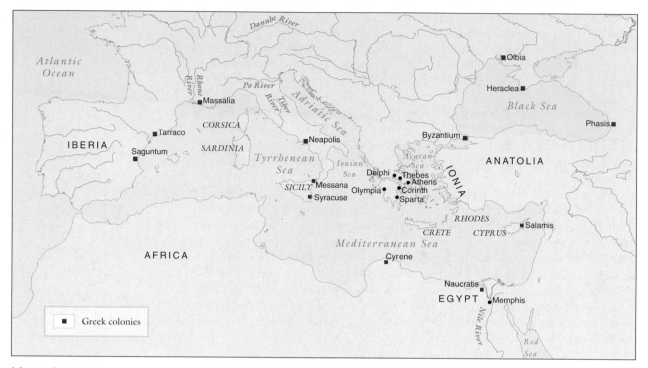

MAP [10.2]

Classical Greece and the Mediterranean basin, 800–500 B.C.E.

For an interactive version of this map, go to www.mhhe.com/bentley3ch10maps.

Greek Colonies

centuries B.C.E., they founded more than four hundred colonies along the shores of the Mediterranean Sea and the Black Sea.

The Greeks established their first colonies in the central Mediterranean during the early eighth century B.C.E. The most popular sites were Sicily and southern Italy, particularly the region around modern Naples, which was itself originally a Greek colony called Neapolis ("new polis"). These colonies provided merchants not only with fertile fields that yielded large agricultural surpluses but also with convenient access to the copper, zinc, tin, and iron ores of central Italy. By the sixth century B.C.E., Greek colonies dotted the shores of Sicily and southern Italy, and more Greeks lived in these colonies than in the Greek peninsula itself. By 600 B.C.E. the Greeks had ventured even farther west and established the important colony of Massalia (modern Marseilles) in what is now southern France.

Greek colonies arose also in the eastern Mediterranean and the Black Sea. Hundreds of islands in the Aegean Sea beckoned to a maritime people such as the Greeks. Colonists also settled in Anatolia, where their Greek cousins had established communities during the centuries of political turmoil after 1100 B.C.E. During the eighth and seventh centuries B.C.E., Greeks ventured into the Black Sea in large numbers and established colonies all along its shores. These settlements offered merchants access to rich supplies of grain, fish, furs, timber, honey, wax, gold, and amber as well as slaves captured in southern Russia and transported to markets in the Mediterranean.

Unlike their counterparts in classical Persia, China, and India, the Greeks did not build a centralized imperial state. Greek colonization was not a process controlled by a central government so much as an ad hoc response of individual poleis to population pressures. Colonies often did not take guidance from the poleis from which their settlers came but, rather, relied on their own resources and charted their own courses.

Effects of Greek Colonization

Nevertheless, Greek colonization sponsored more communication, interaction, and exchange than ever before among Mediterranean lands and peoples. From the early eighth century B.C.E., colonies facilitated trade between their own regions and the poleis in peninsular Greece and Anatolia. At the same time, colonization spread Greek language and cultural traditions throughout the Mediterranean basin. Moreover, the Greek presence quickened the tempo of social life, especially in the western Mediterranean and the Black Sea. Except for a few urban districts surrounding Phoenician colonies in the western Mediterranean, these regions were home mostly to small-scale agricultural societies organized by clans. As Greek merchants brought wealth into these societies, local clan leaders built small states in areas like Sicily, southern Italy, southern France, the Crimean peninsula, and southern Russia where trade was especially strong. Thus Greek colonization had important political and social effects throughout the Mediterranean basin.

Two Greek ships under sail, a merchant vessel (left) and a galley (right) powered by oars as well as sails.

Conflict with Persia

During the fifth century B.C.E., their links abroad brought the poleis of the Greek peninsula into direct conflict with the Persian empire in a long struggle known as the Persian Wars (500–479 B.C.E.). As the Persian emperors Cyrus and Darius tightened their grip on Anatolia, the Greek cities on the Ionian coast became increasingly restless. In 500 B.C.E. they revolted against Persian rule and expelled the Achaemenid administrators. In support of their fellow Greeks and commercial partners, the Athenians sent a fleet of ships to aid the Ionian effort. Despite this gesture, Darius repressed the Ionian rebellion by 493 B.C.E.

The Persian Wars

To punish the Athenians and forestall future interference in Persian affairs, Darius then mounted a campaign against peninsular Greece. In 490 B.C.E. he sent an army and a fleet of ships to attack Athens. Although greatly outnumbered, the Athenians routed the Persian army at the battle of Marathon and then marched back to Athens in time to fight off the Persian fleet.

Ten years later Darius's successor, Xerxes, decided to avenge the Persian losses. In 480 B.C.E. he dispatched a massive force consisting of perhaps one hundred thousand troops and a fleet of one thousand ships to subdue the Greeks. The Persian army succeeded in capturing and burning Athens, but a Greek fleet led by Athenians shattered the Persian navy at the battle of Salamis. Xerxes himself viewed the conflict from a temporary throne set up on a hillside overlooking the narrow strait of water between Athens and the island of Salamis. The following year a Greek force at Plataea routed the Persian army, whose survivors retreated to Anatolia.

Greeks and Persians continued to skirmish intermittently for more than a century, although their conflict did not expand into full-scale war. The Persian rulers were unwilling to invest resources in the effort to conquer small and distant Greece, and after Xerxes' reign they faced domestic problems that prevented them from undertaking foreign adventures. For their part, the Greeks had neither the resources nor the desire to challenge the Persian empire, and they remained content with maintaining their independence.

Once the Persian threat subsided, however, serious conflict arose among the Greek poleis themselves. After the Persian Wars, the poleis created an alliance known as the Delian League to discourage further Persian actions in Greece. Because of its superior fleet, Athens became the leader of the alliance. In effect, Athens supplied

The Delian League

Pericles organized the construction of numerous marble buildings, partly with funds collected from poleis belonging to the Delian League. Most notable of his projects was the Parthenon, a temple dedicated to the goddess Athena, which symbolizes the prosperity and grandeur of classical Athens.

the league's military force, and the other poleis contributed financial support, which went largely to the Athenian treasury. Indeed, these contributions financed much of the Athenian bureaucracy and the vast construction projects that employed Athenian workers during the era of Pericles' leadership. In the absence of a continuing Persian threat, however, the other poleis resented having to make contributions that seemed to benefit only the Athenians.

The Peloponnesian War

Ultimately, the tensions resulted in a bitter and destructive civil conflict known as the Peloponnesian War (431–404 B.C.E.). Both in peninsular Greece and throughout the larger Greek world, poleis divided into two armed camps under the leadership of Athens and Sparta, the most powerful of the poleis and the principal contenders for hegemony in the Greek world. The fortunes of war favored first one side, then the other, but by 404 B.C.E. the Spartans and their allies had forced the Athenians to unconditional surrender. Sparta's victory soon generated new jealousies, however, and conflicts broke out again. During the decades following Athenian surrender, hegemony in the Greek world passed to Sparta, Thebes, Corinth, and other poleis. As internal struggles weakened the world of the poleis, a formidable power took shape in the north.

The Macedonians and the Coming of Empire

The Kingdom of Macedon

Until the fourth century B.C.E., the kingdom of Macedon was a frontier state north of peninsular Greece. The Macedonian population consisted partly of cultivators and partly of sheepherders who migrated seasonally between the mountains and valleys. Although the Macedonians recognized a king, semiautonomous clans controlled political affairs.

Proximity to the wealthy poleis of Greece brought change to Macedon. From the seventh century B.C.E., the Greek cities traded with Macedon. They imported grain, timber, and other natural resources in exchange for olive oil, wine, and finished products. Macedonian political and social elites, who controlled trade from their side of the border, became well acquainted with Greek merchants and their society.

Philip of Macedon

During the reign of King Philip II (359–336 B.C.E.), Macedon underwent a thorough transformation. Philip built a powerful military machine that enabled him to overcome the traditional clans and make himself the ruler of Macedon. His military force featured an infantry composed of small landowners and a cavalry staffed by aristocrats holding large estates. During the fourth century B.C.E., both elements proved to be hardy, well trained, and nearly invincible.

When Philip had consolidated his hold on Macedon, he turned his attention to two larger prizes: Greece and the Persian empire. During the years following 350 B.C.E., Philip moved into northern Greece, annexing poleis and their surrounding territories. The poleis recognized the Macedonian threat, but the Peloponnesian War had poisoned the atmosphere so much that the poleis could not agree to form an alliance against Philip. Thus as he moved into Greece, Philip faced nothing more than small forces patched together by shifting and temporary alliances. By 338 B.C.E. he had overcome all organized resistance and brought Greece under his control.

Philip intended to use his conquest of Greece as a launching pad for an invasion of Persia. He did not have the opportunity to carry out his plans, however, because an assassin brought him down in 336 B.C.E. The invasion of Persia thus fell to his son, the young Alexander of Macedon, often called Alexander the Great.

Alexander of Macedon

At the age of twenty, Alexander succeeded Philip as ruler of an expanding empire. He soon began to assemble an army of about thirty-seven thousand men to invade the Persian empire. Alexander was a brilliant strategist and an inspired leader, and he inherited a well-equipped, well-disciplined, highly spirited veteran force from his father. By 333 B.C.E. Alexander had subjected Ionia and Anatolia to his control; within another year he held Syria, Palestine, and Egypt; by 331 B.C.E. he controlled Mesopotamia and prepared to invade the Persian homeland. He took Pasargadae and burned the Achaemenid palace at Persepolis late in 331 B.C.E., and he pursued the dispirited Persian army for another year until the last Achaemenid ruler fell to an assassin. Alexander established himself as the new emperor of Persia in 330 B.C.E.

Alexander's Conquests

By 327 B.C.E. Alexander had larger ambitions: he took his army into India and crossed the Indus River, entering the Punjab. He subjected local rulers and probably would have continued to campaign in India except that his troops refused to proceed any further from home. By 324 B.C.E. Alexander and his army had returned to Susa in Mesopotamia, where they celebrated their exploits in almost continuous feasting. Alexander busied himself with plans for governing his empire and for conducting further explorations. In June of 323 B.C.E., however, after an extended round of feasting and drinking, he suddenly fell ill and died at the age of thirty-three.

During the course of a meteoric career, Alexander proved to be a brilliant conqueror, but he did not live long enough to construct a genuine state for his vast realm or to develop a system of administration. He established cities throughout the lands he conquered and reportedly named about seventy of them Alexandria in his own honor. Alexander also toyed with some intriguing ideas about governing his empire, notably a scheme to marry his officers to Persian women and create a new ruling class of Greek, Macedonian, and Persian ancestry, but his early death prevented him from turning this plan into a coherent policy. So long as he lived, he relied on established institutions such as the Persian satrapies to administer the lands he conquered.

Wearing a lion skin around his head, Alexander the warrior plunges into battle with Persian forces in this carving from his sarcophagus.

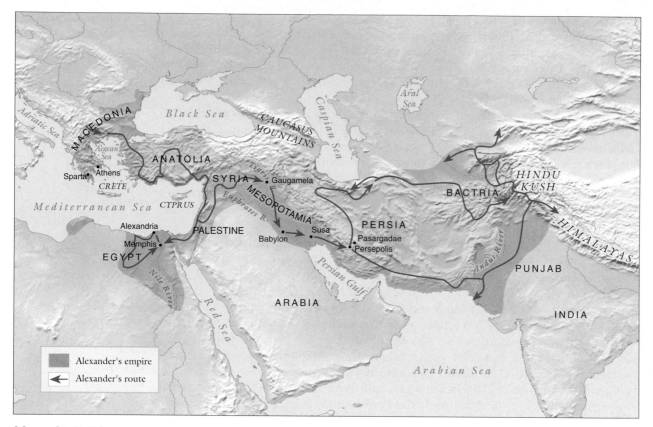

MAP [10.3]
Alexander's empire,
ca. 323 B.C.E.

The Hellenistic Empires

When Alexander died, his generals jockeyed for position in hopes of taking over choice parts of his realm, and by 275 B.C.E. they had divided the empire into three large states. Antigonus took Greece and Macedon, which his Antigonid successors ruled until the Romans established their authority in the eastern Mediterranean during the second century B.C.E. Ptolemy took Egypt, which the Ptolemaic dynasty ruled until the Roman conquest of Egypt in 31 B.C.E. Seleucus took the largest portion, the former Achaemenid empire stretching from Bactria to Anatolia, which his Seleucid successors ruled until the Parthians displaced them during the second century B.C.E.

The Hellenistic Era   Historians refer to the age of Alexander and his successors as the Hellenistic age—an era when Greek cultural traditions expanded their influence beyond Greece itself (*Hellas*) to a much larger world. During the centuries between Alexander's death and the expansion of the Roman empire in the eastern Mediterranean, the Hellenistic empires governed cosmopolitan societies and sponsored interactions between peoples from Greece to India. Like imperial states in classical Persia, China, and India, the Hellenistic empires helped to integrate the economies and societies of distant regions. They facilitated trade, and they made it possible for beliefs, values, and religions to spread over greater distances than ever before.

The Antigonid Empire   Although the Antigonid realm of Greece and Macedon was the smallest of the Hellenistic empires, it benefited handsomely from the new order. There was continual

Sources from the Past

Arrian on the Character of Alexander of Macedon

One of the earliest surviving accounts of Alexander's life and career is that of Flavius Arrianus Xenophon, better known as Arrian. Although Greek, Arrian served in the armies of the early Roman empire and developed a strong interest in military history. About the middle of the second century C.E., he composed his work on Alexander, drawing on contemporary accounts that no longer survive. Here he assesses Alexander's character.

He had great personal beauty, invincible power of endurance, and a keen intellect; he was brave and adventurous, strict in the observance of his religious duties, and hungry for fame. Most temperate in the pleasures of the body, his passion was for glory only, and in that he was insatiable. He had an uncanny instinct for the right course in a difficult and complex situation, and was most happy in his deductions from observed facts. In arming and equipping troops and in his military dispositions he was always masterly. Noble indeed was his power of inspiring his men, of filling them with confidence, and, in the moment of danger, of sweeping away their fear by the spectacle of his own fearlessness. When risks had to be taken, he took them with the utmost boldness, and his ability to seize the moment for a swift blow, before his enemy had any suspicion of what was coming, was beyond praise. No cheat or liar ever caught him off his guard, and both his word and his bond were inviolable. Spending but little on his own pleasures, he poured out his money without stint for the benefit of his friends.

Doubtless, in the passion of the moment Alexander sometimes erred; it is true that he took some steps towards the pomp and arrogance of the Asiatic kings: but I, at least, cannot feel that such errors were very heinous, if the circumstances are taken fairly into consideration. For, after all, he was young; the chain of his successes was unbroken, and, like all kings, past, present, and to come, he was surrounded by courtiers who spoke to please, regardless of what evil their words might do. On the other hand, I do indeed know that Alexander, of all the monarchs of old, was the only one who had the nobility of heart to be sorry for his mistakes . . .

. . . As for his reputed heavy drinking, Aristoboulos [one of Alexander's generals who composed an account of the conqueror that was available to Arrian but that does not survive] declares that his drinking bouts were prolonged not for their own sake—for he was never, in fact, a heavy drinker—but simply because he enjoyed the companionship of his friends.

Anyone who belittles Alexander has no right to do so on the evidence only of what merits censure in him; he must base his criticism on a comprehensive view of his whole life and career. But let such a person, if blackguard Alexander he must, first compare himself with the object of his abuse: himself, so mean and obscure, and, confronting him, the great King with his unparalleled worldly success, the undisputed monarch of two continents [Europe and Asia], who spread the power of his name over all the earth. Will he dare to abuse him then, when he knows his own littleness and the triviality of his own pursuits, which, even so, prove too much for his ability?

It is my belief that there was in those days no nation, no city, no single individual beyond the reach of Alexander's name; never in all the world was there another like him, and therefore I cannot but feel that some power more than human was concerned in his birth; indications of this were, moreover, said to be provided at the time of his death by oracles; many people saw visions and had prophetic dreams; and there is the further evidence of the extraordinary way in which he is held, as no mere man could be, in honour and remembrance. Even today, when so many years have passed, there have been oracles, all tending to his glory, delivered to the people of Macedon.

SOURCE: Arrian. *The Campaigns of Alexander.* Trans. by Aubrey de Sélincourt. Revised by J. R. Hamilton. London: Penguin, 1971, pp. 395–98.

On the basis of Arrian's characterization, do you think Alexander had strong potential to become an effective governor as well as a talented conqueror?

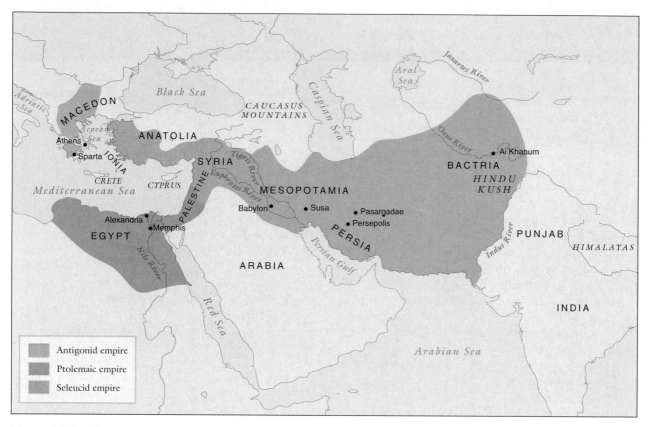

MAP [10.4]

The Hellenistic empires,
ca. 275 B.C.E.

tension between the Antigonid rulers and the Greek cities, which sought to retain their independence by forming defensive leagues that stoutly resisted Antigonid efforts to control the Greek peninsula. The poleis often struck bargains with the Antigonids, offering to recognize their rule in exchange for tax relief and local autonomy. Internal social tensions also flared, as Greeks wrestled with the perennial problem of land and its equitable distribution. Yet cities like Athens and Corinth flourished during the Hellenistic era as enormous volumes of trade passed through their ports. Moreover, the overpopulated Greek peninsula sent large numbers of colonists to newly founded cities, especially in the Seleucid empire.

The Ptolemaic Empire

Perhaps the wealthiest of the Hellenistic empires was Ptolemaic Egypt. Greek and Macedonian overlords did not interfere in Egyptian society, but contented themselves with the efficient organization of agriculture, industry, and tax collection. They maintained the irrigation networks and monitored the cultivation of crops and the payment of taxes. They also established royal monopolies over the most lucrative industries, such as textiles, salt making, and the brewing of beer.

Alexandria

Much of Egypt's wealth flowed to the Ptolemaic capital of Alexandria. Founded by Alexander at the mouth of the Nile, Alexandria served as the Ptolemies' administrative headquarters, but it became much more than a bureaucratic center. Alexandria's enormous harbor was able to accommodate 1,200 ships simultaneously, and the city soon became the most important port in the Mediterranean. Its wealth attracted migrants from all parts of the Mediterranean basin and beyond. Alongside Greeks, Macedonians, and Egyptians lived sizable communities of Phoenicians, Jews, Arabs, and Babylonians. The city was indeed an early megalopolis, where peoples of different ethnic, religious, and cultural traditions conducted their affairs. Under the Ptolemies, Alexandria also became the cultural capital of the Hellenistic world. It was the site of the famous Alexandrian Museum—a state-financed institute of higher learning where philosophical, literary, and scientific scholars carried on advanced research—and of the equally famous Alexandrian Library, which supported the scholarship sponsored by the museum and which, by the first century B.C.E., boasted a collection of more than seven hundred thousand works.

It was in the Seleucid realm, however, that Greek influence reached its greatest extent. The principal channels of this influence were the numerous cities that Alexander and his successors founded in the former Persian empire. Most of them were small settlements intended to serve as fortified sites or administrative centers, though some developed into thriving commercial centers. Greek and Macedonian colonists flocked to these cities, where they joined the ranks of imperial bureaucrats and administrators. Though few in number compared to the native populations, the colonists created a Mediterranean-style urban society that left its mark on lands as distant as Bactria and India. Emperor Ashoka of India himself had his edicts promulgated in Greek and Aramaic, the two most commonly used languages of the Hellenistic empires. *The Seleucid Empire*

Archaeological excavations have thrown considerable light on one of these Greek settlements—the Hellenistic colony at Ai Khanum on the Oxus River in ancient Bactria (modern-day Afghanistan). The colony at Ai Khanum was founded either by Alexander of Macedon himself or by Seleucus shortly after Alexander's death. As an integral part of the Seleucid empire, Bactria was in constant communication with Greece and the Mediterranean world. After about 250 B.C.E. the governors of Bactria withdrew from the Seleucid empire and established an independent Greek kingdom. Excavations at Ai Khanum show that the colony's inhabitants spoke the Greek language, dressed according to Greek fashions, read Greek literature and philosophy, and constructed buildings and produced works of art in Greek styles. At the same time, while honoring Greek gods at Greek shrines, residents of Ai Khanum also welcomed Persian and central Asian deities into their midst. Indeed, some Greeks even converted to Buddhism. Most prominent of the converts was King Menander, who ruled in Bactria approximately 160 to 135 B.C.E. In many ways, like the Achaemenids before them, the Hellenistic ruling classes constituted a thin, supervisory veneer over long-established societies that largely continued to observe their own inherited customs. Nevertheless, like classical states in Persia, China, and India, the Hellenistic empires brought distant lands into interaction by way of trade and cultural exchange. *Greeks in Bactria*

THE FRUITS OF TRADE: GREEK ECONOMY AND SOCIETY

The geography of the Greek peninsula posed difficult challenges for its inhabitants: its mountainous terrain and rocky soil yielded only small harvests of grain, and the southern Balkan mountains hindered travel and communication. Indeed, until the construction of modern roads, much of Greece was more accessible by sea than by land. As a result, early Greek society depended heavily on maritime trade.

Trade and the Integration of the Mediterranean Basin

Although it produced little grain, much of Greece is ideally suited to the cultivation of olives and grapes. After the establishment of the poleis, the Greeks discovered that they could profitably concentrate their efforts on the production of olive oil and *Trade*

Harvesting olives. In this painting on a vase, two men knock fruit off the branches while a third climbs the tree to shake the limbs, and another gathers olives from the ground.

wine. Greek merchants traded these products around the Mediterranean, returning with abundant supplies of grain and other items as well.

By the early eighth century B.C.E., trade had generated considerable prosperity in the Greek world. Merchants and mariners linked Greek communities throughout the Mediterranean world—not only those in the Greek peninsula but also those in Anatolia, the Mediterranean islands, and the Black Sea. The populations of all these communities grew dramatically, encouraging further colonization. In the colonies merchants offered Greek olive oil and wine for local products. Grain came from Egypt, Sicily, and southern Russia, salted fish from Spain and Black Sea lands, timber and pitch from Macedon, tin from Anatolia, and slaves from Egypt and Russia. Merchant ships with a capacity of four hundred tons were common in the classical Mediterranean, and a few vessels had a capacity of one thousand tons. Some cities, such as Athens and Corinth, relied more on commerce than on agriculture for their livelihood and prosperity.

Commercial and Economic Organization

Large volumes of trade promoted commercial and economic organization in the Mediterranean basin. In Greece, for example, shipowners, merchants, and moneylenders routinely formed partnerships to spread the risks of commercial ventures. Usually, a merchant borrowed money from a banker or an individual to purchase cargo and rented space from a shipowner, who transported the goods and returned the profits to the merchant. In the event of a shipwreck, the contract became void, leaving both the merchant and the lender to absorb their losses.

The production of cultivators and manufacturers filled the holds of Mediterranean merchant vessels. Manufacturers usually operated on a small scale, but there are records of pottery workshops with upwards of sixty employees. One factory in fourth-century Athens employed 120 slaves in the manufacture of shields. Throughout the trading world of the Mediterranean basin, entrepreneurs established small businesses and offered their wares in the larger market.

Trade links between the Greek cities and their colonies contributed to a sense of a larger Greek community. Colonists recognized the same gods as their cousins in the Greek peninsula. They spoke Greek dialects, and they maintained commercial relationships with their native communities. Greeks from all parts gathered periodically to participate in panhellenic festivals that reinforced their common bonds. Many of these festivals featured athletic, literary, or musical contests in which individuals sought to win glory for their polis.

Panhellenic Festivals

Best known of the panhellenic festivals were the Olympic games. According to tradition, in 776 B.C.E. Greek communities from all parts of the Mediterranean sent their best athletes to the polis of Olympia to engage in contests of speed, strength, and skill. Events included footracing, long jump, boxing, wrestling, javelin tossing, and discus throwing. Winners of events received olive wreaths, and they became celebrated heroes in their home poleis. The ancient Olympic games took place every four years for more than a millennium before quietly disappearing from Greek life. So, although they were not united politically, by the sixth century B.C.E. Greek communities had nevertheless established a sense of collective identity.

The Olympic Games

During the Hellenistic era, trade drew the Greeks into an even larger world of commerce and communication as colonists and traders expanded the range of their operations throughout Alexander's empire and the realms that succeeded him. Caravan trade linked Persia and Bactria to the western regions of the Hellenistic world. Dependent on horses and donkeys, caravans could not transport heavy or bulky goods, but rather carried luxury products such as gems, jewelry, perfumes, and aromatic oils. These goods all had high value relative to weight so that merchants could feed themselves and their animals, pay the high costs of overland transport, and still turn a profit. Traffic in bulkier goods traveled the sea lanes of the Mediterranean, Red Sea, Persian Gulf, and Arabian Sea.

Family and Society

Homer's works portrayed a society composed of heroic warriors and their outspoken wives. Strong-willed human beings clashed constantly with one another and sometimes even defied the gods in pursuing their interests. These aggressive and assertive characters depended on less flamboyant individuals to provide them with food and other necessities, but Homer had no interest in discussing the humdrum lives of farmers and their families.

With the establishment of poleis in the eighth century B.C.E., the nature of Greek family and society came into clearer focus. Like urban societies in southwest Asia and Anatolia, the Greek poleis adopted strictly patriarchal family structures. Male family heads ruled their households, and fathers even had the right to decide whether or not to keep infants born to their wives. They could not legally kill infants, but they could abandon newborns in the mountains or the countryside where they would soon die of exposure unless found and rescued by others.

Patriarchal Society

Greek women fell under the authority of their fathers, husbands, or sons. Upper-class women living in poleis spent most of their time in the family home, and they ventured outside in the company of servants or chaperones and often wore veils to discourage the attention of men from other families. In most of the poleis, women could not own landed property, but they sometimes operated small businesses such as shops and food stalls. The only public position open to Greek women was that of priestess of a religious cult. Sparta was something of a special case when it came to gender relations: there women participated in athletic contests, went about town by themselves, joined in public festivals, and sometimes even took up arms to defend the polis. Even in Sparta, however, men were family authorities, and men alone determined state policies.

Sappho

Literacy was common among upper-class Greek women, and a few women earned reputations for literary talent. Most famous of them was the poet Sappho, who was active during the years around 600 B.C.E. Sappho, probably a widow from an aristocratic family, invited young women into her home for instruction in music and literature. Critics charged her with homosexual activity, and her surviving verse speaks of her strong physical attraction to young women. Greek society readily tolerated sexual relationships between men but frowned on female homosexuality. As a result, Sappho fell under a moral cloud, and only fragments of her poetry survive.

Aristocratic families with extensive landholdings could afford to provide girls with a formal education, but in less privileged families all hands contributed to the welfare of the household. In rural families, men performed most of the outside work while women took care of domestic chores and wove wool textiles. In artisan families living in the poleis, both men and women often participated in businesses and maintained stands or booths in the marketplace.

Slavery

A slave carrying a lantern guides his drunken master home following a party.

Throughout the Greek world, as in other classical societies, slavery was a prominent means of mobilizing labor. Slaves came from several different backgrounds. Some were formerly free Greeks who entered slavery because they could not pay their debts. Many came from the ranks of soldiers captured in war. A large number came from the peoples with whom the Greeks traded: slave markets at Black Sea ports sold seminomadic Scythians captured in Russia, while Egyptians provided African slaves from Nubia and other southern regions.

Greek law regarded all slaves as the private chattel property of their owners, and the conditions of slaves' lives depended on the needs and the temperament of their owners. Physically powerful slaves with no special skills most often provided heavy labor on the estates of large landholders. Other unskilled slaves worked at lighter tasks as domestic servants or caretakers of their owners' children. Educated slaves and those skilled at some craft or trade had special opportunities. Their owners often regarded them as economic investments, provided them with shops, and allowed them to keep a portion of their earnings as an incentive and a reward for efficient work. In some cases, slaves with entrepreneurial talent succeeded well enough in their businesses to win their freedom. A slave named Pasion, for example, worked first as a porter and then as a clerk at a prominent Athenian bank during the late fifth and early fourth centuries B.C.E. Pasion's owners entrusted him with larger responsibilities and rewarded him for his efforts. Ultimately, Pasion gained his freedom, took over management of the bank, outfitted five warships from his own pocket, and won a grant of Athenian citizenship.

THE CULTURAL LIFE OF CLASSICAL GREECE

During the eighth and seventh centuries B.C.E., as Greek merchants ventured throughout the Mediterranean basin, they became acquainted with the sophisticated cultural traditions of Mesopotamia and Egypt. They learned astronomy, science, mathematics, medicine, and magic from the Babylonians as well as geometry, medicine, and divination from the Egyptians. They also drew inspiration from the myths, religious beliefs, art motifs, and architectural styles of Mesopotamia and Egypt. About 800 B.C.E. they adapted the Phoenician alphabet to their own language. To the Phoenicians' consonants they added symbols for vowels and thus created an exceptionally flexible system for representing human speech in written form.

During the fifth and fourth centuries B.C.E., the Greeks combined these borrowed cultural elements with their own intellectual interests to elaborate a rich cultural tradition. The most distinctive feature of classical Greek culture was the effort to construct a consistent system of philosophy based purely on human reason. Greek cultural figures also exercised enormous influence over art, literature, and moral thought in the Mediterranean basin and western Europe.

Rational Thought and Philosophy

The pivotal figure in the development of philosophy was Socrates (470–399 B.C.E.), a thoughtful and reflective Athenian driven by a powerful urge to understand human beings and human affairs in all their complexity. During his youth Socrates studied the ideas of Greek scientists who pursued the interests of their Mesopotamian and Egyptian predecessors. Gradually, however, he became disenchanted with their

Socrates

Tradition holds that Socrates was not a physically attractive man, but this statue emphasizes his sincerity and simplicity.

Sources from the Past

Socrates' View of Death

In one of his earliest dialogues, The Apology, *Plato offered an account of Socrates' defense of himself during his trial before a jury of Athenian citizens. After the jury had convicted him and condemned him to death, Socrates reflected on the nature of death and reemphasized his commitment to virtue rather than to wealth or fame.*

And if we reflect in another way we shall see that we may well hope that death is a good thing. For the state of death is one of two things: either the dead man wholly ceases to be and loses all sensation; or, according to the common belief, it is a change and a migration of the soul unto another place. And if death is the absence of all sensation, like the sleep of one whose slumbers are unbroken by any dreams, it will be a wonderful gain. For if a man had to select that night in which he slept so soundly that he did not even see any dreams, and had to compare with it all the other nights and days of his life, and then had to say how many days and nights in his life he had slept better and more pleasantly than this night, I think that a private person, nay, even the great king of Persia himself, would find them easy to count, compared with the others. If that is the nature of death, I for one count it a gain. For then it appears that eternity is nothing more than a single night.

But if death is a journey to another place, and the common belief be true, that all who have died dwell there, what good could be greater than this, my judges? Would a journey not be worth taking if at the end of it, in the other world, we should be released from the self-styled judges of this world, and should find the true judges who are said to sit in judgment below? . . . It would be an infinite happiness to converse with them, and to live with them, and to examine them. Assuredly there they do not put men to death for doing that. For besides the other ways in which they are happier than we are, they are immortal, at least if the common belief be true.

And you too, judges, must face death with a good courage, and believe this as a truth, that no evil can happen to a good man, either in life, or after death. His fortunes are not neglected by the gods, and what has come to me today has not come by chance. I am persuaded that it is better for me to die now, and to be released from trouble. . . . And so I am hardly angry with my accusers, or with those who have condemned me to die. Yet it was not with this mind that they accused me and condemned me, but rather they meant to do me an injury. Only to that extent do I find fault with them.

Yet I have one request to make of them. When my sons grow up, visit them with punishment, my friends, and vex them in the same way that I have vexed you if they seem to you to care for riches or for anything other than virtue: and if they think that they are something when they are nothing at all, reproach them as I have reproached you for not caring for what they should and for thinking that they are great men when in fact they are worthless. And if you will do this, I myself and my sons will have received our deserts at your hands.

But now the time has come, and we must go hence: I to die, and you to live. Whether life or death is better is known to God, and to God only.

SOURCE: F. J. Church, trans. *The Trial and Death of Socrates*, 2nd ed. London: Macmillan, 1886, pp. 76–78. (Translation slightly modified.)

How does Socrates' understanding of personal morality and its rewards compare and contrast with the Zoroastrian, Buddhist, and Hindu views discussed in earlier chapters?

efforts to understand the natural world, which he regarded as less important than human affairs.

Socrates did not commit his thought to writing, but his disciple Plato later composed dialogues that represented Socrates' views. Nor did he expound his views assertively: rather, he posed questions that encouraged reflection on human issues, particularly on matters of ethics and morality. He suggested that human beings could lead honest lives and that honor was far more important than wealth, fame, or other superficial attributes. He scorned those who preferred public accolades to personal integrity, and he insisted on the need to reflect on the purposes and goals of life. "The unexamined life is not worth living," he held, implying that human beings had an obligation to strive for personal integrity, behave honorably toward others, and work toward the construction of a just society.

In elaborating these views, Socrates often played the role of a gadfly who subjected traditional ethical teachings to critical scrutiny. This tactic outraged some of his fellow citizens, who brought him to trial on charges that he encouraged immorality and corrupted the Athenian youths who joined him in the marketplace to discuss moral and ethical issues. A jury of Athenian citizens decided that Socrates had indeed passed the bounds of propriety and condemned him to death. In 399 B.C.E. Socrates drank a potion of hemlock sap and died in the company of his friends.

Socrates' influence survived in the work of his most zealous disciple, Plato (430–347 B.C.E.), and in Plato's disciple Aristotle (384–322 B.C.E.). Inspired by his mentor's reflections, Plato elaborated a systematic philosophy of great subtlety. He presented his thought in a series of dialogues in which Socrates figured as the principal speaker. In the earliest dialogues, written shortly after Socrates' death, Plato largely represented his mentor's views. As time passed, Plato gradually formulated his thought into a systematic vision of the world and human society.

Plato

The cornerstone of Plato's thought was his theory of Forms or Ideas. It disturbed Plato that he could not gain satisfactory intellectual control over the world. The quality of virtue, for example, meant different things in different situations, as did honesty, courage, truth, and beauty. Generally speaking, for example, virtue required individuals to honor and obey their parents. But if a parent engaged in illegal behavior, virtue required offspring to denounce the offense and seek punishment. How was it possible,

A mosaic from the Italian town of Pompeii, near Naples, depicts Plato (standing at left) discussing philosophical issues with students. Produced in the early first century C.E., this illustration testifies to the popularity of Greek philosophy in classical Roman society.

then, to understand virtue as an abstract quality? In seeking an answer to this question, Plato developed his belief that the world in which we live was not the only world—indeed, was not the world of genuine reality, but only a pale and imperfect reflection of the world of Forms or Ideas. Displays of virtue or other qualities in the world imperfectly reflected the ideal qualities. Only by entering the world of Forms or Ideas was it possible to understand the true nature of virtue and other qualities. The secrets of this world were available only to philosophers—those who applied their rational faculties to the pursuit of wisdom.

Though abstract, Plato's thought had important political and social implications. In his dialogue *The Republic,* for example, Plato sketched an ideal state that reflected his philosophical views. Because philosophers were in the best position to understand ultimate reality, and hence to design policies in accordance with the Form or Idea of justice, he held that the best state was one where either philosophers ruled as kings or kings were themselves philosophers. In effect, then, Plato advocated an intellectual aristocracy: the philosophical elite would rule, and other, less intelligent classes would work at functions for which their talents best suited them.

Aristotle

During the generation after Plato, Aristotle also elaborated a systematic philosophy that equaled Plato's work in its long-term influence. Though originally a disciple of Plato, Aristotle came to distrust the theory of Forms or Ideas, which he considered artificial intellectual constructs unnecessary for understanding the world. Unlike Plato, Aristotle believed that philosophers could rely on their senses to provide accurate information about the world and then depend on reason to sort out its mysteries. Like Plato, Aristotle explored the nature of reality in subtle metaphysical works, and he devised rigorous rules of logic in an effort to construct powerful and compelling arguments. But he also wrote on biology, physics, astronomy, psychology, politics, ethics, and literature. His work provided such a coherent and comprehensive vision of the world that his later disciples, the Christian scholastic philosophers of medieval Europe, called him "the master of those who know."

The Greek philosophers deeply influenced the development of European and Islamic cultural traditions. Until the seventeenth century C.E., most European philosophers regarded the Greeks as intellectual authorities. Christian and Islamic theologians alike went to great lengths to harmonize their religious convictions with the philosophical views of Plato and Aristotle. Thus, like philosophical and religious figures in other classical societies, Plato and Aristotle provided a powerful intellectual framework that shaped thought about the world and human affairs for two millennia and more.

Popular Religion and Greek Drama

Because most Greeks of the classical era did not have an advanced education and did not chat regularly with the philosophers, they did not rely on systems of formal logic when seeking to understand their place in the larger world. Instead, they turned to traditions of popular culture and popular religion that shed light on human nature and offered guidance for human behavior.

Greek Deities

The Greeks did not recognize a single, exclusive, all-powerful god. Their Indo-European ancestors had attributed supernatural powers to natural elements such as sun, wind, and rain. Over the course of the centuries, the Greeks personified these powers and came to think of them as gods. They constructed myths that related the stories of the gods, their relations with one another, and their roles in bringing the world to its present state.

In the beginning, they believed, there was the formless void of chaos out of which emerged the earth, the mother and creator of all things. The earth then generated the sky, and together they produced night, day, sun, moon, and other natural phenomena. Struggles between the deities led to bitter heavenly battles, and ultimately Zeus, grandson of the earth and sky gods, emerged as paramount ruler of the divine realm. Zeus's heavenly court included scores of subordinate deities who had various responsibilities: the god Apollo promoted wisdom and justice, for example, while the goddess Fortune brought unexpected opportunities and difficulties, and the Furies wreaked vengeance on those who violated divine law.

Like religious traditions in other lands, Greek myths sought to explain the world and the forces that shape it. They served also as foundations for religious cults that contributed to a powerful sense of community in classical Greece. Many of the cults conducted ritual observances that were open only to initiates. One especially popular cult known as the Eleusinian mysteries, for example, sponsored a ritual community meal and encouraged initiates to observe high moral standards. *Religious Cults*

Some cults admitted only women. Because women could not participate in legal and political life, the cults provided opportunities for them to play roles in society outside the home. The fertility cult of Demeter, goddess of grain, excluded men. In honor of Demeter women gathered on a hill for three days, offered sacrifices to the goddess, and took part in a celebratory feast. This event occurred in October or November before the planting of grain and sought to ensure bountiful harvests.

Women were also the most prominent devotees of Dionysus, the god of wine, also known as Bacchus, although men sometimes joined in his celebration. During the spring of the year, when the vines produced their fruit, devotees retreated into the hills to celebrate Dionysus with song and dance. The dramatist Euripides offered an account of one such Dionysian season in his play *The Bacchae*. Euripides described the preparations for the festival and the celebrants' joyful march to the mountains. Spirited music and dance brought the devotees to such a state of frenzy that they fell upon a sacrificial goat—and also a man hiding in the brush in an unwise effort to observe the proceedings—ripped the victims apart, and presented them as offerings to Dionysus. Though he was a skeptic who regarded much of Greek religion as sham and hypocrisy, Euripides nonetheless recognized that powerful emotional bonds held together the Dionysian community. *The Cult of Dionysus*

During the fifth century B.C.E., as the poleis strengthened their grip on public and political life, the religious cults became progressively more tame. The cult of Dionysus, originally one of the most unrestrained, became one of the most thoroughly domesticated. The venue of the rituals shifted from the mountains to the polis, and the nature of the observances changed dramatically. Instead of emotional festivals, the Dionysian season saw the presentation of plays that honored the traditions of the polis, examined relations between human beings and the gods, or reflected on problems of ethics and morality.

This transformation of Dionysus's cult set the stage for the emergence of Greek dramatic literature as dramatists composed plays for presentation at annual theatrical festivals. Of the thousands of plays written in classical Greece, only a few survive: thirty-two tragedies and a dozen comedies have come down to the present in substantially complete form. Yet this small sample shows that the dramatists engaged audiences in subtle reflection on complicated themes. The great tragedians—Aeschylus, Sophocles, and Euripides—whose lives spanned the fifth century B.C.E., explored the possibilities and limitations of human action. To what extent could human beings act as responsible agents in society? What was their proper role when they confronted the limits that the gods or other humans placed on their activity? How should they proceed when the gods and human authorities presented them with conflicting demands? *Tragic Drama*

Comic dramatists such as Aristophanes also dealt with serious issues of human striving and responsible behavior. They took savage delight in lampooning the public and political figures of their time. The comedians aimed to influence popular attitudes by ridiculing the foibles of prominent public figures and calling attention to the absurd consequences of ill-considered action.

Hellenistic Philosophy and Religion

As the Hellenistic empires seized the political initiative in the Mediterranean basin and eclipsed the poleis, Greek philosophy and religion lost their civic character. Because the poleis no longer controlled their own destinies but, rather, figured as small elements in a large administrative machine, residents ceased to regard their polis as the focus of individual loyalties. Instead, they inclined toward cultural and religious alternatives that ministered to the needs and interests of individuals living in a large, cosmopolitan society.

The Hellenistic Philosophers

The most popular Hellenistic philosophers—the Epicureans, Skeptics, and Stoics—addressed individual needs by searching for personal tranquility and serenity. Epicureans, for example, identified pleasure as the greatest good. By *pleasure* they did not mean unbridled hedonism but, rather, a state of quiet satisfaction that would shield them from the pressures of the Hellenistic world. Skeptics refused to take strong positions on political, moral, and social issues because they doubted the possibility of certain knowledge. Rather than engage in fruitless disputes, they sought equanimity and left contentious issues to others.

The most respected and influential of the Hellenistic philosophers were the Stoics, who considered all human beings members of a single, universal family. Unlike the Epicureans and Skeptics, the Stoics did not seek to withdraw from the pressures of the world. Rather, they taught that individuals had the duty to aid others and lead virtuous lives. The Stoics believed that individuals could avoid anxieties caused by the pressures of Hellenistic society by concentrating their attention strictly on the duties that reason and nature demanded of them. Thus, like the Epicureans and Skeptics, the Stoics sought ways to bring individuals to a state of inner peace and tranquility.

Religions of Salvation

While the philosophers' doctrines appealed to educated elites, religions of salvation enjoyed surging popularity in Hellenistic society. Mystery religions promised eternal bliss for initiates who observed their rites and lived in accordance with their doctrines. Some of these faiths spread across the trade routes and found followers far from their homelands. The Egyptian cult of Osiris, for example, became extraordinarily popular because it promised salvation for those who led honorable lives. Cults from Persia, Mesopotamia, Anatolia, and Greece also attracted disciples throughout the Hellenistic world.

Many of the mystery religions involved the worship of a savior whose death and resurrection would lead the way to eternal salvation for devoted followers. Some philosophers and religious thinkers speculated that a single, universal god might rule the entire universe—just as Alexander and his successors governed enormous empires on earth—and that this god had a plan for the salvation of all humankind. Like the Hellenistic philosophies, then, religions of salvation addressed the interests of individuals searching for security in a complex world.

Greek travelers linked the regions of the Mediterranean basin in classical times. Although they did not build a centralized empire, the Greeks dotted the Mediterranean and Black Sea shorelines with their colonies, and their merchant fleets stimulated both commercial and cultural interactions between peoples of distant lands. Greek merchants, soldiers, and administrators also played prominent roles in the massive empires of Alexander and the Hellenistic rulers. Quite apart from their political and economic significance, the Greeks also left a remarkably rich cultural legacy. Greek philosophy, literature, and science profoundly influenced the intellectual and cultural development of peoples from southwest Asia to western Europe. The Greek poleis and the Hellenistic cities provided nurturing environments for rational thought and academic pursuits, and the frequent travels of the Greeks promoted the spread of popular religious faiths throughout the Mediterranean basin and beyond. Like classical Persia, China, and India, the Mediterranean basin became an integrated world.

CHRONOLOGY

2200–1100 B.C.E.	Minoan society
1600–1100 B.C.E.	Mycenaean society
800–338 B.C.E.	Era of the classical Greek polis
around 600 B.C.E.	Life of Sappho
500–479 B.C.E.	Persian Wars
490 B.C.E.	Darius's invasion of Greece
490 B.C.E.	Battle of Marathon
480 B.C.E.	Xerxes' invasion of Greece
480 B.C.E.	Battle of Salamis
479 B.C.E.	Battle of Plataea
470–399 B.C.E.	Life of Socrates
443–429 B.C.E.	Pericles' leadership in Athens
431–404 B.C.E.	Peloponnesian War
430–347 B.C.E.	Life of Plato
384–322 B.C.E.	Life of Aristotle
359–336 B.C.E.	Reign of Philip II of Macedon
336–323 B.C.E.	Reign of Alexander of Macedon

FOR FURTHER READING

Martin Bernal. *Black Athena: The Afroasiatic Roots of Classical Civilization*. 2 vols. to date. New Brunswick, 1987–. Provocative and controversial study arguing for Egyptian and Semitic influences on early Greek society.

Sue Blundell. *Women in Ancient Greece*. Cambridge, Mass., 1995. A comprehensive survey of women and their roles in ancient Greek society, solidly based on recent scholarship.

Walter Burkert. *The Orientalizing Revolution: Near Eastern Influence on Greek Culture in the Early Archaic Age*. Trans. by M. E. Pinder and W. Burkert. Cambridge, Mass., 1992. An important scholarly work tracing Mesopotamian influence in early Greece.

Lionel Casson. *The Ancient Mariners: Seafarers and Sea Fighters of the Mediterranean in Ancient Times*. 2nd ed. Princeton, 1991. Draws heavily on discoveries of underwater archaeologists in reconstructing the maritime history of the ancient Mediterranean.

F. M. Cornford. *Before and after Socrates*. Cambridge, 1965. A short but brilliant synthesis of classical Greek philosophy.

C. R. Dodds. *The Greeks and the Irrational*. Berkeley, 1968. An influential study of Greek religion in light of modern psychological and anthropological theories.

Kenneth Dover. *The Greeks*. Austin, 1980. An engaging personal interpretation of classical Greece.

M. I. Finley. *Ancient Slavery and Modern Ideology*. Expanded ed. Princeton, 1998. Presents a thoughtful analysis of Greek and Roman slavery in light of modern slavery and contemporary debates.

Frank J. Frost. *Greek Society*. 2nd ed. Lexington, 1980. Concentrates on economic and social history from Myceanean to Hellenistic times.

Frederick C. Grant, ed. *Hellenistic Religions: The Age of Syncretism*. Indianapolis, 1953. Fascinating collection of translated documents and texts that throw light on religious and philosophical beliefs of the Hellenistic era.

N. G. L. Hammond. *The Genius of Alexander the Great*. Chapel Hill, 1997. The best recent work on Alexander of Macedon.

William H. McNeill and Jean W. Sedlar, eds. *The Classical Mediterranean World*. New York, 1969. Primary sources from classical Greece and the Hellenistic world in English translation.

Sarah B. Pomeroy. *Goddesses, Whores, Wives, and Slaves: Women in Classical Antiquity*. New York, 1995. Outstanding study analyzing the status and role of women in classical Greece and Rome.

Susan Sherwin-White and Amélie Kuhrt. *From Samarkhand to Sardis: A New Approach to the Seleucid Empire*. Berkeley, 1993. Detailed scholarly analysis of the Seleucid empire concentrating on political and economic matters.

Mortimer Wheeler. *Flames over Persepolis*. New York, 1968. Examines the influence of Hellenistic artists in Persia, Bactria, and India.

See our **Online Learning Center** at www.mhhe.com/bentley3 for additional readings, practice maps, quizzes, and internet activities.

Unfamiliar words? Check out the **Primary Source Investigator CD-ROM** for an interactive glossary, interactive maps, more images, and primary sources.

A marble relief sculpture of about 100 C.E. depicts a crew of men working in a treadmill that powers a crane used in construction of a Roman temple.

CHAPTER 11

MEDITERRANEAN SOCIETY: THE ROMAN PHASE

About 55 C.E. Roman guards transported a prisoner named Paul of Tarsus from the port of Caesarea in Palestine to the city of Rome. The journey turned out to be more eventful than the travelers had planned. The party boarded a sailing ship loaded with grain and carrying 276 passengers as well. The ship departed in the fall—after the main sailing season, which ran from May through September—and soon encountered a violent storm. For two frightening weeks crew and passengers alike worked furiously to keep the ship afloat, jettisoning baggage, tackle, and cargo to lighten the load as wind and rain battered the vessel. Eventually, the ship ran aground on the island of Malta, where storm-driven waves destroyed the craft. Yet most of the passengers and crew survived, including Paul and his guards, who spent three months on Malta before catching another ship to Rome.

Paul had become embroiled in a dispute between Jews and early proponents of the fledgling Christian religion. Christianity first emerged as a sect of Judaism accepted only by a small number of individuals who regarded Jesus of Nazareth as a savior for the Jewish community. By the mid-first century C.E., Christianity was attracting numerous converts throughout the Mediterranean basin. Paul himself was a devout Jew from Anatolia who accepted Christian teachings and became a zealous missionary seeking converts from outside as well as within the Jewish community. Indeed, he was the principal figure in the development of Christianity from a Jewish sect to an independent religious faith. When a crowd of Paul's enemies attacked him in Jerusalem, where he was promoting his recently adopted faith, the resulting disturbance became so severe that authorities of the Roman imperial government intervened to restore order. Under normal circumstances Roman authorities would deliver an individual like Paul to the leaders of his own ethnic community, and the laws and customs of that community would determine the person's fate.

Paul's case, however, was different. Knowing that Jewish leaders would condemn him and probably execute him, Paul asserted his rights as a Roman citizen. Although he had never traveled west of Greece, Paul had inherited Roman citizenship from his father. As a result, he had the right to appeal his case to Rome, and he did so. His appeal did not succeed. No record of his case survives, but tradition holds that imperial authorities executed him out of concern that Christianity threatened the peace and stability of the Roman state.

Paul's experience reflects the cosmopolitan character of the early Roman empire, which by the first century C.E. dominated the entire Mediterranean basin. Roman administrators oversaw affairs from Anatolia and Palestine in the east to Spain and

Morocco in the west. Roman military forces maintained order in an empire with scores of different and sometimes conflicting ethnic and religious groups. Like many others, Paul of Tarsus traveled freely through much of the Roman empire in an effort to attract converts to Christianity. Indeed, except for the integration of the Mediterranean basin by the Roman empire, Paul's message and his faith might never have expanded beyond the small community of early Christians in Jerusalem.

Like the Phoenicians and Greeks before them, the Romans established close links between the various Mediterranean regions. As they conquered new lands, pacified them, and brought them into their empire, the Romans enabled merchants, missionaries, and others to travel readily throughout the Mediterranean basin. The Romans differed from their Phoenician and Greek predecessors, however, by building an extensive land empire and centralizing the administration of their realm. At its high point the Roman empire dominated the entire Mediterranean basin and parts of southwest Asia, including Anatolia, Mesopotamia, Syria, Egypt, and north Africa, besides much of continental Europe, and even parts of Britain as well.

The Roman empire also served as a vehicle for the spread of Christianity. The early Christians encountered harsh opposition and persecution from Roman officials. Yet the new faith took advantage of the Romans' well-organized imperial holdings and spread rapidly throughout the Mediterranean basin and beyond. Eventually, Christianity became the official religion of the Roman empire, and imperial sponsorship enabled Christianity to spread more effectively than before.

FROM KINGDOM TO REPUBLIC

Founded in the eighth century B.C.E., the city of Rome was originally a small city-state ruled by a single king. Late in the sixth century B.C.E., the city's aristocrats deposed the king, ended the monarchy, and instituted a republic—a form of government in which delegates represented the interests of various constituencies. The Roman republic survived for more than five hundred years, and it was under the republican constitution that Rome established itself as the dominant power in the Mediterranean basin.

The Etruscans and Rome

Romulus and Remus

The city of Rome arose from origins both obscure and humble. According to the ancient legends, the city owed its existence to the flight of Aeneas, a refugee from Troy who migrated to Italy when Greek invaders destroyed his native land. Two of his descendants, the twins Romulus and Remus, almost did not survive infancy because an evil uncle abandoned them by the flooded Tiber River, fully expecting them to drown or die of exposure. But a kindly she-wolf found them and nursed them to health. The boys grew strong and courageous, and in 753 B.C.E. Romulus founded the city of Rome and established himself as its first king.

Modern scholars do not tell so colorful a tale, but they agree that Rome grew from humble beginnings. Beginning about 2000 B.C.E., bands of Indo-European migrants crossed the Alps and settled throughout the Italian peninsula. Like their distant cousins in India, Greece, and northern Europe, these migrants blended with the neolithic inhabitants of the region, adopted agriculture, and established tribal federations. Sheepherders and small farmers occupied much of the Italian peninsula, including the future site of Rome itself. Bronze metallurgy appeared about 1800 B.C.E. and iron about 900 B.C.E.

Paintings in Etruscan tombs often represent scenes from daily life. Illustrations in the Tomb of the Leopards in Tarquinia depict musicians playing pipes and lyre during a banquet.

During the middle centuries of the first millennium B.C.E., Italy underwent rapid political and economic development. The agents of this development were the Etruscans, a dynamic people who dominated much of Italy between the eighth and fifth centuries B.C.E. The Etruscans probably migrated to Italy from Anatolia. They settled first in Tuscany, the region around modern Florence, but they soon controlled much of the territory from the Po River valley in northern Italy to the region around modern Naples in the south. They built thriving cities and established political and economic alliances between their settlements. They manufactured high-quality bronze and iron goods, and they worked gold and silver into jewelry. They built a fleet and traded actively in the western Mediterranean. During the late sixth century B.C.E., however, the Etruscans encountered a series of challenges from other peoples, and their society began to decline. Greek fleets defeated the Etruscans at sea while Celtic peoples attacked them from Gaul (modern France).

The Etruscans

The Etruscans deeply influenced the early development of Rome. Like the Etruscan cities, Rome was a monarchy during the early days after its foundation, and several Roman kings were Etruscans. The kings ruled Rome through the seventh and sixth centuries B.C.E., and they provided the city with paved streets, public buildings, defensive walls, and large temples.

The Kingdom of Rome

Etruscan merchants drew a large volume of traffic to Rome, thanks partly to the city's geographical advantages. Rome enjoyed easy access to the Mediterranean by way of the Tiber River, but since it was not on the coast, it did not run the risk of invasion or attack from the sea. Already during the period of Etruscan dominance, trade routes from all parts of Italy converged on Rome. When Etruscan society declined, Rome was in a strong position to play a more prominent role both in Italy and in the larger Mediterranean world.

The Roman Republic and Its Constitution

Establishment of the Republic

In 509 B.C.E. the Roman nobility deposed the last Etruscan king and replaced the monarchy with an aristocratic republic. At the heart of the city, they built the Roman forum, a political and civic center filled with temples and public buildings where leading citizens tended to government business. They also instituted a republican constitution that entrusted executive responsibilities to two consuls who wielded civil and military power. Consuls were elected by an assembly dominated by hereditary aristocrats and wealthy classes, known in Rome as the patricians, and they served one-year terms. The powerful Senate, whose members were mostly aristocrats with extensive political experience, advised the consuls and ratified all major decisions. Because the consuls and Senate both represented the interests of the patricians, there was constant tension between the wealthy classes and the common people, known as the plebeians.

Conflicts between Patricians and Plebeians

During the early fifth century B.C.E., relations between the classes became so strained that the plebeians threatened to secede from Rome and establish a rival settlement. In order to maintain the integrity of the Roman state, the patricians granted plebeians the right to elect officials, known as tribunes, who represented their interests in the Roman government. Originally plebeians chose two tribunes, but the number eventually rose to ten. Tribunes had the power to intervene in all political matters, and they possessed the right to veto measures that they judged unfair.

Ruins of the Roman forum, where political leaders conducted public affairs during the era of the republic, still stand today.

Although the tribunes provided a voice in government for the plebeians, the patricians continued to dominate Rome. Tensions between the classes persisted for as long as the republic survived. During the fourth century B.C.E., plebeians became eligible to hold almost all state offices and gained the right to have one of the consuls come from their ranks. By the early third century, plebeian-dominated assemblies won the power to make decisions binding on all of Rome. Thus, like fifth-century Athens, republican Rome gradually broadened the base of political participation.

Constitutional compromises eased class tensions, but they did not solve all political problems confronted by the republic. When faced with civil or military crises, the Romans appointed an official, known as a dictator, who wielded absolute power for a term of six months. By providing for strong leadership during times of extraordinary difficulty, the republican constitution enabled Rome to maintain a reasonably stable society throughout most of the republic's history. Meanwhile, by allowing various constituencies a voice in government, the constitution also helped to prevent the emergence of crippling class tensions.

The Expansion of the Republic

While the Romans dealt constructively with internal problems, external challenges mounted. During the fifth century B.C.E., for example, Rome faced threats not only from peoples living in the neighboring hills but also from the Etruscans. Beyond Italy itself were the Gauls, a powerful Celtic people who on several occasions invaded Italy. Between the fourth and second centuries B.C.E., however, a remarkable expansion of power and influence transformed Rome from a small and vulnerable city-state to the center of an enormous empire.

First the Romans consolidated their position in central Italy. During the fifth and early fourth centuries B.C.E., the Romans founded a large regional state in central

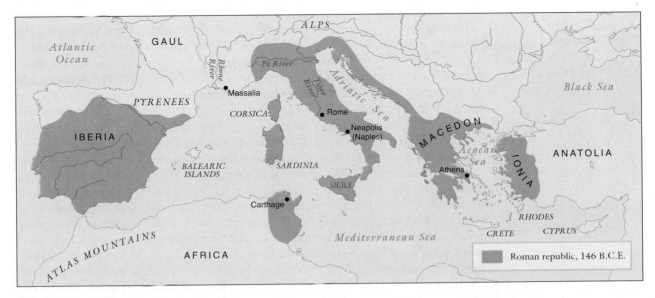

MAP [11.1]

Expansion of the Roman republic to 146 B.C.E.

Italy at the expense of the declining Etruscans and other neighboring peoples. Their conquests gave them access to the iron industry built by the Etruscans and greatly expanded the amount of land under Roman control.

During the later fourth century, the Romans built on their early conquests and emerged as the predominant power in the Italian peninsula. The Romans secured control of the peninsula partly because they established military colonies in regions they overcame and partly because of a generous policy toward the peoples they conquered. Instead of ruling them as vanquished subjects, the Romans often exempted them from taxation and allowed them to govern their own internal affairs. Conquered peoples in Italy enjoyed the right to trade in Rome and take Roman spouses. Some gained Roman citizenship and rose to high positions in Roman society. The Romans forbade conquered peoples from making military or political alliances except with Rome itself and required them to provide soldiers and military support. These policies provided the political, military, and diplomatic support Rome needed to put down occasional rebellions and to dominate affairs throughout the Italian peninsula.

Expansion in the Mediterranean

With Italy under its control, Rome began to play a major role in the affairs of the larger Mediterranean basin and to experience conflicts with other Mediterranean powers. The principal power in the western Mediterranean during the fourth and third centuries B.C.E. was the city-state of Carthage, located near modern Tunis. Originally established as a Phoenician colony, Carthage enjoyed a strategic location that enabled it to trade actively throughout the Mediterranean. From the wealth generated by this commerce, Carthage became the dominant political power in north Africa (excluding Egypt), the southern part of the Iberian peninsula, and the western region of grain-rich Sicily as well. Meanwhile, the three Hellenistic empires that succeeded Alexander of Macedon continued to dominate the eastern Mediterranean: the Antigonids ruled Macedon, the Ptolemies ruled Egypt, and the Seleucids included wealthy Syria and Anatolia among their many possessions. The prosperity of the Hellenistic realms supported a thriving network of maritime commerce in the eastern Mediterranean, and as in the case of Carthage, commercial wealth enabled rulers to maintain powerful states and armies.

The Punic Wars

The Romans clashed first with Carthage. Between 264 and 146 B.C.E., they fought three devastating conflicts known as the Punic Wars with the Carthaginians. Friction first arose from economic competition, particularly over Sicily, the most important source of grain in the western Mediterranean. Later on, Romans and Carthaginians struggled for supremacy in the region. The rivalry ended after Roman forces subjected Carthage to a long siege, conquered the city, burned much of it to the ground, and forced some fifty thousand survivors into slavery. The Romans then annexed Carthaginian possessions in north Africa and Iberia—rich in grain, oil, wine, silver, and gold—and used these resources to finance continued imperial expansion.

Shortly after the beginning of the Carthaginian conflict, Rome became embroiled in disputes in the eastern Mediterranean. Conflict arose partly because pirates and ambitious local lords ignored the weakening Hellenistic rulers and threatened regional stability. On several occasions Roman leaders dispatched armies to protect the interests of Roman citizens and merchants, and these expeditions brought them into conflict with the Antigonids and Seleucids. Between 215 and 148 B.C.E., Rome fought five major wars, mostly in Macedon and Anatolia, against Antigonid and Seleucid opponents. The Romans did not immediately annex lands in the eastern Mediterranean but, rather, entrusted them to allies in the region. Nevertheless, by the middle of the second century B.C.E., Rome clearly ranked as the preeminent power in the eastern as well as the western Mediterranean.

Roman expansion depended on well-equipped and highly disciplined military forces. In this detail from Trajan's Column, troops assume the siege formation known as the *testudo* (literally, the "tortoise") by surrounding themselves with their shields to avoid defenders' missiles while approaching city walls.

FROM REPUBLIC TO EMPIRE

Imperial expansion brought wealth and power to Rome, but wealth and power brought problems as well as benefits. Unequal distribution of wealth aggravated class tensions and gave rise to conflict over political and social policies. Meanwhile, the need to administer conquered lands efficiently strained the capacities of the republican constitution. During the first century B.C.E. and the first century C.E., Roman civil and military leaders gradually dismantled the republican constitution and imposed a centralized imperial form of government on the city of Rome and its empire.

Imperial Expansion and Domestic Problems

In Rome, as in classical China and Greece, patterns of land distribution caused serious political and social tensions. Conquered lands fell largely into the hands of wealthy elites, who organized enormous plantations known as *latifundia*. Because they enjoyed economies of scale and often employed slave labor, owners of *latifundia* operated at lower costs than did owners of smaller holdings, who often had to mortgage their lands or sell out to their wealthier neighbors.

The Gracchi Brothers

During the second and first centuries B.C.E., relations between the classes became so strained that they led to violent social conflict and civil war. The chief proponents of social reform in the Roman republic were the brothers Tiberius and Gaius Gracchus. Just as Wang Mang, the imperial usurper of the Han dynasty, tried to bring about a redistribution of land resources in classical China, the Gracchi brothers worked to limit the amount of conquered land that any individual could hold. Those whose lands exceeded the limit would lose some of their property, which officials would then allocate to small farmers. Again, as in the case of Wang Mang, the Gracchi had little success because most members of the wealthy and ruling classes considered them dangerous radicals and found ways to stymie their efforts. Indeed, fearing that the brothers might gain influence over Roman affairs, their enemies had them both assassinated—Tiberius in 132 B.C.E. and Gaius in 121 B.C.E.

The experiences of the Gracchi brothers clearly showed that the constitution of the Roman republic, originally designed for a small city-state, was not suitable for a large and growing empire. Formal political power remained in the hands of a small, privileged class of people in Rome, and their policies often reflected the interests of their class rather than the concerns of the empire as a whole. For the century following the assassinations of the Gracchi brothers, Roman politicians and generals jockeyed for power and position as they sought to mobilize support. Several military commanders began to recruit personal armies not from the ranks of small farmers—traditionally the core of the Roman army—but from landless rural residents and urban workers. Because these troops had no economic cushion to fall back on, they were intensely loyal to their generals and placed the interests of the army before those of the state. Most important of these generals were Gaius Marius, who sided with social reformers who advocated redistribution of land, and Lucius Cornelius Sulla, a veteran of several foreign campaigns who allied with the conservative and aristocratic classes.

Civil War   During the early first century B.C.E., Rome fell into civil war. In 87 B.C.E. Marius marched on Rome, placed the city under military occupation, and hunted down his political enemies. After Marius died the following year, Sulla made plans to take his place. In 83 B.C.E. he seized Rome and initiated a grisly slaughter of his enemies. Sulla posted lists naming "proscribed" individuals whom he labeled enemies of the

A bust of Julius Caesar depicts a trim conqueror and a canny political leader.

state, and he encouraged the Roman populace to kill these individuals on sight and confiscate their properties. During a reign of terror that lasted almost five years, Sulla brought about the murder or execution of some ten thousand individuals. By the time Sulla died in 78 B.C.E., he had imposed an extremely conservative legislative program that weakened the influence of the lower classes and strengthened the hand of the wealthy in Roman politics.

Because Sulla's program did not address Rome's most serious social problems, however, it had no chance to succeed over a long term. *Latifundia* continued to pressure small farmers, who increasingly left the countryside and swelled the ranks of the urban lower classes. Poverty in the cities, especially Rome, led to periodic social eruptions when the price of grain rose or the supply fell. Meanwhile, the urban poor increasingly joined the personal armies of ambitious generals, who themselves posed threats to social and political stability. In this chaotic context Gaius Julius Caesar inaugurated the process by which Rome replaced its republican constitution with a centralized imperial form of government.

The Foundation of Empire

A nephew of the general Marius, Julius Caesar favored liberal policies and social reform. In spite of these well-known political sympathies, he escaped danger during the reign of Sulla and the conservatives who followed him. Caesar's survival was due in some measure to his youth—Sulla and his supporters simply did not consider Caesar to be a serious threat—but partly also to a well-timed excursion to Greece and the eastern Mediterranean. During the decade of the 60s B.C.E., Caesar played an active role in Roman politics. He spent enormous sums of money sponsoring public spectacles—such as battles between gladiators and wild animals—which helped him build a reputation and win election to posts in the republican government. This activity kept him in

In this statue, which emphasizes his civil and military leadership in Rome, Augustus wears the uniform of a Roman general.

the public eye and helped to publicize his interest in social reform. During the next decade Caesar led a Roman army to Gaul, which he conquered and brought into the still-growing Roman empire.

The conquest of Gaul helped to precipitate a political crisis. As a result of his military victories, Caesar had become extremely popular in Rome. Conservative leaders sought to maneuver him out of power and regain the initiative for their own programs. Caesar refused to stand aside, and in 49 B.C.E. he turned his army toward Rome. By early 46 B.C.E. he had made himself master of the Roman state and named himself dictator—an office that he claimed for life rather than for the constitutional six-month term. Caesar then centralized military and political functions and brought them under his own control. He confiscated property from conservatives and distributed it to veterans of his armies and other supporters. He launched large-scale building projects in Rome as a way to provide employment for the urban poor. He also extended Roman citizenship to peoples in the imperial provinces, and he even appointed Gauls to the Roman Senate.

Caesar's policies pointed the way toward a centralized, imperial form of government for Rome and its possessions, but the consolidation of that government had to wait for a new generation of leaders. Caesar's rule alienated many members of the Roman elite classes, who considered him a tyrant. In 44 B.C.E. they organized a plot to assassinate Caesar and restore the republic. They attacked Caesar and stabbed him to death in the Roman forum, but the restoration of an outmoded form of government was beyond their powers. Instead, they plunged Rome into a fresh round of civil conflict that persisted for another thirteen years.

When the struggles ended, power belonged to Octavian, a nephew and protégé of Julius Caesar and the dictator's adopted son. In a naval battle at Actium in Greece

Augustus

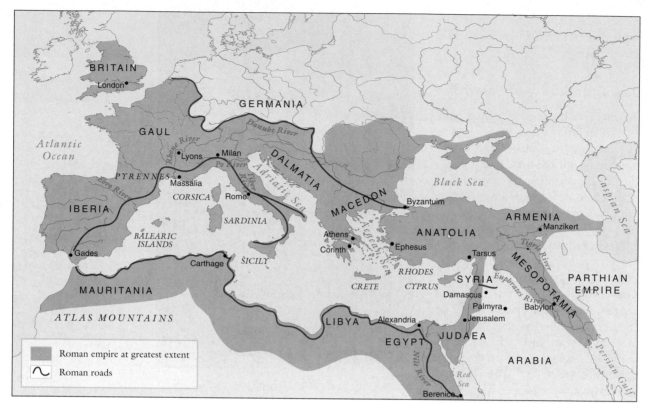

MAP [11.2]

The Roman empire about
117 C.E.

(31 B.C.E.), Octavian defeated his principal rival, Mark Antony, who had joined forces
with Cleopatra, last of the Ptolemaic rulers of Egypt. He then moved quickly and efficiently to consolidate his rule. In 27 B.C.E. the Senate bestowed upon him the title Augustus, a term with strong religious connotations suggesting the divine or semidivine nature of its holder. During his forty-five years of virtually unopposed rule, Augustus
fashioned an imperial government that guided Roman affairs for the next three centuries.

*Augustus's
Administration*

Augustus's government was a monarchy disguised as a republic. Like Julius Caesar, Augustus ruled by centralizing political and military power. Yet he proceeded
more cautiously than had his patron: Augustus preserved traditional republican offices and forms of government and included members of the Roman elite in his government. At the same time, though, he fundamentally altered the nature of that government. He accumulated vast powers for himself and ultimately took responsibility
for all important governmental functions. He reorganized the military system, creating a new standing army with commanders who owed allegiance directly to the emperor—a reform that eliminated problems caused during the late republic by generals with personal armies. He also was careful to place individuals loyal to him in all
important positions. Augustus served as emperor until his death in 14 C.E. During
his long reign he stabilized a land racked by civil war and enabled the institutions of
empire to take root.

Continuing Expansion and Integration of the Empire

During the two centuries following Augustus's rule, Roman armies conquered distant lands and integrated them into a larger economy and society. During republican

times Rome already held Italy, Greece, Syria, Gaul, and most of the Iberian peninsula, with small outposts in north Africa and Anatolia. By Augustus's reign imperial holdings included much of southeastern Europe, most of north Africa, including Egypt, and sizable territories in Anatolia and southwest Asia. At its high point, during the early second century C.E., the Roman empire embraced much of Britain as well as a continuous belt of possessions surrounding the Mediterranean and extending to rich agricultural regions inland, including Mesopotamia. After Octavian's conquest of Egypt in 30 B.C.E., Roman forces even made forays deep into the kingdom of Kush, and for more than three centuries they occupied a stretch of the Nile valley about 110 kilometers (70 miles) south of the river's first cataract near Aswan.

Roman expansion had especially dramatic effects in European lands embraced by the empire. Egypt, Anatolia, Syria, and Mesopotamia had long been sites of complex city-based societies, but Gaul, Germany, Britain, and Spain were sparsely populated lands occupied by cultivators who lived in small villages. When Roman soldiers, diplomats, governors, and merchants began to arrive in large numbers, they stimulated the development of local economies and states. They sought access to resources like tin, and they encouraged local inhabitants to cultivate wheat, olives, and grapes. Local ruling elites allied with Roman representatives and used the wealth that came into their communities to control natural resources and build states on a much larger scale than ever before. Cities emerged where administrators and merchants conducted their business, and the tempo of European society noticeably quickened: Paris, Lyons, Cologne, Mainz, London, Toledo, and Segovia all trace their origins to Roman times.

Roman engineers built paved roads far from home. This road served as the main street through the bustling city of Ephesus in Anatolia (modern-day Turkey).

Tacitus on Corruption in the Early Roman Empire

Augustus's imperial regime and the pax romana *brought peace and stability to the Roman empire, but some contemporaries thought there was a darker side to the new imperial order. Cornelius Tacitus (56–120 C.E.) was a prominent aristocrat and the most important historian of the early Roman empire. In his* Annals, *written in the early second century C.E., Tacitus did not deny the "gift of peace," but he deplored the loss of political courage among Roman leaders after the establishment of the imperial regime.*

Famous writers have recorded Rome's early glories and disasters. The Augustan Age, too, had its distinguished historians. But then the rising tide of flattery exercised a deterrent effect. The reigns of [Augustus's successors as emperor] Tiberius, Gaius, Claudius, and Nero were described during their lifetimes in fictitious terms, for fear of the consequences; whereas the accounts written after their deaths were influenced by raging animosities. So I have decided to say a little about Augustus, with special attention to his last period, and then go on to the reign of Tiberius [14–37 C.E.] and what followed. . . .

[Augustus] seduced the army with bonuses, and his cheap food policy was successful bait for civilians. Indeed, he attracted everybody's goodwill by the enjoyable gift of peace. Then he gradually pushed ahead and absorbed the functions of the senate, the officials, and even the law. Opposition did not exist. War or judicial murder had disposed of all men of spirit. Upper-class survivors found that slavish obedience was the way to succeed, both politically and financially. They had profited from the revolution [the replacement of the republic by an imperial form of government], and so now they liked the security of the existing arrangement better than the dangerous uncertainties of the old regime. Besides, the new order was popular in the provinces. There, government by Senate and People was looked upon skeptically as a matter of sparring dignitaries and extortionate officials. The legal system had provided no remedy against these, since it was wholly incapacitated by violence, favouritism, and—most of all—bribery. . . .

Nobody had any immediate worries as long as Augustus retained his physical powers, and kept himself going, and his House, and the peace of the empire. But when old age incapacitated him, his approaching end brought hopes of change. A few people started idly talking of the blessings of freedom [i.e., discussing a return to the republic]. Some, more numerous, feared civil war; others wanted it. The great majority, however, exchanged critical gossip about candidates for the succession. . . .

Then two pieces of news became known simultaneously: Augustus was dead, and Tiberius was in control.

The new reign's first crime was the assassination of Agrippa Postumus [grandson of Augustus]. He was killed by a staff-officer—who found it a hard task, though he was a persevering murderer and the victim [was] taken by surprise unarmed. Tiberius said nothing about the matter in the senate. He pretended that the orders came from Augustus, who was alleged to have instructed the colonel in charge to kill Agrippa Postumus as soon as Augustus himself was dead. It is true that Augustus' scathing criticisms of the young man's behavior were undoubtedly what had prompted the senate to decree his banishment. But the emperor had never been callous enough to kill any of his relations, and that he should murder his own grandchild to remove the worries of a stepson seemed incredible. It would be nearer the truth to suppose that Tiberius because he was afraid, and Livia [Augustus's widow and mother of Tiberius by another man, but not the grandmother of Agrippa] through stepmotherly malevolence, loathed and distrusted the young Agrippa Postumus and got rid of him at the first opportunity. . . .

Meanwhile at Rome consuls, senate, knights, precipitately became servile. The more distinguished men were, the greater their urgency and insincerity. They must show neither satisfaction at the death of one emperor, nor gloom at the accession of another: so their features were carefully arranged in a blend of tears and smiles, mourning and flattery.

SOURCE: Tacitus. *The Annals of Imperial Rome.* Rev. ed. Trans. by Michael Grant. Harmondsworth: Penguin, 1977, pp. 31–35.

How might a spokesperson from the Roman imperial court have responded to these views of Tacitus?

Within the boundaries of the Roman empire itself, a long era of peace facilitated economic and political integration from the first to the middle of the third century C.E. Augustus brought peace not only to Rome, by ending the civil disturbances that had plagued the city for more than a century, but also to the empire. His reign inaugurated the era known as the *pax romana* ("Roman peace") that persisted for two and a half centuries. In spite of occasional flareups, especially among conquered peoples who resented Roman rule, the *pax romana* facilitated trade and communication throughout the region from Mesopotamia to the Atlantic Ocean.

The Pax Romana

Like their Persian, Chinese, Indian, and Hellenistic counterparts, the Romans integrated their empire by building networks of transportation and communication. Since ancient times, Roman engineers have enjoyed a reputation as outstanding road builders. Roman engineers prepared a deep bed for their roads, edged them with curbs, provided for drainage, and then topped them off with large, flat paving stones. Their main roads were 6 to 8 meters wide (20 to 26 feet)—large enough to accommodate two-way traffic—while even roads winding through mountains were 2 to 3 meters wide (6 to 10 feet). Builders placed milestones along the roads, and the imperial postal system maintained stations for couriers. The roads and postal system permitted urgent travel and messages to proceed with remarkable speed: Tiberius, successor of Augustus as Roman emperor, once traveled 290 kilometers (180 miles) in a single day over Roman roads.

Roman Roads

Roads linked all parts of the Roman empire. One notable highway of more than 2,500 kilometers (1,554 miles) stretched along the northeast imperial frontier from the Black Sea to the North Sea, parallel to the Danube and Rhine Rivers. Another road linked Rome to the city of Gades (modern Cadiz) in southern Spain. A road of 4,800 kilometers (2,983 miles) ran parallel to the coast of north Africa, and numerous spurs reached south, enabling merchants and soldiers to range deep into the Sahara desert. Romans also built new roads that facilitated travel and trade in the eastern Mediterranean region. One route linked the port of Berenice on the Red Sea to Alexandria, while others linked the towns and ports of the eastern Mediterranean seaboard to Palmyra, a principal way station of caravan traffic coming west from central Asia.

Under conditions of political stability and the *pax romana*, jurists constructed an elaborate system of law. Romans began a tradition of written law about 450 B.C.E., when they promulgated the Twelve Tables as a basic law code for citizens of the early republic. As armies spread Roman influence throughout the Mediterranean, jurists worked to construct a rational body of law that would apply to all peoples under Roman rule. During the late republic and especially during the empire, the jurists articulated standards of justice and gradually applied them throughout Roman territory. They established the principle that defendants were innocent until proven guilty, and they ensured that defendants had a right to challenge their accusers before a judge in a court of law. They also permitted judges to set aside laws that were inequitable or unfair. Like transportation and communication networks, Roman law helped to integrate the diverse lands that made up the empire, and the principles of Roman law continued to shape Mediterranean and European society long after the empire had disappeared.

Roman Law

ECONOMY AND SOCIETY IN THE ROMAN MEDITERRANEAN

The rapid expansion of Roman influence and the imposition of Roman imperial rule brought economic and social changes to peoples throughout the Mediterranean basin.

A wall painting from Stabiae (a small community near Pompeii destroyed by the eruption of Vesuvius in 79 C.E.) depicts an Italian harbor with ships, wharves, warehouses, markets, and decorative columns topped by statues.

Good roads and the *pax romana* encouraged trade between regions. Existing cities benefited handsomely from the wealth generated by trade, and in the lands they conquered, the Romans founded new cities to serve as links between local regions and the larger Mediterranean economy. Meanwhile, like most other peoples of classical times, the Romans built a strictly patriarchal society and made extensive use of slave labor.

Trade and Urbanization

Commercial Agriculture

Like other classical societies, the Roman Mediterranean experienced economic development and social change as the state expanded and brought new regions into its network of trade and communication. Agricultural production, the economic foundation of the Roman empire, also underwent transformation with the expansion of empire and the growth of trade. Instead of planting crops for immediate local use, owners of *latifundia* concentrated on production for export. Grain from *latifundia* in north Africa, Egypt, and Sicily routinely found its way to the large cities of the empire. The ship that Paul of Tarsus boarded at Caesarea, for example, carried several hundred tons of wheat destined for consumers in Rome.

Commercial agriculture played an important role in the economic specialization and integration of the empire. Because it was possible to import grain at favorable prices from lands that routinely produced large surpluses, other regions could concentrate on the cultivation of fruits and vegetables or on the production of manufactured items. Greece, for example, concentrated on olives and vines. Syria and Palestine produced fruits, nuts, and wool fabrics. Gaul produced grain, supplied copper, and began to experiment with the cultivation of vines. Spain produced high-quality olive oil as well as wine, horses, and most of the precious metal used in the Roman empire. Italy became a center for the production of pottery, glassware, and bronze goods. Archaeologists have uncovered one pottery factory north of Rome that might have employed hundreds of workers and that had a mixing vat capable of holding more than 40,000 liters (10,568 gallons) of clay.

Mediterranean Trade

Specialized production of agricultural commodities and manufactured goods set the stage for vigorous trade. Sea lanes linked ports from Syria and Palestine to Spain and north Africa. Roman military and naval power kept the seas largely free of pirates so that sizable cargoes could move safely over long distances, barring foul weather. Indeed, the Mediterranean became essentially a Roman lake, which the Romans called *mare nostrum* ("our sea"). As Roman military forces, administrators, tax collectors, and other officials traveled throughout the empire carrying out their duties, they joined the merchants in linking the Mediterranean's regions into a well-integrated network of communication and exchange.

The City of Rome

Cities benefited handsomely from Mediterranean integration and played a prominent role in promoting economic and social change. Along with taxes, tributes, booty, and other wealth generated by military expansion, much of the profit from Mediterranean trade flowed to Rome, where it fueled remarkable urban development. In the

Many Roman aqueducts survive to the present day. This one carried water to the city of Nemausus in Gaul (modern Nîmes in France). The water flowed through a trough supported by the top layer of arches.

first century C.E., some ten thousand statues decorated the city, along with seven hundred pools, five hundred fountains, and thirty-six monumental marble arches celebrating military victories and other achievements. The Roman state financed the construction of temples, bath houses, public buildings, stadiums, and perhaps most important of all, aqueducts that brought fresh water into the city from the neighboring mountains. Construction projects benefited from the use of concrete, invented by Roman engineers during the republican era, which strengthened structures and allowed builders to meet high standards of precision required for plumbing and water control.

Construction provided employment for hundreds of thousands of workers. As a result, the population of Rome surged, and the city's economy experienced rapid growth. Shopkeepers, artisans, merchants, and bankers proliferated in the imperial capital. Economic development attracted large numbers of migrants from the countryside and from foreign lands. Most received low wages as laborers, construction workers, or servants, but those with skills sometimes found good employment as craftsmen. Some who went to Rome with a bit of money established successful businesses, and by hard work or good fortune, a few entrepreneurs became wealthy and respected businessmen.

Urban growth and development also took place beyond the capital. Some parts of the empire, such as Greece and Syria, had long-standing urban traditions. There trade and economic development brought additional prosperity. Elsewhere the Romans founded cities at strategic sites for purposes of government and administration, especially in Spain, Gaul, and Britain, which encouraged economic and social development at the far reaches of the empire.

Roman Cities and Their Attractions

As wealth concentrated in the cities, urban residents came to expect a variety of comforts not available in rural areas. Merchants traveling the roads and sea lanes brought delicacies and luxury items from all parts of the Roman empire: Spanish hams, oysters from British waters, fine wool cloaks from Gaul, and Syrian nuts, dates, and figs all made their way to consumers in Rome and other prosperous cities. Roman cities enjoyed abundant supplies of fresh water, sometimes brought from distant mountains by aqueducts, and elaborate sewage and plumbing systems. All sizable cities and even many smaller towns had public baths featuring hot and cold rooms, and often swimming pools and gymnasia as well. Underground sewers carried away waste waters.

Enormous circuses, stadiums, and amphitheaters provided sites for the entertainment of the urban masses. Circuses were oval structures with tracks for chariot races, which were wildly popular in the Roman empire. The Circus Maximus at Rome accommodated about 250,000 spectators. Entertainment in stadiums often took forms now considered coarse and cruel—battles to the death between gladiators or between humans and wild animals—but urban populations flocked to such events, which they looked upon as exciting diversions from daily routine. The Roman Colosseum, a magnificent marble stadium and sports arena opened in 80 C.E., provided seating for about 50,000 spectators. The structure had a multicolored awning that protected viewers from sun and rain, and its construction was so precise that it was possible to flood the arena with water and stage mock naval battles within its walls.

Family and Society in Roman Times

The Pater Familias

Roman law vested immense authority in male heads of families. The Roman family consisted of an entire household, including slaves, free servants, and close relatives who lived together. Usually the eldest male ruled the household as *pater familias*— "father of the family." Roman law gave the *pater familias* the authority to arrange marriages for his children, determine the work or duties they would perform, and punish them for offenses as he saw fit. He had rights also to sell them into slavery and even to execute them.

From the days of the republic, residents of Rome consumed subsidized grain imported from distant territories. In this painting from a tomb, workers load grain onto a boat at the port of Ostia, at the mouth of the Tiber River, for transport upriver to the city of Rome.

Although legally endowed with extraordinary powers, the Roman *pater familias* rarely ruled tyranically over his charges. In fact, women usually supervised domestic affairs in Roman households, and by the time they reached middle age, women generally wielded considerable influence within their families. They helped select marriage partners for their offspring, and they sometimes played large roles in managing their families' financial affairs. Although Roman law placed strict limits on the ability of women to receive inheritances, enforcement was inconsistent, and clever individuals found ways to evade the law or take advantage of its loopholes. During the third and second centuries B.C.E., as Roman expansion in the Mediterranean brought wealth to the capital, women came to possess a great deal of property. By the first century B.C.E., in spite of the authority legally vested in the *pater familias,* many women supervised the financial affairs of family businesses and wealthy estates.

Wealth and Social Change

Increasing wealth had important consequences for Roman society. New classes of merchants, landowners, and construction contractors accumulated enormous private wealth and rivaled the old nobility for prominence. The newly rich classes built palatial houses with formal gardens and threw lavish banquets with rare and exotic foods such as boiled ostrich, parrot-tongue pie, and tree fungus served in a sauce of fish fat, jellyfish, and eggs. While wealthy classes probed culinary frontiers, cultivators and urban masses subsisted largely on porridge and vegetables occasionally supplemented by eggs, fish, sausage, or meat.

By the first century B.C.E., poverty had become a considerable problem in Rome and other large cities of the empire. Often unemployed, the urban masses sometimes rioted to express their dissatisfaction and seek improved conditions, and they readily provided recruits for private armies of ambitious generals like Marius and Sulla. Imperial authorities never developed a true urban policy but, rather, sought to keep the masses contented with "bread and circuses"—subsidized grain and spectacular public entertainments.

Slavery

Roman society made extensive use of slave labor: by the second century C.E., slaves may have represented as much as one-third of the population of the Roman empire. In the countryside they worked mostly on *latifundia,* though many labored in state quarries and mines. Rural slaves worked under extremely harsh conditions, often chained together in teams. Discontent among rural slaves led to several massive

Contexts & Connections

Resistance to Slavery

Writing about 100 C.E., the Greek biographer Plutarch told the story of a Roman senator, Pupius Piso, who instructed his slaves not to speak unless he addressed them first. One evening Piso put on a lavish dinner party to honor a distinguished guest named Clodius. At the ap-

pointed hour, all the guests arrived except for Clodius. Piso sent a slave to find the guest of honor, but still Clodius did not appear. Puzzled, Piso asked the slave if he had delivered an invitation to Clodius. When the slave responded that he had, Piso asked why Clodius had not

A relief carving on a Roman monument depicts some slaves serving guests at a banquet (above), while others work in the kitchen (below).

revolts, especially during the second and first centuries B.C.E. During the most serious uprising, in 73 B.C.E., the escaped slave Spartacus assembled an army of seventy thousand rebellious slaves. The Roman army dispatched eight legions, comprising more than forty thousand well-equipped, veteran troops, to quell the revolt.

In the cities, conditions were much less difficult than in the countryside. Female slaves commonly worked as domestic servants while males toiled as servants, laborers, craftsmen, shopkeepers, or business agents for their owners. Slaves who had an education or possessed some particular talent had the potential to lead comfortable lives. The first-century Anatolian slave Epictetus even became a prominent Stoic philosopher. He joined the dinner party. The slave replied that Clodius had declined the invitation. In exasperation, Piso demanded to know why the slave had not informed him earlier. The slave's response: because Piso had not asked him.

Throughout history, many societies have recognized some form of institutional slavery. The conditions of slavery varied wildly from one society to another and even within individual societies. In the Roman-dominated Mediterranean basin, for example, some slaves had relatively light chores as household servants, while others provided heavy labor on *latifundia,* and some worked in mines under brutal, dangerous, and hellish conditions. In the Roman empire as in other societies that made extensive use of slave labor, most slaves worked hard and benefited little from the fruits of their labors.

It is not surprising, then, that resistance to slavery has been a prominent feature of most if not all societies that have permitted slavery. Resistance has taken several forms. In many cases it involved sabotage of slave owners' interests. Piso's slave, for example, withheld important information and thus embarrassed his master. Other slaves broke tools, injured farm animals, destroyed crops, or simply worked very slowly in efforts to retaliate against masters who appropriated their energy. Another form of resistance involved escape from slavery and flight to freedom. During the era of the Atlantic slave trade, from the early sixteenth to the early nineteenth centuries, African-American slaves frequently escaped and fled to mountains, swamps, or forests where their masters could not easily recapture them. In Roman society, escape was often easier because most slaves resembled the larger population in physical appearance.

By far the most serious and feared form of resistance to slavery was rebellion. Because slaves were fighting for their lives as well as their freedom, slave revolts often became exceptionally brutal conflicts. Over the centuries, thousands of slaves followed in the footsteps of the Roman slave rebel Spartacus by attacking their masters in a bid for freedom. To mention only a few of the more notable uprisings: the Zanj revolt in Mesopotamia (869–883), in which African slaves defied their Muslim masters for fourteen years; the Haitian revolution (1791–1804), in which slave rebellion contributed to the establishment of an independent Haiti; the Stono rebellion in South Carolina (1739) and Nat Turner's insurrection in Virginia (1831), both of which terrified slave owners in the American south. These and other desperate rebellions testify eloquently to the bitterness that has flowed from the institution of slavery.

spent much of his life studying with Rome's leading intellectuals, and he lectured to large audiences that included high Roman officials and perhaps even emperors.

More than their counterparts in rural areas, urban slaves could hope for manumission as a reward for a long term of loyal service: it was common, though not mandatory, for masters to free urban slaves about the time they reached thirty years of age. Until freed, however, slaves remained under the strict authority of their masters, who had the right to sell them, arrange their family affairs, punish them, and even execute them for serious offenses.

THE COSMOPOLITAN MEDITERRANEAN

The integration of the Mediterranean basin had important effects not only for the trade and economy of the Roman empire but also for its cultural and religious traditions. As travelers ventured throughout the Mediterranean basin, they became acquainted with

Roman Deities

Built between 118 and 125 C.E., the Pantheon in Rome was a temple honoring all gods, and it survives as one of the outstanding examples of Roman architecture. With a diameter of 43 meters (141 feet), the building's dome was the largest constructed until the twentieth century.

other cultural and religious traditions. When migrants moved to Rome and other large cities, they often continued to observe their inherited traditions and thus contributed to the cosmopolitan cultural atmosphere of the empire. Roads and communication networks favored the spread of new popular religions. Most important of these over the long run was Christianity, which originated as a small and persecuted Jewish sect. Within three centuries, however, Christianity had become the official religion of the Roman empire and the predominant faith of the Mediterranean basin.

Greek Philosophy and Religions of Salvation

During the early days of their history, the Romans recognized many gods and goddesses, who they believed intervened directly in human affairs. Jupiter was the principal god, lord of the heavens, while Mars was the god of war, Ceres the goddess of grain, Janus the god who watched the threshold of individual houses, and Vesta the goddess of the hearth. In addition to these major deities, most Roman households also honored tutelary deities, gods who looked after the welfare of individual families.

As the Romans expanded their political influence and built an empire, they encountered the religious and cultural traditions of other peoples. Often they adopted the deities of other peoples and used them for their own purposes. From the Etruscans, for example, they learned of Juno, the moon goddess, and Minerva, the goddess of wisdom, as well as certain religious practices, such as divination of the future through examination of the internal organs of ritually sacrificed animals.

Greek Influence   The Romans also drew inspiration from the Greek tradition of rational thought and philosophy. When the Romans established political hegemony in the eastern Mediterranean in the third and second centuries B.C.E., the most prominent school of thought in Hellenistic Greece was Stoicism. Recognizing that they lived in a large and interdependent world, the Stoics sought to identify a set of universal moral standards based on nature and reason that would transcend local ethical codes.

Cicero and Stoicism   This approach to moral thought appealed strongly to Roman intellectuals, and thinkers such as Marcus Tullius Cicero (106–43 B.C.E.) readily adopted Stoic values. Cicero studied in Greece and became thoroughly acquainted with both classical and Hellenistic schools of thought. He was a persuasive orator, and he wrote clear, elegant, polished Latin prose. In adapting Hellenistic thought to Roman needs, Cicero drew heavily from the Stoics' moral and ethical teachings. His letters and treatises emphasized the individual's duty to live in accordance with nature and reason. He argued that the pursuit of justice was the individual's highest public duty, and he scorned those who sought to accumulate wealth or to become powerful through immoral, illegal, or unjust means. Through his speeches and especially his writings, Cicero helped to establish Stoicism as the most prominent school of moral philosophy in Rome.

Religions of Salvation

While educated thinkers drew inspiration from the Greeks, the masses found comfort in religions of salvation that established their presence throughout the Mediterranean basin and beyond. Like Stoicism, these religions clearly reflected the political and social conditions of the Hellenistic period: in an imperial era, when close-knit city-states no longer served as a focus for individual loyalties, religions of salvation appealed to the popular masses by providing a sense of purpose and the promise of a glorious future existence.

These religions became prominent features of Mediterranean society during Hellenistic times and became increasingly noticeable in Rome during the late republic as migrants settled in the capital and brought their faiths with them. Under the Roman empire, religions of salvation flourished both in Rome and throughout the Mediterranean basin. Merchants, soldiers, and administrators carried their cults as they conducted their business, and missionaries traveled alongside them in search of converts. The roads of the empire and the sea lanes of the Mediterranean thus served not only as trade routes and lines of official communication but also as highways for religions of salvation, which traveled to all the ports and large cities of the empire.

Mithraism

Among the most popular of these religions of salvation was the cult dedicated to Mithras. In Zoroastrian mythology, Mithras was a god closely identified with the sun and light. Roman soldiers serving in the Hellenistic world, particularly Anatolia, encountered the cult of Mithras and adapted it to their interests. They associated Mithras less with the sun than with military virtues such as strength, courage, and discipline, and the cult of Mithras quickly became exceptionally popular among the Roman armed forces.

This mithraeum—a shrine to the god Mithras—survives beneath the church of San Clemente in Rome. Benches accommodated worshipers. The sculpture on the altar depicts Mithras sacrificing a bull to the god Apollo.

The Mithraic religion provided divine sanction for human life and especially for purposeful moral behavior. It brought together a community that welcomed and nurtured like-minded individuals. Finally, it offered hope for individuals who conscientiously observed the cult's teachings by promising them ecstatic and mysterious union with Mithras himself. During the late republic, Mithraic altars and temples appeared in military garrisons throughout the empire. During the early centuries C.E., administrators and merchants also became enchanted with Mithras, and his cult attracted followers among the male populations of all sizable communities and commercial centers in the Roman empire.

Cult of Isis

The cult of Mithras did not admit women, but cults dedicated to the Anatolian mother goddess Cybele, the Egyptian goddess Isis, and other deities made a place for both men and women. Indeed, the cult of Isis may have been the most popular of all the Mediterranean religions of salvation before the rise of Christianity. Devotees built temples to Isis throughout the Roman empire, and they adored the Egyptian goddess as a benevolent and protective deity who nurtured her worshipers and helped them cope with the stresses of life in cosmopolitan society. Like the Mithraic religion, the cult of Isis and other religions of salvation attracted followers in Rome and other cities throughout the Mediterranean basin. The immense popularity of these religions of salvation provides a context that helps to explain the remarkable success of Christianity in the Roman empire.

Judaism and Early Christianity

The Jews and the Empire

After the dissolution of the Jewish kingdom of David and Solomon in the early tenth century B.C.E., the Jewish people maintained their faith and their communities under various imperial regimes: Babylonian, Achaemenid, Alexandrian, Seleucid, and Roman. All these empires embraced many different ethnic and religious groups and mostly tolerated the cultural preferences of their subjects, providing that communities paid their taxes and refrained from rebellious activities. In an effort to encourage political loyalty, these empires often created state cults that honored their emperors as gods, and they sometimes called for subjects to participate in the cults and revere the emperor-gods. This requirement created a serious problem for the strictly monotheistic Jews, who recognized only their own god, Yahweh, as divine. Jews considered the pretensions of the state cults to be blasphemy, and many of them refused to pay homage to a mortal being who laid claim to divinity. Sometimes they even declined to pay taxes to regimes that required subjects to revere their emperors. Relations between Jews and imperial authorities became especially tense as the Romans extended their empire in the eastern Mediterranean region. Between the third century B.C.E. and the first century C.E., Jews in Palestine mounted several rebellions against their Seleucid and Roman overlords. Ultimately the resistance failed, and Roman forces decisively defeated the rebels during the Jewish War of 66 to 70 C.E.

The Essenes

While some Jews actively fought the Romans, others founded new sects that looked for saviors to deliver them from subjection. The Essenes formed one such sect. In 1947 shepherds accidentally discovered some Essene writings known as the Dead Sea scrolls, which have shed fascinating light on the sect and its beliefs. The Essenes formed their community in Palestine during the first century B.C.E. They observed a strict moral code and participated in rituals designed to reinforce a sense of community: they admitted new members after a rite of baptism in water, and they took part in ritual community meals. They also looked for a savior who would deliver them from Roman rule and lead them in the establishment of a community in which they could practice their faith without interference.

Sources from the Past

Jesus' Moral and Ethical Teachings

Several accounts of Jesus' life record the Sermon on the Mount in which Jesus challenged his followers to honor God and observe a demanding code of ethics. Here Jesus explicitly instructed his listeners to reject moral and legal principles that southwest Asian peoples had followed since the third millennium B.C.E. and that the Babylonian emperor Hammurabi had enshrined in his famous code of laws about 1750 B.C.E. Jesus enjoined them to refrain from revenge against those who had caused them harm, for example, and instead to repay harm with kindness.

Blessed are the poor in spirit: for theirs is the kingdom of heaven. Blessed are they that mourn: for they shall be comforted. Blessed are the meek: for they shall inherit the earth. Blessed are they which do hunger and thirst after righteousness: for they shall be filled. Blessed are the merciful: for they shall obtain mercy. Blessed are the pure in heart: for they shall see God. Blessed are the peacemakers: for they shall be called the children of God. Blessed are they which are persecuted for righteousness's sake: for theirs is the kingdom of heaven. Blessed are ye when men shall revile you and persecute you and shall say all manner of evil against you falsely for my sake. Rejoice, and be exceeding glad: for great is your reward in heaven. . . .

Ye have heard that it hath been said, "An eye for an eye, and a tooth for a tooth." But I say unto you that ye resist not evil: but whosoever shall smite thee on thy right cheek, turn to him the other also. And if any man will sue thee at the law, and take away thy coat, let him have thy cloak also. And whosoever shall compel thee to go a mile, go with him two. Give to him that asketh thee, and from him that would borrow of thee turn not thou away.

Ye have heard that it hath been said, "Thou shalt love thy neighbour, and hate thine enemy." But I say unto you, love your enemies, bless them that curse you, do good to them that hate you, and pray for them which despitefully use you and persecute you, that ye may be the children of your Father which is in heaven: for he maketh his sun to rise on the evil and on the good, and sendeth rain on the just and on the unjust. . . .

Ask, and it shall be given you; seek, and ye shall find; knock, and it shall be opened unto you. For every one that asketh receiveth; and he that seeketh findeth; and to him that knocketh it shall be opened. What man is there of you, whom if his son ask bread, will he give him a stone? Or if he ask a fish, will he give him a serpent? If ye then, being evil, know how to give good gifts unto your children, how much more shall your Father which is in heaven give good things to them that ask him? Therefore all things whatsoever ye would that men should do to you, do ye even so to them.

SOURCE: Matthew 5:3–13, 5:38–45, 7:7–12 (Authorized Version). (Translation slightly modified.)

Compare and contrast Jesus' moral teachings with the Zoroastrian, Confucian, Daoist, Buddhist, Hindu, and Socratic views discussed in earlier chapters.

Jesus of Nazareth

The early Christians probably had little contact with the Essenes, but they shared many of the same concerns. The Christians formed their community around Jesus of Nazareth, a charismatic Jewish teacher whom they recognized as their savior. Born about the year 4 B.C.E., Jesus grew up at a time of high tension between Roman overlords and their Jewish subjects. He was a peaceful man who taught devotion to God and love for fellow human beings. He attracted large crowds because of a reputation for wisdom and miraculous powers, especially the ability to heal the sick.

Yet Jesus alarmed the Romans because he also taught that "the kingdom of God is at hand." To Jesus, the kingdom of God was a spiritual realm in which God would gather those faithful to him. To Roman administrators, however, his message carried political overtones: an impending kingdom of God sounded like a threat to Roman rule in Palestine, especially since enthusiastic crowds routinely accompanied Jesus. In an effort to forestall a new round of rebellion, Roman administrators executed Jesus by fixing him to a cross in the early 30s C.E.

Jesus' Early Followers   Jesus' crucifixion did not put an end to his movement. Even after his execution Jesus' close followers strongly felt his presence and proclaimed that he had triumphed over death by rising from his grave. They called him "Christ," meaning "the anointed one," the savior who would bring individuals into the kingdom of God. They taught that he was the son of God and that his sacrifice served to offset the sins of those who had faith in him. They taught further that like Jesus, the faithful would survive death and would experience eternal life in the spiritual kingdom of God. Following Jesus' teachings, the early Christians observed a demanding moral code and devoted themselves uncompromisingly to God. They also compiled a body of writings—accounts of Jesus' life, reports of his followers' works, and letters outlining Christian teachings—that gained recognition as the New Testament. Together with the Jews' Hebrew scriptures, which Christians referred to as the Old Testament, the New Testament became the holy book of Christianity.

Paul of Tarsus   Jesus and his earliest followers were all Jews. Beginning about the middle of the first century C.E., however, some Christians avidly sought converts from non-Jewish communities in the Hellenistic world and the Roman empire. The principal figure in the expansion of Christianity beyond Judaism was Paul of Tarsus, a Jew from Anatolia who zealously preached his faith, especially in the Greek-speaking eastern region of the Roman empire. Paul taught a Christianity that attracted the urban masses in the same way as other religions of salvation that spread widely in the Roman empire. His doctrine called for individuals to observe high moral standards and to place their faith ahead of personal and family interests. His teaching also explained the world and human history as the results of God's purposeful activity so that it provided a framework of meaning for individuals' lives. Furthermore, Paul's doctrine promised a glorious future existence for those who conscientiously observed the faith.

Like missionaries of other faiths, Paul was no stranger to Roman roads and Mediterranean sea lanes. He traveled widely in search of converts and made several journeys through Greece, Anatolia, Syria, and Palestine to visit fledgling Christian communities and offer them guidance. His last journey took him by ship from Palestine to Rome, where he took the opportunity to promote Christianity and seek converts for about two years before losing his appeal to the emperor and suffering execution.

Early Christian Communities   For two centuries after the crucifixion of Jesus, there was no central authority for the fledgling church. Rather, individual communities selected their own supervisors, known as *bishops,* who oversaw priests and governed their jurisdictions according to their own best understanding of Christian doctrine. As a result, until the emergence of Rome as the principal seat of church authority in the third century C.E., Christians held doctrinal views and followed practices that varied considerably from one community to the next. Some religious leaders taught that Jesus had literally risen from the dead and come back to life, while others held that his resurrection was a spiritual rather than physical matter. Some communities forbade women from playing active public roles in the church, while others allowed women to serve as priests. Some congregations permitted individuals to seek their own understanding of spiritual matters, while others insisted that access to spiritual truth was available only through properly ordained priests and bishops. Early Christianity was indeed a remarkably diverse faith. Only gradually did believers agree to recognize certain texts as authoritative scripture—the New Testament—and adopt them as fundamental guides for Christian doctrine and practice.

The Growth of Early Christianity

Like the Jews from whose ranks they had sprung, the early Christians refused to honor the Roman state cults or revere the emperor as a god. As a result, Roman imperial authorities launched sporadic campaigns of persecution designed to eliminate Christianity as a threat to the empire. In spite of this repression, Christian numbers grew rapidly. During the first three centuries of the faith's existence, Christianity found its way to almost all parts of the Roman empire, and Christians established thriving communities throughout the Mediterranean basin and farther east in Mesopotamia and Iran. Rome itself had a sizable Christian population by 300 C.E.

The remarkable growth of Christianity reflected the new faith's appeal particularly to the lower classes, urban populations, and women. Christianity accorded honor and dignity to individuals who did not enjoy high standing in Roman society, and it endowed them with a sense of spiritual freedom more meaningful than wealth, power, or social prominence. Unlike the popular cult of Mithras, which admitted only men, Christianity taught the spiritual equality of the sexes and welcomed the contributions of both men and women. Like Mithraism and other religions of salvation, Christianity provided a sense of purpose and a promise of future glory for those who placed their faith in Jesus. Thus, although Christianity originated as a minor sect of Judaism, urban populations in the Roman empire embraced the new faith with such enthusiasm that by the third century C.E. it had become the most dynamic and influential religious faith in the Mediterranean basin.

Under Roman influence Mediterranean lands became a tightly integrated society. The Roman empire provided a political structure that administered lands as distant as Mesopotamia and Britain. Highly organized trade networks enabled peoples throughout the empire to concentrate on specialized agricultural or industrial production and to import foods and other goods that they did not produce themselves. Popular religions spread widely and attracted enthusiastic converts. Like Confucianism and Buddhism in classical China and India, rational philosophy and Christianity became prominent sources of intellectual and religious authority in the classical Mediterranean and continued to influence cultural development in the Mediterranean, Europe, and southwest Asia over the long term.

CHRONOLOGY

753 B.C.E.	Founding of Rome, according to tradition
509 B.C.E.	Establishment of the Roman republic
264–146 B.C.E.	Roman expansion in the Mediterranean basin
106–43 B.C.E.	Life of Marcus Tullius Cicero
first century B.C.E.	Civil war in Rome
46–44 B.C.E.	Rule of Gaius Julius Caesar as dictator
31 B.C.E.–14 C.E.	Rule of Augustus
4 B.C.E.–early 30s C.E.	Life of Jesus of Nazareth
first century C.E.	Life of Paul of Tarsus
66–70 C.E.	Jewish War

FOR FURTHER READING

Henry C. Boren. *Roman Society.* 2nd ed. Lexington, 1992. An authoritative synthesis that places social and economic history in its political context.

Keith R. Bradley. *Discovering the Roman Family: Studies in Roman Social History.* New York, 1991. A provocative analysis of Roman family life with illustrations from individual experiences.

———. *Slavery and Society at Rome.* Cambridge, 1994. An engaging and readable essay on slavery and its role in Roman society, with special attention to individual experiences.

Peter Brown. *The Rise of Western Christendom: Triumph and Diversity, A.D. 200–1000.* 2nd ed. Oxford, 2003. A landmark analysis of early Christian history that incorporates the findings of recent scholarship.

Barry Cunliffe. *Greeks, Romans, and Barbarians: Spheres of Interaction.* New York, 1988. Draws on archaeological evidence in assessing the effects of the Roman presence in Gaul, Britain, and Germany.

M. I. Finley. *Ancient Slavery and Modern Ideology.* Expanded ed. Princeton, 1998. A thoughtful analysis of Greek and Roman slavery in light of modern slavery and contemporary debates.

Michael Grant. *Cities of Vesuvius: Pompeii and Herculaneum.* London, 1971. Fascinating glimpse of Roman society as reconstructed by archaeologists working at sites destroyed by the eruption of Vesuvius in 79 C.E.

A. H. M. Jones. *Augustus.* New York, 1970. A distinguished historian of ancient Rome provides the best study of Augustus and his career.

Naphtali Lewis and Meyer Reinhold, eds. *Roman Civilization: Selected Readings.* 2 vols. 3rd ed. New York, 1990. A rich collection of translated texts and documents that illuminate Roman history and society.

Paul MacKendrick. *The Mute Stones Speak: The Story of Archaeology in Italy.* New York, 1960. An older but engaging work with still valuable information on Roman architecture and construction techniques.

Ramsay MacMullen. *Christianizing the Roman Empire.* New Haven, 1984. Scholarly study of the processes by which Christianity became established in the Roman empire.

Harold Mattingly. *The Man in the Roman Street.* New York, 1966. An engaging study of popular culture and religion in the Roman empire.

Elaine Pagels. *Adam, Eve, and the Serpent.* New York, 1988. Provocative and fascinating analysis of early Christianity and its relationship with the Roman state.

———. *The Gnostic Gospels.* New York, 1979. Fascinating reconstruction of some little-known early Christian communities.

Sarah B. Pomeroy. *Goddesses, Whores, Wives, and Slaves: Women in Classical Antiquity.* New York, 1975. Outstanding study analyzing the status and role of women in classical Greece and Rome.

Geza Vermes. *The Dead Sea Scrolls: Qumran in Perspective.* Revised ed. London, 1994. A reliable introduction to scholarship on the Dead Sea scrolls and the community that produced them.

———. *The Dead Sea Scrolls in English.* 4th ed. London, 1995. Translations of the major texts from the Dead Sea scrolls that throw light on the Essenes and their beliefs.

See our **Online Learning Center at www.mhhe.com/bentley3** for additional readings, practice maps, quizzes, and internet activities.

Unfamiliar words? Check out the **Primary Source Investigator CD-ROM** for an interactive glossary, interactive maps, more images, and primary sources.

Ruins of the ancient city of Khocho (Gaochang), near Turpan on the northern silk road.

CROSS-CULTURAL EXCHANGES ON THE SILK ROADS

In the year 139 B.C.E., the Chinese emperor Han Wudi sent an envoy named Zhang Qian on a mission to lands west of China. The emperor's purpose was to find allies who could help combat the nomadic Xiongnu, who menaced the northern and western borders of the Han empire. From captives he had learned that other nomadic peoples in far western lands bore grudges against the Xiongnu, and he reasoned that they might ally with Han forces to pressure their common enemy.

The problem for Zhang Qian was that to communicate with potential allies against the Xiongnu, he had to pass directly through lands they controlled. Soon after Zhang Qian left Han territory, Xiongnu forces captured him. For ten years the Xiongnu held him in comfortable captivity: they allowed him to keep his personal servant, and they provided him with a Xiongnu wife, with whom he had a son. When suspicions about him subsided, however, Zhang Qian escaped with his family and servant. He even had the presence of mind to keep with him the yak tail that Han Wudi had given him as a sign of his ambassadorial status. He fled to the west and traveled as far as Bactria, but he did not succeed in lining up allies against the Xiongnu. While returning to China, Zhang Qian again fell into Xiongnu hands but managed to escape after one year's detention when the death of the Xiongnu leader led to a period of turmoil. In 126 B.C.E. Zhang Qian and his party returned to China and a warm welcome from Han Wudi.

Although his diplomatic efforts did not succeed, Zhang Qian's mission had far-reaching consequences. Apart from political and military intelligence about western lands and their peoples, Zhang Qian also brought back information of immense commercial value. While in Bactria about 128 B.C.E., he noticed Chinese goods—textiles and bamboo articles—offered for sale in local markets. Upon inquiry he learned that they had come from southwest China by way of Bengal. From this information he deduced the possibility of establishing trade relations between China and Bactria through India.

Han Wudi responded enthusiastically to this idea and dreamed of trading with peoples inhabiting lands west of China. From 102 to 98 B.C.E., he mounted a massive campaign that broke the power of the Xiongnu and pacified central Asia. His conquests simplified trade relations, since it became unnecessary to route commerce through India. The intelligence that Zhang Qian gathered during his travels thus contributed to the opening of the silk roads—the network of trade routes that linked

287

lands as distant as China and the Roman empire—and more generally to the establishment of relations between China and lands to the west.

China and other classical societies imposed political and military control over vast territories. They promoted trade and communication within their own empires, bringing regions that had previously been self-sufficient into a larger economy and society. They also fostered the spread of cultural and religious traditions to distant regions, and they encouraged the construction of institutional frameworks that promoted the long-term survival of those traditions.

The influence of the classical societies did not stop at the imperial boundaries. Nearby peoples regarded their powerful neighbors with a mixture of envy and suspicion, and they sought to share the wealth that those neighbors generated. They pursued this goal by various means, both peaceful and violent, and relations with neighboring peoples, particularly nomadic peoples, became a major preoccupation of all the classical societies.

Beyond their relations with neighboring peoples, the classical societies established a broad zone of communication and exchange throughout much of the earth's eastern hemisphere. Trade networks crossed the deserts of central Asia and the depths of the Indian Ocean. Long-distance trade passed through much of Eurasia and north Africa, from China to the Mediterranean basin, and to parts of sub-Saharan Africa as well.

This long-distance trade profoundly influenced the experiences of peoples and the development of societies throughout the eastern hemisphere. It brought wealth and access to foreign products, and it enabled peoples to concentrate their efforts on economic activities best suited to their regions. It facilitated the spread of religious traditions beyond their original homelands, since merchants carried their beliefs and sometimes attracted converts in the lands they visited. It also facilitated the transmission of disease: pathogens traveled the trade routes alongside commercial wares and religious faiths. Indeed, the transmission of disease over the silk roads helped bring an end to the classical societies, since infectious and contagious diseases sparked devastating epidemics that caused political, social, and economic havoc. Long-distance trade thus had deep political, social, and cultural as well as economic and commercial implications for classical societies.

LONG-DISTANCE TRADE AND THE SILK ROADS NETWORK

Ever since the earliest days of history, human communities have traded with one another, sometimes over long distances. Before classical times, however, long-distance trade was a risky venture. Ancient societies often policed their own realms effectively, but since they were relatively small and compact, extensive regions lay beyond their control. Trade passing between societies was therefore liable to interception by bandits or pirates. This risk increased the costs of long-distance transactions in ancient times.

During the classical era, two developments reduced the risks associated with travel and stimulated long-distance trade. In the first place, rulers invested heavily in the construction of roads and bridges. They undertook these expensive projects primarily for military and administrative reasons, but roads also had the effect of encouraging trade within individual societies and facilitating exchanges between different societies. In the second place, classical societies built large imperial states that sometimes expanded to the point that they bordered on one another: the campaigns of Alexander of Macedon, for example, brought Hellenistic and Indian societies into direct contact, and only small buffer states separated the Roman and Parthian empires. Even when they did not encounter each other so directly, classical empires pacified large stretches of Eurasia and north Africa. As a result, merchants did not face such great risk as in previous eras, the costs of long-distance trade dropped, and its volume rose dramatically.

Trade Networks of the Hellenistic Era

The tempo of long-distance trade increased noticeably during the Hellenistic era, partly because of the many colonies established by Alexander of Macedon and the Seleucid rulers in Persia and Bactria. Though originally populated by military forces and administrators, these settlements soon attracted Greek merchants and bankers who linked the recently conquered lands to the Mediterranean basin. The Seleucid rulers worked diligently to promote trade. They controlled land routes linking Bactria, which offered access to Indian markets, to Mediterranean ports in Syria and Palestine. Archaeologists have unearthed hundreds of coins, pieces of jewelry, and other physical remains, including Greek-style sculptures and buildings, that testify to the presence of Greek communities in Persia and Bactria during the Hellenistic era.

Like the Seleucids, the Ptolemies maintained land routes—in their case, routes going south from Egypt to the kingdom of Nubia and Meroë in east Africa—but they also paid close attention to sea lanes and maritime trade. They ousted pirates from sea lanes linking the Red Sea to the Arabian Sea and the Indian Ocean. They also built several new ports, the most important being Berenice on the Red Sea, while Alexandria served as their principal window on the Mediterranean.

Even more important, perhaps, mariners from Ptolemaic Egypt learned about the monsoon winds that governed sailing and shipping in the Indian Ocean. During the summer the winds blow regularly from the southwest, whereas in the winter they come from the northeast. Knowledge of these winds enabled mariners to sail safely

The Monsoon System

Parthian merchants and other travelers like the soldiers depicted here followed in the footsteps of their Achaemenid and Seleucid predecessors and became regular visitors to northern India. This gray schist carving from Gandhara dates from the second century B.C.E.

and reliably to all parts of the Indian Ocean basin. During the second century B.C.E., Hellenistic mariners learned the rhythm of these winds from Arab and Indian seamen whose ancestors had sailed before the monsoons for centuries. Merchant seamen then established regular links by way of the Red Sea between India and Arabia in the east and Egypt and the Mediterranean basin in the west.

Establishment and maintenance of these trade routes was an expensive affair calling for substantial investment in military forces, construction, and bureaucracies to administer the commerce that passed over the routes. But the investment paid handsome dividends. Long-distance trade stimulated economic development within the Hellenistic realms themselves, bringing benefits to local economies throughout the empires. Moreover, Hellenistic rulers closely supervised foreign trade and levied taxes on it, thereby deriving income even from foreign products.

Trade in the Hellenistic World

With official encouragement, a substantial trade developed throughout the Hellenistic world, from Bactria and India in the east to the Mediterranean basin in the west. Spices, pepper, cosmetics, gems, and pearls from India traveled by caravan and ship to Hellenistic cities and ports. Grain from Persia and Egypt fed urban populations in distant lands. Mediterranean wine, olive oil, jewelry, and works of art made their way to Persia and Bactria. And throughout the region from India to the Mediterranean, merchants conducted a brisk trade in slaves recruited largely from the ranks of kidnapping victims or prisoners of war.

Indeed, maritime trade networks through the Indian Ocean linked not only the large classical societies of Eurasia and north Africa but also smaller societies in east Africa. During the late centuries B.C.E., the port of Rhapta emerged as the principal commercial center on the east African coast. Archaeologists have not discovered the precise location of Rhapta, but it probably was located near modern Dar es Salaam in Tanzania. With increasing trade, groups of professional merchants and entrepreneurs emerged at Rhapta, and coins came into general use on the east African coast. Merchants of Rhapta imported iron goods such as spears, axes, and knives from southern Arabia and the eastern Mediterranean region in exchange for ivory, rhinoceros horn, tortoise shell, and slaves obtained from interior regions. Just as trade in the Mediterranean basin encouraged economic and political development in regions like western Europe, far-flung commercial networks of the Hellenistic era fostered economic organization and the emergence of states in the distant lands that they brought into interaction.

The Silk Roads

The establishment of classical empires greatly expanded the scope of long-distance trade, as much of Eurasia and north Africa fell under the sway of one classical society or another. The Han empire maintained order in China and pacified much of central Asia, including a sizable corridor offering access to Bactria and western markets. The Parthian empire displaced the Seleucids in Persia and extended its authority to Mesopotamia. The Roman empire brought order to the Mediterranean basin. With the decline of the Mauryan dynasty, India lacked a strong imperial state, but the Kushan empire and other regional states provided stability and security, particularly in northern India, that favored long-distance trade.

Overland Trade Routes

As the classical empires expanded, merchants and travelers created an extensive network of trade routes that linked much of Eurasia and north Africa. Historians refer to these routes collectively as the silk roads, since high-quality silk from China was one of the principal commodities exchanged over the roads. The overland silk roads took caravan trade from China to the Roman empire, thus linking the extreme ends of the Eurasian landmass. From the Han capital of Chang'an, the main silk road went west

A cave painting from the late seventh century C.E. depicts the Chinese emperor Han Wudi (seated on horse) as he dispatches Zhang Qian (kneeling at left) on his mission to western lands in search of an alliance against the Xiongnu.

until it arrived at the Taklamakan desert, also known as the Tarim Basin. This desert is one of the most dangerous and inhospitable regions of the earth: its very name, Takla-makan, warns that "he who enters does not come back out." The silk road then split into two main branches that skirted the desert proper and passed through oasis towns that ringed it to the north and south. The branches came together at Kashgar (now known as Kashi, located in the westernmost corner of modern China). From there the reunited road went west to Bactria, where a branch forked off to offer access to Taxila and northern India, while the principal route continued across northern Iran. There it joined with roads to ports on the Caspian Sea and the Persian Gulf and proceeded to Palmyra (in modern Syria), where it met roads coming from Arabia and ports on the Red Sea. Continuing west, it terminated at the Mediterranean ports of Antioch (in modern Turkey) and Tyre (in modern Lebanon).

The silk roads also included a network of sea lanes that sustained maritime commerce throughout much of the eastern hemisphere. From Guangzhou in southern China, sea lanes through the South China Sea linked the east Asian seaboard to the mainland and the islands of southeast Asia. Routes linking southeast Asia with Ceylon (modern Sri Lanka) and India were especially busy during classical times. From India, sea lanes passed through the Arabian Sea to Persia and Arabia, and through the Persian

Sea Lanes and Maritime Trade

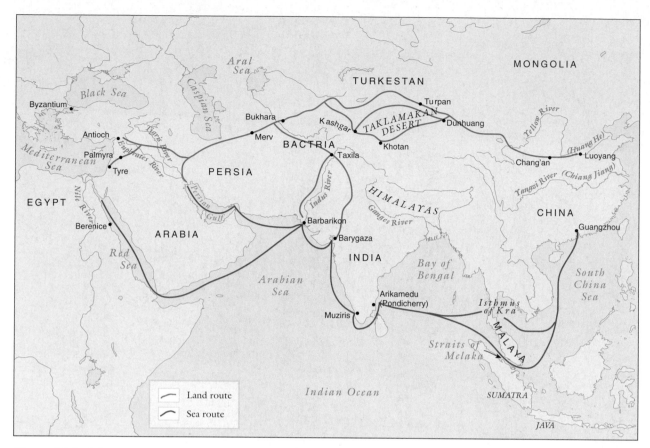

M A P [1 2 . 1]

The silk roads,
200 B.C.E.–300 C.E.

For an interactive version
of this map, go to
www.mhhe.com/
bentley3ch12maps.

Trade Goods

Gulf and the Red Sea they offered access to land routes and the Mediterranean basin, which already possessed a well-developed network of trade routes.

A wide variety of manufactured products and agricultural commodities traveled over the silk roads. Generally speaking, silk and spices traveled west from producers in southeast Asia, China, and India to consumers in central Asia, Iran, Arabia, and the Roman empire (including Egypt and north Africa as well as the European regions of the empire). Silk came mostly from China, the only land in classical times where cultivators and weavers had developed techniques for producing high-quality silk fabrics. The fine spices—cloves, nutmeg, mace, and cardamom—all came from southeast Asia. Ginger came from China, cinnamon from China and southeast Asia, pepper from India, and sesame oil from India, Arabia, and southwest Asia. Spices were extremely important commodities in classical times because they had many more uses than they do in the modern world. They served not only as condiments and flavoring agents but also as drugs, anesthetics, aphrodisiacs, perfumes, aromatics, and magical potions. Apart from spices, India also exported cotton textiles and valuable exotic items such as pearls, coral, and ivory.

Central Asian and Mediterranean lands exchanged a variety of manufactured goods and other commodities for the silks and spices that they imported. Central Asia produced large, strong horses and high-quality jade, much prized in China by stone carvers. From the Roman empire came glassware, jewelry, works of art, decorative items, perfumes, bronze goods, wool and linen textiles, pottery, iron tools, olive oil, wine, and gold and silver bullion. Mediterranean merchants and manufacturers often imported raw materials such as uncut gemstones, which they exported as finished products in the form of expensive jewelry and decorative items.

Some individuals made very long journeys during classical times: Zhang Qian ventured from China as far west as Bactria; Chinese merchants traveled regularly to central Asia and Persia; several Indian embassies called on Roman emperors; Roman merchants traveled by sea at least as far east as southern India; and Malay merchant mariners sailed from the islands of southeast Asia to India and east Africa. On a few occasions individuals even traveled across much or all of the eastern hemisphere between China and the Roman empire. A Chinese ambassador named Gang Ying embarked on a mission to distant western lands in 97 C.E. and proceeded as far as Mesopotamia before reports of the long and dangerous journey ahead persuaded him to return home. And Chinese sources reported the arrival in 166 C.E. of a delegation claiming to represent the Roman emperor Marcus Aurelius. No information survives to throw light on the experiences of this party—or even to confirm its identity—but Roman subjects from Egypt or Syria might well have traveled as far as China in search of trading opportunities.

During the first century B.C.E. Romans developed advanced glass-blowing techniques that enabled them to produce wares like this jar that were popular with wealthy consumers.

Individual merchants did not usually travel from one end of Eurasia to the other. Instead, they handled long-distance trade in stages. On the caravan routes between China and Bactria, for example, Chinese and central Asian nomadic peoples dominated trade. Rarely if ever did they go farther west, however, because the Parthians

A Roman coin dated 189 C.E. depicts a merchant ship near the lighthouse at Alexandria. Ships like this one regularly picked up pepper and cinnamon from India along with other cargoes.

The Organization of Long-Distance Trade

took advantage of their power and geographic position to control overland trade within their boundaries and to reserve it for their own subjects. Once it reached Palmyra, merchandise passed mostly into the hands of Roman subjects such as Greeks, Jews, and Armenians, who were especially active in the commercial life of the Mediterranean basin.

Meanwhile, on the seas, other peoples became involved in long-distance trade. From south China through southeast Asia to Ceylon and India, the principal figures were Malay and Indian mariners. In the Arabian Sea, Persians joined Egyptian and Greek subjects of the Roman empire as the most prominent trading peoples. The Parthian empire largely controlled trade in the Persian Gulf, whereas the Ptolemaic dynasty and later the Roman empire dominated affairs in the Red Sea. After Roman emperors absorbed Egypt in the first century C.E., their subjects carried on an especially brisk trade between India and the Mediterranean. The Greek geographer Strabo reported in the early first century C.E. that as many as 120 ships departed annually from the Red Sea for India. Archaeologists have unearthed the remains of a Roman trading outpost at Arikamedu, near modern Pondicherry in southern India, and literary sources report that merchants subject to Roman rule established Indian colonies also at Muziris (near modern Cranganore), Barygaza (near modern Broach), Barbarikon (near modern Karachi), and other sites as well. Meanwhile, since the mid-first century C.E., the Romans also had dominated both the eastern and western regions of *mare nostrum,* the Mediterranean.

It is impossible to determine the quantity or value of trade that passed over the silk roads in classical times, but it clearly made a deep impression on contemporaries. By the first century C.E., pepper cinnamon, and other spices graced the tables of the wealthy classes in the Roman empire, where silk garments had become items of high fashion. Indeed, silk was in such demand that Roman merchants often stretched their supplies by unraveling the densely woven fabrics that came from China and then reweaving them into larger numbers of sheer garments that were sometimes so light as to be transparent. Some Romans fretted that see-through silk attire would lead to moral decay, while others worried that hefty expenditures for luxury items would ruin the imperial economy. In both cases their anxieties testified to the powerful attraction of imported silks and spices for Roman consumers.

As it happened, long-distance trade did not cause moral or economic problems for the Roman empire or any other state in classical times. Indeed, it more likely stimulated rather than threatened local economies. Yet long-distance trade did not occur in a vacuum. Commercial exchanges encouraged cultural and biological exchanges, some of which had large implications for classical societies.

CULTURAL AND BIOLOGICAL EXCHANGES ALONG THE SILK ROADS

The silk roads served as magnificent highways for merchants and their commodities, but others also took advantage of the opportunities they offered to travel in relative safety over long distances. Merchants, missionaries, and other travelers carried their beliefs, values, and religious convictions to distant lands: Buddhism, Hinduism, and Christianity all traveled the silk roads and attracted converts far from their original homelands. Meanwhile, invisible travelers such as disease pathogens also crossed the silk roads and touched off devastating epidemics when they found fresh populations to infect. Toward the end of the classical era, epidemic disease that was spread over the silk roads caused dramatic demographic decline especially in China and the Mediterranean basin and to a lesser extent in other parts of Eurasia as well.

The Spread of Buddhism and Hinduism

By the third century B.C.E., Buddhism had become well established in northern India, and with the sponsorship of the emperor Ashoka the faith spread to Bactria and Ceylon. Buddhism was particularly successful in attracting merchants as converts. When they traveled, Buddhist merchants observed their faith among themselves and explained it to others. Gradually, Buddhism made its way along the silk roads to Iran, central Asia, China, and southeast Asia.

A mosaic of the second century C.E. depicts a musician playing flutes and a dancer wearing a thin and revealing silk garment.

Buddhism in Central Asia

Buddhism first established a presence in the oasis towns along the silk roads—notably Merv, Bukhara, Samarkand, Kashgar, Khotan, Kuqa, Turpan, and Dunhuang—where merchants and their caravans found food, rest, lodging, and markets. The oases depended heavily on trade for their prosperity, and they allowed merchants to build monasteries and invite monks and scribes into their communities. Because they hosted travelers who came from different lands, spoke different languages, and observed different religious practices, the oasis towns became cosmopolitan centers. As early as the second century B.C.E., many residents of the oases themselves adopted Buddhism, which was the most prominent faith of silk roads merchants for almost a millennium, from about 200 B.C.E. to 700 C.E.

From the oasis communities Buddhism spread to the steppe lands of central Asia and to China. Nomadic peoples from the steppes visited the oases regularly to trade animal products from their herds for grains and manufactured items. They often found Buddhism intriguing, and in the early centuries C.E. they increasingly responded to its appeal. By the fourth century C.E., they had sponsored the spread of Buddhism throughout much of central Asia.

Buddhism in China

By the first century B.C.E., Buddhism had also established a foothold in China. The earliest Buddhists in China were foreign merchants—Indians, Parthians, and central Asian peoples—who observed their faith in the enclaves that Han dynasty officials

Buddhism and Hinduism in Southeast Asia

Early Buddhist sculpture in Bactria reflected the influence of Mediterranean and Greek artistic styles. This seated Buddha from the first or second century C.E. bears Caucasian features and wears Mediterranean-style dress.

allowed them to inhabit in Chang'an and other major cities. For several centuries Buddhism remained the faith largely of these expatriate merchants, and it did not appeal very strongly to native Chinese. Yet the presence of monasteries and missionaries offered Buddhism the potential to attract Chinese converts. Beginning about the fifth century C.E., Chinese began to respond enthusiastically to Buddhism, which during the postclassical era became the most popular religious faith throughout all of east Asia, including Japan and Korea as well as China.

As Buddhism spread north from India into central Asia and China, both Buddhism and Hinduism also began to attract a following in southeast Asia. Once again, merchants traveling the silk roads—in this case the sea lanes through the Indian Ocean—played prominent roles in spreading these faiths. Merchant mariners regularly plied the waters between India and southeast Asia during the late centuries B.C.E. By the first century C.E., clear signs of Indian cultural influence had appeared in southeast Asia. In Java, Sumatra, and other islands, as well as in the Malay peninsula and territories embraced by modern Vietnam and Cambodia, rulers of southeast Asian states called themselves *rajas* ("kings"), in the manner of Indian rulers, and they adopted Sanskrit as a means of written communication. Many rulers converted to Buddhism, while others promoted the Hindu cults of Shiva and Vishnu. They built walled cities around lavish temples constructed in the Indian style. They appointed Buddhist or Hindu advisors, and they sought to enhance their authority by associating themselves with honored religious traditions.

The Spread of Christianity

Early Christians faced intermittent persecution from Roman officials. During the early centuries C.E., Roman authorities launched a series of campaigns to stamp out Christianity, since most Christians refused to observe the state cults that honored emperors as divine beings. Paradoxically, imperial officials viewed Christians as irreligious because they declined to participate in state-approved religious ceremonies. They also considered Christianity a menace to society because zealous missionaries attacked other religions and generated sometimes violent conflict. Nevertheless, Christian missionaries took full advantage of the Romans' magnificent network of

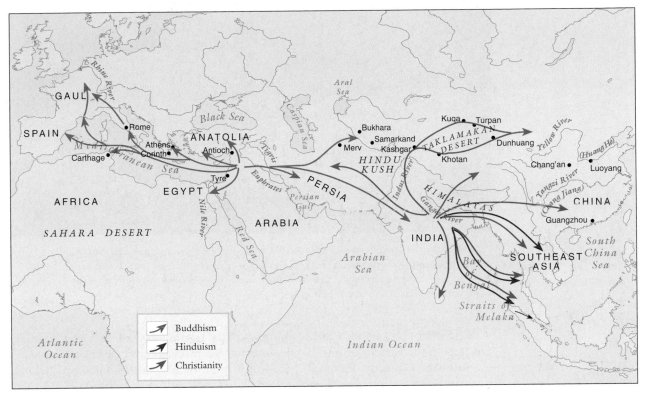

MAP [12.2]
The spread of Buddhism, Hinduism, and Christianity, 200 B.C.E.–400 C.E.

roads and sea lanes, which enabled them to carry their message throughout the Roman empire and the Mediterranean basin.

During the second and third centuries C.E., countless missionaries took Paul of Tarsus as their example and worked zealously to attract converts. One of the more famous was Gregory the Wonderworker, a tireless missionary with a reputation for performing miracles, who popularized Christianity in central Anatolia during the mid-third century C.E. Contemporaries reported that Gregory not only preached Christian doctrine but also expelled demons, moved boulders, diverted a river in flood, and persuaded observers that he had access to impressive supernatural powers. Gregory and his fellow missionaries helped to make Christianity an enormously popular religion of salvation in the Roman empire. By the late third century C.E., in spite of continuing imperial opposition, devout Christian communities flourished throughout the Mediterranean basin in Anatolia, Syria, Palestine, Egypt, and north Africa as well as in Greece, Italy, Spain, and Gaul.

As Christianity became a prominent source of religious inspiration within the Roman empire, the young faith also traveled the trade routes and found followers beyond the Mediterranean basin. By the second century C.E., sizable Christian communities flourished throughout Mesopotamia and Iran, and a few Christian churches had appeared as far away as India. Christians did not dominate eastern lands as they did the Roman empire, but they attracted large numbers of converts in southwest Asia. Indeed, alongside Jews and Zoroastrians, Christians constituted one of the major religious communities in the region, and they remained so even after the seventh century C.E., when the Islamic faith of Arab Muslim conquerors began to displace the older religious communities.

MAP [12.2]
The spread of Buddhism, Hinduism, and Christianity, 200 B.C.E.–400 C.E.

Christianity in the Mediterranean Basin

Christianity in Southwest Asia

Chinese military leaders placed high value on the large, strong horses bred in central Asia, and they imported as many of the animals as possible. The fortunate owners of these horses often commissioned artists to prepare representations of their animals, as in this wall tile from an aristocratic tomb in central China dating to the second or first century B.C.E.

Christian communities in Mesopotamia and Iran deeply influenced Christian practices in the Roman empire. To demonstrate utter loyalty to their faith, Christians in southwest Asia often followed strict ascetic regimes: inspired by Indian traditions, they abstained from sexual contact, refused fine foods and other comforts, and sometimes even withdrew from family life and society. These practices impressed devout Christians in the Roman empire. By the third century C.E., some Mediterranean Christians had begun to abandon society altogether and live as hermits in the deserts of Egypt, the mountains of Greece, and other isolated locations. Others withdrew from lay society but lived in communities of like-minded individuals who devoted their efforts to prayer and praise of God. Thus ascetic practices of Christians living in lands east of the Roman empire helped to inspire the formation of Christian monastic communities in the Mediterranean basin.

After the fifth century C.E., Christian communities in southwest Asia and the Mediterranean basin increasingly went separate ways. Most of the faithful in southwest Asia became Nestorians—followers of the Greek theologian Nestorius, who lived during the early fifth century and emphasized the human as opposed to the divine nature of Jesus. Mediterranean church authorities rejected Nestorius's views, and many of his disciples departed for Mesopotamia and Iran. They soon became prominent in local Christian communities, and they introduced a strong organizational framework to the church in southwest Asia. Although they had limited dealings with Mediterranean Christians, the Nestorians spread their faith east across the silk roads. Nestorian merchants took their faith with them on trade missions, and by the early seventh century they had established communities in central Asia, India, and China.

The Spread of Manichaeism

Mani and Manichaeism

The explosive spread of Manichaeism dramatically illustrated how missionary religions made effective use of the silk roads trading network. Manichaeism was the faith derived from the prophet Mani (216–272 C.E.), a devout Zoroastrian from Babylon in Mesopotamia. Apart from Zoroastrianism, Mani drew deep influence from Christianity and Buddhism. He regarded Zarathustra as the prophet of Persia, Buddha as

A cave painting from about the seventh century C.E. depicts a group of devout Manichaean faithful, whose austere regimen called for them to dress in plain white garments and keep their hair uncut and untrimmed.

the prophet of India, and Jesus as the prophet of the Mediterranean world. Because of the intense interaction between peoples of different societies, Mani saw a need for a prophet for all humanity, and he promoted a syncretic blend of Zoroastrian, Christian, and Buddhist elements as a religious faith that would serve the needs of a cosmopolitan world.

Mani was a dualist: he viewed the world as the site of a cosmic struggle between the forces of light and darkness, good and evil. He associated light with spiritual awareness and darkness with the material world. He urged his followers to reject worldly pleasures, which entangled the spirit in matter, and rise toward the light. His doctrine had strong appeal because it offered a rational explanation for the presence of good and evil in the world while also providing a means for individuals to achieve personal salvation and contribute to the triumph of good over evil.

Mani promoted an ascetic lifestyle and insisted that disciples observe high ethical standards. Devout Manichaeans, known as "the elect," abstained from marriage, sexual

Manichaean Ethics

relations, fine clothing, meat, rich foods, and other personal comforts, dedicating themselves instead to prayer, fasting, and ritual observances. Less zealous Manichaeans, known as "hearers," led more conventional lives, but they followed a strict moral code and provided food and gifts to sustain the elect. All Manichaeans looked forward to individual salvation and eternal association with the forces of light and good.

Mani was a fervent missionary: he traveled widely to promote his faith, corresponded tirelessly with Manichaean adherents, and dispatched disciples to lands that he could not visit himself. He also created a Manichaean church with its own services, rituals, hymns, and liturgies. His doctrine attracted converts first in Mesopotamia, and before Mani's death it had spread throughout the Sasanid empire and into the eastern Mediterranean region. In spite of its asceticism, Manichaeism appealed especially strongly to merchants, who adopted the faith as hearers and supported the Manichaean church. By the end of the third century C.E., Manichaean communities had appeared in all the large cities and trading centers of the Roman empire.

Decline of Manichaeism

Manichaeism soon came under tremendous pressure. Zoroastrian leaders urged the Sasanid rulers to suppress Mani's movement as a threat to public order. Mani himself died in chains as a prisoner of the Sasanid emperor, who sought to use Zoroastrianism as a cultural foundation for the unification of his realm. Authorities in the Roman empire also persecuted Manichaeans, whom they suspected because of the religion's origins in the rival Sasanid empire. Indeed, during the fifth and sixth centuries, political authorities largely exterminated Manichaeism in the Mediterranean basin. Yet Manichaeism survived in central Asia, where it attracted converts among nomadic Turkish peoples who traded with merchants from China, India, and southwest Asia. Like Buddhism, Hinduism, and Christianity, then, Manichaeism relied on the trade routes of classical times to extend its influence to new lands and peoples.

The Spread of Epidemic Disease

Like religious faiths, infectious and contagious diseases also spread along the trade routes of the classical world. Aided by long-distance travelers, pathogens had opportunities to spread beyond their original environments and attack populations with no inherited or acquired immunities to the diseases they caused. The resulting epidemics took a ferocious toll in human lives.

Information about human populations in classical times is scanty and full of gaps. Scholars often do not have records to work with and must draw inferences about population size from the area enclosed by city walls, the number of houses discovered in a settlement, the agricultural potential of a region, and similar considerations. As a result, population estimates for premodern societies are rough approximations rather than precise figures. Moreover, within a single society, individual regions often had very different demographic experiences. Nevertheless, even for classical times, the general outlines of population history are reasonably clear.

Epidemic Diseases

During the second and third centuries C.E., the Han and Roman empires suffered large-scale outbreaks of epidemic disease. The most destructive of these diseases were probably smallpox and measles, and epidemics of bubonic plague may also have erupted. All three diseases are devastating when they break out in populations without resistance, immunities, or medicines to combat them. As disease ravaged the two empires, Chinese and Roman populations declined sharply.

During the reign of Augustus, the population of the Roman empire stood at about sixty million people. During the second century C.E., epidemics reduced Roman population by about one-quarter, to forty-five million. Most devastating was an outbreak of smallpox that spread throughout the Mediterranean basin during the years 165 to

Sources from the Past

St. Cyprian on Epidemic Disease in the Roman Empire

St. Cyprian, bishop of Carthage, was an outspoken proponent of Christianity during the early and middle decades of the third century C.E. When epidemic disease struck the Roman empire in 251 C.E., imperial authorities blamed the outbreak on Christians who refused to honor pagan gods. Cyprian refuted this charge in his treatise On Mortality, *which described the symptoms of epidemic disease and reflected on its significance for the Christian community.*

It serves as validation of the [Christian] faith when the bowels loosen and drain the body's strength, when fever generated in bone marrow causes sores to break out in the throat, when continuous vomiting roils the intestines, when blood-shot eyes burn, when the feet or other bodily parts are amputated because of infection by putrefying disease, when through weakness caused by injuries to the body either mobility is impeded, or hearing is impaired, or sight is obscured. It requires enormous greatness of heart to struggle with resolute mind against so many onslaughts of destruction and death. It requires great loftiness to stand firm amidst the ruins of the human race, not to concede defeat with those who have no hope in God, but rather to rejoice and embrace the gift of the times. With Christ as our judge, we should receive this gift as the reward of his faith, as we vigorously affirm our faith and, having suffered, advance toward Christ by Christ's narrow path. . . .

Many of us [Christians] are dying in this epidemic—that is, many of us are being liberated from the world. The epidemic is a pestilence for the Jews and the pagans and the enemies of Christ, but for the servants of God it is a welcome event. True, without any discrimination,

the just are dying alongside the unjust, but you should not imagine that the evil and the good face a common destruction. The just are called to refreshment, while the unjust are herded off to punishment: the faithful receive protection, while the faithless receive retribution. We are unseeing and ungrateful for divine favors, beloved brethren, and we do not recognize what is granted to us. . . .

How suitable and essential it is that this plague and pestilence, which seems so terrible and ferocious, probes the justice of every individual and examines the minds of the human race to determine whether the healthy care for the ill, whether relatives diligently love their kin, whether masters show mercy to their languishing slaves, whether physicians do not abandon those seeking their aid, whether the ferocious diminish their violence, whether the greedy in the fear of death extinguish the raging flames of their insatiable avarice, whether the proud bend their necks, whether the shameless mitigate their audacity, whether the rich will loosen their purse strings and give something to others as their loved ones perish all around them and as they are about to die without heirs.

SOURCE: Wilhelm von Hartel, ed. *S. Thasci Caecili Cypriani opera omnia* in *Corpus scriptorum ecclesiasticorum latinorum.* Vienna: 1868, vol. 3, pp. 305–6. (Translation by Jerry H. Bentley.)

To what extent do you think St. Cyprian was effective in his efforts to bring inherited Christian teachings to bear on the unprecedented conditions he and his followers faced?

180 C.E. The epidemic was especially virulent in cities, and it even claimed the life of the Roman emperor Marcus Aurelius (180 C.E.). In combination with war and invasions, continuing outbreaks caused a significant population decline during the third and fourth centuries: by 400 C.E. the number of Romans had fallen to perhaps forty million. By the sixth century C.E., population had probably stabilized or perhaps even begun to expand in the eastern Mediterranean, but western Mediterranean lands experienced demographic stagnation until the tenth century.

Effects of Epidemic Diseases

Epidemics appeared slightly later in China than in the Mediterranean region. From fifty million people at the beginning of the millennium, Chinese population rose to sixty million in 200 C.E. As diseases found their way east, however, Chinese numbers fell back to fifty million by 400 C.E. and to forty-five million by 600 C.E. Thus by 600 C.E. both Mediterranean and Chinese populations had fallen by a quarter to a third from their high points during classical times.

Demographic decline in turn brought economic and social change. Trade within the empires declined, and both the Chinese and Roman economies contracted. Both economies also moved toward regional self-sufficiency: whereas previously the Chinese and Roman states had integrated the various regions of their empires into a larger network of trade and exchange, after about 200 C.E. they increasingly embraced several smaller regional economies that concentrated on their own needs instead of the larger imperial market. In the Roman empire, for example, the eastern Mediterranean regions of Anatolia, Egypt, and Greece continued to form a larger, integrated society, but regional economies increasingly emerged in western Mediterranean lands, including Italy, Gaul, Spain, and northwest Africa.

The demographic histories of classical Persia, India, and other lands are not so clear as they are for China and the Roman empire. Persia most likely experienced demographic, economic, and social problems similar to those that afflicted China and the Mediterranean basin. India may well have suffered from epidemic disease and population losses, although there is limited evidence for these troubles in south Asia. In east Asia and the Mediterranean basin, however, it is clear that epidemic disease seriously weakened Chinese and Roman societies. Indeed, epidemic disease contributed to serious instability in China after the collapse of the Han dynasty, and in weakening Mediterranean society, it helped bring about the decline and fall of the western Roman empire.

CHINA AFTER THE HAN DYNASTY

By the time epidemic diseases struck China, internal political problems had already begun to weaken the Han dynasty. By the late second century C.E., Han authorities had largely lost their ability to maintain order. Early in the third century C.E., the central government dissolved, and a series of autonomous regional kingdoms took the place of the Han state. With the disappearance of the Han dynasty, China experienced significant cultural change, most notably an increasing interest in Buddhism.

Internal Decay of the Han State

The Han dynasty collapsed largely because of internal problems that its rulers could not solve. One problem involved the development of factions within the ranks of the ruling elites. Marriage alliances between imperial and aristocratic families led to the formation of many factions whose members sought to advance their own prospects in the imperial government and exclude others from important positions. This atmosphere led to constant infighting and backstabbing among the ruling elites, which in turn reduced the effectiveness of the central government.

An even more difficult problem had to do with the perennial issue of land and its equitable distribution. At the turn of the millennium, the usurper Wang Mang had attempted to redistribute land in China, but his program did not survive his own brief reign (9–23 C.E.). During the last two centuries of the Han dynasty, large landowners gained new influence in the government. They managed to reduce their share of taxes and shift the burden onto peasants. They even formed private armies to advance the interests of their class.

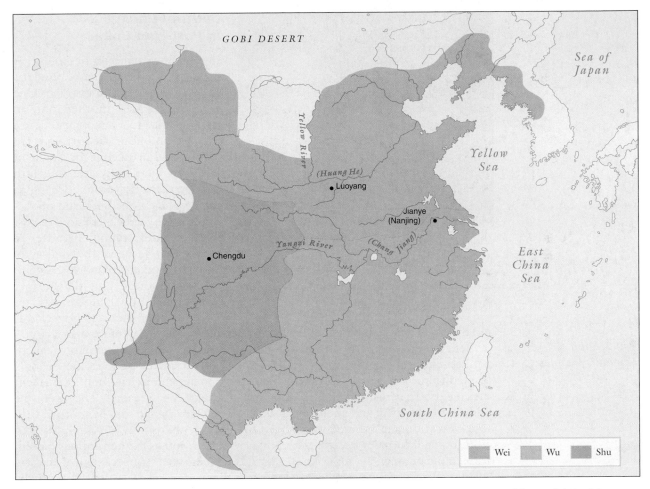

Peasant Rebellion

These developments provoked widespread unrest, particularly among peasants, who found themselves under increasing economic pressure with no means to influence the government. Pressures became particularly acute during the late second and third centuries when epidemics began to take their toll. In 184 C.E. peasant discontent fueled a massive uprising known as the Yellow Turban rebellion, so called because the rebels wore yellow headbands that represented the color of the Chinese earth and symbolized their peasant origins. Although quickly suppressed, the rebellion proved to be only the first in a series of insurrections that plagued the late Han dynasty.

*Collapse of
the Han Dynasty*

Meanwhile, Han generals increasingly usurped political authority. By 190 C.E. the Han emperor had become a mere puppet, and the generals effectively ruled the regions controlled by their armies. They allied with wealthy landowners of their regions and established themselves as warlords who maintained a kind of rough order based on force of arms. The generals continued to recognize an emperor for a short time, but in 220 C.E. they formally abolished the Han dynasty and divided the empire into three large kingdoms.

Once the dynasty had disappeared, large numbers of nomadic peoples migrated into China, especially the northern regions, and they helped to keep China disunited for more than 350 years. Between the fourth and sixth centuries C.E., nomadic peoples established large kingdoms that dominated much of northern China as well as the steppe lands.

After the collapse of the Han dynasty, China experienced social and economic difficulty. Wealthy classes often traveled in ox carts instead of more expensive, horse-drawn carriages. Archaeologists found this ceramic model of an ox cart in a tomb from the sixth century C.E.

Cultural Change in Post-Han China

In some ways the centuries following the fall of the Han dynasty present a spectacle of chaos and disorder. One kingdom toppled another, only to fall in its turn to a temporary successor. War and nomadic invasions led to population decline in much of northern China. By the mid-fifth century, the region around Chang'an and Luoyang—the heartland of classical China—had experienced almost complete devastation because of armies that ravaged the region in search of food and plunder. Contemporaries reported that the Former Han capital of Chang'an had no more than one hundred households and that the Later Han capital of Luoyang resembled a trash heap more than a city.

Sinicization of Nomadic Peoples

Beneath the disorderly surface of political events, however, several important social and cultural changes were taking place. First, nomadic peoples increasingly adapted to the Chinese environment. They took up agriculture and built permanent settlements. They married Chinese spouses and took Chinese names. They wore the clothes, ate the food, and adopted the customs of China. Some sought a formal Chinese education and became well versed in Chinese philosophy and literature. In short, nomadic peoples became increasingly sinicized, and as the generations passed, distinctions between peoples of nomadic and Chinese ancestry became less and less obvious. Partly because of this development, a new imperial dynasty was eventually able to reconstitute a centralized imperial state in north China.

Second, with the disintegration of political order, the Confucian tradition lost much of its credibility. The original goal of Confucius and his early followers was to find some means to move from chaos to stability during the Period of the Warring States. As long as Confucian methods and principles helped to maintain order, ruling elites and intellectual classes honored the Confucian tradition. When the Han dynasty collapsed, Confucianism seemed irrelevant.

Individuals who in earlier centuries might have committed themselves to Confucian values turned instead to Daoism and Buddhism. As in the Period of the Warring States, Daoism once again offered a way to find peace in a turbulent world. Originally, Daoism was a school of speculative philosophical thought that appealed mostly to an educated elite. After the fall of the Han, however, it became more a religious than a philosophical doctrine. Daoist sages not only promised salvation to those who observed their doctrines and rituals but also experimented with spices, herbs, and drugs to concoct elixirs or potions that supposedly conferred health and immortality. Daoism attracted widespread interest among a population afflicted by war and disease and became much more popular than before, especially because it faced less competition from the Confucian tradition.

Popularity of Buddhism

Even more important than Daoism for Chinese cultural history was Buddhism. Until about the fourth century C.E., Buddhism was largely the faith of foreign merchants in China and attracted little interest on the part of native Chinese. After the fall of the Han empire, however, Buddhism received strong support from nomadic peoples who migrated into northern China and who in many cases had long been familiar with Buddhism in central Asia. Meanwhile, as a result of missionary efforts, the Indian faith began to attract a following among native Chinese as well. Indeed, between the fourth and sixth centuries C.E., Buddhism became well established in China. When a centralized imperial state took shape in the late sixth century C.E., Buddhism provided an important cultural foundation for the restoration of a unified political order.

THE FALL OF THE ROMAN EMPIRE

Moralists have often interpreted the fall of the Roman empire as a symbol of the transitory nature of human creations. Fascination with imperial Rome has encouraged the proliferation of theories—many of them quite silly—seeking to explain the fall of the empire as the result of some single, simple cause. By various accounts, the Roman empire declined and fell because of lead poisoning, radiation given off by bricks, immorality, or the rise of Christianity. Notwithstanding the zeal with which proponents have promoted pet theories, there was no single cause for the decline and fall of the Roman empire. Instead, a combination of internal problems and external pressures weakened the empire and brought an end to Roman authority in the western portion of the empire, whereas in the eastern Mediterranean imperial rule continued until the fifteenth century C.E. In the Mediterranean basin as in China, imperial weakness and collapse coincided with significant cultural change, notably the increasing popularity of Christianity.

The Barracks Emperors

Internal Decay in the Roman Empire

As in the case of the Han dynasty, internal political problems go a long way toward explaining the fall of the Roman empire. Like their Han counterparts, the Roman emperors faced internal opposition. During the half century from 235 to 284 C.E., there were no fewer than twenty-six claimants to the imperial throne. Known as the "barracks emperors," most of them were generals who seized power, held it briefly, and then suddenly lost it when they were displaced by rivals or their own mutinous troops. Not surprisingly, most of the barracks emperors died violently: only one is known for sure to have succumbed to natural causes.

Apart from divisions and factions, the Roman empire also faced problems because of its sheer size. Even during the best of times, when the

Sculpture of the tetrarchs, or four corulers of the Roman empire, during the late third century C.E.; from left, Galerius, Constantius, Diocletian, and Maximian.

Diocletian

Only the colossal head of Constantine survives from a statue that originally stood about 14 meters (46 feet) tall.

emperors could count on abundant revenues and disciplined armed forces, the sprawling empire posed a challenge for central governors. After the third century, as epidemics spread throughout the empire and its various regions moved toward local, self-sufficient economies, the empire as a whole became increasingly unmanageable.

The emperor Diocletian (reigned 284–305 C.E.) attempted to deal with this problem by dividing the empire into two administrative districts. The eastern district included the wealthy lands of Anatolia, Syria, Egypt, and Greece, and the western district embraced Italy, Gaul, Spain, Britain, and north Africa. A coemperor ruled each district with the aid of a powerful lieutenant, and the four officials, known as the tetrarchs, were able to administer the vast empire more effectively than an individual emperor could. Diocletian was a skillful administrator. He managed to bring Rome's many armies, including unpredictable maverick forces, under firm imperial control. He also tried to deal with a crumbling economy by strengthening the imperial currency, forcing the government to adjust its expenditures to its income, and imposing price caps to dampen inflation. His economic measures were less successful than his administrative reforms, but they helped stabilize an economy ravaged by half a century of civil unrest.

Yet Diocletian's reforms also encouraged ambition among the four top corulers and their generals, and his retirement from the imperial office in 305 C.E. set off a round of internal struggles and bitter civil war. Already in 306 C.E. Constantine, son of Diocletian's coruler Constantius, moved to stake his claim as sole emperor. By 313 C.E. he had defeated most of his enemies, although he overcame his last rivals only in 324 C.E. Once he had consolidated his grip on power, Constantine ordered the construction of a new capital city, Constantinople, at a strategic site overlooking the Bosporus, the strait linking the Black Sea to the Sea of Marmara and beyond to the wealthy eastern Mediterranean. After 340 C.E. Constantinople became the capital of a united Roman empire.

Constantine

Constantine himself was an able emperor. With the reunion of the eastern and western districts of the empire, however, he and his successors faced the same sort of administrative difficulties that Diocletian had attempted to solve by dividing the empire. As population declined and the economy contracted, emperors found it increasingly difficult to marshall the resources needed to govern and protect the vast Roman empire. The need for protection against external threats became especially acute during the late fourth and early fifth centuries C.E.

Germanic Invasions and the Fall of the Western Roman Empire

Apart from internal problems, the Roman empire also faced a formidable military threat from migratory Germanic peoples. Indeed, during the fifth century C.E., Germanic in-

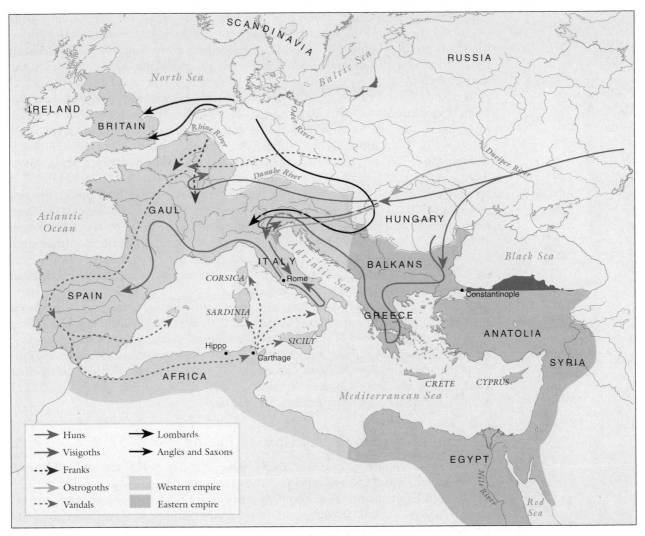

Huns
Visigoths
Franks
Ostrogoths
Vandals
Lombards
Angles and Saxons
Western empire
Eastern empire

MAP [12.4]
Germanic invasions and the
fall of the western Roman
empire, 450–476 C.E.

For an interactive version
of this map, go to
www.mhhe.com/
bentley3ch12maps.

Germanic Migrations

The Huns

vasions brought an end to Roman authority in the western half of the empire, although imperial rule survived for an additional millennium in the eastern Mediterranean.

Germanic peoples had migrated from their homelands in northern Europe and lived on the eastern and northern borders of the Roman empire since the second century C.E. Most notable were the Visigoths, who came originally from Scandinavia and Russia. Like the nomadic peoples who moved into northern China after the fall of the Han dynasty, the Visigoths settled, adopted agriculture, and drew deep inspiration from Roman society. They adapted Roman law to the needs of their own society, for example, converted to Christianity, and translated the Bible into the Visigothic language. They also contributed large numbers of soldiers to the Roman armies. In the interests of social order, however, the Romans discouraged settlement of the Visigoths and other Germanic peoples within the empire, preferring that they constitute buffer societies outside imperial borders.

During the late fourth century, the relationship between Visigoths and Romans changed dramatically when the nomadic Huns began an aggressive westward migration from their homeland in central Asia. The Huns spoke a Turkish language, and they probably were cousins of the nomadic Xiongnu who inhabited the central Asian steppe lands west of China. During the mid-fifth century C.E., the warrior-king Attila organized the Huns into a virtually unstoppable military juggernaut. Under Attila, the Huns invaded Hungary, probed Roman frontiers in the Balkan region, menaced Gaul and northern Italy, and attacked Germanic peoples living on the borders of the Roman empire.

Collapse of the Western Roman Empire

Attila did not create a set of political institutions or a state structure, and the Huns disappeared as a political and military force soon after his death in 453 C.E. By that time, however, the Huns had placed such pressure on Visigoths, Ostrogoths, Vandals, Franks, and other Germanic peoples that they streamed en masse into the Roman empire in search of refuge. Once inside imperial boundaries, they encountered little effective resistance and moved around almost at will. They established settlements throughout the western half of the empire—Italy, Gaul, Spain, Britain, and north Africa—where populations were less dense than in the eastern Mediterranean. Under the command of Alaric, the Visigoths even stormed and sacked Rome in 410 C.E. By the middle of the fifth century, the western part of the Roman empire was in shambles. In 476 C.E. imperial authority came to an ignominious end when the Germanic general Odovacer deposed Romulus Augustulus, the last of the Roman emperors in the western half of the empire.

Unlike the Han dynasty, the Roman empire did not entirely disintegrate: imperial authority survived for another millennium in the eastern half of the empire, known after the fifth century C.E. as the Byzantine empire. In the western half, however, Roman authority dissolved, and nomadic peoples built successor states in regions formerly subject to Rome. Vandals and then Visigoths governed Spain, Franks ruled Gaul, Angles and Saxons invaded Britain, and Italy fell under the sway of a variety of peoples, including Visigoths, Vandals, and Lombards.

Cultural Change in the Late Roman Empire

In the Roman empire, as in China, the collapse of the imperial state coincided with important social and cultural changes. The Germanic peoples who toppled the empire looked to their own traditions for purposes of organizing society and government. When they settled in the regions of the former empire, however, they absorbed a good deal of Roman influence. They adapted Roman law to their own needs, for example, thus preserving one of the most important features of Roman society. Over time, the mingling of Roman and Germanic traditions led to the emergence of an altogether new society—medieval Europe.

Prominence of Christianity

Christianity was perhaps the most prominent survivor of the western Roman empire. During the fourth century C.E., several developments enhanced its influence throughout the Mediterranean basin. In the first place, Christianity won recognition as a legitimate religion in the Roman empire. In 312 C.E., while seeking to establish himself as sole Roman emperor, Constantine experienced a vision that impressed upon him the power of the Christian God. He believed that the Christian God helped him to prevail over his rivals, and he promulgated the Edict of Milan, which allowed Christians to practice their faith openly in the Roman empire. At some point during his reign, perhaps after his edict, Constantine himself converted to Christianity, and in 380 C.E. the emperor Theodosius proclaimed Christianity the official religion of the Roman empire. By the mid-fourth century, Christians held important political and military positions, and imperial sponsorship helped their faith to attract more converts than ever before.

Christianity also began to attract thoughtful and talented converts who articulated a Christian message for the intellectual elites of the Roman empire. The earliest

Christians had come largely from the ranks of ordinary working people, and their doctrine struck philosophers and the educated elites as both unsophisticated and unbelievable. During its first three centuries, the new faith grew as a popular religion of salvation favored by the masses, rather than as a reasoned doctrine of intellectual substance. During the fourth century, however, intellectual elites began to take more interest in Christianity.

St. Augustine

The most important and influential of these figures was St. Augustine (354–430 C.E.), bishop of the north African city of Hippo (modern-day Annaba in Algeria). Augustine had a fine education, and he was conversant with the leading intellectual currents of the day. During his youth he drew great inspiration from Stoicism and Platonism, and for nine years he belonged to a community of Manichaeans. Eventually he became disillusioned with both Hellenistic philosophical school and Manichaeism, and in 387 C.E., while studying in Italy, he converted to Christianity. For the remainder of his life he worked to reconcile Christianity with Greek and Roman philosophical traditions, especially Platonism, and to articu-

Portrait of St. Augustine holding a copy of his most famous work, *The City of God*, which sought to explain the meaning of history and the world from a Christian point of view.

late Christianity in terms that were familiar and persuasive to the educated classes. More than any others, Augustine's writings made Christianity an intellectually respectable alternative to Hellenistic philosophy and popular religions of salvation.

Besides winning the right to practice their faith openly and attracting intellectual talent, Christian leaders constructed an institutional apparatus that transformed a popular religion of salvation into a powerful church. In the absence of recognized leadership, the earliest Christians generated a range of conflicting and sometimes contradictory doctrines. Some taught that Jesus was a mortal human being, others that he was a god, and yet others that he was both human and divine. Some allowed women to serve as priests and attributed great powers to Jesus' mother Mary, while others restricted church offices to men and conceived of Christian deities as males.

To standardize their faith, Christian leaders instituted a hierarchy of church officials. At the top were five religious authorities—the bishop of Rome and the patriarchs of Jerusalem, Antioch, Alexandria, and Constantinople—who resided in the most important spiritual and political centers of the Roman empire. These five authorities wielded roughly equal influence in the larger Christian community, although the bishop of Rome enjoyed somewhat greater prestige than the others. (His enhanced status derived both from his claim to be the spiritual descendant of Jesus' chief disciple, St. Peter, and from the fact that he had his seat at Rome, the original imperial capital.)

The Institutional Church

Subordinate to the five principal authorities were bishops, who presided over religious affairs in their districts, known as dioceses, which included all the prominent cities of the Roman empire. When theological disputes arose, the patriarchs and bishops assembled in church councils to determine which views would prevail as official doctrine. The councils at Nicaea (325 C.E.) and Chalcedon (451 C.E.), for example, took up the difficult and contentious issue of Jesus' nature. Delegates at these councils proclaimed that Jesus was both fully human and fully divine at the same time, in contrast to Nestorians, Arians, and other Christian groups who held that Jesus was either primarily human or primarily divine.

As Roman imperial authority crumbled, the bishop of Rome, known as the pope (from the Latin *papa,* meaning "father"), emerged as spiritual leader of Christian communities in the western regions of the empire. As the only sources of established and recognized authority, the popes and the bishops of other important cities organized local government and defensive measures for their communities. They also mounted missionary campaigns to convert Germanic peoples to Christianity. Although Roman imperial authority disappeared, Roman Christianity survived and served as a foundation for cultural unity in lands that had formerly made up the western half of the Roman empire.

By 500 C.E. classical societies in Persia, China, India, and the Mediterranean basin had either collapsed or fallen into decline. Yet all the classical societies left rich legacies that shaped political institutions, social orders, and cultural traditions for centuries to come. Moreover, by sponsoring commercial and cultural relations between different peoples, the classical societies laid a foundation for intensive and systematic cross-cultural interaction in later times. After the third century C.E., the decline of the Han and Roman empires resulted in less activity over the silk roads than in the preceding three hundred years. But the trade routes survived, and when a new series of imperial states reestablished order throughout much of Eurasia and north Africa in the sixth century C.E., the peoples of the eastern hemisphere avidly resumed their crossing of cultural boundary lines in the interests of trade and communication.

CHRONOLOGY

third century B.C.E.	Spread of Buddhism and Hinduism to southeast Asia
second century B.C.E.	Introduction of Buddhism to central Asia
139–126 B.C.E.	Travels of Zhang Qian in central Asia
first century B.C.E.	Introduction of Buddhism to China
second century C.E.	Spread of Christianity in the Mediterranean basin and southwest Asia
184 C.E.	Yellow Turban rebellion
216–272 C.E.	Life of Mani
220 C.E.	Collapse of the Han dynasty
284–305 C.E.	Reign of Diocletian
313–337 C.E.	Reign of Constantine
313 C.E.	Edict of Milan and the legalization of Christianity in the Roman empire
325 C.E.	Council of Nicaea
451 C.E.	Council of Chalcedon
476 C.E.	Collapse of the western Roman empire

FOR FURTHER READING

Thomas J. Barfield. *The Perilous Frontier: Nomadic Empires and China.* Cambridge, Mass., 1989. Provocative study of the Xiongnu and other central Asian peoples.

Jerry H. Bentley. *Old World Encounters: Cross-Cultural Contacts and Exchanges in Pre-Modern Times.* New York, 1993. Studies the spread of cultural and religious traditions before 1500 C.E.

Luce Boulnois. *The Silk Road.* Trans. by D. Chamberlain. New York, 1966. Popular account of trade and travel over the silk roads.

Peter Brown. *The Making of Late Antiquity.* Cambridge, Mass., 1978. Brilliant and evocative analysis of the cultural and religious history of the late Roman empire.

———. *The World of Late Antiquity, A.D. 150–750.* London, 1971. Well-illustrated essay concentrating on social and cultural themes.

Averil Cameron. *The Later Roman Empire, A.D. 284–430.* Cambridge, Mass., 1993. A lively synthesis.

———. *The Mediterranean World in Late Antiquity, A.D. 395–600.* London, 1993. Like its companion volume just cited, a well-informed synthesis.

Philip D. Curtin. *Cross-Cultural Trade in World History.* New York, 1984. A synthetic work that concentrates on merchant communities in distant lands and their roles in facilitating cross-cultural trade.

Edward Gibbon. *The Decline and Fall of the Roman Empire.* Many editions available. A classic account, still well worth reading, by a masterful historical stylist of the eighteenth century.

C. D. Gordon, ed. *The Age of Attila: Fifth-Century Byzantium and the Barbarians.* Ann Arbor, 1972. Translations of primary sources on the society and history of nomadic and migratory peoples.

A. H. M. Jones. *The Decline of the Ancient World.* New York, 1966. Synthetic study of the Roman empire in decline by a foremost scholar of the subject.

J. Innes Miller. *The Spice Trade of the Roman Empire, 29 B.C. to A.D. 641.* Oxford, 1969. Scholarly study of long-distance trade during classical times.

Samuel Hugh Moffett. *A History of Christianity in Asia,* vol. 1. San Francisco, 1992. An important volume that surveys the spread of early Christianity east of the Roman empire.

C. G. F. Simkin. *The Traditional Trade of Asia*. London, 1968. Survey of Eurasian trade with a chapter on the classical era.

Joseph A. Tainter. *The Collapse of Complex Societies*. Cambridge, 1988. Scholarly review of theories and evidence bearing on the fall of empires and societies.

Mortimer Wheeler. *Flames over Persepolis*. New York, 1968. Well-illustrated volume dealing with the interactions of Greek, Persian, and Indian peoples during the Hellenistic era.

Susan Whitfield. *Life along the Silk Road*. Berkeley, 1999. Focuses on the experiences of ten individuals who lived or traveled along the silk roads.

Francis Wood. *The Silk Road: Two Thousand Years in the Heart of Asia*. Berkeley, 2002. A brilliantly illustrated volume discussing the history of the silk roads from antiquity to the twentieth century.

See our **Online Learning Center at www.mhhe.com/bentley3** for additional readings, practice maps, quizzes, and internet activities.

Unfamiliar words? Check out the **Primary Source Investigator CD-ROM** for an interactive glossary, interactive maps, more images, and primary sources.

PART III

THE POSTCLASSICAL ERA, 500 TO 1000 C.E.

The postclassical era was a period of major readjustment for societies throughout the eastern hemisphere. The early centuries C.E. brought turbulence and instability to classical societies in China, India, southwest Asia, and the Mediterranean basin. Most of the classical empires collapsed under the strain of internal power struggles, external invasions, or a combination of the two. During the postclassical era the settled societies of the eastern hemisphere underwent political, social, economic, and cultural change that would shape their experiences over the long term. Indeed, the influence of the postclassical era continues to the present day.

The first task that settled societies faced in the postclassical era was the need to restore political and social order. They went about this task in very different ways. In the eastern Mediterranean the eastern half of the Roman empire survived as the Byzantine empire—the only empire that outlasted the difficulties of the late classical era—but underwent political and social reorganization in order to deal with external pressures. In southwest Asia, Arab conquerors inspired by the recently founded Islamic faith overcame the Sasanid empire of Persia. In China the Sui and Tang dynasties restored centralized imperial authority after almost four centuries of rule by competing regional kingdoms and nomadic conquerors. In India, by contrast, centralized imperial rule did not return: authority devolved instead to a series of regional kingdoms, some of them quite large. In western Europe centralized imperial rule returned only for a brief moment during the eighth and ninth centuries under the Carolingian empire. Economic difficulties and new rounds of invasions, however, brought down the empire and encouraged devolution of authority to local rulers: the result was the development of a decentralized political order in western Europe. In different ways, then, all the settled societies of the eastern hemisphere embarked upon a quest for political and social order during the centuries after the collapse of the classical empires.

The reestablishment of political and social order enabled postclassical societies to revive networks of long-distance trade and participate more actively in processes of cross-cultural communication and exchange. As a result, the postclassical era was a time of rapid economic growth in most of the eastern hemisphere. The volume of long-distance trade increased dramatically, and manufacturers began to produce goods explicitly for export rather than local consumption. Meanwhile, increased trade facilitated biological and technological as well as commercial exchanges: agricultural crops migrated far beyond the lands of their origin, and improved techniques of irrigation and cultivation spread through much of Eurasia. New crops and improved agricultural techniques led to enlarged harvests and enriched diets particularly in China, India, and southwest Asia.

As agricultural production increased, so did human population. Growing numbers of people devoted their efforts to trade and manufacturing rather than cultivation. China, India, and the eastern Mediterranean region were especially prominent sites for the production of textiles, ceramics, and metal goods. Increased trade and manufacturing activity encouraged a remarkable round of technological invention and innovation. The magnetic compass, printing technologies, and gunpowder, for example, first appeared in postclassical China and then diffused to other lands. These inventions and others of the era have profoundly influenced the course of human history since their first appearance.

The postclassical era was also crucially important for the formation and development of cultural and religious traditions. Islam first appeared during the postclassical era, and it soon became the cultural and religious foundation of an expansive empire stretching from north Africa to northern India. Buddhism expanded beyond the Indian subcontinent and central Asia, attracting converts in China, Korea, Japan, and southeast Asia. Christianity was the official faith of the Byzantine empire, where the Eastern Orthodox church emerged and gave shape to a distinctive form of Christianity. Orthodox missionaries also spread their faith to formerly pagan lands throughout much of eastern Europe and Russia. Farther west, Christianity spread from the Mediterranean basin to western and northern Europe, where papal leadership guided the emergence of the Roman Catholic church. For a millennium and more, Roman Catholic Christianity served as the foundation for cultural unity in the politically disunited world of western and northern Europe. Meanwhile, quite apart from the expansion of religious faiths, the postclassical era also witnessed the spread of literacy and formal education throughout much of the eastern hemisphere.

The empires and regional states of the postclassical era disappeared long ago, but the social, economic, and cultural legacies of the age are noticeable even today. Long-distance trade surged in postclassical times and helped to structure economic and social development throughout much of the eastern hemisphere. Even more notable, perhaps, religious and cultural traditions continue to flourish in lands where they first attracted converts in postclassical times. In some ways, then, the postclassical age survives even in the modern world.

A sixth-century icon depicting an enthroned Virgin Mary and infant Jesus attended by angels and saints.

THE COMMONWEALTH OF BYZANTIUM

According to the Byzantine historian Procopius, two Christian monks from Persia set out on a momentous journey about the middle of the sixth century C.E. The result of their travels was the introduction of high-quality silk production to the eastern Mediterranean. Although local crafts workers had long produced coarse fabrics from the cocoons of wild silkworms, fine silks had come to the Mediterranean only from China, where manufacturers closely guarded both their carefully bred strains of silkworms and the complex technology that yielded high-quality textiles. Mediterranean consumers did not obtain silk directly from Chinese producers but, rather, through intermediaries subject to the Sasanid empire of Persia.

According to Procopius's account, the two Christian monks observed the techniques of silk production during the course of a mission to China. Upon departure they hollowed out their walking staffs and filled them with silkworm eggs, which they smuggled out of China, through their native land of Persia, and into the Byzantine empire.

The monks' motives are unknown. Perhaps they resented Sasanid religious policies favoring Zoroastrians and sought to aid Christians in the Byzantine empire. Perhaps they hoped to receive a handsome reward for their efforts. Whatever their motives may have been, though, it is certain that the monks by themselves could not have introduced a full-blown silk industry to Byzantium. The production of fine, Chinese-style silks required more than a few silkworm eggs. It called also for understanding of sophisticated technologies and elaborate procedures that must have reached the Byzantine empire by several different routes. Thus it seems that Procopius simplified a complex story by focusing attention on the monks.

In any case, Byzantine crafts workers soon learned how to breed silkworms, feed them mulberry leaves, unravel their cocoons, and produce high-quality silk fabrics. By the late sixth century, Byzantine silks matched the quality of Chinese products. Mediterranean consumers no longer relied on Chinese producers and Persian intermediaries, and local production of high-quality silk greatly strengthened the Byzantine economy. Thus Procopius's anonymous monks participated in a momentous transfer of technology between distant lands. Their efforts contributed to the vibrance of Byzantine society, and their story highlights the significance of cross-cultural interactions during the postclassical era.

During the centuries after 200 C.E., most of the classical societies faced a series of problems—epidemic disease, declining population, economic contraction, political turmoil, social unrest, and military threats from outside—that brought about their collapse. Only in the eastern Mediterranean did a classical empire survive. The eastern half of the Roman empire, known as the Byzantine empire, withstood the various problems that brought down other classical societies and survived for almost a millennium after the collapse of the western Roman empire in the fifth century C.E.

The Byzantine empire did not reconstitute the larger Mediterranean society of classical times. The Roman empire had dominated an integrated Mediterranean basin; the Byzantine empire mostly faced a politically and culturally fragmented Mediterranean region. After the seventh century C.E., Islamic states controlled lands to the east and south of the Mediterranean, Slavic peoples dominated lands to the north, and western Europeans organized increasingly powerful states in lands to the west.

Although it was more compact than the Roman empire, the Byzantine empire was a political and economic powerhouse of the postclassical era. Until the twelfth century, Byzantine authority dominated the wealthy and productive eastern Mediterranean region. Manufactured goods from the Byzantine empire enjoyed a reputation for high quality in markets from the Mediterranean basin to India. The Byzantine empire also deeply influenced the historical development of the Slavic peoples of eastern Europe and Russia. Byzantine missionaries and diplomats introduced writing, Christianity, codified law, and sophisticated political organization into lands settled by Slavic peoples. Because Byzantine political, economic, and cultural influence stretched so far, historians often refer to it as the "Byzantine commonwealth." Just as Greek and Roman initiative brought Mediterranean lands into a larger integrated society during classical times, Byzantine policies led to the formation of a large, multicultural zone of trade, communication, interaction, and exchange in eastern Europe and the eastern Mediterranean basin during the postclassical era.

THE EARLY BYZANTINE EMPIRE

The Byzantine empire takes its name from Byzantion—latinized as Byzantium—a modest market town and fishing village that occupied a site of enormous strategic significance. Situated on a defensible peninsula and blessed with a magnificent natural harbor known as the Golden Horn, Byzantion had the potential to control the Bosporus, the strait of water leading from the Black Sea to the Sea of Marmara and beyond to the Dardanelles, the Aegean Sea, and the Mediterranean. Apart from its maritime significance, Byzantion also offered convenient access to the rich lands of Anatolia, southwestern Asia, and southeastern Europe. Trade routes linked Byzantion to ports throughout the Mediterranean basin.

Because of its strategic value, the Roman emperor Constantine designated Byzantion as the site of a new imperial capital, which he named Constantinople ("city of Constantine"). He built the new capital partly because the eastern Mediterranean was the wealthier and more productive part of the Roman empire and partly because relocation enabled the imperial court to maintain close watch over both the Sasanid empire in Persia and the Germanic peoples who lived along the lower stretches of the Danube River. The imperial government moved to Constantinople in 340 C.E., and the new capital rapidly reached metropolitan dimensions. By the late fourth century, it was the most important political and military center of the eastern Roman empire, and it soon became the dominant economic and commercial center in the eastern Mediterranean basin. The city kept the name Constantinople until 1453 C.E., when it fell to the Ottoman Turks, who renamed it Istanbul. By convention, however, historians refer to the realm governed from Constantinople between the fifth and fifteenth centuries C.E. as the Byzantine empire, or simply as Byzantium, in honor of the original settlement.

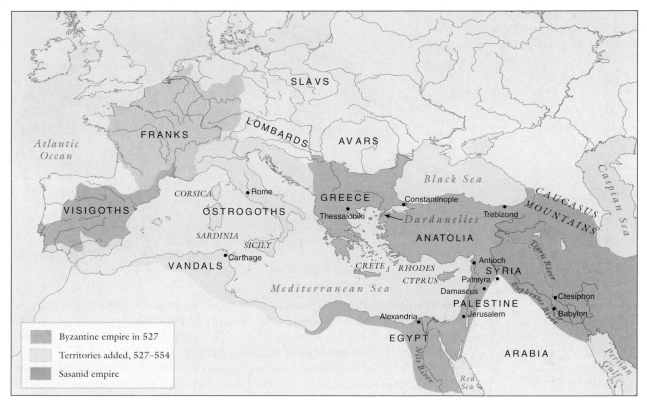

M A P [1 3 . 1]
The Byzantine empire and
its neighbors, 527–554 C.E.

The Later Roman Empire and Byzantium

The Byzantine empire originated as the eastern half of the classical Roman empire, which survived the collapse of the western Roman empire in the fifth century C.E. In its early days the Byzantine empire embraced Greece, the Balkan region, Anatolia, Syria, Palestine, Egypt, and northeast Africa. Byzantine rulers occasionally expanded their boundaries, and neighboring peoples sometimes seized portions of the Byzantine empire for themselves. During the seventh and eighth centuries C.E., for example, the southern regions of the empire fell into the hands of Arab Muslim conquerors. Generally speaking, however, Byzantium figured as a major power of the eastern Mediterranean basin until the thirteenth century C.E.

As the western Roman empire crumbled in the fifth century C.E., the eastern half of the empire remained intact, complete with roads, communications, lines of authority, and a set of functioning imperial institutions, all inherited from Roman predecessors. Yet the early Byzantine emperors faced challenges different from those of their predecessors, and they built a state significantly different from the classical Roman empire.

The principal challenges that confronted the late Roman and early Byzantine empires were the consolidation of the dynamic Sasanid dynasty (226–641 C.E.) in Persia and the invasions of migratory peoples from the north and east. The Sasanid emperors sought to rebuild the Achaemenid empire of classical Persia, a goal that brought them into conflict with Roman forces in Mesopotamia and Syria. By the late third century, Roman armies had largely stabilized their eastern borders, but until their fall in the seventh century, the Sasanids remained the principal foreign threat to the eastern Roman empire. Germanic invasions also menaced the late Roman empire. Because they did

*The Later
Roman Empire*

In 260 C.E. the Sasanid emperor Shapur I (right) captured the Roman emperor Valerian, as depicted in this cameo medallion of the fourth century.

not have adequate resources to respond strongly to the threat on all fronts, Roman authorities concentrated on maintaining the integrity of the wealthy eastern portion of the empire. As a result, migratory peoples were rarely a serious threat to Constantinople or the other heavily defended cities of the eastern empire.

The Early Byzantine State

Having secured their realm against Sasanids and migratory invaders, the Byzantine emperors built a distinctive tradition of statecraft. The most important feature of the Byzantine state was tightly centralized rule that concentrated power in the hands of a highly exalted emperor. This characteristic was noticeable already in the time of Constantine, who built his new capital to lavish standards. He filled it with libraries, museums, and artistic treasures, and he constructed magnificent marble palaces, churches, baths, and public buildings—all in an effort to create a new Rome fit for the ruler of a mighty empire.

Caesaropapism

Constantine also set a precedent by hedging his rule with an aura of divinity. As protector of the Christians and a baptized Christian himself, Constantine could not claim the divine status that some of his imperial predecessors had sought to appropriate. As the first Christian emperor, however, Constantine claimed divine favor and sanction for his rule. He intervened in theological disputes and used his political position to support views that he considered orthodox and condemn those that he regarded as heretical. Constantine initiated a policy that historians call "caesaropapism," whereby the emperor not only ruled as secular lord but also played an active and prominent role in ecclesiastical affairs.

Particularly after the sixth century, Byzantine emperors became exalted, absolute rulers. According to Roman law, emperors stood above the law: theoretically, they wielded absolute authority in political, military, judicial, financial, and religious matters. They also enjoyed the services of a large and complex bureaucracy. Indeed, its intricacy gave rise to the adjective *byzantine,* which suggests unnecessary complexity and convolution. In combination, law and bureaucracy produced an exceptionally centralized state.

The Byzantine Court

Even dress and court etiquette drew attention to the lofty status of Byzantine rulers. The emperors wore heavily bejeweled crowns and dressed in magnificent silk robes dyed a dark, rich purple—a color reserved for imperial use and strictly forbidden to those not associated with the ruling house. High officials presented themselves to the emperor as slaves, not subjects. When approaching him, they prostrated themselves three times and then ceremoniously kissed the imperial hands and feet before taking up matters of business. By the tenth century, engineers had contrived a series of mechanical devices that worked dazzling effects and impressed foreign envoys at the Byzantine court: imitation birds sang as ambassadors approached the emperor while mechanical lions roared and swished their tails. During an audience the imperial throne itself sometimes moved up and down to emphasize the awesome splendor of the emperor.

Justinian and His Legacy

The most important of the early Byzantine emperors was Justinian (527–565 C.E.), an energetic and tireless worker known to his subjects as "the sleepless emperor," who profoundly influenced the development of the Byzantine empire with the aid of his ambitious wife Theodora. The imperial couple came from obscure origins: Justinian was born into a Macedonian peasant family, and Theodora, the daughter of a bear keeper in the circus, worked as a striptease artist before meeting the future emperor. Yet both Justinian and Theodora were intelligent, strong willed, and disciplined. Thanks to these qualities, Justinian received an excellent education, found a position in the imperial bureaucracy, and soon mastered the intricacies of Byzantine finance. Theodora proved to be a sagacious advisor: she offered Justinian advice on sensitive political, diplomatic, and theological issues, and she contributed to the formation of a grand imperial court.

Justinian and Theodora

Like Constantine, Justinian lavished resources on the imperial capital. During the early years of his rule, riots against high taxes had destroyed much of Constantinople. After Theodora persuaded him to deploy the imperial army and quash the disturbances, Justinian embarked on an ambitious construction program that thoroughly remade the city. The most notable building erected during this campaign was the church of Hagia Sophia, a magnificent domed structure that later became a mosque and a museum and that ranks as one of the world's most important examples of Christian architecture. Visitors marveled at the church's enormous dome, which they likened to the heavens encircling the earth, and they expressed awe at the gold, silver, gems, precious stones, and thousands of lamps that decorated and illuminated Hagia Sophia. Over time, the church even acquired a reputation for working miraculous cures: its columns and doors reportedly healed the illnesses of people who stood beside them or rubbed against them.

Justinian's most significant political contribution was his codification of Roman law. The origins of Roman law go back to the time of the kings of Rome, and legal scholars worked to systematize Roman law during the Roman republic and the early empire. Almost immediately upon taking the throne, Justinian ordered a systematic review of Roman law that was more thorough than any that had taken place before. On the basis of this work, he issued the *Corpus iuris civilis (Body of the Civil Law)*, which immediately won recognition as the definitive codification of Roman law. Later emperors updated Roman law by adding new provisions, but Justinian's code continued to serve as a source of legal inspiration. Through Justinian's code, for example, Roman law influenced civil law codes throughout much of western Europe.

Justinian's Code

Justinian's most ambitious venture was his effort to reconquer the western Roman empire from Germanic peoples and reestablish Roman authority throughout the Mediterranean basin. Beginning in 533 he sent his brilliant general Belisarius on military campaigns that returned Italy, Sicily, northwestern Africa, and southern Spain to imperial hands. By the end of his reign in 565, Justinian had reconstituted a good portion of the classical Roman empire.

Belisarius and Byzantine Conquests

Justinian's accomplishment, however, did not long survive his own rule. Byzantium simply did not possess the resources to sustain Belisarius's conquests. Reconstitution of

Justinian wears imperial purple robes in this mosaic from the church of San Vitale in Ravenna, which depicts him in the company of ecclesiastical, military, and court officials.

the Roman empire would have required a long-term occupation of reconquered regions and a costly reassertion of imperial authority. Yet Byzantine forces were unable to hold Rome itself for very long, and the city of Ravenna on Italy's Adriatic coast became the headquarters of Byzantine authority in the western Mediterranean. As a result, Ravenna possesses magnificent Byzantine art and architecture. But Justinian's dream of restoring Roman authority throughout the Mediterranean basin soon faded.

Indeed, Justinian's efforts clearly showed that the classical Roman empire was beyond recovery. While Justinian devoted his attention to the western Mediterranean, the Sasanids threatened Byzantium from the east and Slavic peoples approached from the north. Justinian's successors had no choice but to withdraw their resources from the western Mediterranean and redeploy them in the east. Even though Belisarius's reconquest of the western Roman empire was a spectacular military accomplishment, it was also something of an anachronism, since the lands of the eastern and western Mediterranean had already begun to follow different historical trajectories.

Islamic Conquests and Byzantine Revival

After the seventh century C.E., the emergence of Islam and the development of a powerful and expansive Islamic state (topics discussed in chapter 14) posed a serious challenge to Byzantium. Inspired by their Islamic faith, Arab peoples conquered the Sasanid empire and overran large portions of the Byzantine empire as well. By the mid-seventh century, Byzantine Syria, Palestine, Egypt, and north Africa had fallen

The interior of the church of Hagia Sophia ("Holy Wisdom"), built by Justinian and transformed into a mosque in the fifteenth century. The dome rises almost 60 meters (197 feet) above the floor, and its windows allow abundant light to enter the massive structure.

under Islamic rule. During the late seventh and early eighth centuries, Islamic forces threatened the heart of the empire and subjected Constantinople itself to prolonged siege (in 674–678 and again in 717–718). Byzantium resisted this northern thrust of Islam partly because of military technology. Byzantine forces used a weapon known as "Greek fire"—a devastating incendiary weapon compounded of sulphur, lime, and petroleum—which they launched at both the fleets and the ground forces of the invaders. Greek fire burned even when floating on water and thus created a serious hazard when deployed around wooden ships. On land it caused panic among enemy forces, since it was very difficult to extinguish and often burned troops to death. As a result of this defensive effort, the Byzantine empire retained its hold on Anatolia, Greece, and the Balkan region.

Though much reduced by the Islamic conquests, the Byzantine empire was more compact and manageable after the eighth century than was the far-flung realm of Justinian. Byzantine rulers responded to the challenge of Islam with political and social adjustments that strengthened the empire that remained in their hands. The most important innovation was the reorganization of Byzantine society under the *theme* system, which Byzantine rulers had tentatively experimented with during earlier periods of hostility with Sasanid Persia. The *theme* system placed an imperial province (*theme*) under the jurisdiction of a general, who assumed responsibility for both its

Imperial Organization

Illustration in a manuscript depicts Byzantine naval forces turning Greek fire on their Arab enemies.

military defense and its civil administration. Generals received their appointments from the imperial government, which closely supervised their activities to prevent decentralization of power and authority. Generals recruited armies from the ranks of free peasants, who received allotments of land in exchange for military service. The armies proved to be effective military forces, and the system as a whole strengthened the class of free peasants, which in turn solidified Byzantium's agricultural economy. The *theme* system enabled Byzantine forces to mobilize quickly and resist further Islamic advances and also undergirded the political order and social organization of the empire from the eighth through the twelfth century.

Indeed, strengthened by the *theme* system, Byzantium vastly expanded its influence between the late ninth and the late eleventh century. During the tenth century Byzantine forces shored up defenses in Anatolia and reconquered Syria from Arab Muslims. During the reign of Basil II (976–1025 C.E.), known as "Basil the Bulgar-Slayer," Byzantine armies turned west and crushed the neighboring Bulgars, who had built a large and expansive kingdom in the Balkans. After his victory at the battle of Kleidion in 1014 C.E., Basil reportedly commanded his forces to blind fourteen thousand Bulgarian survivors, though he spared one eye in a few who then guided the others home. By the mid-eleventh century the Byzantine empire embraced lands from Syria and Armenia in the east to southern Italy in the west, from the Danube River in the north to Cyprus and Crete in the south. Byzantine expansion brought in so much wealth that Basil was able to waive the collection of taxes for two years. Once again, Byzantium dominated the eastern Mediterranean.

Byzantium and Western Europe

Tensions between Byzantium and Western European States

While they went to war with their Arab Muslim and pagan Slavic neighbors, Byzantines also experienced tense ecclesiastical and political relations with their Christian counterparts in the western Mediterranean. The Christian church of Constantinople conducted its affairs in Greek and bowed to the will of the caesaropapist emperors, whereas the Christian church of Rome conducted its affairs in Latin and rejected imperial claims to oversee ecclesiastical matters. Ecclesiastical authorities in Byzantium regarded Roman Christians as poorly educated and uncouth. Church leaders in Rome considered their Byzantine counterparts subtle and learned but insincere and insufficiently wary of heresy.

Political grievances also strained relations between Byzantium and western European lands. During the fifth and sixth centuries, imperial authorities could do little more than watch as Germanic peoples established successor states to the western Roman empire. Visigoths, Vandals, Franks, and others imposed their rule on lands that Byzantine emperors regarded as their rightful inheritance. Worse yet, some of the upstart powers claimed imperial authority for themselves. In 800, for example, the Frankish ruler Charlemagne received an imperial crown from the pope in Rome, thereby directly challenging Byzantine claims to imperial authority over western lands. Charlemagne's empire soon dissolved, but in 962 Otto of Saxony lodged his own claim to rule as emperor over the western lands of the former Roman empire. Adding injury to insult, Otto then attacked lands in southern Italy that had been in Byzantine possession since the days of Justinian.

Liudprand of Cremona

The tenor of relations between Byzantium and western European lands emerges clearly from the report of an ambassador named Liudprand of Cremona, whom Otto sent on a diplomatic mission to Constantinople in 968. Liudprand described the Byzantine emperor as "a monstrosity of a man, a dwarf, fat-headed and with tiny mole's eyes; disfigured by a short, broad, thick beard half going gray; disgraced by a neck scarcely an inch long; piglike by reason of the big close bristles on his head." Liudprand despised Byzantine food, drink, dress, and shelter, and he denounced his diplomatic counterparts as slippery, scheming liars. He described Constantinople itself as a formerly prosperous and illustrious city that had become shabby, sleazy, and pretentious. In light of these attitudes, it is hardly surprising that Byzantium and western European lands experienced almost continuously strained relations until the fall of the Byzantine empire.

BYZANTINE ECONOMY AND SOCIETY

Byzantium dominated the political and military affairs of the eastern Mediterranean largely because of its strong economy. Ever since classical times, the territories embraced by the Byzantine empire had produced abundant agricultural surpluses, supported large numbers of crafts workers, and participated in trade with lands throughout the Mediterranean. The economic and social assets of the eastern Mediterranean did not disappear with the classical Roman empire. Instead, they continued to provide a solid material foundation for Byzantium, and they helped to make the Byzantine empire an economic powerhouse of the postclassical era.

Rural Economy and Society

Until its conquest by Arab forces, Egypt was the major source of grain for Byzantium. Afterward, Anatolia and the lower Danube region served as the imperial breadbasket. All these lands produced abundant harvests of wheat, which supported large populations in Constantinople, Thessaloniki, Antioch, Trebizond, and other major cities. Throughout most of Byzantium's existence, Constantinople was the largest city in Europe: between the fifth and the early thirteenth century, its population approached or exceeded one million people. Only on the basis of a reliable and productive agricultural economy was it possible for a city of this size to survive and flourish.

The Peasantry

Byzantine economy and society were strongest when the empire supported a large class of free peasants who owned small plots of land. Besides serving as the backbone of the Byzantine military system, free peasants cultivated their land intensively in hopes of improving their families' fortunes. As in other societies, however, wealthy individuals

Peasants—probably sharecroppers—receive seeds and tend to vineyards in this painting from a Byzantine manuscript.

and families sought to accumulate land, the principal source of wealth in Byzantium as elsewhere. Especially in the early centuries of the Byzantine empire, wealthy cultivators ran large estates and supervised the peasantry as a dependent class. Peasants did not become slaves, but neither did they remain entirely free. Sometimes they were bound to the land, forbidden to depart without permission of their lords. Other times they worked under sharecropping arrangements, whereby landlords contracted landless peasants to cultivate their lands in exchange for a large portion of the yield. Rarely did sharecroppers accumulate enough wealth to gain their independence: often they worked the same holdings for years—or for life—on terms set by the landlords.

The invasions of the sixth and seventh centuries broke up many large estates and afforded peasants an opportunity to rebuild small holdings. The *theme* system strengthened the free peasantry by making land available to those who performed military service. The imperial government also made periodic efforts to support free peasants and prevent wealthy landowners from gaining control over their lands. During the sixth, eighth, and tenth centuries in particular, Byzantine authorities limited the accumulation of land by wealthy classes and thereby strengthened the peasantry. Over the long term, however, wealthy landowners built ever larger estates. From the eleventh century onward, they transformed the peasants into an increasingly dependent class, and by the thirteenth century free peasants accounted for only a small portion of the rural population.

Decline of the Free Peasantry

Quite apart from its social effects, the accumulation of landholdings had important implications for financial and military affairs. Large estates did not contribute to imperial tax coffers at the rate of small peasants' holdings, since wealthy landowners had the influence to obtain concessions and exemptions. Moreover, the decline of the free peasantry diminished the pool of recruits available for service in military forces organized under the *theme* system. Large landowners raised forces from their estates, but they often deployed them to advance their own interests rather than those of the imperial government. Concentration of land and rural resources worked against the financial interests of the central government, and it caused political, military, and economic difficulties for the Byzantine state during the last three centuries of its existence.

Industry and Trade

In spite of social and economic problems, Byzantium remained a wealthy land. Byzantine prosperity derived both from the empire's productive capacity and from the importance of Constantinople as a center of trade.

Manufacturing Enterprises

Constantinople was already a major site of crafts and industry in classical times, and it became even more important as capital of the Byzantine empire. The city was home to many artisans and crafts workers, not to mention thousands of imperial officials and bureaucrats. Byzantine crafts workers enjoyed a reputation especially for their glassware, linen and woolen textiles, gems, jewelry, and fine work in gold and silver.

By the late sixth century, after the arrival of silkworms in monks' walking staffs and no doubt by other routes as well, crafts workers had added high-quality silk textiles to the list of products manufactured in the Byzantine empire. Silk was a most

A manuscript illustration depicts one Byzantine woman weaving cloth (left), while another spins thread (right). Both women veil their hair for modesty. Women workers were prominent in Byzantine textile production.

important addition to the economy, and Byzantium became the principal supplier of this fashionable fabric to lands in the Mediterranean basin. The silk industry was so important to the Byzantine economy that the government closely supervised every step in its production and sale. Regulations allowed individuals to participate in only one activity—such as weaving, dyeing, or sales—to prevent the creation of a monopoly in the industry by a few wealthy or powerful entrepreneurs.

Trade

Trade also helped to sustain the Byzantine economy. Situated astride routes going east and west as well as north and south, Constantinople served as the main clearinghouse for trade in the western part of Eurasia. The merchants of Constantinople maintained direct commercial links with manufacturers and merchants in central Asia, Russia, Scandinavia, northern Europe, and the lands of the Black Sea and the Mediterranean basin. Even after the early Islamic conquests, Byzantine merchants dealt regularly with their Muslim counterparts in Persia, Syria, Palestine, and Egypt except during periods of outright war between Byzantium and Islamic states. Byzantium dominated trade to such an extent that trading peoples recognized the Byzantine gold coin, the *bezant,* as the standard currency of the Mediterranean basin for more than half a millennium, from the sixth through the twelfth centuries.

Byzantium drew enormous wealth simply from the control of trade and the levying of customs duties on merchandise that passed through its lands. More important, Byzantium served as the western anchor of a Eurasian trading network that revived the silk roads of classical times. Silk and porcelain came to Constantinople from China, spices from India and southeast Asia. Carpets arrived from Persia, woolen textiles from western Europe, and timber, furs, honey, amber, and slaves came from Russia and Scandinavia. Byzantine subjects consumed some commodities from distant lands, but they redistributed most merchandise, often after adding to its value by further processing—by fashioning jewelry out of gems imported from India, for example, or by dyeing raw woolen cloth imported from western Europe.

The Organization of Trade

Banks and business partnerships helped to fuel Byzantine trade. Banks advanced loans to individuals seeking to launch business ventures and thus made trade possible even when merchants did not personally possess large supplies of liquid wealth. Byzantine merchants often formed partnerships, which allowed them to pool their resources and limit their risks. Neither banking nor partnership was an altogether new technique: both had origins in classical Mediterranean business practices. Yet Byzantine businessmen made much more extensive use than their predecessors had of banking and cooperative partnerships, which provided both support and stimulus for a dynamic commercial economy.

Urban Life

Constantinople had no rival among Byzantine cities. Subjects of the Byzantine empire referred to it simply as "the City." The heart of the City was the imperial palace, which

A manuscript illustration from the ninth century depicts Byzantine shipbuilders at work.

Sources from the Past

The Wealth and Commerce of Constantinople

The Spanish rabbi Benjamin of Tudela traveled throughout Europe, north Africa, and southwest Asia between 1165 and 1173 C.E. He may have ventured as far as India, and he mentioned both India and China in his travel account. His main purpose was to record the conditions of Jewish communities, but he also described the many lands and about three hundred cities that he visited. His travels took place during an era of political decline for the Byzantine empire, yet he still found Constantinople a flourishing and prosperous city.

The circumference of the city of Constantinople is eighteen miles; half of it is surrounded by the sea, and half by land, and it is situated upon two arms of the sea, one coming from the sea of Russia [the Black Sea], and one from the sea of Sepharad [the Mediterranean].

All sorts of merchants come here from the land of Babylon, from the land of Shinar [Mesopotamia], from Persia, Media [western Iran], and all the sovereignty of the land of Egypt, from the land of Canaan [Palestine], and the empire of Russia, from Hungary, Patzinakia [Ukraine], Khazaria [southern Russia], and the land of Lombardy [northern Italy] and Sepharad [Spain].

Constantinople is a busy city, and merchants come to it from every country by sea or land, and there is none like it in the world except Baghdad, the great city of Islam. In Constantinople is the church of Hagia Sophia, and the seat of the pope of the Greeks, since Greeks do not obey the pope of Rome. There are also as many churches as there are days of the year. . . . And in this church [Hagia Sophia] there are pillars of gold and silver, and lamps of silver and gold more than a man can count.

Close to the walls of the palace is also a place of amusement belonging to the emperor, which is called the Hippodrome, and every year on the anniversary of the birth of Jesus the emperor gives a great entertainment there. And in that place men from all the races of the world come before the emperor and empress with jugglery and without jugglery, and they introduce lions, leopards, bears, and wild asses, and they engage them in combat with one another; and the same thing is done with birds. No entertainment like this is to be found in any other land. . . .

From every part of the Byzantine empire tribute is brought here every year, and they fill strongholds with garments of silk, purple, and gold. Like unto these storehouses and this wealth there is nothing in the whole world to be found. It is said that the tribute of the city amounts every year to 20,000 gold pieces, derived both from the rents of shops and markets and from the tribute of merchants who enter by sea or land.

The Greek inhabitants are very rich in gold and precious stones, and they go clothed in garments of silk and gold embroidery, and they ride horses and look like princes. Indeed, the land is very rich in all cloth stuffs and in bread, meat, and wine.

Wealth like that of Constantinople is not to be found in the whole world. Here also are men learned in all the books of the Greeks, and they eat and drink, every man under his vine and his fig-tree.

SOURCE: Benjamin of Tudela. *The Itinerary of Benjamin of Tudela*. Trans. by M. N. Adler. London: H. Frowde, 1907. (Translation slightly modified.)

How is it possible to account for the prosperity that Benjamin of Tudela found in Constantinople?

employed twenty thousand workers as palace staff. Peacocks strutted through gardens filled with sculptures and fountains. Most famous was a gold fountain in the shape of a pineapple that spouted wine for imperial guests.

Aristocrats maintained enormous palaces that included courtyards, reception halls, libraries, chapels, and quarters for members of the extended family as well as servants and slaves. Women lived in separate apartments and did not receive male visitors from

Housing in Constantinople

outside the household. Indeed, women often did not participate in banquets and parties, especially when wine flowed freely or when the affairs were likely to become so festive that they could compromise a woman's honor.

The less privileged classes of Constantinople occupied less splendid dwellings. Artisans and crafts workers usually lived in rooms above their shops, while clerks and government officials lived in multistory apartment buildings. Workers and the poor occupied dangerous and rickety tenements, sharing kitchens and sanitary facilities with their neighbors.

Attractions of Constantinople

Even for the poor, though, the City had its attractions. As the heir to Rome, Constantinople was a city of baths, which were sites of relaxation and exercise as well as hygienic bathing. Taverns and restaurants offered settings for social gatherings—checkers, chess, and dice games were especially popular activities at taverns—and theaters provided entertainment in the form of song, dance, and striptease. Mass entertainment took place in the Hippodrome, a large stadium adjacent to the imperial palace. There Byzantine subjects watched athletic matches, contests between wild animals, and circuses featuring clowns, jugglers, acrobats, and dwarfs.

Greens and Blues

Most popular of the City's pastimes were the chariot races that took place in the Hippodrome. Spectators' passions for chariot teams ran high, and until the seventh century they often contributed to public disturbances. Racing fans formed two factions—the Greens and the Blues—that pursued their rivalry well beyond the Hippodrome. Greens and Blues frequently fought in the streets and constantly sought to influence imperial officials to favor one group over the other. On one occasion, Greens and Blues united and mounted a serious popular uprising against the high taxes imposed by Justinian. In 532 they seized the Hippodrome and proclaimed a new emperor. Belisarius's army quelled the disturbance, but only after killing thousands of rioters. The rebellion left Constantinople in shambles, and Justinian took the opportunity to rebuild the city on a lavish scale. By the late seventh century, the rivalry between Greens and Blues had faded. The parties remained, but they increasingly took on the character of civic societies, and leaders of the two groups became respected officials at the imperial court.

CLASSICAL HERITAGE AND ORTHODOX CHRISTIANITY

The first Christian emperor of the Roman empire gave both his name and his faith to Constantinople. Like the Byzantine state, however, Byzantine Christianity developed along distinctive lines, and it became a faith different from the early Christianity of the Roman empire. The philosophy and literature of classical Greece had a much deeper influence in Byzantium than in western Europe, and the classical legacy helped to shape Byzantine education and cultural development as well as Orthodox Christianity. Byzantine church leaders disagreed with their western counterparts on matters of doctrine, ritual, and church authority. By the mid-eleventh century, differences between the eastern and western churches had become so great that their leaders formally divided Mediterranean Christianity into the Eastern Orthodox and Roman Catholic churches.

The Legacy of Classical Greece

Although local inhabitants spoke Greek, the official language of early Constantinople was Latin, the language of Rome. The connection between Byzantium and Rome was apparent in Justinian's code of laws, which appeared in Latin. After the sixth century, however, Greek replaced Latin as the language of government in the Byzantine empire. Byzantine scholars often did not learn to read Latin, and they drew intellectual inspiration from the New Testament (originally composed in Greek) and the philosophy and literature of classical Greece rather than classical Rome.

Byzantine Education

The legacy of classical Greece was especially noticeable in Byzantine education. An educational system was necessary because of the large bureaucracy that administered the empire: government machinery called for large numbers of literate and intelligent individuals. Byzantine aristocrats often hired tutors to provide private instruction for their children, girls as well as boys. But the bureaucratic workforce emerged mostly from a state-organized school system that offered a primary education in reading, writing, and grammar, followed by studies of classical Greek literature, philosophy, and science.

Although most peasants and many urban workers had no formal education, basic literacy was widespread in Byzantine society. Alongside the bureaucrats, Byzantine merchants, manufacturers, clergy, and military personnel usually had at least a primary education. At the pinnacle of the state educational system was a school of higher learning in Constantinople that offered advanced instruction in law, medicine, and philosophy. This school functioned almost continuously from its founding in 425 C.E. until the end of the Byzantine empire more than one thousand years later in 1453.

Byzantine Scholarship

Like the educational system, Byzantine scholarship also reflected the cultural legacy of classical Greece. Byzantine scholars concentrated on the humanities—literature, history, and philosophy—rather than on the natural sciences or medicine. They produced commentaries on Homer, Plato, Aristotle, and other prominent figures, and their works served as textbooks studied in schools alongside writings from classical times. Byzantines with a literary education considered themselves the direct heirs of classical Greece, and they went to great lengths to preserve and transmit the classical legacy. Indeed, almost all literary and philosophical works of classical Greece that survive have come down to the present in copies made between the tenth and twelfth centuries in the Byzantine empire.

The Byzantine Church

Church and State

The most distinctive feature of Byzantine Christianity was its close relationship with the imperial government. From the time of Constantine on, caesaropapist emperors participated actively in religious and theological matters. Constantine himself intervened in theological debates, even when the issues at stake had little or no direct political implication. In 325 C.E., for example, Constantine organized the Council of Nicaea, which brought together bishops, spokesmen, and leaders from all the important Christian churches in order to consider the views of the Arians. Followers of a priest from Alexandria named Arius (250–336 C.E.), the Arians taught that Jesus had been a mortal human being and that he was a creation of God rather than a divine being coeternal with God. Yet many Christian theologians held to the contrary: that in a unique and mysterious way Jesus was both a mortal human being and a manifestation of God himself, that Jesus simultaneously possessed fully human and fully divine natures. Although he originally favored Arian views, Constantine came to accept the alternative and personally attended sessions of the Council of Nicaea in order to support it. His presence encouraged the council to endorse his preferred view as orthodox and to condemn Arianism as heresy.

Throughout Byzantine history the emperors treated the church as a department of state. They appointed individuals to serve as patriarch of Constantinople—the highest ecclesiastical official in the Byzantine church, counterpart of the pope in

Rome—and they instructed patriarchs, bishops, and priests to deliver sermons that supported imperial policy and encouraged obedience to imperial authorities. This caesaropapism was a source of constant conflict between imperial and ecclesiastical authorities, and it also had the potential to generate large-scale dissent and protest when imperial views clashed with those of the larger society.

Iconoclasm

The most divisive ecclesiastical policy implemented by Byzantine emperors was iconoclasm, inaugurated by Emperor Leo III (reigned 717–741 C.E.). By the time of Leo's rule, Byzantium had a long tradition of producing icons—paintings of Jesus, saints, and other figures of religious significance—many of which were splendid works of art. For most theologians these icons served a useful purpose in that they inspired the popular imagination and encouraged reverence for holy personages. Leo, however, became convinced that the veneration of religious images was sinful, tantamount to the worship of physical idols. In 726 C.E. he embarked on the policy of iconoclasm (which literally means "the breaking of icons"), destroying religious images and prohibiting their use in churches. The policy immediately sparked protests and riots throughout the empire, since icons were extremely popular among the laity. Debates about iconoclasm raged in Byzantium for more than a century. Only in 843 did the iconoclasts abandon their efforts. Meanwhile, the controversy demonstrated once again the willingness of Byzantine emperors to involve themselves directly in religious and theological matters.

In its theology, Byzantine Christianity reflected the continuing influence of classical Greek philosophy. Christianity had originally emerged from Jewish sources. As it attracted adherents in the Roman empire, theologians sought ways to harmonize

This illustration from a psalter prepared about 900 C.E. depicts an iconoclast whitewashing an image of Jesus painted on a wall.

Christianity with other, long-established cultural traditions, notably Greek philosophy. A faith embracing both Christian revelation and Greek reason, they recognized, would have a powerful appeal.

Greek Philosophy and Byzantine Theology

The influence of Greek philosophy in Christian theology was especially prominent in Greek-speaking Byzantium. Theologians invested a great deal of time and intellectual energy in the examination of religious questions from a philosophical point of view. They looked to classical philosophy, for example, when seeking to understand the nature of Jesus and the extent to which he possessed both human and divine characteristics. Although these debates often became extremely technical, they illustrate the continuing influence of classical Greek philosophy. Debates about Jesus' nature represented an effort to understand Christian doctrine in light of the terms and concepts that classical philosophers had employed in their analysis of the world. A school maintained by the patriarch of Constantinople provided instruction for clergy and church officials in advanced theology of this sort. Though it differed in many ways from Mediterranean society of classical times, Byzantium built its own cultural and religious traditions on a solid classical foundation.

Monasticism and Popular Piety

Caesaropapist emperors, powerful patriarchs, and other high church officials concerned themselves with theological and ritual matters and rarely dealt directly with the lay population of the Byzantine church. For their part the Byzantine laity had little interest in fine points of theology or high-level church administration, and they positively resented policies like iconoclasm that infringed on cherished patterns of worship. For religious inspiration, the laity looked less to the church hierarchy than to the local monasteries.

Asceticism

Byzantine monasticism grew out of the efforts of devout individuals to lead especially holy lives. Drawing inspiration from early Christian ascetics in Egypt, Mesopotamia, and Persia, these individuals observed regimes of extreme asceticism and self-denial. Some abandoned society altogether and went to live in the desert or in caves as hermits. Others dedicated themselves to celibacy, fasting, and prayer. During the fifth century a few men and at least two women demonstrated their ascetic commitments by perching for years at a time atop tall pillars. St. Simeon Stylite, the first and most famous of these "pillar saints," attracted the attention of admirers from as far away as Gaul.

Byzantine Monasticism and St. Basil

Because of the extreme dedication of hermits and ascetics, disciples often gathered around them and established communities of men and women determined to follow their example. These communities became the earliest monasteries of the Byzantine church. They had few rules until St. Basil of Caesarea (329–379 C.E.), the patriarch of Constantinople during the mid-fourth century, urged them to adopt reforms that enhanced their effectiveness. In Basilian monasteries, monks and nuns gave up their personal possessions and lived communally. They obeyed the rule of elected superiors, and all community members devoted themselves to work and prayer. After the fourth century, Basilian monasticism spread rapidly throughout the Byzantine empire.

Mt. Athos

Unlike their counterparts in western Europe and other lands, Byzantine monasteries for the most part did not become centers of education, study, learning, and scholarship. Yet monasteries under the rule of St. Basil had a reputation for piety and devotion that endeared them to the Byzantine laity. Basilian monks went to great lengths in search of mystical union with God through meditation and prayer. Some employed special techniques such as controlled breathing and intensely focused gazing to bring divine illumination. Others retired to remote destinations to lead a strict

Sources from the Past

Anna Comnena on the Suppression of Bogomil Heretics

Anna Comnena (1083–1148), daughter of the Byzantine emperor Alexius I (reigned 1081–1118), wrote the Alexiad, *a laudatory history of her father's reign. In the following selection, she discusses his prosecution in 1110 of Bogomil heretics, who revived the dualist teachings of the Manichaeans. Her account makes it clear that the caesaropapist Byzantine emperors took seriously their commitment to the Orthodox church and their obligation to protect its interests.*

Later . . . there arose an extraordinary "cloud of heretics," a new hostile group, hitherto unknown to the Church . . . Apparently it was in existence before my father's time, but was unperceived (for the Bogomils' sect is most adept at feigning virtue). No worldly hairstyles are to be seen among Bogomils: their wickedness is hidden beneath cloak and cowl. Your Bogomil wears a somber look; muffled up to the nose, he walks with a stoop, quietly muttering to himself—but inside he's a ravening wolf. This unpleasant race, like a serpent lurking in its hole, was brought to the light and lured out by my father with magical incantations. . . .

The fame of the Bogomils had by now spread to all parts, for the impious sect was controlled with great cunning by a certain monk called Basil. He had twelve followers whom he called "apostles" and also dragged along with him certain female disciples, women of bad character, utterly depraved. In all quarters he made his wicked influence felt and when the evil, like some consuming fire, devoured many souls, the emperor could no longer bear it. He instituted a thorough inquiry into the heresy. . . .

. . . Alexius condemned the heretics out of hand: chorus and chorus-leader alike were to suffer death by burning. When the Bogomils had been hunted down and brought together in one place, some clung to the heresy, but others denied the charges completely, protesting strongly against their accusers and rejecting the Bogomilian heresy with scorn. . . .

The emperor glared at them and said, "Two pyres will have to be lit today. By one a cross will be planted firmly in the ground. Then a choice will be offered to all: those who are prepared to die for their Christian faith will sepa-

rate themselves from the rest and take up position by the pyre with the cross; the Bogomilian adherents will be thrown on the other. Surely it is better that even Christians should die than live to be hounded down as Bogomils and offend the conscience of the majority. Go away, then, all of you, to whichever pyre you choose". . .

A huge crowd gathered and stood all about them. Fires were then lit, burning seven times more fiercely than usual. . . . The flames leapt to the heavens. By one pyre stood the cross. Each of the condemned was given his choice, for all were to be burnt. Now that escape was clearly impossible, the orthodox to a man moved over to the pyre with the cross, truly prepared to suffer martyrdom; the godless adherents of the abominable heresy went off to the other. Just as they were about to be thrown on the flames, all the bystanders broke into mourning for the Christians; they were filled with indignation against the emperor (they did not know of his plan). But an order came from him just in time to stop the executioners. Alexius had in this way obtained firm evidence of those who were really Bogomils. The Christians, who were victims of calumny, he released after giving them much advice; the rest [i.e., the Bogomils] were committed once again to prison, but the [Bogomil] "apostles" were kept apart. Later he sent for some of these men every day and personally taught them, with frequent exhortations to abandon their abominable cult. . . . And some did change for the better and were freed from prison, but others died in their heresy, still incarcerated, although they were supplied with plentiful food and clothing.

SOURCE: Anna Comnena. *The Alexiad of Anna Comnena.* Trans. by E. R. A. Sewter. Harmondsworth: Penguin, 1969, pp. 496–505. (Translation slightly modified.)

Why did Byzantine rulers go to such lengths to suppress heresy?

existence. Most famous of the austere monasteries are those of Mt. Athos, a cold and windswept peninsula in northern Greece that has been the site of monasteries since the ninth century C.E. Since the eleventh century, monastic authorities have made Mt. Athos off-limits for all females, both human and animal, out of concern that they might inspire carnal thoughts among the monks. The strict devotion of the monks of Mt. Athos and other Basilian monasteries inspired piety among the Byzantine laity because the monks represented a religious faith more immediate and meaningful than that of the theologians and ecclesiastical bureaucrats of Constantinople.

Monks and nuns also provided social services to their communities. They provided spiritual counsel to local laity, and they organized relief efforts by bringing food and medical attention to communities struck by disasters. They won the support of the Byzantine populace, too, when they vigorously opposed the policy of iconoclasm and fought to restore icons to churches and monasteries. Tensions sometimes arose between clergy and laity because monasteries often owned extensive tracts of land, and the monks had different economic interests from the peasants who worked the land. Nevertheless, by setting examples of devotion and by tending to the needs and interests of the laity, monks helped to maintain support for their faith in the Byzantine empire.

Tensions between Eastern and Western Christianity

Byzantine Christianity developed in tension particularly with the Christian faith of western Europe. During the centuries following Constantine's legalization of Christianity, church leaders in Jerusalem, Alexandria, Antioch, Constantinople, and Rome exercised great influence in the larger Christian community. After Arab peoples conquered most of southwest Asia and introduced Islam there in the seventh century, the influence of the patriarchs in Jerusalem, Alexandria, and Antioch declined, leaving only Constantinople and Rome as the principal centers of Christian authority.

The tensions that developed between Constantinople and Rome mirrored political strains between Byzantine and western European societies. The specific issues that divided the two Christian communities, however, were religious and theological. One of them was the iconoclastic movement of the eighth and ninth centuries. Western theologians regarded religious images as perfectly appropriate aids to devotion and resented Byzantine claims to the contrary, whereas the iconoclasts took offense at the efforts of their Roman counterparts to have images restored in Byzantium.

Constantinople and Rome

In later centuries, Christian churches based in Constantinople and Rome disagreed on many other points. Some ritual and doctrinal differences concerned forms of worship and the precise wording of theological teachings—relatively minor issues that by themselves need not have caused deep division in the larger Christian community. Byzantine theologians objected, for example, to the fact that western priests shaved their beards and used unleavened instead of leavened bread when saying Mass. Other differences concerned substantive theological matters such as the precise relationship between God, Jesus, and the Holy Spirit—all regarded as manifestations of God by most Christian theologians.

Alongside these ritual and doctrinal differences, the Byzantine patriarchs and Roman popes disputed their respective rights and powers. Patriarchs argued for the autonomy of all major Christian jurisdictions, including that of Constantinople, while popes asserted the primacy of Rome as the sole seat of authority for all Christendom. Ultimately, relations became so strained that the eastern and western churches went separate ways. In 1054 C.E. the patriarch and pope mutually excommunicated each other, each refusing to recognize the other's church as properly Christian. Despite

Schism

efforts at reconciliation, the resulting schism between eastern and western churches persists to the present day. In recognition of the split, historians refer to the eastern Christian church after 1054 as the Eastern Orthodox church and its western counterpart as the Roman Catholic church.

THE INFLUENCE OF BYZANTIUM IN EASTERN EUROPE

Byzantines called themselves *Romaioi* ("Romans"), and aristocrats sometimes traced their lineage to ancestors who went to Constantinople with Constantine himself. Yet by about 1000 C.E., Byzantium differed profoundly from Mediterranean society of classical times. Under Roman rule the Mediterranean basin had formed a coherent political and economic unit, as trade and cultural exchanges linked all lands and peoples of the region. By the second millennium C.E., however, a dynamic society founded on the Islamic faith had seized control of the lands on the Mediterranean's southern and eastern rims, and Byzantines and western Europeans contested the northern rim. Hemmed in and increasingly pressured by Islamic and western European societies, Byzantium entered a period of decline beginning about the late eleventh century.

As its Mediterranean influence waned, however, Byzantium turned its attention to eastern Europe and Russia. Through political, commercial, and cultural relations, Byzantium decisively influenced the history of Slavic peoples. The Byzantine state itself came to an end in the fifteenth century C.E. But because of the Byzantine commonwealth—the larger collection of societies in eastern Europe and the eastern Mediterranean basin that developed under Byzantine political, economic, and cultural influence during the postclassical era—the legacy of Byzantium survives and continues to shape the lives of millions of people in Russia and eastern Europe.

Domestic Problems and Foreign Pressures

When Basil II, "the Bulgar-Slayer," died in 1025 C.E., the Byzantine empire was a political, military, and economic dynamo. Within fifty years, however, the empire was suffering from serious internal weaknesses and had endured a series of military reverses. In fact, it had entered a long period of gradual but sustained decline from which it never fully recovered. Both domestic and foreign problems help to explain this decline.

Social Problems   Domestic problems arose, ironically, from the success of the *theme* system. Generals who governed the *themes* were natural allies of local aristocrats who held large tracts of land. Generals and their offspring intermarried with the local aristocracies, creating an elite class with tremendous military, political, social, and economic power. Some of these powerful families resisted the policies of the imperial government and even mounted rebellions against central authorities. The rebels never managed to defeat the imperial forces, but their revolts seriously disrupted local economies. Moreover, the elite class accumulated vast estates that placed the free peasantry under increasing pressure. Formerly the backbone of Byzantium's military system and its agricultural economy, by the mid-eleventh century the free peasantry was declining both in numbers and in prosperity. As a result, Byzantine military forces had fewer recruits available for service, and declining tax receipts from free peasants caused fiscal problems for the imperial government.

Challenges from the West   As domestic problems mounted, Byzantium also faced fresh foreign challenges. From the west came representatives of a dynamic and expanding western European so-

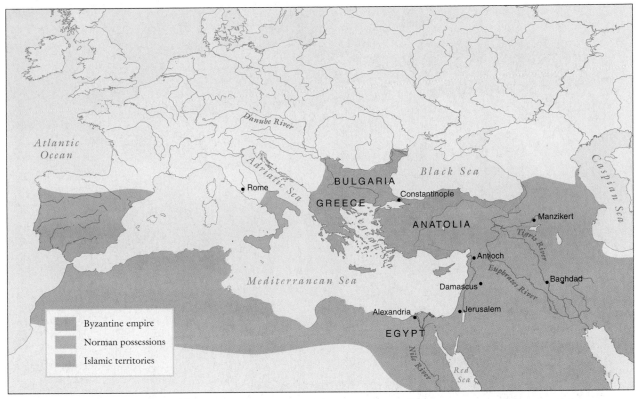

MAP [13.2]
The Byzantine empire and its neighbors, about 1100 C.E.

For an interactive version of this map, go to www.mhhe.com/bentley3ch13maps.

ciety. Beginning in the eleventh century, vigorous economic development in western Europe supported a remarkable round of military and political expansion. During the early eleventh century, the Normans—a Scandinavian people who had seized Normandy (in northern France) and settled there—established themselves as an independent power in southern Italy. By midcentury Norman adventurers led by Robert Guiscard had taken control of southern Italy and expelled Byzantine authorities there.

During the twelfth and thirteenth centuries, the Normans and other western European peoples mounted a series of crusades—vast military campaigns intended to recapture Jerusalem and other sites holy to Christians from Muslims—and took the opportunity to carve out states in the heart of the Byzantine empire. Venetian merchants even managed to divert the fourth crusade (1202–1204) from its original mission in the eastern Mediterranean to Constantinople. Venetians had become prominent in the commercial life of the eastern Mediterranean, and they viewed the fourth crusade as an opportunity to strengthen their position against Byzantine competition. As it happened, the expedition never got beyond Constantinople, which crusaders conquered and sacked in 1204. Byzantine forces recaptured the capital in 1261, but the destruction of Constantinople dealt the Byzantine empire a blow from which it never completely recovered.

As Europeans expanded into Byzantine territory from the west, nomadic Turkish peoples invaded from the east. Most important among them were the Muslim Saljuqs, who beginning in the eleventh century sent waves of invaders into Anatolia. Given the military and financial problems of the Byzantine empire, the Saljuqs found Anatolia ripe for plunder. In 1071 they subjected the Byzantine army to a demoralizing defeat at the battle of Manzikert. Byzantine factions then turned on each other

Challenges from the East

During the sack of Constantinople in 1204, crusading forces seized and carted away Byzantine treasures of all sorts—including the great bronze horses that now stand over the entrance to St. Mark's basilica in Venice.

in civil war, allowing the Saljuqs almost free rein in Anatolia. By the late twelfth century, the Saljuqs had seized much of Anatolia, and crusaders from western Europe held most of the remainder.

The loss of Anatolia—the principal source of Byzantine grain, wealth, and military forces—sealed the fate of the Byzantine empire. A territorially truncated Byzantium survived until the mid-fifteenth century, but the late Byzantine empire enjoyed little autonomy and continually faced fresh challenges from Italian merchants, western European adventurers, and Turkish nomads. In 1453, after a long era of decline, the Byzantine empire came to an end when Ottoman Turks captured Constantinople and absorbed its territories into their own expanding realm.

Early Relations between Byzantium and Slavic Peoples

By the time Constantinople fell, Byzantine traditions had deeply influenced the political and cultural development of Slavic peoples in eastern Europe and Russia. Close relations between Byzantium and Slavic peoples date from the sixth century. When Justinian deployed Byzantium's military resources in the western Mediterranean, Slavic peoples from the north took advantage of the opportunity to move into Byzantine territory. Serbs and Croats moved into the Balkan peninsula, and Bulgars established a powerful kingdom in the lower Danube region.

Relations between Byzantium and Bulgaria were especially tense. By the eighth century, however, as a result of its wealth and sophisticated diplomacy, Byzantium had begun to influence Bulgarian politics and society. Byzantine emperors recognized Bulgarian rulers, enhancing their status as legitimate sovereigns. Byzantium and Bulgaria entered into political, commercial, and cultural relations. Members of Bulgarian ruling families often went to Constantinople for a formal education in Greek language and literature and followed Byzantine examples in organizing their court and capital.

Byzantium also sent missionaries to Balkan lands, and Bulgars and other Slavic peoples began to convert to Orthodox Christianity. The most famous of the missionaries to the Slavs were Saints Cyril and Methodius, two brothers from Thessaloniki in Greece. During the mid-ninth century Cyril and Methodius conducted missions in Bulgaria and Moravia (which in-

Cyril and Methodius

This illustration from a twelfth-century manuscript depicts ninth-century incursions of Bulgarians into Byzantine territory, culminating in a lecture by the Bulgarian king to the Byzantine emperor, shown here with bound hands.

cluded much of the modern Czech, Slovakian, and Hungarian territories). While there, they devised an alphabet, known as the Cyrillic alphabet, for the previously illiterate Slavic peoples. Though adapted from written Greek, the Cyrillic alphabet represented the sounds of Slavic languages more precisely than did the Greek, and it remained in use in much of eastern Europe until supplanted by the Roman alphabet in the twentieth century. In Russia and most other parts of the former Soviet Union, the Cyrillic alphabet survives to the present day.

Missions to the Slavs

The creation of a written Slavic language enabled Slavic peoples to organize complex political structures and develop sophisticated traditions of thought and literature. More immediately, the Cyrillic alphabet stimulated conversion to Orthodox Christianity. Missionaries translated the Christian scriptures and church rituals into Slavonic, and Cyrillic writing helped them explain Christian values and ideas in Slavic terms. Meanwhile, schools organized by missionaries ensured that Slavs would receive religious instruction alongside their introduction to basic literacy. As a result, Orthodox Christianity deeply influenced the cultural traditions of many Slavic peoples.

Byzantium and Russia

North of Bulgaria another Slavic people began to organize large states: the Russians. About the mid-ninth century Russians created several principalities governed from thriving trading centers, notably Kiev. Strategically situated on the Dnieper River along the main trade route linking Scandinavia and Byzantium, Kiev became a wealthy and powerful center, and it dominated much of the territory between the Volga and the Dnieper from the tenth to the thirteenth century. Russian merchants visited Constantinople in large numbers and became well acquainted with Byzantine society. Russian princes sought alliances with Byzantine rulers and began to express an interest in Orthodox Christianity.

The Conversion of Prince Vladimir

About 989 Prince Vladimir of Kiev converted to Orthodox Christianity and ordered his subjects to follow his example. Vladimir was no paragon of virtue: he lauded drunkenness and reportedly maintained a harem of eight hundred girls. After his conversion, however, Byzantine influences flowed rapidly into Russia. Cyrillic writing, literacy, and Orthodox missions all spread quickly throughout Russia. Byzantine teachers traveled north to establish schools, and Byzantine priests conducted services for Russian converts. For two centuries Kiev served as a conduit for the spread of Byzantine cultural and religious influence in Russia.

Byzantine art and architecture dominated Kiev and other Russian cities. Icons in the Byzantine style encouraged popular piety, and religious images became a principal form of Russian artistic expression. The onion domes that are a distinctive feature of early Russian churches were the result of architects' efforts to imitate the domed structures of Constantinople using wood as their principal building material.

The Growth of Kiev

The princes of Kiev established firm, caesaropapist control over the Russian Orthodox church—so called to distinguish it from the Eastern Orthodox church of the Byzantine empire. They also drew inspiration from Byzantine legal tradition and compiled a written law code for their lands. By controlling trade with Byzantium and other lands, they gained financial resources to build a flourishing society. In the eleventh century Kiev reportedly had four hundred churches and eight large marketplaces. By the early twelfth century its population approached thirty thousand, and a fire in 1124 consumed six hundred churches.

Eventually, Russians even claimed to inherit the imperial mantle of Byzantium. According to a popular theory of the sixteenth century, Moscow was the world's third Rome: the first Rome had fallen to Germanic invaders in the fifth century, whereas the second Rome, Constantinople, had fallen to the Turks a thousand years later. Moscow survived as the third Rome, the cultural and religious beacon that would guide the world to Orthodox Christian righteousness. Inspired by this theory, missionaries took their Russian Orthodox faith to distant lands. During the sixteenth and later centuries, they brought Siberia into the fold of the Orthodox church, crossed the Bering Strait, and dispatched missions to Alaska and even northern California. Thus, long after the collapse of the eastern Roman empire, the Byzantine legacy continued to work its influence through the outward reach of the Russian Orthodox church.

The Byzantine empire originated as a survivor of the classical era. Byzantium inherited a hardy economy, a set of governing institutions, an imperial bureaucracy, an official religion, an established church, and a rich cultural tradition from classical Mediterranean society and the Roman empire. Byzantine leaders drew heavily on this legacy as they dealt with new challenges. Throughout Byzantine history, classical inspiration was especially noticeable in the imperial office, the bureaucracy, the church, and the educational system. Yet in many ways Byzantium changed profoundly over the course of its thousand-year history. After the seventh century the Byzantine empire shrank dramatically in size, and after the eleventh century it faced relentless foreign pressure from western Europeans and nomadic Turkish peoples. Changing times also brought transformations in Byzantine social and economic organization. Yet from the fifth to the twelfth century and beyond, Byzantium brought political stability and economic prosperity to the eastern Mediterranean basin, and Byzantine society served as a principal anchor supporting commercial and cultural exchanges in the postclassical world. Through its political, economic, and cultural influence, Byzantium also helped shape the development of the larger Byzantine commonwealth in eastern Europe and the eastern Mediterranean basin.

CHRONOLOGY

313–337	Reign of Constantine
325	Council of Nicaea
329–379	Life of St. Basil of Caesarea
340	Transfer of Roman government to Constantinople
527–565	Reign of Justinian
717–741	Reign of Leo III
726–843	Iconoclastic controversy
ninth century	Missions of St. Cyril and St. Methodius to the Slavs
976–1025	Reign of Basil II, "the Bulgar-Slayer"
989	Conversion of Prince Vladimir of Kiev to Orthodox Christianity
1054	Beginning of the schism between the eastern and western Christian churches
1071	Battle of Manzikert
1202–1204	Fourth crusade
1453	Fall of Constantinople

FOR FURTHER READING

Peter Arnott. *The Byzantines and Their World*. New York, 1973. A lively, popular, personal vision of Byzantine history.

Louis Bréhier. *The Life and Death of Byzantium*. Trans. by M. Vaughan. Amsterdam, 1977. A detailed political history of the Byzantine empire.

Averil Cameron. *The Mediterranean World in Late Antiquity, A.D. 395–600*. London, 1993. A thoughtful synthesis that places Byzantium in the context of the late Roman empire.

Francis Dvornik. *Byzantine Missions among the Slavs: SS. Constantine-Cyril and Methodius*. New Brunswick, 1970. Deals with the spread of Orthodox Christianity to eastern Europe.

John V. A. Fine Jr. *The Early Medieval Balkans: A Critical Survey from the Sixth to the Late Twelfth Century*. Ann Arbor, 1983. An excellent introduction to Balkan history in the postclassical era.

Garth Fowden. *Empire to Commonwealth: Consequences of Monotheism in Late Antiquity*. Princeton, 1993. A provocative volume that interprets Byzantine political and cultural development as a monotheist Christian society.

Deno John Geanakoplos. *Byzantium: Church, Society, and Civilization Seen through Contemporary Eyes*. Chicago, 1984. Rich collection of translated documents that throw light on all aspects of Byzantine society.

J. M. Hussey. *The Byzantine World*. London, 1982. A brief and reliable survey.

Liudprand of Cremona. *The Works of Liudprand of Cremona*. Trans. by F. A. Wright. London, 1930. Translations that include accounts of tenth-century Byzantium and of Liudprand's diplomatic mission to Constantinople.

Dimitri Obolensky. *The Byzantine Commonwealth: Eastern Europe, 500–1453*. New York, 1971. A well-informed overview of early Slavic history and relations between Byzantine and Slavic peoples.

George Ostrogorsky. *History of the Byzantine State*. Rev. ed. Trans. by J. Hussey. New Brunswick, 1969. Comprehensive and detailed survey emphasizing political developments.

Procopius. *History of the Wars, Secret History, and Buildings*. Trans. by A. Cameron. New York, 1967. Translations of writings by the most important historian in the time of Justinian.

Michael Psellus. *Fourteen Byzantine Rulers*. Trans. by E. R. A. Sewter. Harmondsworth, 1966. Memoirs of eleventh-century Byzantium by a highly placed advisor to several emperors.

Steven Runciman. *Byzantine Civilization*. Cleveland, 1965. An authoritative overview concentrating on Byzantine institutions by a distinguished scholar.

———. *The Byzantine Theocracy*. Cambridge, 1977. Set of engaging lectures on the Orthodox church.

Speros Vryonis Jr. *Byzantium and Europe*. London, 1967. Well-illustrated and well-written perusal of Byzantine history and Byzantine relations with western Europe.

———. *The Decline of Medieval Hellenism in Asia Minor and the Process of Islamization from the Eleventh through the Fifteenth Century*. Berkeley, 1971. Authoritative analysis of the Turkish conquest of the Byzantine empire.

Mark Whittow. *The Making of Byzantium, 600–1025*. Berkeley, 1996. Concentrates on Byzantine military and political relations with neighboring societies.

Serge A. Zenkovsky, ed. *Medieval Russia's Epics, Chronicles, and Tales*. New York, 1963. A rich collection of literary and historical sources in English translation.

See our **Online Learning Center** at www.mhhe.com/bentley3 for additional readings, practice maps, quizzes, and internet activities.

Unfamiliar words? Check out the **Primary Source Investigator CD-ROM** for an interactive glossary, interactive maps, more images, and primary sources.

A fifteenth-century Persian manuscript depicts pilgrims praying at Mecca in the mosque surrounding the Ka'ba.

THE EXPANSIVE REALM OF ISLAM

In 632 C.E. the prophet Muhammad visited his native city of Mecca from his home in exile at Medina, and in doing so he set an example that devout Muslims have sought to emulate ever since. The *hajj*—the holy pilgrimage to Mecca—draws Muslims by the hundreds of thousands from all parts of the world to Saudi Arabia. Each year Muslims travel to Mecca by land, sea, and air to make the pilgrimage and visit the holy sites of Islam.

In centuries past the numbers of pilgrims were smaller, but their observance of the hajj was no less conscientious. By the ninth century, pilgrimage had become so popular that Muslim rulers went to some lengths to meet the needs of travelers passing through their lands. With the approach of the pilgrimage season—the last month of the Islamic lunar calendar—crowds gathered at major trading centers like Baghdad, Damascus, and Cairo. There they lived in tent cities, surviving on food and water provided by government officials, until they could join caravans bound for Mecca. Muslim rulers invested considerable sums in the maintenance of roads, wells, cisterns, and lodgings that accommodated pilgrims—as well as castles and police forces that protected travelers—on their journeys to Mecca and back.

The hajj was not only solemn observance but also an occasion for joy and celebration. Muslim rulers and wealthy pilgrims often made lavish gifts to caravan companions and others they met en route to Mecca. During her famous hajj of 976–977, for example, the Mesopotamian princess Jamila bint Nasir al-Dawla provided food and fresh green vegetables for her fellow pilgrims and furnished five hundred camels for handicapped travelers. She also purchased freedom for five hundred slaves and distributed fifty thousand fine robes among the common people of Mecca.

Most pilgrims did not have the resources to match Jamila's generosity, but for common travelers, too, the hajj became a special occasion. Merchants and craftsmen made acquaintances and arranged business deals with pilgrims from other lands. Students and scholars exchanged ideas during their weeks of traveling together. For all pilgrims, participation in ritual activities lent new meaning and significance to their faith.

The word *Islam* means "submission," signifying obedience to the rule and will of Allah, the only deity recognized in the strictly monotheistic Islamic religion. An individual who accepts the Islamic faith is a *Muslim*, meaning "one who has submitted." Though it began as one man's expression of unqualified faith in Allah, Islam quickly attracted followers and took on political and social as well as religious significance. During the first century of the new faith's existence, Islam reached far beyond its Arabian homeland, bringing Sasanid Persia and parts of the Byzantine empire into its orbit. By the eighth century the realm of Islam stood alongside the Byzantine empire as a political and economic anchor of the postclassical world.

Islamic society originally reflected the nomadic and mercantile Arabian society from which Islam arose. Yet over time, Muslims drew deep inspiration from other societies as well. After toppling the Sasanid dynasty, Muslim conquerors adopted Persian techniques of government and finance to administer their lands. Persian literature, science, and religious values also found a place in Islamic society. During later centuries Muslims drew inspiration from Greek and Indian traditions as well. Thus Muslims did not invent a new Islamic society but, rather, fashioned it by blending elements from Arab, Persian, Greek, and Indian societies.

While drawing influence from other societies, however, the Islamic faith thoroughly transformed the cultural traditions that it absorbed. The expansive realm of Islam eventually provided a political framework for trade and diplomacy over a vast portion of the eastern hemisphere, from west Africa to the islands of southeast Asia. Many lands of varied cultural background thus became part of a larger society often called the *dar al-Islam*—an Arabic term that means the "house of Islam" and that refers to lands under Islamic rule.

A PROPHET AND HIS WORLD

Islam arose in the Arabian peninsula, and the new religion faithfully reflected the social and cultural conditions of its homeland. Desert covers most of the peninsula, and agriculture is possible only in the well-watered area of Yemen in the south and in a few other places, such as the city of Medina, where oases provide water. Yet human communities have occupied Arabia for millennia. Nomadic peoples known as bedouin kept herds of sheep, goats, and camels, migrating through the deserts to find grass and water for their animals. The bedouin organized themselves in family and clan groups. Individuals and their immediate families depended heavily on their larger kinship networks for support in times of need. In an environment as harsh and unforgiving as the Arabian desert, cooperation with kin often made the difference between death and survival. Bedouin peoples developed a strong sense of loyalty to their clans and guarded their common interests with determination. Clan identities and loyalties survived for centuries after the appearance of Islam.

Arabia also figured prominently in the long-distance trade networks of the postclassical era. Commodities arrived at ports on the Persian Gulf (near modern Bahrain), the Arabian Sea (near modern Aden), and the Red Sea (near Mecca), and then traveled overland by camel caravan to Palmyra or Damascus, which offered access to the Mediterranean basin. After the third century C.E., Arabia became an increasingly important link in trade between China and India in the east and Persia and Byzantium in the west. With the weakening of classical empires, trade routes across central Asia had become insecure. Merchants abandoned the overland routes in favor of sea lanes connecting with land routes in the Arabian peninsula. Trade passing across the peninsula was especially important for the city of Mecca, which became an important site of fairs and a stopping point for caravan traffic.

Muhammad and His Message

Muhammad's Early Life

The prophet Muhammad came into this world of nomadic bedouin herders and merchants. Born about 570 C.E. into a reputable family of merchants in Mecca, Muhammad ibn Abdullah lost both of his parents by the time he was six years old. His

Some northern Arabs went to great lengths to demonstrate their devotion to Christianity. This structure, carved out of sheer rock along the wall of a ravine at Petra in modern-day Jordan, served as a monastery.

grandfather and uncle cared for him and provided him with an education, but Muhammad's early life was difficult. As a young man, he worked for a woman named Khadija, a wealthy widow whom he married about the year 595. Through this marriage he gained a position of some prominence in Meccan society, although he did not by any means enter the ranks of the elite.

By age thirty Muhammad had established himself as a merchant. He made a comfortable life for himself in Arabian society, where peoples of different religious and cultural traditions regularly dealt with one another. Most Arabs recognized many gods, goddesses, demons, and nature spirits whose favor they sought through prayers and sacrifices. Large communities of Jewish merchants also worked throughout Arabia, and especially in the north, many Arabs had converted to Christianity by

Muhammad's time. Although he was not deeply knowledgeable about Judaism or Christianity, Muhammad had a basic understanding of both faiths. He may even have traveled by caravan to Syria, where he would certainly have dealt with Jewish and Christian merchants.

Muhammad's Spiritual Transformation

About 610 C.E., as he approached age forty, Muhammad underwent a profound spiritual experience that transformed his life and left a deep mark on world history. His experience left him with the convictions that in all the world there was only one true deity, Allah ("God"), that he ruled the universe, that idolatry and the recognition of other gods amounted to wickedness, and that Allah would soon bring his judgment on the world, rewarding the righteous and punishing the wicked. Muhammad experienced visions, which he understood as messages or revelations from Allah, delivered through the archangel Gabriel (also recognized by Jews and Christians as a special messenger of God), instructing him to explain his faith to others. He did not set out to construct a new religion by combining elements of Arab, Jewish, and Christian beliefs. In light of his cultural context, however, it is not surprising that he shared numerous specific beliefs with Jews and Christians—and indeed also with Zoroastrians, whose views had profoundly influenced the development of both Judaism and Christianity. In any case, in accordance with instructions transmitted to him by Gabriel, Muhammad began to expound his faith to his family and close friends. Gradually, others showed interest in his message, and by about 620 C.E. a zealous and expanding minority of Mecca's citizenry had joined his circle.

The Quran

Muhammad originally presented oral recitations of the revelations he received during his visions. As the Islamic community grew, his followers prepared written texts of his teachings. During the early 650s devout Muslims compiled these written versions of Muhammad's revelations and issued them as the Quran ("recitation"), the holy book of Islam. A work of magnificent poetry, the Quran communicates in powerful and moving terms Muhammad's understanding of Allah and his relation to the world, and it serves as the definitive authority for Islamic religious doctrine and social organization.

Apart from the Quran, several other sources have provided moral and religious guidance for the Islamic community. Most important after the Quran itself are traditions known as *hadith,* which include sayings attributed to Muhammad and accounts of the prophet's deeds. Several collections of *hadith* appeared between the ninth and eleventh century C.E., and Muslim scholars have often taken them as guides for interpretation of the Quran. Regarded as less authoritative than the Quran and the *hadith,* but still important as inspirations for Islamic thought, were early works describing social and legal customs, biographies of Muhammad, and pious commentaries on the Quran.

Muhammad's Migration to Medina

Conflict at Mecca

The growing popularity of Muhammad's preaching brought him into conflict with the ruling elites at Mecca. Conflict centered on religious issues. Muhammad's insistence that Allah was the only divine power in the universe struck many polytheistic Arabs as offensive and dangerous as well, since it disparaged long-recognized deities and spirits thought to wield influence over human affairs. The tensions also had a personal dimension. Mecca's ruling elites, who were also the city's wealthiest merchants, took it as a personal affront and a threat to their position when Muhammad denounced greed as moral wickedness that Allah would punish.

Muhammad's attack on idolatry also represented an economic threat to those who owned and profited from the many shrines to deities that attracted merchants

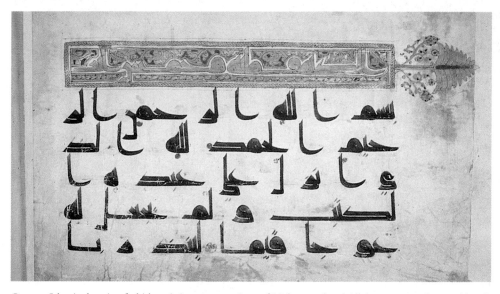

Current Islamic doctrine forbids artistic representations of Muhammad and Allah to prevent the worship of their images as idols. Although artists of previous centuries occasionally produced paintings of Muhammad, Islamic art has emphasized geometric design and calligraphy. This handsome page from a Quran written on vellum dates from the ninth or early tenth century.

and pilgrims to Mecca. The best known of these shrines was a large black rock long considered to be the dwelling of a powerful deity. Housed in a cube-shaped building known as the Ka'ba, it drew worshipers from all over Arabia and brought considerable wealth to Mecca. As Muhammad relentlessly condemned the idolatry officially promoted at the Ka'ba and other shrines, the ruling elites of Mecca began to persecute the prophet and his followers.

The pressure became so great that some of Muhammad's followers fled to Abyssinia (modern Ethiopia). Muhammad himself remained in Mecca until 622 C.E., when he too fled and joined a group of his followers in Yathrib, a rival trading city 345 kilometers (214 miles) north of Mecca. Muslims called their new home Medina ("the city," meaning "the city of the prophet"). Known as the *hijra* ("migration"), Muhammad's move to Medina serves as the starting point of the official Islamic calendar.

The Hijra

In Mecca Muhammad had lived within the established political framework and concentrated on the moral and religious dimensions of his faith. In Medina he found himself at the head of a small but growing society in exile that needed guidance in practical as well as spiritual affairs. He organized his followers into a cohesive community called the *umma* ("community of the faithful") and provided it with a comprehensive legal and social code. He led this community both in daily prayers to Allah and in battle with enemies at Medina, Mecca, and other places. He looked after the economic welfare of the *umma*—sometimes by organizing commercial ventures and sometimes by launching raids against caravans from Mecca. Remembering the difficult days of his own youth, he provided relief for widows, orphans, and the poor, and he made almsgiving a prime moral virtue.

The Umma

Muhammad's understanding of his religious mission expanded during his years at Medina. He began to refer to himself as a prophet, indeed as the "seal of the prophets"—the final prophet through whom Allah would reveal his message to humankind. Muhammad accepted the authority of earlier Jewish and Christian prophets,

The "Seal of the Prophets"

Sources from the Past

The Quran on Allah and His Expectations of Humankind

The foundation of the Islamic faith is the understanding of Allah, his nature, and his plan for the world as outlined in the Quran. Through his visions Muhammad came to understand Allah as the one and only god, the creator and sustainer of the world in the manner of the Jews' Yahweh and the Christians' God. Those who rejected Allah and his message would suffer eternal punishment, while those who recognized and obeyed him would receive his mercy and secure his blessings.

In the name of Allah, most benevolent, ever-merciful.
All praise be to Allah,
Lord of all the worlds,
Most beneficent, ever-merciful,
King of the Day of Judgement.
You alone we worship, and to You
alone turn for help.
Guide us (O Lord) to the path that is straight,
The path of those You have blessed,
Not of those who have earned Your anger,
nor those who have gone astray. . . .

Verily men and women who have come to submission,
men and women who are believers,
men and women who are devout,
truthful men and women,
men and women with endurance,
men and women who are modest,
men and women who give alms,
men and women who observe fasting,
men and women who guard their private parts,
and those men and women who remember God a great deal,
for them God has forgiveness and a great reward.
No believing men and women have any choice in a matter
after God and His Apostle [i.e., Muhammad] have decided it.
Whoever disobeys God and His Apostle
has clearly lost the way and gone astray. . . .

O you who believe, remember God a great deal,
And sing His praises morning and evening.
It is He who sends His blessings on you,
as (do) His angels, that He may lead you out of darkness into light,
for He is benevolent to the believers. . . .

I call to witness
the early hours of the morning,
And the night when dark and still,
Your Lord has neither left you,
nor despises you.
What is to come is better for you
than what has gone before;
For your Lord will certainly give you,
and you will be content.
Did He not find you an orphan
and take care of you?
Did He not find you poor
and enrich you?
So do not oppress the orphan,
And do not drive
the beggar away,
And keep recounting the favours of your Lord. . . .

Say: "He is God
the one the most unique,
God the immanently indispensable.
He has begotten no one,
and is begotten of none.
There is no one comparable to Him."

SOURCE: *Al-Qur'an: A Contemporary Translation.* Trans. by Ahmed Ali. Princeton: Princeton University Press, 1984, pp.11, 358, 359, 540, 559.

Compare the Quran's teachings on the relationship between Allah and human beings with the views of Zoroastrians, Jews, and Christians discussed in earlier chapters.

including Abraham, Moses, and Jesus, and he held the Hebrew scriptures and the Christian New Testament in high esteem. He also accepted his predecessors' monotheism: Allah was the same omnipotent, omniscient, omnipresent, and exclusive deity as the Jews' Yahweh and the Christians' God. Muhammad taught, however, that the message entrusted to him offered a more complete revelation of Allah and his will than Jewish and Christian faiths had made available. Thus, while at Medina, Muhammad came to see himself consciously as Allah's final prophet: not simply as a devout man who explained his spiritual insights to a small circle of family and friends, but as the messenger who communicated Allah's wishes and his plan for the world to all humankind.

The Establishment of Islam in Arabia

Throughout their sojourn at Medina, Muhammad and his followers planned ultimately to return to Mecca, which was both their home and the leading city of Arabia. In 629 C.E. they arranged with the authorities to participate in the annual pilgrimage to the Ka'ba, but they were not content with a short visit. In 630 they attacked Mecca and conquered the city. They forced the elites to adopt Muhammad's faith, and they imposed a government dedicated to Allah. They also destroyed the pagan shrines and replaced them with mosques, buildings that sought to instill a sense of sacredness and community where Muslims gathered for prayers. Only the Ka'ba escaped their efforts to cleanse Mecca of pagan monuments.

Muhammad's Return to Mecca

Muhammad and his followers denied that the Ka'ba was the home of a deity, but they preserved the black rock and its housing as a symbol of Mecca's greatness. They allowed only the faithful to approach the shrine, and in 632 Muhammad himself led the first Islamic pilgrimage to the Ka'ba, thus establishing the hajj as an example for all devout Muslims. Building on the conquest of Mecca, Muhammad and his followers launched campaigns against other towns and bedouin clans, and by the time of the prophet's death in 632, shortly after his hajj, they had brought most of Arabia under their control.

Muhammad's faith and his personal leadership decisively shaped the values and the development of the Islamic community. The foundation of the Islamic faith as elaborated by Muhammad consists of obligations known as the Five Pillars of Islam: (1) Muslims must acknowledge Allah as the only god and Muhammad as his prophet. (2) They must pray to Allah daily while facing Mecca. (3) They must observe a fast during the daylight hours of the month of Ramadan. (4) They must contribute alms for the relief of the weak and poor. (5) Finally, in honor of Muhammad's visits to Mecca in 629 and 632, those who are physically and financially able must undertake the hajj and make at least one pilgrimage to Mecca. During the centuries since its appearance, Islam has generated many schools and sects, each with its own particular legal, social, and doctrinal features. The Five Pillars of Islam, however, constitute a simple but powerful framework that has bound the *umma* as a whole into a cohesive community of faith.

The Five Pillars of Islam

Some Muslims, though by no means all, have taken *jihad* as an additional obligation for the faithful. The term *jihad* literally means "struggle," and Muslims have understood its imperatives in various ways. In one sense, *jihad* imposes spiritual and moral obligations on Muslims by requiring them to combat vice and evil. In another sense, *jihad* calls on Muslims to struggle against ignorance and unbelief by spreading the word of Islam and seeking converts to the faith. In some circumstances, *jihad* also involves physical struggle, obliging Muslims to take up the sword and wage war against unbelievers who threaten Islam.

Jihad

Context & Connections

The Hajj, Past and Present

"Announce the Pilgrimage to the people," proclaimed the Islamic scriptures. "They will come to you on foot and riding along distant roads on lean and slender beasts" (Quran 22:27). Over the centuries, Muslims obeying the Quran's teachings have turned the hajj into the world's largest public gathering. It is impossible to know how many pilgrims made the hajj in premodern times, but it is clear that within two or three centuries of Muhammad's death, thousands of Muslims traveled each year to Mecca.

In the earliest days, pilgrims approached Mecca by one of the camel caravans that organized travelers into groups departing from Cairo, Damascus, and Baghdad, as well as from various points within the Arabian peninsula itself. As Islam became popular in India, southeast Asia, and east Africa, pilgrims increasingly arrived aboard ships sailing through

Modern-day pilgrims circle the Ka'ba in hajj observations.

the Indian Ocean and the Red Sea. In the late nineteenth and twentieth centuries, steamships and railroads enabled larger and larger numbers of pilgrims to visit

Islamic Law: The Sharia

Beyond the general obligations prescribed by the Five Pillars, Islamic holy law, known as the *sharia*, emerged during the centuries after Muhammad and offered detailed guidance on proper behavior in almost every aspect of life. Elaborated by jurists and legal scholars, the *sharia* drew its inspiration especially from the Quran and the early historical accounts of Muhammad's life and teachings. It offered precise guidance on matters as diverse as marriage and family life, inheritance, slavery, business and commercial relationships, political authority in the *dar al-Islam,* and crime. Through the *sharia,* Islam became more than a religious doctrine: it developed into a way of life complete with social and ethical values derived from Islamic religious principles.

THE EXPANSION OF ISLAM

After Muhammad's death the Islamic community might well have unraveled and disappeared. Muhammad had made no provision for a successor, and there was serious

Mecca: in 1965 participants numbered 294,000. Since the introduction of jumbo jets in the 1970s, pilgrim numbers have reached a new order of magnitude: in recent years, more than two million pilgrims have traveled annually to Mecca.

While methods of travel and numbers of participants have changed dramatically over the years, hajj rituals themselves have remained remarkably stable since the time of Muhammad. Since Muhammad's conquest of Mecca (630 C.E.), the hajj has been open only to Muslims, although from time to time a very few non-Muslims have managed to sneak into the observances. To prepare for hajj rituals, pilgrims enter a state of consecration by removing their usual attire and donning simple white garments that symbolize the equality of all Muslims. The ceremonies of the hajj itself take place in a five-day period during the last month of the Islamic lunar calendar. Pilgrims first undertake a circular procession around the Ka'ba, then visit several sites near Mecca, where they perform a precisely defined set of rituals that symbolize the most important tenets of Islam and com-memorate the experiences of the patriarch Abraham. Hajj observances conclude with another circular procession around the Ka'ba. Some pilgrims then depart from Mecca, while others visit Medina and other sites sacred to Islam.

The hajj places formidable logistical demands on the Saudi Arabian government, which has hosted the annual pilgrimage since its conquest of the Hijaz (the western region of the Arabian peninsula, including the cities of Mecca and Medina) in 1926. Thousands of volunteers work to provide food, water, lodging, sanitation facilities, health care, transportation, and guide services for the masses of pilgrims who inundate Mecca. Servicing the hajj and the needs of pilgrims constitutes one of the world's most challenging exercises in public administration.

For devout Muslims the significance of the hajj lies not in logistical proficiency but, rather, in the intensification of their Islamic faith. According to tradition, Muhammad taught that as a reward for their efforts, those who performed the hajj properly would emerge from the experience as newly born babies free of sin.

division within the *umma* concerning the selection of a new leader. Many of the towns and bedouin clans that had recently accepted Islam took the opportunity of Muhammad's death to renounce the faith, reassert their independence, and break free from Mecca's control. Within a short time, however, the Islamic community had embarked on a stunningly successful round of military expansion that extended its political and cultural influence far beyond the boundaries of Arabia. These conquests laid the foundation for the rapid growth of Islamic society.

The Early Caliphs and the Umayyad Dynasty

The Caliph

Because Muhammad was the "seal of the prophets," it was inconceivable that another prophet should succeed him. Shortly after Muhammad's death his advisors selected Abu Bakr, a genial man who was one of the prophet's closest friends and most devoted disciples, to serve as *caliph* ("deputy"). Thus Abu Bakr and later caliphs led the *umma* not as prophets, but as lieutenants or substitutes for Muhammad. Abu Bakr became head of state for the Islamic community as well as chief judge, religious

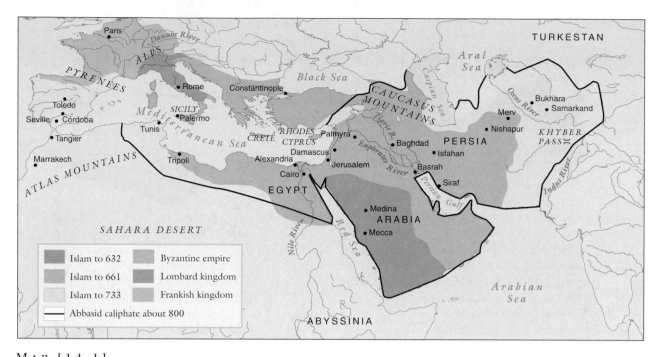

MAP [14.1]
The expansion of Islam,
632–733 C.E.

*The Expansion
of Islam*

leader, and military commander. Under the new caliph's leadership, the *umma* went on the offensive against the towns and bedouin clans that had renounced Islam after Muhammad's death, and within a year it had compelled them to recognize the faith of Islam and the rule of the caliph.

Indeed, during the century after Muhammad's death, Islamic armies ranged well beyond the boundaries of Arabia, carrying their religion and their authority to Byzantine and Sasanid territories and beyond. Although much less powerful than either the Byzantine empire or the Sasanid empire, early Islamic warriors fought with the zeal of new converts. Moreover, they attacked at a moment when the larger empires—both of them already exhausted because of perennial conflicts with each other—also faced internal uprisings by overtaxed peasants and oppressed ethnic or religious minorities. Between 633 and 637 C.E., taking advantage of these difficulties, Muslim forces seized Byzantine Syria and Palestine and took most of Mesopotamia from the Sasanids. During the 640s they conquered Byzantine Egypt and north Africa. In 651 they toppled the Sasanid dynasty and incorporated Persia into their expanding empire. In 711 they conquered the Hindu kingdom of Sind in northwestern India. Between 711 and 718 they extended their authority to northwest Africa and crossed the Strait of Gibraltar, conquering most of the Iberian peninsula and threatening the Frankish kingdom in Gaul. By the mid-eighth century an immense Islamic empire ruled lands from India and the central Asian steppe lands in the east to northwest Africa and Iberia in the west.

During this rapid expansion the empire's rulers encountered difficult problems of governance and administration. One problem had to do with the selection of caliphs. During the early decades after Muhammad's death, leaders of the most powerful Arab clans negotiated among themselves and appointed the first four caliphs. Political ambitions, personal differences, and clan loyalties complicated their deliberations, however, and disputes soon led to the rise of factions and parties within the Islamic community.

Disagreements over succession led to the emergence of the Shia sect, the most important and enduring of all the alternatives to the faith observed by the majority of Muslims, known as Sunni Islam. The Shia sect originated as a party supporting the appointment of Ali and his descendants as caliphs. A cousin and son-in-law of Muhammad, Ali was a candidate for caliph when the prophet died, but support for Abu Bakr was stronger. Ali served briefly as the fourth caliph (656–661 C.E.), but his enemies assassinated him, killed many of his relatives, and imposed their own candidate as caliph. Partisans of Ali then organized the Shia ("party"), furiously resisted the victorious faction, and struggled to return the caliphate to the line of Ali. Although persecuted, the Shia survived and strengthened its identity by adopting doctrines and rituals distinct from those of the Sunnis ("traditionalists"), who accepted the legitimacy of the early caliphs. Shia partisans, for example, observed holy days in honor of their leaders and martyrs to their cause, and they taught that descendants of Ali were infallible, sinless, and divinely appointed to rule the Islamic community.

The Shia

Shia Muslims also advanced interpretations of the Quran that support the party's views, and the Shia itself has often served as a source of support for those who oppose the policies of Sunni leaders.

After the assassination of Ali, the establishment of the Umayyad dynasty (661–750 C.E.) solved the problem of succession, at least temporarily. The Umayyads ranked among the most prominent of the Meccan merchant clans, and their reputation and network of alliances helped them bring stability to the Islamic community. Despite their association with Mecca, the Umayyads established their capital at Damascus, a thriving commercial city in Syria, whose central location enabled them to maintain better communication with the vast and still-expanding Islamic empire.

The Umayyad Dynasty

Although the Umayyads' dynasty solved the problem of succession, their tightly centralized rule and the favor they showed to their fellow Arabs generated an administrative problem. The Umayyads ruled the *dar al-Islam* as conquerors, and their policies reflected the interests of the Arab military

The early expansion of Islam was a bloody affair. This illustration from an Arabic manuscript of the thirteenth century depicts a battle between Muhammad's cousin Ali and his adversaries.

Policy toward Conquered Peoples

aristocracy. The Umayyads appointed members of this elite as governors and administrators of conquered lands, and they distributed the wealth that they extracted among this privileged class.

This policy contributed to high morale among Arab conquerors, but it caused severe discontent among the scores of ethnic and religious groups embraced by the Umayyad empire. Apart from Muslims the empire included Christians, Jews, Zoroastrians, and Buddhists. Apart from Arabs and bedouin, it included Indians, Persians, Mesopotamians, Greeks, Egyptians, and nomadic Berbers in north Africa. The Arabs mostly allowed conquered peoples to observe their own religions—particularly Christians and Jews—but they levied a special head tax, called the *jizya*, on those who did not convert to Islam. Even those who converted did not enjoy access to wealth and positions of authority, which the Umayyads reserved almost exclusively for members of the Arab military aristocracy. These policies caused deep resentment among conquered peoples and led to restiveness against Umayyad rule.

Umayyad Decline

Beginning in the early eighth century, the Umayyad caliphs became alienated even from other Arabs. They devoted themselves increasingly to luxurious living rather than to zealous leadership of the *umma*, and they scandalized devout Muslims by their casual attitudes toward Islamic doctrine and morality. By midcentury the Umayyad caliphs faced not only the resistance of the Shia faction, whose members continued to promote descendants of Ali for caliph, but also the discontent of conquered peoples throughout their empire and even the disillusionment of Muslim Arab military leaders.

The Abbasid Dynasty

Abu al-Abbas

Rebellion in Persia brought the Umayyad dynasty to an end. The chief leader of the rebellion was Abu al-Abbas, a descendant of Muhammad's uncle. Although he was a Sunni Arab, Abu al-Abbas allied readily with Shias and with Muslims who were not Arabs, such as converts to Islam from southwest Asia. Particularly prominent among his supporters were Persian converts who resented the preference shown by the Umayyads to Arab Muslims. During the 740s Abu al-Abbas's party rejected Umayyad authority and seized control of Persia and Mesopotamia. In 750 his army shattered Umayyad forces in a massive battle. Afterward Abu al-Abbas invited the remaining members of the Umayyad clan to a banquet under the pretext of reconciling their differences. During the festivities his troops arrested the Umayyads and slaughtered them, effectively annihilating the clan. Abu al-Abbas then founded the Abbasid dynasty, which was the principal source of authority in the *dar al-Islam* until the Mongols toppled it in 1258 C.E.

The Abbasid Dynasty

The Abbasid dynasty differed considerably from the Umayyad. For one thing the Abbasid state was far more cosmopolitan than its predecessor. Even though they sprang from the ranks of conquering Arabs, Abbasid rulers did not show special favor to the Arab military aristocracy. Arabs continued to play a large role in government, but Persians, Egyptians, Mesopotamians, and others also rose to positions of wealth and power.

The Abbasid dynasty differed from the Umayyad also in that it was not a conquering dynasty. The Abbasids sparred intermittently with the Byzantine empire, they clashed frequently with nomadic peoples from central Asia, and in 751 they defeated a Chinese army at Talas River near Samarkand. The battle of Talas River was exceptionally important: it ended the expansion of China's Tang dynasty into central Asia (discussed in chapter 15), and it opened the door for the spread of Islam among

Turkish peoples. Only marginally, however, did the Abbasids expand their empire by conquest. The *dar al-Islam* as a whole continued to grow during the Abbasid era, but the caliphs had little to do with the expansion. During the ninth and early tenth centuries, for example, largely autonomous Islamic forces from distant Tunisia mounted naval expeditions throughout the Mediterranean, conquering Crete, Sicily, and the Balearic Islands while seizing territories also in Cyprus, Rhodes, Sardinia, Corsica, southern Italy, and southern France.

Instead of conquering new lands, the Abbasids largely contented themselves with administering the empire they inherited. Fashioning a government that could administer a sprawling realm with scores of linguistic, ethnic, and cultural groups was a considerable challenge. In designing their administration, the Abbasids relied heavily on Persian techniques of statecraft. Central authority came from the court at Baghdad (capital of modern Iraq), the magnificent new city that the early Abbasid caliphs built near the Sasanid capital of Ctesiphon. Baghdad was a round city protected by three round walls. At the heart of the city was the caliph's green-domed palace from which instructions flowed to the distant reaches of the Abbasid realm. In the provinces, governors represented the caliph and implemented his political and financial policies.

Abbasid Administration

Learned officials known as *ulama* ("people with religious knowledge") and *qadis* ("judges") set moral standards in local communities and resolved disputes. *Ulama* and *qadis* were not priests—Islam does not recognize priests as a distinct class of religious specialists—but they had a formal education that emphasized study of the Quran and the *sharia*. *Ulama* were pious scholars who sought to develop public policy in accordance with the Quran and *sharia*. *Qadis* heard cases at law and rendered decisions based on the Quran and *sharia*. Because of their moral authority, *ulama* and *qadis* became extremely influential officials who helped to ensure widespread observance of Islamic values. Apart from provincial governors, *ulama*, and *qadis,* the Abbasid caliphs kept a standing army, and they established bureaucratic ministries in charge of taxation, finance, coinage, and postal services. They also maintained the magnificent network of roads that the Islamic empire inherited from the Sasanids.

The high point of the Abbasid dynasty came during the reign of the caliph Harun al-Rashid (786–809 C.E.). By the late eighth century, Abbasid authority had lost some of its force in provinces distant from Baghdad, but it remained strong enough to bring reliable tax revenues from most parts of the empire. Flush with wealth, Baghdad became a center of banking, commerce, crafts, and industrial production, a metropolis with a population of several hundred thousand people. According to stories from his own time, Harun al-Rashid provided liberal support for artists and writers, bestowed lavish and luxurious gifts on his favorites, and distributed money to the poor and the common classes by tossing coins into the streets of Baghdad. Once he sent an elephant and a collection of rich presents as gifts to his contemporary Charlemagne, who ruled the Carolingian empire of western Europe.

Harun al-Rashid

Soon after Harun al-Rashid's reign, the Abbasid empire entered a period of decline. Civil war between Harun's sons seriously damaged Abbasid authority, and disputes over succession rights became a recurring problem for the dynasty. Provincial governors took advantage of disorder in the ruling house by acting independently of the caliphs: instead of implementing imperial policies and delivering taxes to Baghdad, they built up local bases of power and in some cases actually seceded from the Abbasid state. Meanwhile, popular uprisings and peasant rebellions, which often enjoyed the support of dissenting sects and heretical movements, further weakened the empire.

Abbasid Decline

Sources from the Past

Benjamin of Tudela on the Caliph's Court at Baghdad

Like Constantinople, Baghdad was in a period of decline when the Spanish rabbi Benjamin of Tudela visited in the later twelfth century. Nevertheless, again like the Byzantine capital, Baghdad remained an immensely prosperous city. Benjamin's report on Baghdad concentrated largely on the court and palace of the Abbasid caliph.

The caliph is the head of the Muslim religion, and all the kings of Islam obey him; he occupies a similar position to that held by the pope over the Christians. He has a palace in Baghdad three miles in extent, wherein there is a great park with all varieties of trees, fruit-bearing and otherwise, and all manner of animals. The whole is surrounded by a wall, and in the park there is a lake whose waters are fed by the river Hiddekel. Whenever the king desires to indulge in recreation and to rejoice and feast, his servants catch all manner of birds, game, and fish, and he goes to his palace with his counsellors and princes. . . .

Each of his brothers and the members of his family has an abode in his palace, but they are all fettered in chains of iron, and guards are placed over each of their houses so that they may not rise against the great caliph. For once it happened to a predecessor that his brothers rose up against him and proclaimed one of themselves as caliph; then it was decreed that all the members of his family should be bound, that they might not rise up against the ruling caliph. Each one of them resides in his palace in great splendor, and they own villages and towns, and their stewards bring them the tribute thereof, and they eat and drink and rejoice all the days of their life.

Within the domains of the palace of the caliph there are great buildings of marble and columns of silver and gold, and carvings upon rare stones are fixed in the walls. In the caliph's palace are great riches and towers filled with gold, silken garments, and all precious stones. . . .

The caliph is a benevolent man. On the other side of the river, on the banks of an arm of the Euphrates which

there borders the city, he built a hospital consisting of blocks of houses and hospices for the sick poor who come to be healed. Here there are about sixty physicians' stores which are provided from the caliph's house with drugs and whatever else may be required. Every sick man who comes is maintained at the caliph's expense and is medically treated. Here is a building which is called Dar-al-Maristan, where they keep charge of the demented people who have become insane in the towns through the great heat in the summer, and they chain each of them in iron chains until their reason becomes restored to them in the winter. While they abide there, they are provided with food from the house of the caliph, and when their reason is restored they are dismissed and each one of them goes to his house and his home. Money is given to those that have stayed in the hospices on their return to their homes. Every month the officers of the caliph inquire and investigate whether they have regained their reason, in which case they are discharged. All this the caliph does out of charity to those that come to the city of Baghdad, whether they be sick or insane. The caliph is a righteous man, and all his actions are for good. . . .

The city of Baghdad is twenty miles in circumference, situated in a land of palms, gardens, and plantations, the like of which is not to be found in the whole land of Mesopotamia. People come thither with merchandise from all lands. Wise men live there, philosophers who know all manner of wisdom, and magicians expert in all manner of witchcraft.

SOURCE: Benjamin of Tudela. *The Itinerary of Benjamin of Tudela.* Trans. by M. N. Adler. London: H. Frowde, 1907, pp.35–42. (Translation slightly modified.)

Compare Baghdad and Constantinople on the basis of descriptions provided by Benjamin of Tudela.

As a result of these difficulties, the Abbasid caliphs became mere figureheads long before the Mongols extinguished the dynasty in 1258. In 945 members of a Persian noble family seized control of Baghdad and established their clan as the power behind the Abbasid throne. Later, imperial authorities in Baghdad fell under the control of the Saljuq Turks, a nomadic people from central Asia who also invaded the Byzantine empire. In response to rebellions mounted by peasants and provincial governors, authorities in Baghdad allied with the Saljuqs, who began to enter the Abbasid realm and convert to Islam about the mid-tenth century. By the mid-eleventh century the Saljuqs effectively controlled the Abbasid empire. During the 1050s they took possession of Baghdad, and during the following decades they extended their authority to Syria, Palestine, and Anatolia. They retained Abbasid caliphs as nominal sovereigns, but for two centuries, until the arrival of the Mongols, the Saljuq *sultan* ("ruler") was the true source of power in the Abbasid empire.

ECONOMY AND SOCIETY OF THE EARLY ISLAMIC WORLD

In the *dar al-Islam*, as in other agricultural societies, peasants tilled the land as their ancestors had done for centuries before them while manufacturers and merchants supported a thriving urban economy. Here, as in other lands, the creation of large empires had dramatic economic implications. The Umayyad and Abbasid empires created a zone of trade, exchange, and communication stretching from India to Iberia. Commerce throughout this zone served as a vigorous economic stimulus for both the countryside and the cities of the early Islamic world.

New Crops, Agricultural Experimentation, and Urban Growth

As soldiers, administrators, diplomats, and merchants traveled throughout the *dar al-Islam*, they encountered plants, animals, and agricultural techniques peculiar to the empire's various regions. They often introduced particularly useful crops to new regions. The most important of the transplants traveled west from India to Persia, southwest Asia, Arabia, Egypt, north Africa, Spain, and the Mediterranean islands of Cyprus, Crete, Sicily, and Sardinia. They included staple crops such as sugarcane, rice, and new varieties of sorghum and wheat; vegetables such as spinach, artichokes, and eggplants; fruits such as oranges, lemons, limes, bananas, coconuts, watermelons, and mangoes; and industrial crops such as cotton, indigo, and henna.

The Spread of Food and Industrial Crops

The introduction of these crops into the western regions of the Islamic world had wide-ranging effects. New food crops led to a richer and more varied diet. They also increased quantities of food available because they enabled cultivators to extend the growing season. In much of the Islamic world, summers are so hot and dry that cultivators traditionally left their fields fallow during that season. Most of the transplanted crops grew well in high heat, however, so cultivators in southwest Asia, north Africa, and other hot zones could till their lands year-round. The result was a dramatic increase in food supplies.

Effects of New Crops

Some new crops had industrial uses. The most important of these was cotton, which became the basis for a thriving textile industry throughout much of the Islamic world. Indigo and henna yielded dyes that textile manufacturers used in large quantities.

Travel and communication in the *dar al-Islam* also encouraged experimentation with agricultural methods. Cultivators paid close attention to methods of irrigation, fertilization, crop rotation, and the like, and they outlined their findings in hundreds of

Agricultural Experimentation

Urban Growth

In a thirteenth-century manuscript illustration, a fictional Muslim traveler passes a lively agricultural village. On the left a woman spins cotton thread. Sheep, goats, chickens, and date palms figure prominently in the local economy.

agricultural manuals. Copies of these works survive in numerous manuscripts that circulated widely throughout the Islamic world. The combined effect of new crops and improved techniques was a far more productive agricultural economy, which in turn supported vigorous economic growth throughout the *dar al-Islam*.

Increased agricultural production contributed to the rapid growth of cities in all parts of the Islamic world from India to Spain. Delhi, Samarkand, Bukhara, Merv, Nishapur, Isfahan, Basra, Baghdad, Damascus, Jerusalem, Cairo, Alexandria, Palermo, Tunis, Tangier, Córdoba, and Toledo were all bustling cities, some with populations of several hundred thousand people. All these cities had flourishing markets supporting thousands of artisans, craftsmen, and merchants. Most of them were also important centers of industrial production, particularly of textiles, pottery, glassware, leather, iron, and steel.

One new industry appeared in Islamic cities during the Abbasid era: paper manufacture. Chinese craftsmen had made paper since the first century C.E., but their technology did not spread far beyond China until Arab forces defeated a Chinese army at the battle of Talas River in 751 and took prisoners skilled in paper production. Paper was cheaper and easier to use than writing materials such as vellum sheets made from calfskin, and it soon became popular throughout the Islamic world. Paper facilitated the keeping of administrative and commercial records, and it made possible the dissemination of books and treatises in larger quantities than ever before. By the tenth century, mills produced paper in Persia, Mesopotamia, Arabia, Egypt, and Spain, and the industry soon spread to western Europe.

The Formation of a Hemispheric Trading Zone

From its earliest days Islamic society drew much of its prosperity from commerce. Muhammad himself was a merchant, and he held merchants in high esteem. According to early accounts of his life, Muhammad once said that honest merchants would stand alongside martyrs to the faith on the day of judgment. By the time of the

Abbasid caliphate, elaborate trade networks linked all the regions of the Islamic world and joined it to a larger, hemispheric economy.

Overland Trade

When they overran the Sasanid empire, Muslim conquerors brought the prosperous trading cities of central Asia under control of the expanding *dar al-Islam*. Merv, Nishapur, Bukhara, and Samarkand were long-established commercial centers, and they made it possible for Muslim merchants to trade over a revived silk roads network extending from China in the east to the Mediterranean in the west. Thus Muslim merchants were able to take advantage of the extensive road networks originally built during the classical era by imperial authorities in India, Persia, and the Mediterranean basin. Umayyad and Abbasid rulers maintained the roads that they inherited because they provided splendid routes for military forces and administrative officials traveling through the *dar al-Islam*. But these same roads

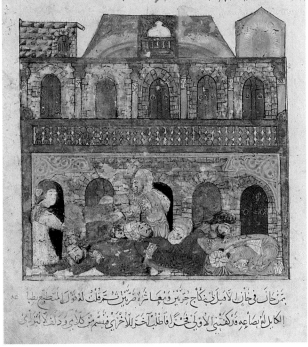

Caravanserais offered splendid facilities for caravan merchants, but they sometimes harbored dangers. In this illustration from a thirteenth-century manuscript, drugged merchants sleep soundly while burglars relieve them of their valuables.

also made excellent highways for merchants as well as missionaries and pilgrims. Travel along these roads could be remarkably speedy and efficient. After the tenth century, for example, the Muslim rulers of Egypt regularly imported ice from the mountains of Syria to their palace in Cairo. Even during the summer months, they received five camel loads of ice weekly to cool their food and drink.

Camels and Caravans

Overland trade traveled mostly by camel caravan. Although they are unpleasant and often uncooperative beasts, camels endure the rigors of desert travel much better than horses or donkeys. Moreover, when fitted with a well-designed saddle, camels can carry heavy loads. During the early centuries C.E., the manufacture of camel saddles spread throughout Arabia, north Africa, southwest Asia, and central Asia, and camels became the favored beasts of burden in deserts and other dry regions. As camel transport became more common, the major cities of the Islamic world and central Asia built and maintained caravanserais—inns offering lodging for caravan merchants as well as food, water, and care for their animals.

Maritime Trade

Meanwhile, innovations in nautical technology contributed to a steadily increasing volume of maritime trade in the Red Sea, Persian Gulf, Arabian Sea, and Indian Ocean. Arab and Persian mariners borrowed the compass from its Chinese inventors and used it to guide them on the high seas. From southeast Asian and Indian mariners, they

A map produced in the eleventh century by the Arab geographer al-Idrisi shows the lands known and reported by Muslim merchants and travelers. Note that, in accordance with Muslim cartographic convention, this map places south at the top and north at the bottom.

borrowed the lateen sail, a triangular sail that increased a ship's maneuverability. From the Hellenistic Mediterranean they borrowed the astrolabe, an instrument that enabled them to calculate latitude.

Thus equipped, Arab and Persian mariners ventured throughout the Indian Ocean basin, calling at ports from southern China to southeast Asia, Ceylon, India, Persia, Arabia, and the eastern coast of Africa. The twelfth-century Persian merchant Ramisht of Siraf (a flourishing port city on the Persian Gulf) amassed a huge fortune from long-distance trading ventures. One of Ramisht's clerks once returned to Siraf from a commercial voyage to China with a cargo worth half a million dinars—gold coins that were the standard currency in the Islamic world. Ramisht himself was one of the wealthiest men of his age, and he spent much of his fortune on pious causes. He outfitted the Ka'ba with a Chinese silk cover that reportedly cost him eighteen thousand dinars, and he also founded a hospital and a religious sanctuary in Mecca.

Banks

Banking also stimulated the commercial economy of the Islamic world. Banks had operated since classical antiquity, but Islamic banks of the Abbasid period conducted business on a much larger scale and provided a more extensive range of services than did their predecessors. They not only lent money to entrepreneurs but also served as brokers for investments and exchanged different currencies. They established multiple branches that honored letters of credit known as *sakk*—the root of the modern word for "check"—drawn on the parent bank. Thus merchants could draw letters of credit in one city and cash them in another, and they could settle accounts with distant business partners without having to deal in cash.

The Organization of Trade

Trade benefited also from techniques of business organization. Like banking, these techniques had precedents in classical Mediterranean society, but increasing volumes of trade enabled entrepreneurs to refine their methods of organization. Furthermore, Islamic law provided security for entrepreneurs by explicitly recognizing certain forms of business organization. Usually Islamic businessmen preferred not to embark on solo ventures, since an individual could face financial ruin if an entire cargo of commodities fell prey to pirates or went down with a ship that sank in a storm. Instead, like their counterparts in other postclassical societies, Abbasid entrepreneurs often pooled their resources in group investments. If several individuals invested in several cargoes, they could distribute their risks and more easily absorb losses. Furthermore, if several groups of investors rented cargo space on several different ships, they spread their risks even more. Entrepreneurs entered into a variety of legally recognized joint endeavors during the Abbasid caliphate. Some involved simply the investment of money in an enterprise, whereas others called for some or all of the partners to play active roles in their business ventures.

As a result of improved transportation, expanded banking services, and refined techniques of business organization, long-distance trade surged in the early Islamic

In this thirteenth-century manuscript illustration, merchants at a slave market in southern Arabia deal in black slaves captured in sub-Saharan Africa. Slaves traded in Islamic markets also came from Russia and eastern Europe.

world. Muslim merchants dealt in silk and ceramics from China, spices and aromatics from India and southeast Asia, and jewelry and fine textiles from the Byzantine empire. Merchants also ventured beyond settled societies in China, India, and the Mediterranean basin to distant lands that previously had not engaged systematically in long-distance trade. They crossed the Sahara desert by camel caravan to trade salt, steel, copper, and glass for gold and slaves from the kingdoms of west Africa. They visited the coastal regions of east Africa, where they obtained slaves and exotic local commodities such as animal skins. They engaged in trade with Russia and Scandinavia by way of the Dnieper and Volga rivers and obtained high-value commodities such as animal skins, furs, honey, amber, and slaves as well as bulk goods such as timber and livestock. The vigorous economy of the Abbasid empire thus helped to establish networks of communication and exchange throughout much of the eastern hemisphere.

Al-Andalus

The prosperity of Islamic Spain, known as al-Andalus, illustrates the far-reaching effects of long-distance trade during the Abbasid era. Most of the Iberian peninsula had fallen into the hands of Muslim Berber conquerors from north Africa during the early eighth century. As allies of the Umayyads, the governors of al-Andalus refused to recognize the Abbasid dynasty, and beginning in the tenth century they styled themselves caliphs in their own right rather than governors subject to Abbasid authority. Despite political and diplomatic tensions, al-Andalus participated actively in the commercial life of the larger Islamic world. The merchant-scholar al-Marwani of Córdoba, for example, made his hajj in 908 and then traveled to Iraq and India on commercial ventures. His profits amounted to thirty thousand dinars—all of which

Interior of the mosque at Córdoba, originally built in the late eighth century and enlarged during the ninth and tenth centuries. One of the largest structures in the *dar al-Islam*, the mosque rests on 850 columns and features nineteen aisles.

he lost in a shipwreck during his return home.

Imported crops increased the supply of food and enriched the diet of al-Andalus, enabling merchants and manufacturers to conduct thriving businesses in cities like Córdoba, Toledo, and Seville. Ceramics, painted tiles, lead crystal, and gold jewelry from al-Andalus enjoyed a reputation for excellence and helped pay for imported goods and the building of a magnificent capital city at Córdoba. During the tenth century Córdoba had more than 16 kilometers (10 miles) of publicly lighted roads as well as free Islamic schools, a gargantuan mosque, and a splendid library with four hundred thousand volumes.

The Changing Status of Women

A patriarchal society had emerged in Arabia long before Muhammad's time, but Arab women enjoyed rights not accorded to women in many other lands. They could legally inherit property, divorce husbands on their own initiative, and engage in business ventures. Khadija, the first of Muhammad's four wives, managed a successful commercial business.

The Quran and Women

In some respects the Quran enhanced the security of women in Arabian society. It outlawed female infanticide, and it provided that dowries went directly to brides rather than to their husbands and male guardians. It portrayed women not as the property of their menfolk, but as honorable individuals, equal to men before Allah, with their own rights and needs. Muhammad's own kindness and generosity toward his wives, as related in early accounts of the prophet's life, also served as an example that may have improved the lives of Muslim women.

For the most part, however, the Quran—and later the *sharia* as well—reinforced male dominance. The Quran and Islamic holy law recognized descent through the male line, and to guarantee proper inheritance, they placed a high premium on genealogical purity. To ensure the legitimacy of heirs, they subjected the social and sexual lives of women to the strict control of male guardians—fathers, brothers, and husbands. While teaching that men should treat women with sensitivity and respect, the Quran and the *sharia* permitted men to follow Muhammad's example and take up to four wives, whereas women could have only one husband. The Quran and the *sharia* thus provided a religious and legal foundation for a decisively patriarchal society.

When Islam expanded into the Byzantine and Sasanid empires, it encountered strong patriarchal traditions, and Muslims readily adopted long-standing customs such as the veiling of women. Social and family pressures had induced upper-class urban women to veil themselves in Mesopotamia as early as the thirteenth century B.C.E., and long before Muhammad the practice of veiling had spread to Persia and the eastern Mediterranean. As a sign of modesty, upper-class urban women covered their faces and ventured outside their homes only in the company of servants or chaperones so as to discourage the attention of men from other families. When Muslim Arabs conquered Mesopotamia, Persia, and eastern Mediterranean lands, they adopted the practice. A conspicuous symbol of male authority thus found a prominent place in the early Islamic community.

Veiling of Women

The Quran served as the preeminent source of authority in the world of Islam, and it provided specific rights for Muslim women. Over the centuries, however, jurists and legal scholars interpreted the Quran in ways that progressively limited those rights and placed women increasingly under the control of male guardians. To a large extent the increased emphasis on male authority in Islamic law reflected the influence of the strongly hierarchical and patriarchal societies of Mesopotamia, Persia, and eastern Mediterranean lands as Islam developed from a local faith to a large-scale complex society.

ISLAMIC VALUES AND CULTURAL EXCHANGES

Since the seventh century C.E., the Quran has served as the cornerstone of Islamic society. Arising from a rich tradition of bedouin poetry and song, the Quran established Arabic as a flexible and powerful medium of communication. Even today Muslims regard the Arabic text of the Quran as the only definitive and reliable scripture: translations do not possess the power and authority of the original. When carrying their faith to new lands during the era of Islamic expansion, Muslim missionaries spread the message of Allah and provided instruction in the Quran's teachings, although usually they also permitted continued observance of pre-Islamic traditions. Muslim intellectuals drew freely from the long-established cultural traditions of Persia, India, and Greece, which they became acquainted with during the Umayyad and Abbasid eras.

The Formation of an Islamic Cultural Tradition

Muslim theologians and jurists looked to the Quran, stories about Muhammad's life, and other sources of Islamic doctrine in their efforts to formulate moral guidelines appropriate for their society. The body of civil and criminal law embodied in the *sharia* provided a measure of cultural unity for the vastly different lands of the Islamic world. Islamic law did not by any means erase the differences, but it established a common cultural foundation that facilitated dealings between peoples of various Islamic lands and that lent substance to the concept of the *dar al-Islam.*

On a more popular level, *ulama, qadis,* and missionaries helped to bridge differences in cultural traditions and to spread Islamic values throughout the *dar al-Islam.* *Ulama* and *qadis* held positions at all Islamic courts, and they were prominent in the

Promotion of Islamic Values

In this manuscript illustration a Muslim teacher (the figure with the open book) instructs students in the fine points of Islamic law in a library near Baghdad.

public life of all cities in the Islamic world. By resolving disputes according to Islamic law and ordering public observance of Islamic social and moral standards, they helped to bring the values of the Quran and the *sharia* into the lives of peoples living far from the birthplace of Islam.

Formal educational institutions also helped promote Islamic values. Many mosques maintained schools that provided an elementary education and religious instruction, and wealthy Muslims sometimes established schools and provided endowments for their support. By the tenth century institutions of higher education known as *madrasas* had begun to appear, and by the twelfth century they had become established in the major cities of the Islamic world. Muslim rulers often supported the *madrasas* in the interests of recruiting literate and learned students with an advanced education in Islamic theology and law for administrative positions. Inexpensive paper enhanced scholars' ability to instruct students and disseminate their views.

Sufis   Among the most effective Islamic missionaries were mystics known as Sufis. The term *Sufi* probably came from the patched woolen garments favored by the mystics. Sufis did not deny Islamic doctrine, and indeed many of them had an advanced education in Islamic theology and law. But they also did not find formal religious teachings to be especially meaningful. Thus, instead of concerning themselves with fine points of doctrine, Sufis worked to deepen their spiritual awareness. Most Sufis led pious and ascetic lives. Some devoted themselves to helping the poor. A few gave up their possessions and lived as mendicant beggars. Many sought a mystical, ecstatic union with Allah, relying on rousing sermons, passionate singing, or spirited dancing to bring them to a state of high emotion. Muslim theologians sometimes mistrusted Sufis, fearing that in their lack of concern for doctrine they would adopt erroneous beliefs. Nevertheless, after the ninth century Sufis became increasingly popular in Muslim societies because of their piety, devotion, and eagerness to minister to the needs of their fellow human beings.

Al-Ghazali   Most important of the early Sufis was the Persian theologian al-Ghazali (1058–1111), who argued that human reason was too frail to understand the nature of Allah and hence could not explain the mysteries of the world. Only through devotion and guidance from

Through song, dance, and ecstatic experiences, sometimes enhanced by wine, Persian Sufis expressed their devotion to Allah, as in this sixteenth-century painting.

the Quran could human beings begin to appreciate the uniqueness and power of Allah. Indeed, al-Ghazali held that philosophy and human reasoning were vain pursuits that would inevitably lead to confusion rather than understanding.

Sufis were especially effective as missionaries because they emphasized devotion to Allah above mastery of doctrine. They sometimes encouraged individuals to revere Allah in their own ways, even if their methods did not have a basis in the Quran. They tolerated the continued observance of pre-Islamic customs, for example, as well as the

Sufi Missionaries

Hajj

association of Allah with deities recognized and revered in other faiths. The Sufis themselves led ascetic and holy lives, which won them the respect of the peoples to whom they preached. Because of their kindness, holiness, tolerance, and charismatic appeal, Sufis attracted numerous converts particularly in lands like Persia and India, where long-established religious faiths such as Zoroastrianism, Christianity, Buddhism, and Hinduism had enjoyed a mass following for centuries.

The symbol of Islamic cultural unity was the Ka'ba at Mecca, which from an early date attracted pilgrims from all parts of the Islamic world. The Abbasid caliphs especially encouraged observance of the hajj: they saw themselves as supreme leaders of a cohesive Islamic community, and as a matter of policy they sought to enhance the cultural unity of their realm. They built inns along the main roads to Mecca for the convenience of travelers, policed the routes to ensure the safety of pilgrims, and made lavish gifts to shrines and sites of pilgrimage. Individuals from far-flung regions of the Abbasid empire made their way to Mecca, visited the holy sites, and learned first hand the traditions of Islam. Over the centuries these pilgrims helped to spread Islamic beliefs and values to all parts of the Islamic world, and alongside the work of *ulama, qadis,* and Sufi missionaries, their efforts helped to make the *dar al-Islam* not just a name, but a reality.

Islam and the Cultural Traditions of Persia, India, and Greece

As the Islamic community expanded, Muslims of Arab ancestry interacted regularly with peoples from other cultural traditions, especially those of Persia, India, and Greece. In some cases, particularly in lands ruled by the Umayyad and Abbasid dynasties, large numbers of conquered peoples converted to Islam, and they brought elements of their inherited cultural traditions into Islamic society. In other cases, particularly in lands beyond the authority of Islamic rulers, Muslims became acquainted with the literary, artistic, philosophical, and scientific traditions of peoples who chose not to convert. Nevertheless, their traditions often held considerable interest for Muslims, who adapted them for their own purposes.

Persian Influences on Islam

Persian traditions quickly found a place in Islamic society, since the culturally rich land of Persia fell under Islamic rule at an early date. Especially after the establishment of the Abbasid dynasty and the founding of its capital at Baghdad, Persian traditions deeply influenced Islamic political and cultural leaders. Persian administrative techniques, which Muslim conquerors borrowed from the Sasanid empire, were crucial for the organization of the imperial structure through which Umayyad and Abbasid rulers governed their vast empire. Meanwhile, Persian ideas of kingship profoundly influenced Islamic political thought. Muslim caliphs and regional governors drew readily on Persian views of kings as wise and benevolent but nonetheless absolute rulers.

Persian influence was also noticeable in literary works from the Abbasid dynasty. While Arabic served as the language of religion, theology, philosophy, and law, Persian was the principal language of literature, poetry, history, and political reflection. The verses of Omar Khayyam entitled the *Rubaiyat* ("quatrains") are widely known, thanks to a popular English translation by the Victorian poet Edward Fitzgerald, but many other writers composed works that in Persian display even greater literary elegance and originality. The marvelous collection of stories known as *The Arabian Nights* or *The Thousand and One Nights,* for example, presented popular tales of adventure and romance set in the Abbasid empire and the court of Harun al-Rashid.

Indian Influences on Islam

Indian mathematics, science, and medicine captured the attention of Arab and Persian Muslims who established Islamic states in northern India. The sophisticated mathematical tradition of Gupta India was attractive to Muslims both as a field of scholarship and for the practical purposes of reckoning and keeping accounts. Muslims readily adopted what they called "Hindi" numerals, which European peoples later called "Arabic" numerals, since they learned about them through Arab Muslims. Hindi numerals enabled Muslim scholars to develop an impressive tradition of advanced mathematics, concentrating on algebra (an Arabic word) as well as trigonometry and geometry. From a more practical point of view, Indian numerals vastly simplified bookkeeping for Muslim merchants working in the lively commercial economy of the Abbasid dynasty.

Muslims also found much to appreciate in the scientific and medical thought they encountered in India. With the aid of their powerful and flexible mathematics, Indian scholars were able to carry out precise astronomical calculations, which helped inspire the development of Muslim astronomy. Similarly, Indian medicine appealed to Muslims because of its treatments for specific ailments and its use of antidotes for poisons. Muslim visitors often railed against Indian religious beliefs—both Hindu and Buddhist—but they uniformly praised Indian mathematical, scientific, and medical thought, which they avidly adopted for their own uses and purposes.

Greek Influences on Islam

Muslims also admired the philosophical, scientific, and medical writings of classical Greece. They became especially interested in Plato and Aristotle, whose works they translated and interpreted in commentaries. During the tenth and eleventh centuries, some Muslim philosophers sought to synthesize Greek and Muslim thought by harmonizing Plato with the teachings of Islam. They encountered resistance among conservative theologians like the Sufi al-Ghazali, who considered Greek philosophy a completely unreliable guide to ultimate truth, since it relied on frail human reason rather than the revelation of the Quran.

Partly in response to al-Ghazali's attacks, twelfth-century Muslim philosophers turned their attention more to Aristotle than Plato. The most notable figure in this development was Ibn Rushd (1126–1198), *qadi* of Seville in the caliphate of Córdoba, who followed Aristotle in seeking to articulate a purely rational understanding of the world. Ibn Rushd's work not only helped to shape Islamic philosophy but also found its way to the schools and universities of western Europe, where Christian scholars knew Ibn Rushd as Averroes. During the thirteenth century his work profoundly influenced the development of scholasticism, the effort of medieval European philosophers to harmonize Christianity with Aristotelian thought.

Ibn Rushd's reliance on natural reason went too far for many Muslims, who placed more value on the revelations of the Quran than on the fruits of human logic. After the thirteenth century, Muslim philosophers and theologians who dominated the *madrasas* drew inspiration more from Islamic sources than from Greek philosophy. Platonic and Aristotelian influences did not disappear, but they lost favor in official seats of learning and fell increasingly under the shadow of teachings from the Quran and Sufi mystics. As they did with political and cultural traditions from Persia and India, Muslim thinkers absorbed Greek philosophy, reconsidered it, and used it to advance the interests of their own society.

Quite apart from philosophy, Greek mathematics, science, and medicine also appealed strongly to Muslims. Like their Indian counterparts, scholars in classical Greek and Hellenistic societies had developed elaborate traditions of scientific thought. Greek mathematics did not make use of Indian numerals, but it offered a solid body of powerful reasoning, particularly when dealing with calculations in algebra and geometry. Greek mathematics supported the development of astronomical and geographical scholarship, while studies of anatomy and physiology served as foundations for medical thought. Muslim scholars quickly absorbed these Greek traditions, combined them with influences from India, and used them all as points of departure for their own studies. The result was a brilliant flowering of mathematical, scientific, and medical scholarship that provided Muslim societies with powerful tools for understanding the natural world.

The prophet Muhammad did not intend to found a new religion. Instead, his intention was to express his faith in Allah and perfect the teachings of earlier Jewish and Christian prophets by announcing a revelation more comprehensive than those Allah had entrusted to his predecessors. His message soon attracted a circle of devout and committed disciples, and by the time of his death most of Arabia had accepted Islam, the faith founded on the individual's submission to Allah and his will. During the two centuries following the prophet's death, Arab conquerors spread Islam throughout southwest Asia and north Africa and introduced their faith to central Asia, India, the Mediterranean islands, and Iberia. This rapid expansion of Islam encouraged the development of a massive trade and communication network: merchants, diplomats, and other travelers moved easily throughout the Islamic world exchanging goods and introducing agricultural crops to new lands. Rapid expansion also led to encounters between Islam and long-established religious and cultural traditions such as Hinduism, Judaism, Zoroastrianism, Christianity, Persian literature and political thought, and classical Greek philosophy and science. Muslim rulers built a society that made a place for those of different faiths, and Muslim thinkers readily adapted earlier traditions to their own needs. As a result of its expansion, its extensive trade and communication networks, and its engagement with other religious and cultural traditions, the *dar al-Islam* became one of the most prosperous and cosmopolitan societies of the postclassical world.

CHRONOLOGY

570–632	Life of Muhammad
622	The *hijra*
632	Muhammad's *hajj*
650s	Compilation of the Quran
661–750	Umayyad dynasty
750–1258	Abbasid dynasty
786–809	Reign of Harun al-Rashid
1050s	Establishment of Saljuq control over the Abbasid dynasty
1058–1111	Life of al-Ghazali
1126–1198	Life of Ibn Rushd

FOR FURTHER READING

Muhammad Manazir Ahsan. *Social Life under the Abbasids.* New York, 1979. Draws on a wide range of sources in discussing dress, food, drink, housing, and daily life during the Abbasid era.

Richard W. Bulliet. *The Camel and the Wheel.* New York, 1990. Fascinating study of the domestication of camels and transportation technologies based on camels.

Richard C. Foltz. *Spirituality in the Land of the Noble: How Iran Shaped the World's Religions.* Oxford, 2004. Includes an accessible discussion of Persian influences on the Islamic faith.

Abu Hamid Muhammad al-Ghazzali. *The Alchemy of Happiness.* Trans. by Claude Field. Rev. by Elton L. Daniel. New York, 1991. Translation of one of the classic works of early Islamic religious and moral thought.

H. A. R. Gibb. *Mohammedanism.* 2nd ed. London, 1953. A short, analytical overview of the Islamic faith and its history by a prominent scholar.

Ahmad Y. al-Hassan and Donald R. Hill. *Islamic Technology: An Illustrated History.* Cambridge, 1986. Thorough survey of Islamic science and technology, with attention both to original inventions and to elements borrowed by Muslims from other societies.

Mahmood Ibrahim. *Merchant Capital and Islam.* Austin, 1990. Examines the role of trade in Arabia during Muhammad's time and in early Islamic society.

Salma Khadra Jayyusi, ed. *The Legacy of Muslim Spain.* Leiden, 1992. Important collection of scholarly essays on Muslim influences at the western end of the Islamic world.

Ira M. Lapidus. *A History of Islamic Societies.* Cambridge, 1988. Authoritative survey of Islamic history, concentrating on social and cultural issues.

Ilse Lichtenstadter. *Introduction to Classical Arabic Literature.* New York, 1974. A brief overview, accompanied by an extensive selection of texts in English translation.

M. Lombard. *The Golden Age of Islam.* Princeton, 2004. Concentrates on the social and economic history of the Abbasid period.

William H. McNeill and Marilyn R. Waldman, eds. *The Islamic World.* New York, 1973. An excellent collection of primary sources in translation.

F. E. Peters. *The Hajj: The Muslim Pilgrimage to Mecca and the Holy Places.* Princeton, 1994. Draws on scores of travelers' reports in studying the Muslim practice through the ages of making a pilgrimage to Mecca.

———. *Muhammad and the Origins of Islam.* Albany, 1994. Excellent introduction to Muhammad's life and thought and the early days of his movement.

Al Qur'an: A Contemporary Translation. Trans. by Ahmed Ali. Princeton, 1984. A sensitive translation of the holy book of Islam.

Francis Robinson, ed. *The Cambridge Illustrated History of the Islamic World.* Cambridge, 1996. An excellent and lavishly illustrated introduction to Islam and the Muslim world.

Maxime Rodinson. *Islam and Capitalism.* Trans. by B. Pearce. New York, 1973. An influential volume that examines Islamic teachings on economic matters as well as economic practice in the Muslim world.

————. *Mohammed*. Trans. by Anne Carter. New York, 1971. Places Muhammad in his social and economic context.

Andrew M. Watson. *Agricultural Innovation in the Early Islamic World: The Diffusion of Crops and Farming Techniques, 700–1100.* Cambridge, 1983. Important scholarly study of the diffusion of food and industrial crops throughout the early Islamic world.

Frances Wood. *The Silk Road: Two Thousand Years in the Heart of Asia.* Berkeley, 2002. A brilliantly illustrated volume discussing the history of the silk roads from antiquity to the twentieth century.

See our **Online Learning Center** at **www.mhhe.com/bentley3** for additional readings, practice maps, quizzes, and internet activities.

Unfamiliar words? Check out the **Primary Source Investigator CD-ROM** for an interactive glossary, interactive maps, more images, and primary sources.

唐太宗真像

帝名世民高祖次子在位二十三年號貞觀

The features of the emperor Tang Taizong reflect his Turkish and Chinese ancestry.

CHAPTER 15

THE RESURGENCE OF EMPIRE IN EAST ASIA

Early in the seventh century C.E., the emperor of China issued an order forbidding his subjects to travel beyond Chinese borders into central Asia. In 629, however, in defiance of the emperor, a young Buddhist monk slipped past imperial watchtowers under cover of darkness and made his way west. His name was Xuanzang, and his destination was India, homeland of Buddhism. Although educated in Confucian texts as a youth, Xuanzang had followed his older brother into a monastery where he became devoted to Buddhism. While studying the Sanskrit language, Xuanzang noticed that Chinese writings on Buddhism contained many teachings that were confusing or even contradictory to those of Indian Buddhist texts. He decided to travel to India, visit the holy sites of Buddhism, and study with the most knowledgeable Buddhist teachers and sages to learn about his faith from the purest sources.

Xuanzang could not have imagined the difficulties he would face. Immediately after his departure from China, his guide abandoned him in the Gobi desert. After losing his water bag and collapsing in the heat, Xuanzang made his way to the oasis town of Turpan on the silk roads. The Buddhist ruler of Turpan provided the devout pilgrim with travel supplies and rich gifts to support his mission. Among the presents were twenty-four letters of introduction to rulers of lands on the way to India, each one attached to a bolt of silk, five hundred additional bolts of silk and two carts of fruit for the most important ruler, thirty horses, twenty-five laborers, and five hundred bolts of silk along with gold, silver, and silk clothes for Xuanzang to use as travel funds. After departing from Turpan, Xuanzang crossed three of the world's highest mountain ranges—the Tian Shan, Hindu Kush, and Pamir ranges—and lost one-third of his party to exposure and starvation in the Tian Shan. He crossed yawning gorges thousands of meters deep on footbridges fashioned from rope or chains, and he faced numerous attacks by bandits as well as confrontations with demons, dragons, and evil spirits.

Yet Xuanzang persisted and arrived in India in 630. He lived there for more than twelve years, visiting the holy sites of Buddhism and devoting himself to the study of languages and Buddhist doctrine, especially at Nalanda, the center of advanced Buddhist education in India. He also amassed a huge collection of relics and images as well as some 657 books, all of which he packed into 527 crates and transported back to China in order to advance the understanding of Buddhism in his native land.

By the time of his return in 645, Xuanzang had logged more than 16,000 kilometers (10,000 miles) on the road. News of the holy monk's efforts had reached the imperial court, and even though Xuanzang had violated the ban on travel, he received a

375

hero's welcome and an audience with the emperor. Until his death in 664, Xuanzang spent his remaining years translating Buddhist treatises into Chinese and promoting his faith. His efforts helped to popularize Buddhism and bring about nearly universal adoption of the faith throughout China.

Xuanzang undertook his journey at a propitious time. For more than 350 years after the fall of the Han dynasty, war, invasion, conquest, and foreign rule disrupted Chinese society. Toward the end of the sixth century, however, centralized imperial rule returned to China. The Sui and Tang dynasties restored order and presided over an era of rapid economic growth in China. Agricultural yields rose dramatically, and technological innovations boosted the production of manufactured goods. China stood alongside the Byzantine and Abbasid empires as a political and economic anchor of the postclassical world.

For China the postclassical era was an age of intense interaction with other peoples. Chinese merchants participated in trade networks that linked most regions of the eastern hemisphere. Buddhism spread beyond its homeland of India, attracted a large popular following in China, and even influenced the thought of Confucian scholars. A resurgent China made its influence felt throughout east Asia: diplomats and armed forces introduced Chinese ways into Korea and Vietnam, and rulers of the Japanese islands looked to China for guidance in matters of political organization. Korea, Vietnam, and Japan retained their distinctiveness, but all three lands drew deep inspiration from China and participated in a larger east Asian society centered on China.

THE RESTORATION OF CENTRALIZED IMPERIAL RULE IN CHINA

During the centuries following the Han dynasty, several regional kingdoms made bids to assert their authority over all of China, but none possessed the resources to dominate its rivals over the long term. In the late sixth century, however, Yang Jian, an ambitious ruler in northern China, embarked on a series of military campaigns that brought all of China once again under centralized imperial rule. Yang Jian's Sui dynasty survived less than thirty years, but the tradition of centralized rule outlived his house. The Tang dynasty replaced the Sui, and the Song succeeded the Tang. The Tang and Song dynasties organized Chinese society so efficiently that China became a center of exceptional agricultural and industrial production. Indeed, much of the eastern hemisphere felt the effects of the powerful Chinese economy of the Tang and Song dynasties.

The Sui Dynasty

Establishment of the Dynasty

Like Qin Shihuangdi some eight centuries years earlier, Yang Jian imposed tight political discipline on his own state and then extended his rule to the rest of China. Yang Jian began his rise to power when a Turkish ruler appointed him duke of Sui in northern China. In 580 Yang Jian's patron died, leaving a seven-year-old son as his heir. Yang Jian installed the boy as ruler but forced his abdication one year later, claiming the throne and the Mandate of Heaven for himself. During the next decade Yang Jian sent military expeditions into central Asia and southern China. By 589 the house of Sui ruled all of China.

Like the rulers of the Qin dynasty, the emperors of the Sui dynasty (589–618 C.E.) placed enormous demands on their subjects in the course of building a strong, centralized government. The Sui emperors ordered the construction of palaces and granaries,

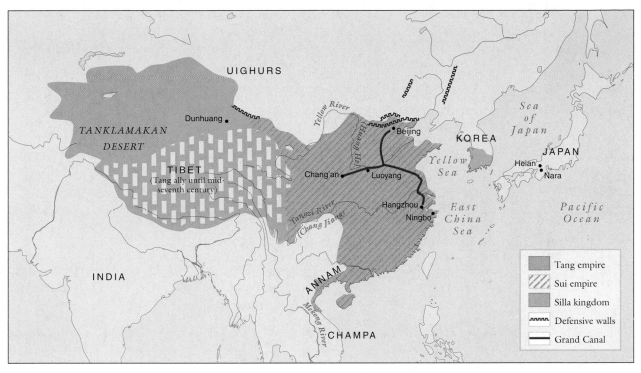

MAP [15.1]
The Sui and Tang dynasties,
589–907 C.E.

carried out extensive repairs on defensive walls, dispatched military forces to central Asia and Korea, levied high taxes, and demanded compulsory labor services.

The most elaborate project undertaken during the Sui dynasty was the construction of the Grand Canal, which was one of the world's largest waterworks projects before modern times. The second emperor, Sui Yangdi (reigned 604–618 C.E.), completed work on the canal to facilitate trade between northern and southern China, particularly to make the abundant supplies of rice and other food crops from the Yangzi River valley available to residents of northern regions. The only practical and economical way to transport food crops in large quantities was by water. But since Chinese rivers generally flow from west to east, only an artificial waterway could support a large volume of trade between north and south.

The Grand Canal was really a series of artificial waterways that ultimately reached from Hangzhou in the south to the imperial capital of Chang'an in the west to a terminus near modern Beijing in the north. Sui Yangdi used canals dug as early as the Zhou dynasty, but he linked them into a network that served much of China. When completed, the Grand Canal extended almost 2,000 kilometers (1,240 miles) and reportedly was forty paces wide, with roads running parallel to the waterway on either side.

Though expensive to construct, Sui Yangdi's investment in the Grand Canal paid dividends for more than a thousand years. It integrated the economies of northern and southern China, thereby establishing an economic foundation for political and cultural unity. Until the arrival of railroads in the twentieth century, the Grand Canal served as the principal conduit for internal trade. Indeed, the canal continues to function even today, although mechanical transport has diminished its significance as a trade route.

Sui Yangdi's construction projects served China well over a long term, but their dependence on high taxes and forced labor generated hostility toward his rule. The

The Grand Canal

In a painting that dates probably from about the seventeenth century, workers build dikes to hold back a river. Construction of the Grand Canal also involved heavy work by large numbers of conscripted laborers.

Grand Canal alone required the services of conscripted laborers by the millions. Military reverses in Korea prompted discontented subjects to revolt against Sui rule. During the late 610s, rebellions broke out in northern China when Sui Yangdi sought additional resources for his Korean campaign. In 618 a disgruntled minister assassinated the emperor and brought the dynasty to an end.

The Tang Dynasty

Tang Taizong

Soon after Sui Yangdi's death, a rebel leader seized Chang'an and proclaimed himself emperor of a new dynasty that he named Tang after his hereditary title. The dynasty survived for almost three hundred years (618–907 C.E.), and Tang rulers organized China into a powerful, productive, and prosperous society.

Much of the Tang's success was due to the energy, ability, and policies of the dynasty's second emperor, Tang Taizong (reigned 627–649 C.E.). Taizong was both ambitious and ruthless: in making his way to the imperial throne, he murdered two of his brothers and pushed his father aside. Once on the throne, however, he displayed a high sense of duty and strove conscientiously to provide an effective, stable government. He built a splendid capital at Chang'an, and he saw himself as a Confucian ruler who heeded the interests of his subjects. Contemporaries reported that banditry ended during his reign, that the price of rice remained low, and that taxes levied on peasants amounted to only one-fortieth of the annual harvest—a 2.5 percent tax rate—although required rent payments and compulsory labor services meant that the effective rate of taxation was somewhat higher. These reports suggest that China enjoyed an era of unusual stability and prosperity during the reign of Tang Taizong.

Three policies in particular help to explain the success of the early Tang dynasty: maintenance of a well-articulated transportation and communications network, distribution of land according to the principles of the equal-field system, and reliance on a bureaucracy based on merit. All three policies originated in the Sui dynasty, but Tang rulers applied them more systematically and effectively than their predecessors had.

Apart from the Grand Canal, which served as the principal route for long-distance transportation within China, Tang rulers maintained an extensive communications network based on roads, horses, and sometimes human runners. Along the main routes, Tang officials maintained inns, postal stations, and stables, which provided rest and refreshment for travelers, couriers, and their mounts. Using couriers traveling by horse, the Tang court could communicate with the most distant cities in the empire in about eight days. Even human runners provided impressively speedy services: relay teams of some 9,600 runners supplied the Tang court at Chang'an with seafood delivered fresh from Ningbo, more than 1,000 kilometers (620 miles) away!

Transportation and Communications

The equal-field system governed the allocation of agricultural land. Its purpose was to ensure an equitable distribution of land and to avoid the concentration of landed property that had caused social problems during the Han dynasty. The system allotted land to individuals and their families according to the land's fertility and the recipients' needs. About one-fifth of the land became the hereditary possession of the recipients, while the rest remained available for redistribution when the original recipients' needs and circumstances changed.

The Equal-Field System

For about a century, administrators were able to apply the principles of the equal-field system relatively consistently. By the early eighth century, however, the system showed signs of strain. A rapidly rising population placed pressure on the land available for distribution. Meanwhile, through favors, bribery, or intimidation of administrators, influential families found ways to retain land scheduled for redistribution. Furthermore, large parcels of land fell out of the system altogether when Buddhist monasteries acquired them. Nevertheless, during the first half of the Tang dynasty, the system provided a foundation for stability and prosperity in the Chinese countryside.

The Tang dynasty also relied heavily on a bureaucracy based on merit, as reflected by performance on imperial civil service examinations. Following the example of the Han dynasty, Sui and Tang rulers recruited government officials from the ranks of candidates who had progressed through the Confucian educational system and had mastered a sophisticated curriculum concentrating on the classic works of Chinese literature and philosophy. Although powerful families used their influence to place relatives in positions of authority, most officeholders won their posts because of intellectual ability. Members of this talented class were generally loyal to the dynasty, and they worked to preserve and strengthen the state. The Confucian educational system and the related civil service served Chinese governments so well that with modifications and an occasional interruption, they survived for thirteen centuries, disappearing only after the collapse of the Qing dynasty in the early twentieth century.

Bureaucracy of Merit

Soon after its foundation, the powerful and dynamic Tang state began to flex its military muscles. In the north, Tang forces brought Manchuria under imperial authority and forced the Silla kingdom in Korea to acknowledge the Tang emperor as overlord. To the south, Tang armies conquered the northern part of Vietnam. To the west they extended Tang authority as far as the Aral Sea and brought a portion of the high plateau of Tibet under Tang control. Territorially, the Tang empire ranks among the largest in Chinese history.

Military Expansion

*Tang Foreign
Relations*

In an effort to fashion a stable diplomatic order, the Tang emperors revived the Han dynasty's practice of maintaining tributary relationships between China and neighboring lands. According to Chinese political theory, China was the Middle Kingdom, a powerful realm with the responsibility to bring order to subordinate lands through a system of tributary relationships. Neighboring lands and peoples would recognize Chinese emperors as their overlords. As tokens of their subordinate status, envoys from these states would regularly deliver gifts to the court of the Middle Kingdom and would perform the kowtow—a ritual prostration during which subordinates knelt before the emperor and touched their foreheads to the ground. In return, tributary states received confirmation of their authority as well as lavish gifts. Because Chinese authorities often had little real influence in these supposedly subordinate lands, there was always something of a fictional quality to the system. Nevertheless, it was extremely important throughout east Asia and central Asia because it institutionalized relations between China and neighboring lands, fostering trade and cultural exchanges as well as diplomatic contacts.

Tang Decline

Under able rulers such as Taizong, the Tang dynasty flourished. During the mid-eighth century, however, casual and careless leadership brought the dynasty to a crisis from which it never fully recovered. In 755, while the emperor neglected public affairs in favor of music and his favorite concubine, one of the dynasty's foremost military commanders, An Lushan, mounted a rebellion and captured the capital at Chang'an, as well as the secondary capital at Luoyang. His revolt was short-lived: in 757 a soldier murdered An Lushan, and by 763 Tang forces had suppressed An Lushan's army and recovered their capitals. But the rebellion left the dynasty in a gravely weakened state. Tang commanders had to invite a nomadic Turkish people,

In this wall painting from the tomb of a Tang prince, three Chinese officials (at left) receive envoys from foreign lands who pay their respects to representatives of the Middle Kingdom. The envoys probably come from the Byzantine empire, Korea, and Siberia.

Sources from the Past

The Poet Du Fu on Tang Dynasty Wars

The eighth century was a golden age of Chinese poetry. Among the foremost writers of the era was Du Fu (712–770 C.E.), often considered China's greatest poet. Born into a prominent Confucian family, Du Fu wrote in his early years about the beauty of the natural world. After the rebellion of An Lushan, however, he fell into poverty and experienced difficulties. Not surprisingly, poetry of his later years lamented the chaos of the late eighth century. In the following verses, Du Fu offered a bitter perspective on the wars that plagued China in the 750s and 760s.

A Song of War Chariots

The war-chariots rattle,
The war-horses whinny.
Each man of you has a bow and a quiver at his belt.
Father, mother, son, wife, stare at you going,
Till dust shall have buried the bridge beyond Chang'an.
They run with you, crying, they tug at your sleeves,
And the sound of their sorrow goes up to the clouds;
And every time a bystander asks you a question,
You can only say to him that you have to go.
. . . We remember others at fifteen sent north to guard
     the river
And at forty sent west to cultivate the camp-farms.
The mayor wound their turbans for them when they
     started out.
With their turbaned hair white now, they are still at the
     border,
At the border where the blood of men spills like the
     sea—
And still the heart of Emperor Wu is beating for war.

. . . Do you know that, east of China's mountains, in
     two hundred districts
And in thousands of villages, nothing grows but weeds,
And though strong women have bent to the ploughing,
East and west the furrows all are broken down?
. . . Men of China are able to face the stiffest battle,
But their officers drive them like chickens and dogs.
Whatever is asked of them,
Dare they complain?
For example, this winter
Held west of the gate,
Challenged for taxes,
How could they pay?
. . . We have learned that to have a son is bad luck—
It is very much better to have a daughter
Who can marry and live in the house of a neighbour,
While under the sod we bury our boys.
. . . Go to the Blue Sea, look along the shore
At all the old white bones forsaken—
New ghosts are wailing there now with the old,
Loudest in the dark sky of a stormy day.

SOURCE: Cyril Birch, ed. *Anthology of Chinese Literature,* 2 vols. New York: Grove Press, 1965, pp. 1:240–41.

Assess the effects of war in the late Tang dynasty from the viewpoints of imperial rulers and individual subjects.

the Uighurs, to bring an army into China to oust An Lushan from the imperial capitals. In return for their services, the Uighurs demanded the right to sack Chang'an and Luoyang after the expulsion of the rebels.

The Tang imperial house never regained control of affairs after this crisis. The equal-field system deteriorated, and dwindling tax receipts failed to meet dynastic needs. Imperial armies were unable to resist the encroachments of Turkish peoples in the late eighth century. During the ninth century a series of rebellions devastated the Chinese countryside. One uprising, led by the military commander Huang Chao, embroiled much of eastern China for almost a decade from 875 to 884. Huang Chao's revolt reflected and fueled popular discontent: he routinely pillaged the wealthy and distributed a portion of his plunder among the poor. In an effort to control the rebels, the Tang emperors granted progressively greater power and authority to regional military commanders, who gradually became the effective rulers of China. In 907 the last Tang emperor abdicated his throne, and the dynasty came to an end.

The Song Dynasty

Following the Tang collapse, warlords ruled China until the Song dynasty reimposed centralized imperial rule in the late tenth century. Though it survived for more than three centuries, the Song dynasty (960–1279 C.E.) never built a very powerful state. Song rulers mistrusted military leaders, and they placed much more emphasis on civil administration, industry, education, and the arts than on military affairs.

Song Taizu

The first Song emperor, Song Taizu (reigned 960–976 C.E.), himself inaugurated this policy. Song Taizu began his career as a junior military officer serving one of the most powerful warlords in northern China. He had a reputation for honesty and effectiveness, and in 960 his troops proclaimed him emperor. During the next several years, he and his army subjected the warlords to their authority and consolidated Song control throughout China. He then persuaded his generals to retire honorably to a life of leisure so that they would not seek to displace him, and he set about organizing a centralized administration that placed military forces under tight supervision.

Song Taizu regarded all state officials, even minor functionaries in distant provinces, as servants of the imperial government. In exchange for their loyalty, Song rulers rewarded these officials handsomely. They vastly expanded the bureaucracy based on merit by creating more opportunities for individuals to seek a Confucian education and take civil service examinations. They accepted many more candidates into the bureaucracy than their Sui and Tang predecessors, and they provided generous salaries for those who qualified for government appointments. They even placed civil bureaucrats in charge of military forces.

Song Weaknesses

The Song approach to administration resulted in a more centralized imperial government than earlier Chinese dynasties had enjoyed. But it caused two big problems that weakened the dynasty and eventually brought about its fall. The first problem was financial: the enormous Song bureaucracy devoured China's surplus production. As the number of bureaucrats and the size of their rewards grew, the imperial treasury came under tremendous pressure. Efforts to raise taxes aggravated the peasants, who mounted two major rebellions in the early twelfth century. By that time, however, bureaucrats dominated the Song administration to the point that it was impossible to reform the system.

The second problem was military. Scholar bureaucrats generally had little military education and little talent for military affairs, yet they led Song armies in the field and made military decisions. It was no coincidence that nomadic peoples flourished along China's northern border throughout the Song dynasty. From the early tenth through the early twelfth century, the Khitan, a seminomadic people from Manchuria, ruled a vast empire stretching from northern Korea to Mongolia. During the first half of the Song dynasty, the Khitan demanded and received large tribute payments of silk and silver from the Song state to the south. In the early twelfth century, the nomadic Jurchen conquered the Khitan, overran northern China, captured the Song capital at Kaifeng, and proclaimed establishment of the Jin empire. Thereafter the Song dynasty moved its capital to the prosperous port city of Hangzhou and survived only in southern China so that the latter part of the dynasty is commonly known as the Southern Song. This

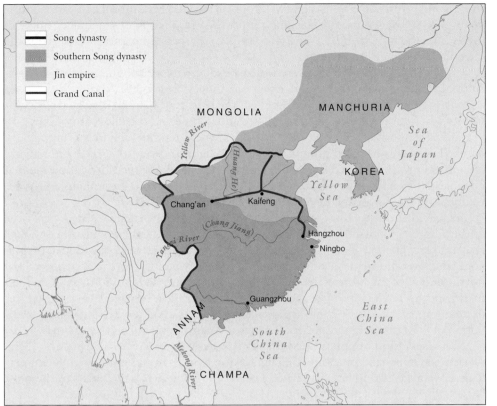

MAP [15.2]
The Song dynasty,
960–1279 C.E.

For an interactive version
of this map, go to
www.mhhe.com/
bentley3ch15maps.

truncated Southern Song shared a border with the Jin empire about midway between
the Yellow River and the Yangzi River until 1279, when Mongol forces ended the dynasty and incorporated southern China into their empire.

THE ECONOMIC DEVELOPMENT
OF TANG AND SONG CHINA

Although the Song dynasty did not develop a particularly strong military capacity, it
benefited from a remarkable series of agricultural, technological, industrial, and commercial developments that transformed China into the economic powerhouse of
Eurasia. This economic development originated in the Tang dynasty, but its results
became most clear during the Song, which presided over a land of enormous prosperity. The economic surge of Tang and Song times had implications that went well
beyond China, since it stimulated trade and production throughout much of the
eastern hemisphere for more than half a millennium, from about 600 to 1300 C.E.

Agricultural Development

The foundation of economic development in Tang and Song China was a surge in
agricultural production. Sui and Tang armies prepared the way for increased agricultural productivity when they imposed their control over southern China and ventured into Vietnam. In Vietnam they encountered new strains of fast-ripening rice

Fast-Ripening Rice

that enabled cultivators to harvest two crops per year. When introduced to the fertile fields of southern China, fast-ripening rice quickly resulted in an expanded supply of food. Like the *dar al-Islam*, Tang and Song China benefited enormously from the introduction of new food crops.

New Agricultural Techniques

Chinese cultivators also increased their productivity by adopting improved agricultural techniques. They made increased use of heavy iron plows, and they harnessed oxen (in the north) and water buffaloes (in the south) to help prepare land for cultivation. They enriched the soil with manure and composted organic matter. They also organized extensive irrigation systems. These included not only reservoirs, dikes, dams, and canals but also pumps and water wheels, powered by both animal and human energy, that moved water into irrigation systems. Artificial irrigation made it possible to extend cultivation to new lands, including terraced mountainsides—a development that vastly expanded China's agricultural potential.

Population Growth

Increased agricultural production had dramatic results. One was a rapid expansion of the Chinese population. After the fall of the Han dynasty, the population of China reached a low point at about 45 million in 600 C.E. By 800 it had rebounded to 50 million, and two centuries later to 60 million. By 1127, when the Jurchen conquered the northern half of the Song state, the Chinese population had passed the 100 million mark, and by 1200 it stood at about 115 million. This rapid population growth reflected both the productivity of the agricultural economy and the well-organized distribution of food through transportation networks built during Sui and Tang times.

Urbanization

Increased food supplies encouraged the growth of cities. During the Tang dynasty the imperial capital of Chang'an was the world's most populous city with perhaps as many as two million residents. During the Song dynasty, China was the most

A wall painting in a Buddhist cave depicts a peasant plowing his field in the rain with the aid of an ox and a heavy plow. Other peasants have found shelter from the rain and consume a midday meal brought to them by their wives.

urbanized land in the world. In the late thirteenth century, Hangzhou, capital of the Southern Song dynasty, had more than one million residents. They supported hundreds of restaurants, taverns, teahouses, brothels, music halls, theaters, clubhouses, gardens, markets, craft shops, and specialty stores dealing in silk, gems, porcelain, lacquerware, and other goods. Hangzhou residents, like those in most cities, observed peculiar local customs. Taverns often had several floors, for example, and patrons gravitated to higher or lower stories according to their plans: those desiring only a cup or two of wine sat at street level, whereas those planning an extended evening of revelry sought tables on the higher floors.

As a capital, Hangzhou was something of a special case among cities, but during the Tang and Song eras, scores of Chinese cities boasted populations of one hundred thousand or more. Li Bo (701–761 C.E.), who was perhaps the most popular poet of the Tang era, took the social life of these Chinese cities as one of his principal themes. Li Bo mostly wrote light, pleasing verse celebrating life, friendship, and especially wine. (Tradition holds that he died by drowning when the drunken poet fell out of a boat while attempting to embrace the moon's reflection in the water.) The annual spring festival was an occasion dear to the heart of urban residents, who flocked to the streets to shop for new products, have their fortunes told, and eat tasty snacks from food vendors.

Another result of increased food production was the emergence of a commercialized agricultural economy. Because fast-ripening rice yielded bountiful harvests, many cultivators could purchase inexpensive rice and raise vegetables and fruits for sale on the commercial market. Cultivators specialized in crops that grew well in their own regions, and they often exported their harvests to distant regions. By the twelfth century, for example, the wealthy southern province of Fujian imported rice and devoted its land to the production of lychees, oranges, and sugarcane, which fetched high prices in northern markets. Indeed, market-oriented cultivation went so far that

A twelfth-century painting depicts the spring festival as observed in the northern Song capital of Kaifeng. Porters, shopkeepers, peddlers, fortune tellers, and Confucian scholars deep in conversation are all in view.

authorities tried—with only limited success—to require Fujianese to grow rice so as to avoid excessive dependence on imports.

Patriarchal Social Structures

Alongside increasing wealth and agricultural productivity, Tang and especially Song China experienced a tightening of patriarchal social structures, which perhaps represented an effort to preserve family fortunes through enhanced family solidarity. During the Song dynasty the veneration of family ancestors became much more elaborate than before. Instead of simply remembering ancestors and invoking their aid in rituals performed at home, descendants diligently sought the graves of their earliest traceable forefathers and then arranged elaborate graveside rituals in their honor. Whole extended families often traveled great distances to attend annual rituals venerating deceased ancestors—a practice that strengthened the sense of family identity and cohesiveness.

Foot Binding

Strengthened patriarchal authority also helps to explain the popularity of foot binding, which spread among privileged classes during the Song era. Foot binding involved the tight wrapping of young girls' feet with strips of cloth that prevented natural growth of the bones and resulted in tiny, malformed, curved feet. Women with bound feet could not walk easily or naturally. Usually they needed canes to walk by themselves, and sometimes they depended on servants to carry them around in litters. Foot binding never became universal in China—it was impractical for peasants or lower-class working women in the cities—but wealthy families often bound the feet of their daughters to enhance their attractiveness, display their high social standing, and gain increased control over the girls' behavior. Like the practice of veiling women in the Islamic world, foot binding placed women of privileged classes under tight supervision of their husbands or other male guardians, who then managed the women's affairs in the interests of the larger family.

Technological and Industrial Development

Porcelain

Abundant supplies of food enabled many people to pursue technological and industrial interests. During the Tang and Song dynasties, Chinese crafts workers generated a remarkable range of technological innovations. During Tang times they discovered techniques of producing high-quality porcelain, which was lighter, thinner, and adaptable to more uses than earlier pottery. When fired with glazes, porcelain could also become an aesthetically appealing utensil and even a work of art. Porcelain technology gradually diffused to other societies, and Abbasid crafts workers in particular produced porcelain in large quantities. Yet demand for Chinese porcelain remained high, and the Chinese exported vast quantities of porcelain during the Tang and Song dynasties. Archaeologists have turned up Tang and Song porcelain at sites all along the trade networks of the postclassical era: Chinese porcelain graced the tables of wealthy and refined households in southeast Asia, India, Persia, and the port cities of east Africa. Tang and Song products gained such a reputation that fine porcelain has come to be known generally as *chinaware*.

Metallurgy

Tang and Song craftsmen also improved metallurgical technologies. Production of iron and steel surged during this era, due partly to techniques that resulted in stronger and more useful metals. Chinese craftsmen discovered that they could use coke instead of coal in their furnaces and produce superior grades of metal. Between the early ninth and the early twelfth century, iron production increased almost tenfold according to official records, which understate total production. Most of the increased supply of iron and steel went into weaponry and agricultural tools: during the early Song dynasty, imperial armaments manufacturers produced 16.5 million iron arrowheads per year. Iron and steel also went into construction projects involving large structures such as bridges and pagodas. As in the case of porcelain technology, metallurgical techniques soon diffused to lands beyond China. Indeed, Song military difficulties stemmed partly from the fact that nomadic peoples quickly learned Chinese techniques and fashioned their own iron weapons for use in campaigns against China.

Quite apart from improving existing technologies, Tang and Song craftsmen also invented entirely new products, tools, and techniques, most notably gunpowder, printing, and naval technologies. Daoist alchemists discovered how to make gunpowder during the Tang dynasty, as they tested the properties of various experimental concoctions while seeking elixirs to prolong life. They soon learned that it was unwise to mix charcoal, saltpeter, sulphur, and arsenic, because the volatile compound often resulted in singed beards and destroyed buildings. Military officials, however, recognized opportunity in the explosive mixture. By the mid-tenth century they were using gunpowder in bamboo "fire lances," a kind of flamethrower, and by the eleventh century they had fashioned primitive bombs.

Gunpowder

The earliest gunpowder weapons had limited military effectiveness: they probably caused more confusion because of noise and smoke than damage because of their destructive potential. Over time, however, refinements enhanced their effectiveness. Knowledge of gunpowder chemistry quickly diffused through Eurasia, and by the late thirteenth century peoples of southwest Asia and Europe were experimenting with metal-barreled cannons.

The precise origins of printing lie obscured in the mists of time. Although some form of printing may have predated the Sui dynasty, only during the Tang era did printing become common. The earliest printers employed block-printing techniques: they carved a reverse image of an entire page into a wooden block, inked the block, and then pressed a sheet of paper on top. By the mid-eleventh century, printers had begun to experiment with reusable, movable type: instead of carving images into blocks, they fashioned dies in the shape of ideographs, arranged them in a frame, inked them, and pressed the frame over paper sheets. Because formal writing in the Chinese language involved as many as forty thousand different characters, printers often found movable type to be unwieldy and inconvenient, so they continued to print from wooden blocks long after movable type became available.

Printing

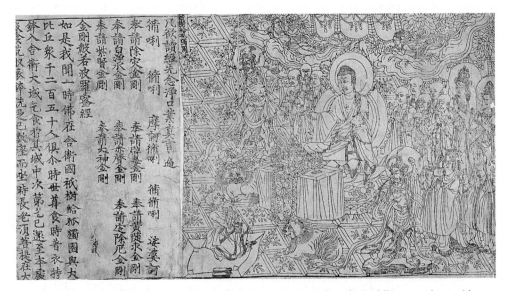

A printed book from the twelfth century presents a Chinese translation of a Buddhist text along with a block-printed illustration of the Buddha addressing his followers.

Contexts & Connections

The Spread of Printing Technology

It is not surprising that China was the birthplace of printing. Paper had been in use there at least since the second century C.E., so early Chinese artisans had a strong but cheap material to use as a surface for printed characters and images. For many centuries Chinese had also fashioned seals from wood, stone, metal, and clay to make impressions of names or words on paintings, letters, and documents. It was a relatively short step from the impressment of individual characters onto paper with a seal to the printing of whole pages, documents, and books from carved blocks of wood.

By the ninth century, printing had made its way to Japan and Korea. Buddhism favored the adoption of printing throughout east Asia because Mahayana Buddhists regarded the copying and distribution of sacred texts as a highly meritorious act. Indeed, in Japan printers worked only in monasteries and produced only religious texts until the late sixteenth century.

Beyond east Asia, however, printing won acceptance only gradually. Knowledge of Chinese printing did not reach Christian Europe until the thirteenth century. In any event, printing was not a practical possibility there until the arrival of paper-making technology. The principal material used in early European book production was parchment or vellum, a very expensive writing surface specially prepared from the skins of young sheep, calves, or goats. If they had only parchment or vellum to work with, Europeans would not have been able to afford the quantities of books that printing presses were capable of churning out.

Paper production reached Islamic Spain about 1150 but did not come into widespread use in Christian Europe until the fifteenth century. About 1450 the German craftsman Johannes Gutenberg independently invented a system of printing with movable type. From that time forward, the European printing press and paper-making industry mutually reinforced one another, and Europe was soon awash in a sea of books, pamphlets, announcements, flyers, news sheets, and other printed matter.

What about the Islamic world? Paper was in use in Muslim central Asia at least from the eighth century, and the Abbasid caliph Harun al-Rashid built a paper mill in Baghdad about 794. Paper quickly displaced parchment and vellum as a writing material in the Islamic world, yet printing did not come into widespread use there until the nineteenth century, at least partly because of aesthetic considerations. Among the most highly prized art forms in the Islamic world was calligraphy: for many readers, printing presses offered a very poor substitute for elegant, handwritten texts. Muslims expected their copies of the Quran in particular to be finely crafted volumes, not cheap, mass-produced books. The absence of printing meant that many texts were inaccessible to Muslim readers. Yet thousands of manuscript books circulated throughout the realm of Islam and served the needs of Muslim societies tolerably well. Only in the context of political, military, and financial difficulties in modern times did the efficiencies of printing come to outweigh the aesthetics of calligraphy in the Islamic world.

Printing made it possible to produce texts quickly, cheaply, and in huge quantities. By the late ninth century, printed copies of Buddhist texts, Confucian works, calendars, agricultural treatises, and popular works appeared in large quantities, particularly in southwestern China (modern Sichuan province). Song dynasty officials disseminated printed works broadly by visiting the countryside with pamphlets that outlined effective agricultural techniques.

Naval Technology   Chinese inventiveness extended also to naval technology. Before Tang times, Chinese mariners did not venture very far from land. They traveled the sea lanes to Korea, Japan, and the Ryukyu Islands but relied on Persian, Arab, Indian, and Malay mariners for long-distance maritime trade. During the Tang dynasty, however, Chinese consumers developed a taste for the spices and exotic products of southeast Asian islands, and Chinese mariners increasingly visited those lands in their own ships. By the time of the Song dynasty, Chinese seafarers sailed ships fastened with iron nails, waterproofed with oils, furnished with watertight bulkheads, driven by canvas and bamboo sails, steered by rudders, and navigated with the aid of the "south-pointing needle"— the magnetic compass. Larger ships sometimes even had small rockets powered by gunpowder. Chinese ships mostly plied the waters between Japan and the Malay peninsula, but some of them ventured into the Indian Ocean and called at ports in India, Ceylon, Persia, and east Africa. These long-distance travels helped to diffuse elements of Chinese naval technology, particularly the compass, which soon became the common property of mariners throughout the Indian Ocean basin.

The Emergence of a Market Economy

Increased agricultural production, improved transportation systems, population growth, urbanization, and industrial production combined to stimulate the Chinese economy. China's various regions increasingly specialized in the cultivation of particular food crops or the production of particular manufactured goods, trading their own products for imports from other regions. The market was not the only influence on the Chinese economy: government bureaucracies played a large role in the distribution of staple foods such as rice, wheat, and millet, and dynastic authorities closely watched militarily sensitive enterprises such as the iron industry. Nevertheless, millions of cultivators produced fruits and vegetables for sale on the open market, and manufacturers of silk, porcelain, and other goods supplied both domestic and foreign markets. The Chinese economy became more tightly integrated than ever before, and foreign demand for Chinese products fueled rapid economic expansion.

Financial Instruments

Indeed, trade grew so rapidly during Tang and Song times that China experienced a shortage of the copper coins that served as money for most transactions. To alleviate the shortage, Chinese merchants developed alternatives to cash that resulted in even more economic growth. Letters of credit came into common use during the early Tang dynasty. Known as "flying cash," they enabled merchants to deposit goods or cash at one location and draw the equivalent in cash or merchandise elsewhere in China. Later developments included the use of promissory notes, which pledged payment of a given sum of money at a later date, and checks, which entitled the bearer to draw funds against cash deposited with bankers.

Paper Money

The search for alternatives to cash also led to the invention of paper money. Wealthy merchants pioneered the use of printed paper money during the late ninth century. In return for cash deposits from their clients, they issued printed notes that the clients could redeem for merchandise. In a society short of cash, these notes greatly facilitated commercial transactions. Occasionally, however, because of temporary economic reverses or poor management, merchants were not able to honor their notes. The resulting discontent among creditors often led to disorder and sometimes even to riots.

By the eleventh century, however, the Chinese economy had become so dependent on alternatives to cash that it was impractical to banish paper money altogether. To preserve its convenience while forestalling public disorder, government authorities forbade private parties from issuing paper money and reserved that right for the state. The first paper money printed under government auspices appeared in 1024 in Sichuan province, the most active center of early printing. By the end of the century, government authorities throughout most of China issued printed paper money—complete with serial numbers and dire warnings against the printing of counterfeit notes. Rulers of nomadic peoples in central Asia soon began to adopt the practice in their own states.

Sources from the Past

The Arab Merchant Suleiman on Business Practices in Tang China

The Arab merchant Suleiman made several commercial ventures by ship to India and China during the early ninth century C.E. In 851 an Arab geographer wrote an account of Suleiman's travels, describing India and China for Muslim readers in southwest Asia. His report throws particularly interesting light on the economic conditions and business practices of Tang China.

Young and old Chinese all wear silk clothes in both winter and summer, but silk of the best quality is reserved for the kings. . . . During the winter, the men wear two, three, four, five pairs of pants, and even more, according to their means. This practice has the goal of protecting the lower body from the high humidity of the land, which they fear. During the summer, they wear a single shirt of silk or some similar material. They do not wear turbans. . . .

In China, commercial transactions are carried out with the aid of copper coins. The Chinese royal treasury is identical to that of other kings, but only the king of China has a treasury that uses copper coins as a standard. These copper coins serve as the money of the land. The Chinese have gold, silver, fine pearls, fancy silk textiles, raw silk, and all this in large quantities, but they are considered commodities, and only copper coins serve as money.

Imports into China include ivory, incense, copper ingots, shells of sea turtles, and rhinoceros horn, with which the Chinese make ornaments. . . .

The Chinese conduct commercial transactions and business affairs with equity. When someone lends money to another person, he writes up a note documenting the loan. The borrower writes up another note on which he affixes an imprint of his index finger and middle finger together. Then they put the two notes together, roll them up, and write a formula at the point where one touches the other [so that part of the written formula appears on each note]. Next, they separate the notes and entrust to the lender the one on which the borrower recognizes his debt. If the borrower denies his debt later on, they say to him, "Present the note that the lender gave to you." If the borrower maintains that he has no such note from the lender, and denies that he ever agreed to the note with his fingerprints on it, and if the lender's note has disappeared, they say to him, "Declare in writing that you have not contracted this debt, but if later the lender brings forth proof that you have contracted this debt that you deny, you will receive twenty blows of the cane on the back and you will be ordered to pay a penalty of twenty million copper coins." This sum is equal to about 2,000 dinars [gold coins used in the Abbasid empire]. Twenty blows of the cane brings on death. Thus no one in China dares to make such a declaration for fear of losing at the same time both life and fortune. We have seen no one who has agreed when invited to make such a declaration. The Chinese are thus equitable to each other. No one in China is treated unjustly.

SOURCE: Gabriel Ferrand, trans. *Voyage du marchand arabe Sulayman en Inde et en Chine*. Paris, 1922, pp. 45, 53–54, 60–61. (Translated into English by Jerry H. Bentley.)

In what ways might Chinese policies have encouraged business and trade during the Tang dynasty?

Printed paper money caused serious problems for several centuries after its appearance. Quite apart from contamination of the money supply by counterfeit notes, government authorities frequently printed currency representing more value than they actually possessed in cash reserves—a practice not unknown in more recent times. The result was a partial loss of public confidence in paper money. By the late eleventh century, some notes of paper money would fetch only 95 percent of their face value in cash. Not until the Qing dynasty (1644–1911 C.E.) did Chinese authorities place the issuance of printed money under tight fiscal controls. In spite of abuses, however, printed paper money provided a powerful stimulus to the Chinese economy.

Trade and urbanization transformed Tang and Song China into a prosperous, cosmopolitan society. Trade came to China both by land and by sea. Muslim merchants from the Abbasid empire and central Asia helped to revive the silk roads network and flocked to large Chinese trading centers. Even subjects of the Byzantine empire made their way across the silk roads to China. Residents of large Chinese cities like Chang'an and Luoyang became quite accustomed to merchants from foreign lands. Indeed, musicians and dancers from Persia became popular entertainers in the cosmopolitan cities of the Tang dynasty. Meanwhile, Arab, Persian, Indian, and Malay mariners arriving by way of the Indian Ocean and South China Sea established sizable merchant communities in the bustling southern Chinese port cities of Guangzhou and Quanzhou. Contemporary reports said that the rebel general Huang Chao massacred 120,000 foreigners when he sacked Guangzhou and subjected it to a reign of terror in 879.

Indeed, high productivity and trade brought the Tang and Song economy a dynamism that China's borders could not restrain. Chinese consumers developed a taste for exotic goods that stimulated trade throughout much of the eastern hemisphere. Spices from the islands of southeast Asia made their way to China, along with products as diverse as kingfisher feathers and tortoise shell from Vietnam, pearls and incense from India, and horses and melons from central Asia. These items became symbols of a refined, elegant lifestyle—in many cases because of attractive qualities inherent in the commodities themselves but sometimes simply because of their scarcity and foreign provenance. In exchange for such exotic items, Chinese sent abroad vast quantities of silk, porcelain, and laquerware. In central Asia, southeast Asia, India, Persia, and the port cities of east Africa, wealthy merchants and rulers wore Chinese silk and set their tables with Chinese porcelain. China's economic surge during the Tang and Song dynasties thus promoted trade and economic growth throughout much of the eastern hemisphere.

A Cosmopolitan Society

China and the Hemispheric Economy

Foreign music and dance were very popular in the large cities of Tang China. This ceramic model depicts a troupe of musicians from southwest Asia performing on a platform mounted on a camel. Many such models survive from Tang times.

CULTURAL CHANGE IN TANG AND SONG CHINA

Interactions with peoples of other societies encouraged cultural change in postclassical China. The Confucian and Daoist traditions did not disappear. But they made way for a foreign religion—Mahayana Buddhism—and they developed along new lines that reflected the conditions of Tang and Song society.

The Establishment of Buddhism

Buddhist merchants traveling the ancient silk roads visited China as early as the second century B.C.E. During the Han dynasty their faith attracted little interest there: Confucianism, Daoism, and cults that honored family ancestors were the most popular cultural alternatives. After the fall of the Han, however, the Confucian tradition suffered a loss of credibility. The purpose and rationale of Confucianism was to maintain public order and provide honest, effective government. But in an age of warlords and nomadic invasions, it seemed that the Confucian tradition had simply failed. Confucian educational and civil service systems went into decline, and rulers sometimes openly scorned Confucian values.

Foreign Religions in China

During the unsettled centuries following the fall of the Han dynasty, several foreign religions established communities in China. Nestorian Christians and Manichaeans settled in China, followed later by Zoroastrians fleeing the Islamic conquerors of Persia. Nestorians established communities in China by the late sixth century. The emperor Tang Taizong himself issued a proclamation praising their doctrine, and he allowed them to open monasteries in Chang'an and other cities. By the mid-seventh century, Arab and Persian merchants had also established Muslim communities in the port cities of south China. Indeed, legend holds that an uncle of Muhammad himself built a small red mosque in the port city of Guangzhou. These religions of salvation mostly served the needs of foreign merchants trading in China and converts from nomadic societies. Sophisticated residents of Chinese cities appreciated foreign music and dance as well as foreign foods and trade goods, but most foreign religious faiths attracted little interest.

Dunhuang

Yet Mahayana Buddhism gradually found a popular following in Tang and Song China. Buddhism came to China over the silk roads. Residents of oasis cities in central Asia had converted to Buddhism as early as the first or second century B.C.E., and the oases became sites of Buddhist missionary efforts. By the fourth century C.E., a sizable Buddhist community had emerged at Dunhuang in western China (modern Gansu province). Between about 600 and 1000 C.E., Buddhists built hundreds of cave temples in the vicinity of Dunhuang and decorated them with murals depicting events in the lives of the Buddha and the *boddhisatvas* who played prominent roles in Mahayana Buddhism. They also assembled libraries of religious literature and operated scriptoria to produce Buddhist texts. Missions supported by establishments such as those at Dunhuang helped Buddhism to establish a foothold in China.

Buddhism in China

Buddhism attracted Chinese interest partly because of its high standards of morality, its intellectual sophistication, and its promise of salvation. Practical concerns also help to account for its appeal. Buddhists established monastic communities in China and accumulated sizable estates donated by wealthy converts. They cultivated these lands intensively and stored a portion of their harvests for distribution among local residents during times of drought, famine, or other hardship. Buddhist monasteries thus became important elements in the local economies of Chinese communities.

In some ways Buddhism posed a challenge to Chinese cultural and social traditions. Buddhist theologians typically took written texts as points of departure for elaborate, speculative investigations into metaphysical themes such as the nature of the soul. Among Chinese intellectuals, however, only the Confucians placed great emphasis on written texts, and they devoted their energies mostly to practical rather than metaphysical issues. Meanwhile, Daoists had limited interest in written texts of any kind. Buddhist morality called for individuals to strive for perfection by observing an ascetic ideal, and it encouraged serious Buddhists to follow a celibate, monastic lifestyle. By contrast, Chinese morality centered on the family unit and the obligations of filial piety, and it strongly encouraged procreation so that generations of offspring would be available to venerate family ancestors. Some Chinese held that Buddhist monasteries were economically harmful, since they paid no taxes, whereas others scorned Buddhism as an inferior creed because of its foreign origins.

Buddhism and Daoism

Because of these differences and concerns, Buddhist missionaries sought to tailor their message to Chinese audiences. They explained Buddhist concepts in vocabulary borrowed from Chinese cultural traditions, particularly Daoism. They translated the Indian term *dharma* (the basic Buddhist doctrine) as *dao* ("the way" in the Daoist sense of the term), and they translated the Indian term *nirvana* (personal salvation

A tenth-century painting in a cave at Dunhuang depicts a monastery on Mt. Wutai in southern China, reputedly the earthly home of an influential *boddhisatva* and the site of numerous Buddhist monasteries.

that comes after an individual soul escapes from the cycle of incarnation) as *wuwei* (the Daoist ethic of noncompetition). While encouraging the establishment of monasteries and the observance of celibacy, they also recognized the validity of family life and offered Buddhism as a religion that would benefit the extended Chinese family: one son in the monastery, they taught, would bring salvation for ten generations of his kin.

Chan Buddhism

The result was a syncretic faith, a Buddhism with Chinese characteristics. One of the more popular schools of Buddhism in China, for example, was the Chan (also known by its Japanese name, Zen). Chan Buddhists had little interest in written texts but, instead, emphasized intuition and sudden flashes of insight in their search for spiritual enlightenment. In this respect they resembled Daoists as much as they did Buddhists.

During the Tang and Song dynasties, this syncretic Buddhism became an immensely popular and influential faith in China. Monasteries appeared in all the major cities, and stupas dotted the Chinese landscape. The monk Xuanzang (602–664) was only one of many devout pilgrims who traveled to India to visit holy sites and learn about Buddhism in its homeland. Many of these pilgrims returned with copies of treatises that deepened the understanding of Buddhism in China. Xuanzang and other pilgrims played roles of enormous significance in establishing Buddhism as a popular faith in China.

Hostility to Buddhism

In spite of its popularity, Buddhism met determined resistance from Daoists and Confucians. Daoists resented the popular following that Buddhists attracted, which resulted in diminished resources available for their own tradition. Confucians despised Buddhists' exaltation of celibacy, and they denounced the faith as an alien superstition. They also condemned Buddhist monasteries as wasteful, unproductive burdens on society.

Persecution

During the late Tang dynasty, Daoist and Confucian critics of Buddhism found allies in the imperial court. Beginning in the 840s the Tang emperors ordered the

This scroll painting depicts the return of the monk Xuanzang to China. His baggage included 657 books, mostly Buddhist treatises but also a few works on grammar and logic, as well as hundreds of relics and images.

closure of monasteries and the expulsion of Buddhists as well as Zoroastrians, Nestorian Christians, and Manichaeans. Motivated largely by a desire to seize property belonging to foreign religious establishments, the Tang rulers did not implement their policy in a thorough way. While it discouraged further expansion, Tang policy did not eradicate foreign faiths from China. Buddhism in particular enjoyed popular support that enabled it to survive. Indeed, it even influenced the development of the Confucian tradition during the Song dynasty.

Neo-Confucianism

The Song emperors did not persecute Buddhists, but they actively supported native Chinese cultural traditions in hopes of limiting the influence of foreign religions. They contributed particularly generously to the Confucian tradition. They sponsored the studies of Confucian scholars, for example, and subsidized the printing and dissemination of Confucian writings.

Confucians and Buddhism

Yet the Confucian tradition of the Song dynasty differed from that of earlier times. The earliest Confucians had concentrated resolutely on practical issues of politics and morality, since they took the organization of a stable social order as their principal concern. Confucians of the Song dynasty studied the classic works of their tradition, but they also became familiar with the writings of Buddhists. They found much to admire in Buddhist thought. Buddhism not only offered a tradition of logical thought and argumentation but also dealt with issues, such as the nature of the soul and the individual's relationship with the cosmos, not systematically explored by Confucian thinkers. Thus Confucians of the Song dynasty drew a great deal of inspiration from Buddhism. Because their thought reflected the influence of Buddhism as well as original Confucian values, it has come to be known as neo-Confucianism.

Zhu Xi

The most important representative of Song neo-Confucianism was the philosopher Zhu Xi (1130–1200 C.E.). A prolific writer, Zhu Xi maintained a deep commitment to Confucian values emphasizing proper personal behavior and social harmony. Among his writings was an influential treatise entitled *Family Rituals* that provided detailed instructions for weddings, funerals, veneration of ancestors, and other family ceremonies. As a good Confucian, Zhu Xi considered it a matter of the highest importance that individuals play their proper roles both in their family and in the larger society.

Yet Zhu Xi became fascinated with the philosophical and speculative features of Buddhist thought. He argued in good Confucian fashion for the observance of high moral standards, and he believed that academic and philosophical investigations were important for practical affairs. But he concentrated his own efforts on abstract and abstruse issues of more theoretical than practical significance. He wrote extensively on metaphysical themes such as the nature of reality. He argued in a manner reminiscent of Plato that two elements accounted for all physical being: *li*, a principle somewhat similar to Plato's Forms or Ideas that defines the essence of the being, and *qi*, its material form.

Neo-Confucianism ranks as an important cultural development for two reasons. First, it illustrates the deep influence of Buddhism in Chinese society. Even though the neo-Confucians rejected Buddhism as a faith, their writings adapted Buddhist themes and reasoning to Confucian interests and values. Second, neo-Confucianism influenced east Asian thought over a very long term. In China, neo-Confucianism enjoyed the status of an officially recognized creed from the Song dynasty until the early twentieth century, and in lands that fell within China's cultural orbit—particularly Korea, Vietnam, and Japan—neo-Confucianism shaped philosophical, political, and moral thought for half a millennium and more.

Neo-Confucian Influence

CHINESE INFLUENCE IN EAST ASIA

Like societies in Byzantium and the *dar al-Islam*, Chinese society influenced the development of neighboring lands during postclassical times. Chinese armies periodically invaded Korea and Vietnam, and Chinese merchants established commercial relations with Japan as well as with Korea and Vietnam. Chinese techniques of government and administration helped shape public life in Korea, Vietnam, and Japan, and Chinese values and cultural traditions won a prominent place alongside native traditions. By no means did these lands become absorbed into China: all maintained distinctive identities and cultural traditions. Yet they also drew deep inspiration from Chinese examples and built societies that reflected their participation in a larger east Asian society revolving around China.

Korea and Vietnam

Chinese armies ventured into Korea and Vietnam on campaigns of imperial expansion as early as the Qin and Han dynasties. As the Han dynasty weakened, however, local aristocrats organized movements that ousted Chinese forces from both lands. Only during the powerful Tang dynasty did Chinese resources once again enable military authorities to mount large-scale campaigns. Although the two lands responded differently to Chinese imperial expansion, both borrowed Chinese political and cultural traditions and used them in their own societies.

During the seventh century, Tang armies conquered much of Korea before the native Silla dynasty rallied to prevent Chinese domination of the peninsula. Both Tang and Silla authorities preferred to avoid a long and costly conflict, so they agreed to a political compromise: Chinese forces withdrew from Korea, and the Silla king recognized the Tang emperor as his overlord. In theory, Korea was a vassal state in a vast Chinese empire. In practice, however, Korea was in most respects an independent kingdom, although the ruling dynasty prudently maintained cordial relations with its powerful neighbor.

The Silla Dynasty

Thus Korea entered into a tributary relationship with China. Envoys of the Silla kings regularly delivered gifts to Chinese emperors and performed the kowtow, but these concessions brought considerable benefits to the Koreans. In return for their recognition of Chinese supremacy, they received gifts more valuable than the tribute they delivered to China. Moreover, the tributary relationship opened the doors for Korean merchants to trade in China.

Chinese Influence in Korea

Meanwhile, the tributary relationship facilitated the spread of Chinese political and cultural influences to Korea. Embassies delivering tribute to China included Korean royal officials who observed the workings of the Chinese court and bureaucracy and then organized the Korean court on similar lines. The Silla kings even built a new capital at Kumsong modeled on the Tang capital at Chang'an. Alongside royal officials, tribute embassies included scholars who studied Chinese thought and literature and who took copies of Chinese writings back to Korea. Their efforts helped to build Korean interest in the Confucian tradition, particularly among educated aristocrats. While Korean elite classes turned to Confucius, Chinese schools of Buddhism attracted widespread popular interest. Chan Buddhism, which promised individual salvation, won the allegiance of peasants and commoners.

China and Korea differed in many respects. Most notably, perhaps, aristocrats and royal houses dominated Korean society much more than was the case in China. Although the Korean monarchy sponsored Chinese schools and a Confucian examination system, Korea never established a bureaucracy based on merit such as that of Tang and Song China. Political initiative remained firmly in the hands of the ruling classes. Nevertheless, extensive dealings with its powerful neighbor ensured that Korea reflected the influence of Chinese political and cultural traditions.

China and Vietnam

Tang dynasty pottery figure of a Vietnamese dancer. Commercial and tributary relationships introduced southeast Asian performers to China, where sophisticated urban communities appreciated their exotic entertainment.

Chinese relations with Vietnam were far more tense than with Korea. When Tang armies ventured into the land that Chinese called Nam Viet, they encountered spirited resistance on the part of the Viet people, who had settled in the region around the Red River. Tang forces soon won control of Viet towns and cities, and they launched efforts to absorb the Viets into Chinese society, just as their predecessors had absorbed the indigenous peoples of the Yangzi River valley. The Viets readily adopted Chinese agricultural methods and irrigation systems as well as Chinese schools and administrative techniques. Like their Korean counterparts, Viet elites studied Confucian texts and took examinations based on a Chinese-style education, and Viet traders marketed their wares in China. Vietnamese authorities even entered into tributary relationships with the Chinese court. Yet the Viets resented Chinese efforts to dominate the southern land, and they mounted a series of revolts against Tang authorities. As the Tang dynasty fell during the early tenth century, the Viets won their independence and successfully resisted later Chinese efforts at imperial expansion to the south.

Like Korea, Vietnam differed from China in many ways. Many Vietnamese retained their indigenous religions in preference to Chinese cultural traditions. Women played a much more prominent role in Vietnamese society and economy than did their Chinese counterparts. Southeast Asian women had dominated local and regional markets for centuries, and they participated actively in business ventures closed to women in the more rigidly patriarchal society of China.

Nevertheless, Chinese traditions found a place in the southern land. Vietnamese authorities established an administrative system and bureaucracy modeled on that of China, and Viet ruling classes prepared for their careers by pursuing a Confucian education. Furthermore, Buddhism came to Vietnam from China as well as India and won a large popular following. Thus, like Korea, Vietnam absorbed political and cultural influence from China and reflected the development of a larger east Asian society centered on China.

Chinese Influence in Vietnam

Early Japan

Chinese armies never invaded Japan, but Chinese traditions deeply influenced Japanese political and cultural development. The earliest inhabitants of Japan were nomadic peoples from northeast Asia. They migrated to Japan, perhaps across land bridges that formed during an ice age, about two hundred thousand years ago. Their language, material culture, and religion derived from their parent society in northeast Asia. Later migrants, who arrived in several waves from the Korean peninsula, introduced cultivation of rice, bronze and iron metallurgy, and horses into Japan. As the population of the Japanese islands grew and built a settled agricultural society, small states dominated by aristocratic clans emerged. By the middle of the first millennium C.E., several dozen states ruled small regions.

The establishment of the powerful Sui and Tang dynasties in China had repercussions in Japan, where they suggested the value of centralized imperial government. One of the aristocratic clans in Japan insisted on its precedence over the others, although in fact it had never wielded effective authority outside its own territory in central Japan. Inspired by the Tang example, this clan claimed imperial authority and introduced a series of reforms designed to centralize Japanese politics. The imperial house established a court modeled on that of the Tang, instituted a Chinese-style bureaucracy, implemented an equal-field system, provided official support for Confucianism and Buddhism, and in the year 710 moved to a new capital city at Nara (near modern Kyoto) that was a replica of the Tang capital at Chang'an. Never was Chinese influence more prominent in Japan than during the Nara period (710–794 C.E.).

Nara Japan

Yet Japan did not lose its distinctive characteristics or become simply a smaller model of Chinese society. While adopting Confucian and Buddhist traditions from China, for example, the Japanese continued to observe the rites of Shinto, their indigenous religion, which revolved around the veneration of ancestors and a host of nature spirits and deities. Japanese society reflected the influence of Chinese traditions but still developed along its own lines.

The experiences of the Heian, Kamakura, and Muromachi periods clearly illustrate this point. In 794 the emperor of Japan transferred his court from Nara to a newly constructed capital at nearby Heian (modern Kyoto). During the next four centuries, Heian became the seat of a refined and sophisticated society that drew inspiration from China but also elaborated distinctively Japanese political and cultural traditions.

During the Heian period (794–1185 C.E.), local rulers on the island of Honshu mostly recognized the emperor as Japan's supreme political authority. Unlike their Chinese counterparts, however, Japanese emperors rarely ruled but, rather, served as ceremonial figureheads and symbols of authority. Effective power lay in the hands of

Heian Japan

the Fujiwara family, an aristocratic clan that controlled affairs from behind the throne through its influence over the imperial house and manipulation of its members.

Since the ninth century the Japanese political order has almost continuously featured a split between a publicly recognized imperial authority and a separate agent of effective rule. This pattern helps to account for the remarkable longevity of the Japanese imperial house. Because emperors have not ruled, they have not been subject to deposition during times of turmoil: ruling parties and factions have come and gone, but the imperial house has survived.

The cultural development of Heian Japan also reflected both the influence of Chinese traditions and the elaboration of peculiarly Japanese ways. Most literature imitated Chinese models and indeed was written in the Chinese language. Boys and young men who received a formal education in Heian Japan learned Chinese, read the classic works of China, and wrote in the foreign tongue. Officials at court conducted business and kept records in Chinese, and literary figures wrote histories and treatises in the style popular in China. Even Japanese writing reflected Chinese influence, since scholars borrowed many Chinese characters and used them to represent Japanese words. They also adapted some Chinese characters into a Japanese syllabic script, in which symbols represent whole syllables rather than a single sound, as in an alphabetic script.

The Tale of Genji

Because Japanese women rarely received a formal Chinese-style education, in Heian times aristocratic women made the most notable contributions to literature in the Japanese language. Of the many literary works that have survived from this era, none reflects Heian court life better than *The Tale of Genji*. Composed by Murasaki Shikibu, a lady-in-waiting at the Heian court who wrote in Japanese syllabic script rather than Chinese characters, this sophisticated work relates the experiences of a fictitious imperial prince named Genji. Living amid gardens and palaces, Genji and his friends devoted themselves to the cultivation of an ultrarefined lifestyle, and they became adept at mixing subtle perfumes, composing splendid verses in fine calligraphic hand, and wooing sophisticated women.

The Tale of Genji also offers a meditation on the passing of time and the sorrows that time brings to sensitive human beings. As Genji and his friends age, they reflect

Samurai depart from a palace in Kyoto after capturing it, murdering the guards, seizing an enemy general there, and setting the structure ablaze. The armor and weaponry of the samurai bespeak the militarism of the Kamakura era.

on past joys and relationships no longer recoverable. Their thoughts suffuse *The Tale of Genji* with a melancholy spirit that presents a subtle contrast to the elegant atmosphere of their surroundings at the Heian court. Due to her limited command of Chinese, Lady Murasaki created one of the most remarkable literary works in the Japanese language.

Decline of Heian Japan

As the charmed circle of aristocrats and courtiers led elegant lives at the imperial capital, the Japanese countryside underwent fundamental changes that brought an end to the Heian court and its refined society. The equal-field system gradually fell into disuse in Japan as it had in China, and aristocratic clans accumulated most of the islands' lands into vast estates. By the late eleventh century, two clans in particular—the Taira and the Minamoto—overshadowed the others. During the mid-twelfth century the two engaged in outright war, and in 1185 the Minamoto emerged victorious. The Minamoto did not seek to abolish imperial authority in Japan but, rather, claimed to rule the land in the name of the emperor. They installed the clan leader as *shogun*—a military governor who ruled in place of the emperor—and established the seat of their government at Kamakura, near modern Tokyo, while the imperial court remained at Kyoto. For most of the next four centuries, one branch or another of the Minamoto clan dominated political life in Japan.

Medieval Japan

Historians refer to the Kamakura and Muromachi periods as Japan's medieval period—a middle era falling between the age of Chinese influence and court domination of political life in Japan, as represented by the Nara and Heian periods, and the modern age, inaugurated by the Tokugawa dynasty in the sixteenth century, when a centralized government unified and ruled all of Japan. During this middle era, Japanese society and culture took on increasingly distinctive characteristics.

Political Decentralization

In the Kamakura (1185–1333 C.E.) and Muromachi (1336–1573 C.E.) periods, Japan developed a decentralized political order in which provincial lords wielded effective power and authority in local regions where they controlled land and economic affairs. As these lords and their clans vied for power and authority in the countryside, they found little use for the Chinese-style bureaucracy that Nara and Heian rulers had instituted in Japan and still less use for the elaborate protocol and refined conduct that prevailed at the courts. In place of etiquette and courtesy, they valued military talent and discipline. The mounted warrior, the *samurai,* thus played the most distinctive role in Japanese political and military affairs.

The Samurai

The samurai were professional warriors, specialists in the use of force and the arts of fighting. They served the provincial lords of Japan, who relied on the samurai both to enforce their authority in their own territories and to extend their claims to other lands. In return for these police and military services, the lords supported the samurai from the agricultural surplus and labor services of peasants working under their jurisdiction. Freed of obligations to feed, clothe, and house themselves and their families, samurai devoted themselves to hunting, riding, archery, and martial arts.

Thus, although it had taken its original inspiration from the Tang empire in China, the Japanese political order developed along lines different from those of the Middle Kingdom. Yet Japan clearly had a place in the larger east Asian society centered on China. Japan borrowed from China, among other things, Confucian values, Buddhist religion, a system of writing, and the ideal of centralized imperial rule. Though somewhat suppressed during the Kamakura and Muromachi periods, these elements of Chinese society not only survived in Japan but also decisively influenced Japanese development during later periods.

The revival of centralized imperial rule in China had profound implications for all of east Asia and indeed for most of the eastern hemisphere. When the Sui and Tang dynasties imposed their authority throughout China, they established a powerful state that guided political affairs throughout east Asia. Tang armies extended Chinese influence to Korea, Vietnam, and central Asia. They did not invade Japan, but the impressive political organization of China prompted the islands' rulers to imitate Tang examples. Moreover, the Sui and Tang dynasties laid a strong political foundation for rapid economic development. Chinese society prospered throughout the postclassical era, partly because of technological and industrial innovation. Tang and Song prosperity touched all of China's neighbors, since it encouraged surging commerce in east Asia. Chinese silk, porcelain, and lacquerware were prized commodities among trading peoples from southeast Asia to east Africa. Chinese inventions such as paper, printing, gunpowder, and the magnetic compass found a place in societies throughout the eastern hemisphere as they diffused across the silk roads and sea lanes. The postclassical era was an age of religious as well as commercial and technological exchanges: Nestorian Christians, Zoroastrians, Manichaeans, and Muslims all maintained communities in Tang China, and Buddhism became the most popular religious faith in all of east Asia. During the postclassical era, Chinese social organization and economic dynamism helped to sustain interactions between the peoples of the eastern hemisphere on an unprecedented scale.

CHRONOLOGY

589–618	Sui dynasty (China)
602–664	Life of Xuanzang
604–618	Reign of Sui Yangdi
618–907	Tang dynasty (China)
627–649	Reign of Tang Taizong
669–935	Silla dynasty (Korea)
710–794	Nara period (Japan)
755–757	An Lushan's rebellion
794–1185	Heian period (Japan)
875–884	Huang Chao's rebellion
960–1279	Song dynasty (China)
960–976	Reign of Song Taizu
1024	First issuance of government-sponsored paper money
1130–1200	Life of Zhu Xi
1185–1333	Kamakura period (Japan)
1336–1573	Muromachi period (Japan)

FOR FURTHER READING

Kenneth Ch'en. *Buddhism in China: A Historical Survey.* Princeton, 1964. A clear and detailed account by an eminent scholar.

Hugh R. Clark. *Community, Trade, and Networks: Southern Fujian Province from the Third to the Thirteenth Century.* Cambridge, 1991. Excellent scholarly study exploring the transformation of a region by trade and market forces.

Peter Duus. *Feudalism in Japan.* 2nd ed. New York, 1976. A brief survey of early Japanese political history, concentrating on the Kamakura and Muromachi periods.

Patricia Buckley Ebrey. *Chinese Civilization: A Sourcebook.* 2nd ed. New York, 1993. A splendid collection of documents in translation.

Patricia Buckley Ebrey and Peter N. Gregory, eds. *Religion and Society in T'ang and Sung China.* Honolulu, 1993. Important collection of scholarly essays dealing with the early entry of Buddhism in China.

Mark Elvin. *The Pattern of the Chinese Past.* Stanford, 1973. A brilliant analysis of Chinese history, concentrating particularly on economic, social, and technological themes.

Jacques Gernet. *Buddhism in Chinese Society: An Economic History from the Fifth to the Tenth Century.* Trans. by F. Verellen. New York, 1995. An important study emphasizing the economic and social significance of Buddhist monasteries in the Chinese countryside.

———. *Daily Life in China on the Eve of the Mongol Invasion, 1250–1276.* Trans. by H. M. Wright. New York, 1962. Rich portrait of Southern Song China, emphasizing social history.

Ivan Morris. *The World of the Shining Prince: Court Life in Ancient Japan.* Harmondsworth, 1964. Vividly reconstructs the court life of Heian Japan.

Joseph Needham. *Science in Traditional China.* Cambridge, Mass., 1981. Essays on the history of Chinese science and technology.

Edward H. Schafer. *The Golden Peaches of Samarkand: A Study of T'ang Exotics.* Berkeley, 1963. Deals with relations between China and central Asian lands during the Tang dynasty.

———. *The Vermilion Bird: T'ang Images of the South.* Berkeley, 1967. Evocative study of relations between China and Vietnam during the Tang dynasty.

Murasaki Shikibu. *The Tale of Genji*. 2 vols. Trans. by E. Seiden-sticker. New York, 1976. Fresh and readable translation of Lady Murasaki's classic work.

H. Paul Varley. *Japanese Culture*. 4th ed. Honolulu, 2000. An authoritative analysis of Japanese cultural development from early times to the present.

Susan Whitfield. *Life along the Silk Road*. Berkeley, 1999. Focuses on the experiences of ten individuals who lived or traveled on the silk roads during the postclassical era.

Sally Hovey Wriggins. *Xuanzang: A Buddhist Pilgrim on the Silk Road*. Boulder, 1996. A fascinating and well-illustrated account of Xuanzang's journey to India and his influence on the development of Buddhism in China.

Arthur F. Wright. *Buddhism in Chinese History*. Stanford, 1959. A brief and incisive study of Buddhism in China by an eminent scholar.

———. *The Sui Dynasty: The Unification of China*, A.D. 581–617. New York, 1978. A useful survey that places the Sui dynasty in its larger historical context.

See our **Online Learning Center** at www.mhhe.com/bentley3 for additional readings, practice maps, quizzes, and internet activities.

Unfamiliar words? Check out the **Primary Source Investigator CD-ROM** for an interactive glossary, interactive maps, more images, and primary sources.

Kabir, the blind guru, weaves cloth while discussing religious matters with disciples.

INDIA AND THE INDIAN OCEAN BASIN

Buzurg ibn Shahriyar was a tenth-century shipmaster from Siraf, a prosperous and bustling port city on the Persian Gulf coast. He probably sailed frequently to Arabia and India, and he may have ventured also to Malaya, the islands of southeast Asia, China, and east Africa. Like all sailors, he heard stories about the distant lands that mariners had visited, the different customs they observed, and the adventures that befell them during their travels. About 953 C.E. he compiled 136 such stories in his *Book of the Wonders of India*.

Buzurg's collection included a generous proportion of tall tales. He told of a giant lobster that seized a ship's anchor and dragged the vessel through the water, of mermaids and sea dragons, of creatures born from human fathers and fish mothers who lived in human society but had flippers that enabled them to swim through the water like fish, of serpents that ate cattle and elephants, of birds so large that they crushed houses, of a monkey that seduced a sailor, and of a talking lizard. Yet alongside the tall tales, many of Buzurg's stories accurately reflected the conditions of his time. One recounted the story of a king from northern India who converted to Islam and requested translations of Islamic law. Others reported on Hindu customs, shipwrecks, encounters with pirates, and slave trading.

Several of Buzurg's stories tempted readers with visions of vast wealth attainable through maritime trade. Buzurg mentioned fine diamonds from Kashmir, pearls from Ceylon, and a Jewish merchant who left Persia penniless and returned from India and China with a shipload of priceless merchandise. Despite their embellishments and exaggerations, his stories faithfully reflected the trade networks that linked the lands surrounding the Indian Ocean in the tenth century. While Buzurg clearly thought of India as a distinct land with its own customs, he also recognized a larger world of trade and communication that extended from east Africa to southeast Asia and beyond to China.

Just as China served as the principal inspiration of a larger east Asian society in the postclassical era, India influenced the development of a larger cultural zone in south and southeast Asia. Yet China and India played different roles in their respective spheres of influence. In east Asia, China was the dominant power, even if it did not always exercise authority directly over its neighbors. In south and southeast Asia, however, there emerged no centralized imperial authority like the Tang dynasty in China. Indeed, although several states organized large regional kingdoms, no single state was able to extend its authority to all parts of the Indian subcontinent, much less to the mainland and islands of southeast Asia.

Though politically disunited, India remained a coherent and distinct society as a result of powerful social and cultural traditions: the caste system and the Hindu religion shaped human experiences and values throughout the subcontinent during the postclassical era. Beginning in the seventh century Islam also began to attract a popular following in India, and after the eleventh century Islam deeply influenced Indian society alongside the caste system and Hinduism.

Beyond the subcontinent Indian traditions helped to shape a larger cultural zone extending to the mainland and islands of southeast Asia. Throughout most of the region, ruling classes adopted Indian forms of political organization and Indian techniques of statecraft. Indian merchants took their Hindu and Buddhist faiths to southeast Asia, where they first attracted the interest of political elites and then of the popular masses. Somewhat later, Indian merchants also helped introduce Islam to southeast Asia.

While Indian traditions influenced the political and cultural development of southeast Asia, the entire Indian Ocean basin began to move toward economic integration during the postclassical era, as Buzurg ibn Shahriyar's stories suggest. Lands on the rim of the Indian Ocean retained distinctive political and cultural traditions inherited from times past. Yet innovations in maritime technology, development of a well-articulated network of sea lanes, and the building of port cities and entrepôts enabled peoples living around the Indian Ocean to trade and communicate more actively than ever before. As a result, peoples from east Africa to southeast Asia and China increasingly participated in the larger economic, commercial, and cultural life of the Indian Ocean basin.

ISLAMIC AND HINDU KINGDOMS

Like the Han and Roman empires, the Gupta dynasty came under severe pressure from nomadic invaders. From the mid-fourth to the mid-fifth century C.E., Gupta rulers resisted the pressures and preserved order throughout much of the Indian subcontinent. Beginning in 451 C.E., however, White Huns from central Asia invaded India and disrupted the Gupta administration. By the mid-sixth century the Gupta state had collapsed, and effective political authority quickly devolved to invaders, local allies of the Guptas, and independent regional power brokers. From the end of the Gupta dynasty until the sixteenth century, when a Turkish people known as the Mughals extended their authority and their empire to most of the subcontinent, India remained a politically divided land.

The Quest for Centralized Imperial Rule

Northern and southern India followed different political trajectories after the fall of the Gupta empire. In the north, politics became turbulent and almost chaotic. Local states contested for power and territory, and northern India became a region of continuous tension and intermittent war. Nomadic Turkish-speaking peoples from central Asia frequently took advantage of this unsettled state of affairs to cross the Khyber Pass and force their way into India. They eventually found niches for themselves in the caste system and became completely absorbed into Indian society. Until processes of social absorption worked themselves out, however, the arrival of nomadic peoples caused additional disruption in northern India.

Harsha

Even after the collapse of the Gupta dynasty, the ideal of centralized imperial rule did not entirely disappear. During the first half of the seventh century, King Harsha (reigned 606–648 C.E.) temporarily restored unified rule in most of northern India and sought to revive imperial authority. Harsha came to the throne of his kingdom in the lower Ganges valley at the age of sixteen. Full of energy and ambition, he led his army throughout northern India. His forces included twenty thousand cavalry, fifty thousand infantry, and five thousand war elephants, and by about 612 he had subdued those who refused to recognize his authority.

Harsha enjoyed a reputation for piety, liberality, and even scholarship. He was himself a Buddhist, but he looked kindly on other faiths as well. He built hospitals and provided free medical care for his subjects. The

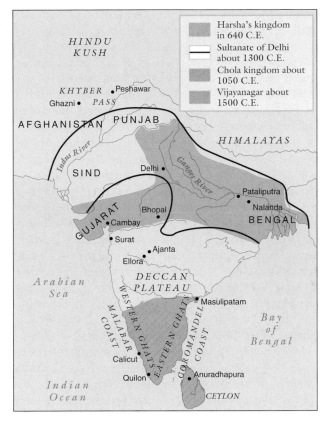

MAP [16.1]
Major states of postclassical India, 600–1600 C.E.

For an interactive version of this map, go to www.mhhe.com/bentley3ch16maps.

Chinese pilgrim Xuanzang lived in northern India during his reign and reported that Harsha liberally distributed wealth to his subjects. On one occasion, Xuanzang said, the king and his aides doled out resources continuously for seventy-five days, making gifts to half a million people. Harsha also generously patronized scholars and even wrote three plays.

Collapse of Harsha's Kingdom

Despite his energy and his favorable reputation, Harsha was unable to restore permanent centralized rule. Since the fall of the Gupta dynasty, local rulers had established their authority too securely in India's regions for Harsha to overcome them. Harsha spent much of his reign on horseback traveling throughout his realm to solidify alliances with local rulers, who were virtually kings in their own lands. He managed to hold his loose empire together mainly by the force of his personality and his constant attention to political affairs. Ultimately, however, he fell victim to an assassin and left no heir to maintain his realm. His empire immediately disintegrated, and local rulers once again turned northern India into a battleground as they sought to enlarge their realms at the expense of their neighbors.

The Introduction of Islam to Northern India

The Conquest of Sind

Amid nomadic incursions and contests for power, northern India also experienced the arrival of Islam and the establishment of Islamic states. Islam reached India by several routes. One was military: Arab forces entered India as early as the mid-seventh century, even before the establishment of the Umayyad caliphate, although their first expeditions were exploratory ventures rather than campaigns of conquest. In 711, however, a well-organized expedition conquered Sind, the Indus River valley in northwestern India, and incorporated it as a province of the expanding Umayyad empire. At mid-century, along with most of the rest of the *dar al-Islam,* Sind passed into the hands of the Abbasid caliphs.

Sind stood on the fringe of the Islamic world, well beyond the effective authority of the Abbasid caliphs. Much of its population remained Hindu, Buddhist, or Parsee, and it also sheltered a series of unorthodox Islamic movements. Infighting between Arab administrators eventually offered opportunities for local political elites to re-assert Hindu authority over much of Sind. Yet the region remained nominally under the jurisdiction of the caliphs until the collapse of the Abbasid dynasty in 1258.

Merchants and Islam

While conquerors brought Islam to Sind, Muslim merchants took their faith to coastal regions in both northern and southern India. Arab and Persian mariners had visited Indian ports for centuries before Muhammad, and their Muslim descendants dominated trade and transportation networks between India and western lands from the seventh through the fifteenth centuries. Muslim merchants formed small communities in all the major cities of coastal India, where they played a prominent role in Indian business and commercial life. They frequently married local women, and in many cases they also found places for themselves in Indian society. Thus Islam entered India's port cities in a more gradual but no less effective way than was the case in Sind. Well before the year 1000, for example, the Gujarat region housed a large Muslim population. Muslim merchants congregated there because of the port city of Cambay, the most important trading center in India throughout the millennium from 500 to 1500 C.E.

Turkish Migrants and Islam

Islam also entered India by a third route: the migrations and invasions of Turkish-speaking peoples from central Asia. During the tenth century, several Turkish groups had become acquainted with Islam through their dealings with the Abbasid caliphate and had converted to the faith. Some of these Muslim Turks entered the Abbasid realm as mercenary soldiers or migrated into Byzantine Anatolia, while others moved into Afghanistan, where they established an Islamic state.

Mahmud of Ghazni

Mahmud of Ghazni, leader of the Turks in Afghanistan, soon turned his attention to the rich land to the south. Between 1001 and 1027 he mounted seventeen raiding expeditions into India. Taking advantage of infighting between local rulers, he annexed several states in northwestern India and the Punjab. For the most part, however, Mahmud had less interest in conquering and ruling India than in plundering the wealth stored in its many well-endowed temples. Mahmud and his forces demolished hundreds of sites associated with Hindu or Buddhist faiths, and their campaigns hastened the decline of Buddhism in the land of its birth. They frequently established mosques or Islamic shrines on the sites of Hindu and Buddhist structures that they destroyed. Not surprisingly, however, Mahmud's raids did not encourage Indians to turn to Islam.

The Sultanate of Delhi

During the late twelfth century, Mahmud's successors mounted a more systematic campaign to conquer northern India and place it under Islamic rule. By the early thirteenth century, they had conquered most of the Hindu kingdoms in northern India and established an Islamic state known as the sultanate of Delhi. The sultans established their capital at Delhi, a strategic site controlling access from the Punjab to the Ganges valley, and they ruled northern India at least in name for more than three centuries, from 1206 to 1526.

During the fourteenth century the sultans of Delhi commanded an army of three hundred thousand, and their state ranked among the most powerful in the Islamic world. Yet for the most part, the authority of the sultans did not extend far beyond Delhi. They often conducted raids in the Deccan region of southern India, but they never overcame Hindu resistance there. They had no permanent bureaucracy or administrative apparatus. Even in northern India, they imposed a thin veneer of Islamic

A fourteenth-century painting depicts the Turkish conqueror Mahmud of Ghazni as he dons a robe bestowed upon him as a gift by the Abbasid caliph. Although Mahmud pursued independent policies, he always recognized the caliph as his overlord.

political and military authority on a land populated mostly by Hindus, and they depended on the goodwill of Hindu kings to carry out their policies and advance their interests in local regions. Indeed, they did not even enjoy comfortable control of their own court: of the thirty-five sultans of Delhi, nineteen perished at the hands of assassins. Nevertheless, the sultans prominently sponsored Islam and helped to establish a secure place for their faith in the cultural landscape of India.

The Hindu Kingdoms of Southern India

Although it too remained politically divided, the southern part of the Indian subcontinent largely escaped the invasions, chronic war, and turmoil that troubled the north. Most Hindu rulers in the south presided over small, loosely administered states. Competition between states sometimes resulted in regional wars, but southern conflicts were less frequent, less intense, and less damaging than those that plagued the north.

The Chola Kingdom

While many regional states organized affairs in local jurisdictions, two kingdoms expanded enough to exercise at least nominal rule over much of southern India. The first was the Chola kingdom, situated in the deep south, which ruled the Coromandel coast for more than four centuries, from 850 to 1267 C.E. At its high point, during the eleventh century, Chola forces conquered Ceylon and parts of southeast Asia. Financed by the profits of trade, the Chola navy dominated the waters from the South China Sea to the Arabian Sea.

Chola rulers did not build a tightly centralized state: they allowed considerable autonomy for local and village institutions as long as they maintained order and delivered tax revenues on time. By the twelfth century, however, the Chola state was in decline. Native Sinhalese forces expelled Chola officials from Ceylon, and revolts erupted within southern India. The Chola realm did not entirely collapse, but by the early thirteenth century, much reduced in size and power, it had reverted to the status of one regional kingdom among many others in southern India.

The kings of Vijayanagar endowed their capital with splendid buildings and even provided these handsome domed stables for their elephants.

The Kingdom of Vijayanagar

The second state that dominated much of southern India was the kingdom of Vijayanagar, based in the northern Deccan. The kingdom owed its origin to efforts by the sultans of Delhi to extend their authority to southern India. Exploratory forays by Turkish forces provoked a defensive reaction in the south. Officials in Delhi dispatched two brothers, Harihara and Bukka, to represent the sultan and implement court policies in the south. Although they had converted from their native Hinduism to Islam, Harihara and Bukka recognized an opportunity to establish themselves as independent rulers. In 1336 they renounced Islam, returned to their original Hindu faith, and proclaimed the establishment of an independent empire of Vijayanagar (meaning "city of victory"). Their unusual coup did not lead to hostilities between Muslims and Hindus: Muslim merchants continued to trade unmolested in the ports of southern India, as they had for more than half a millennium. But the Hindu kingdom of Vijayanagar was the dominant state in southern India from the mid-fourteenth century until 1565 when it fell to Mughal conquerors from the north.

As in northern India, then, political division and conflict between states in southern India characterized its political history in postclassical times. India did not generate the sort of large-scale, centralized, imperial state that guided the fortunes of postclassical societies in the eastern Mediterranean, southwest Asia, or China. States like the sultanate of Delhi in northern India and the kingdoms of Chola and Vijayanagar in the south were not powerful enough to organize political life throughout the subcontinent. Nevertheless, on the basis of trade, common social structures, and inherited cultural traditions, a coherent and distinctive society flourished in postclassical India.

PRODUCTION AND TRADE IN THE INDIAN OCEAN BASIN

As in the Mediterranean, southwest Asia, and China, agricultural yields increased significantly in postclassical India, enabling large numbers of people to devote themselves to trade and manufacturing rather than the production of food. Trade forged links between the various regions of the subcontinent and fostered economic development in southern India. Trade also created links between India and distant lands, as merchants and manufacturers transformed the Indian Ocean basin into a vast zone of communication and exchange. The increasing prominence of trade and industry brought change to Indian society, as merchant and artisan guilds became stronger and more influential than before. Yet caste identities and loyalties also remained strong, and the caste system continued to serve as the most powerful organizing feature of Indian society.

Agriculture in the Monsoon World

Because of the rhythms of the monsoons, irrigation was essential for the maintenance of a large, densely populated, agricultural society. During the spring and summer, warm, moisture-laden winds from the southwest bring most of India's rainfall. During the autumn and winter, cool and very dry winds blow from the northeast. To achieve their agricultural potential, Indian lands required a good watering by the southern monsoon, supplemented by irrigation during the dry months. Light rain during the spring and summer months or short supplies of water for irrigation commonly led to drought, reduced harvests, and widespread famine.

The Monsoons

In northern India, irrigation had been a fixture of the countryside since Harappan times, when cultivators tapped the waters of the Indus River. Later, as Aryans migrated into the Ganges River valley, they found plentiful surface water and abundant opportunities to build irrigation systems. For the most part, however, southern India is an arid land without rivers like the Indus or Ganges that can serve as sources for large-scale irrigation. Thus, as southern India became more densely populated, irrigation systems became crucial, and a great deal of energy and effort went into the construction of waterworks. Dams, reservoirs, canals, wells, and tunnels appeared in large numbers. Particularly impressive were monumental reservoirs lined with brick or stone that captured the rains of the spring and summer months and held them until the dry season, when canals carried them to thirsty fields. One such reservoir—actually an artificial lake constructed near Bhopal during the eleventh century—covered some 650 square kilometers (250 square miles). Projects of this size required enormous investments of human energy, both for their original construction and for continuing maintenance, but they led to significant increases in agricultural productivity.

Irrigation Systems

As a result of this increased productivity, India's population grew steadily throughout the postclassical era. In 600 C.E., shortly after the fall of the Gupta dynasty, the subcontinent's population stood at about 53 million. By 800 it had increased almost 20 percent to 64 million, and by 1000 it had grown by almost another 25 percent to 79 million. During the following centuries the rate of growth slowed, as Indian numbers increased by 4 to 5 million individuals per century. Toward 1500, however, the rate of growth increased again, and by 1500 the subcontinent's population had reached 105 million.

Population Growth

This demographic surge encouraged the concentration of people in cities. During the fourteenth century, the high point of the sultanate of Delhi, the capital city had a population of about four hundred thousand, which made it second only to Cairo among Muslim cities. Many other cities—particularly ports and trading centers like Cambay, Surat, Calicut, Quilon, and Masulipatam—had populations well over one hundred thousand. Cities in southern India grew especially fast, partly as a result of increasing agricultural productivity in the region.

Urbanization

Trade and the Economic Development of Southern India

Political fragmentation of the subcontinent did not prevent robust trade between the different states and regions of India. As the population grew, opportunities for specialized work became more numerous. Increased trade was a natural result of this process.

Internal Trade

Most regions of the Indian subcontinent were self-sufficient in staple foods such as rice, wheat, barley, and millet. The case was different, however, with iron, copper, salt, pepper, spices, condiments, and specialized crops that grew well only in certain regions. Iron came mostly from the Ganges River valley near Bengal, copper mostly from the Deccan Plateau, salt mostly from coastal regions, and pepper from southern India. These and other commodities sometimes traveled long distances to consumers in remote parts of the subcontinent. Pepper, saffron, and sugar were popular commodities in subcontinental trade, and even rice sometimes traveled as a trade item to northern and mountainous regions where it did not grow well.

Southern India and Ceylon benefited especially handsomely from this trade. As invasions and conflicts disrupted northern India, southern regions experienced rapid economic development. The Chola kingdom provided relative stability in the south, and Chola expansion in southeast Asia opened markets for Indian merchants and producers. Coastal towns like Calicut and Quilon flourished, and they attracted increasing numbers of residents.

Temples and Society

The Chola rulers allowed considerable autonomy to their subjects, and the towns and villages of southern India largely organized their own affairs. Public life revolved around Hindu temples that served as economic and social centers. Southern Indians used their growing wealth to build hundreds of elaborate Hindu temples, which organized agricultural activities, coordinated work on irrigation systems, and maintained reserves of surplus production for use in times of need. These temples also provided basic schooling for boys in the community, and larger temples offered advanced instruction as well. Temples often possessed large tracts of agricultural land, and they sometimes employed hundreds of people, including brahmins, attendants, musicians, servants, and slaves. To meet their financial obligations to employees, temple administrators collected a portion of the agricultural yield from lands subject to temple authority. Administrators were also responsible for keeping order in their communities and delivering tax receipts to the Cholas and other political authorities.

Temple authorities also served as bankers, made loans, and invested in commercial and business ventures. As a result, temples promoted the economic development of southern India by encouraging production and trade. Temple authorities cooperated closely with the leaders of merchant guilds in seeking commercial opportunities to exploit. The guilds often made gifts of land or money to temples by way of consolidating their relationship with the powerful economic institutions. Temples thus grew prosperous and became crucial to the economic health of southern India.

Cross-Cultural Trade in the Indian Ocean Basin

Indian prosperity sprang partly from the productivity of Indian society, but it depended also on the vast wealth that circulated in the commercial world of the Indian Ocean basin. Trade in the Indian Ocean was not new in postclassical times: Indian merchants had already ventured to southeast Asia during the classical era, and they dealt regularly with mariners from the Roman empire who traveled to India in search of pepper. During the postclassical era, however, larger ships and improved commercial organization supported a dramatic surge in the volume and value of trade in the Indian Ocean basin.

Dhows and Junks

The earliest voyaging in the Indian Ocean followed the coastlines, but already in classical times mariners recognized the rhythms of the monsoons. Over time they built larger ships, which enabled them to leave the coasts behind and ply the blue waters of the Indian Ocean: the dhows favored by Indian, Persian, and Arab sailors averaged about one hundred tons burden in 1000 and four hundred tons in 1500. After the naval and commercial expansion of the Song dynasty, large Chinese and

During the eighth century C.E., workers carved a massive temple out of sheer rock at Ellora in central India. Temple communities like the one that grew up at Ellora controlled enormous resources in postclassical India.

southeast Asian junks also sailed the Indian Ocean: some of them could carry one thousand tons of cargo.

As large, stable ships came into use, mariners increasingly entrusted their crafts and cargoes to the reasonably predictable monsoons and sailed directly across the Arabian Sea and the Bay of Bengal. In the age of sail, it was impossible to make a round trip across the entire Indian Ocean without spending months at distant ports waiting for the winds to change, so merchants usually conducted their trade in stages.

Because India stood in the middle of the Indian Ocean basin, it was a natural site   *Emporia* for emporia and warehouses. Merchants coming from east Africa or Persia exchanged their cargoes at Cambay, Calicut, or Quilon for goods to take back west with the winter monsoon. Mariners from China or southeast Asia called at Indian ports and traded their cargoes for goods to ship east with the summer monsoon. Merchants also built emporia outside India: the storytelling mariner Buzurg ibn Shahriyar came from the emporium of Siraf on the Persian Gulf, a port city surrounded by desert that nevertheless enjoyed fabulous wealth because of its trade with China, India, and east Africa. Because of their central location, however, Indian ports became the principal clearinghouses of trade in the Indian Ocean basin, and they became remarkably cosmopolitan centers. Hindus, Buddhists, Muslims, Jews, and others who inhabited the Indian port cities did business with counterparts from all over the eastern hemisphere and swapped stories like those recounted by Buzurg ibn Shahriyar.

Dhows fitted with lateen sails skim across the Indian Ocean much like their ancestors of the postclassical era.

Specialized Production

Particularly after the establishment of the Umayyad and Abbasid dynasties in southwest Asia and the Tang and Song dynasties in China, trade in the Indian Ocean surged. Indian merchants and mariners sometimes traveled to distant lands in search of marketable goods, but the carrying trade between India and points west fell mostly into Arab and Persian hands. During the Song dynasty, Chinese junks also ventured into the western Indian Ocean and called at ports as far away as east Africa. In the Bay of Bengal and the China seas, Malay and Chinese vessels were most prominent.

As the volume of trade in the Indian Ocean basin increased, lands around the ocean began to engage in specialized production of commodities for the commercial market. For centuries Indian artisans had enjoyed a reputation for the manufacture of fine cotton textiles, which they produced in small quantities for wealthy consumers. In postclassical times their wares came into high demand throughout the trading world of the Indian Ocean basin. In response to that demand, Indian artisans built thriving local industries around the production of high-quality cotton textiles. These industries influenced the structure of the Indian economy: they created a demand for specific agricultural products, provided a livelihood for thousands of artisans, and enabled consumers to import goods from regions that specialized in the production of other commodities.

Alongside textiles other specialized industries that emerged in postclassical India included sugar refining, leather tanning, stone carving, and carpet weaving. Iron and steel production also emerged as prominent industries. Indian artisans became well known especially for the production of high-carbon steel that held a lethal cutting edge and that consequently came into high demand for use in knives and swords. Other lands concentrated on the production of different manufactured goods and agricultural commodities: China produced silk, porcelain, and lacquerware, southeast Asian lands provided fine spices, while incense, horses, and dates came from southwest Asia, and east Africa contributed gold, ivory, and slaves. Thus trade en-

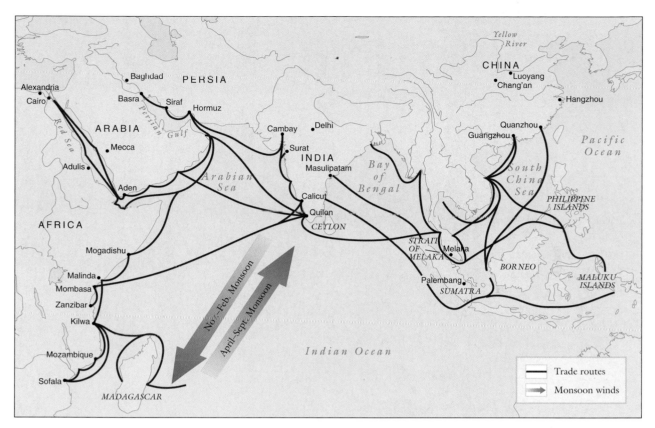

MAP [16.2]

The trading world of the Indian Ocean basin, 600–1600 C.E.

couraged specialized production and economic development in all lands participating in the trade networks of the Indian Ocean basin: cross-cultural trade in postclassical times influenced the structure of economies and societies throughout much of the eastern hemisphere.

The Kingdom of Axum

The experience of the kingdom of Axum (sometimes spelled Aksum) well illustrates the potential of trade to support political as well as economic development. Founded in the highlands of northern Ethiopia about the first century C.E., Axum was originally a small kingdom whose merchants traded from the port of Adulis on the Red Sea. Axum soon displaced Kush as Egypt's principal link to southern lands and sent the Nubian kingdom into economic and political decline: about 360 C.E. Axumite forces even invaded Kush and destroyed the capital city of Meroë. During the fourth and fifth centuries, Axumites adopted Christianity and established a distinctive church that maintained relations with Christian communities in Egypt and the Mediterranean basin. During the sixth century Axum embarked on a round of territorial expansion, building an empire that included most of modern-day Ethiopia as well as Yemen in southern Arabia. Indeed, an Axumite army and elephant corps campaigned as far north as Mecca in the year 571 C.E., birth year of the prophet Muhammad.

During the seventh and eighth centuries, Arab conquerors sought to bring Axum into the expanding realm of Islam, but the kingdom maintained its independence and its Christian religion. Because neighboring lands mostly adopted Islam, Axum fell out of communication with other Christian societies. Nevertheless, Axumite merchants

Mealtime for a Persian merchant and his two companions served by three women attendants in this ceiling decoration from the Ajanta caves in central India.

not only maintained commercial ties with distant lands, as ships from Adulis routinely sailed for India and the islands of southeast Asia, but also traded regularly with Muslim merchants in neighboring lands. From the sixth to ninth centuries C.E., Adulis was perhaps the most prominent port in east Africa, funneling gold, ivory, and slaves from sub-Saharan Africa to Egypt, the eastern Mediterranean region, and the Indian Ocean basin. Thus, even though challenged by Muslim forces, Axum was able to maintain its independence and prosperity, largely because of its participation in trading networks of the Indian Ocean and Mediterranean Sea.

Caste and Society

The political, economic, and social changes of the postclassical era brought a series of challenges for India's caste system. Migrations, the growing prominence of Islam, economic development, and urbanization all placed pressures on the caste system as it had developed during the Vedic and classical eras. But the caste system has never been a rigid, unchanging structure. Rather, individuals and groups have continuously adjusted it and adapted it to new circumstances. Adjustments and adaptations of the postclassical era resulted in a caste system that was more complex than in earlier ages and that also extended its geographic reach deeper into southern India than ever before. In the absence of strong central governments, the caste system helped

Sources from the Past

Cosmas Indicopleustes on Trade in Southern India

Cosmas Indicopleustes was a Christian monk from Egypt who lived during the sixth century C.E. and traveled widely throughout north Africa and southwest Asia. On one of his trips, he ventured as far as India and Ceylon, which he described at some length in a work entitled The Christian Topography. *Cosmas's account clearly shows that sixth-century India and Ceylon played prominent roles in the larger economy of the Indian Ocean basin.*

Ceylon lies on the other side of the pepper country [southern India]. Around it are numerous small islands all having fresh water and coconut trees. They nearly all have deep water close up to their shores. . . . Ceylon is a great market for the people in those parts. The island also has a church of Persian Christians who have settled there, and a priest who is appointed from Persia, and a deacon and a complete ecclesiastical ritual. But the natives and their kings are heathens. . . .

Since the island of Ceylon is in a central position, it is much frequented by ships from all parts of India and from Persia and Ethiopia, and it likewise sends out many of its own. And from the remotest countries—I mean China and other trading places—it receives silk, aloes, cloves, sandalwood, and other products, and these again are passed on to markets on this side, such as Male [the western coast of southern India], where pepper grows, and to Calliana [a port city near modern Bombay], which exports copper and sesame logs and cloth for making dresses, for it also is a great place of business.

And also to Sind [Gujarat], where musk and castor and spice are procured, and to Persia and the Homerite country [Anatolia], and to Adule [in Ethiopia]. And this island [Ceylon] receives imports from all these markets that we have mentioned and passes them on to the remoter ports, while at the same time exporting its own produce in both directions. . . .

The kings of various places in India keep elephants. . . . They may have six hundred each, or five hundred, some more, some fewer. Now the king of Ceylon gives a good price both for the elephants and for the horses that he has. The elephants he pays for by the cubit [a unit of measurement equivalent to about half a meter or twenty inches]. For the height is measured from the ground, and the price is reckoned at so many gold coins for each cubit—fifty [coins] it may be, or a hundred, or even more. Horses they bring to him from Persia, and he buys them, exempting the importers of them from paying custom duties. The kings of the Indian subcontinent tame their elephants, which are caught wild, and employ them in war.

SOURCE: Cosmas Indicopleustes. *The Christian Topography of Cosmas, an Egyptian Monk.* Trans. by J. W. McCrindle. London: Hakluyt Society, 1897, pp. 364–72. (Translation slightly modified.)

How did Ceylon compare as a commercial center with Constantinople and Baghdad, as described by Benjamin of Tudela?

maintain to order in local communities by providing guidance on individuals' roles in society and their relationships with others.

Caste and Migration

The caste system closely reflected changes in Indian society. It adapted to the arrival of migrants, for example, and helped to integrate them into Indian society. As Turkish peoples or Muslim merchants pursued opportunities in India, they gained recognition as distinct groups under the umbrella of the caste system. They established codes of conduct both for the regulation of behavior within their own groups and for guidance in dealing with members of other castes. Within a few generations their descendants had become absorbed into Indian society.

*Caste and
Social Change*

The caste system also accommodated the social changes brought about by trade and economic development. Indeed, the caste system influenced the lives of most people by helping to order their work and their relationships with other workers. The castes that individuals most closely identified with were the subcastes *(jati)*, which often took the form of workers' guilds. As merchants and manufacturers became increasingly important in the larger economy, they organized powerful guilds to represent their interests. Merchant guilds in particular wielded political and economic influence, since their members enjoyed access to considerable wealth and contributed in large measure to the economic health of their states. Guild members forged group identities by working within the caste system. Merchants specializing in particular types of commerce, such as the silk, cotton, or spice trade, established themselves as distinct subcastes, as did artisans working in particular industries, such as the iron, steel, or leather business.

*Expansion of
the Caste System*

Besides becoming more complex, the caste system also extended its geographic reach. Caste distinctions first became prominent in northern India following Aryan migrations into the subcontinent. During the postclassical era, the caste system became securely established in southern India as well. Economic development aided this process by encouraging commercial relationships between southern merchants and their caste-conscious counterparts in the north. The emergence of merchant and craft guilds in southern regions strengthened the caste system, since guild members usually organized as a subcaste. Powerful temples also fostered caste distinctions. Caste-conscious brahmins who supervised the temples were particularly effective promoters of the system, since temples provided the only formal education available in most regions and also served as centers of local social life. By about the eleventh century C.E., caste had become the principal basis of social organization in southern India.

THE MEETING OF HINDU
AND ISLAMIC TRADITIONS

The Indian cultural landscape underwent a thorough transformation during the postclassical era. Jainism and Buddhism lost much of their popular following. Neither belief completely disappeared from India, and indeed, a small community continues to observe each faith there even today. After 1000 C.E., however, Hindu and Islamic traditions increasingly dominated the cultural and religious life of India.

Hinduism and Islam differed profoundly as religious traditions. The Hindu pantheon made places for numerous gods and spirits, for example, whereas Islamic theology stood on the foundation of a firm and uncompromising monotheism. Yet both religions attracted large popular followings throughout the subcontinent, with Hinduism predominating in southern India and Islam in the north.

The Development of Hinduism

Toward the end of the first millennium C.E., Buddhism flourished in east Asia, central Asia, and parts of southeast Asia but came under great pressure in India. Like Mahayana Buddhism, both Hinduism and Islam promised salvation to devout individuals, and they gradually attracted Buddhists to their own communities. Invasions of India by Turkish peoples hastened the decline of Buddhism because the invaders looted and destroyed Buddhist stupas and shrines. In 1196 Muslim forces overran the city of Nalanda and ravaged the schools where Xuanzang and other foreign pilgrims had studied with the world's leading Buddhist philosophers and theologians. The conquerors torched Buddhist libraries and either killed or exiled thousands of monks living at Nalanda. Buddhism soon became a minor faith in the land of its birth.

Vishnu and Shiva

Hinduism benefited from the decline of Buddhism. One reason for the increasing popularity of Hinduism was the remarkable growth of devotional cults, particularly those dedicated to Vishnu and Shiva, two of the most important deities in the Hindu pantheon. Vishnu was the preserver of the world, a god who observed the universe from the heavens and who occasionally entered the world in human form in order to resist evil or communicate his teachings. By contrast, Shiva was both a god of fertility and a destructive deity: he brought life but also took it away when its season had passed. Hindus associated many gods and goddesses with Vishnu and Shiva, and they recognized other cults that were altogether independent of these two. But the most popular devotional cults focused on veneration of Vishnu or Shiva.

Devotional Cults

Hindus embraced the new cults warmly because they promised salvation. Devotional cults became especially popular in southern India, where individuals or family groups went to great lengths to honor their chosen deities. Often cults originated when individuals identified Vishnu or Shiva with a local spirit or deity associated with a particular region or a prominent geographic feature. The famous cult of Shiva as lord of the dancers arose, for example, about the fifth or sixth century C.E. when devotees identified a stone long venerated locally in a southern Indian village as a symbol of Shiva. In the tenth century Chola kings took the dancing Shiva as their family god and spread the cult's popularity throughout southern India. By venerating images of Vishnu or Shiva, offering them food and drink, and meditating on the deities and their qualities, Hindus hoped to achieve a mystic union with the gods that would bring grace and salvation. As the cults proliferated, temples and shrines dotted the landscape of southern India. Veneration of Vishnu and Shiva gradually became popular among Hindus in northern as well as southern India.

The significance of Hinduism extended well beyond popular religion: it also influenced philosophy. Just as Buddhism, Christianity, and Islam influenced moral thought and philosophy in other lands, devotional Hinduism guided

Southern Indian artists often portrayed Shiva in bronze sculptures as a four-armed lord of dancers. In this figure from the Chola dynasty, Shiva crushes with his foot a dwarf demon symbolizing ignorance. One hand holds a bell to awaken his devotees, another bears the fire used by Shiva as creator and destroyer of the world, and a third gestures Shiva's benevolence toward his followers.

Shankara

An elaborate open-air rock carving at Mamallapuram, south of modern Madras, celebrates the Ganges River as a gift from Shiva and other gods.

the efforts of the most prominent philosophers in postclassical India. Brahmin philosophers such as Shankara and Ramanuja took the Upanishads as a point of departure for subtle reasoning and sophisticated metaphysics. Shankara, a southern Indian devotee of Shiva who was active during the early ninth century C.E., took it upon himself to digest all sacred Hindu writings and harmonize their sometimes contradictory teachings into a single, consistent system of thought. In a manner reminiscent of Plato, Shankara held that the physical world was illusion—a figment of the imagination—and that ultimate reality lay beyond the physical senses. Although he was a worshiper of Shiva, Shankara mistrusted emotional services and ceremonies, insisting that only by disciplined logical reasoning could human beings understand the ultimate reality of Brahman, the impersonal world-soul of the Upanishads. Only then could they appreciate the fundamental unity of the world, which Shankara considered a perfectly understandable expression of ultimate reality, even though to human physical senses that same world appears chaotic and incomprehensible.

Ramanuja
Ramanuja, a devotee of Vishnu who was active during the eleventh and early twelfth centuries C.E., challenged Shankara's uncompromising insistence on logic. Also a brahmin philosopher from southern India, Ramanuja's thought reflected the deep influence of devotional cults. According to Ramanuja, intellectual understanding of ultimate reality was less important than personal union with the deity. Ramanuja granted that intellectual efforts could lead to comprehension of reality, but he held that genuine bliss came from salvation and identification of individuals with their gods. He followed the *Bhagavad Gita* in recommending intense devotion to Vishnu, and he taught that by placing themselves in the hands of Vishnu, devotees would win the god's grace and live forever in his presence. Thus, in contrast to Shankara's consistent, intellectual system of thought, Ramanuja's philosophy pointed toward a Hindu theology of salvation. Indeed, his thought inspired the development of devotional cults throughout India, and it serves even today as a philosophical foundation for Hindu popular religion.

Islam and Its Appeal

The Islamic faith did not attract much immediate interest among Indians when it arrived in the subcontinent. It won gradual acceptance in merchant communities where foreign Muslim traders took local spouses and found a place in Indian society. Elsewhere, however, circumstances did not favor its adoption, since it often arrived in the cultural baggage of conquering peoples. Muslim conquerors generally reserved important political and military positions for their Arab, Persian, and Turkish companions. Only rarely did they allow Indians—even those who had converted to Islam—to hold sensitive posts. Thus, quite apart from the fact that they introduced a foreign religion radically different from those of the subcontinent, conquerors offered little incentive for Indians to convert to Islam.

Conversion to Islam
Gradually, however, many Indians converted to Islam. By 1500 C.E. Indian Muslims numbered perhaps twenty-five million—about one-quarter of the subcontinent's population. Some Indians adopted Islam in hope of improving their positions in society:

Sources from the Past

The *Bhagavata Purana* on Devotion to Vishnu

With the development of devotional Hinduism in the postclassical era, religious leaders produced a body of literature known as the puranas, *texts that told stories about the gods and offered instructions in proper methods of worship. The most influential of these works is the* Bhagavata Purana *("Purana of the Lord"), composed about the eighth or ninth century C.E. In the following selection the god Vishnu sometimes refers to himself in the third person as "the lord" and sometimes speaks in the first person while instructing devotees how to worship him and support his cult.*

The teachers consider the utterance of the Lord's name as destructive of sin completely, even when the utterance is due to the name being associated with something else, or is done jocularly, or as a result of involuntary sound, or in derision. . . .

One should therefore resort to a teacher, desiring to know what constitutes the supreme welfare. . . . Taking the teacher as the deity, one should learn from him the practices characteristic of the Lord's devotees. . . . First, detachment from all undesirable associations, then, association with the good souls, compassion, friendliness, and due humility toward all beings, purity, penance, forbearance, silence, study of sacred writings, straightforwardness, continence, nonviolence, equanimity, seeing one's own Self and the Lord everywhere, seeking solitude, freedom from home, wearing clean recluse robes, satisfying oneself with whatever comes to one, faith in the scriptures of devotion and refraining from censure of those of other schools, subjugation of mind, speech, and action, truthfulness, quietude, restraint, listening to accounts of the Lord's advents, exploits, and qualities, singing of the Lord, contemplation of the Lord of wonderful exploits, engaging in acts only for His sake, dedicating unto the Lord everything—the rites one does, gifts, penance, sacred recital, righteous conduct and whatever is dear to one like one's wife, son, house, and one's own life—cultivating friendship with those who consider the Lord as their soul and master, service to the Lord and to the world and especially to the great and good souls, sharing in the company of fellow devotees the sanctifying glory of the Lord, sharing with them one's delight, satisfaction and virtues of restraint, remembering oneself and reminding fellow-worshipers of the Lord who sweeps away all sin; bearing a body thrilled with devotion and ecstatic experience of the Lord, now in tears with some thought of the Lord, now laughing, now rejoicing, now speaking out, now dancing, now singing, now imitating the Lord acts, and now becoming quiet with the blissful experience of the Supreme—such are the devotees, who behave like persons not of this world. . . .

One should engage himself in singing of Me, praising Me, dancing with My themes, imitating My exploits and acts, narrating My stories or listening to them.

With manifold hymns of praise of Me, taken from the *Puranas* or from the local languages . . . , the devotee should praise and pray to Me that I bless him and prostrate himself completely before Me. With his head and hands at My feet, he should pray, "My lord, from the clutches of death [i.e., the cycle of birth and death], save me who have taken refuge under You." . . .

Whenever and wherever one feels like worshiping Me in images, etc., one should do so; I am, however, present in oneself and in all beings; for I am the Soul of everything. . . .

Having consecrated an image of Me one should build a firm temple for Me, and beautiful flower gardens around for conducting daily worship and festivals. For the maintenance of My worship, etc., in special seasons as well as every day, one should bestow fields, bazaars, townships, and villages, and thereby attain to My own lordship.

SOURCE: Ainslie T. Embree and Stephen Hay, eds. *Sources of Indian Tradition*, 2 vols., 2nd ed. New York: Columbia University Press, 1988, 1: 325–26, 328.

Assess the extent to which the Bhagavata Purana *builds on devotional teachings offered in the* Bhagavad Gita *discussed earlier.*

Hindus of lower castes, for example, hoped to escape discrimination by converting to a faith that recognized the equality of all believers. In fact, Hindus rarely improved their social standing by conversion. Often members of an entire caste or subcaste adopted Islam en masse, and after conversion they continued to play the same social and economic roles that they had before.

Sufis

In India as elsewhere, the most effective agents of conversion to Islam were Sufi mystics. Sufis encouraged a personal, emotional, devotional approach to Islam. They did not insist on fine points of doctrine, and they sometimes even permitted their followers to observe rituals or venerate spirits not recognized by the Islamic faith. Because of their piety and sincerity, however, Sufi missionaries attracted individuals searching for a faith that could provide comfort and meaning for their personal lives.

In India as in other lands, Sufi mystics were the most effective Muslim missionaries. This eighteenth-century painting depicts the Sufi Khwaja Khidr, beloved in Muslim communities throughout northern India as one associated with springtime, fertility, and happiness.

Thus, like Hinduism, Indian Islam emphasized piety and devotion. Even though Hinduism and Islam were profoundly different religions, they encouraged the cultivation of similar spiritual values that transcended the social and cultural boundary lines of postclassical India.

The Bhakti Movement

In some ways the gap between Hinduism and Islam narrowed in postclassical India because both religions drew on long-established and long-observed cultural traditions. Sufis, for example, often attracted schools of followers in the manner of Indian gurus, spiritual leaders who taught Hindu values to disciples who congregated around them. Even more important was the development of the *bhakti* movement, a cult of love and devotion that ultimately sought to erase the distinction between Hinduism and Islam. The bhakti movement emerged in southern India during the twelfth century, and it originally encouraged a traditional piety and devotion to Hindu values. As the movement spread to the north, bhakti leaders increasingly encountered Muslims and became deeply attracted to certain Islamic values, especially monotheism and the notion of spiritual equality of all believers.

Guru Kabir

The bhakti movement gradually rejected the exclusive features of both Hinduism and Islam. Thus guru Kabir (1440–1518), a blind weaver who was one of the most famous bhakti teachers, went so far as to teach that Shiva, Vishnu, and Allah were all manifestations of a single, universal deity, whom all devout believers could find within their own hearts. The bhakti movement did not succeed in harmonizing Hinduism and Islam. Nevertheless, like the Sufis, bhakti teachers promoted values that helped to build bridges between India's social and cultural communities.

THE INFLUENCE OF INDIAN SOCIETY IN SOUTHEAST ASIA

Just as China stood at the center of a larger east Asian society, India served as the principal source of political and cultural traditions widely observed throughout south and southeast Asia. For a millennium and more, southeast Asian peoples adapted Indian political structures and religions to local needs and interests. Although Indian armed forces rarely ventured into the region, southeast Asian lands reflected the influence of Indian society, as merchants introduced Hinduism, Buddhism, Sanskrit writings, and Indian forms of political organization. Beginning about the twelfth century, Islam also found solid footing in southeast Asia, as Muslim merchants, many of them Indians, established trading communities in the important port cities of the region. During the next five hundred years, Islam attracted a sizable following and became a permanent feature in much of southeast Asia.

The States of Southeast Asia

Indian Influence in Southeast Asia

Indian merchants visited the islands and mainland of southeast Asia from an early date, perhaps as early as 500 B.C.E. By the early centuries C.E., they had become familiar figures throughout southeast Asia, and their presence brought opportunities for the native ruling elites of the region. In exchange for spices and exotic products such as pearls, aromatics, and animal skins, Indian merchants brought textiles, beads, gold, silver, manufactured metal goods, and objects used in political or religious rituals. Southeast Asian rulers used the profits from this trade to consolidate their political control.

Meanwhile, southeast Asian ruling elites became acquainted with Indian political and cultural traditions. Without necessarily giving up their own traditions, they borrowed Indian forms of political organization and accepted Indian religious faiths. On the model of Indian states, for example, they adopted kingship as the principal form of political authority. Regional kings in southeast Asia surrounded themselves with courts featuring administrators and rituals similar to those found in India.

Ruling elites also sponsored the introduction of Hinduism or Buddhism—sometimes both—into their courts. They embraced Indian literature like the *Ramayana* and the *Mahabharata,* which promoted Hindu values, as well as treatises that explained Buddhist views on the world. They did not show much enthusiasm for the Indian caste system and continued to acknowledge the deities and nature spirits that southeast Asian peoples had venerated for centuries. But ruling elites readily adopted Hinduism and Buddhism, which they found attractive because the Indian faiths reinforced the principle of monarchical rule.

Funan

The first state known to have reflected Indian influence in this fashion was Funan, which dominated the lower reaches of the Mekong River (including parts of modern Cambodia and Vietnam) between the first and the sixth century C.E. The rulers of Funan consolidated their grip on the Mekong valley and built a capital city at the port of Oc Eo. Funan grew wealthy because it dominated the Isthmus of Kra, the narrow portion of the Malay peninsula where merchants transported trade goods between China and India. (The short portage enabled them to avoid a long voyage around the Malay peninsula.) The rulers of Funan drew enormous wealth by controlling trade between China and India. They used their profits to construct an elaborate system of water storage and irrigation—so extensive that aerial photography still reveals its lines—that served a productive agricultural economy in the Mekong delta.

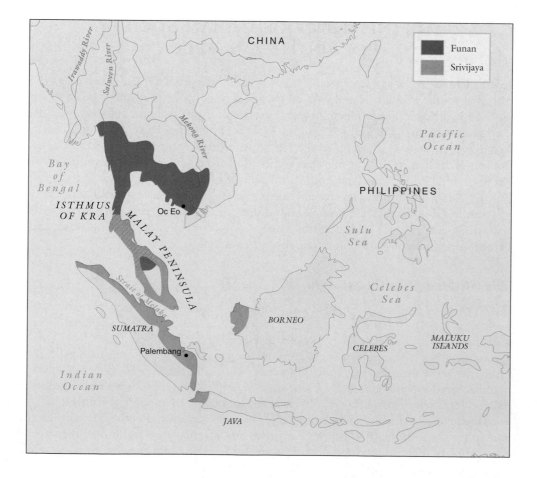

MAP [16.3]
Early states of southeast Asia: Funan and Srivijaya, 100–1025 C.E.

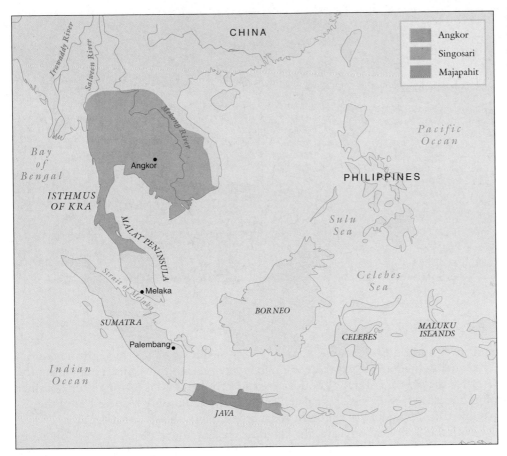

MAP [16.4]
Later states of southeast
Asia: Angkor, Singosari, and
Majapahit, 889–1520 C.E.

As trade with India became an increasingly important part of Funan's economy, the ruling classes adopted Indian political, cultural, and religious traditions. They took the Sanskrit term *raja* ("king") for themselves and claimed divine sanction for their rule in the manner of Hindu rulers in India. They established positions for administrators and bureaucrats such as those found at Indian courts and conducted official business in Sanskrit. They introduced Indian ceremonies and rituals and worshiped Vishnu, Shiva, and other Hindu deities. They continued to honor local deities, particularly water spirits venerated widely throughout southeast Asia, but they eagerly welcomed Hinduism, which offered additional recognition and divine legitimacy for their rule. At first, Indian cultural and religious traditions were most prominent and most often observed at ruling courts. Over the longer term, however, these traditions extended well beyond ruling elites and won a secure place in southeast Asian society.

During the sixth century C.E., a bitter power struggle weakened Funan internally. Peoples from the north took advantage of this weakness, migrated to the lower Mekong valley in large numbers, and overwhelmed Funan. Chams settled in the southern portion of modern Vietnam, and Khmers dominated in the region occupied by modern Cambodia. By the late sixth century, Funan's intricate irrigation system had fallen into ruins, and Funan itself soon passed into oblivion.

After the fall of Funan, political leadership in southeast Asia passed to the kingdom of Srivijaya (670–1025 C.E.) based on the island of Sumatra. The kings of Srivijaya built a powerful navy and controlled commerce in southeast Asian waters. They compelled port cities in southeast Asia to recognize their authority, and they financed

Srivijaya

Maritime trade flourished in southeast Asia during postclassical times. This ninth-century relief carving from the Buddhist temple at Borobodur in Java depicts a typical southeast Asian ship.

their navy and bureaucracy from taxes levied on ships passing through the region. They maintained an all-sea trade route between China and India, eliminating the need for the portage of trade goods across the Isthmus of Kra. As the volume of shipping increased in the postclassical era, the Srivijaya kingdom prospered until the expansive Chola kingdom of southern India eclipsed it in the eleventh century.

With the decline of Srivijaya, the kingdoms of Angkor (889–1431 C.E.), Singosari (1222–1292 C.E.), and Majapahit (1293–1520 C.E.) dominated affairs in southeast Asia. Many differences characterized these states. Funan had its base of operations in the Mekong valley, Srivijaya at Palembang in southern Sumatra, Angkor in Cambodia, and Singosari and Majapahit on the island of Java. Funan and Angkor were land-based states that derived most of their wealth from productive agricultural economies, whereas Srivijaya, Singosari, and Majapahit were island-based states that prospered because they controlled maritime trade. Funan and Majapahit were largely Hindu states, but the kings of Srivijaya and Angkor made deep commitments to Buddhism. Native southeast Asian traditions survived in all these states, and at the court of Singosari, religious authorities fashioned a cultural blend of Hindu, Buddhist, and indigenous values. Sculptures at the Singosari court depicted Hindu and Buddhist personalities, for example, but used them to honor local deities and natural spirits rather than Indian deities.

Angkor   The magnificent monuments of Angkor testify eloquently to the influence of Indian traditions in southeast Asia. Beginning in the ninth century, kings of the Khmers began to build a capital city at Angkor Thom. With the aid of brahmin advisors from India, the kings designed the city as a microcosmic reflection of the Hindu world order. At the center, they built a temple representing the Himalayan Mount Meru, the sacred abode of Shiva, and surrounded it with numerous smaller temples representing other parts of the Hindu universe.

As the Khmers turned to Buddhism during the twelfth and thirteenth centuries, they added Buddhist temples to the complex, though without removing the earlier structures inspired by Hinduism. The entire complex formed a square with sides of about three kilometers (two miles), surrounded by a moat filled from the nearby Tonle Sap River. During the twelfth century the Khmer kings constructed a smaller

General view of the temple complex dedicated to Vishnu at Angkor Wat.

but even more elaborate temple center at Angkor Wat, about one kilometer (just over half a mile) from Angkor Thom.

The Khmers abandoned Angkor in 1431 after Thai peoples invaded the capital and left much of it in ruins. Soon the jungle reclaimed both Angkor Thom and Angkor Wat, which remained largely forgotten until French missionaries and explorers rediscovered the sites in the mid-nineteenth century. Rescued from the jungle, the temple complexes of Angkor stand today as vivid reminders of the influence of Indian political, cultural, and religious traditions in southeast Asia.

The Arrival of Islam

Muslim merchants had ventured into southeast Asia by the eighth century, but only during the tenth century did they become prominent in the region. Some came from southern Arabia or Persia, but many were Indians from Gujarat or the port cities of southern India. Thus Indian influence helped to establish Islam as well as Hinduism and Buddhism in southeast Asia.

For several centuries Islam maintained a quiet presence in southeast Asia. Small communities of foreign merchants observed their faith in the port cities of the region but attracted little interest on the part of the native inhabitants. Gradually, however, ruling elites, traders, and others who had regular dealings with foreign Muslims became interested in the faith. During the late thirteenth century, the Venetian traveler Marco Polo visited the island of Sumatra and noted that many residents of the towns and cities had converted to Islam, while those living in the countryside and the hills retained their inherited traditions.

Conversion to Islam

Like Hinduism and Buddhism, Islam did not enter southeast Asia as an exclusive faith. Ruling elites who converted to Islam often continued to honor Hindu, Buddhist, or native southeast Asian traditions. They adopted Islam less as an exclusive and absolute creed than as a faith that facilitated their dealings with foreign Muslims and provided additional divine sanction for their rule. Rarely did they push their subjects to convert to Islam, although they allowed Sufi mystics to preach their faith before popular audiences. As in India, Sufis in southeast Asia appealed to a large public because of their reputation for sincerity and holiness. They allowed converts to retain inherited customs while adapting the message of Islam to local needs and interests.

Melaka

During the fifteenth century the spread of Islam gained momentum in southeast Asia, largely because the powerful state of Melaka sponsored the faith throughout the region. Founded during the late fourteenth century by Paramesvara, a rebellious prince from Sumatra, Melaka took advantage of its strategic location in the Strait of Melaka, near modern Singapore, and soon became prominent in the trading world of southeast Asia. During its earliest days Melaka was more a lair of pirates than a legitimate state. By the mid-fifteenth century, however, Melaka had built a substantial navy that patrolled the waters of southeast Asia and protected the region's sea lanes. Melakan fleets compelled ships to call at the port of Melaka, where ruling authorities levied taxes on the value of their cargoes. Thus, like southeast Asian states of earlier centuries, Melaka became a powerful state through the control of maritime trade.

In one respect, though, Melaka differed significantly from the earlier states. Although it began as a Hindu state, Melaka soon became predominantly Islamic. About the mid-fifteenth century the Melakan ruling class converted to Islam. It welcomed theologians, Sufis, and other Islamic authorities to Melaka and sponsored missionary campaigns to spread Islam throughout southeast Asia. By the end of the fifteenth century, mosques had begun to define the urban landscapes of Java, Sumatra, and the Malay peninsula, and Islam had made its first appearance in the spice-bearing islands of Maluku and in the southern islands of the Philippine archipelago.

Thus, within several centuries of its arrival, Islam was a prominent feature in the cultural landscape of southeast Asia. Along with Hinduism and Buddhism, Islam helped link southeast Asian lands to the larger cultural world of India and to the larger commercial world of the Indian Ocean basin.

With respect to political organization, India differed from postclassical societies in China, southwest Asia, and the eastern Mediterranean basin: India did not experience a return of centralized imperial rule such as that provided by the Tang and Song dynasties, the Umayyad and Abbasid dynasties, and the Byzantine empire. In other respects, however, India's development was similar to that of other postclassical societies. Increased agricultural production fueled population growth and urbanization while trade encouraged specialized industrial production and rapid economic growth. The vigorous and voluminous commerce of the Indian Ocean basin influenced the structure of economies and societies from east Asia to east Africa. It brought prosperity especially to India, which not only contributed cotton, pepper, sugar, iron, steel, and other products to the larger hemispheric economy but also served as a major clearinghouse of trade. Like contemporary societies, postclassical India experienced cultural change, and Indian traditions deeply influenced the cultural development of other lands. Hinduism and Islam emerged as the two most popular religious faiths within the subcontinent, while Indian merchants helped to establish Hinduism, Buddhism, and Islam in southeast Asian lands. Throughout the postclassical era, India participated fully in the larger hemispheric zone of cross-cultural communication and exchange.

CHRONOLOGY

1st to 6th century	Kingdom of Funan
606–648	Reign of Harsha
670–1025	Kingdom of Srivijaya
711	Conquest of Sind by Umayyad forces
early 9th century	Life of Shankara
850–1267	Chola kingdom
889–1431	Kingdom of Angkor
1001–1027	Raids on India by Mahmud of Ghazni
11th to 12th century	Life of Ramanuja
12th century	Beginning of the bhakti movement
1206–1526	Sultanate of Delhi
1336–1565	Kingdom of Vijayanagar
1440–1518	Life of guru Kabir

FOR FURTHER READING

Aziz Ahmad. *Studies in Islamic Culture in the Indian Environment.* Oxford, 1964. A scholarly analysis of the arrival of Islam and its effects in India.

A. L. Basham. *The Wonder That Was India.* New York, 1954. A popular survey by a leading scholar of ancient India.

Al-Biruni. *Alberuni's India.* 2 vols. Trans. by E. Sachau. London, 1910. English translation of al-Biruni's eleventh-century description of Indian customs, religion, philosophy, geography, and astronomy.

Buzurg ibn Shahriyar. *The Book of the Wonders of India: Mainland, Sea and Islands.* Trans. by G. S. P. Freeman-Grenville. London, 1981. Stories and tall tales of a tenth-century mariner who sailed frequently between Persia and India.

K. N. Chaudhuri. *Asia before Europe: Economy and Civilisation of the Indian Ocean from the Rise of Islam to 1750.* Cambridge, 1990. Controversial and penetrating analysis of economic, social, and cultural structures shaping societies of the Indian Ocean basin.

———. *Trade and Civilisation in the Indian Ocean: An Economic History from the Rise of Islam to 1750.* Cambridge, 1985. Brilliant analysis of the commercial life of the Indian Ocean basin by a prominent scholar.

Georges Coedès. *The Indianized States of Southeast Asia.* Trans. by S. B. Cowing. Honolulu, 1968. A careful survey that is still useful, though somewhat dated.

Ainslie T. Embree and Stephen Hay, eds. *Sources of Indian Tradition.* 2 vols. 2nd ed. New York, 1988. An important collection of primary sources in English translation.

Bernard Groslier and Jacques Arthaud. *Angkor: Art and Civilization.* Rev. ed. Trans. by E. E. Smith. New York, 1966. Well-illustrated summary, concentrating on the magnificent temple complexes at Angkor.

Kenneth R. Hall. *Maritime Trade and State Development in Early Southeast Asia.* Honolulu, 1985. Examines the link between long-distance trade and state building in southeast Asia.

Charles Higham. *The Civilization of Angkor.* London, 2001. Draws usefully on recent archaeological research in placing Angkor in historical context.

S. M. Ikram. *Muslim Civilization in India.* Ed. by A. T. Embree. New York, 1964. Important survey of Islam and its impact in India.

Hermann Kulke and Dietmar Rothermund. *A History of India.* Totowa, N.J., 1986. A valuable interpretative synthesis of Indian history.

Eleanor Mannikka. *Angkor Wat: Time, Space, and Kingship*. Honolulu, 1996. A detailed analysis of the magnificent Cambodian temple complex from an architectural point of view.

Patricia Risso. *Merchants and Faith: Muslim Commerce and Culture in the Indian Ocean*. Boulder, 1995. Surveys the activities of Muslim merchants in the Indian Ocean basin from the seventh to the nineteenth centuries.

Kernial Singh Sandhu. *Early Malaysia*. Singapore, 1973. Survey concentrating on the periods of Indian and Islamic influence in southeast Asia.

Burton Stein. *Vijayanagara*. Cambridge, 1989. A study of the southern Hindu kingdom concentrating on political and economic history.

Romila Thapar. *A History of India*. Harmondsworth, 1966. A sound, popular survey by one of the world's leading students of early Indian history.

 See our **Online Learning Center** at **www.mhhe.com/bentley3** for additional readings, practice maps, quizzes, and internet activities.

 Unfamiliar words? Check out the **Primary Source Investigator CD-ROM** for an interactive glossary, interactive maps, more images, and primary sources.

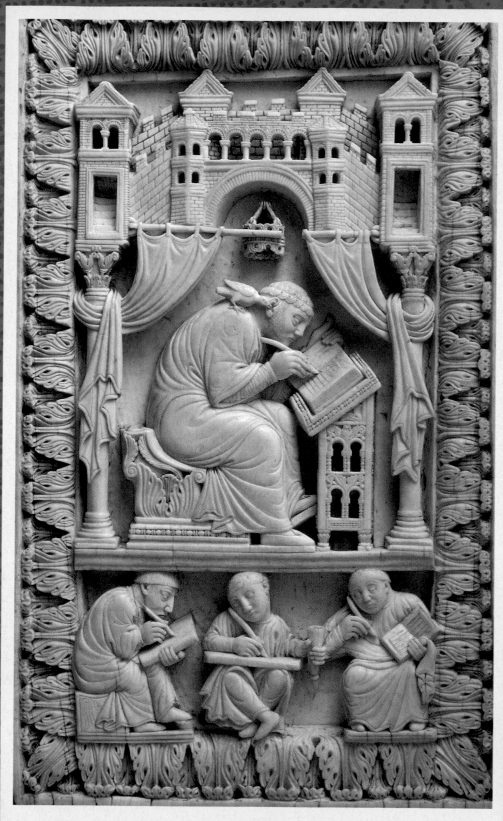

An ivory book cover carved in the tenth century depicts Pope Gregory I at his writing desk.

THE FOUNDATIONS OF CHRISTIAN SOCIETY IN WESTERN EUROPE

In 802 C.E. a most unusual traveler made his way from Baghdad to Aachen (in modern Germany), capital of the western European empire ruled by Charlemagne. The traveler was an albino elephant, a diplomatic gift from the Abbasid caliph Harun al-Rashid to Charlemagne. The elephant—whom Harun named Abu al-Abbas, in honor of the Abbasid dynasty's founder—was born in India and went to Baghdad as a present from an Indian king. From Baghdad the animal accompanied an embassy overland to Syria, then traveled by ship from Beirut to Malta and Rome, and finally went overland north to Charlemagne's court. Abu al-Abbas must have shivered through the cold, damp winters of western Europe, yet he overawed and amazed all who beheld him until his death in 810.

Charlemagne was not friendly to Islam. At the battle of Tours (732 C.E.) his grandfather, Charles Martel, had defeated a Muslim army that ventured into Frankish territory after Muslim forces had conquered most of the Iberian peninsula. Charlemagne himself fought Muslim forces in northern Spain. One of the battles from his campaign—in a much fictionalized version—provided the story line in later centuries for a popular poetic work called the *Song of Roland*. Nevertheless, in spite of his personal religious preferences, Charlemagne found it both necessary and convenient to have diplomatic dealings with Harun al-Rashid.

Charlemagne dispatched at least three embassies to Baghdad and received three in return. The embassies dealt with several issues: the safety of Christian pilgrims and merchants traveling in Abbasid-controlled Syria and Palestine, relations between Charlemagne's realm and neighboring Muslim Spain, and policy toward the Byzantine empire, which stood between western Europe and the Abbasid caliphate. Charlemagne's realm was weak and poor compared to the Abbasid empire, and by the mid-ninth century it was well on the way to dissolution. For about half a century, however, it seemed that Charlemagne and his successors might be able to establish a centralized imperial state in western Europe. His dealings with Harun al-Rashid—and the unusual odyssey of the elephant Abu al-Abbas—indicated that Charlemagne had the potential and the ambition to establish a western European empire similar to the Byzantine and Abbasid realms.

Historians refer to the era from about 500 to 1500 C.E. as the medieval period of European history—the "middle ages" falling between the classical era and modern times. During the early medieval period, from about 500 to 1000 C.E., European peoples recovered from the invasions that brought the Roman empire to an end and laid the political, economic, and cultural foundations for a new society. Europeans did not rebuild a powerful society as quickly as did the Abbasids in southwest Asia or the Tang and Song emperors of China: like India during the postclassical era, early medieval Europe was a politically disunited and disorganized region. Unlike India, though, Europe mostly disengaged from hemispheric communication and exchange. Only about the tenth century, after the establishment of effective political authority and a productive agricultural economy, were western European peoples able to reenter the larger trading world of the eastern hemisphere.

Three developments of the early medieval era served as foundations for the development of the powerful European society that emerged after 1000 C.E. First, following the disruption caused by invasions and depopulation, the peoples of western Europe restored political order. Unlike their counterparts in southwest Asia and China, they did not return to centralized imperial rule but, instead, resorted to a decentralized political order that vested public authority mostly in local and regional rulers. Second, European peoples began a process of economic recovery. They did not build large cities or generate a powerful industrial economy like those of the Byzantine, Abbasid, Tang, and Song empires. But they boosted agricultural production by increasing the amount of land under cultivation and introducing new tools and techniques, thus laying an agricultural foundation for trade and rapid economic development after the tenth century. Third, European peoples built an institutional framework that enabled the Christian church based in Rome to provide religious leadership and maintain cultural unity throughout western Europe. Thus, just as Confucianism, Buddhism, Hinduism, Islam, and eastern Christianity shaped cultural values in other lands, western Christianity emerged as the principal source of cultural authority in western Europe.

THE QUEST FOR POLITICAL ORDER

After toppling Rome's authority in the late fifth century C.E., Germanic invaders established successor states throughout the western Roman empire. From the fifth through the eighth century, continuing invasions and conflicts among the invaders themselves left western Europe in shambles. For a brief moment during the late eighth and early ninth centuries, it looked as though one group of Germanic invaders, the Franks, might reestablish imperial authority in western Europe. If they had succeeded, they might have played a role similar to that of the Sui and Tang dynasties in China by reviving centralized imperial rule after a hiatus of several centuries. By the late ninth century, however, the Frankish empire had fallen victim to internal power struggles and a fresh series of invasions by Muslims, Hungarian Magyars, and Vikings. Political authority in early medieval Europe then devolved to local and regional jurisdictions, and Europeans fashioned a decentralized political order.

Germanic Successor States

In 476 C.E. the Germanic general Odoacer deposed the last of the western Roman emperors, but the administrative apparatus of the Roman empire did not immediately disappear. Provincial governors continued to rule in their territories, aided by Roman bureaucrats and tax collectors, and Roman generals continued to field armies throughout the crumbling empire. Cities of the western Roman empire, however, lost population during the fifth century, as invasions and contests for power disrupted trade and manufacturing. This decay of Roman cities hastened imperial decline. De-

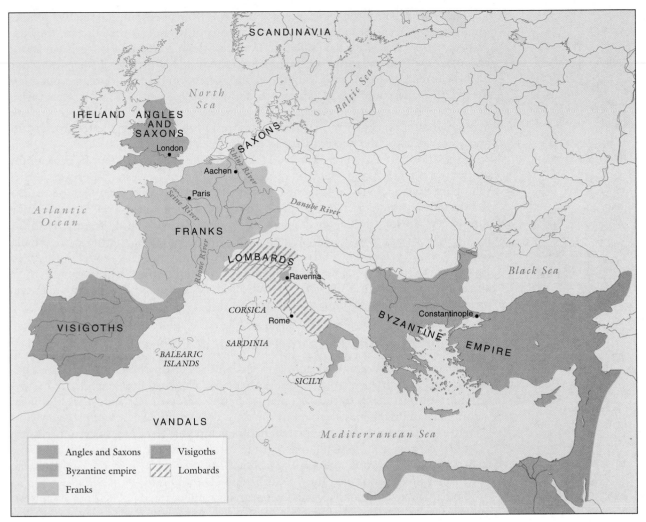

MAP [17.1]

Successor states to the Roman empire, ca. 600 C.E.

Germanic Kingdoms

prived of legitimacy and resources supplied from Rome and the other major cities of the empire, imperial institutions progressively weakened.

By the late fifth century, the invaders had organized a series of Germanic kingdoms as successor states in place of the Roman empire. Visigoths conquered Spain during the 470s, for example, and established a kingdom there that survived until the Muslim invasions of the early eighth century. Ostrogoths dominated Italy from the fifth century until Justinian's forces reasserted imperial authority there during the 530s. The departure of Byzantine armies from Italy created a power vacuum, which the Lombard people quickly moved to fill. Although they did not establish a tightly centralized monarchy, the Lombards maintained their hegemony throughout most of Italy from the mid-sixth until the mid-eighth century. Meanwhile, beginning about the mid-fifth century, Gaul fell under the control of other Germanic peoples, including the Burgundians, who settled in the southern and eastern regions, and the Franks, who brought the more northerly and westerly regions under their control. Angles, Saxons, and other Germanic peoples from Germany and Denmark crossed the English Channel and established regional kingdoms in Britain.

Thus, throughout the western portion of the Roman empire, Germanic peoples gradually displaced the authority and institutions of Rome. As they did so, they absorbed a great deal of Roman influence. Many of them converted to Christianity, for example, while others adapted Roman law to the needs of their own societies. None of the Germanic peoples possessed the economic and military resources—much less the political and social organization—to dominate all the others and establish their hegemony throughout western Europe. Nevertheless, the Franks built an impressive imperial state that organized, at least temporarily, about half of the territories formerly embraced by the western Roman empire.

The Franks

Even though their empire survived for only a short time, the Franks profoundly influenced the political, social, and cultural development of western Europe. Rather than participate actively in the commercial world of the Mediterranean basin, the Franks constructed a society that drew on the agricultural resources of continental Europe. As a result, the center of gravity in western Europe shifted from Italy to the northern lands of France, Germany, and the Low Countries. Furthermore, the Franks oversaw the development of decentralized political institutions, which influenced European politics and society for a millennium and more. Finally, they made a firm alliance with the western Christian church and helped Roman Christianity maintain its cultural and religious primacy in western Europe.

The Franks and the Temporary Revival of Empire

As Roman authority crumbled during the late fifth century, the Franks appeared unlikely to play a prominent role in European affairs. They had little experience in government and little exposure to Roman society. Some of their ancestors had lived within Roman boundaries since about the third century, and a few had probably converted to Christianity. But the Franks had developed a group identity only during the third century C.E., much later than the other Germanic peoples. Not until the fifth century did a strong military and political leader emerge from their midst. That leader was Clovis, who ruled the Franks from 481 until his death in 511.

Clovis

Under Clovis the Franks became the preeminent military and political power in western Europe. In 486 Clovis led Frankish forces on a campaign that wiped out the last vestiges of Roman authority in Gaul. Then he imposed his authority on the Franks themselves. Finally, he organized campaigns against other Germanic peoples whose states bordered the Frankish realm in Gaul. By the time of his death, Clovis had thoroughly transformed the Franks. No longer were they just one among many Germanic peoples inhabiting a crumbling Roman empire. Instead, they ranked as the most powerful and dynamic of the peoples building new states in western Europe.

One reason for the Franks' rapid rise had to do with re-

Clovis's Conversion

A manuscript illustration depicts the baptism of Clovis witnessed by church officials (left) and Frankish nobles (right), while a dove descends from above, indicating divine approval of the event.

ligion. Originally, all the Germanic invaders of the Roman empire were polytheists who honored a pantheon of warlike gods and other deities representing elements of nature such as the sun, moon, and wind. As they settled in and around the Roman empire, many Germanic peoples converted to Christianity. Most of them accepted Arian Christianity, which was popular in much of the eastern Roman empire. In both Rome and Constantinople, however, church authorities followed the decisions of church councils at Nicaea and Constantinople and condemned Arian views as heretical. Unlike other Germanic peoples, the Franks remained mostly pagan until the time of Clovis, who converted to Roman rather than to Arian Christianity along with his army. Clovis's conversion probably reflected the influence of his wife, Clotilda, a devout Christian who had long urged her husband to adopt her faith.

The Franks' conversion had large political implications. By adopting Roman rather than Arian Christianity, the Franks attracted the allegiance of the Christian population of the former Roman empire as well as recognition and support from the pope and the hierarchy of the western Christian church. Alliance with the church of Rome greatly strengthened the Franks, who became the most powerful of the Germanic peoples between the fifth and ninth centuries.

The Carolingians

After Clovis's death the Frankish kings lost much of their authority, as aristocratic warriors seized effective control of affairs in their own regions. Nevertheless, Clovis's successors ruled the Frankish kingdom until the early eighth century, when the aristocratic clan of the Carolingians displaced the line of Clovis and asserted the authority of the central government. The Carolingian dynasty takes its name from its founder, Charles (*Carolus* in Latin)—known as Charles Martel ("Charles the Hammer") because of his military prowess. In 732 at the battle of Tours (in the central part of modern France), he turned back a Muslim army that had ventured from Spain—recently conquered by Muslim warriors from north Africa—in order to reconnoiter lands north of the Pyrenees mountains. His victory helped persuade Muslim rulers of Spain that it was not worthwhile for them to seek further conquests in western Europe. Charles Martel himself never ruled as king of the Franks but, rather, served as deputy to the last of Clovis's descendants. In 751, however, Charles's son claimed the throne for himself.

Charlemagne

The Frankish realm reached its high point under Charles Martel's grandson Charlemagne ("Charles the Great"), who reigned from 768 to 814. Like King Harsha in India, Charlemagne temporarily reestablished centralized imperial rule in a society disrupted by invasion and contests for power between ambitious local rulers. Like Harsha again, Charlemagne possessed enormous energy, and the building of the Carolingian empire was in large measure his personal accomplishment. Although barely literate, Charlemagne was extremely intelligent. He spoke Latin, understood some Greek, and regularly conversed with theologians and other learned men. He maintained diplomatic relations with the Byzantine empire and the Abbasid caliphate. The

A bronze statue depicts Charlemagne riding a horse and carrying an orb symbolizing his imperial authority.

Sources from the Past

Gregory of Tours on the Conversion of Clovis

St. Gregory (538–594 C.E.) was bishop of Tours in central Gaul for the last twenty-one years of his life. During this period he composed a History of the Franks, *which is the chief source of information about the early Franks. Gregory clearly embellished the story of Clovis's conversion to Christianity, but his account indicates the significance of the event both for Clovis and for the Roman church.*

The queen [Clotilda] did not cease to urge him [Clovis] to recognize the true God and cease worshiping idols. But he could not be influenced in any way to this belief, until at last a war arose with the Alamanni, in which he was driven by necessity to confess what before he had of his free will denied. It came about that as the two armies were fighting fiercely, there was much slaughter, and Clovis's army began to be in danger of destruction. He saw it and raised his eyes to heaven, and with remorse in his heart he burst into tears and cried: "Jesus Christ, whom Clotilda asserts to be the son of the living God, who art said to give aid to those in distress and to bestow victory on those who hope in thee, I beseech the glory of thy aid, with the vow that if thou wilt grant me victory over these enemies, and I shall know that power which she says that people dedicated in thy name have had from thee, I will believe in thee and be baptized in thy name. For I have invoked my own gods, but, as I see, they have withdrawn from aiding me; and therefore I believe that they possess no power, since they do not help those who obey them. I now call upon thee, I desire to believe thee, only let me be rescued from my adversaries." And when he said this, the Alamanni turned their backs, and began to disperse in flight. And when they saw that their king was killed, they submitted to the dominion of Clovis, saying: "Let not the people perish further, we pray; we are yours now." And he stopped the fighting, and after encouraging his men retired in peace and told the queen how he had had merit to win the victory by calling on the name of Christ. . . .

Then the queen asked saint Remi, bishop of Rheims, to summon Clovis secretly, urging him to introduce the king to the word of salvation. And the bishop sent for him secretly and began to urge him to believe in the true God, maker of heaven and earth, and to cease worshiping idols, which could help neither themselves nor any one else. But the king said: "I gladly hear you, most holy father; but there remains one thing: the people who follow me cannot endure to abandon their gods; but I shall go and speak to them according to your words." He met with his followers, but before he could speak, the power of God anticipated him, and all the people cried out together: "O pious king, we reject our mortal gods, and we are ready to follow the immortal God whom Remi preaches." This was reported to the bishop, who was greatly rejoiced, and bade them get ready the baptismal font. . . . And the king was the first to ask to be baptized by the bishop. . . . And so the king confessed all-powerful God in the Trinity and was baptized in the name of the Father, Son, and Holy Spirit, and was anointed with the holy ointment with the sign of the cross of Christ. And of his army more than 3,000 were baptized.

SOURCE: Gregory of Tours. *History of the Franks.* Trans. by E. Brehaut. New York: Columbia University Press, 1916, pp. 39–41. (Translation slightly modified.)

To what extent was Clovis's conversion a case of religious transformation and to what extent a political act?

gift of the white elephant Abu al-Abbas symbolized relations between the Carolingian and Abbasid empires, and the animal accompanied Charlemagne on many of his travels until its death.

When Charlemagne inherited the Frankish throne, his realm included most of modern France as well as the lands that now form Belgium, the Netherlands, and southwestern Germany. Charlemagne was a conqueror in the mold of the Germanic peoples who invaded the Roman empire. By the time of his death in 814, Charlemagne had extended his authority to northeastern Spain, Bavaria, and Italy as far south as Rome. He campaigned for thirty-two years to impose his rule on the Saxons of northern Germany and repress their rebellions. Beyond the Carolingian empire proper, rulers in eastern Europe and southern Italy paid tribute to Charlemagne as imperial overlord.

Charlemagne's Administration

Charlemagne established a court and capital at Aachen (in modern Germany), but like Harsha in India, he spent most of his reign traveling throughout his realm in order to maintain his authority. Such constant travel was necessary because Charlemagne did not have the financial resources to maintain an elaborate bureaucracy or an administrative apparatus that could implement his policies. Instead, Charlemagne relied on aristocratic deputies, known as counts, who held political, military, and legal authority in local jurisdictions.

The counts often had their own political ambitions, and they sometimes pursued policies contrary to the interests of the central government. In an effort to bring the counts under tighter control, Charlemagne instituted a new group of imperial officials known as *missi dominici* ("envoys of the lord ruler"), who traveled every year to all local jurisdictions and reviewed the accounts of local authorities.

Charlemagne built the Frankish kingdom into an empire on the basis of military expeditions and began to outfit it with some centralized institutions. Yet he hesitated

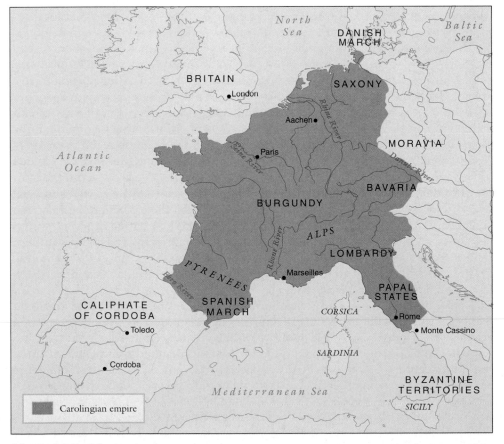

For an interactive version of this map, go to www.mhhe.com/bentley3ch17maps.

M A P [1 7 . 2]
The Carolingian empire, 814 C.E.

*Charlemagne
as Emperor*

to call himself emperor because the imperial title would constitute a direct challenge to the authority of the Byzantine emperors, who regarded themselves as the sole and legitimate successors of the Roman emperors.

Only in the year 800 did Charlemagne accept the title of emperor. While campaigning in Italy, Charlemagne attended religious services on Christmas Day conducted by Pope Leo III. During the services, the pope proclaimed Charlemagne emperor and placed an imperial crown on his head. It is not certain, but it is at least possible that Charlemagne did not know of the pope's plan and that Leo surprised him with an impromptu coronation: Charlemagne had no desire for strained relations with Byzantine emperors, who deeply resented the use of the imperial title in western Europe as a pretentious affront to their own dignity and authority. In any case, Charlemagne had already built an imperial state, and his coronation constituted public recognition of his accomplishments.

Decline and Dissolution of the Carolingian Empire

If Charlemagne's empire had endured, Carolingian rulers might well have built a bureaucracy, used the *missi dominici* to enhance the authority of the central government, and permanently reestablished centralized imperial rule in western Europe. As it happened, however, internal disunity and external invasions brought the Carolingian empire to an early end.

Louis the Pious

Charlemagne's only surviving son, Louis the Pious (reigned 814–840), succeeded his father and kept the Carolingian empire together. Lacking Charlemagne's strong will and military skills, however, Louis lost control of the counts and other local authorities, who increasingly pursued their own interests and ignored the central government. Moreover, even before Louis's death his three sons disputed the inheritance of the empire and waged bitter wars against each other. In 843 they agreed to divide the empire into three roughly equal portions, and each of them took one portion to rule as king. Thus, less than a century after its creation, the Carolingian empire dissolved.

Invasions

Even if internal disunity had not resulted in the dismemberment of the Carolingian empire, external pressures might well have brought it down. Beginning in the early ninth century, three groups of invaders pillaged the Frankish realm in search of wealth stored in towns and monasteries. From the south came Muslims, who raided towns, villages, churches, and monasteries in Mediterranean Europe from the mid-ninth to the late tenth century. Muslim invaders also seized Sicily as well as several territories in southern Italy and southern France. From the east came the Magyars, descendants of nomadic peoples from central Asia who had settled in Hungary. Expert horsemen, the Magyars raided settlements in Germany, Italy, and southern France from the late ninth to the mid-tenth century. From the north came the Vikings, most feared of all the invaders, who began mounting raids in northern France even during Charlemagne's reign.

Norse Expansion

Viking invasions represented one dimension of a larger process of Norse expansion that began around 800 C.E. Motives for this expansion included population pressure in Scandinavian lands, some of which offered limited opportunities for agriculture, and resistance to Christian missions that sought to abolish pagan gods and beliefs. During the eighth century C.E., Norse mariners developed a remarkable set of shipbuilding techniques and seafaring skills that enabled them to travel safely and reliably through the open ocean. Venturing from their Scandinavian homelands of Norway, Denmark, and Sweden, they reconnoitered much of the north Atlantic Ocean and established settlements in the Shetland Islands, the Faeroes, Iceland, and Greenland. About the year 1000 C.E., a small group even established a colony at Newfoundland in modern Canada and explored the Atlantic coast of North America at least as far south as modern-day Maine in the United States. Norse colonies in North America survived no more than a few decades, and even the colony in Greenland eventually disappeared around 1500 C.E. after a cooling global climate made it difficult to cultivate food crops there. Nevertheless, the colonies in Greenland and North America demonstrate the ability of Norse peoples to travel safely over long stretches of open ocean. These remarkable seafaring skills made it possible for Norse cultivators to migrate from their homelands and establish new agricultural communities in the north Atlantic basin.

Most Norse seafarers were merchants seeking commercial opportunities or migrants seeking lands to settle and cultivate. Some, however, turned their maritime skills more toward raiding and plundering than trading or raising crops. These were the Vikings. The term *Viking* originally referred to a group that raided the British Isles from their home at Vik in southern Norway. Over time, however, the term came to refer more generally to Norse mariners who mounted invasions and plundered settlements from eastern Europe to Mediterranean lands.

The Vikings sailed shallow-draft boats that could cross heavy seas, but then could also navigate the many rivers offering access to interior regions of Europe. Viking sailors carefully coordinated their ships' movements and timed their attacks to take advantage of the tides. Fleets of Viking boats with ferocious dragon heads mounted on their prows could sail up a river, arrive unexpectedly at a village or monastery far from the sea, and then spill

Danish Vikings prepare to invade England in this manuscript illustration produced at an English monastery about 1130.

The Vikings

The Oseberg ship, pictured here, is the best-preserved Viking vessel from the early middle ages. Built around 800 C.E., it served as a royal tomb until its discovery in 1903. A ship this size would accommodate about forty men.

M A P [1 7 . 3]
The dissolution of the Carolingian empire (843 C.E.) and the invasions of early medieval Europe in the ninth and tenth centuries.

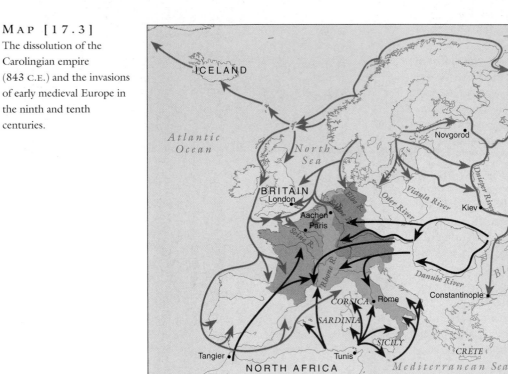

Kingdom of Charles the Bald   → Vikings

Kingdom of Louis the German   → Magyars

Kingdom of Lothar I   → Muslims

out crews of warriors who conducted lightning raids on unprepared victims. In 844 C.E. more than 150 Viking ships sailed up the Garonne River in southern France, plundering settlements along the way. Sometimes large fleets of Viking ships even attacked sizable cities. In 845 a menacing fleet of some 800 vessels materialized without warning before the city of Hamburg in northern Germany; in 885 a Viking force consisting of at least 700 ships sailed up the Seine River and besieged Paris; and in 994 an armada of about 100 ships sprinted up the Thames River and raided London. Bypassing relatively close targets in Russia, Germany, England, Ireland, France, and Spain, some Vikings ventured into the Mediterranean, where they plundered sites in the Balearic Islands, Sicily, and southern Italy. By following the Russian rivers to the Black Sea, other Vikings made their way to Constantinople, which they raided at least three times during the ninth and tenth centuries.

The Establishment of Regional Authorities

The Carolingians had no navy, no means to protect vulnerable sites, and no way to predict the movements of Viking raiders. Defense against the Magyars and Muslims as well as the Vikings rested principally with local forces that could respond rapidly to invasions. Because imperial authorities were unable to defend their territory, the Carolingian empire became the chief casualty of the invasions. After the ninth century, political and military initiative in western Europe passed increasingly to regional and local authorities.

Responses to ninth-century invasions took different forms in different lands. In England, which bore the brunt of the earliest Viking raids, invasions prompted the series of small kingdoms established earlier by Angles, Saxons, and other Germanic peoples to merge into a single larger realm. The leader of this effort was King Alfred (reigned 871–899), who expanded from his base in southern England to territories farther north held by Danish invaders. Alfred built a navy to challenge the Vikings at sea and constructed fortresses on land to secure areas that he conquered from the invaders. Danish settlers continued to occupy agricultural lands, but by the mid-tenth century Alfred's successors had established themselves as kings of all England.

England

In Germany the response to invasion brought the end of Carolingian rule and the formation of a more effective state under a new dynasty. When Carolingian authorities were unable to prevent invasions by the Magyars, local lords took matters into their own hands. The most successful of them was King Otto I of Saxony (reigned 936–973). In 955 he faced a large Magyar army at Lechfeld near Augsburg and inflicted a crushing defeat that effectively ended the Magyar threat. Otto also imposed his authority throughout Germany, and twice he led armies into Italy to support the papacy against Lombard magnates. On his second venture there in 962, the pope proclaimed him emperor and bestowed an imperial crown upon him. Otto's realm was really a German kingdom rather than an empire, but the imperial title survived until the nineteenth century, and later rulers of the Holy Roman Empire dated the foundation of their state to Otto's coronation in 962. In Germany, as in England, then, response to ninth-century invasions led to the organization of an effective regional state.

Germany

In France the end of Carolingian rule led to the proliferation of local authorities. Counts and other subordinates of the Carolingians withdrew allegiance from the central government, ruled their territories in their own interests, and usurped royal rights and prerogatives for themselves. They collected taxes, organized armed forces, built castles, and provided justice without reference to the Carolingians or other central authorities. Meanwhile, Vikings established many settlements in northern France, where they carved out small, independent states. The devolution of political and military responsibility to local authorities in tenth-century France encouraged the development of a decentralized political order.

France

The emergence of effective regional kingdoms and local authorities prevented the return of centralized imperial rule like that of the Carolingians or postclassical societies in China, southwest Asia, and the eastern Mediterranean region. Like postclassical India, medieval Europe became a society of competing regional states. By putting an end to the ninth-century invasions and establishing a stable political order, these states laid a foundation for social, economic, and cultural development.

EARLY MEDIEVAL SOCIETY

Historians once used the term *feudalism* to refer to the political and social order of medieval Europe. They spoke of a "feudal system" based on a neat hierarchy of lords and vassals, who collectively took charge of political and military affairs. Increasingly, however, scholars are abandoning the term *feudalism* because it distorts and oversimplifies the understanding of a complicated society. It is more helpful to view early medieval Europe as a society in which local political and military elites worked out various ad hoc ways to organize their territories and maintain order in the absence of effective central authorities. The arrangements they adopted had deep implications for the lives of political and military elites themselves and also for their relationships with commoners.

Organizing a Decentralized Society

After the dissolution of the Carolingian empire, European nobles built a decentralized society as they sought to protect their lands and maintain public order during a period of weak central authority and periodic invasions from outside. Local nobles, such as the Carolingian counts or other authorities, took responsibility for maintaining order in their own territories. These nobles usually owed at least nominal allegiance to a higher authority, most often a Carolingian king descended from Louis the Pious. In fact, though, the nobles acted with growing independence: they collected rents and fees, administered local affairs, mobilized armed forces, decided legal disputes, and sought to enhance their own authority at the expense of their superiors.

Lords and Retainers   To organize their territories the local nobles built military and political relationships with other prominent individuals in their territories. In doing so, they drew on military talent during the later Roman empire and the early Frankish kingdom, and they mobilized small private armies by attracting armed retainers into their service with grants of land or money. During the ninth and tenth centuries, as the Carolingian empire dissolved, local authorities revived these recruitment practices. Local lords provided grants that enabled their retainers to support themselves and their families. Usually these grants were parcels of land, but they sometimes took other forms, such as the right to income generated by a mill, the right to receive rents or payments from a village, or even a payment of money. These grants enabled retainers to devote their time and energy to the service of their lords rather than the domestic tasks of cultivating food and providing for families. The grants also provided resources that retainers needed to maintain horses and acquire expensive military equipment such as armor and weapons. In exchange for their grants, retainers owed loyalty, obedience, respect, counsel, and military service to their lords.

Military retainers receive swords that indicate their close relationship with a local lord who accepts them as partners in authority.

Indeed, relationships between lords and retainers became stronger because political leaders increasingly attracted followers by offering them rights over land and they increasingly recognized the prerogative of their supporters to pass these rights along to their heirs. In effect, these ties established close relationships between local political and military authorities. These relationships became extremely important for the larger social order because retainers increasingly exercised political and legal rights over their holdings. Retainers became responsible for the organizations of local public works projects, the resolution of disputes, and the administration of justice. As a result, political authorities and military specialists merged into a hereditary noble class that lived off the surplus agricultural production that it extracted from cultivators.

This decentralized political order developed into a complicated and sometimes even confusing network of relationships between lords and retainers. A lord with several retainers might himself be a retainer to a higher lord, who in turn might be one of several retainers to a yet greater lord in a web of relationships extending from local communities to a king. In some ways, dependence on the personal relationship between lord and retainer introduced an element of instability into the political order, since retainers—particularly those with many retainers of their own—sometimes decided unpredictably to pursue their own interests rather than those of their lords. Unless lords could discipline and control their retainers, this decentralized political order had strong potential to lead to political chaos, as in post–Carolingian France, where ambitious local authorities largely ignored central authorities and pursued their own interests.

Potential for Instability

Yet it was also possible for high-ranking lords to build powerful states on the foundation of relationships between lords and retainers. The tenth-century rulers of England and Germany, for example, monitored their retainers and prevented them from becoming too independent. And during the high middle ages (discussed in chapter 20), the kings of both England and France depended on relationships with their retainers in building powerful, centralized monarchies.

Serfs and Manors

Military, political, and legal affairs were the business of a small governing elite composed of lords and their retainers. But the establishment of a decentralized political order in early medieval Europe had important implications for the lives of all classes of people. Benefices held by political elites consisted most often of land cultivated by peasants who lived on the land and delivered a portion of their production to their superiors. Only by tapping this surplus agricultural production could lords and their retainers secure the material resources they needed to maintain their control over military, political, and legal affairs.

The development of a decentralized political order accompanied fundamental changes in European society, particularly for slaves and free peasants. Both Roman and Germanic societies had recognized enslaved and free classes, and for several centuries after the fall of the western Roman empire the population of western Europe consisted mostly of slaves and free peasants. As European society regained stability following the collapse of the Roman empire and the Germanic invasions, these slaves and free peasants worked at the same kinds of agricultural tasks and frequently intermarried. Free peasants often sought protection from a lord and pledged their labor and obedience in exchange for security and land to cultivate. Beginning about the mid-seventh century, rulers and administrators recognized intermediate categories of individuals neither fully slave nor fully free. Though not chattel slaves subject to sale on a master's whim, these semifree individuals, known as *serfs,* owed obligations to the lords whose lands they cultivated.

Serfs

Serfs usually had the right to work certain lands and to pass rights to those lands along to their heirs, so long as they observed their obligations to landlords. These obligations included both labor services and payments of rents in kind, such as a portion of a serf's own harvest, a chicken, or a dozen eggs, at specified times during the year. Male serfs typically worked three days a week in the fields of their lords and provided additional labor services during planting and harvesting seasons, while women churned butter, made cheese, brewed beer, spun thread, wove cloth, or sewed clothes

Serfs' Obligations

for the lords and their families. Some women also kept sheep and cattle, and their obligations to lords included products from their herds. Because landlords provided them with land to cultivate and sometimes with tools and animals as well, serfs had little opportunity to move to different lands. Indeed, they were able to do so only with the permission of their lord. They even had to pay fees for the right to marry a serf who worked for a different lord.

Manors

During the early middle ages, the institution of serfdom encouraged the development of the manor as the principal form of agricultural organization in western Europe. A manor was a large estate consisting of fields, meadows, forests, agricultural tools, domestic animals, and sometimes lakes or rivers, as well as serfs bound to the land. The lord of the manor was a prominent political or military figure. He and his deputies provided government, administration, police services, and justice for the manor. If a dispute arose between serfs, for example, the lord and his deputies restored order, conducted an investigation, and determined how to resolve the conflict. Many lords had the authority to execute serfs for serious misconduct such as murder or other violent crimes.

By the Carolingian era, manors dominated rural regions in much of France, western Germany, and the Low Countries, as well as southern England and northern Italy. In the absence of thriving cities, manors became largely self-sufficient communities. Lords of the manors maintained mills, bakeries, breweries, and wineries, and serfs produced most of the iron tools, leather goods, domestic utensils, and textiles that the manorial community needed. Small local markets, often organized near monasteries, supplied the products that residents of manors could not conveniently manufacture for themselves. During the high middle ages, craft skills developed on manors would help fuel an impressive round of economic development in western Europe.

The Economy of Early Medieval Europe

During the early middle ages, economic activity in western Europe was considerably slower than in China, India, southwest Asia, and the eastern Mediterranean region. Agricultural production suffered from repeated invasions by Germanic peoples, Magyars, Muslims, and Vikings, which seriously disrupted European economy and society. The decay of urban centers resulted in diminished industrial production and trade. By the tenth century, however, political stability served as a foundation for economic recovery, and western Europeans began to participate more actively in the larger trading world of the eastern hemisphere.

Agriculture

With the establishment of the Frankish kingdom and the Carolingian empire, the European center of gravity shifted from the Mediterranean to more northern lands, particularly France. But the agricultural tools and techniques inherited from the classical Mediterranean world did not transfer very well. In light, well-drained Mediterranean soils, cultivators used small wooden plows that basically broke the surface of the soil, created a furrow, and disrupted weeds. This type of plow made little headway in the heavy, moist soils of the north.

Heavy Plows

After the eighth century a more serviceable plow became available: a heavy tool equipped with iron tips that dug into the earth and with a mould-board that turned the soil so as to aerate it thoroughly and break up the root networks of weeds. Though known as early as the second century, this heavy northern plow did not see widespread use until the Carolingian era. The heavy plow was a more expensive piece of equipment than the light Mediterranean plow, and it required cultivators to harness much more energy to pull it through moist northern soils. Once hitched to oxen or draft horses, however, the heavy plow contributed to significantly increased agricultural production.

In this twelfth-century manuscript illustration, a peasant guides a heavy, wheeled plow while his wife prods the oxen that pull the plow.

As the heavy plow spread throughout western Europe, cultivators took several additional steps that increased agricultural production. Under the direction of their lords, serfs cleared new lands for cultivation. They constructed watermills, which enabled them to take advantage of a ready and renewable source of inanimate energy, thus freeing human and animal energy for other work. They developed a special horse collar, which enabled them to rely less on slow-moving oxen and more on much speedier horses to draw their heavy plows. As a result, they were able to increase the amount of land under cultivation. They also experimented with new methods of rotating crops that enabled them to cultivate land more intensively than before.

A Rural Society

The agricultural surplus of early medieval Europe was sufficient to sustain political elites like lords and their retainers, but not substantial enough to support cities with large populations of artisans, crafts workers, merchants, and professionals. Whereas cities had thrived and trade had linked all regions of the Roman empire, early medieval Europe was almost entirely a rural society that engaged in little commerce. Manors and local communities produced most of the manufactured goods that they needed, including textiles and heavy tools, and they provided both the materials and the labor for construction and other large-scale projects. Towns were few and sparsely populated, and they served as economic hubs for the areas immediately surrounding them rather than as vibrant centers integrating the economic activities of distant regions.

Mediterranean Trade

By no means did trade entirely disappear from western Europe. Local markets and fairs offered opportunities for small-scale exchange, while itinerant peddlers shopped their wares from one settlement to another. Maritime trade flourished in the Mediterranean despite Muslim conquests in the region. Christian merchants from Italy and Spain regularly traded across religious boundary lines with Muslims of Sicily, Spain, and north Africa, who linked Europe indirectly with the larger Islamic world of communication and exchange. By the end of the early medieval era, about 1000 C.E., food crops that in earlier centuries had made their way throughout much of the Islamic world were beginning to take root also in Mediterranean Europe. Hard durum

Sources from the Past

Life on an Early Medieval Manor

Some useful insights into the lives and experiences of common people come from a decree known as the "Capitulary de Villis" issued by the emperor Charlemagne in 807 C.E. as a guide for stewards of Carolingian estates. The decree envisions a community with sophisticated agricultural and craft skills. Probably few estates observed all provisions of Charlemagne's decree, but the capitulary nonetheless communicates clearly how lords hoped to control their manors and profit from their production.

Each steward shall make an annual statement of all our income: an account of our lands cultivated by the oxen which our ploughmen drive and of our lands which the tenants of farms ought to plough; an account of the pigs, of the rents, of the obligations and fines; of the game taken in our forests without our permission; . . . of the mills, of the forest, of the fields, of the bridges, and ships; of the free men and the hundreds who are under obligations to our treasury; of markets, vineyards, and those who owe wine to us; of the hay, firewood, torches, planks, and other kinds of lumber; of the waste lands; of the fruits of the trees, of the nut trees, larger and smaller; of the grafted trees of all kinds; of the gardens; of the turnips; of the fish ponds; of the hides, skins, and horns; of the honey, wax; of the fat, tallow and soap; of the mulberry wine, cooked wine, mead, vinegar, beer, wine new and old; of the new grain and the old; of the hens and eggs; of the geese; the number of fishermen, [metal] smiths, sword-makers, and shoemakers; . . . of the forges and mines, that is iron and other mines; of the lead mines; . . . of the colts and fillies; they shall make all these known to us, set forth separately and in order, at Christmas, in order that we may know what and how much of each thing we have. . . .

[Stewards] must provide the greatest care, that whatever is prepared or made with the hands, that is, lard, smoked meat, salt meat, partially salted meat, wine, vinegar, mulberry wine, cooked wine . . . mustard, cheese, butter, malt, beer, mead, honey, wax, flour, all should be prepared and made with the greatest cleanliness. . . .

[Stewards should ensure] that in each of our estates, the chambers [living quarters] shall be provided with counterpanes, cushions, pillows, bed clothes, coverings for the tables and benches; vessels of brass, lead, iron and wood; andirons, chains, pot-hooks, adzes, axes, augers, cutlasses and all other kinds of tools, so that it shall never be necessary to go elsewhere for them, or to borrow them. And the weapons, which are carried against the enemy, shall be well cared for, so as to keep them in good condition; and when they are brought back they shall be placed in the chamber.

For our women's work they are to give at the proper time, as has been ordered, the materials, that is the linen, wool, woad, vermillion, madder, wool-combs, teasels, soap, grease, vessels and the other objects which are necessary.

Of the food products other than meat, two-thirds shall be sent each year for our own use, that is of the vegetables, fish, cheese, honey, mustard, vinegar, millet, panic [a grain similar to millet], dried and green herbs, radishes, and in addition of the wax, soap and other small products; and they shall tell us how much is left by a statement, as we have said above; and they shall not neglect this as in the past; because from those two-thirds, we wish to know how much remains.

Each steward shall have in his district good workmen, namely, blacksmiths, goldsmiths, silversmiths, shoemakers, [wood] turners, carpenters, sword-makers, fishermen, foilers [fine metalworkers], soap-makers, men who know how to make beer, cider, berry, and all other kinds of beverages, bakers to make pastry for our table, net-makers who know how to make nets for hunting, fishing and fowling, and the others who are too numerous to be designated.

SOURCE: *Translations and Reprints from the Original Sources of European History*, vol. 2. Philadelphia: University of Pennsylvania Press, 1900. (Translation slightly modified.)

On the basis of the "Capitulary de Villis," how would you characterize the conditions of material life in the Carolingian countryside?

wheat, rice, spinach, artichokes, eggplant, lemons, limes, oranges, and melons all made their way to Sicily, southern Italy, and Spain because of European participation in the larger trading world of the eastern hemisphere, even if western European merchants were not nearly so prominent as their Byzantine, Arab, Persian, Indian, Malay, and Chinese counterparts.

Maritime trade flourished also in the North Sea and the Baltic Sea. Most active among the early medieval merchants in the northern seas were Norse seafarers, kinsmen of the Vikings who raided lands from eastern Europe to the Mediterranean. Norse traders followed the same routes as Viking raiders, and many individual mariners no doubt turned from commerce to plunder and back again as opportunities arose. Norse merchants called at ports from Russia to Ireland, carrying cargoes of fish and furs from Scandinavia, honey from Poland, wheat from England, wine from France, beer from the Low Countries, and swords from Germany. By traveling down the Russian rivers to the Black Sea, they were able to trade actively in both the Byzantine and Abbasid empires. Thus, like Mediterranean merchants, Norse mariners linked western Europe with the Islamic world. Indeed, the Carolingian empire depended heavily on this connection: Norse merchants took Scandinavian products to the Abbasid empire and brought back silver, which they traded at Carolingian ports for wine, jugs, glassware, and other products. This silver transported from the Abbasid empire by Norse merchants was a principal source of bullion used for minting coins in early medieval Europe and hence a crucially important element of the western European economy.

Norse Merchant-Mariners

By 900 the results of political stability and agricultural innovation were clearly evident in population figures as well as trade. In 200 C.E., before the Roman empire began to experience serious difficulties, the European population stood at about thirty-six million. It fell sharply over the next four centuries, to thirty-one million in 400 and twenty-six million in 600—a decline that reflected both the ravages of epidemic diseases and the unsettled conditions of the early middle ages. Then, gradually, the population recovered, edging up to twenty-nine million in 800 and thirty-two million in 900. By 1000 European population once again amounted to thirty-six million—the level it had reached some eight centuries earlier. By the end of the early middle ages, western Europe was poised to experience remarkable economic and demographic expansion that vastly increased European influence in the eastern hemisphere.

Population

THE FORMATION OF CHRISTIAN EUROPE

By the time the Roman empire collapsed, Christianity was the principal source of religious, moral, and cultural authority throughout the Mediterranean basin. In the northern lands of Gaul, Germany, the British isles, and Scandinavia, however, Christianity had attracted few converts. Germanic invaders of the Roman empire sometimes embraced Arian Christianity, but not until the conversion of Clovis and the Franks did Roman Christianity enjoy a powerful and energetic sponsor in lands beyond the Mediterranean rim. One of the most important developments of the early middle ages was the conversion of western Europe to Roman Christianity. The Franks, the popes, and the monasteries played important roles in bringing about this conversion. The adoption of Roman Christianity ensured that medieval Europe would inherit crucial cultural elements from classical Roman society, including the Latin language and the institutional Roman church.

The Politics of Conversion

Clovis and the Franks won the support of the church hierarchy as well as the Christian population of the former Roman empire when they converted to the Roman faith. Their alliance with the Roman church also provided them with access to educated and literate individuals who could provide important political services. Scribes, secretaries, and record keepers for the Frankish kingdom came largely from the ranks of churchmen—priests, monks, bishops, and abbots—since very few others received a formal education during the early middle ages.

The Franks and the Church

A deep commitment to Roman Christianity became a hallmark of Frankish policy. Clovis, his successors, and the Carolingians viewed themselves as protectors of the papacy. Charlemagne mounted a military campaign that destroyed the power of the Lombards, who had threatened the popes and the city of Rome since the sixth century, and brought most of central and northern Italy into the expanding Carolingian empire. In exchange for this military and political support, the Carolingians received recognition and backing from the popes, including the award of Charlemagne's imperial crown at the hands of Pope Leo III.

Charlemagne not only supported the church in Italy but also worked to spread Christianity in northern lands. He maintained a school at his court in Aachen where he assembled the most prominent scholars from all parts of his empire. They corrected texts, made careful copies of the Bible and classical Latin literature, and taught Christian doctrine to men preparing for careers as priests or church officials. Charlemagne ordered monasteries throughout his empire to establish elementary schools, and he even tried to persuade village priests to provide free instruction in reading and writing. These efforts had limited success, but they certainly increased literacy in the Latin language as well as popular understanding of basic Christian doctrine. Charlemagne's efforts also resulted in an explosion of writing: not since the fall of the Roman empire had western Europe produced so much writing.

The Spread of Christianity

Charlemagne sometimes promoted the spread of Christianity by military force. Between 772 and 804 he waged a bitter campaign against the Saxons, a pagan people inhabiting northern Germany. Alongside his claim to political hegemony, he insisted that the Saxons adopt Roman Christianity. The Saxons violently resisted both the political and the religious dimensions of Charlemagne's campaign. In the end, though, Charlemagne prevailed: the Saxons not only acknowledged Charlemagne as their political lord but also replaced their pagan traditions with Christianity.

Pagan ways did not immediately disappear from western Europe. Even within the Carolingian empire, pockets of paganism survived for several centuries after the arrival of Christianity, particularly in out-of-the-way areas that did not attract the immediate attention of conquerors or missionaries. Moreover, beyond the Carolingian empire were the Scandinavian lands, whose peoples resisted Christianity until the end of the millennium. By the year 1000, however, Christianity had won the allegiance of most people throughout western Europe and even in the Nordic lands. By sponsoring the Roman church and its missionaries, Charlemagne helped establish Christianity as the dominant religious and cultural tradition in western Europe.

The Papacy

Apart from the political support it received from the Franks, the Roman church benefited from strong papal leadership. When the western Roman empire collapsed, the papacy survived and claimed spiritual authority over all the lands formerly embraced by the empire. For a century after the dissolution of the western Roman empire, the popes cooperated closely with the Byzantine emperors, who seemed to be the nat-

Pope Leo III crowns Charlemagne emperor in a manuscript illustration. The coronation symbolized the firm alliance between the Franks and the western Christian church.

ural heirs to the emperors of Rome. Beginning in the late sixth century, however, the popes acted more independently and devoted their efforts to strengthening the western Christian church based at Rome and clearly distinguishing it from the eastern Christian church based at Constantinople. The two churches differed on many issues by the eleventh century, and in 1054 the pope and patriarch mutually excommunicated each other. After the eleventh century the two branches of Christianity formed distinct identities as the Roman Catholic and Eastern Orthodox churches.

Pope Gregory I

The individual most important for providing the Roman church with its sense of direction was Pope Gregory I (590–604 C.E.), also known as Gregory the Great. As pope, Gregory faced an array of difficult challenges. During the late sixth century the Lombards consolidated their hold on the Italian peninsula, menacing Rome and the Roman church in the process. Gregory ensured the survival of both the city and the church by mobilizing local resources and organizing the defense of Rome. He also faced difficulties within the church, since bishops frequently acted independently of the pope, as though they were supreme ecclesiastical authorities within their own dioceses. To regain the initiative, Gregory reasserted papal primacy—the claim that the bishop of Rome was the ultimate authority in the Christian church. Gregory also made contributions as a theologian: he strongly emphasized the sacrament of penance, which required individuals to confess their sins to their priests and then to atone for their sins by penitential acts prescribed by the priests—a practice that enhanced the influence of the Roman church in the lives of individuals.

The Conversion of England

Gregory strengthened the Roman church further by extending its appeal and winning new converts in western Europe. The most important of his many missionary campaigns was one directed at England, recently conquered by Angles, Saxons, and other Germanic peoples. He aimed his efforts at the kings who ruled the various regions of England, hoping that their conversion would induce their subjects to adopt Christianity. This tactic largely succeeded: by the early seventh century Christianity had established a stable foothold in England, and by 800 England was securely within the fold of the Roman church.

Gregory's successors continued his policy of expanding the Roman church through missionary activity. France and Germany offered plentiful opportunities to win converts, particularly as the Frankish kingdom and the Carolingians brought those lands under their control. Some of the popes' most effective missionaries were monks. Pope Gregory himself was a monk, and he relied heavily on the energies of his fellow monks in seeking converts in England and elsewhere.

Monasticism

Christian monasticism had its origin in Egypt. During the second and third centuries, many devout Christians sought to lead ascetic and holy lives in the deserts of Egypt. Some lived alone as hermits, and others formed communes where they devoted themselves to the pursuit of holiness rather than worldly success. When Christianity became legal during the fourth century, the monastic lifestyle became an increasingly popular alternative throughout the Roman empire. Monastic communities cropped up in Italy, Spain, Gaul, and the British isles as well as in the eastern Mediterranean region.

Monastic Rules

During the early days of monasticism, each community developed its own rules, procedures, and priorities. Some communities demanded that their inhabitants follow extremely austere lifestyles that sapped the energy of the monks. Other communities did not establish any clear expectations of their recruits, with the result that monks frittered away their time or wandered aimlessly from one monastic house to another. These haphazard conditions prevented monasteries from mounting effective Christian missions.

St. Benedict

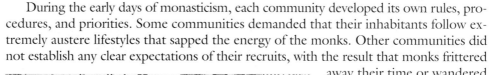

St. Benedict of Nursia (480–547 C.E.) strengthened the early monastic movement by providing it with discipline and a sense of purpose. In 529 St. Benedict prepared a set of regulations known as Benedict's *Rule* for the monastic community that he had founded at Monte Cassino, near Rome. The *Rule* did not permit extreme asceticism, but it required monks to take vows to lead commu-

A fourteenth-century manuscript illustration shows St. Benedict presenting his rule to a group of nuns.

nal, celibate lives under the absolute direction of the abbot who supervised the monastery: poverty, chastity, and obedience became the prime virtues for Benedictine monks. The *Rule* also called for monks to spend their time in prayer, meditation, and work. At certain hours monks came together for religious services and prayer, and they divided the remainder of the day into periods for study, reflection, and manual labor.

St. Scholastica

Monasteries throughout Europe began to adopt Benedict's *Rule* as the standard for their own houses. Through the influence of St. Benedict's sister, the nun St. Scholastica (482–543), an adaptation of the *Rule* soon provided guidance for the religious life of women living in convents. Within a century most European monasteries and convents observed the Benedictine *Rule*. During the following centuries the Roman church generated many alternatives to Benedictine monasticism. Yet even today most Roman Catholic monasteries observe rules that reflect the influence of the Benedictine tradition.

Strengthened by the discipline that the Benedictine *Rule* introduced, monasteries became a dominant feature in the social and cultural life of western Europe throughout the middle ages. Monasteries helped to provide order in the countryside, for example, and to expand agricultural production. Monasteries accumulated large landholdings—as well as authority over serfs working their lands—from the bequests of wealthy individuals seeking to contribute to the church's work and thereby to merit salvation. Particularly in France and Germany, abbots of monasteries dispatched teams of monks and serfs to clear forests, drain swamps, and prepare lands for cultivation. Indeed, monasteries organized much of the labor that brought about the expansion of agricultural production in early medieval Europe.

Monasticism and Society

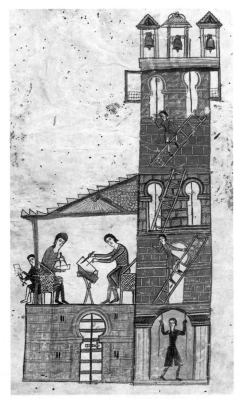

Like Buddhist monasteries in Asian lands and charitable religious foundations in Muslim lands, European monasteries provided a variety of social services. They served as inns for travelers and places of refuge for individuals suffering from natural or other calamities. They served as orphanages and provided medical treatment for the ill and injured. They often set up schools and offered at least some rudimentary educational services for local regions, and large monasteries provided more advanced instruction for those preparing for the priesthood or high ecclesiastical positions. Some monasteries maintained libraries and scriptoria, where monks copied works of classical literature and philosophy as well as the scriptures and other Christian writings. Almost all works of Latin literature that have come down to the present survive because of copies made by medieval monks. Finally, monasteries served as a source of literate, educated, and talented individuals whose secretarial and administrative services were crucial for the organization of effective government in early medieval Europe.

Monasteries were the principal centers of literacy in western Europe during the early middle ages. In this manuscript illustration, one monk copies a manuscript, another makes geometric calculations, a third cuts parchment, while two work on the building, and one more rings the bells that call monks and members of the surrounding community to religious services.

Because of the various roles they played in the larger society, monasteries were particularly effective agents in the spread of Christianity. While they organized life in the countryside and provided social services, monks also zealously preached Christianity and tended to the spiritual needs of rural populations. For many people a neighboring monastery was the only source of instruction in Christian doctrine, and a local monastic church offered the only practical opportunity for them to take part in religious services. Monks patiently and persistently served the needs of rural populations, and over the decades and centuries they helped to instill Christian values in countless generations of European peasants.

Like societies in China, India, southwest Asia, and the eastern Mediterranean region, western European society experienced massive change during the postclassical era. In some ways western Europe had the most difficult experience of all the postclassical societies. In China, southwest Asia, and the eastern Mediterranean, societies were able to preserve or reestablish centralized imperial rule that maintained order and stability while also facilitating trade and encouraging economic development. India did not generate an imperial form of government, but because of the subcontinent's geographic location and productive capacity, India participated actively in the larger economic and commercial life of the eastern hemisphere. In contrast, rulers of early medieval Europe did not reinstate an imperial form of government—except for the short-lived Carolingian empire—and western Europeans did not participate actively in the larger trading world of the eastern hemisphere. The standards of material life in early medieval Europe—as measured by agricultural and industrial production, volume of trade, and the extent of urban settlement—stood well below those of other postclassical societies.

Yet, just as postclassical developments deeply influenced the evolution of societies in other lands, the early medieval era was a crucial period for the development of western Europe. In the absence of a durable centralized empire, western Europeans found ways to maintain relative order and stability by decentralizing political responsibilities and relying on local authorities for political organization. Over the longer term the decentralized political order of medieval Europe discouraged the revival of empire and encouraged the emergence of regional states that organized their communities into powerful societies. During the early middle ages, western Europeans experimented with agricultural techniques that enabled them to expand production dramatically, conduct increased trade, and rebuild urban centers. Finally, western Christianity preserved elements of classical Roman society and established a foundation for cultural unity in western Europe, just as Buddhism, Hinduism, Islam, and eastern Christianity served as sources of cultural authority in other societies.

CHRONOLOGY

476	Fall of the western Roman empire
480–547	Life of St. Benedict of Nursia
481–511	Reign of Clovis
482–543	Life of St. Scholastica
590–604	Reign of Pope Gregory I
751–843	Carolingian kingdom
768–814	Reign of Charlemagne
800	Coronation of Charlemagne as emperor
814–840	Reign of Louis the Pious
843	Dissolution of the Carolingian empire
871–899	Reign of King Alfred
936–973	Reign of King Otto I of Saxony
955	Battle of Lechfeld
962	Coronation of Otto I

FOR FURTHER READING

Geoffrey Barraclough. *The Crucible of Europe.* Berkeley, 1976. A brilliant, brief analysis of early medieval Europe concentrating on the Carolingian era and its aftermath.

Robert-Henri Bautier. *The Economic Development of Medieval Europe.* New York, 1971. An excellent and well-illustrated survey, which examines the economic and social history of western Europe in the context of the larger Mediterranean basin.

Marc Bloch. *Feudal Society.* 2 vols. Trans. by L. A. Manyon. Chicago, 1961. A classic interpretation concentrating on social and economic history that has decisively influenced the way historians think about medieval Europe.

Peter Brown. *The Rise of Western Christendom: Triumph and Diversity, A.D. 200–1000.* 2nd ed. Oxford, 2003. A landmark analysis of early Christian history that incorporates the findings of recent scholarship.

Einhard and Notker the Stammerer. *Two Lives of Charlemagne.* Ed. and trans. by Lewis Thorpe. New York, 1969. Excellent translations of two early biographies of Charlemagne.

F. L. Ganshof. *Frankish Institutions under Charlemagne.* Trans. by B. and M. Lyon. New York, 1970. Concise synthesis of research on Charlemagne's government.

Patrick J. Geary. *Before France and Germany: The Creation and Transformation of the Merovingian World.* 2nd ed. New York, 1997. Draws usefully on recent research in reconstructing early medieval Europe.

———, ed. *Readings in Medieval History.* Lewiston, N.Y., 1989. Offers substantial English translations of primary sources.

Louis Halphen. *Charlemagne and the Carolingian Empire.* Trans. by G. de Nie. Amsterdam, 1977. Thorough discussion of Charlemagne's imperial creation and its larger importance in European history.

David Herlihy. *Opera Muliebra: Women and Work in Medieval Europe.* New York, 1990. Examines women's roles both in their own households and in the larger society of medieval Europe.

Richard Hodges and David Whitehouse. *Mohammed, Charlemagne, and the Origins of Europe: Archaeology and the Pirenne Thesis.* Ithaca, 1983. Draws on archaeological discoveries in placing the early medieval European economy in hemispheric context.

Edward James. *The Franks.* Oxford, 1988. A concise account.

Gwyn Jones. *A History of the Vikings.* Rev. ed. Oxford, 1984. The best general work on Viking society and Viking expansion.

Ferdinand Lot. *The End of the Ancient World and the Beginnings of the Middle Ages.* Trans. by P. and M. Leon. New York, 1961. A masterful survey of the Germanic invasions and their results for western Europe.

Michael McCormick. *Origins of the European Economy: Communications and Commerce,* A.D. *300–900.* Cambridge, Mass., 2001. A thorough and comprehensive analysis that emphasizes the participation of early medieval Europe in a larger Mediterranean economy.

Rosamond McKitterick. *The Frankish Kingdoms under the Carolingians, 751–987.* New York, 1983. Comprehensive survey of the Carolingian dynasty with special attention to political, cultural, and religious developments.

Susan Reynolds. *Fiefs and Vassals: The Medieval Evidence Reinterpreted.* Oxford, 1994. A powerful scholarly critique of the concept of feudalism.

———. *Kingdoms and Communities in Western Europe, 900–1300.* Oxford, 1984. An imaginative study focusing on the political and social values that undergirded western European society.

J. M. Wallace-Hadrill. *The Barbarian West: The Early Middle Ages,* A.D. *400–1000.* New York, 1962. A powerful and insightful synthesis by a leading scholar.

See our **Online Learning Center at www.mhhe.com/bentley3** for additional readings, practice maps, quizzes, and internet activities.

Unfamiliar words? Check out the **Primary Source Investigator CD-ROM** for an interactive glossary, interactive maps, more images, and primary sources.

GLOSSARY AND PRONUNCIATION KEY

AH *a* sound, as in *car, father*
IH short *i* sound, as in *fit, his, mirror*
OO long *o* sound, as in *ooze, tool, crew*
UH short *u* sound, as in *up, cut, color*
A short *a* sound, as in *asp, fat, parrot*
EE long *e* sound, as in *even, meet, money*
OH long *o* sound, as in *open, go, tone*
EH short *e* sound, as in *ten, elf, berry*
AY long *a* sound, as in *ape, date, play*
EYE long *i* sound, as in *ice, high, bite*
OW dipthong *o* sound, as in *cow, how, bow*
AW dipthong *a* sound, as in *awful, paw, law*

Note on emphasis: Syllables in capital letters receive the accent. If there is no syllable in capitals, then all syllables get equal accent.

Abbasid (ah-BAH-sihd) Cosmopolitan Arabic dynasty (750–1258) that replaced the Umayyads; founded by Abu al-Abbas and reached its peak under Harun al-Rashid.

Abolitionism Antislavery movement.

Absolutism Political philosophy that stressed the divine right theory of kingship: the French king Louis XIV was the classic example.

Abu Bakr (ah-BOO BAHK-uhr) First caliph after the death of Muhammad.

Achaemenid empire (ah-KEE-muh-nid) First great Persian empire (558–330 B.C.E.), which began under Cyrus and reached its peak under Darius.

Aeshylus (ES-kuh-luhs) Greek tragedian, author of the *Oresteia.*

Age grades Bantu institution in which individuals of roughly the same age carried out communal tasks appropriate for that age.

Ahimsa (uh-HIM-suh) Jain term for the principle of nonviolence to other living things or their souls.

Ahmosis (AH-moh-sis) Egyptian pharaoh (c. 1500 B.C.E.), founder of the New Kingdom.

Ahura Mazda (uh-HOORE-uh MAHZ-duh) Main god of Zoroastrianism who

represented truth and goodness and was perceived to be in an eternal struggle with the malign spirit Angra Mainyu.

Al-Andalus (al-ANN-duh-luhs) Islamic Spain.

Allah (AH-lah) God of the monotheistic religion of Islam.

Ali'i nui Hawaiian class of high chiefs.

Amon-Re (AH-muhn RAY) Egyptian god, combination of the sun god Re and the air god Amon.

Angkor (AHN-kohr) Southeast Asian Khmer kingdom (889–1432) that was centered around the temple cities of Angkor Thom and Angkor Wat.

Anti-Semitism Term coined in late nineteenth century that was associated with a prejudice against Jews and the political, social, and economic actions taken against them.

Antonianism African syncretic religion, founded by Dona Beatriz, that taught that Jesus Christ was a black African man and that heaven was for Africans.

Apartheid (ah-PAHR-teyed) South African system of "separateness" that was implemented in 1948 and that maintained the black majority in a position of political, social, and economic subordination.

Appeasement British and French policy in the 1930s that tried to maintain peace in Europe in the face of German aggression by making concessions.

Arianism Early Christian heresy that centered around teaching of Arius (250–336 C.E.) and contained the belief that Jesus was a mortal human being and not coeternal with God; Arianism was the focus of Council of Nicaea.

Artha Hindu concept for the pursuit of economic well-being and honest prosperity.

Arthashastra (AR-thah-sha-strah) Ancient Indian political treatise from the time of Chandragupta Maurya; its authorship was traditionally ascribed to Kautalya, and it stressed that war was inevitable.

Aryans (AIR-ee-anns) Indo-European tribes who settled in India after 1500 B.C.E.; their union with indigenous Dravidians formed the basis of Hinduism.

Association of Southeast Asian Nations (ASEAN.) Regional organization established in 1967 by Thailand, Malaysia, Singapore, Indonesia, and the Philippines; the organization was designed to promote economic progress and political stability; it later became a free-trade zone.

Assyrians (uh-SEAR-ee-uhns) Southwest Asian people who built an empire that reached its height during the eighth and seventh centuries B.C.E.; it was known for a powerful army and a well-structured state.

Astrolabe Navigational instrument for determining latitude.

Aten Monotheistic god of Egyptian pharaoh Akhenaten (r. 1353–1335 B.C.E.) and a very early example of monotheism.

Audiencias Spanish courts in Latin America.

Australopithecus (ah-strah-loh-PITH-uh-kuhs) "Southern ape," oldest known ancestor of humans; it lived from around four million down to around one million years ago, and it could walk on hind legs, freeing up hands for use of simple tools.

Austronesians People who as early as 2000 B.C.E. began to explore and settle islands of the Pacific Ocean basin.

Avesta Book that contains the holy writings of Zoroastrianism.

Aztec empire Central American empire constructed by the Mexica and expanded greatly during the fifteenth century during the reigns of Itzcoatl and Motecuzoma I.

Axum African kingdom centered in Ethiopia that became an early and lasting center of Coptic Christianity.

Balfour Declaration British declaration from 1917 that supported the creation of a Jewish homeland in Palestine.

Bantu (BAN-too) African peoples who originally lived in the area of present-day Nigeria; around 2000 B.C.E. they began a centuries-long migration that took them to most of sub-Saharan Africa; the Bantu were very influential, especially linguistically.

Bedouins (BEHD-oh-ihnz) Nomadic Arabic tribespeople.

Benefice Grant from a lord to a vassal, usually consisting of land, which supported the vassal and signified the relationship between the two.

Berlin Conference Meeting organized by German chancellor Otto von Bismarck in 1884–1885 that provided the justification for European colonization of Africa.

Bhagavad Gita (BUH-guh-vahd GEE-tuh) "Song of the Lord," an Indian short poetic work drawn from the lengthy *Mahabharata* that was finished around 400 C.E. and that expressed basic Hindu concepts such as karma and dharma.

Bhakti (BAHK-tee) Indian movement that attempted to transcend the differences between Hinduism and Islam.

Black Hand Pre–World War I secret Serbian society; one of its members, Gavrilo Princip, assassinated Austrian archduke Francis Ferdinand and provided the spark for the outbreak of the Great War.

Blitzkrieg German style of rapid attack through the use of armor and air power that was used in Poland, Norway, Denmark, Belgium, the Netherlands, and France in 1939–1940.

Boddhisatvas (BOH-dih-SAT-vuhs) Buddhist concept regarding individuals who had reached enlightenment but who stayed in this world to help people.

Bolshevik (BOHL-shih-vehk) Russian communist party headed by Lenin.

Bourgeoisie Middle class in modern industrial society.

Boyars (BOY-ahrs) Russian nobles.

Brahmins (BRAH-minz) Hindu caste of priests.

Brezhnev Doctrine Policy developed by Leonid Brezhnev (1906–1982) that claimed for the Soviet Union the right to invade any socialist country faced with internal or external enemies; the doctrine was best expressed in Soviet invasion of Czechoslovakia.

Buddha (BOO-duh) The "enlightened one," the term applied to Siddhartha Gautama after his discoveries that would form the foundation of Buddhism.

Buddhism (BOO-diz'm) Religion, based on Four Noble Truths, associated with Siddhartha Gautama (563–483 B.C.E.), or the Buddha; its adherents desired to eliminate all distracting passion and reach nirvana.

Bunraku (boon-RAH-koo) Japanese puppet theater.

Bushido (BOH-shee-DOH) The "way of the warrior," the code of conduct of the Japanese samurai that was based on loyalty and honor.

Byzantine Empire (BIHZ-ann-teen) Long-lasting empire centered at Constantinople; it grew out of the end of the Roman empire and carried legacy of Roman greatness and was the only classical society to survive into the early modern age; it reached its early peak during the reign of Justinian (483–565).

Caesaropapism Concept relating to the mixing of political and religious authority, as with the Roman emperors, that was central to the church versus state controversy in medieval Europe.

Cahokia (kuh-HOH-kee-uh) Large structure in modern Illinois that was constructed by the mound-building peoples; it was the third largest structure in the Americas before the arrival of the Europeans.

Caliph (KAL-ihf) "deputy," Islamic leader after the death of Muhammad.

Capetian (cah-PEE-shuhn) Early French dynasty that started with Hugh Capet.

Capitalism An economic system with origins in early modern Europe in which private parties make their goods and services available on a free market.

Capitulation Highly unfavorable trading agreements that the Ottoman Turks signed with the Europeans in the nineteenth century that symbolized the decline of the Ottomans.

Carolingians Germanic dynasty that was named after its most famous member, Charlemagne.

Carthage Northern African kingdom, main rival to early Roman expansion, that was defeated by Rome in the Punic Wars.

Çatal Hüyük Important Neolithic settlement in Anatolia (7250–6150 B.C.E.).

Cathars Medieval heretics, also known as the Albigensians, who considered the material world evil; their followers renounced wealth and marriage and promoted an ascetic existence.

Catholic Reformation Sixteenth-century Catholic attempt to cure internal ills and confront Protestantism; it was inspired by the reforms of the Council of Trent and the actions of the Jesuits.

Caudillos (KAW-dee-ohs) Latin American term for nineteenth-century local military leaders.

Central Powers World War I term for the alliance of Germany, Austria-Hungary, and the Ottoman empire.

Chaghatai One of Chinggis Khan's sons, whose descendants ruled central Asia through the Chaghatai khanate.

Chan Buddhism (CHAHN BOO-diz'm) Most popular branch of Buddhism in China, with an emphasis on intuition and sudden flashes of insight instead of textual study.

Chanchan (chahn-chahn) Capital of the pre-Incan, South American Chimu society that supported a large population of fifty thousand.

Chavín cult Mysterious but very popular South American religion (1000–300 B.C.E.).

Chimu Pre-Incan South American society that fell to Incas in the fifteenth century.

Chinampas Agricultural gardens used by Mexica (Aztecs) in which fertile muck from lake bottoms was dredged and built up into small plots.

Chivalry European medieval code of conduct for knights based on loyalty and honor.

Chola Southern Indian Hindu kingdom (850–1267), a tightly centralized state that dominated sea trade.

Chucuito Pre-Incan South American society that rose in the twelfth century and fell to the Incas in the fifteenth century.

City-state Urban areas that controlled surrounding agricultural regions and that were often loosely connected in a broader political structure with other city-states.

Cohong Specially licensed Chinese firms that were under strict government regulation.

Collectivization Process beginning in the late 1920s by which Stalin forced the Russian peasants off their own land and onto huge collective farms run by the state; millions died in the process.

COMECON The Council for Mutual Economic Assistance, which offered increased trade within the Soviet Union and eastern Europe; it was the Soviet alternative to the United States's Marshall Plan.

Communalism A term, usually associated with India, that placed an emphasis on religious rather than national identity.

Communism Philosophy and movement that began in middle of the nineteenth century with the work of Karl Marx; it has the same general goals as socialism, but it includes the belief that violent revolution is necessary to destroy the bourgeois world and institute a new world run by and for the proletariat.

Confucianism (kuhn-FYOO-shuhn-iz'm) Philosophy, based on the teachings of the Chinese philosopher Kong Fuzi (551–479 B.C.E.), or Confucius, that emphasizes order, the role of the gentleman, obligation to society, and reciprocity.

Congress of Vienna Meeting in 1815 of the victorious powers (England, Russia, Prussia, and Austria) in order to determine the settlement of Europe after the defeat of Napoleon; the congress established a system of international diplomacy for the nineteenth century and beyond.

Conquistadores (kohn-KEE-stah-dohr-ayz) Spanish adventurers like Cortés and Pizarro who conquered Central and South America in the sixteenth century.

Constitutionalism Movement in England in the seventeenth century that placed power in Parliament's hands as part of a constitutional monarchy and that increasingly limited the power of the monarch; the movement was highlighted by the English Civil War and the Glorious Revolution.

Containment Concept associated with the United States and specifically with the Truman Doctrine during the cold war that revolved around the notion that the United States would contain the spread of communism.

Corporation A concept that reached mature form in 1860s in England and France; it entailed private business owned by thousands of individual and institutional investors who financed the business through the purchase of stocks.

Corpus iuris civilis (KOR-puhs yoor-uhs sih-VEE-lihs) *Body of the Civil Law,* the Byzantine emperor Justinian's attempt to codify all Roman law.

Criollos (kree-OH-lohs) Creoles, people born in the Americas of Spanish or Portuguese ancestry.

Cro-Magnon (CROW MAG-nuhn) *Homo sapiens sapiens,* who appeared forty thousand years ago during the Paleolithic age and were the first human beings of the modern type.

Cross staff Device that sailors used to determine latitude by measuring the angle of the sun or pole star above the horizon.

Cuneiform Written language of the Sumerians, probably the first written script in the world.

Daimyo (DEYEM-yoh) Powerful territorial lords in early modern Japan.

Dao Key element in Chinese philosophy that means the "way of nature" or the "way of the cosmos."

Daodejing (DOW-DAY-JIHNG) Book that is the fundamental work of Daoism.

Daoism (DOW-i'zm) Chinese philosophy with origins in the Zhou dynasty; it is associated with legendary philosopher Laozi, and it called for a policy of non-competition.

Dar al-Islam The "house of Islam," a term for the Islamic world.

Declaration of Independence Written by Thomas Jefferson in 1776; the document expressed the ideas of John Locke and the Enlightenment, represented the idealism of the American rebels, and influenced other revolutions.

Declaration of the Rights of Man and the Citizen Document from the French Revolution (1789) that was influenced by the American Declaration of Independence and in turn influenced other revolutionary movements.

Decolonization Process by which former colonies achieved their independence, as with the newly emerging African nations in the 1950s and 1960s.

Deism (DEE-iz'm) An Enlightenment view that accepted the existence of a god but denied the supernatural aspects of Christianity; in deism, the universe was an orderly realm maintained by rational and natural laws.

Descamisados "Shirtless ones," Argentine poor who supported Juan and Eva Peron.

Détente A reduction in cold war tension between the United States and the Soviet Union from 1969 to 1973.

Devshirme Ottoman requirement that the Christians in the Balkans provide young boys to be slaves of the sultan.

Dharma (DAHR-muh) Hindu concept of obedience to religious and moral laws and order.

Dhimmi (dihm-mee) Islamic concept of a protected people that was symbolic of Islamic toleration during the Mughal and Ottoman empires.

Dhow Indian, Persian, and Arab ships, one hundred to four hundred tons, that sailed and traded throughout the Indian Ocean basin.

Diaspora People who have settled far from their original homeland but who still share some measure of ethnic identity.

Dionysus Greek god of wine, also known as Bacchus; Greek plays were performed in his honor.

Dravidians Peoples who produced the brilliant Harappan society in India, 3000–1500 B.C.E.

Dreadnoughts A class of British battleships whose heavy armaments made all other battleships obsolete overnight.

Duma Russian parliament, established after the Revolution of 1905.

Dutch learning European knowledge that reached Tokugawa Japan.

East India Company British joint-stock company that grew to be a state within a state in India; it possessed its own armed forces.

Eight-legged essay Eight-part essays that an aspiring Chinese civil servant had to compose, mainly based on a knowledge of Confucius and the Zhou classics.

Encomienda (ehn-KOH-mee-ehn-dah) System that gave the Spanish settlers *(encomenderos)* the right to compel the indigenous peoples of the Americas to work in the mines or fields.

Engenho Brazilian sugar mill; the term also came to symbolize the entire complex world relating to the production of sugar.

Enlightenment Eighteenth-century philosophical movement that began in France; its emphasis was on the preeminence of reason rather than faith or tradition; it spread concepts from the Scientific Revolution.

Epicureans (ehp-ih-kyoo-REE-uhns) Hellenistic philosophers who taught that pleasure—as in quiet satisfaction—was the greatest good.

Equal-field system Chinese system during the Han dynasty in which the goal was to ensure an equitable distribution of land.

Essenes Jewish sect that looked for the arrival of a savior; they were similar in some of their core beliefs to the early Christians.

Etruscans (ih-TRUHS-kuhns) Northern Italian society that initially dominated the Romans; the Etruscans helped convey Greek concepts to the expanding Romans.

Eunuchs (YOO-nihks) Castrated males, originally in charge of the harem, who grew to play major roles in government; eunuchs were common in China and other societies.

European Community (EC) Organization of European states established in 1957; it was originally called the European Economic Community and was renamed the EC in 1967; it promoted economic growth and integration as the basis for a politically united Europe.

European Union Established by the Maastricht Treaty in 1993, a supranational organization for even greater European economic and political integration.

Fascism Political ideology and mass movement that was prominent in many parts of Europe between 1919 and 1945; it sought to regenerate the social, political, and cultural life of societies, especially in contrast to liberal democracy and socialism; fascism began with Mussolini in Italy, and it reached its peak with Hitler in Germany.

Five Pillars The foundation of Islam; (1) profession of faith, (2) prayer, (3) fasting during Ramadan, (4) alms, and (5) pilgrimage, or hajj.

Five-year plans First implemented by Stalin in the Soviet Union in 1928; five-year plans were a staple of communist regimes in which every aspect of production was determined in advance for a five-year period; five-year plans were opposite of the free market concept.

Four Noble Truths The foundation of Buddhist thought: (1) life is pain, (2) pain is caused by desire, (3) elimination of desire will bring an end to pain, (4) living a life based on the Noble Eightfold Path will eliminate desire.

Front de Libération Nationale (FLN) The Algerian organization that fought a bloody guerilla war for freedom against France.

Fulani (foo-LAH-nee) Sub-Saharan African people who, beginning in the seventeenth century, began a series of wars designed to impose their own strict interpretation of Islam.

Gathas (GATH-uhs) Zoroastrian works believed to be compositions by Zarathustra.

Gauchos (GOW-chohz) Argentine cowboys, highly romanticized figures.

General Agreement on Tariffs and Trade (GATT) Free trade agreement first signed in 1947; by 1994 it had grown to 123 members and formed the World Trade Organization (WTO).

Ghana (GAH-nuh) Kingdom in west Africa during the fifth through the thirteenth centuries whose rulers eventually converted to Islam; its power and wealth was based on dominating trans-Saharan trade.

Ghaznavids Turkish tribe under Mahmud of Ghazni who moved into northern India in the eleventh century and began a period of greater Islamic influence in India.

Ghazi (GAH-zee) Islamic religious warrior.

Gilgamesh Legendary king of the Mesopotamian city-state of Uruk (ca. 3000 B.C.E.), subject of the *Epic of Gilgamesh*, world's oldest complete epic literary masterpiece.

Glasnost (GLAHS-nohst) Russian term meaning "openness" introduced by Mikhail Gorbachev in 1985 to describe the process of opening Soviet society to dissidents and public criticism.

Globalization The breaking down of traditional boundaries in the face of increasingly global financial and cultural trends.

Global warming The emission of greenhouse gases, which prevents solar heat from escaping the earth's atmosphere and leads to the gradual heating of the earth's environment.

Golden Horde Mongol tribe that controlled Russia from the thirteenth to the fifteenth centuries.

Greater East Asia Co-Prosperity Sphere Japanese plan for consolidating east and southeast Asia under their control during World War II.

Great Game Nineteenth-century competition between Great Britain and Russia for the control of central Asia.

Great Zimbabwe Large sub-Saharan African kingdom in the fifteenth century.

Greenpeace An environmental organization founded in 1970 and dedicated to the preservation of earth's natural resources.

Guomindang (GWOH-mihn-dahng) Chinese nationalist party founded by Sun Yatsen (1866–1925) and later led by Jiang Jieshi; it has been centered in Taiwan since the end of the Chinese civil war.

Gupta (GOOP-tah) Indian dynasty (320–550 C.E.) that briefly reunited India after the collapse of the earlier Mauryan dynasty.

Hacienda (HAH-see-ehn-dah) Large Latin American estates.

Hagia Sophia (HAH-yah SOH-fee-uh) Greek orthodox temple constructed by the Byzantine emperor Justinian and later converted into a mosque.

Hajj (HAHJ) Pilgrimage to Mecca.

Hammurabi's Code (hahm-uh-RAH-beez) Sophisticated law code associated with the Babylonian king Hammurabi (r. 1792–1750 B.C.E.).

Harappan (hah-RAP-puhn) Early brilliant Indian society centered around Harappa and Mohenjo-Daro.

Harijans "Children of God," Gandhi's term for the Untouchables.

Hebrews Semitic-speaking nomadic tribe influential for monotheistic belief in Yahweh.

Heian (HAY-ahn) Japanese period (794–1185), a brilliant cultural era notable for the world's first novel, Murasaki Shikibu's *The Tale of Genji*.

Hellenic Era Phase in Greek history (ca. 800–328 B.C.E.), which was highlighted by the Golden Age of Athens in the fifth century B.C.E.

Hellenistic Era Phase in Greek history (328–146 B.C.E.), from the conquest of Greece by Philip of Macedon until Greece's fall to the Romans; this era was a more cosmopolitan age facilitated by the conquests of Alexander the Great.

Hieroglyphics (heye-ruh-GLIPH-iks) Ancient Egyptian written language.

Hijra Muhammad's migration from Mecca to Medina in 622, which is the beginning point of the Islamic calendar and is considered to mark the beginning of the Islamic faith.

Hinayana (HEE-nah-yah-nuh) Branch of Buddhism known as the "lesser vehicle," also known as Theravada Buddhism; its beliefs include strict, individual path to enlightenment, and it is popular in south and southeast Asia.

Hinduism Main religion of India, a combination of Dravidian and Aryan concepts; Hinduism's goal is to reach spiritual purity and union with the great world spirit; its important concepts include dharma, karma, and samsara.

Holocaust German attempt in World War II to exterminate the Jews of Europe.

Home front Term made popular in World War I and World War II for the civilian "front" that was symbolic of the greater demands of total war.

Hominid (HAWM-ih-nihd) A creature belonging to the family Hominidae, which includes human and humanlike species.

Homo erectus (HOH-MOH ee-REHK-ruhs) "Upright-walking human," which existed from two million to two hundred thousand years ago; *Homo erectus* used cleavers and hand axes and learned how to control fire.

Homo sapiens (HOH-MOH SAY-pee-uhns) "Consciously thinking human," which first appeared around two hundred fifty thousand years ago and used sophisticated tools.

Homo sapiens sapiens (HOH-MOH SAY-pee-uhns SAY-pee-uhns) First human being of the modern type, which appeared roughly one hundred thousand years ago; Cro-Magnon falls into this category.

Hundred Days of Reform Chinese reforms of 1898 led by Kang Youwei and Liang Qichao in their desire to turn China into a modern industrial power.

Huitzilopochtli (wee-tsee-loh-pockt-lee) Sun god and patron deity of the Aztecs.

Hyksos (HICK-sohs) Invaders who seized the Nile delta and helped bring an end to the Egyptian Middle Kingdom.

Iconoclasts (eye-KAHN-oh-klasts) Supporters of the movement, begun by the Byzantine Emperor Leo III (r. 717–741), to destroy religious icons because their veneration was considered sinful.

Ilkhanate (EEL-kahn-ate) Mongol state that ruled Persia after abolition of the Abbasid empire in the thirteenth century.

Imperialism Term associated with the expansion of European powers and their conquest and colonization of African and Asian societies, mainly from the sixteenth through the nineteenth centuries.

Inca empire Powerful South American empire that would reach its peak in the fifteenth century during the reigns of Pachacuti Inca and Topa Inca.

Indentured labor Labor source for plantations; wealthy planters would pay the European poor to sell a portion of their working lives, usually seven years, in exchange for passage.

Indo-Europeans Series of tribes from southern Russia who, over a period of millennia, embarked on a series of migrations from India through western Europe; their greatest legacy was the broad distribution of Indo-European languages throughout Eurasia.

Indra Early Indian god associated with the Aryans; Indra was the king of the gods and was associated with warfare and thunderbolts.

Investiture (ihn-VEHST-tih-tyoor) One aspect of the medieval European church-versus-state controversy, the granting of church offices by a lay leader.

Iroquois (EAR-uh-kwoi) Eastern American Indian confederation made up of the Mohawk, Oneida, Onondaga, Cayuga, and Seneca tribes.

Islam Monotheistic religion announced by the prophet Muhammad (570–632); influenced by Judaism and Christianity, Muhammad was considered the final prophet because the earlier religions had not seen the entire picture; the Quran is the holy book of Islam.

Jainism (JEYEN-iz'm) Indian religion associated with the teacher Vardhamana Mahavira (ca. 540–468 B.C.E.) in which every physical object possessed a soul; Jains believe in complete nonviolence to all living beings.

Jati Indian word for a Hindu subcaste.

Jizya (JIHZ-yuh) Tax in Islamic empires that was imposed on non-Muslims.

Joint-stock companies Early forerunner of the modern corporation; individuals who invested in a trading or exploring venture could make huge profits while limiting their risk.

Ka'ba (KAH-buh) Main shrine in Mecca, goal of Muslims embarking on the hajj.

Kabuki (kah-BOO-kee) Japanese theater in which actors were free to improvise and embellish the words.

Kama Hindu concept of the enjoyment of physical and sexual pleasure.

Kamikaze (KAH-mih-kah-zee) A Japanese term meaning "divine wind" that is related to the storms that destroyed Mongol invasion fleets; the term is symbolic of Japanese isolation and was later taken by suicide pilots in World War II.

Kanun (KAH-noon) Laws issued by the Ottoman Süleyman the Magnificent, also known as Süleyman Kanuni, "the Lawgiver."

Kapu Hawaiian concept of something being taboo.

Karma (KAHR-mah) Hindu concept that the sum of good and bad in a person's life will determine his or her status in the next life.

Khoikhoi South African people referred to pejoratively as the Hottentots by Europeans.

Kongo Central African state that began trading with the Portuguese around 1500; although their kings, such as King Affonso I (r. 1506–1543), converted to Christianity, they nevertheless suffered from the slave trade.

Koumbi-Saleh Important trading city along the trans-Saharan trade route from the eleventh to the thirteenth centuries.

Kshatriayas (KSHAHT-ree-uhs) Hindu caste of warriors and aristocrats.

Kulaks Land-owning Russian peasants who benefited under Lenin's New Economic Policy and suffered under Stalin's forced collectivization.

Kush Nubian African kingdom that conquered and controlled Egypt from 750 to 664 B.C.E.

Lamaist Buddhism (LAH-muh-ihst BOO-diz'm) Branch of Buddhism that was similar to shamanism in its acceptance of magic and supernatural powers.

La Reforma Political reform movement of Mexican president Benito Juárez (1806–1872) that called for limiting the power of the military and the Catholic church in Mexican society.

Latifundia (LAT-ih-FOON-dee-uh) Huge state-run and slave-worked farms in ancient Rome.

League of Nations Forerunner of the United Nations, the dream of American president Woodrow Wilson, although its potential was severely limited by the refusal of the United States to join.

Lebensraum (LAY-behnz-rowm) German term meaning "living space"; the term is associated with Hitler and his goal of carving out territory in the east for an expanding Germany.

Legalism Chinese philosophy from the Zhou dynasty that called for harsh suppression of the common people.

Levée en Masse (leh-VAY on MASS) A term signifying universal conscription during the radical phase of the French revolution.

Lex talionis (lehks tah-lee-oh-nihs) "Law of retaliation," laws in which offenders suffered punishments similar to their crimes; the most famous example is Hammurabi's Laws.

Li (LEE) Confucian concept, a sense of propriety.

Linear A Minoan written script.

Linear B Early Mycenaean written script, adapted from the Minoan Linear A.

Luddites Early-nineteenth-century artisans who were opposed to new machinery and industrialization.

Machismo (mah-CHEEZ-moh) Latin American social ethic that honored male strength, courage, aggressiveness, assertiveness, and cunning.

Madrasas (MAH-drahs-uhs) Islamic institutions of higher education that originated in the tenth century.

Magyars (MAH-jahrs) Hungarian invaders who raided towns in Germany, Italy, and France in the ninth and tenth centuries.

Mahabharata (mah-hah-BAH-rah-tah) Massive ancient Indian epic that was developed orally for centuries; it tells of an epic civil war between two family branches.

Mahayana (mah-huh-YAH-nah) The "greater vehicle," a more metaphysical and more popular northern branch of Buddhism.

Majapahit Southeast Asian kingdom (1293–1520) centered on the island of Java.

Mali (MAH-lee) West African kingdom founded in the thirteenth century by Sundiata; it reached its peak during the reign of Mansa Musa.

Manchus Manchurians who conquered China, putting an end to the Ming dynasty and founding the Qing dynasty (1644–1911).

Mandate of Heaven Chinese belief that the emperors ruled through the mandate, or approval, of heaven contingent on their ability to look after the welfare of the population.

Mandate system System that developed in the wake of World War I when the former colonies ended up mandates under European control, a thinly veiled attempt at continuing imperialism.

Manichaeism (man-ih-KEE-iz'm) Religion founded by the prophet Mani in the third century C.E., a syncretic version of Zoroastrian, Christian, and Buddhist elements.

Manor Large estates of the nobles during the European middle ages, home for the majority of the peasants.

Maori (MAY-oh-ree) Indigenous people of New Zealand.

Marathon Battlefield scene of the Athenian victory over the Persians in 490 B.C.E.

Marae Polynesian temple structure.

Maroons Runaway African slaves.

Marshall Plan U.S. plan, officially called the European Recovery Program, that offered financial and other economic aid to all European states that had suffered from World War II, including Soviet bloc states.

Mauryan empire Indian dynasty (321–185 B.C.E.) founded by Chandragupta Maurya and reaching its peak under Ashoka.

Maya (Mye-uh) Brilliant Central American society (300–1100) known for math, astronomy, and a sophisticated written language.

May Fourth Movement Chinese movement that began 4 May 1919 with a desire to eliminate imperialist influences and promote national unity.

Medes (meeds) Indo-European branch that settled in northern Persia and eventually fell to another branch, the Persians, in the sixth century B.C.E.

Meiji Restoration (MAY-jee) Restoration of imperial rule under Emperor Meiji in 1868 by a coalition led by Fukuzawa Yukichi and Ito Hirobumi; the restoration enacted western reforms to strengthen Japan.

Melaka (may-LAH-kah) Southeast Asian kingdom that was predominantly Islamic.

Mesopotamia Term meaning "between the rivers," in this case the Tigris and Euphrates; Sumer and Akkad are two of the earliest societies.

Mestizo (mehs-TEE-zoh) Latin American term for children of Spanish and native parentage.

Métis (may-TEE) Canadian term for individuals of mixed European and indigenous ancestry.

Millet An autonomous, self-governing community in the Ottoman empire.

Ming Chinese dynasty (1368–1644) founded by Hongwu and known for its cultural brilliance.

Minoan (mih-NOH-uhn) Society located on the island of Crete (ca. 2000–1100 B.C.E.) that influenced the early Mycenaeans.

Missi dominici (mihs-see doh-mee-nee-chee) "Envoys of the lord ruler," the noble and church emissaries sent out by Charlemagne.

Mithraism (MITH-rah-iz'm) Mystery religion based on worship of the sun god Mithras; it became popular among the Romans because of its promise of salvation.

Mochica (moh-CHEE-kuh) Pre-Incan South American society (300–700) known for their brilliant ceramics.

Moksha Hindu concept of the salvation of the soul.

Monotheism (MAW-noh-thee-iz'm) Belief in only one god, a rare concept in the ancient world.

Monroe Doctrine American doctrine issued in 1823 during the presidency of James Monroe that warned Europeans to keep their hands off Latin America and that expressed growing American imperialistic views regarding Latin America.

Mughals (MOO-guhls) Islamic dynasty that ruled India from the sixteenth through the eighteenth centuries; the construction of the Taj Mahal is representative of their splendor; with the

exception of the enlightened reign of Akbar, the increasing conflict between Hindus and Muslims was another of their legacies.

Muhammad (muh-HAH-mehd) Prophet of Islam (570–632).

Muslim A follower of Islam.

Mycenaean (meye-seh-NEE-uhn) Early Greek society on the Peloponese (1600–1100 B.C.E.) that was influenced by the Minoans; the Mycenaeans' conflict with Troy is immortalized in Homer's *Odyssey*.

Nara era Japanese period (710–794), centered around city of Nara, that was the highest point of Chinese influence.

National Policy Nineteenth-century Canadian policy designed to attract migrants, protect industries through tariffs, and build national transportation systems.

NATO The North Atlantic Treaty Organization, which was established by the United States in 1949 as a regional military alliance against Soviet expansionism.

Ndongo (n'DAWN-goh) Angolan kingdom that reached its peak during the reign of Queen Nzinga (r. 1623–1663).

Neandertal (nee-ANN-duhr-tawl) Early humans (100,000 to 35,000 years ago) who were prevalent during the Paleolithic period.

Negritude (NEH-grih-tood) "Blackness," a term coined by early African nationalists as a means of celebrating the heritage of black peoples around the world.

Neo-Confucianism (nee-oh-kuhn-FYOO-shuhn-iz'm) Philosophy that attempted to merge certain basic elements of Confucian and Buddhist thought; most important of the early Neo-Confucianists was the Chinese thinker Zhu Xi (1130–1200).

Neolithic New Stone Age (10,000–4000 B.C.E.), which was marked by the discovery and mastery of agriculture.

Nestorian (neh-STOHR-ee-uhn) Early branch of Christianity, named after the fifth-century Greek theologian Nestorius, that emphasized the human nature of Jesus Christ.

New Economic Policy (NEP) Plan implemented by Lenin that called for minor free market reforms.

Nirvana (nuhr-VAH-nuh) Buddhist concept of a state of spiritual perfection and enlightenment in which distracting passions are eliminated.

Noble Eightfold Path Final truth of the Buddhist Four Noble Truths that called for leading a life of balance and constant contemplation.

North American Free Trade Agreement (NAFTA) Regional accord established in 1993 between the United States, Canada, and Mexico; it formed world's second largest free-trade zone.

Nubia (NOO-bee-uh) Area south of Egypt; the kingdom of Kush in Nubia invaded and dominated Egypt from 750 to 664 B.C.E.

Oceania Term referring to the Pacific Ocean basin and its lands.

Olmecs Early Mesoamerican society (1200–100 B.C.E.) that centered around sites at San Lorenzo, La Venta, and Tres Zapotes and that influenced later Maya.

Oprichnina (oh-PREEK-nee-nah) A Russian term meaning the "land apart," Muscovite territory that the Russian Tsar Ivan IV (r. 1533–1584) demanded to control; the tsar created a new class of nobles called the *oprichniki* for this territory.

Oracle bones Chinese Shang dynasty (1766–1122 B.C.E.) means of foretelling the future.

Organization of African Unity (OAU) An organization started in 1963 by thirty-two newly independent African states and designed to prevent conflict that would lead to intervention by former colonial powers.

Organization of Petroleum Exporting Countries (OPEC) An organization begun in 1960 by oil-producing states originally for purely economic reasons but that later had more political influence.

Osiris Ancient Egyptian god that represented the forces of nature.

Ottoman empire Powerful Turkish empire that lasted from the conquest of Constantinople (Istanbul) in 1453 until 1918 and reached its peak during the reign of Süleyman the Magnificent (r. 1520–1566).

Paleolithic Old Stone Age, a long period of human development before the development of agriculture.

Palestinian Liberation Organization (PLO) Organization created in 1964 under the leadership of Yasser Arafat to champion Palestinian rights.

Paris Peace Accords Agreement reached in 1973 that marked the end of the United States's role in the Vietnam War.

Parsis (pahr-SEES) Indian Zoroastrians.

Parthians Persian dynasty (247 B.C.E.–224 C.E.) that reached its peak under Mithradates I.

Pater familias (PAH-tur fuh_MEE-lee-ahs) Roman term for the "father of the family," a theoretical implication that gave the male head of the family almost unlimited authority.

Patriarch (PAY-tree-ahrk) Leader of the Greek Orthodox church, which in 1054 officially split with the Pope and the Roman Catholic church.

Patricians Roman aristocrats and wealthy classes.

Pax Americana "American Peace," a term that compares American domination in the years after World War II with the power of Rome at its peak.

Pax Romana (Pahks roh-MAH-nah) "Roman Peace," a term that relates to the period of political stability, cultural brilliance, and economic prosperity beginning with unification under Augustus and lasting through the first two centuries C.E.

Peninsulares (pehn-IHN-soo-LAH-rayz) Latin American officials from Spain or Portugal.

Perestroika (PAYR-eh-stroy-kuh) "Restructuring," a Russian term associated with Gorbachev's effort to reorganize the Soviet state.

Pharaohs (FARE-ohs) Egyptian kings considered to be gods on earth.

Plebians (plih-BEE-uhns) Roman common people.

Polis (POH-lihs) Greek term for the city-state.

Popol Vuh (paw-pawl vuh) Mayan creation epic.

Prehistory The period before the invention of writing.

Proletariat Urban working class in a modern industrial society.

Protestant Reformation Sixteenth-century European movement during which Luther, Calvin, Zwingli, and others broke away from the Catholic church.

Putting-out system Method of getting around guild control by delivering unfinished materials to rural households for completion.

Ptolemaic (TAWL-oh-may-ihk) Term used to signify both the Egyptian kingdom founded by Alexander the Great's general Ptolemy and the thought of the philosopher Ptolemy of Alexandria (second century C.E.), who used mathematical formulas in an attempt to prove Aristotle's geocentric theory of the universe.

Qadi Islamic judges.

Qanat (kah-NAHT) Persian underground canal.

Qi (chee) Chinese concept of the basic material that makes up the body and the universe.

Qin (chihn) Chinese dynasty (221–207 B.C.E.) that was founded by Qin Shihuangdi and was marked by the first unification of China and the early construction of defensive walls.

Qing (chihng) Chinese dynasty (1644–1911) that reached its peak during the reigns of Kangxi and Qianlong.

Quetzalcoatl (keht-zahl-koh-AHT'l) Aztec god, the "feathered serpent," who was borrowed originally from the Toltecs; Quetzalcoatl was believed to have been defeated by another god and exiled, and he promised to return.

Quinto (KEEN-toh) The one-fifth of Mexican and Peruvian silver production that was reserved for the Spanish monarchy.

Quipu (KEE-poo) Incan mnemonic aid comprised of different colored strings and knots that served to record events in the absence of a written text.

Qizilbash (gih-ZIHL-bahsh) Term meaning "red heads," Turkish tribes that were important allies of Shah Ismail in the formation of the Safavid empire.

Quran (koo-RAHN) Islamic holy book that is believed to contain the divine revelations of Allah as presented to Muhammad.

Ramayana (rah-mah-yah-nah) Ancient Indian masterpiece about the hero Rama that symbolized the victory of *dharma* (order) over *adharma* (chaos).

Rape of Nanjing Japanese conquest and destruction of the Chinese city of Nanjing in the 1930s.

Realpolitik (ray-AHL-poh-lih-teek) The Prussian Otto von Bismarck's "politics of reality," the belief that only the willingness to use force would actually bring about change.

Reconquista (ray-kohn-KEE-stah) Crusade, ending in 1492, to drive the Islamic forces out of Spain.

Reconstruction System implemented in the American South (1867–1877) that was designed to bring the Confederate states back into the union and also extend civil rights to freed slaves.

Repartimiento (reh-PAHR-tih-mehn-toh) Spanish labor system in Latin America, supposed to replace the *encomienda* system, in which native communities were compelled to provide laborers for the farms or mines and the Spanish employers were expected to pay fair wages.

Romanov (ROH-mah-nahv) Russian dynasty (1610–1917) founded by Mikhail Romanov and ending with Nicholas II.

Rubaiyat (ROO-bee-aht) "Quatrains," famous poetry of Omar Khayyam that was later translated by Edward Fitzgerald.

Safavid (SAH-fah-vihd) Later Persian empire (1501–1722) that was founded by Shah Ismail and that became a center for Shiism; the empire reached its peak under Shah Abbas the Great and was centered around the capital of Isfahan.

Sakk Letters of credit that were common in the medieval Islamic banking world.

Saljuqs (sahl-JYOOKS) Turkish tribe that gained control over the Abbasid empire and fought with the Byzantine empire.

Samsara (sahm-SAH-ruh) Hindu term for the concept of transmigration, that is, the soul passing into a new incarnation.

Samurai (SAM-uhr-eye) A Japanese warrior who lived by the code of *bushido*.

Sasanids (suh-SAH-nids) Later powerful Persian dynasty (224–651) that would reach its peak under Shapur I and later fall to Arabic expansion.

Sati (SOO-TEE) Also known as *suttee*, Indian practice of a widow throwing herself on the funeral pyre of her husband.

Satraps (SAY-traps) Persian administrators, usually members of the royal family, who governed a satrapy.

Satyagraha (SAH-tyah-GRAH-hah) "Truth and firmness," a term associated with Gandhi's policy of passive resistance.

Scholasticism Medieval attempt of thinkers like St. Thomas Aquinas to merge the beliefs of Christianity with the logical rigor of Greek philosophy.

Scientific racism Nineteenth-century attempt to justify racism by scientific means; an example would be Gobineau's *Essay on the Inequality of the Human Races.*

Self-determinism Belief popular in World War I and after that every people should have the right to determine their own political destiny; the belief was often cited but ignored by the Great Powers.

Self-strengthening movement Chinese attempt (1860–1895) to blend Chinese cultural traditions with European industrial technology.

Seleucids (sih-LOO-sihds) Persian empire (323–83 B.C.E.) founded by Seleucus after the death of Alexander the Great.

Semitic (suh-miht-ihk) A term that relates to the Semites, ancient nomadic herders who spoke Semitic languages; examples of Semites were the Akkadians, Hebrews, Aramaics, and Phoenicians, who often interacted with the more settled societies of Mesopotamia and Egypt.

Sepoys Indian troops who served the British.

Seppuku A Japanese term for ritual suicide committed by the samurai when he had been dishonored.

Serfs Peasants who, while not chattel slaves, were tied to the land and who owed obligation to the lords on whose land they worked.

Shamanism (SHAH-mah-niz'm) Belief in shamans or religious specialists who possessed supernatural powers and who communicated with the gods and the spirits of nature.

Shari'a (shah-REE-ah) The Islamic holy law, drawn up by theologians from the Quran and accounts of Muhammad's life.

Shia (SHEE-ah) Islamic minority in opposition to the Sunni majority; their belief is that leadership should reside in the line descended from Ali.

Shintoism (SHIHN-toh-iz'm) Indigenous Japanese religion that emphasizes purity, clan loyalty, and the divinity of the emperor.

Shiva (SHEE-vuh) Hindu god associated with both fertility and destruction.

Shogun (SHOH-gun) Japanese military leader who ruled in place of the emperor.

Shudras (SHOO-druhs) Hindu caste of landless peasants and serfs.

Siddhartha Gautama (sih-DHAR-tuh GOW-tau-mah) Indian *kshatriya* who achieved enlightenment and became known as the Buddha, the founder of Buddhism.

Sikhs (SIHKS) Indian syncretic faith that contains elements of Hinduism and Islam.

Silk roads Ancient trade routes that extended from the Roman empire in the west to China in the east.

Social Darwinism Nineteenth-century philosophy, championed by thinkers such as Herbert Spencer, that attempted to apply Darwinian "survival of the fittest" to the social and political realm; adherents saw the the elimination of weaker nations as part of a natural process and used the philosophy to justify war.

Socialism Political and economic theory of social organization based on the collective ownership of the means of production; its origins were in the early nineteenth century, and it differs from communism by a desire for slow or moderate change compared to the communist call for revolution.

Solidarity Polish trade union and nationalist movement in the 1980s that was headed by Lech Walesa.

Song (SOHNG) Chinese dynasty (960–1279) that was marked by an increasingly urbanized and cosmopolitan society.

Soviets Russian elected councils that originated as strike committees during the 1905 St. Petersburg disorders; they represented a form of local self-government that went on to become the primary unit of government in the Union of Soviet Socialist Republics. The term was also used during the cold war to designate the Soviet Union.

Spanish Inquisition Institution organized in 1478 by Fernando and Isabel of Spain to hunt out heretical or contrary opinions; subjects of persecution included Protestants, Jews, Muslims, and witches.

Srivijaya (sree-VIH-juh-yuh) Southeast Asian kingdom (670–1025), based on the island of Sumatra, that used a powerful navy to dominate trade.

Stateless societies Term relating to societies such as those of sub-Saharan Africa after the Bantu migrations that featured decentralized rule through family and kinship groups instead of strongly centralized hierarchies.

Stoics (STOH-ihks) Hellenistic philosophers who encouraged their followers to lead active, virtuous lives and to aid others.

Strabo (STRAH-boh) Greek geographer (first century C.E.).

Strategic Arms Limitations Talk (SALT) Agreement in 1972 between the United States and the Soviet Union.

Stupas (STOO-pahs) Buddhist shrines.

Sufis (SOO-fees) Islamic mystics who placed more emphasis on emotion and devotion than on strict adherence to rules.

Sui (SWAY) Chinese dynasty (589–618) that constructed Grand Canal, reunified China, and allowed for the splendor of the Tang dynasty that followed.

Süleyman (SOO-lee-mahn) Ottoman Turkish ruler Süleyman the Magnificent (r. 1520–1566), who was the most powerful and wealthy ruler of the sixteenth century.

Sumerians (soo-MEHR-ee-uhns) Earliest Mesopotamian society.

Sundiata (soon-JAH-tuh) Founder of the Mali empire (r. 1230–1255), also the inspiration for the *Sundiata*, an African literary and mythological work.

Sunni (SOON-nee) "Traditionalists," the most popular branch of Islam; Sunnis believe in the legitimacy of the early caliphs, compared to the Shiite belief that only a descendent of Ali can lead.

Suu Kyi, Aung San (SOO KEY, AWNG SAHN) Opposition leader (1945–) in Myanmar; she was elected leader in 1990 but she was not allowed to come to power; she was a Nobel Peace Prize recipient in 1991.

Swahili (swah-HEE-lee) East African city-state society that dominated the coast from Mogadishu to Kilwa and was active in trade.

Taino (TEYE-noh) A Caribbean tribe who were the first indigenous peoples from the Americas to come into contact with Christopher Columbus.

Taiping rebellion (TEYE-pihng) Rebellion (1850–1864) in Qing China led by Hong Xiuquan, during which twenty to thirty million were killed; the rebellion was symbolic of the decline of China during the nineteenth century.

Taliban Strict Islamic organization that ruled Afghanistan from 1996 to 2002.

Tang Taizong (TAHNG TEYE-zohng) Chinese emperor (r. 627–649) who founded the Tang dynasty (618–907).

Tanzimat "Reorganization" era (1839–1876), an attempt to reorganize the Ottoman empire on Enlightenment and constitutional forms.

Temüjin (TEM-oo-chin) Mongol conqueror (ca. 1167–1227) who later took the name Chinggis Khan, "universal ruler."

Tenochtitlan (the-NOCH-tee-tlahn) Capital of the Aztec empire, later Mexico City.

Teotihuacan (tay-uh-tee-wah-KAHN) Central American society (200 B.C.E.–750 C.E.); its Pyramid of the Sun was the largest structure in Mesoamerica.

Teutonic Knights Crusading European order that was active in the Baltic region.

Third Rome Concept that a new power would rise up to carry the legacy of Roman greatness after the decline of the Second Rome, Constantinople; Moscow was referred to as the Third Rome during the fifteenth century.

Three Principles of the People Philosophy of Chinese Guomindang leader Sun Yatsen (1866–1925) that emphasized nationalism, democracy, and people's livelihood.

Tian (TEE-ehn) Chinese term for heaven.

Tikal (tee-KAHL) Maya political center from the fourth through the ninth centuries.

Timur-i lang (tee-MOOR-yee LAHNG) "Timur the Lame," known in English as Tamerlane (ca. 1336–1405), who conquered an empire ranging from the Black Sea to Samarkand.

Tokugawa (TOH-koo-GAH-wah) Last shogunate in Japanese history (1600–1867); it was founded by Tokugawa Ieyasu who was notable for unifying Japan.

Toltecs Central American society (950–1150) that was centered around the city of Tula.

Trail of Tears Forced relocation of the Cherokee from the eastern woodlands to Oklahoma (1837–1838); it was symbolic of U.S. expansion and destruction of indigenous Indian societies.

Triangular trade Trade between Europe, Africa, and the Americas that featured finished products from Europe, slaves from Africa, and American products bound for Europe.

Triple Alliance Pre–World War I alliance of Germany, Austria-Hungary, and Italy.

Triple Entente (ahn-TAHNT) Pre–World War I alliance of England, France, and Russia.

Truman Doctrine U.S. policy instituted in 1947 by President Harry Truman in which the United States would follow an interventionist foreign policy to contain communism.

Tsar (ZAHR) Old Russian term for king that is derived from the term *caesar.*

Twelver Shiism (SHEE'i'zm) Branch of Islam that stressed that there were twelve perfect religious leaders after Muhammad and that the twelfth went into hiding and would return someday; Shah Ismail spread this variety through the Safavid empire.

Uighurs (WEE-goors) Turkish tribe.

Ukiyo Japanese word for the "floating worlds," a Buddhist term for the insignificance of the world that came to represent the urban centers in Tokugawa Japan.

Ulama Islamic officials, scholars who shaped public policy in accordance with the Quran and the *sharia.*

Ulaanbaatar (OO-lahn-bah-tahr) Mongolian city.

Umayyad (oo-MEYE-ahd) Arabic dynasty (661–750), with its capital at Damascus, that was marked by a tremendous period of expansion to Spain in the west and India in the east.

Umma (UM-mah) Islamic term for the "community of the faithful."

United Nations (UN) Successor to the League of Nations, an association of sovereign nations that attempts to find solutions to global problems.

Upanishads (oo-PAHN-ee-shahds) Indian reflections and dialogues (800–400 B.C.E.) that reflected basic Hindu concepts.

Urdu (OOR-doo) A language that is predominant in Pakistan.

Uruk (OO-rook) Ancient Mesopotamian city from the fourth millennium B.C.E. that was allegedly the home of the fabled Gilgamesh.

Vaishyas (VEYES-yuhs) Hindu caste of cultivators, artisans, and merchants.

Vaqueros (vah-KEHR-ohs) Latin American cowboys, similar to the Argentine gaucho.

Varna (VAHR-nuh) Hindu word for caste.

Varuna (vuh-ROO-nuh) Early Aryan god who watched over the behavior of mortals and preserved the cosmic order.

Vedas (VAY-duhs) "Wisdom," early collections of prayers and hymns that provide information about the Indo-European Aryans who migrated into India around 1500 B.C.E.; *Rig Veda* is most important collection.

Velvet revolution A term that describes the nonviolent transfer of power in Czechoslovakia during the collapse of Soviet rule.

Venta, La (VEHN-tuh, lah) Early Olmec center (800–400 B.C.E.).

Venus figurines Small Paleolithic statues of women with exaggerated sexual features.

Vernacular (ver-NA-kyoo-lar) The language of the people; Martin Luther translated the Bible from the Latin of the Catholic church into the vernacular German.

Versailles (vehr-SEYE) Palace of French King Louis XIV.

Viet Minh North Vietnamese nationalist communists under Ho Chi Minh.

Vijayanagar (vee-juh-yah-NAH-gahr) Southern Indian kingdom (1336–1565) that later fell to the Mughals.

Vishnu (VIHSH-noo) Hindu god, preserver of the world, who was often incarnated as Krishna.

Vodou (voh-DOW) Syncretic religion practiced by African slaves in Haiti.

Volksgeist (FOHLKS-geyest) "People's spirit," a term that was coined by the

German philosopher Herder; a nation's volksgeist would not come to maturity unless people studied their own unique culture and traditions.

Volta do mar (VOHL-tah doh MAHR) "Return through the sea," a fifteenth-century Portuguese sea route that took advantage of the prevailing winds and currents.

Voltaire (vohl-TAIR) Pen name of French philosophe Francois-Marie Arouet (1694–1778), author of *Candide*.

Walesa, Lech (WAH-lehn-sah, LEHK) Leader of the Polish Solidarity movement.

Waldensians Twelfth-century religious reformers who criticized the Roman Catholic church and who proposed that the laity had the right to preach and administer sacraments; they were declared heretics.

Wanli (wahn-LEE) Chinese Ming emperor (r. 1572–1620) whose refusal to meet with officials hurried the decline of Ming dynasty.

War Communism The Bolshevik policy of nationalizing industry and seizing private land during the civil war.

Warsaw Pact Warsaw Treaty Organization, a military alliance formed by Soviet bloc nations in 1955 in response to rearmament of West Germany and its inclusion in NATO.

Wind wheels Prevailing wind patterns in the Atlantic and Pacific Oceans north and south of the equator; their discovery made sailing much safer and quicker.

Witte, Sergei (VIHT-tee, SAYR-gay) Late-nineteenth-century Russian minister of finance who pushed for industrialization.

World Health Organization (WHO) United Nation organization designed to deal with global health issues.

World Trade Organization (WTO) An organization that was established in

1995 with more than 120 nations and whose goal is to loosen barriers to free trade.

Wuwei (woo-WAY) Daoist concept of a disengagement from the affairs of the world.

Xia (shyah) Early Chinese dynasty (2200–1766 B.C.E.) that is known mainly from legend.

Xianyang (SHYAHN-YAHNG) Capital city of Qin empire.

Xiao (SHAYOH) Confucian concept of respect for one's parents and ancestors.

Xinjiang (shin-jyahng) Western Chinese province.

Xuanzang (SHWEN-ZAHNG) Seventh-century Chinese monk who made a famous trip to India to collect Buddhist texts.

Yahweh (YAH-way) God of the monotheistic religion of Judaism that influenced later Christianity and Islam.

Yangshao (YAHNG-show) Early Chinese society (2500–2200 B.C.E.).

Yangzi (YAHNG-zuh) River in central China.

Yongle (YAWNG-leh) Chinese Ming emperor (r. 1403–1424) who pushed for foreign exploration and promoted cultural achievements such as the *Yongle Encyclopedia*.

Young Turks Nineteenth-century Turkish reformers who pushed for changes within the Ottoman empire, such as universal suffrage and freedom of religion.

Yu (yoo) Legendary founder of the Xia dynasty (ca. 2200 B.C.E.).

Yuan (yoo-AHN) Chinese dynasty (1279–1368) that was founded by the Mongol ruler Khubilai Khan.

Yucatan (yoo-kuh-TAN) Peninsula in Central America, home of the Maya.

Yurts (yuhrts) Tents used by nomadic Turkish and Mongol tribes.

Zaibatsu (zeye-BAHT-soo) Japanese term for "wealthy cliques," which are similar to American trusts and cartels but usually organized around one family.

Zambos (ZAHM-bohs) Latin American term for individuals born of indigenous and African parents.

Zamudio, Adela (ZAH-moo-dee-oh, ah-DEH-lah) Nineteenth-century Bolivian poet, author of "To Be Born a Man."

Zarathustra (zar-uh-THOO-struh) Persian prophet (ca. 628–551 B.C.E.) who founded Zoroastrianism.

Zen Buddhism Japanese version of Chinese Chan Buddhism, with an emphasis on intuition and sudden flashes of insight instead of textual study.

Zhou (JOH) Chinese dynasty (1122–256 B.C.E.) that was the foundation of Chinese thought formed during this period: Confucianism, Daoism, Zhou Classics.

Zhu Xi (ZHOO-SHEE) Neo-Confucian Chinese philosopher (1130–1200).

Ziggurats (ZIG-uh-rahts) Mesopotamian temples.

Zimbabwe (zihm-BAHB-way) Former colony of Southern Rhodesia that gained independence in 1980.

Zemstvos (ZEHMST-voh) District assemblies elected by Russians in the nineteenth century.

Zoroastrianism (zohr-oh-ASS-tree-ahn-iz'm) Persian religion based on the teaching of the sixth-century-B.C.E. prophet Zarathustra; its emphasis on the duality of good and evil and on the role of individuals in determining their own fate would influence later religions.

CREDITS

〜⚬〜

CHAPTER 1

Text Credits From *The Making of Mankind* by Richard E. Leakey (Michael Joseph, 1981). Copyright © B. V. Sherma 1981. Reprinted with permission of Richard E. Leakey. **Photo Credits p. 4,** Courtesy Ministere de la Culture et de la Communication, Direction Régionale des Affaires Culturelles de Rhône-Alpes, Service Régional de Archéologie; **p. 7,** © John Reader/Photo Researchers, Inc.; **p. 15,** © The Field Museum, Neg. #76851c; **p. 16,** © Damian Andrus/Maxwell Museum, University of New Mexico; **p. 17T,** © Victor Boswell/National Geographic Image Collection; **p. 17B,** © Erich Lessing/Art Resource, NY; **p. 18,** © Francois Ducasse/Photo Researchers, Inc.; **p. 20,** © Erich Lessing/Art Resource, NY; **p. 25,** © Arlete Mellaart.

CHAPTER 2

Text Credits Pritchard, James B.: *Ancient Near Eastern Texts Relating to the Old Testament.* © 1950 Princeton University Press, 1978 renewed, 2nd. edition 1955, 1983 renewed PUP. Reprinted by permission of Princeton University Press. **Photo Credits p. 30,** © Erich Lessing/Art Resource, NY; **p. 34,** © Georg Gerster/Photo Researchers, Inc.; **p. 36,** © Iraq Museum, Baghdad/Hirmer Fotoarchiv; **p. 37,** © Réunion des Musées Nationaux/Art Resource, NY; **p. 39,** © Werner Foreman/Art Resource, NY; **p. 41T,** © Nik Wheeler; **p. 41B,** © Oriental Institute, University of Chicago; **p. 44,** © The British Museum; **p. 47,** © Erich Lessing/Art Resource, NY; **p. 49,** © Réunion des Musées Nationaux/Art Resource, NY.

CHAPTER 3

Text Credits Miriam Lichtheim, ed., *Ancient Egyptian Literature*, three Vols.: Vol. 1, Berkeley: University of California Press, 1973. Copyright © 1973–1980 Regents of the University of California. Reprinted by permission. **Photo Credits**

p. 58, © Will & Demi McIntyre/Getty Images/Stone; **p. 63,** © Erich Lessing/Art Resource, NY; **p. 64,** © Hirmer Fotoarchiv; **p. 67,** Stela of the Nubian soldier Nenu, Egypt (Geblein), about 2130–1980 B.C. First Intermediate Period; Limestone, painted; $14\frac{5}{8} \times 17\frac{3}{4}$ in. (37.1×45 cm). Purchased by A.M. Lythgoe, 03.1848. Courtesy, Museum of Fine Arts, Boston. Reproduced with permission. © 2004 Museum of Fine Arts, Boston. All rights reserved; **p. 69,** © Robert Partridge/The Ancient Egypt Picture Library; **p. 71,** © The British Museum, London/Bridgeman Art Library; **p. 72,** © Michael Holford; **p. 74,** © Werner Foreman/Art Resource, NY; **p. 75,** By permission of the British Library; **p. 76,** © Art Resource, NY; **p. 78,** © The British Museum, London/Bridgeman Art Library; **p. 80,** © Bildarchiv Preussischer Kulturbesitz/Art Resource, NY.

CHAPTER 4

Text Credits From *The Upanishads*, Juan Mascaró, trans. (Penguin Classics, 1965). Copyright © Juan Mascaró, 1965. **Photo Credits p. 86,** © Josephine Powell Photograph, Courtesy of Historic Photographs, Fine Arts Library, Harvard College Library; **p. 91, 92,** © MacQuitty International Collection; **p. 93,** © National Museum of India, New Delhi/Bridgeman Art Library; **p. 95,** © The British Museum; **p. 99,** Los Angeles County Museum of Art, From the Nasli and Alice Heeramaneck Collection, Museum Associates Purchase, Photograph © 2001 Museum Associates/LACMA; **p. 101,** By permission of the British Library; **p. 103,** © V.I. Thayil/DPA/VIT/The Image Works.

CHAPTER 5

Photo Credits p. 108, © The British Museum; **p. 111,** Cultural Relics Publishing House, Beijing; **p. 113,** © ChinaStock; **p. 114,** Cultural Relics Publishing House, Beijing; **p. 117,** © 1995 Wang Lu/China

Stock; **p. 118,** © The British Museum; **p. 119,** Ritual vessel (chia), Chinese, Shang Dynasty, 12th century B.C., Bronze, 52.8×30.5 cm. Freer Gallery of Art, Smithsonian Institution, Washington, DC: Purchase F1923.1; **p. 121,** Wang-go Wen, Inc.; **p. 123,** Cultural Relics Publishing House, Beijing; **p. 125,** © Werner Foreman Archive/Art Resource, NY; **p. 129,** © Keren Su/Corbis.

CHAPTER 6

Text Credits Reprinted with the permission of Simon & Schuster Adult Publishing Group from *Popol Vuh* by Dennis Tedlock. Copyright © 1985, 1996 by Dennis Tedlock; Low, Drury and Timi Koro, "The Story of Ru's Canoe and the Discovery and Settlement of Aitutaki," *Journal of the Polynesian Society* 43 (1934): 17–24. Reprinted by permission of The Polynesian Society, University of Auckland. **Photo Credits p. 132,** © Werner Foreman/Art Resource, NY; **p. 137,** © Andrew Rakaczy/Photo Researchers, Inc.; **p. 138,** Courtesy Department of Library Services, American Museum of Natural History, Neg. #1298(3). Photo by Denis Finnin; **p. 139,** © Richard Steedman/Corbis; **p. 140,** Mural, Room 1, Bonampak, Chiapas, Mexico, Mayan. Classic Period c. 700–900 A.D. Watercolor copy by Antonio Tejada. Peabody Museum, Harvard University. Photo by Hillel Burger; **p. 141,** © Justin Kerr; **p. 142,** Courtesy Arthur A. Demarest; **p. 144,** © Robert Frerck/Odyssey; **p. 148,** Osterreichische Nationalbibliothek; **p. 150,** By permission of the British Library (ADD. 23921 fol. 20); **p. 151,** © Carl Bento/Nature Focus.

CHAPTER 7

Photo Credits p. 158, © The British Museum; **p. 162,** © The Oriental Institute, University of Chicago; **p. 163,** © Fred J. Maroon/Photo Researchers, Inc.; **p. 165,** © The Oriental Institute, University of

Chicago; **p. 166,** Courtesy Museum of Fine Arts, Boston. Reproduced with permission. Gift of Mrs. George M. Brett. © 2004 Museum of Fine Arts, Boston. All rights reserved; **p. 167,** The State Hermitage Museum, St. Petersburg, Russia; **p. 170,** © Fred J. Maroon/Photo Researchers, Inc.; **p. 172,** © The Oriental Institute, University of Chicago; **p. 175,** The State Hermitage Museum, St. Petersburg, Russia; **p. 177,** © SEF/Art Resource, NY.

CHAPTER 8

Photo Credits p. 180, Bibliotheque Nationale, Paris, France/© The Bridgeman Art Library; **p. 183,** © AKG London; **p. 187, 193,** © O. Louis Mazzatenta/NGS Image Collection; **p. 195,** © ChinaStock; **p. 198,** The Nelson-Atkins Museum of Art, Kansas City, Missouri, Purchase: Nelson Trust; **p. 199,** Tales from History and Legends (detail: single male figure), late 1st century B.C. China; Western Han Dynasty. Hollow tiles of a tomb lintel and pediment; ink and color on whitened ground. Total 73.8 × 204.7 cm. Denman Waldo Ross Collection. 25.10-13. Courtesy Museum of Fine Arts, Boston. Reproduced with permission. © 2004 Museum of Fine Arts, Boston. All rights reserved.; **p. 200,** © Erich Lessing/ Art Resource, NY; **p. 201,** Wang-go Wen, Inc.; **p. 202,** Cultural Relics Publishing House, Beijing.

CHAPTER 9

Text Credits Strong, John, *The Legend Of King Asoka.* © 1983 Princeton University Press. Reprinted by permission of Princeton University Press; from *The Campaigns of Alexander* by Arrian, Aubrey de Sélincourt, trans., revised by J. R. Hamilton (Penguin Classics 1958, Revised edition 1971). Copyright © the Estate of Aubrey de Sélincourt, 1958, 1971. **Photo Credits p. 206,** Indian, Andhra Pradesh Amaravati, Head of Buddha, 2nd century, limestone, 34.3 × 21.7 × 10.2 cm, The James W. and Marilynn Alsdorf Collection AL.353. © The Art Institute of Chicago. All rights reserved.; **p. 210,** Sarnath, Uttar Pradesh, India/ © The Bridgeman Art Library; **p. 211,** By permission of the British Library; **p. 212,** © Underwood & Underwood/Corbis; **p. 214,** © The Art Archive; **p. 215,** Buddha, Coin of Kaniska, 2nd century A.D., India, gold. Seth K. Sweetser Fund. Courtesy Museum of Fine Arts, Boston.

(31.895). Reproduced with permission. © 2004 Museum of Fine Arts, Boston. All rights reserved; **p. 216,** © Borromeo/Art Resource, NY; **p. 218,** © The British Museum; **p. 220,** © Borromeo/Art Resource, NY; **p. 221,** Foto Features; **p. 222,** © Borromeo/Art Resource, NY; **p. 224,** Pakistani (ancient Gandhara), Bodhisattva, 2nd–3rd century, schist, 150.5 × 53.3 × 19 cm, The James W. and Marilynn Alsdorf Collection, 198.1997. © The Art Institute of Chicago. All rights reserved.

CHAPTER 10

Photo Credits p. 230, © Corbis; **p. 233,** © Erich Lessing/Art Resource, NY; **p. 235,** © Walter S. Clark/Photo Researchers, Inc.; **p. 236,** © Réunion des Musées Nationaux/ Art Resource, NY; **p. 237,** © Scala/Art Resource, NY; **p. 239,** © The British Museum; **p. 240,** © Corbis; **p. 241,** © C. M. Dixon; **p. 246, 248, 249,** © The British Museum; **p. 251,** © Corbis.

CHAPTER 11

Text Credits From *The Annals of Imperial Rome* by Tacitus, translated by Michael Grant (Penguin Classics 1956, sixth revised edition 1989). Copyright © Michael Grant Publications Ltd., 1956, 1956, 1971, 1973, 1975, 1977, 1989. **Photo Credits p. 258,** © Scala/Art Resource, NY; **p. 261,** © Hirmer Fotoarchiv; **p. 262,** © Comstock; **p. 265,** © C. M. Dixon; **p. 266,** © Vatican Museum/Robert Harding Picture Library; **p. 267, 269, 272,** © Erich Lessing/Art Resource, NY; **p. 273,** © Michael Holford; **p. 275,** © C. M. Dixon; **p. 276,** © Alinari/ Art Resource, NY; **p. 278,** © Robert Frerck/ Corbis; **p. 279,** © Alinari/Art Resource, NY.

CHAPTER 12

Photo Credits p. 286, © Royal Geographic Society; **p. 289,** Stair-riser with Parthian men, Pakistan, Gandharan school. With permission of the Royal Ontario Museum. © ROM (939.17.19); **p. 291,** Cultural Relics Publishing House, Beijing; **p. 293T,** © The British Museum; **p. 293B,** With permission of the Royal Ontario Museum. © ROM (910.159.644); **p. 295,** © Scala/Art Resource, NY; **p. 296,** © AKG London; **p. 298,** With permission of the Royal Ontario Museum. © ROM (931.13.127); **p. 299,** © Iris Papadopuolos/Staatliche Museen zu Berlin/Preussischer Kulturbesitz Museum für Indische

Kunst/Art Resource, NY; **p. 304,** Cultural Relics Publishing House, Beijing; **p. 305,** © Michael Holford; **p. 306,** © Erich Lessing/Art Resource, NY; **p. 309,** © Ancient Art & Architecture Collection.

CHAPTER 13

Text Credits From *The Alexiad of Anna Comnenea*, E. R. A. Sewter, trans. (Penguin Classics, 1969). Copyright © E. R. A. Sewter, 1969. **Photo Credits p. 316, 320,** © Erich Lessing/Art Resource, NY; **p. 322,** © Scala/Art Resource, NY; **p. 323,** © Robert Frerck/Odyssey; **p. 324,** © The Granger Collection, New York; **p. 326,** © Giraudon/Art Resource, NY; **p. 327,** © Bibliotheque Nationale de France, Paris (RCA12523); **p. 328,** © Bibliotheque Nationale de France (GREC 923 Fol 206v, RCC 10078); **p. 332,** Historical Museum, Moscow; **p. 338,** © Erich Lessing/Art Resource, NY; **p. 339,** © Biblioteca Apostolica, Vatican Library/Index S.A.S.

CHAPTER 14

Photo Credits p. 344, By permission of the British Library (Ms. add. 27261, f. 363a); **p. 347,** © Robert Harding Picture Library; **p. 349,** Reproduced by kind permission of the Trustees of the Chester Beatty Library, Dublin; **p. 352,** © The Granger Collection, New York; **p. 355,** © Archivo Iconografico S.A./Corbis; **p. 360,** © Bibliotheque Nationale de France, Paris (Ms Arabe 5847 fol 138); **p. 361,** © Bibliotheque Nationale de France, Paris (Ms Arabe 5847 fol 89); **p. 362,** © Bodleian Library, University of Oxford, MS. Pococke 275 folios 3v-4r; **p. 363,** © Bibliotheque Nationale de France, Paris (Ms Arabe 5847 fol 105); **p. 364,** © Benjamin Rondel/Corbis; **p. 366,** © Bibliotheque Nationale de France, Paris (Ms Arabe 5847 fol 5v); **p. 367,** Courtesy of the Arthur M. Sackler Museum, Harvard University Art Museums. Promise gift of Mr. and Mrs. Stuart Cary Welch, Jr.. Partially owned by the Metropolitan Museum of Art and the Arthur M. Sackler Museum, Harvard University, 1988. In honor of the students of Harvard University and Radcliffe College (1988.460.3).

CHAPTER 15

Text Credits From "A Song of War Chariots," *Anthology of Chinese Literature,* Cyril

INDEX